A NEW HANDBOOK OF CHRISTIAN THEOLOGIANS

Donald W. Musser
AND
Joseph L. Price
EDITORS

D0188488

ABINGDON PRESS
Nashville

A NEW HANDBOOK OF CHRISTIAN THEOLOGIANS

Library of Congress Cataloging-in-Publication Data

A new handbook of Christian theologians / Donald W. Musser and Joseph L. Price, editors.
    p. cm.
   Includes bibliographical references.
   ISBN 0-687-27803-1 (alk. paper)
    1. Theology, Doctrinal—History—20th century—Handbooks, manuals, etc. 2. Theologians—Biography—Dictionaries. I. Musser, Donald W., 1942– . II. Price, Joseph L., 1949– .
BT28.N48   1996
230'.092'2—dc20   96–12801
[B]   CIP

96 97 98 99 00 01 02 03 04 05—10 9 8 7 6 5 4 3 2 1

MANUFACTURED IN THE UNITED STATES OF AMERICA

A NEW HANDBOOK
OF CHRISTIAN
THEOLOGIANS

ACKNOWLEDGMENTS

Selecting the most significant theologians at the turn of the century was a formidable task. We sought advice from many people. Perhaps the most important input to our selection process came from thirty-nine anonymous consulting theologians who were solicited by our editor. Our most important decisions were made during a balmy January in Whittier, California, when we poured over the thick file of responses from these thoughtful and perceptive respondents. They remain a silent but ever-present company over this volume.

Our editor gave us just the right amount of freedom and structure in which to do our work. She never interfered in our work; she always supported our efforts. We could not be more grateful for the support of her and her colleagues at Abingdon Press.

Don Musser solicited advice from three of his former students who were in the trenches of doctoral studies in theology. He appreciates the salient comments of Dan Bell, D. Gregory Sapp, and Luis Pedraja. His colleague at Stetson, D. Dixon Sutherland, exploited his knowledge of European theology and provided sage advice that we accepted to our benefit. He has had more influence on this project than even he knows. Don's secretaries, Liz Clark and Kim Loadholtz, the Greg Maddux and John Smoltz of word processing, receive Most Valuable Player Awards for their tactile efficiency. Don is also grateful for the collegiality of his Stetson environment, especially his colleagues in the Department of Religious Studies, who provide personal and professional support beyond that experienced by most teaching scholars.

Joe Price benefits from personal and professional support at Whittier College, which awarded him a Faculty Research Grant to facilitate consultation with contributors and collaboration with editors working on this volume. Institutional support was directed by former deans of faculty Wendy Furman and Lisa Rossacher, and professional support was sustained by departmental colleague Glenn Yocum. Joe especially appreciates the fine counsel of his theological colleague and friend,

James R. Price III, and of his former theological student Pamela Hill Park; and he is also grateful for the efficacious clerical work of John Maki, his student research assistant.

Without the extensive and enduring support of our spouses, Ruth Musser and Bonnie Price, this volume would not have been possible. They worked "our" way through graduate school, reared children with us, forged careers of their own, and provided us the freedom to nurture our personal and professional friendship that has born this volume.

To our theological mentors throughout the past two millennia.
To our theological colleagues and collaborators during the past quarter of a century.
To inquiring theological students in the next decade.

CONTENTS

PREFACE

As one of the standard resources for theological education during the last three decades, *A Handbook of Christian Theologians*, edited by Martin Marty and Dean Peerman, introduced a generation of students to theologians whose voices and visions had shaped the midcentury course of Christian theology. Since its initial publication the current of theology has taken new directions, diverging into several distinct streams. Although various works and series of separate texts have occasionally sought to present essays about sets of current theologians, and although an enlarged edition of the Marty and Peerman volume appeared more than a decade ago, we have sensed the need to provide a more expansive volume focusing on the shapers of Christian theology at the turn of the millennium.

The earlier Marty and Peerman collection will continue to be a viable resource because the persons whom it considers—Friedrich Schleiermacher and Søren Kierkegaard, Albrecht Ritschl and Adolf von Harnack, Rudolf Bultmann, Teilhard de Chardin, among others—are identified with main currents of Protestant and Roman Catholic thought in this century. Christian theology has proliferated beyond the liberal, neoorthodox, neothomist, and conservative camps that had dominated the European and North American models and concerns through the middle of this century. From groups whose issues and perspectives had often been ignored or suppressed by the predominantly white, male group of theologians, new voices have begun to clarify, articulate, and direct expressions of Christian thought. In recent years, the flow of Christian theology has been channeled in diverse streams of thought represented by such trends and movements as black theology, liberation theology, feminist theology, and womanist theology—all of which have sprung forth since the publication of the Marty and Peerman handbook.

Some familiar names do not appear in the roster of theologians who are treated in this volume. In some cases, because of the usual limits imposed on length, representatives of the various traditions and trends in developing Christian theology had to be selected. In other cases, authoritative contributors could not make commitments to write about important figures. And regrettably, in still other cases, such as the anticipated essay on Bernard Lonergan, contracted authors had to withdraw from the project at such a late date that publication had to move forward without substitutions.

Because Christian theology has become so diverse in its expressions, the issue arises, of course, as to whether or not Christian theology as a unified "discipline" or discourse continues to exist in the multifarious forms that distinguish it (often so radically) from its sources. But even as the powerful and ancient current of the Mississippi River splits and spreads out to empty effectively into the Gulf of Mexico, so too the testimonies of various Christian theologians pursue a common goal—to make sense of their experience of divine revelation and human hope.

Perhaps Christian theology no longer can be identified with the single channel of a mighty river coursing toward its mouth; instead, Christian theology might be compared to the separate, rich repositories of silt in a delta created by the diverging channels of distributaries as they pursue the common goal of emptying into the sea. The very presence and richness of the delta deposits result from their soil having been transported by the river itself. In a like manner, the divergent courses created by current Christian theologians draw their power from the traditional stream of Christian theology that has fed them, even as they distinctly and separately course toward the single sea.

One of the possible ways to survey the delta of current Christian theology is to navigate the streams through which its identity is shaped—to examine the theologies of representative theologians. In that regard, we have identified various routes for reading, in part to offer alternate ways to utilize this resource and also to suggest the possibility of undertaking a preliminary exploration of comparative Christian theologies. To facilitate this possible exploration, we have identified several common themes or issues within many of the essays, thus demarcating such recurrent concerns as the ways in which the theologians consider the sources and goals for theology, their variant assumptions and conclusions about the nature of God, their divergent approaches to understanding the person and purpose of the Christ, and their distinct expectations for the destiny of history and faith.

Joseph L. Price
Donald W. Musser
January 1996

ROUTES FOR READING

In today's fermentive and eclectic theological context, readers may be helped by some routing guidelines as they peruse the essays in this book. To some extent all maps of the theological terrain distort as well as clarify. We therefore provide these "routes" with some apprehension, knowing that in many cases the categories are fluid.

One can locate the essays according to the geographic region in which the theologian works, the ecclesial tradition of the theologian, and the theological family with which the theologian is identified. Geographic location may provide some clues to the cultural context in which an author writes. The ecclesial tradition locates the theologian within a church, and the theological family identifies the theological rubric or rubrics by which some people designate the author's thought.

Geographical Region

North America—Altizer, Bloesch, Cobb, Cone, Daly, Dulles, Frei, Gilkey, Griffin, Gustafson, Hartshorne, Henry, Hick, Hodgson, Isasi-Diaz, Kaufman, Lindbeck, McFague, Merton, Meyendorff, Neville, H. R. Niebuhr, Reinhold Niebuhr, Oden, Ogden, Ruether, Taylor, Thurman, Tillich, Tracy, van Buren, West

Latin America—Boff, Gutiérrez, Segundo, Sobrino

Europe—Barth, Berdyaev, Bonhoeffer, Brunner, Ebeling, Jüngel, Küng, Pannenberg, Rahner, Schillebeeckx, Tillich, Torrance, von Balthasar

Asia and Africa—Asian Theologians (Koyama, Minjung theology, Pieris, Samartha, Song), Panikkar, Tutu

Ecclesial Tradition

Roman Catholic—Boff, Dulles, Küng, Merton, Rahner, Ruether, Schillebeeckx, Tracy, von Balthasar

Eastern Orthodox—Berdyaev, Meyendorff

Reformed/Presbyterian—Barth, Bloesch, Moltmann, H. R. Niebuhr, Reinhold Niebuhr, Torrance

Lutheran—Bonhoeffer, Ebeling, Lindbeck, Pannenberg, Tillich

Free Church—Gilkey, Henry, Kaufman

Wesleyan/Methodist—Cobb, Griffin, Hodgson, Neville, Oden, Ogden

Ecumenical—Gilkey, Gustafson, Lindbeck, Moltmann, Tracy, Pannenberg, Panikkar

Episcopal—Frei, Tutu, van Buren

Theological Family

Barthian—Barth, Bloesch, Frei, Jüngel, Küng, Torrance

Black—Cone, Thurman, Tutu, West, Womanist Theologians (Grant, Williams)

Deconstructive—Altizer, Daly, Taylor

Ecological—Cobb, Gustafson, McFague, Moltmann, Ruether

Evangelical—Bloesch, Henry, Oden

Feminist—Daly, Isasi-Diaz, McFague, Ruether, Womanist Theologians (Grant, Williams)

Liberation—Asian Theologians, Boff, Cone, Daly, Grant, Gutiérrez, Isasi-Diaz, McFague, Ruether, Segundo, Sobrino, Song, Tutu, West, Womanist Theologians (Grant, Williams)

Minjung—Asian Theologians

Mujerista—Isasi-Diaz

Narrative—Frei, Lindbeck, Ricoeur

Neoorthodox—Barth, Bonhoeffer, Brunner, H. R. Niebuhr, Reinhold Niebuhr, Tillich

Philosophical—Cobb, Griffin, Hartshorne, Hodgson, Neville, Ogden, Rahner, Ricoeur, Taylor

Pluralistic—Asian Theologians (Koyama, Minjung theology, Pieris, Samartha, Song), Hick, Panikkar

Post-Holocaust—Küng, Moltmann, van Buren

Postliberal—Frei, Lindbeck, Oden

Postmodern—Altizer, Daly, Neville, Taylor

Process—Cobb, Griffin, Hartshorne, Ogden

Public—Gilkey, Ogden, Tracy, West

Systematic—Barth, Bloesch, Brunner, Cobb, Ebeling, Gilkey, Gutiérrez, Henry, Küng, Moltmann, Ogden, Pannenberg, Ruether, Torrance, van Buren

Womanist—Womanist Theologians (Grant, Williams)

THOMAS J. J. ALTIZER
1927–

Life and Career

Thomas Jonathan Jackson Altizer was born in Cambridge, Massachusetts, in 1927 and grew up in Charlottesville, Virginia. After briefly attending St. John's College in Annapolis, Maryland, he went to the University of Chicago where he received the A.B. in 1948, the A.M. (with a thesis on Augustine) in 1951, and the Ph.D. (with a thesis on Greek and Eastern religious philosophy) in 1955. After teaching at Wabash College (1954–1956), he moved to Emory University where he remained until 1968, serving as Professor of Bible and Religion as well as teaching in the Institute of Liberal Arts and the Graduate Division of Religion.

It was during this time that the distinctive themes of Altizer's radical theology came to initial expression. His book *Oriental Mysticism and Biblical Prophecy* (1961) launched a dialogue with Buddhism that continues to characterize his work, and *Mircea Eliade and the Dialectic of the Sacred* (1963) makes clear both that Eliade is for Altizer the principle "theologian" of archaic religion and, as such, also the one who brings to expression the religious perspective that is transcended by biblical perspectives. Already in these books Altizer regards the work of the Christian theologian as properly engaged in the clarification of the distinctiveness of biblical religions (Judaism, Christianity, and Islam) over against the archaic "other" of "primitive" religions and the contemporary "other" of Buddhism.

Although many of the themes of his radical theology come to expression in these books, the publication of *The Gospel of Christian Atheism* and of the essays collected in *Radical Theology and the Death of God* (both in 1966) brought his views to scholarly and public attention. At first the popular and scholarly discussion linked him with other radical theologians like Gabriel Vahanian, Paul van Buren, and William Hamilton as the "death of God movement." But it became increasingly clear that Altizer was moving in a way that distinguished him from them. The central difference is the way in which the "death of God" is, for Altizer, the affirmation of loyalty to the Christian gospel and is by no means either a temporary slogan or a resignation from the tasks of a specifically Christian theology.

The "death of God controversy" raged furiously for a time, especially in the religious climate of the South. Although Emory withstood the demand for Altizer's removal from its faculty, he accepted a position at the State University of New York at Stony Brook in 1968 as Professor of English after his publication of *The New Apocalypse: The Radical Christian Vision of William Blake* (1967). Although his position there has sometimes included religion or, more recently, "Comparative Studies," he remains one of the few outstanding theologians who are neither ordained nor teach in a confessional context or even in a department of religion. Despite this anomaly, Altizer's theological work has continued to deepen and develop. On the one hand, he has continued to teach introduction to the Bible, and his work continues to be an attempt to devise a theological language that is at once biblical and current (see *The Self-Embodiment of God,* 1977). On the other hand, his immersion in the study of literature, especially the tradition of epic poetry, has funded some of his deepest insights into Western imagination and sensibility. Although Blake remains a pivotal figure in all of his subsequent work, Altizer has also engaged in a growing discussion of Milton, Dante, and James Joyce (*History as Apocalypse,* 1985). Altizer's theology, then, is characterized as a reflection on poetic vision as the place where the experience of modernity most decisively comes to expression.

Theological Voice and Poetic Vision

But Altizer does not restrict himself either to biblical voices or to poetic visions in his attempt to develop a theological perspective appropriate for our time. His theology may also be understood as a profound appropriation and transformation of Hegel, above all in his determination to view history as the history of God (*Genesis and Apocalypse,* 1990). This appropriation of a Hegelian perspective and style makes Altizer's work challenging reading, for the tracing of oppositions that negate themselves and move forward by a process of self-negation means that a simple expository prose is rejected in favor of a dialectical style that requires great concentration on the part of writer and reader alike. In his attempt to think the divine, Altizer aligns himself with a history of "pure thinking" with antecedents in Jakob Böhme and Meister Eckhart, in Spinoza and Hegel, in Kierkegaard and Nietzsche. Hence, Altizer's style is often characterized as prophetic, poetic, mystical, or incantatory, as well as speculative and dialectical.

Another way to try to locate the theology of Altizer is to connect it with perhaps better-known theological orientations in the twentieth century. Like several contemporary theologians, Altizer supposes that theism is no longer a possible way for thinking about God. In this way he is joined with others who would regard themselves as atheists. Unlike most of these, however, Altizer supposes that atheism is or should be Christian, that is, grounded in the biblical witness to the God who negates Godself in Christ. Like Kierkegaard and the early Barth, Altizer supposes that Christian theology attempts to think Christian faith through a subversion of Christendom. Like Barth, Altizer's theology may be said to be christocentric to the point of "Christomonism," but without entailing the proposal of a sectarian Christianity in correspondence to the revelation of a transcendent God. Instead, Altizer's "Christomonism" must mean the dissolution of separate Christian identity in correspondence with the full immanence of God.

For Altizer, the task of theology is above all the attempt to reflect adequately on the character of God. No theologian of the modern period has so sharply focused upon the question of God as has Altizer. This concentration on the subject of God or the Godhead means that Altizer has not engaged in a reflection on the church or on "social issues" or on a range of Christian doctrines. His entire concern is to find a way to speak adequately and clearly about God from the standpoint of the current epoch as the epoch in which God has disappeared as an object of cultural consciousness.

God in Christ

But it is not simply an anonymous divinity or sacred reality that is at the center of Altizer's reflection; rather, it is specifically the Christian God, which is to say, the God who is fully in Christ, the God who becomes flesh, who speaks and who is crucified in Jesus. Altizer's "christomonistic" theology accepts the supposition that God is, without remainder, in Christ. Indeed this is the basic and literal meaning of the death of God, since Altizer supposes that God has not only entered into history in Christ but has done so irreversibly and irrevocably and without remainder. In this connection Altizer is deeply suspicious of trinitarian frameworks that provide the possibility of asserting a remainder of the divine that escapes the fate or avoids the commitment of incarnation and death. His view is closer in this respect to the ancient patripassian or Sabellian perspectives, or to the late-medieval speculations of Joachim of Fiore. In Altizer's view the development of orthodox views of God and Christ may best be understood as a subversion of the radical nature of the primitive Christian gospel; and they are subversive precisely in their attempt to affirm the transcendence of God after the incarnation and death of God in Christ.

Essential to Altizer's project is the attempt to link the basic Christian affirmation of incarnation and crucifixion with the experience today of the absence, disappearance, or "death of God" in such a way that the situation now is the consequence of the action of God in Christ, a consequence that works itself out in the course of Western history and consciousness through a complex but intelligible process of subversions, reversals, and negations. Tracing this history involves Altizer in the attempt to discern in the intellectual and cultural history of the West the traces of the evolving realization of God's determination to be present in Christ in such a way as to negate the transcendent otherness or separateness of God. Hence, Altizer reflects on biblical language, the achievement of Augustine, and the emergence, from Aquinas and Dante forward, of the distinctively modern world, which is even yet coming to ever greater awareness of the apocalyptic character of reality.

The Self-Negation of God

In this view the basic character of God is God's act or decision, an act which may best be understood as an act of self-negation. This act is indeed the "genesis" of God in the sense that God distinguishes Godself from a quiescent nothingness (such as that which is the subject of Buddhist reflection). This act of negation is the act of genesis in which God becomes God and so is the genesis of world as well. This act of self-differentiation continues in the act of revelation in which, by coming to speech as I AM, God negates an original silence. The revelation of the divine I AM is at the same time the constitution of Israel as a historical subject and so is the beginning of history itself as an irreversible forward movement in which the eternal return of archaic religion becomes impossible.

This same act of self-negation is decisively actualized within history by the incarnation of God in Christ, an incarnation that becomes "word" in the worldly speech of Jesus concerning the kingdom of God (*Total Presence,* 1980); the incarnation also becomes the self-annihilation of the divine in the crucifixion and resurrection of Christ (understood as one event as in Paul and John). Altizer notes that the image of the cross disappears in postbiblical Christianity, only gradually reappearing in medieval art, and becoming the explicit theme of theological reflection only with Luther and of philosophical reflection with Hegel and, ultimately, Nietzsche.

In the New Testament the event of incarnation, cross, and resurrection is understood as occurring within an apocalyptic horizon, meaning that it entails the end of world as world and of God as God. This apocalyptic end produces self-consciousness (in Paul) as a divided consciousness in which the person stands riven by the division between the two eons of a "before" and an "after," and as a consciousness that is both flesh and spirit, both bound and free. Altizer regards this self-consciousness as the first aftereffect of the self-annihilation of the divine. Although the apocalyptic horizon recedes in Christianity after Paul, the consciousness of self as a divided self reappears in Augustine's recognition of the freedom and the bondage of the will. This "dichotomous" self is the ground of an interior awareness of the self that is characteristic of Western Christian culture coming to expression in modernity in Rembrandt and Dostoyevsky. But late modernity sees a growing disappearance of this interiority in art (Picasso) and literature (Beckett) and so a coming to an end (apocalypse) of the distinctive form of Western Christian selfhood.

Linked to the reemergence of a dichotomous selfhood and so of a Christian interiority in Augustine is also the reemergence of an apparent dualism of good and evil in the will of God through the doctrines of providence and, especially, double predestination. Biblical language increasingly posits Satan as the "other" of God. But the insistence on reconstituting the transcendence of God characteristic of nonapocalyptic Christianity ends by attributing all that occurs to the eternal will of God, including the ultimate evil of final damnation. The emergence of modernity witnesses the logical triumph of this dichotomous divine will (as in Calvin and Zwingli). The vigorous portrait of Satan in Milton and the identification of Satan with the transcendent creator (Urizen) in Blake signify the rebirth of an apocalyptic consciousness that both repudiates the divine transcendence of Christendom and affirms the divine immanence of Jesus and the kingdom of God. In late modernity both the divine and the demonic become fully immanent historical realities (Joyce), unleashing not only apocalyptic hope but also the full horror of our history. In a sense, then, Altizer views the horrors of our history as a consequence of the divine act of self-negation and so as analogous to the damnation that is the necessary complement to, or antecedent condition of, complete redemption.

Altizer's reading of Western history is thus a reading of the traces of the positing and overcoming of dichotomy in the direction of the apocalypse that was announced and enacted in Jesus and whose goal is God's becoming "all in all." Increasingly this world-historical process of the realization of the act of God in Christ takes place outside and over against Christendom; hence the importance of the "heretical" tradition of Eckhart and Böhme, of Spinoza, Hegel, and Nietzsche, of Dante, Milton, Blake, and Joyce. But it is not only within such presumably heretical perspectives that Altizer traces the realization of the self-negation of God, for Augustine, Aquinas, Luther, and Barth play significant roles in this history as well.

Apocalypse and the Kingdom of God

What is the goal of this process? The biblical symbols for the end of the world or its consummation are apocalypse and kingdom of God, both of which Altizer discerns as the emerging reality of our time. Yet it is undeniably more difficult to see where we are going than to see where we have been. Thus a few decisive characteristics of our time may be all that can be clearly represented here. The modern period is to be understood as apocalypse, which is above all the end of God as a separate or speakable transcendence. This apocalypse occurs in several realms of our experience. With the emergence of the Newtonian world, God no longer stands over against the world as its other. Indeed for Newton it was possible to speak of God as the infinite extension of space or the world, but increasingly it is the infinity of the universe alone that we can name. Similarly, our political history is increasingly a history of revolution in which the absolute ground or basis of the political ordering of the world disappears, at least since the French Revolution. In literature we are confronted not only with the disappearance of the divine subject but also, increasingly, of a human interior subject. Indeed all the arts bear witness to the disappearance of the human face and interiority.

In important respects the period of late modernity may be understood as the triumph of nihilism, a time during which the power of nothingness spreads throughout the imagination (Kafka, Beckett), during which science itself describes the order of chaos (the aggregate of indeterminacy), and during which history opens out to a seemingly chaotic mixture of unspeakable horrors and of celebrative affirmations.

Altizer regards the attempt to speak meaningfully of faith within this nihilistic world as a decided risk or gamble. Often his language emphasizes the unlikelihood of finding a way to speak of faith that is decisively Christian faith within this context. This search is all the more difficult precisely because Altizer rejects the sectarian tendency to speak of Christian faith apart from or over against this world of late modernity. Rather, he is determined to see precisely this world as the consummation of the act of God and so as apocalypse. It is then a world in which the God who is love is wholly immanent, without reserve or remainder, and thus given over to death. But the death of God that is now appearing in our history and culture and experience is the same death that Christianity has seen to be good news and thus redemption for the world. To be sure, this redemption has always been inseparable from damnation. And it cannot be denied that damnation has in all too many ways become an immanent reality within our historical world. But just for that reason the radical Christian knows intimations not only of hope but also of joy. For the realization of the kingdom of God occurs within the uttermost darkness and chaos, but is itself light and joy.

The symbol of the kingdom of God permits Altizer to anticipate the complete immanence of God within the everyday world of everyone, a world in which the alienation and estrangement of the historical subject is ever more overcome. The way to that consummation cannot by any means short-circuit the nothingness and darkness that is the path through which immanence is accomplished, any more than there can be a resurrection that is not first and foremost crucifixion.

Conclusion

One of the most remarkable features of Altizer's theology is the way in which, despite its emphatic focus on the theme of God and its essential continuity with ideas already announced in his earliest publications, it has continued to develop in subtlety and complexity. His wager that it is possible to think of God in connection with the history of the emergence and dissolution of Western Christian consciousness and to clarify this thinking about God and dissolution through a continuing comparison with other religious traditions continues to produce fresh insight and vigorous reformulation.

The radical theology of Altizer may not seem congenial to persons who wish to engage in theology as a churchly, or in his terms, sectarian enterprise; nor will it appeal to persons who wish theology to pronounce directly on the moral or political quandaries of our time. But in its single-minded insistence that the chief task of theology is to *think God*, and that the chief task of Christian theology is to *think God in Christ* and to do so resolutely and radically, Altizer's theology continues to be both fruitful and provocative.

Theodore W. Jennings, Jr.

Selected Primary Works

1961   *Oriental Mysticism and Biblical Eschatology.*
1962   *Truth, Myth, and Symbol,* ed. Altizer, William A. Beardslee, and J. Harvey Young.
1963   *Mircea Eliade and the Dialectic of the Sacred.*
1966   *Radical Theology and the Death of God,* ed. Altizer and William Hamilton.
1966   *The Gospel of Christian Atheism.*
1967   *The New Apocalypse: The Radical Christian Vision of William Blake.*
1970   *The Descent into Hell.*
1977   *The Self-Embodiment of God.*
1980   *Total Presence: The Language of Jesus and the Language of Today.*
1985   *History as Apocalypse.*
1990   *Genesis and Apocalypse: A Theological Voyage Toward Authentic Christianity.*
1993   *The Genesis of God: A Theological Genealogy.*

Selected Secondary Sources

1970   John B. Cobb, Jr., ed., *The Theology of Altizer: Critique and Response.*
1982   Thomas J. J. Altizer, ed., *Deconstruction and Theology.*
1990   R. P. Scharlemann, ed., *Theology at the End of the Century.*

ASIAN THEOLOGIANS

Kosuke Koyama, Minjung Theology, Aloysius Pieris,
Stanley J. Samartha, Choan Seng Song

Introduction

Writing about "Asian" theologies and "Asian" theologians is problematic in many ways. First is the problem of definition: What counts as an "Asian" theology? Anything written by an Asian? If so, we run into an irony because most of what is written by Asian theologians 'today still remains largely European and North American in its approach and content, a more or less faithful reproduction of the contents, issues, and methodologies of Western theology. It is Asian by author but Western by spirit and content. On the other hand, a growing minority of theologians are not only Asian by origin but also by theological content and approach, and they consciously try to draw their inspiration from Asian sources and to "theologize" in the specific context of Asian cultures and problems. In this essay the designation "Asian theologians" refers precisely to this vocal, creative, and increasingly influential minority of Asian theologians.

A second problem is that of the selection of representative Asian theologians. Although Asian theology has not yet been as productive or creative as Western theology, it has been developing rather rapidly since the 1960s as more and more Asian theologians, originally trained in the West, turn their creative talents to the challenge of constructing Christian theologies in specifically Asian contexts. A number of Asian theologians have received international recognition. Also a new generation of theologians who were trained in the emerging pluralist and liberationist theological culture of the late 1970s and 1980s is now coming to theological maturity. Given the limits of space, this essay discusses five pioneers of specifically Asian theologies of the older generation: Kosuke Koyama, Minjung theology, Aloysius Pieris, Stanley J. Samartha, and Choan Seng Song. The theologians included have been chosen not only for the significance of their theological achievements but also for their accessibility to English-speaking readers. (The author's hope is that the next edition of this *Handbook* would include many of those of the older generation not included here as well as many of the emerging voices of the new generation, especially women.)

A third problem is that of heterogeneity. One would not normally even think of including Barth, Balthasar, Tillich, Rahner, Schillebeeckx, Küng, Moltmann, Cobb, Pannenberg, Tracy, and others all in one essay under the one heading of "Western" theology, not only because their productivity requires separate treatments but also because they are different in their theological methods, contents, and issues, even though all of them write within the orbit of a common Western culture. Asia, however, has no common culture or common religion in the sense in which Christianity has been the common religion of the West. From Palestine (remember, this too is part of Asia) to Central Asia to Indonesia, there is no culture, religion, or *lingua franca* common to them all (ironically, English comes closest to this). At best, we may divide the continent into spheres of different religions, such as Islam, Hinduism, Buddhism, Confucianism, and others. Asia is a continent of a bewildering plurality of races, nations, religions, languages, and inherited problems, and thus also a pluralism of specifically different contexts and challenges to the Christian theologian. It is completely misleading, therefore, to speak of Asian theology in the singular. This essay does not hope to do justice to this heterogeneity of continental size; instead, it seeks to focus on five countries, each with its own contextual challenge: Sri Lanka, India, Japan, Korea, and China.

Kosuke Koyama

1929–

Kosuke Koyama, Professor of Ecumenics and World Christianity at the Union Theological Seminary in New York City since 1980, received the B.D. from Drew University and the Ph.D. from Princeton Theological Seminary. He served as a Japanese Kyodan missionary to the Church of Christ in Thailand from 1960 to 1968, a period during which he taught theology at Thailand Theological Seminary in Chiengmai. From 1968 to 1974, then, he worked as Director of the Association of Theological Schools in Southeast Asia and Dean of the South East Asia Graduate School of Theology, Singapore, from which he went on to teach at the University of Otago in Dunedin, New Zealand, for six years, until his appointment at the Union Theological Seminary in 1980.

His chief works include *Waterbuffalo Theology* (1974) and *Mount Fuji and Mount Sinai: A Critique of Idols* (1984). One of the most traveled theologians of our time, Koyama acknowledges that his theology has been shaped by two experiences, the devastation of Tokyo and Hiroshima in 1945 and his many years of missionary immersion in the multireligious realities of Asia. By means of short biblical and theological meditations full of perceptive intercultural insights and earthy metaphors, Koyama has offered a sustained reflection on the problem of Asian contextual theology, the relation between Christianity and other Asian

23

religions, the theological significance of modernization and technology, and Japanese imperialism, all from the unifying perspective of a theology of the cross, which is also a theology of history.

For Koyama, who rejects all purely intellectualist, academic approaches to theology, theology is authentic only when it is historically relevant to the particularities of its setting in life. Theology should begin not by digesting Western theologians, but by raising issues present in a situation. Theology is possible only as contextual theology. Every theology is a "particular orbit theology"—theology from the perspective of a particular culture and incarnated in its particularities. It is not possible to have raw Christ unseasoned with the "salt" and "pepper" of a particular culture. The only question is what kind of salt and pepper are and should be seasoning Christ. Theology is situated in the dialectic of the Word of God and the culture of a people, which it is essential to know and appreciate on its own terms.

According to Koyama, contextualization means more than indigenization of the gospel in a traditional culture; it also means coming to grips with the challenges of secularity, technology, and the struggle for human rights and social justice. Furthermore, it must carefully distinguish between an authentic form of contextualization, which consists in being rooted in a given historical moment yet also seeking critical, prophetic transformation of the situation, and an inauthentic form, which consists in an uncritical accommodation of the status quo. Contextualization means "letting theology speak in and through that context." This critical, authentic contextualization is not possible except through the cross, by participating in the crosses of the context, just as the cross was God's way of participating in human history.

Theology becomes truly Asian theology when it bears the marks of Jesus in the depths of Asian hearts and Asian kidneys. Asian theology is possible only as the theology of Asian crosses, only as the theology of those crucified and suffering like the servant of Isaiah 53 in the building up of Asian communities. A Chinese theology, for example, is not a matter of recasting theology in Confucian categories from Neoplatonic categories, which would make the work of indigenization and contextualization easy; it means "the emergence of theological work engaged in by a Chinese crucified mind" (*Waterbuffalo Theology*, 1974, p. 24).

An Asian contextual theology must come to grips with the theological significance of the legacy of Western colonialism and modernization. For Koyama, the West has been both destructive "gun" and healing "ointment" in Asia, the former in the sense of colonial exploitation and disruption of Asian culture; the latter in the sense of modernization. Although an ambiguous mixture of good and evil, modernization brought about an emancipation of humanity from toil and suffering and gave humanity a sense of confidence in the human ability to change history, as in Gandhi's movement in India and Mao's proletarian revolution in China. It also produced much technological destruction. The role of the Christian mission, while repenting of its complicity in the colonial exploitation of Asia, is to discern the positive aspects of modernization, especially historical consciousness, ameliorate them with the oil of God's judgment and salvation, and let the ointments of modernization participate in the unfolding history of God's own mission in the world in the form of the crucified One. The Christian mission is not to "Christianize" secular movements but rather to participate in them with the sensibility of God's judgment and hope.

The whole of Koyama's theology is a theology of the cross. His peculiar emphasis in this theology is on the fact that the cross, unlike lunchboxes, has no handle: It cannot be controlled or manipulated. The crucified mind is a mind shaken by the power of God coming from the crucified Lord, and it renounces all control and manipulation, unlike the crusading, aggressive mind whose sole interest is in controlling and conquering others. Christians are to follow the crucified Christ, his self-denial and service for others. In this regard, crusading for Christ is most unchristian. Christians should not call other religions inferior and Christianity superior, not only because there is no objective measure to rank different religions, but also because the "finality" of Christ is that of someone who has been spat upon, mocked, and crucified. It is not triumphant but "crucified finality." It therefore sees God's presence in religions other than Christianity; it sees God's presence, for example, in the common emphases of Honen and Shinran on human depravity and in the mercy and grace of the Buddha.

In this regard, Koyama's indictment of Christian triumphalism is noteworthy. The cross of Christ is the form of God's participation in history, and in failing to follow the crucified Christ, Christianity has also failed to be truly historical, despite its traditional claim that it is historically based while nonbiblical religions are not. Asian Christianity has failed to immerse itself in the sufferings of its people and be spat upon. Asian Christians have been taught to depart from their own historical and cultural contexts, becoming cultural monsters in their own countries and becoming alienated from their own traditions. A truly historical Christianity would have listened to the stories of Asian peoples more seriously. Instead, Christianity suffers from a teacher complex: It seeks to teach but does not want to learn from Asian peoples.

In refusing to become flesh in Asia, this militant Christianity has become docetic. Ignoring God's universal love and impartiality regarding religions, triumphalistic Christianity fails to see the historical efforts that Buddhists make precisely in order to achieve "detachment from history." It sees history from the perspective of self-assertiveness, not self-denial. It is no wonder, therefore, that Christianity has not really listened to the people during the last four hundred years, listening instead to its bishops, theologians, and financial sponsors ten thousand miles away. In fact, for Koyama, "that the Christ crucified is seen as the Christ crucifying is the most serious missiological problem today in Asia" (*No Handle on the Cross*, 1977, p. 109).

The problem of technology is not a problem of technology per se, but that of the relation between human greed and human meaning. Technology is not intrinsically destructive; but it becomes destructive when placed at the service of efficient greed, which has no moral compunction about exploiting others, impoverishing and destroying the meaning of human life. Under the pressure of greed, persons are constantly tempted to subjugate meaning to efficiency, creating the demonic and producing dehumanization. Today persons are confronted with a choice between "demonic" efficiency (which is technological efficiency pursued for its own sake) and "crucified" efficiency (which is efficiency subordinated to meaning, the paradoxical efficiency of God, who moves only "three miles an hour," and of Christ nailed to the cross). Only the efficiency of the crucified Lord will free persons from the obsession with technological efficiency, provide the antidote against the demonic, and enable them to discern how God's purpose is fulfilled in and through the universal technological civilization.

In one of his most celebrated symbolic typologies, Koyama contrasts Mount Fuji and Mount Sinai, Asian and biblical spiritualities, again using the theology of the cross as a way of transcending the excesses of both. Fuji stands for the cosmological, natural orientation toward reality with its emphasis on continuity and harmony, where help is expected from "heaven and earth" or the immanent operations of the cosmos itself, while Sinai stands for the eschatological, historical orientation toward reality with its emphasis on discontinuity between God and humanity, where help is expected from beyond the cosmological, from the "maker" of heaven and earth. The cosmological orientation places continuity over discontinuity, *chronos* over *kairos,* space over time, cosmology over eschatology, the beauty and productivity of the whole of nature over those of its parts.

Each orientation has its own temptation. Without a transcendent basis of historical critique, the temptation of the cosmological is to subordinate all things to a principle of totality embodied in the nation or a person such as the emperor and thus to produce ultranationalist ideologies and imperial cults. The temptation of the eschatological is to take the name of God in vain and fall into self-idolatry. Thus, cosmological Shinto Japan and eschatological Christian Germany found themselves on the same side in World War II. Only the theology of the cross provides a criterion by which one can make a distinction between true God and false gods. The cosmological embraces persons, the eschatological confronts believers, but in a theology of the cross, the eschatological embraces its followers. The crucified Christ exposes and judges the subtle manifestations of idolatry in both types of spiritualities.

Selected Primary Works

1974   *Waterbuffalo Theology.*
1974   *Pilgrim or Tourist?* (also published as *Fifty Meditations,* 1979).
1977   *No Handle on the Cross: An Asian Meditation on the Crucified Mind.*
1980   *Three Mile an Hour God: Biblical Reflections.*
1984   *Mount Fuji and Mount Sinai: A Critique of Idols.*

Minjung Theology

One of the most provocative and controversial of recent theologies, Minjung theology is an independent theological movement originating in South Korea and centered on the theme of *minjung* or people. Its representatives include Byung Mu Ahn (b. 1922), educated at Heidelberg; Nam Dong Suh (1918–1984) of Immanuel College, Canada; Kwang Sun Suh (b. 1931) of Vanderbilt; Young Hak Hyun (b. 1921) from the Union Theological Seminary in New York; Hee Suk Moon (b. 1933) of Emory; and Yong Bock Kim (b. 1938) from Princeton Theological Seminary. *Minjung* theology was born and has matured during the two decades of popular struggles for human rights and social justice under a succession of repressive military regimes since the early 1970s.

Like many of the Latin American liberation theologians, many minjung theologians suffered imprisonment, torture, and dismissal from their academic positions. In addition to the impact of liberation and political theologies, personal participation in the suffering of the *minjung,* especially workers and farmers brutally exploited and displaced during the decades of intensive, planned industrialization, awakened the theologians to the fundamental inadequacy of traditional Western theology and the urgency of a radically new theology that could speak to the new *kairos* in Korea. Like other Asian theologians in this survey, minjung theologians are fiercely critical of Western imperialism and colonialism, both political and theological, deeply disturbed about the ideological role of the established churches in the maintenance of the repressive status quo, and intensely concerned with the development of an independent theology that would be both authentically Korean and prophetic in articulating the perspective of suffering *minjung*.

One of the most crucial and controversial aspects of this theology concerns the very definition of its ruling category, *minjung. Min* means "people," and *jung* means "crowd," "masses," or "multitude." In the context of minjung theology, *minjung* refers to the inclusive category of those who are politically oppressed, economically exploited, culturally deprived, and in general socially alienated and marginalized. As an inclusive category, it must be distinguished from the Marxian "proletariat," which is an economic category. *Minjung* includes not only the working class but also the farmers and other socially marginalized people. As a socially critical category, it must be distinguished from the politically neutral category of "people," as well as from the liberal democratic category of "citizens." It is likewise different from "crowd" or "masses," which is a socially neutral category. As an active political category, *minjung* is also to be distinguished from the North Korean concept of *juche* or the collective subjectivity of the people; the latter is something imposed on the people from above, while *minjung* ceases to be itself when it is not determining itself.

As a critical political category, *minjung* refers to the totality of oppressed, exploited, and alienated peoples precisely in their contradiction to the existing order and its ruling class and therefore in their potential or actual role as subjects of history capable of liberating themselves. As a dynamic, changing, and complex reality, *minjung* includes the subjective, experiential dimension of the oppressed and marginalized in their struggles and sufferings, their triumphs and defeats.

The defining experience of *minjung* in their subjectivity is called *han*, perhaps most powerfully described by the poet Chi Ha Kim. It is the feeling of outrage at blatant injustice, the sense of helplessness to vindicate oneself, the awareness, however indeterminate, of the moral contradictions and inequities of the existing social structure, and the tenacious hope, often suppressed into resignation, in the ultimate triumph of justice. For Koreans, long subjected to foreign invasions and domestic oppressions, *minjung* has expressed the cumulative history of *han* and their cries for the resolution of that *han*. The challenge has been how to resolve this *han* of the *minjung* in a way that does not tranquilize their consciousness like an opium, promote destructive masochism, or perpetuate the vicious circle of hatred and revenge, but channels the energy of the suppressed anger and indignation toward constructive liberating praxis through religious commitment and spiritual transformation.

The task of theology, according to minjung theologians, is precisely to meet this challenge. The overriding issue is not sin as traditional theology insists but *han* and how to resolve it. Sin has been defined from above by the ruling classes and has become an ideological mask that covers up the reality of oppressions and injustices. The concept of *han*, defined from below in terms of the *minjung*'s own experience of oppression, serves as a critical counterpart to the concept of sin.

This central task of theology also defines its method. For minjung theologians, as for other Asian theologians, theology is a reflection on praxis for the sake of praxis; it is never a theory for its own sake, a speculation divorced from life, a theology based on other theologies. It is self-consciously situated in the *minjung*'s struggle for liberation from *han* and to establish justice in society. It reflects on such struggles in light of the biblical tradition. Its method, therefore, includes political hermeneutics to disclose God's liberating presence in the struggles of the *minjung*, as well as reliance on telling stories about their *han*.

The biblical basis of minjung theology, like that of liberation theologies in general, remains the Exodus event and the events of the crucifixion and resurrection of Jesus as paradigms of God's liberating action in history, which also defines who God is. The God of the Bible is not an object of philosophical speculation divorced from life and concrete history, with its endemic tendencies to the dualism of eternal and temporal, sacred and profane. The biblical God reveals Godself in concrete history, in the midst of its contradictions and tensions. Prior to the human and ecclesial mission in the world, God has already been engaged in God's own mission of liberating the oppressed with a preferential love, and the Christian mission is to participate in that mission. This liberating *missio Dei* undercuts all the traditional dualisms including that of church and society to the extent that God's mission is not the monopoly of the Christian churches. In this regard, Nam Dong Suh highlights the role of the Holy Spirit as the universal, eschatological, liberating presence of God beyond the borders of Christian history. The Spirit is at work whenever and wherever selfishness is transcended and the existing order is eschatologically renewed.

Minjung theologians generally do not have much use for speculative doctrines, whether trinitarian or christological. Just as God is more an "event" of liberation in history than a philosophical theory, so Jesus is more an "event" of liberation among the *minjung* than an abstract metaphysical doctrine. The entire emphasis of minjung theology is on the historical, human Jesus, the suffering servant in his concrete solidarity with the outcast of society, and on his crucifixion and resurrection as the paradigmatic events of liberation. Nam Dong Suh goes so far as to say that Jesus is himself the means for understanding *minjung*, not that *minjung* is the conceptual means for understanding Jesus. In any event, the point is to appreciate Jesus in his concrete historical involvement with the suffering people of his day and to discern his continuing presence in the many *minjung*s of history, not to spiritualize and reduce him to his abstract presence in worship and proclamation.

In this regard, it is important to note Ahn's work on the Christology of Mark. For Ahn, in Mark more than anywhere else in the New Testament corpus, the critical, liberating identification of Jesus with *minjung* is seen most clearly. Mark refers to socially alienated and marginalized people by the term *ochlos,* a political category, rather than *laos,* an ethnic category. He presents Jesus as identifying himself with this *ochlos* and makes an explicit critique not only of the religious and political but also of the incipient ecclesiastical authoritarianism of the nascent Christian communities. Ahn identifies the *ochlos* with *minjung*.

Norms of theology are not limited to Scripture. Without denying the foundational importance of Scripture, minjung theology takes as its "norm" or, preferably, "points of reference" (Nam Dong Suh) the whole of human history insofar as it is the locus of God's liberating activity. Not only Scripture and the events recited in it, but also the history of the church and secular movements can be such points of reference for theology. Jesus continues to suffer, die, and rise again in his people. The Holy Spirit has been poured out on all creation even before the arrival of any Christian missionary. The task of theology is to discern this liberating presence of the Spirit and Jesus in the concrete events and struggles of human history.

As a Korean theology, minjung theology is compelled to review the history of the Korean *minjung* for signs of such a liberating and saving presence of God and to explore their experiences such as *han* for theological insights. Thus, there has emerged a "rereading" of Korean history from the perspective of the *minjung* and their struggles for liberation, and a renewed appreciation of the theological significance of such events as the Donghak Revolution of 1894 against colonial powers; the National Independence Movement of March 1, 1919, against Japan; the National Liberation from Japan on August 15, 1945; and the Student Revolution of

April 19, 1960, against the corruption and tyranny of the Rhee regime. A new appreciation of many aspects of Korean culture that used to be condemned as pagan and unchristian has also arisen, thus manifesting a new sensitivity to their liberating potential. These include shamanism, the mask dance, *pansori*, folktales of *han*, and native popular religions such as Chondogyo.

Beyond the Catholic sacramental and the Protestant proclamation models of church, minjung theology provides a third model, the *minjung* church. Nam Dong Suh considers the model as most appropriate to the third age of the Spirit (borrowing a phrase from Joachim of Fiore), and Byung Mu Ahn regards it as the most faithful to the historical Jesus. In both instances church is not an institution, a fixed form, a building; it is an event, the event of the encounter between Jesus and *minjung*. It is a community of life sharing in the struggles of *minjung*, not a cultic community dualistically separated from such struggles. It is a community of which *minjung* remain the subjects, not subjected to hierarchical manipulation; no dualism of sacred and profane, clergy and laity, should prevail. It is a community of equals, in which no social stratification should be accepted. It is an eschatological community awaiting the advent of the kingdom of God with constant *metanoia* (repentant change) and renewal, not only *gathered* to celebrate but also *sent* to proclaim the coming of the Kingdom. It is primarily a prophetic community of liberating praxis, not a priestly community of worship. It is not an end in itself but only a servant of the Kingdom.

Selected Bibliography

1983   Commission on Theological Concerns of the Christian Conference of Asia, ed., *Minjung Theology: People as the Subjects of History*.

1985   Cyris Hee Suk Moon, *A Korean Minjung Theology: An Old Testament Perspective*.

1988   Jung Young Lee, ed., *An Emerging Theology in World Perspective: Commentary on Korean Minjung Theology*.

1989   Peter Schuttke-Scherle, *From Contextual to Ecumenical Theology? A Dialogue Between Minjung Theology and "Theology After Auschwitz."*

Aloysius Pieris

1934–

A Sri Lankan Jesuit, Pieris studied philosophy at the Sacred Heart College, Shembaganur, theology at the Pontifical Theological Faculty of Naples, and music in Venice. He also studied Pali and Sanskrit literature at the University of London and obtained the first doctorate ever awarded a non-Buddhist in Buddhist philosophy from the University of Sri Lanka in 1972. He has taught or lectured at many universities throughout the world including Cambridge University, the Gregorian University, the Graduate Theological Union, Vanderbilt University, Union Theological Seminary (New York), and the East Asian Pastoral Institute in Manila. Since 1974 he has been founding director of the Tulana Research Center promoting the Christian-Buddhist dialogue in Kelaniya, Sri Lanka. For a number of years he has also been serving as editor of *Dialogue,* and has written *Theologie der Befreiung* (1982), *An Asian Theology of Liberation* (1987), and *Love Meets Wisdom: A Christian Experience of Buddhism* (1988) in addition to numerous articles published in many languages.

Pieris tells of two transforming experiences in his life: his immersion in Buddhism and his encounter with the reality of poverty. His experience of Buddhism occurred during his doctoral studies in Buddhism at the University of Sri Lanka, which required complete immersion in Buddhist monastic life, its long meditations and ascetic practices, under the personal guidance of a monk, for one year and a half, to the point of forgetting and denying Christianity. Overwhelming as his experience of complete immersion in Buddhism might have been, it was not to compare to his encounter with poverty. While working in the slums of Colombo with university students in the 1960s and living through the revolution of 1971, he was awakened to the full dimensions of the problem of poverty. He vividly remembers being personally stung by the question put to him by a Marxist student, who later joined the revolution and was killed, "From where do you get your money?" His concern ever since has been an authentically Asian theology that would integrate religion and poverty.

The theology of Pieris comprises certain characteristic themes and emphases. They include the definition of the Asian context as the twin challenge of religion and poverty, the primacy of life and praxis over speculation and theory in theological method, the contrast between Asian *Gnosis* (enlightenment) and Christian *agape* (love) as two primordial orientations of human religiosity, the reciprocity of inculturation and liberation, the imperative of an ecclesiological revolution that the Christian churches be thoroughly rooted in the "soteriological depth" of Asian culture and become churches *of* Asia, not just churches *in* Asia, and such a revolution as a necessary precondition for an authentically Asian Christian church, theology, Christology, and theology of religions. As a theologian duly critical of the colonial and imperialist past of Asian Christianity and in quest for the future of a genuinely Asian theology and church, Pieris produces a theology still largely in process, one consisting of insightful methodological clues and suggestive sketches of responses rather than definitive systematic answers to the fundamental theological questions that must be asked again in the specifically Asian contexts in order to find truly Asian answers, especially to questions about Christology, ecclesiology, and theological method.

31

One of the distinctive features of Pieris' theology is the determining conviction, derived from his familiarity with the monastic, spiritual tradition of both East and West and the Latin American theology of liberation, that life itself and the praxis of life are the sources of all theories—including theology—and that theories are derivative, secondary reflections on and of that life. The tradition of monastic spirituality has always emphasized the unity of theory and praxis, reflection and life, philosophy and religion, "truth" and "path," as, in its political form, the liberation spirituality of Latin America has recently rediscovered for the West. All authentic theories must both originate from and culminate in one's immersion and participation in life, merely "unfolding" and "revealing" (apocalypse) what is already implicit in the experience and praxis of life and promoting its liberating possibilities. This primacy of life also applies to the liturgy and the sacraments: authentic sacramental liturgy is possible only as a moment of the liturgy of life, from which it originates and in which it must also culminate.

For Pieris, this relationship of theory and praxis dictates its own theological method. First of all, theology is contextual; theology must first disclose the context of the life of which it is the self-conscious reflection. For Asian theology, this context is constituted by the double characteristics of profound religiosity and overwhelming poverty, what Pieris loves to call "the Jordan of Asian religions and the Calvary of Asian poverty." Asia is the birthplace of all the principal religions of the world, and the vitality of Asian religions has kept Asia, less than 3 percent Christian, the least Christianized of all the world's continents after some four centuries of colonialism and mission. Asia is also a continent of massive poverty existing side-by-side with its profound religiosity, and it suffers from both the alienating and liberating effects of poverty and religion. Second, theology is practical; it must draw its theoretical challenges precisely from the practical challenges of its context so as to serve the praxis of life. In the Asian context, this means the challenges of inculturation, liberation, and relation to non-Christian religions going beyond the alternatives of exclusivism and inclusivism. Third, theology is an immanent reflection; instead of trying to impose a purely theoretical solution to such challenges from outside, it must thoroughly immerse itself in the context and reflect on the challenges from *within* the context. For Asian theology, this means participating in Asian poverty, Asian culture, and Asian religions, and reflecting from the "depth" of Asian life. Such an immanent reflection is still in its incipient stage, and a truly Asian theology of liberation, ecclesial identity, and religions is possible only as the future of such participation and such reflection.

In approaching the issues of inculturation, liberation, and theology of religions, Pieris is thoroughly organic and holistic, rejecting all purely intellectual, mechanical, and dualistic approaches. Inculturationist theologians often identify inculturation with studying the classical texts of non-Christian religions and borrowing their categories and symbols for the purpose of Christian liturgy and theology. They divorce philosophical concepts from the religious and spiritual matrices in which they have been nourished, as well as from any mediation by the hermeneutics of contemporary religious praxis. This basically Western model of inculturation is based on the separation of culture, philosophy, and religion, where, due to the peculiarities of the historical circumstances, the Christian *religion* was indeed inculturated in Latin *culture*, Greek *philosophy*, North European *religiousness*, and monastic *spirituality*. In the different circumstances of Asia, however, it is not possible to assume only philosophy or culture without its religion. It is dualistic to think of inculturation as insertion of Christianity *without* its European culture and philosophy into Asian cultures with their philosophies but *without* their religions. Philosophies and cultures are not just instruments that can be plucked out of their religious contexts; it is "theological vandalism" to steal certain practices, concepts, and symbols, and use them as theological tools without regard for the soteriological ethos and religious experiences behind them.

Inculturationists assume a mechanical conception of inculturation. They ask whether the churches have been inculturated and how such inculturation should proceed, as though inculturation were something that could be artificially invented, managed, and externally imposed, like an object of a consciously conducted program of action. For Pieris, inculturation is a natural, organic by-product of involvement with a people that creates a culture. The real question is not *whether* but *how* the churches are inculturated. In a real sense the churches are *already* inculturated insofar as they are embodied in a people, who necessarily have a culture of their own. In a class-divided society, churches also reflect the class division of the larger society, the official clerical church being identified with the elitist culture and separated from the general culture of the poor masses, raising the question of how the churches should be inculturated in the life of the poor. The real issue is how the churches should be *properly* inculturated: How should they enter into, participate in, and be *rooted* in, the organic whole of the life of the people? Pieris envisions a process of genuine inculturation in which Christianity would so immerse itself in the depth of Asian reality through liberation and "enreligioniza-tion" as to acquire Asia's own soteriological perspectives from which to reforge its identity as specifically Asian Christianity, born again of the waters of the "Jordan" of Asian religions and the "Calvary" of Asian poverty. In this holistic approach, the paths to inculturation, liberation, and the relation with other religions are one and the same.

This process of holistic inculturation requires humility, courage, and recovery of its own authentic tradition on the part of Christianity. First of all, in imitation of its founder, who was the epitome of *kenosis* and submitted himself to John's baptism, Christianity must be humble enough to immerse or baptize itself in the waters of Asian religions, predominantly religions of *Gnosis*. Gnostic religions seek salvific knowledge and freedom from greed through cultivation of voluntary poverty and renunciation of wealth, which also implies an indirect critique of society. This immersion in the Gnostic religion entails much more than knowing its philosophical self-interpretations or its collective memories such as its traditions and practices; it entails *communicatio in sacris*, not in the conventional sense of sharing the eucharist with that religion, but in the holistic sense of sharing its "core" or "primordial" experiences of redemption by entering into its tradition as deeply as possible, preferably through humble discipleship under a monk. In this self-immersion in Asia's Gnostic experience, however, Christianity is not confronting something wholly other. One of the two biblical axioms, according to Pieris, is the opposition between God and Mammon, the tradition of voluntary poverty and detachment from wealth and greed, and the call to become poor for God, a call institutionalized in the monastic tradition of the early Christian centuries and continuing to our own day. In recovering this tradition of *Gnosis* and voluntary poverty and in building a bridge to Asian *Gnosis,* Pieris considers the works of Christian monks, such as Thomas Merton, especially important.

Inculturation, however, requires more than "enreligionization" or sharing in the "voluntary poverty" of the monks. It also means the courage of sharing in the struggles of the poor masses to liberate themselves from "forced poverty" and all its alienating and enslaving effects. The interior liberation of the monks or becoming poor for God is not enough; it must enter into solidarity with the forced poor and become a concrete political means of bringing about their social emancipation from structural oppression. In this regard, it is important to explore the liberating and socially critical potential of Gnostic religions, which are not, as is so often alleged, world-denying but are only world-relativizing religions. Nevertheless, Pieris notes the distinctive contribution of the Jewish and Christian traditions to highlight the love of neighbor, especially the poor and oppressed, which makes Christianity an *agapeic* religion in contrast to the *Gnostic*.

The second of biblical axioms is God's preferential concern for the poor, a concern normatively manifested in Jesus' special solidarity with the poor and his presence among the poor as both victim and judge (Matthew 25). In a class-divided society, this option for the poor means political struggles, and in a society with long religious and rural traditions of sharing according to need and contributing according to ability, this means struggles for religious socialism, often embodied in "basic human communities," where, as in Latin American "basic Christian communities," struggle for justice is combined with religious sharing. In contrast to the sharing that occurs in Latin American basic Christian communities, however, the Asian sharing must take place across boundaries of different religions.

Regarding Asian Christology and theology of religions, then, Pieris' position is provisional and tentative. Neither exclusivism nor inclusivism is adequate, yet the conditions for a definitive position are not yet mature. In the meantime, many do the preliminary work of Asian Christology by searching for the "sensitive zones" in the Asian soul that would respond to and find Jesus congenial and attractive, encouraging socially committed non-Christians to tell their own stories of him, and presenting his cross as the possible paradigm of renunciation to justify the struggle for complete human liberation, interior and structural, in terms of a salvific encounter with Ultimate Reality. The point of Asian Christology would be to use the Asian perspective to disclose Jesus as experienced by Asians. What counts is not names, titles, concepts, or interpretations, which are culturally specific, but the saving reality itself. Instead of making an absolute claim about the efficacy of salvation brought about by Jesus, it is more important to prove such efficacy through our own transforming praxis and fruits of liberation. For Pieris, the provisional Christology of the crucified Jesus as the symbol of both the struggle to be poor and the struggle for the poor does not compete with Buddhology. Rather, it complements Buddhology by acknowledging the "one" path of liberation on which Christians can join the Buddhists in their voluntary poverty and on which Buddhists join Christians in their struggles against forced poverty, while also engaging in a core-to-core dialogue as in basic human communities. Only at the end of this joint praxis and dialogue will the name of the path be revealed.

Selected Primary Works

1987   *An Asian Theology of Liberation.*
1988   *Love Meets Wisdom: A Christian Experience of Buddhism.*

Stanley J. Samartha

1920–

A presbyter of the Church of South India, Samartha received the B.D. from the United Theological College in Bangalore in 1945, the S.T.M. from Union Theological Seminary in New York City in 1950, and the Ph.D. from Hartford Seminary Foundation in 1958. He taught at the Karnataka Theological College in Mangalore, Serampore College in West Bengal, and the United Theological College, as well as in the United States, Canada, and the Netherlands. His most transforming experiences were his ecumenical activities with fellow Christians of different denominations and especially with neighbors of other faiths. Serving on the staff of the World Council of Churches in charge of its various dialogue programs with other faiths from 1968 to 1981, he was the first director of the Dialogue Program of the World Council of Churches. He then returned to his own Indian roots, gaining not only a global vision of things but also a rare ecumenical sensibility to the theological challenge of other faiths.

These experiences have also defined his life task as a theologian, namely, his enduring preoccupation with interreligious dialogue, especially with Hinduism, theology of religions, and Christology in a religiously plural world, which he worked out in critical dialogue with Hendrik Kraemer, Paul D. Devanandan, and M. M. Thomas. His numerous involvements in ecumenical conferences with other faiths as well as his countless articles and books demonstrate his single-minded, lifelong commitment to interreligious understanding and establish him as a world pioneer, expert, and advocate in matters of interreligious dialogue and religious pluralism. Among his numerous publications are *Hindu Response to the Unbound Christ* (1974), *Courage for Dialogue: Ecumenical Issues in Interreligious Relationships* (1982), and *One Christ—Many Religions: Toward a Revised Christology* (1991).

The defining historical situation today, for Samartha, is the coexistence of different faiths and ideologies in an increasingly interdependent world where collective destinies are inextricably interwoven, and the defining historical and theological challenge is how to bring this irreducible plurality of faiths to live and work together in peace and justice. One might argue that there are many areas of human concern (such as justice and human rights) in which cooperation is possible without settling all the theological issues, but such a cooperation will not be effective in the long run without a coherent solution to the fundamental issues. How is theology to promote genuine dialogue and fellowship, beyond intolerant fanaticism, shallow friendliness, and even practical cooperation, while taking seriously the challenges and tensions of the existential reality of the religiously plural world? For Samartha, this question requires nothing less than rethinking Christian exclusivism, classical Christology, and the traditional conception of mission. The challenge is to reconstruct a Christian identity that is indeed distinctively Christian but also sensitive to the distinctiveness of other faiths and the Indian tradition of religious pluralism. How does one do this without arousing suspicions of surrender on the part of Christians and imperialism on the part of other faiths? Is there a solution that is "theologically credible, spiritually satisfying, and pastorally helpful"?

The first task in this theological reconstruction is to transcend both the exclusivism and inclusivism of Christology. Samartha provides a number of reasons, epistemological, psychological, political, social, and theological. Basically, exclusivism operates with a narrow and fixed conception of truth as a matter of either/or, finding commitment to one faith impossible without rejecting all others. Exclusivism thus divides humanity into two opposed camps, the saved and the damned, "us" and "them," and promotes a cramped, isolationist, and particularist mentality, making cooperation with neighbors of other faiths difficult if not impossible even in matters of common human concern. It is imperialist toward other faiths because it merely universalizes its own particularity. Exclusivism, therefore, necessarily tends to foment social tensions and conflicts, especially when it is combined, as it most often is, with economic, political, and military power. From a theological point of view, exclusivism denies the universality of God's salvific love by raising theological doubts about the eternal fate of the absolute majority of humanity who have died without knowing Christ. Inclusivism is not a viable alternative to exclusivism either; deep down, it is no more than a way of patronizing and coopting other faiths without their permission. Both are forms of "theological violence" against neighbors of other faiths. Christians must shift from the missiological approach, which treats other faiths as objects of mission, to the theological approach, which grants salvific significance to each faith in its autonomy.

Samartha's pluralism might be called ontological, critical pluralism. It is pluralism in the sense that it recognizes a plurality of faiths as the normal reality of human religiosity, without attempting either to impose one particular faith on all others or to invent a new, world faith by a syncretistic mix of different faiths. It appreciates each faith precisely in its distinctive, irreducible particularity with its own conceptions of the absolute, the human predicament, and salvation. It respects the freedom of each faith to define itself on its own terms. And it recognizes each faith as an authentic, even normative way of salvation for its own followers, although not for others.

Samartha's pluralism, however, is critical pluralism in the way that it rejects any relativism that regards all particular faiths as equally valid, making them absolute in their particularity without recognizing a criterion by which to judge among them. It is critical in the way that it regards God or the Mystery alone as absolute and relativizes all faiths as historically and culturally conditioned, particular, and provisional responses to the absolute. Based on the commitment to the absolute through the relative, it rejects the claim of any particular faith to be itself the absolute, it reserves the full critical freedom to judge and reject the demonic elements in any faith or ideology, and it sets each faith free to serve the cause of the ultimate and absolute.

Samartha's arguments for pluralism are in part historical but ultimately ontological. Diversity is inherent in the very structure of being itself, the being of the Mystery, of human nature, and of human historicity. The Mystery, to which Brahman, God, and other divine names are symbolic pointers, transcends our intellectual grasp in principle. No one faith can claim finality and exhaustiveness for its own knowledge of the Mystery; of necessity, there can only be a plurality of different paths to the Mystery, not only of different faiths but also of different approaches such as the intellectual, aesthetic, and spiritual. Furthermore, according to Hindu arguments, human beings have different needs and aptitudes; not all humans are suited for one kind of religion. Diversity of human nature dictates diversity of religions. Finally, the historicity of human existence entails the essential diversity of cultures and perspectives and thus also of religions. People living in different cultures cannot be expected to possess the same religion, and the different religions that have provided enduring spiritual, ethical, and religious meaning and direction for millions of people over many centuries must be accorded positive salvific significance. After centuries of Western Christian colonialism, the affirmation of that pluralism is also a way of recovering and reasserting one's own religious tradition and fighting religious colonialism.

As a way of facilitating and justifying the acceptance of pluralism for Christians, Samartha urges two important turns: (1) the theocentric turn in pneumatology, Christology, and missiology away from the christomonistic preoccupations of the past, *the* source of exclusivism; and (2) the methodological turn to dialogue and praxis as themselves theological *loci* or places of insight and revelation. The theocentric turn is an appeal to a theological ground internal to the Christian tradition itself that would justify pluralism without causing the loss of Christian identity to that tradition. Motivated by the fact that neither Scripture nor tradition provides relevant theological insights for the genuinely new *kairos* constituted by the reality and challenge of religious pluralism, Samartha's methodological turn is an invitation to venture into the unknown in full confidence and hope in the universality of the Mystery operative in all faiths.

Samartha's theocentric turn is best illustrated in his pneumatology. Over against the tradition that has subordinated the role of the Holy Spirit to that of Christ through the *filioque* and confined it to the church through baptism, Samartha tries to understand the Spirit primarily as the Spirit of God the "Father" without the *filioque*, as God's immanent activity in the world, and thus as universal as is God whose Spirit it is. The Spirit is present in all creation and all history, not only in the "religious" life of the Christian churches but also outside, not only in secular experiences in which liberal Christians have recently been trying to see signs of the Spirit but also in non-Christian faiths. The activity of the Spirit is not limited by time, geography, or race. What Scripture says about the relation of the Spirit to Christians should not be interpreted as negative judgments on other faiths. In fact, if the Persian Cyrus could be described by the prophet as "the Lord's shepherd" (Isa. 44:28), why not also Gandhi, Castro, or Mao Tse Tung? The liberations that these leaders brought to India, Cuba, and China should be considered theologically as significant as that of the Exodus under Moses. The Spirit is boundlessly free and just as capable of transforming a *chronos* into a *kairos* in the history of non-Christians as in that of Christians. As the Acts testify (4:17, 18; 10; 19:1-7), the Spirit can be given without baptism. Our understanding of the Spirit must be freed from the traditional christocentric, ecclesiocentric, and Western ethnocentric captivities. What is needed is a definitive break from the paradigm of "salvation history"; what is urgent is to see and clarify the presence of the Spirit in the world, especially in the lives of other faiths.

Samartha's revision of Christology is also based on the theocentric turn, a turn from the classic Christology of Chalcedon (or at least one interpretation of it). This Christology, which he calls "helicopter Christology" in the sense of a Christology from above, is to be rejected for at least four reasons. (1) It compromises the very basis of monotheism by identifying the human Jesus with God as Godself, the "very God of very God," something that denies the ontological priority of God and contradicts Scripture. (2) In a world where humanity is undergoing a crisis of dehumanization, its failure to do justice to the humanity of Jesus is to diminish the Christian resources for supporting the struggles for human freedom and dignity. (3) It seriously underestimates the significance of the historical precisely when historical consciousness is becoming global with its emphasis on historical, experiential foundations. (4) Most important, the claim that God has been revealed "only" in Jesus Christ and "once for all" is a scandal that further divides peoples and makes impossible dialogue and cooperation with neighbors of other faiths as true partners in a larger human community.

What is urgently necessary, then, is to avoid the christomonistic, absolutistic identification of God with the particularities of Jesus Christ, which Samartha does by attempting a *theocentric* Christology that at once centers Christology on God, as he does pneumatology, and thereby also releases the full humanity of Jesus to have its full evangelical impact. For Samartha, one must begin with the ontological priority of God as the *universal* creator and redeemer of all creation. God's universality contradicts the claim that God has been revealed only and once for all in Jesus of Nazareth. It also rules out the exclusive ontological identification of God with Jesus. The Incarnation should be interpreted to mean that the God present in Jesus is indeed God's very self and that Jesus is divine in this sense, not that Jesus in his own being is identical with the God present in him. Jesus was divine, but not God. Neither God nor Christ is limited to Jesus of Nazareth. Christ is also found and witnessed to in other faiths, and it is important to discern and incorporate marks of such witness and presence into new christologies of the future. As Jesus and the whole Bible are theocentric, so it is essential to be God-centered. The only way to be Christ-centered is to be God-centered, but to be God-centered is not necessarily to be Christ-centered. There is no Christology without theology, but theology is wider than Christology. Theocentric Christology can thus recognize the distinctiveness of Jesus Christ—along with that of all other faiths—without being negative to other faiths. The postbiblical attribution of deity to Jesus is a dangerous distortion of the New Testament and must be discarded as excess baggage.

Theocentric Christology frees Christology to be a Christology from below, a "bullock cart Christology" that maintains its contact with the earthy realities of humanity rather than being imposed, like the classic "helicopter Christology," on humanity from above. It is a Christology based on the concrete humanity of Jesus, not on later doctrinal formulations and creeds. It is the story of Jesus who proclaimed the kingdom of God as the center of his message, who was wholly committed to his vocation given by God, with a singular sense of trust in God as his "Father" and freedom from attachments to family, money, and security. He possessed and was possessed by a profound compassion for the poor. He was obedient to the essence of the Torah—the love of God and neighbor—and to God, even unto death as the suffering servant. His resurrection was God's vindication of his entire life, ministry, and death. No triumphalist, Jesus is the way, truth, and life, precisely through the *kenosis* of the cross, through vulnerability and service.

Samartha also applies the theocentric turn to the theology of mission. Inseparable from the gospel and therefore from the identity of the Christian Church, mission raises questions about its practice in a religiously plural world. Is it possible to rethink the theology of mission in such a way that it recognizes the historical reality of global interdependence in which Christians are called upon to cooperate with other faiths and ideologies in the renewal of the world? Is it possible to discern in the renewal movements something of God's own presence? Is it possible to appreciate participation in such movements as a promotion, not as a betrayal, of mission, yet without losing the sense of Christian identity? For Samartha, such a rethinking, the most urgent imperative of our time, is possible only by decentering the theology of mission from ecclesiocentrism and Christocentrism and recentering it on God.

Samartha's theocentric theology of mission begins with the ontological priority of God's own mission in the world as the theological basis of all human missions. God's creating and redeeming activity through the power of the Spirit is prior to and more comprehensive than the mission of Christian churches and should direct our attention beyond the churches to the Kingdom. All human missions are modes of responses to and participations in God's own universal activity of reconciling the world, mending the brokenness of creation, overcoming the fragmentation of humanity, healing the rifts among humanity, nature, and God. This mission of God is comprehensive in scope, for nothing can be excluded from the all-embracing love of God and activities of the Holy Spirit. The contemporary movements of social and political renewal in other religions and ideologies (e.g., Marxism) cannot be considered to be outside the reach of that divine mission, which bears on the totality of human existence in all its concerns, sacred and secular, spiritual and material, without tolerating dualistic restrictions. As a *living* God, God deals with peoples directly, not through the extension of the "history of salvation," acting in ways that are often unfamiliar and surprising.

For Christians, this mission of God is mediated through the divine revelation in Jesus of Nazareth and his own mission in the world. This christological mediation gives the Christian mission its identity, while the promise of the guidance of the Spirit should give Christians a sense of confident adventure into the unknown and the constantly enlarging vision of the kingdom of God. The Christian mission is meant to be a joyful confession of faith, an affirmation of commitment, an invitation to others to share in the good news, not an invidious, negative judgment on other faiths. It does not have to deny that neighbors in other faiths also have their own shares in God's mission in the world. The demand of the contemporary *kairos* is that different faiths and ideologies, inextricably involved as they are in the common struggle for renewal, cooperate with one another in participating in God's own mission of renewing the whole creation.

Selected Primary Works

1964   *Introduction to Radhakrishnan.*
1971   ed., *Dialogue Between Men of Living Faiths.*
1971   ed., *Living Faiths and the Ecumenical Movement.*
1974   *Hindu Response to the Unbound Christ.*
1977   ed., *Faith in the Midst of Faiths: Reflections on Dialogue in Community.*
1982   *Courage for Dialogue: Ecumenical Issues in Interreligious Relationships.*
1983   *The Other Side of the River: Some Reflections on the Theme of the Vancouver Assembly.*
1987   *The Search for New Hermeneutics in Asian Christian Theology.*
1991   *One Christ—Many Religions: Toward a Revised Christology.*

Selected Secondary Source

1992   Eeuwout Klootwijk, *Commitment and Openness: The Interreligious Dialogue and Theology of Religions in the Work of Stanley J. Samartha.*

Choan Seng Song

1929–

Song is Professor of Theology and Asian Cultures at the Pacific School of Religion and Regional Professor of Theology at the South East Asia Graduate School of Theology in Singapore and Hong Kong. He received the B.A. in philosophy from the National Taiwan University, the B.D. from the University of Edinburgh, and in 1965 the Ph.D. from Union Theological Seminary in New York City. He has lectured at the United Theological College (Sydney), McGill University, the Vancouver School of Theology, the University of Edinburgh, and Princeton Theological Seminary. He has also served as President of Taiwan Theological College; Director of Study for the World Alliance of Reformed Churches; Secretary for Asian Ministries, the Reformed Church in America; and Associate Director of the Faith and Order Commission of the World Council of Churches, Geneva. Like other Asian theologians being surveyed here, Song acquired his basic theological awakening and orientation from his exposure to Asia's twin struggles for independence from Western domination and for social justice at home and from his involvement in ecumenical activities. His numerous publications include *Christian Mission in Reconstruction: An Asian Analysis* (1977), *Tell Us Our Names: Story Theology from an Asian Perspective* (1984), and the trilogy (under the general title

41

The Cross in the Lotus World) of *Jesus, the Crucified People* (1990), *Jesus and the Reign of God* (1993), and *Jesus in the Power of the Spirit* (1994).

Song's lifelong passion has been to devise a Christian theology whose Asian identity is unmistakably "enfleshed" in the particularities of the Asian context. The overriding task of Asian theology is to establish its identity as a theology both Asian and Christian, which means radical, critical, and resolute independence from Western theology, its perspectives and categories. Asian theology must become, in the title of one of Song's own books, a theology from the "womb" of Asia, born of Asian experiences, energized by Asian sensibilities, interpreted by Asian herme-neutics and categories, and dedicated to decoding Asian life and discerning and proclaiming the theological meaning of the signs of God's redeeming presence in Asian history and culture. In order to articulate a theology of Asian experience, however, Asian theology must self-consciously immerse itself in Asian realities, becoming "flesh" in Asia's aspirations and sufferings, and identifying itself with the common humanity of Asia beneath its cultural and religious diversity. Asian Christians must be as Asian as their non-Christian neighbors, no longer aliens and external observers in their own countries.

The most fundamental task of a truly Asian theology is to rethink the relationship between creation and redemption, *the* source of all the degrading dualisms of Western theology. Western Christianity has made a sharp separation between creation and redemption, limiting the sphere of redemptive significance to the Christian Church, that is, to those who know of Christ's redemption explicitly. Although recognizing "general" revelation in creation as opposed to the "special" revelation in Christ, the churches have regarded such general revelation as redemp-tively helpless and have relegated the whole of creation—human history, culture, and non-Christian religions—to human self-idolatry deserving only of God's wrath and judgment. Over against this traditional, exclusivist view of salvation, Song insists on the intrinsic unity of universal creation and redemption in Christ and the primacy of God's universal redemptive love over God's judgment, and he places the totality of human existence and history within that unity and love.

For Song, there is an intrinsic relationship between creation and redemption, a unity expressive of God's effective, universal love. The Logos or Word of creation and the Word of incarnation are one and the same and cannot be separated. The Christ who is the mediator of redemption is also the mediator of creation with precisely redemptive intent. Christ is present everywhere in creation in and through the Spirit: "Christ is all and in all" (Col. 3:11). God's saving and revealing activity in Christ is as universal as creation itself. It is crucial to restore the dimension of universality to God's salvific love by integrating creation and redemption. The traditional separation of creation and redemption reduces the universality of re-demption and distorts God's sovereign, comprehensive relation to all creation. Redemption and new creation do not mean destruction, but completion and fulfill-ment of creation, which is intrinsically oriented to redemption. God in Christ is redemptively present in *all* history, not only Western culture or the Judeo-Christian "history of salvation," moving all cultures and all religions toward such fulfillment in Christ.

Song is fully aware of the typically Protestant emphasis that there is much corruption, idolatry, sin, and judgment in the history of creation, but he also insists that there is goodness, truth, grace, and love as well. In a world where God remains sovereign, evil cannot be final, for God's universal salvific love is greater than human sinfulness. The thoroughgoing pessimism of theologians such as the early Karl Barth, Hendrik Kraemer, and Emil Brunner toward the non-Christians must be transcended. Such a pessimism limits either the universality of God's love or the efficacy of God's redemptive work in Christ. To appreciate the *theological* value of non-Christian (i.e., non-Western) cultures and to justify the Christian validity of new theological ventures based on non-Western experiences, one needs a more positive relationship between creation and redemption to enable one to see not only God's wrath and judgment but also God's love and grace in non-Christian cultures. Then one can more thoroughly appreciate truth, goodness, and nobility wherever they may be found, without a priori, negative theological judgments.

For Song, this emancipation of God's redemptive presence from its confinement to Western salvation history, perhaps the single greatest theological scandal of Christianity, is of the utmost theological significance. It means universalizing the liberation of divine grace and the theological justification of all experiences, including the Asian, which have revolutionary implications for all areas of theology: theological method, theology of "enfleshment," theology of culture, theology of religions, theology of mission, and political theology.

That in Christ and through the Spirit, God is redemptively engaged in the whole of creation means, first of all, a Copernican revolution in theological method. Persons are not to look for the raw material of theology only in the biblical history of salvation or to reflect only on the traditional theological themes such as the Trinity, Christology, church, sacraments, ministry, and so on. Christian humanists are to discern and interpret the signs of God's saving presence in the *totality* of human existence and human history, with absolutely no a priori restrictions. Christian theology needs not only a definitive break from the narrowing, ethnocentric captivity of salvation history but also the transcendence of all dualisms, such as the dualism of sacred and profane, individual and social, religious and political, Christian and non-Christian. This definitive break in turn entails radical decentering of our theological attention from the church and Christian history and radical recentering of our theological concern on the universal saving action of God, on God's reign in the whole of creation in Christ and in the power of the Spirit. No human problem is to be considered too humble or too insignificant or too secular for theology. According to the dynamics of the incarnation, Song invites us to see God, especially in the depth of our spiritual quests and the depth of our sufferings and hopes.

Song's theology of God's universal saving presence is a theology of incarnation or enfleshment. The incarnation of God in Jesus Christ remains the central symbol of God's redeeming involvement in the crying needs of the world. God becomes "flesh" by becoming what God has created, sharing Godself with creation and sharing in concrete human joys and sorrows with a redeeming presence, even to the point of risking the loss of self-identity in the otherness of the creature. Because of the incarnation one can no longer encounter God except in and through human beings and their history, one can no longer give witness to God's own agony and hope except in and through the agonies and hopes of suffering humanity. Precisely because of God's incarnate presence in humanity, nothing human can be alien to theology. Enfleshment entails being transposed to and entering into solidarity with the Other. God has become flesh in the otherness of Jesus of Nazareth, crossing the boundaries of divine and human, transposing the divine self into humanity, and enabling persons to cross such boundaries of religions, cultures, and histories in Jesus Christ and to achieve a deeper union with God and a profounder solidarity of destiny with humanity precisely through the otherness, disruptions, and transpositions that they experience. A theology of "enfleshment" is necessarily a theology of "transposition."

That God is redemptively present in all creation means, for Song, that theology is most fundamentally a theology of culture. As the totality of ways of living, culture is the continuation of creation in which God is also redemptively present. Creation is fundamentally good; it not only distorts or corrupts but also reflects God's redemptive love. It is wrong to oppose culture with revelation, as though there is a revelation without cultural conditioning, as though Christianity is not culturally conditioned. Against the Protestant opposition of Christ and culture that is identified in H. R. Niebuhr's typology, Song stresses Christ's role as the "fulfiller," not always the critical "transformer," of culture. Christ is implicitly present in every culture through the power of the Spirit to create and re-create a people, enabling each culture to purge and transform itself from within. The role of the Christian is not so much to try to "transform" a culture from outside as to "resonate" with the power of self-transformation already there within the culture through the presence of the Spirit. Christians should also remain open to new ways of God's being disclosed to that culture although these ways may be hidden from the Christian. Divine grace is not the monopoly of Christianity, but it is operative in all cultures, just as immorality and idolatry are not the monopoly of non-Christians but infect Christianity as well. No culture, not even an atheistic culture, is completely godless. God establishes a direct saving relationship with every culture.

Song's theology of religions, based on the universality of God's creating and redeeming presence, can be called pluralistic inclusivism. It rejects traditional exclusivism based on claims to absoluteness, uniqueness, and finality. Jesus cannot be "absolute" because he would have no relation to finite creation and because he could not be understood. At most, such a claim expresses a strong conviction on the part of the believer. It also generates intolerance and hostility, making dialogue impossible and breeding nothing but contempt for Asian religions. The claim to uniqueness is likewise problematic. On the one hand, such a claim makes it impossible for Jesus to be the medium of God's revelation to persons on their terms. On the other, it does not explain how the uniqueness of Jesus differs from the uniqueness of everything else. And the traditional claim to finality, Song asserts, tends to freeze the process of revelation after Christ and deprive other religions of their intrinsic, existential meaning.

Song's preferred description of the salvific role of Jesus Christ is that Christ is the "decisive" revelation of God. As the creative and redemptive Word of God, Christ is present in other cultures and religions as their foundation, judgment, and fulfillment. In every quest for the absolute, Christ is present with his saving revelation. Christ not only judges religions insofar as they are tempted to absolutize themselves into self-idolatry, but he also inspires and enables them to transcend and fulfill themselves in Christ, evoking positive responses to God's love and justice. Christ brings to light the dialectic of love and judgment at work in history. As a synthesis of particular and universal, Jesus is always relevant to the particular without losing his universal significance. Song pleads ignorance as to why Jesus alone is the decisive revelation of God. Song's theology of religions, then, is christological inclusivism: He insists both on the reality of revelation and salvation outside the Christian Church and on the mediation of that revelation and salvation by the universal presence of Christ in the Spirit.

Song's inclusivism, however, is pluralistic inclusivism because he recognizes the intrinsic and permanent validity of non-Christian religions and does not subordinate non-Christian religions to either the christological or the ecclesiological demand of the Christian Church. He demands a dialectic of the explicit Christ revealed in the Christian revelation and the implicit Christ present in the non-Christian religions, not the subordination of the latter to the former. Faith in Christ does not serve as the sole point of departure for understanding the mystery of God's dealings with human beings to the suppression of other religions; it serves, instead, as the "focal" point and enabling power for interpreting history and responding to God precisely in the particular contexts of non-Christian cultures. A non-Christian religion is not just a "preparation for the gospel" with only a provisional, extrinsic validity to be surrendered on the arrival of the Christian Church. The creative and redemptive Word of God is really present in other religions, even though often in distorted ways. Humans are meant to be saved through the particular religions of their own culture in which they find themselves existentially. Each religion is a particular, partial response to the universality of the absolute, divine reality. No purely objective judgment of religions is possible; each must be evaluated on the basis of its merit in a given culture.

What, then, is the rationale and purpose of the Christian mission in the world? Song's radically theocentric turn in Christ is nowhere more evident than in his theology of mission. He denies that the Christian Church has its own mission. What is theologically primary is God's mission, which the church exists to serve. The mission of the church is secondary and derivative; it is participation in the primary mission of God. This theocentric conception of mission entails radical broadening of the traditional concept of mission. God, not the church, initiates the mission in the world, and God does so through the creation and redemption of the world in Christ in whom God assumed human history as God's own. God's mission did not begin with Abraham, nor will it end with the mission of the church. The world was God's mission field even before the church's missionary work, and it will continue to be so even after and outside that work. Wherever God's redemptive power is at work, even in communist China, for example, there God is involved in God's own mission. The destiny of the world is in the control not of the church but of God. The church should give up the illusion of saving the whole world by itself.

How does the church participate in the mission of God and the world? By revealing, giving witness to, and sharing in God's redeeming presence in all things and thus becoming a "sacrament" of God's mission in the world. In Song's sacramental conception of mission, the church's mission is to make visible and respond to God's saving presence already operative in all things. The purpose of the mission is not to convert non-Christians to Christianity but to make Christians truly sacramental, the explicit and responsive signs of God's love and reconciliation implicitly but really operative in their own societies and the world so that the universe will become a sacrament of God. The Gentiles are already accepted by God, and the mission of the church is to affirm and proclaim the good news. The church must therefore remain sensitive to, discern, and interpret the signs of God's reconciling and renewing presence in the events of the world in light of the Bible and the particular situation, just as ancient Hebrews tried to discern and experience God in the liberating events of the Exodus and other historical events.

In Song's sacramental conception, the Christian mission includes proclaiming explicitly, openly, and publicly the Christ already implicitly present in the context and confronting non-Christians with Christ. The Christ to be presented, however, is not a dogma, proposition, or doctrine, but personal truth—one who provokes hearers to reevaluate themselves as well as their religions, cultures, and political realities. Christ will be proclaimed as the way, the truth, and the life, but the meaning of this proclamation will be interpreted in the dialectic of the Bible and the context. Furthermore, the purpose of such proclamation is conversion not in the sense of making a clean break from one's own religion or culture but in the sense of becoming more deeply immersed in the depth of one's own religion in which one can only encounter God's grace in Christ. In short, the purpose of mission is to produce not Christians but rather, for example, Christian Buddhists, Christian Confucians, and Christian communists.

Song's theology of enfleshment and theology of mission come together in his political Christology of the cross. God's mission of redeeming the world is most "enfleshed" in the sufferings and hopes of the "people," the humiliated and oppressed, whose stories are often suppressed behind the stories of the oppressors and dictators of history. The story of people's sufferings and hopes is the most concrete, incarnate form of God's own story, for it is the story of Jesus himself continuing his crucifixion and resurrection in the agonies and hopes of his "crucified people." It is imperative to unmask the abstract Jesus of statues and doctrines and to restore the concrete Jesus whose suffering on the cross embodies both the passion of his people and the compassion of God.

Selected Primary Works

1973   *Asians and Blacks: Theological Challenges.*
1977   *Christian Mission in Reconstruction: An Asian Analysis.*
1979   *Third-Eye Theology: Theology in Formation in Asian Settings.*
1981   *The Tears of Lady Meng: A Parable of People's Political Theology.*
1982   *The Compassionate God.*
1984   *Tell Us Our Names: Story Theology from an Asian Perspective.*
1986   *Theology from the Womb of Asia.*
1990   *Jesus, the Crucified People.*
1993   *Jesus and the Reign of God.*
1994   *Jesus in the Power of the Spirit.*

Conclusion

This brief survey of five Asian theologies reveals a certain commonality of concerns and issues. The first common concern is to secure independence from the colonial heritage of Western theology, which endures despite the end of formal imperialism and colonialism. The long-ingrained habits and categories of Western theology with all its narrowing and degrading dualisms survive in the minds and hearts of Asian Christians. The first task of an authentically Asian theology is to prepare the ground for theological independence through a critical transcendence of Western theological heritage. This concern for theological independence and the needed preliminary work for that independence has led all five theologians to invest significant energy in issues of theological method.

The second common concern has been the turn to the particularities of the Asian context in which Asian theology must manifest its theological independence from the West. The Asian context reveals the twin challenges of political and economic liberation of the oppressed on the one hand and religious pluralism on the other. A growing consensus concludes that the problems of oppression and religious diversity are not separable in the Asian context.

The third common concern has been the theological avoidance of the ethnocentrism implicit in the perspective of "salvation history," which tends to limit the range of salvific significance to the history of Western Christianity, condemning the rest of the world as the sphere of mere nature and sin. In order to bring about an inclusive theological perspective, Asian theologians have turned away from ecclesiocentrism and Christomonism and toward theocentrism, especially the universal saving presence of the Holy Spirit. In terms of this emphasis on the universality of God's presence, a new Christology, theology of religions, and theology of mission are restructured.

The theological independence of Asian theology is far from achieved, and as a result, Asian theology still suffers from a certain ambivalence. On the one hand, it wants to be independent from Western theological categories and concepts. However, it remains captive to Western categories even in combating the surviving legacy of Western theology, for which it still must use these categories. The precise role of Western theology in relation to Asian theologies remains undecided by Asian theologians. On the other hand, Asian theology seeks to manifest itself in the historical realities of Asia, its cultures, religions, and political-economic contradictions. It still has a long way to go in penetrating those realities before it can theologize from what Pieris called the "soteriological depth" of Asia. Once it has become thoroughly rooted and taken "flesh" in Asian realities, perhaps in the coming Pacific Century, we may hope for a theology that is truly Asian in both content and form and elaborated by mature, sophisticated Asian theologians.

Anselm Kyongsuk Min

Selected Secondary Sources

1976 Gerald H. Anderson, ed., *Asian Voices in Christian Theology.*
1991 R. S. Sugirtharajah, ed., *Voices from the Margins: Interpreting the Bible in the Third World.*
1993 R. S. Sugirtharajah, ed., *Asian Faces of Jesus.*
1994 R. S. Sugirtharajah, ed., *Frontiers in Asian Christian Theology: Emerging Trends.*

Journals

Asia Journal of Theology.
East Asia Journal of Theology.
Dialogue.
Indian Journal of Theology.
Voices from the Third World.

KARL BARTH
1886–1968

Karl Barth undoubtedly changed the course of Christian theology and has even left his mark on cultural and political life. His theology remains a benchmark by which later theological developments are often measured.

Life and Career

Born in Basel, Switzerland, on May 10, 1886, into a family steeped in the Reformed tradition of theology and church, Karl Barth began to show interest in theology by the time of his confirmation, as he sought to understand the truths of the Christian faith, in his words, "from the inside out." He began his theological studies at age eighteen at the University of Bern where his father was a lecturer in church history and New Testament. Exposure to the philosophy of Immanuel Kant and the theology of Friedrich Schleiermacher made a profound impact on the young ministerial student, steering him in the direction of the dominant liberal theology of the day and away from the more conservative theology of his father. He continued his theological studies at the universities of Berlin, Tübingen, and Marburg, eager to learn from such prominent scholars as Adolf von Harnack and Wilhelm Herrmann.

In 1911, at the conclusion of his formal studies, Barth accepted a call to pastor the village church of Safenwil, Switzerland. During this eleven-year pastorate he formed a close friendship with Eduard Thurneysen, whose correspondence and conversations played a significant role in the development of his thought. Also during this time Barth experienced a dramatic shift in many of his most basic convictions regarding the shape and task of Christian theology. Even at the beginning of his work as pastor, Barth was not without misgivings about the adequacy of the liberal theology of the German universities to provide a sufficient foundation for the task of Christian ministry. A single event, however, was to have a lasting effect which helped focus his critical assessment. On August 1, 1914, the day World War I began, a manifesto was issued by ninety-three German intellectuals in support of the war policy of Kaiser Wilhelm II. Much to Barth's dismay, almost all of his German theological teachers were among the signers of the declaration. In their support for the war Barth perceived a profound ethical failure that called into question all of their theological and exegetical assumptions. He identified a fatal alliance between Christian faith and cultural experience as the fundamental error of liberal thought.

Thus, Barth became convinced that a responsible understanding of the Christian faith simply would not stand upon the theological foundation of liberal theology, at least not as it had developed through the writings of theologians like Schleiermacher, Albrecht Ritschl, and Harnack. This concern for foundations and for theological starting points led him and Thurneysen toward a "rediscovery of the Bible." Barth desired to find a new way of reading the Bible that might discern the Word of God within the words of the Bible, a task for which the historical-critical method had shown itself particularly ill-suited. The literary fruit of this concern is most prominently displayed in his first important work, *The Epistle to the Romans,* initially published in 1919. The book resulted in an offer to teach at the University of Göttingen in Germany as associate professor of Reformed theology, a position he assumed in 1921. The following year he produced a thoroughly revised second edition of the book that became the much celebrated cornerstone of the new movement known as "dialectical theology" (see below). The move to an academic post was to mark the beginning of one of the most prolific literary careers in the history of Christian theology.

In 1922, Barth, along with Friedrich Gogarten, Thurneysen, and Georg Merz, founded the journal *Zwischen den Zeiten* (Between the Times), which served as the mouthpiece for the new movement. Rudolf Bultmann was a frequent contributor to the journal and an apparent ally with Barth in his theological revolution. In 1927, as professor of Dogmatics and New Testament Exegesis at the University of Münster, he produced *Christian Dogmatics in Outline,* which marked a period of transition toward his "dogmatic phase," a period more closely associated with the term "neoorthodoxy" (see below) than with dialectical theology. Barth later expressed his dissatisfaction with the book and thoroughly revised it as the first volume of the *Church Dogmatics* in 1932. Clear differences began to emerge between Barth and the other leaders of dialectical theology, particularly Bultmann and Gogarten, resulting in the decision to discontinue *Zwischen den Zeiten* in 1933.

In 1930, Barth left Münster to become professor of systematic theology at the University of Bonn. The distinctive patterns of his mature theology emerged during this time, with Barth differentiating himself not only from liberal theology but also from his former "dialectical" allies. These patterns are particularly evident in two books: *Fides Quarens Intellectum* (Faith Seeking Understanding, 1931), a study of Anselm's proof for the existence of God; and the first half-volume of the *Church*

Dogmatics (1932), subtitled "The Doctrine of the Word of God." Hitler's seizure of power in 1933 and the ensuing "German Church Struggle" occasioned a theological crisis for Barth. He perceived in the pro-Nazi "German Christians" the logical outcome of liberal theology's alliance between culture and faith. He was primary author of the "Barmen Declaration" (1934), a significant theological confession that established the distinction between God's revelation and human experience as the theological rationale for the minority "Confessing Church," a group formed in clear opposition to the nationalist path of the "German Christians." This same theological logic was what led Barth to write the provocative pamphlet "Nein!" (No!) (1934) in response to Emil Brunner, rejecting his postulate of a natural "point of contact" for reception of the gospel. In 1934 he was dismissed from his post in Bonn for his refusal to take the oath of loyalty to the Führer. The publication of his works was subsequently prohibited in Nazi Germany.

The following year Barth was called to the University of Basel, where he taught for the balance of his career. From Basel, the remaining volumes of the *Church Dogmatics* were written, finally totaling thirteen volumes. Ironically, the work, which constitutes one of the longest theological treatises ever produced, remains incomplete according to Barth's original plan, which called for a final volume on redemption. He remained a politically controversial figure due in part to his opposition to German rearmament after the war as well as his refusal to criticize communism with the same vigor he had shown National Socialism. His official teaching career concluded in 1962, although he continued to write and offer seminars until his death in 1968.

Barth's Thought

The theology of Karl Barth may best be understood as an extended response to nineteenth- and early-twentieth-century Protestant liberalism. This is not to suggest that his theology is merely reactionary or polemical, even though many individual passages within his writings could be characterized in this way. Nor is it true that Barth's theology represents a complete rejection of all that is assumed and affirmed by liberal theology. The main thrust of his thought, however, is to offer a positive account of the faith of the Christian church that stands (or falls) on its own merits, while avoiding the hazards of theological liberalism.

The Theological Task

Barth's contribution to Christian theology lies as much (if not more) in his distinctive way of doing theology as it does in the content of his theological reflection. He remained a lifelong opponent of "theological systems" that seek to organize theological truth around a set of controlling concepts or general principles.

Nevertheless, numerous methodological patterns or motifs recur throughout the Barthian corpus, which, taken together, constitute a distinctive approach to the theological task.

The first of these motifs is the belief that Christian theology can proceed only on the assumption of the radical transcendence of God. Liberal theology had taken the reality of religious experience as its starting point for theological reflection. Such an anthropological or humanistic approach to theology, one that took the subjective experience of religious piety as its basic subject matter, was justified in part on the assumption that the divine being was immanently present within human history and experience. Barth, however, rejected this assumption on the grounds that it failed adequately to distinguish the Creator and the creation. This rejection is especially prominent in the early phase of his work known as dialectical theology. In response to liberalism's theology of immanence, dialectical theology emphasized a theology of transcendence. Borrowing the language of Søren Kierkegaard, Barth spoke of the "infinite qualitative distinction" between God and the human being. God is the one who is "wholly other," and if one is to know anything of God, it will not be found by gazing into the world of human experience. In response to liberal theology's affirmation of continuity between God and the world, dialectical theology emphasized the radical discontinuity between such polarities as God and humanity, heaven and earth, and eternity and time.

Barth's emphasis on divine transcendence brought to light in a forceful way the profound obstacles to any human talk of God. The human relationship to God is essentially one of crisis and judgment. Even the best human efforts at religious piety and morality fall ultimately under the resounding "No" of the biblical God. Consequently, human talk about God can never be more than fragmentary. For the early Barth, dialectics seemed to offer the only way toward authentic talk of God. Dialectical method assumes that no single human word or affirmation can bring divine truth to expression in an entirely adequate way. Every affirmation is met with a negation, which paradoxically also directs one toward truth. The fact of the incarnation—that God is in Jesus Christ and is really God, and that Jesus Christ is indeed a human being and a part of creation—both exemplifies and justifies the necessity of dialectics in theology. For the Barth of the *Church Dogmatics,* dialectics played a less obvious role. Here he appealed to the more traditional notion of the analogical character of all talk of God. He allowed that theological language bears an analogy to divine truth, though he denied that this is because of any inherent capacity in human speech to bring God to expression. It is a miracle of divine grace that enables theological language to convey truth about God.

A second methodological motif follows logically from the first. If the gulf between God and humanity is so great, then authentic knowledge of God is possible only on the assumption of divine revelation. Indeed, for Barth this knowledge is available exclusively through the historical self-revelation of God, a series of particular events that have their climax in the person of Jesus Christ. An account of this historical encounter between God and the world is in turn available only within the Bible. Consequently, other sources of theological truth are unconditionally discounted. Natural theology, or the attempt to gain knowledge of God by use of reason alone, is categorically rejected. Christian apologetics, at least in its usual form, remains a fruitless endeavor. The knowledge of God that comes from revelation has the character of self-verifying truth that requires no external support or corroboration. Thus, for Barth, the efforts of theological liberalism to find a basis for theology in the experience of religious devotion were doomed to failure.

The necessity of revelation implies yet a third methodological motif, the centrality of Jesus Christ, or what is often referred to as the christocentric character of Barth's thought. Liberal theology had tended to focus more on the ethical message of Jesus, allowing theological reflection on his person and redemptive work to recede into the background. For Barth, Jesus Christ represents the climax of God's historical self-revelation. The content of revelation comes to its clearest expression in his life and destiny. Jesus Christ is literally the Word of God in the sense that through the God-man Jesus, God communicates God's own self to the world. The prominence of this theme within Barth's writings explains why many early commentators referred to his theological movement as a theology of the Word. Interestingly, Barth's emphasis on the centrality of Christ leads logically to his high view of Scripture and not the other way around. He begins the first volume of the *Church Dogmatics* by unfolding what he calls the doctrine of the threefold Word of God. Jesus Christ is literally and preeminently the Word of God for reasons just stated. The Bible, however, is also the Word of God, though in a secondary and derivative sense. The Bible is and becomes the Word of God insofar as it bears witness to Jesus Christ. Proclamation of the gospel, as in Christian preaching, is yet a third form of the Word of God, insofar as it reflects the biblical witness to the Christ.

The strong emphasis on the Bible as the indispensable source and measure of all that theology wants to say should not be read as an affirmation of fundamentalism or biblical literalism. Barth eschewed readings of Scripture that sought to interpret revelation in terms of propositional truths, and he employed the findings of historical-critical research no less than his liberal opponents. But he also had little use for readings of Scripture that regarded the biblical texts as a compilation of great religious ideas or human aspirations for divine truth, as liberal theology had often done. Barth's rediscovery of Scripture represented a conviction that in spite of the obvious human character of the Bible, God's own Word does indeed confront humanity in its pages.

A fourth methodological feature of Barth's writings is a narrow definition of the ecclesial function of theology. Theological liberalism was greatly concerned to devise a theology acceptable to the scientific and cultural sensibilities of the modern world. By way of contrast, Barth defined theology as a function of the church in service to the church. Theology is a function of the church because it can only properly proceed on the assumption of faith. Theology serves the church because .

it scrutinizes the truthfulness and legitimacy of the church's talk of God. Theology exists in particular to serve the needs of the pastor, who must constantly evaluate the truthfulness of his or her own proclamation of the gospel.

The ecclesial function of theology also implies that the theologian looks to ecclesial sources and traditions for wisdom and guidance. Although these sources bear a secondary authority in relation to Scripture, they offer a profound commentary on Scripture to which the church theologian is bound to give attention. Especially throughout the "dogmatic phase" of his career, Barth drew heavily from the historical tradition of Christian thought, making particular use of the Reformers and the doctrinal themes of Protestant orthodoxy (e.g., the doctrine of the Trinity, the radicality of human sinfulness, the authority of Scripture, the incarnation, predestination, and two-nature Christology, to name but a few). The prominence of his creative and often innovative interaction with orthodox themes explains why the term "neoorthodoxy" has become the most common designation used to describe his distinctive theological approach.

Key Doctrinal Perspectives

Barth resisted the idea that his theology should ever be conceived as a mere set of doctrinal positions. Theology was far too provisional and fragmentary an undertaking to become fixed in particular doctrinal formulations. Nevertheless, the inventive way in which many of the basic themes of Christian belief are brought to expression in his writings is one of the reasons for his continuing popularity even a generation after his death. A sampling of some of these basic themes will offer some indication of the shape of Barth's distinctive formulation of Christian teaching.

Barth's doctrine of God goes to great lengths to identify the Christian God as the living and active God encountered through the history of God's self-revelation. This God has nothing to do with the general principles or static concepts of philosophy or with the theistic ideas of world religions. This God is neither an impersonal force nor a mere reflection of admirable human qualities. Barth took up the classical doctrine of the Trinity, which had become little more than an artifact of Christian history for much modern theology, in order to make the point that the Christian God is the particular God revealed in the particular history that climaxes in Jesus Christ. Dismissing the notion that the Trinity is a speculative or metaphysical construct, Barth developed and interpreted the doctrine in such a way that it answers the question, "Who is God?" by referring one to the biblical story of redemption: The Father is revealed in the reconciling work of the Son that becomes effective within the believer through the activity of the Holy Spirit. Hence the doctrine of the Trinity functions not only to identify the Christian God by pointing to God's unique history with humanity, but it also serves as a reminder that revelation is the only avenue by which this God may be known.

Barth places great emphasis on the dynamic character of the divine being. One may not speak of God in abstraction from the divine activity. God is known concretely only in God's historical acts, preeminently in Jesus Christ. Theology is right to speak of God as personal, not because one knows in advance what a person is and applies this concept to God, but because from God's self-revelation one learns what true personhood is. Revelation shows the personal God to be one who always acts in love and in freedom. In love God acts to show judgment and mercy, and to will and fulfill fellowship with humanity. In freedom God acts unbounded by any external necessity, utterly transcendent to creation, but also free to dwell immanently within the world.

Christology, or the doctrine of Jesus Christ, is a theme that so dominates and permeates the *Church Dogmatics* that no single volume brings together all that Barth would want to say. As noted already, Jesus Christ represents for Barth the only reliable path to genuine knowledge of God, since only Jesus is fully and decisively the self-revelation of God. This affirmation entails the same profound theological insight that the early church brought to light in its Chalcedonian Christology—that Jesus Christ is truly God and truly human. Barth also affirms the orthodox doctrine of the virgin birth as a sign that points to the "miracle of Christmas." Rejecting interpretations of the doctrine that view it as a crude attempt to prove the divinity of Christ, Barth finds in the virgin birth a sign that bears witness to the unique status of Jesus Christ, not by explaining the mystery of the incarnation but by proclaiming it.

Christology offers more than simply a reliable knowledge of God. Jesus Christ in his life, death, and resurrection is the event of reconciliation whereby God takes the initiative to restore fellowship with a lost humanity. This pivotal event of salvation history is best observed in the two decisive moments that compose it: the Lord as servant, and the servant as Lord. The Lord as servant refers to the condescension of God as incarnate Son—what Barth terms "the way of the Son of God into the far country." Here the Son performs his priestly function, moving toward humanity in mercy and love, climaxing in the cross, where through an event of radical substitution the sinless judge of humanity takes the sins of humanity upon himself. The priest becomes the victim, thereby restoring the broken covenant. The servant as Lord refers to the exaltation of the Son—what Barth terms "the home-coming of the Son of Man." In the exaltation manifested preeminently in the resurrection, the event of reconciliation is completed. The public exaltation of the Son includes the exaltation of his humanity that moves homeward toward God. The reconciliation of humanity is completed by virtue of its inclusion within the exalted humanity of the Son.

An aspect of Barth's thought for which he is perhaps best known is his reinterpretation of the Reformed doctrine of election. He recognizes in the church's language of predestination an attempt to bring to expression the sovereign grace of God. For Barth it is quite simply the sum of the gospel—that God elects humanity and that this election is utterly unconditioned by any human merit, preparation, or disposition. But his fresh reinterpretation of the doctrine of election rejects any form of double-predestination whereby some are elected to salvation and others to damnation. He departs from the orthodox Reformed tradition in his refusal to speak of the doctrine in isolation from Jesus Christ. Christ himself, as the electing God, has elected humanity for salvation. But Christ is also the elect man, the one chosen before time to restore the broken covenant between God and humanity. The election of any particular person is always an election "in Christ," and the election "in Christ" is an election of all persons for salvation and eternity. Hence, Barth removes the doctrine of election from the realm of speculation regarding the eternal destiny of any particular person and transforms it into an affirmation of radical grace.

Salvation comes to the human being as an unconditioned act of God's sovereign mercy. The reality and the objectivity of the salvation event can only be fully affirmed if the event is seen to come to humankind as a gift that is already actual and complete. The gift is effective whether or not it is acknowledged by the recipient. The alternative, describing salvation as in some sense dependent on a human response, would imply that salvation is a mere possibility not yet realized in human existence. The gospel would become yet another law by which humanity was condemned. These considerations lead Barth to the tentative and somewhat ambiguous conclusion that, while the promise of a universal salvation cannot be dogmatically proclaimed, it must nevertheless remain an open question and a real possibility of God's grace.

If Christ the Son establishes the objective possibility of human salvation for Barth, the Holy Spirit establishes the subjective possibility. Since response to the gospel is in no sense an inherent capacity of human existence, Barth speaks of the Holy Spirit as the divine act whereby a human being is empowered for encounter with the self-revealing God. Always presented in dynamic categories, the Spirit transforms the ancient words of the Bible into life-changing divine address, just as the Spirit in any given moment transforms a local congregation into Christ's faithful church.

Theological anthropology, says Barth, must conform to the same epistemological restrictions valid for other theological assertions. Only God's revelation in Jesus Christ can offer a reliable starting point for an authentic theological understanding of the human being. Although scientific and philosophical descriptions of human existence can offer helpful insights on many levels, they can never do more than describe the "human phenomenon," which is nothing more than a shadow of the authentic humanity revealed comprehensively only in Jesus Christ. An analysis of the humanity of the Christ reveals for Barth the critical role of *relationality* as a fundamental attribute of existence. Jesus is the Son who lives and acts in intimate fellowship with the Father, which enables Jesus to be "the Man for others." Relationality as the basic form of humanity is already implied by the doctrine of the image of God, which according to Barth's exegesis of Genesis 1 refers to the creation of humanity in the differentiated unity of male and female. Sexuality is a sign of the relationality that defines the ultimate purpose of human existence, the covenant relation between creator and creature. Correspondingly, sin may be interpreted as the negation of one's cohumanity—as the act of the solitary "I am" whereby one violates one's own true humanity. Barth offers a reinterpretation of the traditional doctrine of "original sin." He joins the consensus of much modern theology in rejecting the notion of a biological inheritance, whereby guilt and corruption are passed down from generation to generation as a result of a historical Fall in the garden. Original sin is the first sin of every individual. Yet, he is unswerving in his commitment to the Augustinian-Reformation insistence on the universal and comprehensive effects of sin on humanity. No area of human activity is preserved from sin's corruptive power.

Barth's often-cited discussion of evil departs from the usual pattern of the debate, which focuses on attempts to reconcile the reality of evil with the dual theological claims of divine love and omnipotence. Criticizing this approach as a philosophical abstraction, Barth insists that a Christian view of evil is one that proceeds in retrospect from the cross, where evil has been finally and ultimately refuted. Resisting the temptation of a theological triumphalism, he concedes the mysterious nature of evil—that human suffering of enormous magnitude continues in the present in spite of the victorious claim of the cross. Evil is thus an "impossible possibility" with no claim to perpetuity. Barth prefers the term "nothingness" as a descriptive designation for evil, thereby refusing to allow evil an ontological status that in principle would rival the rule of God. Nothingness derives its reality as something that "is" only as that which God in fact rejects. It is the divine non-willing from which nothingness derives its own perverse reality. Giving the discussion a more practical turn, Barth observes that the defeat of evil is primarily God's affair, and that indeed God has taken up the cause of humanity in the fight with nothingness, not only by defeating evil at the cross, but through the gracious empowerment of men and women to take their part in the conflict.

The relationship of Christianity to other religions is a theme of Barth's theology frequently criticized and unfortunately often misunderstood. His approach is usually described in terms of exclusivism; that is, there is simply no place for divine revelation outside the biblical narrative. The early Barth in particular was fond of describing the idea of religion as a human grasping after the divine in contrast to the divine initiative of self-revelation portrayed in the Bible. On this basis the phenomenon of religion is subject to the harsh critique of self-righteousness and idolatry. What is often neglected in summaries of Barth's position, however, is that he includes Christianity as an instance of human religiosity subject to this divine judgment. In this sense Christianity as a religion is actually one with the religions of the world. Of course, the "false religion" of Christianity can by God's grace point to the "true religion" of faith in the God revealed in Jesus Christ, a claim that Barth would not make for other religions. For this reason, a general discussion on the nature and significance of religion would fit uneasily, if at all, with Barth's emphasis on the revelational boundaries of theological reflection and the universality of the salvation event. At the same time, it should be observed that this is a theme for which Barth simply had little interest.

Impact and Criticism

From approximately 1930 to 1960, the theology of Karl Barth along with that of other representatives of neoorthodoxy enjoyed immense popularity in North America. Barth has been assigned at least partial credit for effecting a number of significant changes on the theological landscape, including a renewed interest among theologians in the role of preaching, a desire to move beyond the historical-critical method to more theologically fruitful ways of reading Scripture, a recovery of the relevance of the doctrine of sin, and a healthy suspicion of cultural ideology's subversion of the theological task.

The most direct continuing influence of Karl Barth's theology is found within the loosely aligned movement of postliberal theology. Barth's interpretation of the ecclesial function of theology parallels in many ways the description of religious doctrines as constituting a grammar of belief normative for a particular community of shared faith, an idea prominent in the writings of Hans Frei and George Lindbeck.

Since the beginnings of his theological career, Barth's theology has also been the target of frequent and often severe criticism. While virtually all of Barth's theological positions are subject to debate on some level, two lines of methodological critique persistently appear in evaluations of his thought. First is the complaint that Barth's theology leads inexorably in the direction of some kind of monism, most commonly designated a "Christomonism." Themes such as the sovereignty and freedom of God, the doctrine of election, and the finality and completeness of salvation combine to overpower the significance of human agency and freedom. Barth's consistent method of deriving all theological truth, even anthropological truth, from what can be said about Jesus Christ would appear to deprive human existence and indeed all of culture and creation of what might be called theological dignity. In response to his critics, Barth consistently affirmed the reality of human freedom and denied any contradiction between human freedom and divine sovereignty—but neither do human and divine freedom compete with each other. Divine freedom always precedes and conditions human freedom. The free agency and dignity of the human being come to full view only as an act of obedient response to the command of God.

Second, the circularity of Barth's theology in basing all of its claims in the faith assertion of divine revelation creates an openness to the charge of "fideism" (Pannenberg) or "revelational positivism" (Bonhoeffer). Critics charge that since Barth allows no external reference points by which theological truth claims might be measured in dialogue with unbelievers, he illegitimately insulates himself from rational critique. In other words, Barth's theology has nothing to offer the inquiring unbeliever interested in the plausibility of Christian faith. At best this implies the irrelevance of his theology for a secular and skeptical world; at worst, it implies its fundamental irrationality. Defenders of Barth counter that the search for a rational basis for Christian faith anywhere outside of God's specific self-revelation amounts to little more than speculation. Christian theology is essentially rational, but its rationality operates on the basis of the unprovable assumption that God's definitive self-revelation has occurred in the person of Jesus Christ.

Benjamin C. Leslie

Selected Bibliography

1957   Karl Barth, *The Word of God and the Word of Man.*
1976   Eberhard Busch, *Karl Barth: His Life from Letters and Autobiographical Texts.*
1986   Eberhard Jüngel, *Karl Barth: A Theological Legacy.*
1991   George Hunsinger, *How to Read Karl Barth.*
1994   ———. *Church Dogmatics: A Selection with Introduction by Helmut Gollwitzer.*

NICHOLAS BERDYAEV
1874–1948

Life and Career

Nicholas Berdyaev's achievements as a philosopher-theologian lead one to regard him as the Eastern Orthodox counterpart to Jacques Maritain, the Roman Catholic thinker, or to the Protestant giant Paul Tillich. Like them, Berdyaev sought to relate religion to culture, to articulate the theological dimension in all forms of modern thought and inquiry, and not least of all to show the relevance and need of Christian faith for the demands and uncertainties of modern human existence. The turbulent quality of Berdyaev's writing reflects the struggle of his early life in Russia and his experiences in Western Europe after he was exiled from Russia in 1922 by the Bolsheviks following the Red Revolution in 1917.

Born in 1874 in Kiev, of an aristocratic family, Berdyaev studied at the University of Kiev, where he came under the influence of Marx's writings and joined the Social Democratic Party, as the Marxists then called themselves, primarily because of their concern for social justice. In 1900, he was arrested by the tsarist government for revolutionary activity and exiled to the northern city of Vologda for three years. During this period of imprisonment Berdyaev and other Marxists began to seek a way to synthesize Marx's social philosophy with German idealism, especially the critical idealism of Kant, whose analysis of truth and freedom they were coming to accept. Berdyaev eventually saw this synthesis as an impossibility because in dialectical materialism the spiritual dimension to existence is denied, and Berdyaev claimed that there could be no freedom without spirit.

Berdyaev finally broke with Marxism because he regarded its political outgrowth in communism as a too rigidly orthodox, literalist, authoritarian sort of religion. The Marxists had no reverence for personality, which Berdyaev was coming to regard as the clue to the meaning of human reality. Despite his rejection of Marxism and communism, he fully accepted Marx's claim that the evolution of society toward the modern industrial state was made possible only by the exploitation of human beings.

Berdyaev began to consider himself a Christian well before his exile from Russia in 1922; but his Christianity was not that of the church in Russia, which he considered as corrupt as the prerevolutionary government. He identified himself with a spiritual Christianity, whose focus was the hero of freedom—the universal Christ portrayed in Dostoyevsky's story of the Grand Inquisitor. The characteristic posture of Berdyaev by temperament and by conviction was that of independence: a Christian, but not of the Russian church; a revolutionary, but not identifying with the Bolsheviks; a socialist, but repudiating Marx. This independence became a part of his theological vision, incorporated into that freedom of spirit, that divine-humanity that is the keynote of his thought.

God

According to Berdyaev, the only idea of God that can have meaning for human beings is that which attributes to God what is most basic and ideal in humanity—the divine possibilities for self-fulfillment in and through others, the divine capacity for love. Hence, the most meaningful understanding of God centers on the social nature of God; this is the divine-human *sobornost*, which is God's spiritual unity with the human, God's need for love, God's desire for the "other" (cf. *Freedom and the Spirit*, 1935, chap. 6).

Berdyaev holds that in seeking to satisfy the need for love, God acted not only to create life, but that God acts decisively within life to redeem creation from its failures to fulfill this need. Berdyaev denies that it makes sense to speak of God as creating for self-glorification in and through the witness of an obedient creation, or to speak of God creating for aesthetic satisfaction. These motives contradict the primacy of love in God's life. God creates and saves creation from sin because God cannot otherwise love and be loved.

The act of creation signifies, for Berdyaev, that God was less than perfect and that God becomes perfect—perfect in love by a creation that realizes its end in loving its creator. Moreover, consistent with God's need for love, God must offer redemption to the world if the integrity of divine love in the divine-human *sobornost* is to be sustained.

The tragedy of God's love is that the creation fails to respond in love, thus frustrating God's purpose in the world. In answer to this failure, God acts to redeem creation by acts of forgiveness and judgment, love and sacrifice, within the creative event of the Christ. Jesus Christ enters history as a continuation and actualization of the possibilities of love established in creation. Thus, the purpose of redemption in Jesus Christ is not the restoration of the world to its original and created relationship to God, but rather the creation of a new reality in the world, bringing the world to a new and more creative relationship to God by virtue of the reality of redemptive grace that is now inseparable from the love of God in creation.

The final tragedy of God's love, Berdyaev says, is that even God's redemptive grace cannot be made real without the cost of suffering and death. The price of humanity's salvation is the crucifixion of Christ. God suffers death out of love for human beings that, in and through his death, he might move humanity to a responsive love.

God's desire for love and humanity's response in love create a spiritual relationship between God and humans. "Spirit," for Berdyaev, means the energy of love, freedom, and creativity within the divine-human *sobornost*. He says at one point:

> It is according to a spiritual plan and within the spiritual life that the creation of the world took place, God desired another self and a reciprocal answer to His love. Then came the Fall, and the New Adam was the restorer of fallen human nature.
>
> *(Freedom and the Spirit, 1935, p. 21)*

And in another place, he adds: "Spirit is not only Divine, it is also divinely human. Divine; it is freedom in God and from God" (*Spirit and Reality,* 1935, p. 33).

Spirit

The spiritual energy that united God and the human contains in its freedom two directions of action. There is the growth of spirit by love, and there is the decay of spirit in the externalization or dissipation of spirit by the absence of love. If spirit grows, it is because the human is able to reach the qualitative depths of God's own being and confront freedom, love, death, sacrifice, suffering, good, evil, sin, joy, and creativeness. For in this depth, humans are truly human, with the human exercising all those capacities within oneself that makes one God's love partner. Hence, for Berdyaev, spirit is not opposed to sin or evil; for both sin and evil are human dimensions inseparable from freedom, and therefore, part of the mystery of God's love and of the divine struggle to discover God's "other self."

The opposite of spirit is dehumanized existence. It is persons living in denial of the divine depths within themselves, living on the surface of life, fearing the task of freedom and therefore not really knowing either good or evil. It is persons dehumanized by absorption into groups and institutions, surrounded by all manner of things or objects, regarded as one among many, a digit or cipher in the world-machine of humanity. This existence, Berdyaev calls "Objectified" existence (cf. *The Beginning and the End,* 1957, pp. 3-80, and *Slavery and Freedom,* 1944). In Plato's terms it is the unreal life of self-deception and illusion. "Objectified" persons are reduced to thing-hood, robbed of the uniqueness that spirit has given them. "Objectified" existence does not recognize God in the human, because it views the human through the quantified conceptions that inhere in the designations

"nations," "law," "race," "economy," and so on. In the "objectified" life, Berdyaev says:

> God, the world, and the soul are separated from one another, and in consequence spiritual experience becomes impossible, for it can only exist when man is regarded as a microcosm in which the whole universe is revealed and in which there are no transcendent limits isolating man from God and from the world.
>
> (*Freedom and the Spirit*, 1935, p. 15)

The agency of spirit makes co-creators of God and humanity. God cannot be the Creator and the Redeemer without the humans, for God cannot love without the human; and humanity cannot be the created and the redeemed without the love of God. Ultimately, beyond the tragedy of freedom in suffering and evil, God and humans are united in both the actualities and possibilities of spirit. This is an indissoluble bond. Persons may oppose God in sin, but in so doing they move God into creative acts of both judgment and grace. Persons cannot fully flee from God, because they cannot finally flee from humanity itself, which can never sever its spiritual roots from the creation in which God is always creatively manifest. By the same token, no person can grow in spirit alone with God. What unites persons with God in spirit unites them with other persons (*Freedom and the Spirit*, p. 19). Berdyaev says that salvation is communal; no human is saved until humanity is saved (*The Destiny of Man*, 1960, p. 281).

Spirit is the ontological structure of creation manifested in the existential "depth" situations of love, freedom, and creativeness. Berdyaev vigorously protests philosophical conceptions that place God at the top of a hierarchy of being. He will have nothing to do with the classical understanding of God in the principle of *analogia entis* (the analogy of being), which, he argues, tends to view the relationship between God and humans as a static order. It externalizes God's basic relationship to the world by replacing spirit with the notions of impermeable and unalterable "substance" and "being." What is most true of God as known by spirit is the real life of God—that is, God's experience of love and tragic suffering. Since the philosophy of being cannot convey this experience, Berdyaev says:

> The Aristotelian conception of God as *actus purus* deprives God of that interior active life, and transforms Him into a lifeless object. God is left without power, that is to say, He is no longer the source of movement and life.

and,

> God is spirit, and for that reason, therefore cannot be substance. The nature of spirit is Heraclitic and not Parmenidean. Spirit is fire and energy.
>
> (*The Destiny of Man*, pp. 1, 15)

Divine and Human Creativeness

For Berdyaev, the meaning of the creative act lies in the conjoining of God's creative and redemptive love with humanity's redemptively transformed life turned toward creative ends. It is God going out to humanity in love and freedom, and persons responding to God in love and freedom. Thus, the creative act is, for Berdyaev, the highest expression of divine-human spirit. As such, human creativeness is the cooperation with all that God does to create the world and creatively to continue the divine creation in and by the redemption of the world from sin. To understand human creativeness is to view it in the wider context of God's struggle with nonbeing to create being, and of God's victory over nonbeing in Christ's reaffirmation of freedom and love. Human creativeness thus is seen through the more primary relationship between creation and redemption.

Berdyaev identifies the relationship between creation and redemption by referring to redemption as "the eighth-day of creation" (*The Meaning of the Creative Act*, 1955, p. 128). Two things are implied by this statement. First, redemption is a continuation of the effort of God to create the world; second, redemption represents in a unique manner the completion of creation.

Berdyaev's entire effort at stating the relationship between creation and redemption centers on the insight that God's forgiveness of sins is insufficient to account for the full scope of God's relation to humanity in love. It is necessary that God offer divine grace to humans, but it is equally necessary that humanity be transformed by grace to offer a creative response to God's love. The sinner must be forgiven, but to what end the forgiveness? Berdyaev answers that

> there can be but one solution for this tragic problem of Christianity: religious awareness of the truth that the religious significance of life and being is not exhausted by the redemption from sin, but that life and being have positive, creative tasks. . . . Salvation from sin, from perdition, is not the final goal of religious life; for salvation is always *from* something, while life should be *for* something. . . . The goal of man is not salvation alone, but a creative ascent; but for the creative ascent salvation from evil and sin is necessary. (*The Meaning of the Creative Act*, p. 99)

It follows, for Berdyaev, that if redemption has as its end the wider creative purpose, then to the degree that humanity has not been fully transformed to become God's love partner, God's purpose in creation remains unfulfilled. Berdyaev holds that the time in which we now find ourselves is the time of unfulfilled creation. This is a peculiarly human era. It is the period of the Holy Spirit, which has been preceded by the revelation of God, the Father, in creation, and God, the Son, in redemption. It is the age of the human under the spirit where both God's creative and redemptive energies converge. Humanity is at the crossroads between answering God and destructively closing humanity to God and to creation as God's expression. The human burden is incredible. It is equal in a sense to God's. Humanity can be god-of-earth, the *microtheos,* in both its positive and negative meanings (cf. *Spirit and Reality,* 1935, p. 149).

Creativeness is a function of human freedom. Humanity is free when it is truly humanity, that is, when it realizes the element of divinity within itself. What is this divinity that is the content of human freedom? God is creator of being out of nonbeing; and humanity is divine in the power to imitate God's creativity. Thus, Berdyaev says, "Creativeness is only possible because the world is created, because there is a Creator. Man, made by God in His own image and likeness, is also a creator and is called to creative work" (*The Destiny of Man,* 1960, p. 127).

Creativeness is human freedom working to bring into the world through all the faculties (imagination, reason, will, freedom, and so on) something that is not a part of its past. But, Berdyaev asks, is something completely new really possible within the historical world? Presumably, God can truly create being out of nonbeing. But humans operate within the world already under the effect of creative action. Can they bring to the world what the world itself has never known? Can they truly create "being"?

Berdyaev answers by examining what we ordinarily mean by "creativeness." In the usual sense of the words, creative becoming always presupposes material antecedents (clay for the potter), formal antecedents (existing ideas influencing the creator's mind), and antecedent creations (already existing works that new creation will to some degree resemble). The creatively "new," Berdyaev argues, does not, then, mean the physically and historically new. However, what is radically new and unique about the creative act is that it is specifically the work of *this* creator, this individual person, and nobody else. The creatively new is the stamp of creation put upon the work by this person as *his* or *her* creation. The criterion of creativeness thus resides in the qualitative region of the projection of human personality. The criterion is intensely subjective, though objective factors will illumine the problem of where the human personality of the creator has broken out and made its impact in the world.

The created work bears witness to creativeness because it points to the personality of the creator. Creativeness is not revolutionary from the point of view of the created work. But it is revolutionary with respect to the element of personality within creativeness. Creative works bear some degree of resemblance to other works, but a creative personality (each human as the unique work of God) does not and cannot, when preserving this uniqueness, resemble another work of God.

The value of each person's creativeness is not equal to, but very similar to, the value revealed by God's creativeness in making the world. Where is the difference? For Berdyaev, the answer lies in the recognition that a person

is not absolute and hence cannot have absolute power. In his creativity man is related to other people and to the whole world of beings: he is not almighty. But in human personality there is original creative force resembling that of God. God is not the master, the lord, the commander. God's management of the world is not an autocracy.

(The Meaning of the Creative Act, 1955, p. 126)

In the biblical myth of creation, what is most important is not that God has brought forth oceans and trees and humans where there were none before, but that through the agency of creativeness, God's own personality as God was expressed. God became "God" in creation. Humans must, therefore, be human where they are most like God—in creativeness.

Thomas A. Idinopulos

Selected Bibliography

1935   *Freedom and the Spirit.*
1935   *Spirit and Reality.*
1944   *Slavery and Freedom.*
1955   *The Meaning of the Creative Act.*
1957   *The Beginning and the End.*
1960   *The Destiny of Man.*

DONALD G. BLOESCH
1928–

Without question, Donald Bloesch is one of the premier thinkers in conservative evangelical theology in North America. When he retired at age sixty-five after teaching at the University of Dubuque Theological Seminary for more than thirty years, Bloesch had written more than twenty-five books and two hundred articles. Through his publications, guest lectures and professorships, and mentoring of hundreds of ministerial students, he exercised a profound influence on a generation of theologians attracted to postfundamentalist, evangelical scholarship.

Bloesch describes his own approach to theology as "progressive evangelicalism," which means that he emphasizes the primacy of the Word of God over cultural and philosophical influences without the narrow, sectarian mind-set that pervaded much fundamentalism. This progressive evangelicalism Bloesch espouses and seeks to develop stands in continuity with the historical church—especially the early church fathers and the Reformers of the sixteenth century. It is not synonymous with emotionalism or scholasticism, but heartily embraces personal transformation through Christ and the life of the mind.

More than anyone else, Bloesch brought the influence of the Swiss theologian Karl Barth to bear on North American evangelical theology. Whereas fundamentalism, and most of conservative evangelical theology, rejected Barth's "neoorthodoxy," Bloesch carefully worked through it. By studying with Barth and reading all of his chief writings, he discovered valuable resources for the evangelical church in his own context. In many ways Bloesch could be considered as standing on the boundary between traditional conservative Protestant theology and twentieth-century neoorthodox (Barthian) theology. From that vantage point he gently but firmly criticized extremes on both conservative and liberal ends of the theological spectrum.

Donald G. Bloesch (which rhymes with *flesh*) was born in Indiana on May 3, 1928. His father and both grandfathers were pastors of the German Evangelical

Church, the North American equivalent of the Prussian Union Church (Lutheran and Reformed). His childhood denomination eventually merged with another denomination to become the Evangelical and Reformed Church, which in turn merged with the Congregational denomination to form the United Church of Christ (UCC). Although he taught at a Presbyterian seminary, Bloesch is an ordained minister with the UCC and actively participates in its evangelical renewal movement, the Biblical Witness Fellowship.

Bloesch grew up in the suburbs of Chicago and attended Elmhurst College. His seminary training was under primarily liberal teachers at Chicago Theological Seminary. Upon completion of his seminary degree in 1953 he was ordained and began doctoral studies in theology at the University of Chicago. Although most of his courses were taught by liberal theologians and biblical scholars, Bloesch found spiritual camaraderie with the evangelical InterVarsity Christian Fellowship. He wrote his dissertation on Reinhold Niebuhr's apologetics, received the Ph.D. in 1956, and then embarked upon postdoctoral studies in Europe (at Oxford and Basel) while teaching and writing. He met his wife, Brenda, in Geneva, Switzerland, and they married in 1962. Trained as a scholar of French language and literature, she became his theological associate in research and writing.

Although he has written numerous influential books and articles, he has twice summed up his entire body of theological thought in systematic theological treatises. In 1978 and 1979 he published his groundbreaking and popular two-volume *Essentials of Evangelical Theology.* Therein he called for evangelicals to turn away from hairsplitting, sectarian disputes over the inerrancy of scripture and the endtimes and to return to the great themes of historical Protestant theology. He argued for a broad, tolerant evangelical theology. In the same volumes Bloesch strongly criticized liberal and neoliberal theologies for capitulating to secularism. He called on liberal theology to rediscover biblical foundations and eschew accommodation to the latest winds of philosophical speculation. On the positive side, Bloesch laid out a trajectory for evangelical theology to follow into the future that began in the past with the church fathers (Tertullian over Justin Martyr), the Protestant Reformers (Luther and Calvin over all others), and the Pietists (over mystics).

In the early 1990s Bloesch began to write a seven-volume systematic theology entitled *Christian Foundations.* The first volume, *Theology of Word and Spirit,* appeared in 1992, and volume two, *Holy Scripture,* appeared in 1994. Each volume of the set is designed to deal with an important locus of Christian theology.

According to Bloesch, the purpose of theology is summed up in the ancient axiom "faith seeking understanding." With Augustine, Anselm, and Calvin, he says that one cannot understand God and God's word, will, and way until one first is transformed by the Spirit of God so that one believes in order to understand: *Credo ut intellegam* ("I believe in order that I may understand"). Faith, which is a gift of God, then provides the light of the mind that opens one to God and drives a person to plumb the depths of understanding of God as far as is humanly possible. Bloesch never tires of refuting all forms of theological rationalism that see theology as a human search for God. The motto of this perennial, rationalistic heresy, according to Bloesch, would be: "I seek to understand [God] in order that I may believe." Such a philosophical approach to theological truth undermines the sovereignty of God, underestimates the negative effects of sin on human reason, and undercuts the prophetic power of the gospel of God's Word, turning it into a message that humans can discover and thus relativizing its truth and power.

As much as he abhors theological rationalism in all its forms (whether liberal or conservative), Bloesch never sides with theology's enemies. For him, mysticism is almost a greater danger than rationalism insofar as it denies the mind's ability to grasp objective truth about God. In fact, Bloesch constantly returns to the theme of twin dangers facing modern Christianity: "philosophism" and "experientialism" (*A Theology of Word and Spirit*, 1992, pp. 108-9). These are *not* equatable with "liberal" and "conservative." They are orientations toward truth and its discovery that underlie all distortions at both ends of the theological spectrum. Philosophism is "the ill-fated confusion of theology with philosophy of religion." In the early centuries of the church, it appeared in some of the apologists' linking of the gospel with Stoicism and Neoplatonism. It reappeared in medieval and post-Reformation Scholasticism's penchant for Aristotelian logic and metaphysics as prolegomena to theology, and in the modern age it can be detected in liberal and conservative attempts to shore up and justify Christian belief with rational apologetics and various "fundamental theologies." According to Bloesch, theology is inevitably corrupted whenever the truth of God's Word is made dependent on coherence with some philosophical source or norm.

The second danger against which Bloesch warns is the perennial temptation of experientialism. Although he values his own Pietist heritage highly, the Iowa theologian has no use for subjectivism that reduces truth to feelings and preferences. Experientialism is prevalent among both liberal and conservative Christians, and it "reduces the content of faith to the vagaries of religious or simply human experiences" (*A Theology of Word and Spirit,* p. 109). The inevitable result of this approach, Bloesch argues, is relativism.

Bloesch defines theology against these twin dangers: "Theology is not the verbalization of religious experience (Schleiermacher), even less of common human experience (David Tracy). Instead, it is the articulation of a divine revelation that breaks into our experience from beyond and transforms it" (*A Theology of Word and Spirit,* p. 118). Because the supreme source and norm for theology is this transcendent, even supernatural, Word of God (which is not identical with the Bible), theology will inevitably express its truths in paradoxical ways that reason, unaided by the Spirit of God, cannot discover or accept.

Clearly, Bloesch's theological method is deeply indebted to Karl Barth. With the Swiss theologian he rejects all forms of natural theology and sees the greatest danger as cultural accommodation of the gospel and theology to secular criteria of truth. Bloesch recognizes this association: "I am not urging a repristination of Barthian theology (some of Barth's conclusions are problematic), but I believe we need to take his way of doing theology over that of Tillich, Küng, and Pannenberg (and I might add Edward John Carnell, Francis Schaeffer, and Carl Henry)" (*A Theology of Word and Spirit*, 1992, p. 271). Bloesch strongly diverges from Barth on several issues, including the existence of a general revelation of God, the inspiration of Scripture, and universalism. Overall, however, he finds Barth's corrective to false and debilitating approaches to theology unsurpassed.

Bloesch labels his own theological method "fideistic revelationism." Although the term itself first appears in volume one of his *Christian Foundations*, the basic approach was laid out in his 1971 alternative to apologetics, *The Ground of Certainty*. Theology begins with the self-authenticating revelation of God—"God's Word," which is neither a mystical experience (subjective) nor a set of descriptive propositions (objective). Rather, it is the personal, historical, objective-subjective self-communication of God from beyond human history that breaks into it, taking human forms. One task of theology is to conform the church's words to the ineffable Word of God that is personal and cannot itself be captured in human language. Perhaps out of necessity, Bloesch (like Barth) is vague about the exact nature of revelation. Sometimes he treats it as "personal encounter" and at other times it becomes the person of Jesus Christ or the Logos in him, and yet again it becomes the gospel message about Christ. In any case, divine revelation is transcendent— from beyond. It cannot be anticipated or judged. It simply comes from God and challenges all historical, cultural thought forms and expressions while also taking them on as its culturally accommodated form (dialectical!).

Revelation, then, is theology's irreducible, unsurpassable, and supreme source and norm. Nothing stands alongside it. It is a message from God and can only be accepted by faith through the work of the Holy Spirit in a person's mind and heart. Bloesch denies that this is "sheer fideism" (blind faith): "What I espouse is not fideism but a faith that is deeper than fideism, for it is anchored in the supreme rationality that constitutes the content and object of faith" (*A Theology of Word and Spirit*, p. 203). Since this "supreme rationality" is only available by faith to the Christian through the Holy Spirit, however, some of Bloesch's (and Barth's) critics see this defense against the charge of "sheer fideism" as specious. Nevertheless, Bloesch is not deterred by such criticism, for he sees all alternatives to his fideistic revelationism as worse than "sheer fideism." According to him, they all end in some degree of cultural captivity of the gospel and theology.

Bloesch's view of the Word of God is sacramental. That is, he believes that the supreme source and norm of theological truth, divine revelation, is never identical with any human, historical reality. For instance, neither the Bible (as a book) nor Jesus Christ (as a human being) is strictly identical with "God's Word." And yet both are necessarily and rightly called "God's Word." The solution to this paradox is the sacramental vision of reality in which transcendent, nonhistorical, divine reality enters into and takes form as some human, historical reality. One must avoid confusing the two realities, however. One is absolute content; the other is relative form. Yet the relative form actually participates to one degree or another, as God's Spirit allows, in the absolute content. Thus, there is a sense in which it is correct to say that the man Christ Jesus *is* God's Word in person. Again, and in a similar way but to a lesser degree, the Bible *is* God's Word written. Finally, following Barth again, Bloesch affirms that the proclamation of the church can *be* God's Word in the present—as God chooses.

The nature of the Bible presents a special problem for theology today. Bloesch is very concerned that two opposite errors be avoided. On the one hand, he contends that liberal higher criticism of Scripture has reduced the Bible to little more than a historical source of dubious information about Israel and the early Christian Church. This, Bloesch is sure, is not truly an "assured result" of higher criticism, but a natural outcome of modernism's naturalistic assumptions. The result is no objective standard of truth for theology. On the other hand, he observes that fundamentalism and much evangelical theology has elevated Scripture nearly to an icon of worship by equating it with God's Word as a set of divinely revealed propositions. Bloesch sees this as problematic in the light of clear cultural conditioning in Scripture. It also, he avers, tends to elevate human words to divine status, robbing God's Spirit of sovereignty.

What is the proper relationship, then, between revelation (God's Word) and the Bible? As an evangelical he wishes to do justice to the *sola scriptura* principle. But as a progressive he wishes to acknowledge the historical and cultural conditioning of Scripture. Bloesch's initial description of the relationship in the second volume of his *Christian Foundations* rings very Barthian: "[Scripture] becomes the revealed Word of God when God himself speaks through the prophetic and apostolic witness, sealing the truth of this witness in our hearts" (*Holy Scripture,* 1994, p. 27). On the other hand, he affirms that this *"becomes"* must be understood in the special sense that Scripture, unlike any other book, is always translucent to God's Word. This perpetual translucency is a work of the Spirit of God, not an autonomous property of the Bible as a book.

Bloesch likens the relation between the Bible and God's Word to that between a light bulb and light. The light bulb is not light itself, but it is the instrument or medium of the light. Of course the question many conservative evangelicals wish to ask at this point is whether this particular light bulb is always glowing? Is the Bible always revealing the Word of God? It seems that Barth was ambiguous on this point, wishing to reserve to Godself the right and power to determine when the light bulb "comes on" and when God's Word breaks forth from the Bible. At this point Bloesch seems to diverge from Barth, but also from traditional evangelical theology. In his particular sacramental understanding of the Bible, it is like a light bulb controlled by a rheostat. To some degree, even if imperceptibly to the unregenerate human eye, the light is there, but the Spirit of God decides its intensity. So, the Bible is *always already* the Word of God (instrumentally), but also *becomes* God's Word as the Spirit wishes to intensify the connection.

Bloesch wrestles with traditional evangelical concepts such as "inspiration" and "inerrancy" of the Bible. He is clearer about the former than the latter. "Inspiration," he avers, "is the divine election and superintendence of particular writers and writings in order to ensure a trustworthy and potent witness to the truth" (*Holy Scripture*, 1994, p. 119). It does *not* mean divine dictation, nor merely the subjective ability to inspire. The Bible is ontologically different from all other books because there alone God's Spirit penetrates and fills a human book, using it to transform lives and lead into divine truth.

The issue of the possible inerrancy of Scripture receives less enthusiastic support from Bloesch. "Inerrancy" is a term that has created a great deal of confusion and turmoil in conservative evangelical circles, and Bloesch believes it can entirely be replaced with "infallibility." The Bible is *not* faultless, but it is "incapable of teaching deception" (*Holy Scripture*, p. 115). Using sound hermeneutics and historical research, Bloesch denies that every single statement of the Bible conforms to the facts of world history and science. This is a function of divine accommodation, however, not of some defect in Scripture.

With regard to theological method, sources, and norms of theology, the nature of divine revelation, and Scripture, Bloesch wishes to stake out a middle ground between classical liberal and conservative theologies. However, his greater sympathy lies with the latter, as he states:

> If required to choose between liberalism and a rigid orthodoxy, my choice would unhesitatingly be the latter. In liberalism truth is dissolved so that only an amorphous experience remains. In orthodoxy truth is frozen into a formula or credo, but there is hope that it can be brought back to life. (*Holy Scripture*, p. 105)

Toward the end of his career Bloesch has come to believe that North American Christianity at the end of the twentieth century is facing a new "church struggle" analogous to the great *Kirchenkampf* of Germany in the Nazi era. In that time and place Christianity was being seduced into an unholy alliance with a cultural quasi-religion of Germanic blood and soil. A few stalwart defenders of transcendent truth such as Barth and Bonhoeffer took an uncompromising stand against the ideological temptation of "German Christianity." According to Bloesch, "Nothing so characterizes the contemporary theological scene as the erosion of transcendence" (*A Theology of Word and Spirit*, 1992, p. 250), and it results in a situation like that in Germany in the 1930s. Christianity, Bloesch fears, is being resymbolized according to various ideologies of the right and left, and in the process it is losing its prophetic character, becoming little more than a cipher for political and social agendas.

In this situation Bloesch calls for a new evangelical confessionalism along the lines of the "Confessing Church" movement of Germany in the decade leading up to World War II. The movement would oppose all claims to any loyalty that challenged loyalty to the transcendent, personal Father, Son, and Holy Spirit. In 1985 Bloesch wrote a stinging attack against "inclusive God-language" arising out of feminist theology entitled *The Battle for the Trinity*. Although he has nothing against using feminine language about God, Bloesch condemns the tendency to *replace* the revealed language of the Bible with *any* socially, politically correct language of the day.

Roger E. Olson

Selected Primary Sources

1971   *The Ground of Certainty: Toward an Evangelical Theology of Revelation.*
1978/1979 *Essentials of Evangelical Theology,* vols. 1 and 2.
1983   *The Future of Evangelical Christianity: A Call for Unity Amid Diversity.*
1985   *The Battle for the Trinity: The Debate Over Inclusive God-Language.*
1992   *A Theology of Word and Spirit: Authority and Method in Theology.*
1994   *Holy Scripture: Revelation, Inspiration, and Interpretation.*

Selected Secondary Source

1988   Leslie R. Keylock, "Evangelical Leaders You Should Know: Meet Donald G. Bloesch," *Moody Monthly* (March).

LEONARDO BOFF
1938–

Life and Career

Born Genezio Darci Fontana Boff on December 14, 1938, in Concordia, Brazil, Leonardo Boff was one of eleven children of Mansueto and Regina Boff, a humble, hard-working Catholic couple. Near his thirteenth birthday, Boff decided to join religious life away from home. From 1952 to 1965 he attended Franciscan high schools and seminaries, where he studied philosophy and theology. On December 15, 1964, at twenty-six, "Neio" (his family nickname) was ordained a Franciscan priest, taking Leonardo as his new name.

From 1965 to 1970, Boff pursued graduate studies in philosophy and theology in Germany, including special courses in anthropology and linguistics in Germany and England. There he honed his skills in nine languages: Greek, Latin, German, Dutch, English, French, Italian, and Spanish, besides his native Portuguese. In 1970, his German dissertation, "The Church as Sacrament," obtained him a Doctorate in Theology *summa cum laude* from the Ludwig-Maximilian University (Munich). Later, in Brazil, he received a Ph.D. in Philosophy of Religion from the Federal University of Rio de Janeiro.

The moving challenge of Brazilian poverty and repression, and the inability of European theology to address the burning questions of the Latin American poor Christian majority, thrust him into a dynamic venture as researcher, author, editor, pastor, lecturer, consultant, and social activist, both in Brazil and around the world. In 1971, he became one of the first Latin Americans, along with Gustavo Gutiérrez, to address a theology of liberation.

From 1970 to 1990 he taught theology at the Franciscan seminary in Petropolis. Among other roles, Boff has served as theological advisor for the Brazilian Conference of Catholic Bishops (CNBB), the Brazilian Conference of Catholic Religious Orders (CRB), the Latin American Conference of Catholic Religious Orders (CLAR), and the Basic Ecclesial Communities of his country. He has been editor-in-chief of the religious journals *Revista Eclesiástica Brasileira* (1971–86), *Concilium* (Brazilian edition, since 1971), *Puebla* (1978–80), *Revista de Cultura*

Vozes (1989–92), and *Cadernos Fé e Política* (since 1992); religious editor-in-chief of the Franciscan publishing house Vozes (Petropolis, Brazil); and editor of many other journals, books, and book series (including the Brazilian version of Carl Jung's works).

Since the 1964–84 military dictatorship, he has been active in the struggle for human rights in Brazil, serving since 1979 as cofounder and president of the Petropolis Center for the Defense of Human Rights, and since 1980 as cofounder and advisor for the National Movement for Human Rights (Brasilia, Brazil).

He rapidly became the leading figure among Brazilian theologians, publishing between 1963 and 1995 nearly seventy books and about five hundred articles (in addition to those translated into many foreign languages). Dissertations on his work are multiplying in universities of Europe and the Americas, with more than two dozen having been written by 1993, and hundreds of articles and books throughout the world have focused on his work. He has also received numerous international awards.

However, since 1971, his has also been a polemic career, bringing as much affliction as awards into his life. In 1984, the Vatican Congregation for the Doctrine of Faith—headed by Cardinal Joseph Ratzinger, an earlier teacher and intellectual inspiration—summoned him to Rome for a colloquy, part of a doctrinal process focusing on his collection of ecclesiological essays, *Church: Charism and Power.* Two Brazilian cardinals and the bishop President of the CNBB accompanied Boff in sign of support. Subsequently, a period of "obsequious silence" was imposed on Boff on May 9, 1985 (unexpectedly lifted eleven months later), his appointments as editor-in-chief and professor curtailed, and ecclesiastical license from both the local bishop and the Franciscan superior required for all his writings.

Ironically, the measure boosted the diffusion of Boff's works and Latin American liberation theology worldwide. Although he declared "I'd rather walk with the church than alone with my theology," his writings were translated into many languages and sold by the tens of thousands, despite the scholarly erudition of many of them.

The loss of his teaching and most editorial functions, as well as the censorship of his writings, prompted him to make the painful decision to leave the Franciscans and resign from the priesthood on June 26, 1993. Since then, Leonardo Boff has been a Roman Catholic lay theologian and full-time Professor of Ethics in the Federal University of Rio de Janeiro, sharing his life with Márcia Miranda—a Roman Catholic theologian in her own right, mother of two adult children by a previous marriage, and one of his longtime friends.

Doing Theology

As for most Latin American liberation theologians, theology is for Boff *a second moment* in the life of faith. The first moment is that of encountering the divine mystery in the concrete circumstances of human existence unique to each faith community—an experience eliciting first of all pleasure, praise, and proclamation, as well as silence and contemplation. Only thereafter come theologies proper: human reflections on the divine and on faith, which is the human experience of the divine; rational attempts to respond to questions raised by the faith experience; explications of faith; and devout reasoning.

In a sense, the object of theology is the entire realm of human experience: All things have a theological dimension in the sense that everything can be perceived in reference to God or as coming from God. Theology, thus, is a human endeavor: dynamic, variegated, socially and historically limited, subject to linguistic and cultural constraints, pregnant with many leanings and debates. Further, it is a human venture tied to a faith experience shared in community. Theology arises from the need to express, without ever entirely succeeding, a faith experience that transcends all explanations and formulae. Theology, for Boff, is not just specialized, academic theology; nor are theologians only those certified and renowned as such. All believers—including the poor and disadvantaged—are theologians in a certain sense and become more so as they think and discuss their faith.

Faithful to the Catholic tradition, and to the innermost spirit of liberation theology, Boff regards theologies not as mere personal undertakings, but as communitarian, ecclesial efforts: dialogical service to the church, attempts to respond from within the church to concrete challenges of a faith community at singular junctures of its history. However, the specific location of each theological attempt within the tendencies and strife marking the life of church and society will influence its preoccupations and perspective, often independently of its author's awareness or intentions. It is no wonder, then, that one finds such a wide variety of theologies and theological conflicts.

For Boff, in fact, conflicts among theological interpretations are an understandable outcome, on the one hand, of the finiteness and limitations of human reason and, on the other hand, of the many forces and constraints (cultural, political, linguistic, ecclesiastical, intellectual, etc.) restricting and orienting the theological task. Thus, each theological tendency, liberation theology included, has contributions to make to the life of the church, as well as risks and limitations. No single theological tendency is enough, then, whereas critical self-understanding and humble dialogical openness are crucial for each and every theological movement without exception.

A problem, however, arises in the fact that some theologies become official doctrines, used not only to justify intolerance toward other theological views, but also to vindicate the excommunication and at times the extermination of people theologizing otherwise. Boff tackles this issue historically and sociologically, finding its roots in the absorption by Christianity of Roman and feudal structures and concepts of authority as inherently divine and hierarchical, thus unchanging and unquestionable. This authoritarian view, tied to an exclusivistic, dogmatic view of revelation and salvation—reinforced by the split of clergy and laity, and by the elite's sway over most churches—is, for Boff, at the root of the violation of human rights in the church.

At its heart, doing theology means reflecting on the demands of the gospel today for our ways of being church, including the service the church owes humankind as a whole, especially the poor. For Boff, complicity with oppression, within and without the churches, appears as the gravest and oldest sin of Christians. Thus, a theology of captivity and liberation, as proposed in his works, requires both a critique of the unfaithfulness of our churches to the good news of Jesus Christ and a pointing out of paths toward greater fidelity to the gospel.

According to Boff, liberation theology is not the final or ultimate theology. It is, more modestly, a humble catalyst and a relatively dynamic element for all theologies; and its mission is achieved when it disappears.

Redefining Theological Sources and Methods

For Boff, as a Catholic theologian, the Bible and the church's tradition are inescapable springs of faith and theology. However, they are not absolute, sacred, exclusively divine points of departure; they are human mediations of God's will, calling both for humble embrace and critical assessment. Only in and through human, historical, social mediations do the Bible and the tradition of the church— and contemporary renditions thereof—emerge. Consequently, a critical judgment of what is valid, in these fountains nourishing and orienting theological production in ecclesial communities, is always needed.

Theologies are part of the long historical journey of believing people striving to understand and live out the implications of God's presence in their midst—a journey that has yielded the Bible (a compilation of writings by different members of this people retelling parts of their experience), created a set of traditions (moral, theological, liturgical, organizational, etc.), and contributed to definitions of certain offices and teachings as endowed with divine authority. These fruits provide essential and inescapable sources for theologians. At the same time, as attested by the church's use of biblical interpretation and traditions to condone slavery and genocide throughout the centuries—these fruits also manifest the finiteness and fallibility of the human condition, thus calling for a critical examination of their consequences for humankind and for the mission of the church in the world. Christian theology, therefore, needs *both* to take up *and* to reflect critically on its own authoritative sources. Liberation theology, as understood and developed by Leonardo Boff, is, among other things, a methodological proposal for tackling and orienting this theological task in a humble, self-critical mode.

Two interconnected facets of that methodology should be emphasized here. First, the sources of faith and theology need to be reexamined, not with the eyes of those in power, but with the eyes of those who have been, like Jesus, abandoned by the powers that be. Consequently, then, a critical social analysis of the history and context of theological production must be undertaken, especially evaluating the ways in which ecclesiastical, doctrinal, and other religious processes have been shaped by and for the benefit of the mightier at the expense of the weaker.

Thus, typically, in examining any theological subject Boff includes erudite references to the history of the theological discussions related to it; he examines the social contexts affecting the theological debates and their concrete implications, especially for the poor and oppressed; and he tries to discern the present-day bearing and prospects of such theological topics, as well as their significance for the defenseless and marginalized in both church and society.

God

For Boff, the divine being transcends any human, theological attempt to define it. Persons can grasp only glimpses of God in their experience of the living Spirit. The reality of God and faith in God surpass all verbal, intellectual formulae attempting to fathom them. As a faithful disciple of St. Francis of Assisi, though, Boff stresses God's reality as a God of life and a God of the poor: creator and sustainer of all living things, lover and companion especially of those whose lives are most vulnerable and subject to unjust suffering. Rather than omnipotent ruler, punishing father, or angry judge, Boff's image of God is one of a maternal nurturer, a loving sibling, One who suffers with those who suffer, a source and defender of joyful life.

Among Latin American liberation theologians, Leonardo Boff has been the first to retrieve the feminine and maternal dimensions of God revealed in the Bible and the history of the church, to analyze and critique the sexist and patriarchal character of most Christian theologies, and to propose, in explicit solidarity with feminist theologies, a trans-sexist theology of God as Maternal Father and Paternal Mother. In this direction, Boff has gone as far as to suggest the possibility of seeing in Mary—Jesus' mother—an incarnation of the Holy Spirit, a revelation of God in the feminine, a recognition of the divine character and call of womanhood.

Acknowledging the inadequacy of our human concepts and expressions in relation to the divine, however, Boff upholds a trinitarian idea of God. The divine as triune is to be grasped not quantitatively, but as a qualitative affirmation that God avoids solitude, defeats separation, and surpasses exclusion. For him, the Trinity is an affirmation of God as unity and diversity, surmounting the limitations while preserving the partial truths of both monotheism and polytheism. Affirming God as Trinity is to accept God as love, community, and relationship, rather than as a hierarchy.

God as Trinity is then a paradigm of how human relations should be reshaped (including relations toward the oppressed, among the genders, within the church) as loving, egalitarian, cooperative, and dialogical. Correspondingly, an integrated, dynamic understanding of the Trinity generates criticism of all injustices and inequalities: the exploitation of the poor, patriarchalism, and the transmutation of the church into an institution for the privileged.

Jesus and the Reign of God

Christology has been at the center of Boff's concerns from the dawn of his research. As visible in *Jesus Christ Liberator* (1972), his first significant work on Christology, Boff strives to remain within the confines of Catholic doctrine and tradition, thoroughly probing the contexts and conflicts marking their history; pushing and testing such boundaries in bold, creative ways, especially when warranted by those whose lives are most aggrieved and vulnerable.

For Boff, a Christology done from within a context of oppression, unjust suffering, and death, such as that of most Latin American Christians, has to be different from one done in a comfortable, affluent setting. Questions, subjects, actors, issues, priorities, emphases, and language, for example, are other. What Christ concretely elicits, challenges, brings, and means is, in each case, different. In this regard Boff proposes a liberation Christology from a Latin American perspective. In it, the historical Jesus—defending the materially poor, denouncing oppression, announcing global liberation, and, for this, suffering unjust persecution, torture, and death at the hands of the powerful—is stressed over an isolated Christ of faith. In Boff's Christology, the historical Jesus and the Christ of faith are unified in a meaningful way for today's Latin American poor.

This Christology affirms clear choices: a primacy of orthopraxis (correct acting in the light of Jesus' spirit and life) over orthodoxy (correct thought and language about Christ); a priority of the social—of our relations and responsibilities toward others, especially toward those suffering the most under our current social arrangements—above the merely private, individual; a precedence of the anthropological—the value of human persons and communities, regardless of religious beliefs—before the ecclesiastical, that is, before the needs and interests of the church as an institution; a preeminence of the utopian element—the best that our community can be in the future in light of Jesus' prophetic call—beyond the factual, that is, beyond what is and what has been already; and a preference for the critical—our capacity to examine and transform our heritage—over the dogmatic element, that is, over our tendency to submit to the ways in which our beliefs, norms, and institutions have thus far been arranged and expressed, to the point of being sacralized.

God made Godself human in Jesus Christ and, in and through Jesus, God reaffirmed the divine filiation of all humankind—that all persons are called to become sisters and brothers in and through Jesus. Through Jesus, God has sided with the poor and oppressed not because of an intrinsic merit of their condition but, rather, because their unjust predicament is a challenge to the justice of God's creation, and a refusal of our divine filiation. Throughout his writings Boff repeats that Jesus preached neither himself nor the church nor even God, but rather the reign of God. The life, death, and resurrection of Jesus centered on preaching, embodying and announcing God's reign. The reign of God "signified for Jesus' listeners the realization of hope at the end of the world, when all human alienation and all evil, be it physical or moral, would be overcome, when the consequence of sin—hate, divisions, pain, death—would be destroyed. . . . This utopia, the longing of all peoples, is the object of the preaching of Jesus. He promises that it will no longer be utopia but a reality introduced by God. . . . [It] is not to be in another world but is the old world transformed into a new one" (*Jesus Christ Liberator*, 1991, pp. 52-53).

Behind this utopia are the Jewish injunctions of the sabbatical and the jubilee (cf. Luke 4:18-21): liberation of slaves and prisoners, egalitarian redistribution of land, and forgiveness of debts, all of which involve a pragmatic recognition of one another as peers and siblings in God.

This reign of God at the center of Jesus' words and actions is not just a new socioeconomic arrangement or a novel political regime, nor is it an exclusively otherworldly or private reality. It is both already here—in Jesus' witness as in our own efforts to live our lives loving one another, treating one another justly, doing away with exploitative relations—and not quite here yet. It has grave social and economic implications, as well as personal and spiritual ones, but it is more than mere intimate conversion or social reform. It begins here and now, but culminates only in the eschatological future.

Preaching the reign of God implies, as in Jesus, critiquing and relativizing any institution, religious or otherwise, that slights or contradicts the divine filiation of human beings through neglect, discrimination, oppression, or violence. Such preaching, indeed, is an invitation to conversion and an occasion for backlash, especially from those who benefit from the present state of affairs. Here lies, for Boff, the root of Jesus' death, neither planned by God, nor sought or accepted resignedly by Jesus: Jesus was persecuted, jailed, tortured, and killed by political and religious elites for heralding a way of life counter to their interests. For choosing not to compromise with the mighty and the privileged in order to survive, Jesus died at their hands. For remaining faithful to the reign of God announced as good news to the poor, he was put to death by the lords of this world. Finally, the complete liberation implied in the resurrection appears only when related to Jesus' efforts to bring God's reign into our world.

Church: Charism and Power

In his ecclesiology, Boff is the most creative, polemical, and renowned. Here, also, history and sociology—especially the history of Christianity and the sociology of religions—show most clearly their import as auxiliary disciplines for theology.

For Boff, Jesus did not preach or found the church. It was born, though, of Jesus' death and resurrection. His death appeared as a failure of his effort to bring about the reign of God, thus creating the possibility for his disciples to assume the continuation of that effort as their own mission. His resurrection provided a confirmation that Jesus had not wholly failed, that the reign of God was possible. "In its essential elements—its message, the Twelve, baptism, the Eucharist—the church was preformed by the historical Jesus. In its *concrete, historical* form, it sprang from the decision of the apostles, as enlightened by the Holy Spirit (cf. Acts 15:28)" (*Ecclesiogenesis*,1986, p. 58).

The church is thus neither God's creation alone nor a bare human artifact. It is both the fruit of a human decision and an extension of Jesus' mission. It is a Spirit-filled human mediation of God's will.

At this point Boff discusses the Protestant contrast of a "Protestant principle" versus a "Catholic" one. The "Catholic principle" hints at the divinization of the visible church as it actually is, without acknowledging its partial origin in social-historical processes—while spurning any attempts to criticize and reform it. The "Protestant principle," on the other hand, radically distinguishes between the divinely ordained Church of Christ and the actual congregations of Christians—the former a creation of God and of God alone, and the latter exclusively human, nondivine artifacts (*Church: Charism and Power*, 1992, pp. 65ff.). Boff recognizes the danger of divinizing the actual church as both a fact and a pathology in church history, and calls for a prophetic critique of facile identifications of actual church traditions with God's presence and will.

Boff, however, goes beyond an extreme, pessimistic opposition of God's will and actual human attempts to live out that will in real institutions, submitting that Christianity can be lived only within human history. Such institutions are necessary for incarnating God's call in real human life (thence a certain *identity* between them and God's will), but they are neither perfect nor the only ones possible nor at all immune to the temptations of power, privilege, or certainty (thence a *nonidentity*, too, between such mediations and the divine plan).

Churches are thus dual, ambiguous realities: sacraments of the Holy Spirit and a frail production of human efforts. This ambiguity allows for churches continually supporting petty human interests as godly, while persecuting church members who reprove such practices or who simply live a different option. The church is always sinful, and it is always in need of self-evaluation, critique, and reform. At the same time, the church is always filled with God's presence, and thus able to reform itself.

Interesting, too, is Boff's discussion of the relation between particular congregations and the universal church:

> The particular church is the church wholly but not the whole church . . . because no particular church exhausts by itself the whole wealth of the mystery of salvation. . . . Historically, the particular Church of Rome has imposed itself upon all the other particular churches. But the Church of Rome has not ceased for all that to be a particular church. (*Ecclesiogenesis*, 1986, p. 18)

For Boff, charisms, which are the free gifts of the Spirit for service to the community, the greatest of which is love, are the organizing principle of the church. Obedience, custom, or hierarchy should never preempt love. In a first moment, a basic equality of all persons is assumed. In a second moment (out of a need for coordination and unity, but also of cultural habits and constraints), an entrenchment and hierarchy of members and their charisms might develop. Position, codes, and customs tend to substitute for charisms—for the free flow of the Spirit in the church. Religious life, then, tends to be stifled by institutional inertia, bureaucratic habits, and authoritarianism. A need for more charismatic, communitarian, egalitarian ways—less subject to custom, codes, career, or commands—might then arise.

According to Boff, this is the case of small ecclesial communities (CEBs) emerging from within the Latin American poor since the 1960s. The CEBs constitute a phenomenon that is compounded by the scarcity of ordained ministers, especially in Roman Catholicism. Boff senses the emergence of CEBs as crucial in church history: a Spirit-filled, salvific event; an "ecclesiogenesis" (birthing the church anew) springing from the laity, the poor, women, and youth; an opportunity for the revitalization of the oldest, deepest, charismatic, and communitarian traditions in Christianity; not a global alternative to the church as an institution, but an impetus for rekindling the liberating breath of the Spirit within the church.

Divine Presence and Human Salvation

Boff's works often betray an exclusivism and supersessionism common to many Christian churches and theologies—partly warranting the charge of anti-Semitism aimed at him and other Latin American liberation theologians. Increasingly, however, Boff has questioned and pushed the limits of Catholic ecumenism to points heretofore unthinkable for most Latin American liberation theologians. In *Ecclesiogenesis*, he dared in the early 1970s to share the opinion that

> the theological reality of church . . . is not restricted to the visible limits of church. . . . Grace, salvation, and the activity of the resurrected One are bestowed on the world itself, and not on that part of the world merely that is consciously Christian, the church. (pp. 10-11)

The debates on the 1992 quincentennial of the European Christian invasion of the Americas, though, compelled Boff to develop both his ecumenism and his critique of Christian imperialism with a boldness that has increased after his resignation from the priesthood. Thus, in *New Evangelization*, he stresses that God, God's revelation, and gospel are already present in all cultures and corners of the earth, even long before Christianity. Religions are unique answers to the antecedent action of God in each culture. For Boff, then, evangelization, which is bringing the good news of God's love to other human beings, has to be mutual, reciprocal, dialogical, or it is not evangelization. A connection with Jesus' person and message can be achieved only by overcoming the dichotomy between evangelist and evangelized. Thus, evangelization is not an exclusively Christian task. Boff reminds us that Jesus was not a Christian, but a Jew. He shared the religion of his people, revering their scriptures, and striving to witness for those around him the good news of God's love for them and its implications. Nor are non-Christians alone to be evangelized. The Christian mission is for all and always. In Latin America, the priority for evangelism today (not the last or the only priority) is saving the lives of the poor: That is good news to the poor.

"We get to God through all paths: that of Umbanda, of Candomblé, of Zen-Buddhism, of Protestants, of Catholics, of secularization, of scientific discourse such as Einstein's." In a 1994 book on mysticism and spirituality, Boff advances this view far beyond an intra-Christian, or even a world-religions' ecumenism. A salient trait of his work is, especially after 1992, a very explicit, positive assessment of the salvific value of the religions of the older, oppressed peoples—including African American and Native American religions, as well as popular Catholicism and Pentecostalism.

In a certain sense, Boff's theology is an optimistic one: uttered from, about, and against captivity, yes, but announcing and trusting that liberation is at hand. Although acknowledging the tragedy of massive oppression, it underscores the God-given capacity for human solidarity and deliverance. Granting and denouncing the collusion of Christian churches with the deadly enterprises of Western imperialism, Boff appreciates the positive contributions that Christianity may yet give to the birth of a new, life-nurturing civilization. Aware of the calamitous dualism typifying much of the churches' perception of human body and sexual love, Boff strives for a positive reunion of body and spirit and finds biblical grounds for reclaiming a joyful sensuality and a positive understanding of sexual love as integral both to a healthy Christian mysticism and to the project of God's reign. Finally, though acutely concerned with the threat of a global catastrophe, Boff takes the Franciscan tradition to its most radical ecological implications—trusting our human capacity to engage in the struggle to save God's creation, a struggle that has to start with that segment of God's creation closest to us and most endangered: the poor, children first.

Otto Maduro

83

Selected Primary Works

1979   *Salvation and Liberation,* with Clodovis Boff.
1984   *When Theology Listens to the Poor.*
1986   *Ecclesiogenesis: The Base Communities Reinvent the Church.*
1987   *The Maternal Face of God.*
1988   *Trinity and Society.*
1991   *Jesus Christ Liberator.*
1991   *New Evangelization.*
1992   *Church: Charism and Power.*
1992   *Introducing Liberation Theology,* with Clodovis Boff.
1993   *The Path to Hope. Fragments of a Theologian's Journey.*

Selected Secondary Sources

1985   Sacred Congregation for the Doctrine of Faith, *Instruction on Certain Aspects of the "Theology of Liberation."*
1986   Joseph Cardinal Ratzinger (W. Vittorio Messori), *The Ratzinger Report.*
1987   Michael Novak, *Will It Liberate? Questions About Liberation Theology.*
1988   Harvey Cox, *The Silencing of Leonardo Boff.*

DIETRICH BONHOEFFER
1906–1945

Few people would ever have predicted during his growing-up years in Berlin that Dietrich Bonhoeffer would become a political conspirator and martyr honored around the world for his heroic witness against the evils of Nazism. Born in Breslau on February 6, 1906, Dietrich was the fourth son and sixth child (his twin sister, Sabine, was born moments later) of Paula von Hase, daughter of Karl-Alfred von Hase, preacher at the court of Kaiser Wilhelm II, and Karl Bonhoeffer, a famous doctor of psychiatry, professor at Berlin University, and director of the psychiatric and neurological clinic at the Charité Hospital.

Student Days

At Berlin University young Bonhoeffer came under the influence of the distinguished church historian, Adolf von Harnack, and the Luther scholar, Karl Holl. To the dismay of von Harnack, who regarded him as a potentially great church historian able one day to step onto his own podium at Berlin, Bonhoeffer steered his scholastic energies, instead, to dogmatics where his main interests lay in the allied fields of Christology and Church. His doctoral dissertation, *The Communion of Saints (Sanctorum Communio),* completed in 1927, was hailed by Karl Barth as a "theological miracle." Bonhoeffer was only twenty-one years old at the time.

In this dissertation Bonhoeffer declares in a ringing phrase that the church is "Christ existing as community" (*Communion of Saints,* 1963, pp. 85, 143, 197, 203). The uniqueness of Bonhoeffer's thesis lay in his attempt to harness social philosophy to the chariot of ecclesiology; hence the subtitle, *A Dogmatic Inquiry into the Sociology of the Church.* First published as a book in 1929, *The Communion of Saints* reflects a spiritual search that would remain a central concern of Bonhoeffer until the end of his life: to discover the concrete Christian community in which the life of following Christ takes shape.

Not yet at the minimum age for "orders" and in need of practical experience to prepare for his eventual ordination to the ministry, Bonhoeffer interrupted his academic career to accept an appointment as assistant curate in a parish tending to the spiritual needs of the German business community in Barcelona, Spain. His ministry there coincided with the initial shock waves of the Great Depression. Parish life in Barcelona gave Bonhoeffer his first grim encounter with poverty and stirred him to become a source of hope to those who had lost their means of livelihood. He helped organize the charity his parish extended to the unemployed and, in desperation, even begged money from his family for this purpose.

Back in Germany, Bonhoeffer turned his attention to the completion of the "second dissertation" required for him to obtain an academic appointment to the university faculty. Published in 1931, *Act and Being* is a studious contrast of how revelation, considered as "being," takes place within the Christian community through Christ's continued incarnate presence. But Bonhoeffer also depicts revelation as the "act" of God's eternal word interrupting a person's life in a direct, transcendental way, intervening, often when least expected, to free that person from the narcissistic tendency to turn in on oneself. Throughout this book Bonhoeffer wishes to avoid what he saw so blatantly done in church and theology: reducing God to a heavenly projection of oneself and reducing God's presence in community to some self-deceiving idolatry whose sole aim was to control God through claims of inerrant biblicism or infallible institutionalism. Bonhoeffer also rejected notions of God's transcendence that placed God in heavenly aloofness from creatures. "God is free," he wrote, "not *from* humans but *for* them. Christ is the Word of God's freedom" (*Act and Being*, 1995, p. 90).

Year in America

Having secured his academic appointment to the university, Bonhoeffer decided to accept a Sloan Fellowship, which offered him a trip to America for an additional year of studies at Union Theological Seminary in New York. This year at Union would have an impact beyond the courses he followed. Trying to explain what had happened to him at Union, Bonhoeffer, in two memorable letters, says simply that he had become a Christian. What was very obvious to his family, friends, and students back in Berlin was the effect Bonhoeffer's close friendships at Union had on him.

Through a black student from Alabama, the Reverend Frank Fisher, Bonhoeffer experienced firsthand the oppressive racism endured by the black community of Harlem. He also reveled in the caring community and joyful liturgies these people had created for themselves even in the midst of the Great Depression's crushing poverty. He spent nearly every Sunday and several evenings with the people of the Abyssinian Baptist Church in Harlem. Admiring their life-affirming church services and enchanted by their soulful spirituals, he took recordings of these spirituals back to Germany to play for his students and seminarians. He spoke to them often of the racial injustice that had falsified the promise of freedom in America.

Gradually, under the influence of another friend, the French pacifist Jean Lasserre, Bonhoeffer began to associate the victimization of peoples with the tendency of nations to resort to violent solutions, even war, in "solving" their political problems. He came to realize that the hardening of hearts required in any war effort makes possible the cruel treatment of dissenters and declared "enemies," by branding them disloyal, unpatriotic, or, in the case of the enemy, less than fully human. Such, he had come to realize, was not Christ's way.

On his return journey from America, Bonhoeffer paused at Bonn University to meet personally with Karl Barth, whose writings had already electrified the theological world. Barth's "Crisis Theology," fired by a love for the biblical word and permeated with his pungent judgment against the idolatries that had corrupted the churches and made World War I possible, had captivated Bonhoeffer during his student days in Berlin. Now in Bonn the two became good friends. Later they would be linked in the church struggle.

Teaching Career

Bonhoeffer's teaching career at the university was cast in the shadows of the political and ecclesiastical turmoil that marked Hitler's ascendency to power. His students admired him for his integrity; some later became his seminarians and colleagues in the church struggle. Those attracted to Nazism avoided him. One student wrote that under Bonhoeffer's guidance, "every sentence went home; here was a concern for what troubled me and, indeed, all of us young people; here was a concern for what we asked and wanted to know" (*I Knew Dietrich Bonhoeffer,* 1966, pp. 60-61).

Ordained on November 15, 1931, Bonhoeffer also found time to teach catechism to a group of young confirmands in the slum section of Prinzlauer-Berg. He left a lasting impression on these children, who were crowded into one of the poorer sections of Berlin and had already been exposed to the drumbeats of the Hitler Youth Movement. To be more involved in their problems he moved into their neighborhood, visited their families, and invited the boys to spend weekends at a rented cottage in the more peaceful mountainous area of Biesenthal.

Those who knew Bonhoeffer recalled his spirited analyses of the nature of Christian faith and freedom in the overarching context of the call to be daring followers of Jesus Christ.

Bonhoeffer's Christology lectures, given in the summer semester of 1933 and published as *Christ the Center,* are, in a way, revealing of how Bonhoeffer influenced his students. In these lectures, he urges his students to answer the disturbing questions: Who is Jesus in the world of 1933? Where is he to be found? These lectures must be set in the context of Bonhoeffer's goading the churches to take the initiative on behalf of the victims of Nazi racist policies.

Church Struggle

Bonhoeffer was appalled at the attempt of Hitler, aided by some enthusiastic Nazis among the church leaders themselves, to integrate racism, militarism, and the denial of the freedom to dissent with official church policy. This led to a schism that split the Protestant churches of Germany into several opposing factions. Those who adopted Hitler's National Socialism as part of their creed became known as "German Christians" and their church, the "German Reich Church."

In one of his six theses of 1934, their spokesman, Hermann Grüner, made it clear what they stood for: "The time is fulfilled for the German people in Hitler. It is because of Hitler that Christ, God the helper and redeemer, has become effective among us. Therefore National Socialism is positive Christianity in action" (*Liberating Faith*, 1984, p. 22). The infamous "Brown Synod" of 1933, so called because so many of the clergy showed up wearing brown shirts and sporting the swastika, elected as National Bishop the Nazi sympathizer, Ludwig Müller. The delegates, not surprisingly, adopted the "Aryan Clause" denying the pulpit to ordained ministers of Jewish blood.

By September 1933, the conflict was out in the open. Even before the church elections, at the beginning of April 1933, Bonhoeffer took steps to pressure the church to resist the government decrees that had excluded Jews from civil service and sponsored the boycott of Jewish stores. Bonhoeffer's talk to the clergy of Berlin, entitled "The Church and the Jewish Question," urged the churches to risk entering into open conflict with the state by, first, boldly challenging the government to justify such flagrantly immoral laws. Second, he demanded that the church come to the aid of the victims and not fret about whether they were baptized or not. Finally, he declared that the church should "jam the spokes of the wheel" of state if the persecution of this people should continue (*Testament to Freedom*, 1995, p. 132). Such an outspoken defense of the Jews was a rarity in Nazi Germany. But Bonhoeffer and his group of "Young Reformers" took the more drastic step of asking their churches to call a General Council to condemn the heresy of the German Reich Church and even to declare spiritual interdict, shutting down the sacramental systems until the racially motivated laws within both church and state were abolished.

A stronger church opposition to Nazi racism was organized shortly after the Brown Synod in the form of the "Pastors Emergency League." Bonhoeffer and the decorated World War I hero, pastor Martin Niemöller, met in Berlin at the home of the young pastor Gerhard Jacobi to declare a state of emergency within the church.

Together they pledged to fight for a repeal of the Aryan Clause and for a confession of faith that would not only attack the rising idolatrous acquiescence to Hitler but also expose the heretical nature of the Reich Church. By late September 1933, at the National Synod of Wittenberg, they had obtained 2,000 signatures. But, to Bonhoeffer's disappointment, the Bishops again remained silent. Only later, at the Barmen Synod of May 29-31, 1934, which marked the official beginning of the Confessing Church, was there a sufficiently robust opposition to the Reich Church. One important clause of the Barmen Confession of Faith, drawn up in large part by Karl Barth, made many of the signers marked men with the Gestapo: "We repudiate the false teaching that there are areas of our life in which we belong not to Jesus Christ but to other lords, areas in which we do not need justification and sanctification through him" (*Testament to Freedom*, 1995, p. 20).

Even prior to Barmen, Bonhoeffer and a fellow "Young Reformer," pastor Hermann Sasse, had been commissioned to withdraw to the retreat center of Bethel and to compose a Confession of Faith that could openly challenge the German Christians. The document, known as the "Bethel Confession," was in its original form a solid, uncompromising declaration of the theological basis of the church struggle and a stirring defense of the Jewish people, now being pilloried by a spurious, official racism in both church and state. This "confession" constituted a clearly crafted repudiation of Hitler's attempt to purge the Christian churches and the German nation of the Jewish presence. Unfortunately, before being circulated, it was watered down to make it less offensive to the Nazi government. In the end Bonhoeffer himself refused to sign the final toothless version (*Testament to Freedom*, pp. 134-37).

The Ecumenist

At this juncture, Bonhoeffer took leave from his teaching post at Berlin, a university that, to him, seemed more and more to have yielded to the popular mood that hailed Hitler as a political savior. He was disturbed, too, by the lack of a protest at the disfranchisement of Jewish professors. He departed for England, therefore, to assume the pastorate of two German-speaking parishes in the Sydenham section of London.

From the more distant vantage point of London, Bonhoeffer intended to bring outside pressure to bear on the German Reich Church, whose acceptance of Nazi ideology was threatening to tear the Christian churches asunder. His ecumenical activities enabled him not only to become an eloquent advocate for the Barmen Confession of Faith but also to rally the churches to take a stronger anti-Nazi stand. Bonhoeffer had been appointed International Youth Secretary of the World Alliance for Promoting International Friendship through the Churches, a forerunner of the World Council of Churches. His activities on this new front led to his lasting friendship with Bishop George Bell of Chichester, President of the "Universal Christian Council for Life and Work." With Bishop Bell's help, Bonhoeffer was able to alert the churches to the "dangers to which the faith of the Protestant Churches was exposed" (*Testament to Freedom*, 1995, p. 399).

Bonhoeffer's attack on the German Reich Church reached a climax at the conference held in 1934 in Fanö, Denmark. Bonhoeffer and other members of the Ecumenical Youth Commission astounded the typically staid delegates by their refusal to couch resolutions in easily ignored, polite diplomatic language. They dared the delegates to behave with uncharacteristic courage on the issue of how churches were allowing themselves to be manipulated and coopted by political ideologies. All the delegates knew that the German Reich Church was the target of the resolutions Bonhoeffer and his group proposed.

In that phase of the history of the ecumenical movement which deals with the Fanö conference, Bonhoeffer is most vividly remembered for his memorable, morning sermon on peace, entitled "The Church and the Peoples of the World." In that sermon he rejected attempts to soften Christ's gospel of peace by appealing to national security or legitimate defense of one's country. God was not to be identified with the idol of national security. The church, he declared, had to be in the vanguard of a movement to establish peace in the world. He added that "this church of Christ exists at one and the same time in all peoples, yet beyond all boundaries, whether national, political, social, or racial." How could the churches ever justify their existence, he asked, if they did not take measures to halt the steady march toward another war? And so he demanded that the ecumenical council speak out, "so that the world, though it gnash its teeth, will have to hear, so that the peoples will rejoice because the church of Christ in the name of Christ has taken the weapons from the hands of their sons, forbidden war, proclaimed the peace of Christ against the raging world." One sentence of that sermon remained forever emblazoned in the memories of Bonhoeffer's students: "Peace must be dared; it is the great venture!" (*Testament to Freedom*, pp. 228-29).

Seminary Director

For a long time Bonhoeffer had been pondering whether his efforts to outlaw war might be better served by adopting as his own the tactics of Gandhi. He began, therefore, to make plans to visit India in order to learn firsthand about Gandhi's way of life and his nonviolent resistance to evil. However, the trip to India would remain a dream never to be realized. Instead, having been approached by leaders of the Confessing Church on the possibility of his becoming director of an illegal seminary to be located in Pomerania, near the Baltic Sea, Bonhoeffer opted for an entirely different kind of adventure.

The young candidates, who gathered first at Zingst on the Baltic Sea and later at an abandoned private school in Finkenwalde, near Stettin, remembered Bonhoeffer's seminary as an "oasis of freedom and peace" (*Liberating Faith*, 1984, p. 24). They soon discovered two things about Bonhoeffer and his understanding of the gospel: his desire that they form themselves into a genuine Christian community and his commitment to pacifism. In order to develop a sense of what living in a faith community entailed for these seminarians, Bonhoeffer structured the typical seminary day around a regimen of common prayer, meditation, biblical readings and reflection, fraternal service, and his own lectures. The highlight of their training remained, however, Bonhoeffer's reflections on the Sermon on the Mount, which his biographer, Eberhard Bethge, has called the "nerve center" of the seminary.

Accused of "catholicizing" the seminary, Bonhoeffer had to defend himself, pointing out that in the short time of their seminary training

the brethren have to learn . . . how to lead a communal life in daily and strict obedience to the will of Christ Jesus, in the exercise of the humblest and highest service one Christian brother can perform for another; they must learn to recognize the strength and liberation to be found in brotherly service and communal life in a Christian community.

Even at the height of the war years, Bonhoeffer again urged them to remain faithful to "the daily, silent meditation upon the Word of God" (*Testament to Freedom*, 1995, p. 27).

These were words of encouragement contained in a letter to his seminarians during the war years. These circular letters were Bonhoeffer's only way to stay in contact with those who had been part of that memorable experience in Christian community. The Gestapo had closed down the seminary in October 1937. The spirit of Finkenwalde has survived, however, in two books that reached the outside world, *The Cost of Discipleship* and *Life Together.*

The Cost of Discipleship was the outgrowth of Bonhoeffer's lectures to his seminarians on the Sermon on the Mount. At the Finkenwalde seminary Bonhoeffer had free range to give more concrete shape to the revolutionary thrust of Christ's challenge to his followers to shape society according to the ideals of the gospel. In this book Bonhoeffer accused Christians of pursuing "cheap grace," a reduction of Christianity to abstract, but nonthreatening doctrines, neatly formulated but easily ignored moral principles, and systems of grace that guaranteed a bargain basement salvation but made no real demands on the people. This was "cheap grace," a poison that had "killed the life of following Christ" (*Cost of Discipleship*, 1963, p. 44). It was a way of calling oneself a Christian while denying Jesus Christ and his cross. Bonhoeffer's book reverberates with the challenge to take one's Christian faith seriously enough to accept even death itself for the sake of the gospel. For him, the words of Christ were unmistakable. Christians were called to accept, not the cheap grace of a thoroughly secularized religion, but the costly grace of a true faith lived in solidarity with the victims of heartless societies.

Life Together, published in 1939, was a recording for posterity of the "experiment in community" that was the concrete form Bonhoeffer and his Finkenwalde seminarians had given to this faith (*Testament to Freedom*, 1995, p. 324). The church, Bonhoeffer believed, needed to promote a genuine sense of community such as he and the seminarians had experienced in order for new life to be breathed into it. This was to be not a congregation closed in on itself but a concrete expression of the discipleship Christ had enjoined on his followers, a refuge for the persecuted, and a new mode of being church in a land of oppression.

Defense of the Jews

During the years 1937 to 1939, Bonhoeffer's essays and lectures brim with bitterness over the failure of nerve on the part of church leaders. He was outraged that these same leaders were willing not only to make peace with a criminal government but also to shirk their responsibility by remaining silent while that government jailed dissenting pastors and decreed even harsher measures against Jews in blatant violation of their basic human rights. He would frequently quote Proverbs 31:8, "Who will speak up for those who have no voice?" to explain why he had to be the "voice" defending the Jews in Nazi Germany ("Dietrich Bonhoeffer and the Jews," 1981, pp. 69-70).

By autumn 1938, however, Bonhoeffer felt that he was a man without a church that he could influence sufficiently to take a courageous stand against a civil government he regarded as inherently evil. But other problems were looming on his horizons as Germany seemed bent on preparation for war.

First, the events of Crystal Night *(Kristallnacht)*, November 9, 1938, in which the full fury of Nazi anti-Semitism was unleashed on the Jewish citizenry, further convinced him of the irrelevancy of the churches when it came to issues of social justice. Bonhoeffer was away from Berlin on that night, but he quickly raced to the scene of the wanton destruction of property and terrorizing of Jewish citizens. He angrily pointed out the maliciousness of attributing this violence to God's so-called curse of the Jews because of the death of Christ. Bonhoeffer's seminarians remember his vehement prediction that, "if the synagogues are set afire today, tomorrow the churches will burn." He insisted that Crystal Night was of a piece with Nazi contempt for Christianity as well as Judaism. In his Bible he underlined the words of Psalm 74:8, "They say to themselves: let us plunder them! They burn all the houses of God in the land," and he marked it with the date of Crystal Night (*Testament to Freedom*, p. 32).

Second Trip to America

Bonhoeffer's disaffection with the spineless leadership he had come to detest in the churches was one of the factors that led him to contemplate a second trip to America. A more pressing reason for leaving Germany was the imminent call to arms of his age group. His friends, who knew of his pacifist leanings and his outspoken rejection of Nazi ideology, could only expect that he would reject military service, though this could mean imprisonment and execution. His refusal of induction into the army would, he realized, tend to bring down more Nazi wrath on his closest colleagues in the Confessing Church. Hence his closest American friend, Paul Lehmann, and his former teacher, Reinhold Niebuhr, formed a committee of two to arrange for a lecture tour. Their goal was to ensure a safe haven in America for Bonhoeffer once the impending war had begun. Bonhoeffer accepted their invitation and embarked for the United States on June 2, 1939.

Having gained the coveted distance from the ecclesiastical and civil turmoil that had clouded his life in recent years, however, Bonhoeffer now longed to be more involved in the anti-Nazi action back home. He soon made up his mind to thank his American hosts and return to Germany as soon as possible, departing on July 8, 1939, a mere month after his arrival. The reasons for his change of mind are expressed in a farewell letter to Reinhold Niebuhr and his American friends. Bonhoeffer's words are an inspiring statement of his heroic decision to accept the dangerous mission in his own country to which God was calling him. "I have made a mistake in coming to America," he wrote. "I must live through this difficult period of our national history with the Christian people of Germany. I will have no right to participate in the reconstruction of Christian life in Germany after the war if I do not share the trials of this time with my people" (*Testament to Freedom,* 1995, p. 479).

Conspirator Against Hitler

On his return home, however, he soon found himself isolated from the public forum he had as a pastor and teacher. Under suspicion for his association with the Confessing Church, he was forbidden to teach, to preach, or to publish without submitting copy for prior approval. He was also ordered to report regularly to the police. The freedom to continue his writing came unexpectedly through his being recruited for the conspiracy by his brother-in-law, Hans von Dohnanyi, and the central figure in the anti-Hitler conspiracy at that time, Colonel Hans Oster, who arranged to have him listed as indispensable for their espionage activities. This move gained him the needed exemption from the military draft and removed him from Gestapo surveillance in Berlin. Bonhoeffer had become officially an unpaid double agent for the *Abwehr,* German Military Intelligence.

Though his ostensible mission was to scout intelligence information through his "pastoral visits" and ecumenical contacts, Bonhoeffer was involved under this cover in secret courier activities. These included "Operation 7," a daring plan by the Abwehr to smuggle Jews out of Germany. It was this rescue attempt in the Abwehr's complex web of anti-Nazi actions that initially attracted the Gestapo's suspicions and eventually led to Bonhoeffer's arrest.

Bonhoeffer's principal mission, however, was to seek terms of surrender from the Allies should the plot against Hitler succeed. The high point of these negotiations between the resistance movement and the Allies came at the secret rendezvous with Bishop Bell in Sigtuna, Sweden, in May 1942. Through Bonhoeffer, Bell was convinced that the conspirators could be trusted to overthrow the Hitler government, restore democracy in Germany, and make war reparations. Unfortunately, both Churchill and Anthony Eden had hardened themselves into what had become the Allied battlecry of those years: "Unconditional Surrender!" Bell would later complain that a more statesmanlike response to Bonhoeffer's proposal could have helped the conspirators, hastened the end of the war, and saved millions of lives.

The Ethics

Bonhoeffer used the cover of his "espionage duties" in another way. Headquartered in the nearby Benedictine monastery of Ettal, he was able to continue writing what he once declared to be his main life's work, his *Ethics*. In this book, Bonhoeffer addresses the great moral dilemmas posed by the war and the need to arouse the Christians of Germany to a greater sense of responsibility in shaping history. Bonhoeffer challenges his readers to set before themselves the example of Christ and to ponder the ethical ramifications of searching for the modes in which Christ takes concrete form in their world. On the question of the Nazi persecution of Jews, he reminds his nation that "an expulsion of the Jews from the West must necessarily bring with it the expulsion of Christ. For Jesus Christ was a Jew" (*Ethics*, 1965, p. 90).

Perhaps the most unsettling section of Bonhoeffer's *Ethics* lies in his "Confession of Guilt" on behalf of the churches. In it Bonhoeffer upbraids the church for witnessing "the lawless application of brutal force," the torture "of countless innocent people, oppression, hatred, and murder," while it did not raise "its voice on behalf of the victims and has not found ways to hasten to their aid." And, in a stinging phrase that demanded the churches own up to their complicity in the Holocaust, he declared the church "guilty of the deaths of the weakest and most defenseless brothers and sisters of Jesus Christ" (ibid., p. 114). This was Bonhoeffer's designation for the Jewish people and the dissenting pastors. What is especially astounding in this "Confession" is that it was composed while Germans were hailing their fearless leader, Adolf Hitler, and wildly celebrating the greatest of all

German victories, the fall of France. In the midst of all the cheering, Bonhoeffer was privately lamenting the church's role in the suffering on which Nazism fed.

The Prison Letters

Bonhoeffer was arrested by the Gestapo on April 5, 1943, and incarcerated at Tegel military prison in Berlin. Though at first the Nazis had only vague charges against him, such as his evading the military draft, his role in "Operation 7," and his prior "disloyalties," the full truth of his part in the plot against Hitler emerged after the failure of the July 20, 1944, assassination attempt. It was in his correspondence from Tegel Prison that Bonhoeffer raised the disturbing questions that would shatter the complacency of the postwar Christian world. In these *Letters and Papers from Prison* Bonhoeffer is harsh on those churches that had diluted the gospel and softened the demands of faith in order to ensure their survival. For Bonhoeffer, the churches' failure to respond to the cry of an oppressed people lost in the killings of a world at war was to deny Christ anew.

The tone of Bonhoeffer's theological reflections in these letters is set in the letter of April 30, 1944, in which he confides that "what is bothering me incessantly is the question of what Christianity really is, or indeed who Christ really is, for us today" *(Letters and Papers from Prison, 1972, p. 279)*. In responding to that question, Bonhoeffer observed that the church, anxious to preserve its clerical privileges and survive the war years with its status intact, had offered people only a self-serving religious haven from personal responsibility. The churches of Nazi Germany were hardly the visible representation of the presence of Christ unafraid to disturb the peace of political overlords. Nor did the churches exhibit any moral credibility for a "world come of age" that no longer needed the tutelage of religion to solve problems once considered to be solely in the domain of the deity and the ecclesiastical establishment. In these letters Bonhoeffer saw the world entering a time of "nonreligious Christianity." This, he said, called for a nonreligious interpretation of biblical concepts in which Christ's lordship of the world could be honestly addressed in terms shorn of their pietistical otherworldliness. The church had to shed forever those "religious trappings" so often mistaken for authentic faith and to face up to the tough question of what it really believed in, and for what cause it was willing to sacrifice its life.

The figure that animates Bonhoeffer's urging the churches to come out of their stagnation and risk entering into controversy is that of Jesus Christ, whom he portrays as "the one for others." For Bonhoeffer, if Jesus is "the man for others," then the church can be the church only when it exists to be of service to people *(Letters and Papers from Prison, pp. 381-83)*. The cutting edge of God's judgment on the church, according to Bonhoeffer, is set in the gospel's radical affirmation of the meaning of the cross of Jesus Christ. The church had to follow Christ to that cross if it were ever to reclaim its credibility and once again proclaim God's word against the idolatries that were murdering the innocent in the battlefields and the death camps. A church, bearing the name of Christ, could not be permitted to play it safe in a time that called for courageous compassion and sacrifice. Bonhoeffer scornfully chided church leaders for failing to speak the prophetic word or to do the responsible deed for fear of losing what the following of Christ most demanded of them, the sacrifice of their privileges and their lives.

Through these letters Bonhoeffer became more famous after his death than he could ever have hoped to be during his brief teaching and preaching career in the years prior to his joining the anti-Hitler conspiracy. After their publication Bonhoeffer seemed to belong to the world at large. In them we can observe a young pastor and teacher deeply in love with his people and brave enough to risk his life in a struggle with both church and country for peace, justice, and fidelity to the gospel.

Martyrdom

What we know of the last days of Bonhoeffer is gleaned from the book *The Venlo Incident*, written by a fellow prisoner, the British Intelligence officer Captain Payne Best. Bonhoeffer and Best were among the "important prisoners" who on April 3, 1945, were loaded into a prison van and transported southward to the extermination camp at Flossenbürg. On April 8, they reached the tiny Bavarian village of Schönberg where the prisoners were herded into the small schoolhouse then being used as a temporary lockup. It was Low Sunday and several of the prisoners prevailed on Bonhoeffer to lead them in a prayer service. He did so, first offering a meditation on Isaiah's words, "With his wounds we are healed." Then he read the opening verses of the First Epistle of Peter: "Blessed be the God and Father of our Lord Jesus Christ! By his great mercy we have been born anew to a living hope through the resurrection of Jesus Christ from the dead." In his book Best recalled that moment: "He reached the hearts of all, finding just the right words to express the spirit of our imprisonment, and the thoughts and resolutions which it had brought" (*Testament to Freedom*, 1995, p. 44).

Their quiet was suddenly interrupted as the door was pushed open and two Gestapo agents entered and demanded that Bonhoeffer follow them. For the prisoners this had come to mean only one thing: He was about to be executed. Bonhoeffer took the time to bid everyone farewell. Drawing Best aside, he spoke his final recorded words, a message to his English friend, Bishop Bell of Chichester: "This is the end—for me, the beginning of life. Tell him . . . with him I believe in the principle of our universal Christian brotherhood which rises above all national interests, and that our victory is certain—tell him, too, that I have never forgotten his words at our last meeting" (*Testament to Freedom*, p. 44).

Early the next morning, Bonhoeffer, Wilhelm Canaris, Hans Oster, and their fellow conspirators were hanged at the extermination camp of Flossenbürg. The camp doctor who had to witness the executions remarked that he watched Bonhoeffer kneel and pray before being led to the gallows. "I was most deeply moved by the way this lovable man prayed, so devout and so certain that God heard his prayer" (ibid.).

In the distance one could hear the cannons of Patton's army. Three weeks later Hitler would commit suicide and the war in Europe would be over. The Nazism Bonhoeffer fought against would linger on in a nazism of the heart, in postwar militarism, blind patriotism, corporation greed, and other forms of systemic evil that continue to crush peoples in the modern world. Bonhoeffer's legacy to the churches is a challenge to view the world through the person of Jesus Christ who made common cause with the poor and the outcast. This is poignantly expressed in a Christmas message in which he reminded his fellow conspirators that they were acting in solidarity with all the victims of Nazi malevolence. "We have for once learned to see the great events of world history from below, from the perspective of the outcast, the suspects, the maltreated, the powerless, the oppressed, the reviled—in short, from the perspective of those who suffer" (*Letters and Papers from Prison*, 1972, p. 17). Such a christocentric identity with those crushed by powerful political, militaristic systems is the centerpiece of Bonhoeffer's life and theology.

Geffrey B. Kelly

Selected Primary Works

1963   *The Communion of Saints,* trans. Ronald Gregor Smith, et al.

1963   *The Cost of Discipleship,* trans. R. H. Fuller.

1965   *Ethics,* trans. Neville Horton Smith.

1966   *Creation and Fall: A Theological Interpretation of Genesis 1–3,* trans. John C. Fletcher.

1972   *Letters and Papers from Prison,* ed. Eberhard Bethge, trans. R. H. Fuller, et al.

1978   *Christ the Center,* rev. translation by Edwin H. Robertson.

1985   *Spiritual Care,* ed. and trans. Jay C. Rochelle.

1995   *Act and Being,* ed. Wayne W. Floyd, Jr., trans. Martin Rumscheidt.

1995   *Life Together,* ed. Geffrey B. Kelly, trans. Daniel W. Bloesch.

1995   *The Prayerbook of the Bible. An Introduction to the Psalms,* ed. Geffrey B. Kelly, trans. James H. Burtness.

1995   *A Testament to Freedom: The Essential Writings of Dietrich Bonhoeffer,* ed. Geffrey B. Kelly and F. Burton Nelson.

Selected Secondary Sources

1966   Wolf-Dieter Zimmermann, ed., *I Knew Dietrich Bonhoeffer.*

1970   Eberhard Bethge, *Dietrich Bonhoeffer: Man of Vision, Man of Courage,* trans. Eric Mosbacher, et al.

1975   Clifford J. Green, *The Sociality of Christ and Humanity: Dietrich Bonhoeffer's Early Theology, 1927–33.*

1981   Eberhard Bethge, "Dietrich Bonhoeffer and the Jews," in John D. Godsey and Geffrey B. Kelly, eds., *Ethical Responsibility: Bonhoeffer's Legacy to the Churches.*

1984   Geffrey B. Kelly, *Liberating Faith: Bonhoeffer's Message for Today.*

1985   James H. Burtness, *Shaping the Future: The Ethics of Dietrich Bonhoeffer.*

1985   Ernst Feil, *The Theology of Dietrich Bonhoeffer,* trans. Martin Rumscheidt.

1986   Keith W. Clements, *A Patriotism for Today: Dialogue with Dietrich Bonhoeffer.*

1992   Wayne W. Floyd and Clifford J. Green have edited a bibliography that contains precise data on all of Bonhoeffer's writings translated into English as well as a listing of all the English language secondary sources. See *Bonhoeffer Bibliography: Primary Sources and Secondary Literature in English.*

1994   Wayne W. Floyd and Charles R. Marsh, eds., *Theology and the Practice of Responsibility: Essays on Dietrich Bonhoeffer.*

1994   Charles R. Marsh, *Reclaiming Dietrich Bonhoeffer: The Promise of His Theology.*

EMIL BRUNNER
1889–1966

Life and Career

Interpreting the thought of the Swiss theologian Emil Brunner requires recalling his historical and theological context. The relative stability of his youth was followed by the crisis of Western civilization occasioned by two cataclysmic world wars. He lived his last decades in the atomic world and the Cold War that divided Western democracies and the Soviet Communist empire. Brunner is among the few theologians whose lifelong experience of diverse world crises challenged him as a committed Christian and church theologian to address the burning issues confronting both the church and the world in the twentieth century.

As early as the 1920s, Brunner was one of the leaders of the new European theology known variously as the "theology of crisis" or "dialectical theology." Later it was called Neo-Reformation or Neoorthodox theology and represented the single most influential Protestant theological movement in Europe and the United States from about 1930 to 1945. Neoorthodoxy opposed Protestant liberalism, which had dominated the nineteenth and early twentieth centuries, for its truncation of the theology of the sixteenth-century Protestant Reformation—especially with respect to the loss of the centrality of the Bible's authority, an overly optimistic view of human nature accompanied by a weak doctrine of human sin, a diminution of the biblical stress on God's transcendence, and the tendency to reduce Jesus' significance to that of a prophet or religious genius. Throughout his career Brunner sought a mediating theological position true to Reformation theology with its focus on God's unique revelation in Jesus Christ, critical of the dogmatism of Protestant orthodoxy, and appreciative of the perspective of the historical-critical study of the Bible developed in modern Protestant liberalism.

In his "Intellectual Autobiography," Brunner speaks appreciatively of Switzerland's democratic heritage. The Swiss stress on the importance of the individual and the personal was deepened through Brunner's childhood and nurture. His godly mother introduced him to the Bible's narrative and to the life of prayer. His father, a schoolteacher, magnified the importance of marriage and family as pillars of society, and showed that he considered his teaching as a calling from, and a service to, God.

Brunner's theological ancestry is the Reformed tradition (Presbyterian) of John Calvin and Ulrich Zwingli, the two most influential Reformed theologians of the sixteenth century whose lives and thought shaped the history of Reformed Christianity both in Switzerland and throughout the world. As a Reformed theologian, Brunner always insisted that a living church and theology cannot be satisfied simply to transmit its revered tradition uncritically. Such an orthodox stance fails to speak responsibly of the Christian faith in conversation with the authority of holy scripture and the tradition of the church in the context of the challenges to faith arising in the modern world.

Brunner's mother introduced their family to the kingdom of God theology of the German pietist pastor Christoph Blumhardt (1842–1919), whose pupils led the movement of Religious Socialism in Switzerland at the beginning of the twentieth century. These Christian socialists championed the cause of labor exploited by rising capitalists. Brunner was impressed with the way Christian socialists interpreted their faith in Jesus Christ as the impetus for calling the church to move beyond personal piety in working for social justice as a sign of the coming kingdom of God. Later during his theological studies Brunner continued to be more influenced by Religious Socialism than by the dominant liberal theology. This influence surely helps account for Brunner's lifelong interest in and contribution to the discipline of Christian ethics.

Brunner also appropriated much from the historical-critical method of biblical studies developed by liberal theology in the nineteenth century. Like many liberals, Brunner searched for a "scientifically satisfying formulation" of his faith in confrontation with challenges raised by developments in modern philosophy and science. Though contending with questions and doubts, Brunner maintained God's reality as a certainty. He credits the "biblical realism" of his theology teacher, Hermann Kutter (1863–1931), and the christological and theological vision of Christoph Blumhardt, for providing him direction and perspective. Brunner's theology was also strongly influenced by Martin Luther and Søren Kierkegaard. Both Lutheran theologians led Brunner to focus on God's saving revelation in Jesus Christ in opposition to all attempts to make Christian faith beholden to any philosophy or ideology. From them Brunner also adopted a strongly existential or personal mode of theologizing rather than an abstract or doctrinaire method.

Before receiving his doctorate in theology from the University of Zürich prior to World War I, Brunner studied for a semester at the University of Berlin where Adolf von Harnack's liberal theology was dominant. Brunner, however, did not fall under his spell. More significant for Brunner's development was his contact with Christian socialists in England while teaching there from 1913 to 1914. His personal friendships and mastery of English figured decisively in the early translation of Brunner's theology into English and his subsequent widespread influence on theology in Great Britain and North America. With the outbreak of World War I, Brunner returned to Switzerland to serve a year in the Swiss military. The "catastrophe of the war" marked the end of Brunner's optimism regarding civilization's inevitable progress and the vision of society's transformation dear to the Religious Socialists. From 1916 to 1924, Brunner served as pastor in a Swiss mountain village. His happy marriage during this time resulted in four sons, two of whom died in young adulthood. Brunner did postdoctoral studies at Union Theological Seminary in New York City during 1919–20, and he lectured widely both in the United States and in England in the early 1920s. By mid-decade, he was called to be professor of Systematic and Practical Theology at the University of Zürich, and he remained there until retirement in 1953. During these three decades Brunner was acknowledged as one of the leading preachers in Switzerland.

In addition to an ever-widening range of publications, Brunner was active ecumenically, especially in the work of the World Council of Churches. Just prior to retirement, Brunner traveled throughout Asia as theological advisor to the international Y.M.C.A. He returned to Japan to teach at the International Christian University of Tokyo from 1953–55, and spoke of that time as the "joyous and fitting culmination of my career as a missionary theologian and churchman." In seeking to communicate something of the meaning of the Christian faith to non-Christians, Brunner sustained his contention—first stated in 1929—that the communication of the gospel to non-Christians should presume a "point of contact" in one's hearers. Brunner held this view consistently against Karl Barth and justified it on the basis of the biblical teaching that all human beings have some awareness of God because they are in God's image. This "point of contact" provides the starting point for the apologetic and missionary task of the church in the modern and largely non-Christian world. Although Brunner suffered a serious stroke on his return from Japan in 1955, through his wife's assistance he was able to publish the third and final volume of his *Christian Dogmatics* (1960).

The Theological Task

As author, teacher, and preacher, Brunner saw his vocation as theologian to be that of a teacher in the service of the church and its mission in the world. This task has two foci. In the first place, from within the church the theologian engages in "believing thinking" in attempting to ascertain true doctrine. These doctrines derive from the theologian's reflection on the witness of holy scripture as the church's primary authority and on the secondary authority of the normative Protestant confessions of faith. In common with most Protestants, Brunner holds that no doctrines or theologies can be considered equal with God or God's revelation, and that all doctrines and theologies are subject to continual revision in light of a better understanding of holy scripture whose center is Jesus Christ.

Theology's second task is apologetic. The theologian's focus is not on the church and its teaching and doctrines, but on non-Christians, both adherents of other religions and the nonreligiously aligned secularists, agnostics, or devotees of some ideology. Brunner's apologetic approach presumed that all persons are created in God's image and therefore have some initial awareness of God. Apologetic theology addresses them in the attempt to show how their preliminary awareness of God is corrected and fulfilled through God's definitive disclosure in Jesus Christ. Or the apologist seeks to uncover some of the inadequacies of agnosticism, secularism, various ideologies, and non-Christian commitments held by those outside the Christian church and to point to the uniqueness of God's self-revelation in Jesus Christ.

Assessing the competing claims of the world's multiple religions is a further apologetic task. On the basis of his view of God's universal revelation, Brunner considers that all religions, from the more primitive to the most highly developed, build upon this universal disclosure of God. Brunner's confessional stance leads him to locate the fulfillment of what the non-Christian religions seek in the revelation in Jesus Christ. Yet that revelation also entails a judgment on all religions for their distortion of God's universal revelation. Judgment is also entailed in the way that all non-Christian religions are finally religions of self-redemption; Christianity is unique among the world's religions with its message of salvation solely through the grace of God in Jesus Christ. To the extent that Christianity distorts the message of God's free grace, it too stands under judgment. In sum, according to Brunner, in order for theology to be relevant today, it must be confessional, ecumenical, and apologetic in nature.

Anthropology, Sin, and Evil

Brunner's comprehensive theology has for its starting point the proper assessment of human nature. This understanding of human nature requires the theologian to assess both humanity's grandeur and misery as revealed supremely in the scriptures and manifested universally in humanity's struggle between its divine destiny and its existential disruption. Among the most significant modern threats to the realization of humanity's potential and divine destiny, Brunner identified all totalitarianisms, technological advances that result in the depersonalization of the self and human community, and a pervasive secularism that denies that human beings are created in God's image and intended to live in right relationship to God, neighbor, creation, and to themselves. Although Brunner recognizes that human institutions along with modern science, philosophy, and technology may all contribute to "making human life more human," they are incapable either individually or collectively of resolving humanity's fundamental alienation and sinfulness.

Brunner concedes that the twin realities of evil and suffering pose a basic question for Christians and non-Christians, but he concludes that non-Christian perspectives fail both to address evil's depths and to approximate the Christian view of God's engagement with evil and human suffering. Brunner admits that the laws of nature are willed by God and make natural evil possible. However, the Bible's concern is with "moral evil" caused by human disobedience to God's will that results in a kingdom of evil opposed to God and a threat to humanity. God confronts and breaks evil's grip on humanity in the life, death, and supremely in the resurrection of Jesus Christ. Henceforth humans need no longer be subject to evil's power, which alienates them from God, others, and themselves. Trusting in God through faith does not exempt Christians from the suffering that results from being human. Yet in faith they are able to interpret both evil and suffering in the light of God's suffering and victorious love revealed in Jesus Christ, and to anticipate God's ultimate victory over evil in the coming kingdom of God.

God, Revelation, and Salvation Through Faith

Central to Brunner's theology are his doctrines of God's nature and of God's revelation made known supremely in Jesus Christ. Brunner contends that God's revelatory activity attested in the Old Testament depicts God as the transcendent, sovereign Lord—the Holy One—while the New Testament focuses on the uniqueness of God as love disclosed in Jesus Christ and made known through the Holy Spirit. God as holy love is thus revealed as Father, Son, and Holy Spirit, but Brunner insists that the development of the doctrine of the Trinity derives from the early church and not from the New Testament. Nevertheless, the confession of God as triune is a true and comprehensive Christian teaching, but theology should avoid speculation about God's transcendent triune nature. Instead, it should follow the Bible's lead in concentrating on the history of God's saving revelation.

The narrative of the history of salvation presupposes God's universal self-revelation as Creator both in creation itself and in the conscience and reason of human beings. By virtue of this universal revelation attesting the imprint of the Creator, all human beings are responsible to God as Creator and have some awareness of God. Brunner's adoption of this position precipitated a painful break with Karl Barth in 1934. Yet both agreed that all human beings fail to honor God as Creator aright and, therefore, that they exist alienated from God. They also concurred that only through God's initiative in Jesus Christ is humanity reconciled to God.

The Bible relates how God established a covenant with Israel and revealed Godself through saving acts and words spoken by the prophets. Although God remained faithful to the covenant, Israel was often unfaithful. Gentiles living outside God's covenant with Israel disobeyed God, their Creator. The New Testament tells how God reconciled both Jews and Gentiles through Jesus Christ, the Son, the Mediator between God and humanity, who in his life, ministry, death, and resurrection fulfilled the will of God, his Father, and established a new covenant between himself and the new humanity. On the basis of the saving work of Jesus Christ in his life and death and validated through his resurrection, the New Testament confesses him to be unique, the only Son of God. Brunner affirms the classical christological confession that Jesus was simultaneously truly and fully human and fully divine, but he warns against the tendency to attempt to reduce this mysterious union to a formula. In confessing faith and living a Christian life, Brunner believes, one is ushered through this response into a communal relationship with God through Christ. When this occurs, God's purpose in creation and redemption is realized.

Brunner construes God's self-revelation to human beings through the living presence of Jesus Christ himself as a person-to-person encounter. He thus rejects the prevalent misconception of faith as being synonymous with believing doctrines or dogmas about God or Jesus Christ, because such a view intellectualizes faith by conceiving the human-divine relationship as analogous to that between a human subject and an object to be known. Brunner follows existentialists like Kierkegaard, Martin Buber, and Friedrich Ebener in interpreting the biblical way of knowing God, in which there is a divine-human encounter initiated by God and responded to by human beings through faith. Hence the movement is from God as a personal subject to human beings as personal subjects related to God. Being responsible to God is the ineradicable sign of being human—whether as sinner or believer. Faith in God through personal trust in Jesus Christ made known through the illumination of the Holy Spirit involves the response of the whole self.

According to the New Testament, faith is always faith in God through Jesus Christ, the Mediator, who continues to reveal himself as the living Lord through the Holy Spirit to his people. Protestant Orthodoxy erred in equating faith with both the acceptance of the Bible's authority and Christian doctrines. For Brunner, the Bible is the primary and indispensable written witness to the historical revelation of God, whose center is the person of Jesus Christ. Christian preaching based on scripture may become the medium through which the Holy Spirit makes God known to the hearer in the present. This relationship to God through faith in Jesus Christ is salvation. God's purpose in revealing Godself as holy love in Jesus Christ is not to judge and condemn sinful humanity, but to save humans by restoring them to communion with God. Though such a relationship is personal, it is mediated through the life and proclamation of the church as the living fellowship of Jesus Christ called into existence through God's grace.

Christian Existence and the Coming Kingdom of God

By virtue of faith in Jesus Christ, the living Lord raised out of death through God's power and made known by the Holy Spirit, Christian believers work for, live for, and hope for the more nearly perfect doing of God's will in the Kingdom that drew near in Jesus Christ, but remains to be consummated. Expressed differently, the believer's transformation into complete conformity to Jesus Christ awaits the consummation when faith gives way to sight in eternal and perfect communion with God. Until that takes place in and through God's gracious initiative, believers are called to faithful and hopeful living and action.

The Christian pilgrimage calls for faith, love, and hope. Faith is fundamental in the sense that it marks both the initiation and the continuation of the believer's relationship to God through Jesus Christ in the church where he rules as Lord. Love is faith in action in relationship both to God and to one's neighbor. Yet in the New Testament both faith and love are inextricably bound together with hope, which looks toward the transcendent fulfillment of God's kingdom anticipated in the resurrection of Jesus Christ from the dead. Hence, Brunner interprets Christian hope seeking to avoid both the view that the consummation of God's kingdom has already taken place in the coming of Jesus Christ as well as that which is so focused on the anticipated future fulfillment as to negate the significance of Christian discipleship in the present. He holds that faith, which has the character of hope, lives in the tension between the "already" and the "not yet." Faith as hope has the resurrection of Jesus Christ behind it and the universal resurrection of the dead before it as it prays and works for the coming and eternal kingdom of God in glory.

David L. Mueller

Selected Primary Works

1936   *Our Faith.*
1947   *Man in Revolt: A Christian Anthropology.*
1950   *The Christian Doctrine of Creation and Redemption. Dogmatics: Vol. 2.*
1961   *The Christian Doctrine of Church, Faith, and the Consummation. Dog-matics: Vol. 3.*
1964   *Truth as Encounter,* 2nd. ed.

Selected Secondary Source

1962   Charles W. Kegley, ed., *The Theology of Emil Brunner.*

JOHN B. COBB, JR.

1925–

Life and Career

Born in Japan of missionary parents, John B. Cobb, Jr., spent his youth in that country—a circumstance that is reflected in one of his interests as an adult, Christian-Buddhist dialogue. He came to America as a high school student in 1939, and entered the University of Chicago as a master's degree student after only two years of undergraduate studies. He received the M.A. in 1949, and the Ph.D. in 1952. Charles Hartshorne directed Cobb's graduate studies, deeply influencing his thinking and the direction of his life's work in process philosophy and theology.

Cobb began his teaching career at Young Harris Junior College in 1950, and in 1953 moved to Candler School of Theology at Emory University. In 1958 Ernest Colwell, a former vice-president at Emory, persuaded Cobb to join the Claremont faculty, where he served throughout the rest of his distinguished teaching career as the Ingraham Professor of Theology. In this capacity he founded the Center for Process Studies, located in Claremont, which publishes the journal *Process Studies* and houses a world-renowned collection of works dealing with process philosophy and theology. Cobb retired in 1990. In the course of his career he has published more than twenty books and several hundred articles.

Cobb's career has been in the church as well as in the academy. Ordained in the Methodist Church (now The United Methodist Church), he has actively served the church on many commissions and consultations. His commitment to the church is evidenced in his deep concern that theology be accessible to the laity of the church. His academic writings are interspersed with books and articles more directly oriented to laypersons.

Cobb's theology draws its inspiration not only from a vital Christian faith, but also from the process philosophies of Alfred North Whitehead and Charles Hartshorne. In Whitehead's organismic system, Cobb finds the fundamental categories that inform his thinking: All existence is a network of interdependent events, each of which becomes itself through its creative response to every element in its past.

In Hartshorne's more rationalistic adaptation of Whitehead, Cobb finds adjustments to Whitehead that slightly shift the understanding of God. In Whitehead, God is a single actual entity, everlastingly relating to all existents in their becoming. Hartshorne changes this concept of God as a single actual entity to make God a series of actual entities that are becoming, after the order of human personhood. Cobb incorporates this change into most of his early thinking.

From the late 1950s through the 1990s, Cobb's works show three somewhat overlapping foci. His books and articles through the mid-1970s concentrate on a reinterpretation of Christian doctrine, particularly the doctrines of God, humanity, and Christ through the categories of process philosophy. The chief works of this period present Cobb's response to what he considered the most pressing problem of Christian existence: adequate reconceptualization of Christian faith given the great shifts in epistemology and science in the nineteenth and twentieth centuries.

But in 1969 Cobb wrote a small book for church study groups, entitled *Is It Too Late? A Theology of Ecology.* At the time, this small text seemed like an interruption in Cobb's main task of reinterpreting Christian faith, but it proved to be prophetic of the ethical themes that would occupy Cobb from the mid-1970s through to the present time. *Is It Too Late?* was Cobb's version of Immanuel Kant's "awakening from his dogmatic slumbers," for the study jolted him into an awareness not simply of epistemological problems, but of existential problems threatening the well-being of the planet Earth and all life within it. The new consciousness did not obliterate Cobb's concern for reconceptualizing faith; rather, it deepened his awareness of the urgency for first-world cultures as a whole to change the way we conceptualize and live our collective lives. He became convinced that we generally live within paradigms of mechanism and individualism that violate the relational interdependence of all life forms; increasingly, the results of living according to mechanistic and individualistic paradigms threaten to destroy the good of earth and its animal and human creatures. Ecology, politics, economics, and education became the urgent themes addressed in the works of this period. Clearly, Cobb understands these problems to be pervasive throughout the world, but they are exacerbated by the American and European paradigms that have so dominated the planet.

The third emphasis of Cobb's thought—lay theology—certainly relates to the first two foci. Changing the culture requires more than changing the minds of academics. Cobb's works addressed to laity within the Christian church must be understood within this ethical framework. They offer laity new ways of conceptualizing Christian faith that can lead the church to address more effectively the wider problems of society. The first of these lay books was the crucial *Is It Too Late?* written in 1969 and published in 1972. The second, *Praying for Jennifer,* was published in 1985, and five additional books appeared in the early 1990s. Through the works addressed to laity, Cobb aims toward a church living responsibly and transformatively within its dominant culture, inexorably changing that culture toward more life-sustaining values.

Although it is helpful to divide Cobb's works into doctrinal, ethical, and lay-oriented categories, in a deep sense the division is somewhat artificial. The earliest doctrinal works certainly contain implications for ethical living, and the ethical works are built up through new ways of reformulating how we think about life and faith. Doctrine and ethics are interwoven. Also, the works addressed to laity are in keeping with the themes addressed in the more academically oriented works. Nonetheless, for purposes of clarity and analysis, I shall proceed first to summarize the Whiteheadian worldview as adapted by Cobb, and then successively to explicate Cobb's works according to these three categories—the doctrinal, the ethical, and the lay-oriented.

A Whiteheadian Worldview

Cobb's initial impetus for the redevelopment of Christian faith stemmed from his own intellectual difficulties with both classical orthodoxy and the twentieth-century neoorthodoxy that was particularly represented by Karl Barth. To Cobb, the sharp distinction between God and the world, the emphasis upon divine power, and the underlying metaphysics that assumed an ideal norm of self-sufficiency seemed inadequate in light of twentieth-century sensitivities. The world of physics had revealed an essential interrelatedness of everything one could measure, bringing the notions of self-sufficient substance and of a God utterly independent of the world sharply into question. The existential horrors of two world wars and the enormity of the Holocaust challenged anew the notion of an all-powerful God of perfect goodness capable of coercive interference in human history. Neoorthodoxy had utilized extreme forms of divine transcendence as a way around the problem of the apparent passivity of God in the face of human evil. For Cobb, such a resolution was suspect.

Alfred North Whitehead's organismic philosophy gave Cobb the means to address more successfully the intellectual problems of Christian faith. A thorough-going relational base displaced the primacy of self-sufficient substance. Process—defined as the internal relatedness of every becoming event to all events in its past—is reality. "Things" emerge from "events": What we call rocks and trees are the result of an intensely complex network of microscopic interchanges of energy. But the network resulting in a tree is itself part of other networks, interconnecting and interdependent, so that all existence is what it is in and through enormous fields of force created by the interchanges of energy.

There is a directional thrust to this dynamic movement of many events. A single event ("actual entity") comes into existence through the force of its past, a directive force from God, and its own emergent decision. It internalizes that which it experiences from others (both God and the world), and having done so it becomes an influence partially determining what its successors can be. Whitehead's way of summarizing this process was to say that "the many become one, and are increased by one." The many influences of the past evoke the becoming of the present, entering into that becoming. But the newly becoming entity unifies those influences, becoming a new "one" in the world of process. Along with its many contemporaries, it then evokes new events into their own becoming. To have become is to have an effect on future becomings. This process constitutes reality.

Clearly, if the influence of God affects each newly becoming event, then God is relationally involved with the world. In the consistency of Whiteheadian thinking, there is no reason to remove God from the universality of relation. God's own being is reconceived as becoming, but in a way somewhat reversed from that of every finite event. God was conceived by Whitehead to be primordially present to the world in the form of infinite possibilities, directively offering to every newly becoming event a possibility for its becoming that was relevant to its past actual world. But if to be is to have an effect, then the world's being cannot exclude God from its effects: God must not only influence the world, but the world must have a return influence upon God. Whitehead developed the notion of the "consequent nature" of God to account for that effect. The Whiteheadian God, then, was dipolar: primordial through being the infinite vision of all possibilities, shaping those possibilities according to the world's capacity to receive them, and consequent through being the receiver of the world's effects in every moment of the world's— the universe's—existence.

God's power in such a conceptuality is clearly not the coercive power of a substance metaphysics. Rather, God's power is persuasive, and it is exerted through the continuous offering to the world of possibilities for its own contextual well-being. Whether or not the world receives those possibilities as offered by God is up to the world's own determinative freedom. Thus the problem of implicating God in the evils of the world is eased by considering God's power as persuasive rather than coercive.

Hartshorne's adaptation of this Whiteheadian view of God was to consider God not as a single everlasting entity, but as a series of successive entities, much as the "soul" of a human person was conceived to be a successive series of entities with a strong degree of continuity through time. By so reconceiving God, Hartshorne addressed what he saw to be a technical inconsistency within Whitehead's development dealing with the inability of entities contemporary to one another to be influenced by one another. One is only influenced by the past; if God is everlasting rather than past, how can one be influenced by God? By reconceiving the relational God as a series rather than as a single event, Hartshorne saw himself as introducing a greater consistency to the relational worldview.

Most of Whitehead's works were devoted to the fundamental metaphysics of a relational world; Hartshorne's works dealt more specifically (though certainly not exclusively) with the reality of God within a relational world. Cobb followed

Hartshorne in this respect, going farther than his teacher by reconsidering a number of Christian doctrines through the framework of process philosophy.

Doctrinal Works

Cobb's earliest books are *Varieties of Protestantism* and *Living Options in Protestant Theology: A Survey of Methods.* In them he presents a critical analysis of theology and theological methods current within midcentury Protestant Christianity in America, uncovering their implicit philosophical suppositions. Cobb then uses this analysis to set the stage for his first significant doctrinal book, *A Christian Natural Theology* (1965), based explicitly on Whiteheadian philosophical suppositions.

The doctrines dealt with are primarily those of humanity and God. With regard to humanity, Cobb quickly established the viability of the concept of "soul," explicating it through Whiteheadian metaphysics. The organism of the body is itself marked by an organizing center of experience that both receives from and affects one's total existence, physical and psychical. This centering is a series of becoming events marked by a capacity for novelty much greater than that of more dominantly physical events. That is, the fundamental distinction between "body" and "soul" is not that the one is physical and the other mental, but the degree of physicality or mentality involved—for all events involve both physicality and mentality within Whitehead's system. Physicality involves the influences received from the past, and mentality involves the novelty with which those influences are integrated in the creation of the becoming event (or "occasion"). Bodily events are dominated by physicality, and soul events are dominated by mentality. The integration of body and soul creates the uniqueness of human existence. The soul receives the influence of those events constituting the body, and it integrates these events in terms of meaning. Consciousness emerges in the intensity of contrasts between physical influences and possible modes of integrating those influences.

Humanity is that peculiar togetherness of body and soul that, due to the organic complexity of the brain, can sustain a high degree of novelty, and hence consciousness. The soul does not exist apart from the body, since the soul requires the stability and sustenance of the environing body for its own existence. But the animation of the body is itself dependent on the creative function of the soul. This composite interdependence is itself an openness to distinctive structures, such as language, that mark all human existence. That the human will have language is part of the structure of what it means to be human, but how that language will be developed is variable, depending on bodily and historical circumstances. The soul, then, is a series of successive events, each of which inherits a common character from its past and from the continuity of its environing body and world. The soul is both integrative and directive, contributing to the uniqueness of human personality.

On this basis, Cobb develops the implications for communal existence. The interdependence of body and soul is itself an echo of the larger interdependence of the person and the environment, both human and nonhuman. Hence each person is called to responsible existence, responding *to* the environing community, and responsible *for* the environing community.

Having established a doctrine of humanity, Cobb then developed the corollary doctrine of God. Following his summary of the Whiteheadian notions as outlined above, he critiqued those notions as insufficiently incorporating Whitehead's own principles of dynamic process. The point of contention was Whitehead's notion of the everlasting God. Cobb, following Hartshorne, argued that an everlasting God violates the relativity principle that no entity can directly experience its contemporaries. Therefore, God must be a succession of entities, much like the succession of events that together create the human soul. Given this, then every becoming finite reality experiences the immediately past event of God. God, defined as person, is the continuously self-surpassing reality, ever succeeding itself.

In any case, the chief import of Cobb's Whiteheadian notion of God is that God is not the sole creator of the world, and therefore God does not have complete control of events in the world. Rather, God *and* the world are responsible for events in the world: God exerts the transformative power of directive possibilities toward the world's good, and the world exerts the often conformative power of perpetuating the values achieved in its own most recent past. The small publication *God and the World* develops these implications even more extensively than does *A Christian Natural Theology.*

Having devised a philosophical basis for understanding humanity and God, Cobb turned to history in *The Structure of Christian Existence* (1967). If existence is relational, then human beings are historical: Each person develops in and through the relations of where and when one is. The structure of humanity is philosophically common, but the way that structure plays out in history is culturally relative. Cobb examined various modes of historical structures, focusing primarily on the period when the leading religions of the world were taking distinctive shape. He focused upon Christian existence, arguing that while it emerges from prophetic existence within Judaism, the main features of Christian existence are its self-transcendence and the radical responsibility that lies at the base of this self-transcendence.

Christ in a Pluralistic Age (1974) is Cobb's last primarily doctrinal work, but unlike the earlier works it begins to show the effects of the 1969 conversion to radical responsibility for the way of the world. It is as if the self-transcendence identified in the 1967 *Structure of Christian Existence* encountered the shock of radical human responsibility for destruction of the world's communal good in *Is It Too Late?* All works written following that shock begin to move away from the intra-Christian doctrinal reformulations, and into world responsibility. Thus *Christ in a Pluralistic Age* not only develops a Christology that logically pulls together the doctrines of humanity, God, and history in the earlier works, it also addresses the interreligious rivalries that disrupt the world's peace and the ecological insensitivities that disrupt the world's sustenance.

The Christology of the work is incarnational in the sense that Cobb derives the "Christ" from the preexistent Logos of God (or, in Whiteheadian terms, the primordial nature of God). All aims given by God to the world stem from the primordial nature, but insofar as those aims call the world toward its own creative transformation, Cobb names those aims as "Christ." Strictly speaking, "Christ" is the incarnation of the transformative Logos into the world. Jesus reveals the supreme incarnation of the Christly aims from God, and his achievement affects the continuing development of human history by opening history to new possibilities for transformation. As human history becomes transformed by the Christ, God's reception of human history within the Consequent Nature becomes the ultimate transformation of history into the Reign of God, which Cobb identifies with Spirit. The whole (Logos and Spirit) constitutes the fullness of God.

The relation to pluralism develops from the pervasiveness of God's creatively transforming aims for the world. Wherever there is transformation toward the good, there is what Cobb calls the "Christ." The effect upon Christian life within a world where religious communities no longer exist in isolated geographic locales is to render the strange familiar. That is, the Christian can approach another religion not from the primacy of the question, "Is it true?" but from the primacy of the question, "Is it transformative toward an increasing good?" Since Christ is identified as the transformation toward good, the very reality one worships as Christ within Christianity can be seen as operative throughout all religions. This in effect gives a new impetus toward an interreligious cooperation that can work toward resolving the pressing problems that hinder peaceful and sustainable existence in the world.

The theme of interreligious dialogue is developed again in *Beyond Dialogue: Toward a Mutual Transformation of Christianity and Buddhism* (1982). This book is a natural consequence of the position described in *Christ in a Pluralistic Age* as Cobb applies the principle of Christ as Creative Transformation to the actual encounter of Christians with persons of other faiths, particularly Buddhists. "Dialogue" implies talking with one another; to move beyond dialogue is to listen creatively to the other, hearing the other's perceptions of truth, and incorporating those perceptions into one's own understanding and selfhood. Insofar as Christians listen in this way to others, Christianity itself is transformed. Likewise, since dialogue is not simply a listening, but a sharing from one's own perspective, the partners in dialogue will hear the Christian perception of the truth given in Jesus Christ, and they will incorporate that into their own transformed understanding of their own religion. Dialogue issues into the creative transformation of all persons engaging in it, yielding new trajectories for ancient traditions. Forms of "Buddhist Christianity" and "Christian Buddhism" can emerge.

Following *Christ in a Pluralistic Age*, Cobb cooperated with his colleague and former student, David Ray Griffin, to write a textbook summarizing the principal themes they had respectively developed. This text, *Process Theology: An Introductory Exposition*, brought Cobb's primarily doctrinal writings to a close.

Ethical Works

The first of Cobb's ethical works is the important text already cited several times, *Is It Too Late? A Theology of Ecology*. The text deals with the enormity of the effects of dualistic thinking on the environment. The separation of mind and nature that became so dominant in the Enlightenment led to the objectification of nature as either a resource for human exploitation or a mystery for human admiration. In either case, the vital interconnections of human beings not only with one another, but with and within a vast ecosystem, were virtually invisible within Enlightenment dualism. The book is a plea for the church study groups for whom it was designed to rethink their dualist suppositions and to begin to live responsibly in the world.

Mind in Nature: Essays on the Interface of Science and Philosophy (1977, edited by Cobb and Griffin) is a collection of essays developed through a conference devoted to exploring academically new paradigms that could displace the dualistic heritage of the Enlightenment. Here the themes of the earlier book on ecology are given new expression as biologists and process philosophers together compared new modes of interrelational thinking with the older paradigms. The culminating expression of these themes emerged in the book that Cobb cowrote with biologist Charles Birch, *The Liberation of Life* (1981). The book deals with molecular, organismic, and population ecology within the web of life. It contrasts various models of living: mechanistic, vitalistic, emergent evolution, and finally the preferred ecological model. Cobb and Birch propose an ethical way of life that follows from the ecological model. The ideal is a just and sustainable world where humans learn to respect life in all its fullness. This ideal is applied to economics and agriculture, to energy use and to transportation, and to peoples marginalized under the mechanistic paradigm of "unlimited growth." Throughout, the concern is to augment the well-being of all the world's peoples through transformative modes of respect and mutuality in more communal lifestyles. The book concludes with a hope-filled answer to the question of the earlier work: "It is not yet too late to shift basic paradigms and act in terms of a new sense of reality. To do that will be very much an act of living and will lead to new possibilities of living" (p. 330).

The norm that emerges throughout Cobb's writings on human responsibility within and toward the environing earth is that of a just, participatory, and sustainable society. This norm serves as a guiding focus in his political, economic, and educational works, as well as in those directed toward laity. In many respects, process thought provided a natural frame of reference to ground such a norm, but insofar as process philosophers and theologians tended to deal with the abstract structure of process philosophy, they too often neglected its pragmatic implications.

Cobb reversed this tendency, making explicit the radical responsibility for a just, participatory, and sustainable society that logically follows from a relational metaphysics.

Cobb's application of process metaphysics to social and public life takes place in *Process Theology as Political Theology* (1982). Here Cobb argues for a stronger engagement with public issues on the part of theologians, both for the sake of calling the church to self-criticism of its own participation in the ills of society, and for the sake of galvanizing the church to exercise its influence in the world toward freedom and justice. Cobb appreciatively and critically interacts with three notable political theologians: John Baptist Metz, Jürgen Moltmann, and Dorothee Soelle. In all three, the notion that God calls the church and the world into more just forms of society is fundamental. Cobb suggests that a process ontology offers a basis for their intuition that all forms of the church are relative to the church's social and temporal location, and that the church is therefore continuously called by God into new modes of being appropriate to its time. "Appropriateness" has to do with the sociological, political, and historical needs of any given time. Process theology as political theology can be a resource to those already working out of political theology, and it can also provide yet another voice that helps the church to determine its most faithful form of influence and action in dealing with political suffering in the world.

Cobb turns toward another dimension of how one achieves a just, participatory, and sustainable society in *For the Common Good: Redirecting the Economy Toward Community, the Environment, and a Sustainable Future* (1989, with Herman Daly). The social gospel theologian Walter Rauschenbusch once simply stated the problem of evil by pointing out that evil is profitable; were it not profitable, it would be easier to control. Cobb's work with Daly could be characterized as pointing out the way in which Western economics builds up profits for the few at the expense of a sustainable world for the many. Such profitability is built into the way the economic system operates; it contains an implicit and often explicit principle of greed.

Cobb and Daly offer an extended critique of Western economic theories under the norm of a just, participatory, and sustainable world. They argue for substituting an Index of Sustainable Economic Well-Being for the prevalent norm of Gross National Product on the grounds that the GNP fails to account for the quality of life and, indeed, that it promotes the deterioration of such quality by ignoring the sociological, psychological, and ecological effects of economic "growth." "Free trade," a corollary of the Gross National Product norm, is also exposed as widening the gap between rich and poor by creating a worldwide pool of cheap labor, thus effectively keeping labor costs down. When all manufacturers have access to the world's labor markets, then the chief form of competition will be poor people competing against one another for jobs. Cobb and Daly advocate national rather than corporate or individual trade, and limitation of any trade that imposes unreasonable debt.

For the Common Good goes beyond critique by proposing that economics as a discipline be more self-consciously dependent on data from the variety of human disciplines, and so become more responsive to the fact of communal well-being. The book further suggests a program for an economic theory that can result in the reorganization of social structures toward smaller, sustainable units. This program includes reorganization of education, local community-building, movement toward self-sufficient national economies, modes of introducing the public to issues of scale and sustainability, and the implementation of the Index of Sustainable Economic Well-Being as the norm measuring our economic condition.

The inclusion of educational reform leads to another significant aspect of Cobb's ethical works. Sustainable societies require modes of education that not only inform citizens of the various disciplines of study developed by the universities, but that also prepare citizens to participate in the creation of just, participatory, and sustainable societies. To this end, educational institutions must foster the interdisciplinary nature of knowledge, breaking down the artificial boundaries that separate the disciplines from one another. Additionally, education must provide students with ways of interpreting the relational structure of reality, and ways of analyzing the global situation of the planet and its inhabitants. Finally, educational institutions must do these things as they themselves participate in society and its goods and ills. Thus they cannot assume the objective stance of the observer; they must instruct with a critical self-consciousness about their own role in the creation of society.

Cobb writes on education in *For the Common Good,* in a number of articles, and in a volume written with Joseph C. Hough, Jr., concerning theological education, *Christian Identity and Theological Education* (1985). As in his other works, his concern in the latter is that education must deal pragmatically with the issues facing the world toward the end of more responsible living. He and Hough argue that theological schools should educate leaders for the church who will be "practical theologians" and "theological practitioners." As such, these leaders will participate in the "creative transformation" that can heighten the church's own contribution toward the creation of communities of well-being.

Lay Theology

Cobb understands theology as the church's critical self-understanding in light of its history and in light of the future to which God calls it. In this sense, theology always stands between the past and the future; it is always itself immersed in the present process of creative transformation. Its foundation is its faith in God through Jesus Christ, who reveals who God is to us and for us. Such an understanding of theology cannot confine theology to the academy, or indeed, to theologians. The task of the theologian is to assist the church in its own theological task of critical self-understanding, toward the end of responsibly contributing to the world's good.

Thus Cobb's writings for laity and his active service within The United Methodist Church are essential to his work as a theologian.

This sensitivity has increased in the last decade. *Is It Too Late?* was written for laity, and published in 1972; this was followed by *Praying for Jennifer* (1985), *Doubting Thomas: Christology in Story Form* (1990), *Can Christ Become Good News Again?* (1991), *Matters of Life and Death* (1991), *Becoming a Thinking Christian* (1993), and *Lay Theology* (1994). Necessarily, given Cobb's understanding of the theologian's task, the themes in these books do not differ significantly from those outlined in the foregoing two sections. Rather, the lay works are an attempt to draw Christians who are not professional theologians into the task of thinking deeply into Christian faith for the sake of living that faith more effectively in the world. For without the involvement of laity as well as professionals in revisioning the nature of the church and its mission, the call to participate in the creation of a more just world will not be answered.

Conclusion

This analysis of Cobb's works has followed the evolving lines of his own thinking, from the primarily doctrinal phase, to the ethical phase, and to his emphasis on lay theology. For Cobb, the task of theology is to deepen Christian understanding for the sake of participating with God in the creative transformation of the world. Cobb's sources and methods are those characteristically used within much of Methodism, including appeal to the authority of scripture, tradition, reason, and experience. "Reason" can lay claim to dominance in Cobb, since he understands that every theologian's suppositions about the nature of reality deeply affect her or his interpretation of scripture and the tradition. Cobb's suppositions are clearly the relational suppositions of process philosophy. However, it is his experience as a Christian in the twentieth century, moving from pietism in his youth toward more rational modes of faith in his maturity, that leads him to find process philosophy such an appropriate tool for the interpretation of the texts and the traditions that also inform him.

God is understood through the revelation of Jesus as the Christ, with this revelation understood through the categories of process thought. God is the one who ever works with the world, calling it toward creative transformation; Jesus was the one in history who in his complete openness to God's aims became the manifestation of God, and therefore the Christ of God. And the "Christ" is the principle of creative transformation.

The problem of evil is on the one hand the world's resistance to God's call toward the good, and on the other hand it is the competition of values that is a concomitant of finitude. Life is such that it involves discord and competition, and God's creative power is persuasive, not coercive. Thus all good is to some extent ambiguous, being interwoven relationally in a world where what is good for one may not necessarily be good for another. God continuously calls the world toward greater good; whether or not the world responds to the divine call rests with the world. The hope of the world is the faithfulness of God. Cobb has devoted his life to explicating Christian faith; in the process, he has continuously empowered others to do the same.

Marjorie Hewitt Suchocki

Selected Bibliography

1960   *Varieties of Protestantism.*

1962   *Living Options in Protestant Theology.*

1965   *A Christian Natural Theology.*

1967   *God and the World.*

1972   *Is It Too Late? A Theology of Ecology.*

1973   *Liberal Christianity at the Crossroads.*

1974   *Christ in a Pluralistic Age.*

1976   *Process Theology: An Introductory Exposition,* with David Ray Griffin.

1977   *Theology and Pastoral Care.*

1981   *The Liberation of Life: From the Cell to the Community,* with Charles Birch.

1982   *Beyond Dialogue: Toward a Mutual Transformation of Christianity and Buddhism.*

1982   *Process Theology as Political Theology.*

1983   *Talking About God: Doing Theology in the Context of Modern Pluralism,* with David Tracy.

1985   *Christian Identity and Theological Education,* with Joseph C. Hough, Jr.

1985   *Praying for Jennifer.*

1989   *Biblical Preaching on the Death of Jesus,* with William A. Beardslee, David J. Lull, Russell Pregeant, Theodore J. Weeden, Sr., and Barry Woodbridge.

1989   *For the Common Good: Redirecting the Economy Toward Community,* with Herman Daly.

1990   *Doubting Thomas: Christology in Story Form.*

1991   *Can Christ Become Good News Again?*

1991   *Matters of Life and Death.*

1993   *Becoming a Thinking Christian.*

1994   *Lay Theology.*

JAMES HAL CONE
1938–

Life and Career

One of the most intellectually daring and creative thinkers on the United States theological scene in the twentieth century is James Hal Cone. Since 1968 he has written eight important books and more than seventy-five articles, as well as having coedited two volumes. As the Charles A. Briggs Professor of Systematic Theology at Union Theological Seminary in New York City, for more than twenty-five years Cone has taught and mentored not only a second generation of black theologians, but students from different racial and cultural groups within the United States and from "the two-thirds world." He is a leader and active participant in the Society for the Study of Black Religion, the Ecumenical Association of Third World Theologians, and the American Academy of Religion. In addition, he is a much sought-after and provocative public lecturer. Although black theology is not exhausted by the work of James Cone, it is inconceivable without his work and cannot be understood properly apart from it.

James Cone was born on August 5, 1938, in Fordyce, Arkansas, about sixty miles southwest of Little Rock; a year later, his parents moved to Bearden. In this small rural community of approximately eight hundred whites and four hundred blacks, Cone was shaped decisively by two powerful forces: daily encounters with the cultural and social (i.e., political, economic, and technological) hegemony of white supremacy *and* the ecstatic and graced religious life of the Black Church. Bearden's segregated schools, Jim Crow seats in movie theaters, and separate water fountains were daily oppressive reminders of the dominance of white supremacy in the South. But when black women and men crossed the threshold of Macedonia African Methodist Episcopal Church, they entered into a faith dimension that sustained their dignity and personhood, reversed the value structures of white supremacy, and mediated the love and compassion of God. Cone responded generously to the experience of the Black Church: At the age of ten, he offered himself for membership, and at the age of sixteen he entered the ministry.

Bearden presented Cone with a dilemma: If God is as good and as powerful as black faith insists, why do blacks suffer so? Cone has recounted how he and his brother Cecil, as quite young children, pondered and discussed this question, literally puzzling themselves into philosophy and theology. This grasp of the tensive situation of black life in Bearden led Cone to a major in religion and philosophy at Philander Smith College in Little Rock, Arkansas, and to seminary studies at Garrett Biblical Institute (now Garrett-Evangelical Theological Seminary) in Evanston, Illinois. If Philander Smith widened Cone's horizon and nurtured his intellectual growth, Garrett, like so many other white graduate schools, exposed him to hurtful instances of flagrant anti-black racism. But Cone's most enduring influence pulled him through: His father's spirit of resistance steeled and centered him. He passed the comprehensive examinations for the bachelor of divinity (now master of divinity) degree with distinction and earned the systematic theology prize. Encouraged by two of his professors, Cone applied for and was admitted to the Ph.D. program in systematic theology at Garrett-Northwestern. Again, he met with blatant anti-black racism from administrators and professors; again, he was undeterred. In the spring of 1965, with a dissertation on Karl Barth's anthropology, James Hal Cone became the first black American to graduate with a doctorate in theology from Garrett-Northwestern.

Cone returned enthusiastically to another year of full-time teaching at his alma mater, Philander Smith College. Here, his life question presented itself again: "What did Barth, Tillich, and Brunner have to do with young black girls and boys coming from the cotton fields of Arkansas, Tennessee, and Mississippi seeking to make a new future for themselves?" Pressured by the college administration, Cone left Philander Smith; his concern for black educational excellence clashed with the interests of white trustees. Cone concluded that if he was "going to teach at a white-controlled school, the control might as well be obvious" (*My Soul Looks Back*, 1982, pp. 38, 40). He left the South for a teaching position at Adrian College in Adrian, Michigan.

The Civil Rights movement made a deep impression on Cone's thinking, and his student years coincided with it. As an undergraduate at Philander Smith, Cone first heard of the Montgomery bus boycott, read about Martin Luther King, Jr., and experienced firsthand the 1957 integration crisis at Little Rock's Central High School. As a seminary student, Cone was an active participant in the movement; but by the early 1960s, he had begun to grapple seriously with Malcolm X's critiques of Christianity. His own study and reflection led him, fairly early on, to endorse the notion of black power.

By 1967 many black Americans had grown disillusioned with the possibility of social change in the United States. With a doctrine of suffering love, peaceful protest, and nonviolence, the Reverend Dr. Martin Luther King, Jr., had demonstrated that a radical Christianity could be effective in the black struggle to win the freedom to exercise their civil and political rights. Although King had exposed the deformed conscience of the nation, he had also uncovered its brutal intransigence. Yet many black pastors and clergy had come to doubt the wisdom of these methods. In the decaying cities of the nation, black men and women vented their anguish and anger in furious street rebellions. The call for "black power" resonated with black suffering in the streets and challenged King's strategies; it also splintered the fragile harmony blacks and whites had achieved under his leadership. Rather than repudiate black power, the National Committee of Negro Churchmen (now the National Committee of Black Churchmen) issued a national statement on it and, thus, inaugurated a new and distinctive stage in African American Christianity.

All this moved Cone deeply, but, as yet, he had no theological structure with which to respond. In fact, theology had lost its currency and power for him; it seemed morally and intellectually bankrupt in the face of black oppression. The assassination of Martin Luther King, Jr., and the bloody rebellions that followed in its wake intensified Cone's sorrow and rage; the racial unrest also galvanized him intellectually. Cone's response was the passionate polemic *Black Theology and Black Power* (*BTBP*, 1969). In that first of several books, Cone intended to show that "the politics of black power was the gospel of Jesus to twentieth-century America" (p. 32). As Jesus gave his life and ministry to the liberating service of the poor, the infirm, the outcast, so too black power was committed to the liberating service of black women and men dominated and oppressed by white racist supremacy. Cone's work met with hostility from critics, white and black alike, who charged him with distorting Christianity; but there were others, white and black alike, who found in his message both a challenge and a springboard for further reflection and action. Perhaps, it would not be too much to say that James Cone began the *liberation of theology* in the United States.

Black theology is a living, changing, developing theology. James Cone is a living theologian who is still developing, still changing his mind. In his comprehensive, excellent study of Cone's theology, Rufus Burrow remarks that even in his earliest writings Cone "did not back himself into a corner" as he was endeavoring to work out black theology (*James H. Cone*, 1994, p. 28). Cone acknowledged that his ideas were provisional and needed to be judged by their fidelity to his community's view of the ultimate. Each of his publications afforded him more structured opportunities to clarify his proposals, and he listened attentively and seriously to his critics.

The Definition, Task, and Authority of Theology

Black theology emerged in the religious, intellectual, and moral vacuum created by the protracted failure of white Christians in the United States to relate the gospel of Jesus to the oppression, suffering, and pain of black people. From the beginning,

Cone grasped the basic task of black theology as analyzing the black human condition in light of God's revelation in Jesus Christ "with the purpose of creating a new understanding of black dignity among black people, and providing the necessary soul in that people, to destroy white racism" (*BTBP,* 1969, p. 117). Black theology, then, is a theology primarily of black people, for black people, and directed in their *authentic* interests. Black theology aims to make sense out of the black religious, cultural, and social experience in the United States: to analyze the nature of Christian faith in such a way that black people can decisively affirm and embrace their black existence and, just as decisively, reject and repudiate all forms of disempowering and debasing white racist supremacy. The binding authority, Cone asserts, for black theology in all matters is the black experience of oppression; in black theology's mediation of faith, this experience is the ultimate test of truth. Moreover, black theology rejects any doctrinal formulation that contradicts "the black demand for freedom now" (*BTBP,* p. 120). All Christian doctrines must be reinterpreted to speak meaningfully to black people living under unbearable oppression.

Although this early statement of the meaning of black theology, its purpose, and its task represents the kernel of Cone's later development, his understanding of black theology shifted most tellingly in the mid-seventies. Cone's second book, *A Black Theology of Liberation,* explicitly works out what had only been implicit in his first: that the message of the gospel is liberation—liberation from racial and social (i.e., political, economic, and technological) oppression. In this work, Cone presents theology as passionate participation in reasoned inquiry on behalf of the oppressed. For theology to be Christian theology, it must be identified with the oppressed and struggle against their condition.

In answer to criticism that his conceptual framework and foundation for theology were not sufficiently emancipated from European and European-American sources, Cone immersed himself in the research and interpretation of the aesthetic mediation of the black experience. The result was *The Spirituals and the Blues* (1972). Cone takes the spirituals and the blues as sources for theologizing the black experience, giving fresh treatment to the significance of these cultural expressions for the black community.

Published in 1975, *God of the Oppressed* (GO) not only demonstrates the extent of the expansion and consolidation of Cone's project, but it stands as his most systematic theological statement. *God of the Oppressed* expands and consolidates Cone's project in the following ways: First, it identifies cultural resources of the black oppressed community as a crucial point of departure for theologizing. Second, it provides an account of the relation between ideas and their social context (sociology of knowledge). Third, it engages the biblical emphasis on the social and political character of divine revelation in history. Fourth, it distinguishes self-critically between divine revelation and human decision (ideology critique). And fifth, it situates the norm for black theology in Jesus Christ as witnessed in Scripture and black experience. As a rigorous theological exercise, *God of the Oppressed,* even twenty years later, remains an impressive example of contextual theology (*Way of the Black Messiah*, 1987, p. 233).

As a movement, black theology has several shortcomings. In the later stages of his work, Cone himself has evaluated the black theology movement and identified some of its inadequacies. These include the absence of a systematic social analysis, which has prevented black theology from addressing the interrelation of racism, sexism, class exploitation, and U. S. global imperialism; the lack of a differentiated understanding of the political, economic, and technological components of social order; an overreaction to white racism and its role in exploitative social, cultural, personal, and ecclesial relations; the failure to attend to sexism in the black oppressed community; the tendency to overlook pressing psychological and affective issues—such as death, dread, despair, sorrow—which are related intimately to the suffering caused by dominative, oppressive, and biased social interpersonal relationships and institutions. Cone squarely acknowledges and confronts the limitations of his theology. He has become seriously attentive to the problem of sexism in the black community, more self-conscious of his methodological dependence on the neoorthodox theology of Karl Barth, and somewhat more analytical regarding economic and class analysis of oppression.

Cone's most recent work bears the marks of his growth. In *Martin & Malcolm & America* (1991), he undertakes an interpretative social history of Martin Luther King, Jr., and Malcolm X. Cone reconstructs the social horizon of their differing and converging responses to the condition of black people and brings their respective appropriations of macro-social analysis to the fore. He turns a sharp eye on the media's power over cultural traditioning. Cone refuses to romanticize Martin Luther King, thus dislodging the liberal icon served up on the national holiday. Likewise, he refuses to romanticize Malcolm X, thus undermining any slick evasion of the ambivalences of nitty-gritty black life. In this work, Cone insinuates the gravity of the crisis black people face at the opening of the twenty-first century and proposes complex models for genuinely transformative social praxis.

God and Christ

Cone asserts that the "reality of God is presupposed" (*GO*, 1975, p. 55). This presupposition, stemming directly from black religious experience, interrupts any attempt, even analogical ones at axioms or proofs for the reality and existence of God. To speak about God in black theology, then, is to do so in relation to the biblical witness to God's self-disclosure in history and the condition of oppressed black people. Thus, first and foremost, Cone understands God as God of the oppressed, the One who takes up their cause and liberates them from suffering and oppression in history. How does God act in history? God acts through the concrete struggles of oppressed people for their liberation. How are we to distinguish God's divine imperatives from mere human motivation? This is the task of black theology: to interpret and impart the Word of God. What can be said of God? Nothing can be said about "God that does not participate in the emancipation of black humanity," that does not directly relate to the liberation of the oppressed (*GO*, 1975, p. 60).

Cone insists that "God is black" (*GO*, p. 63). Because God has taken up the cause of black people as a divine cause, because God has made the liberation of oppressed black people a divine goal, God is black. The assertions that God is black and that Christ is black are among the most controversial in Cone's theology. It is best to distinguish these and take each in turn.

What does it mean to say that *God is black?* Cone argues that the blackness of God signifies that God has made the oppressed's condition God's own. This affirmation is grounded in biblical witness: God elects or chooses an oppressed and enslaved people, takes up their cause, and promises their liberation and flourishing. Thus Cone concludes that liberation characterizes the essence of divine activity. He reasons that the blackness of God means that God is one with, for, and on the side of oppressed black people. The blackness of God manifests liberation as God's *essential* activity. Moreover, God is black, because God loves black people, takes on black oppressed existence, becomes one with black people.

In *Is God a White Racist?* William Jones raises an objection to Cone's argument. Jones contends that the black claim to divine engagement in their liberation is undermined by a lack of supporting evidence. Cone is sympathetic to the importance Jones places on suffering as a category in black theology, but he is not persuaded. Jones overlooks the normative role of Jesus Christ in Cone's formulation of black theology. For Cone, Jesus Christ is the essence of the meaning of liberation: Jesus *is* black.

To say that Jesus is "the Black Christ" is to confirm the Gospel's witness to the life and ministry, death and resurrection of the historical Jesus. Jesus goes where women and men are outcast, downtrodden, and oppressed and becomes one with them in their oppression and suffering; Jesus is the "Oppressed One." He announces to them, in word and sign, the nearness of the inbreaking of the kingdom of God. But Jesus' preaching and ministry bring him to the hostile attention of the religious and political establishment; he is arrested, tried, crucified, and dies. Yet death does not have the last word: God makes Jesus' cause a divine cause; God raises Jesus from the dead. In his suffering, death, and resurrection, Jesus discloses God's liberating presence in the suffering and pain of oppressed black women and men. He is the "Black Christ."

There are further consequences to this proposition. Jesus Christ is "the Incarnate One" in whom God becomes oppressed black humanity: Christ is black. He is black, not because of some cultural or psychological necessity on the part of black people. Christ is black because oppressed black people are God's poor people whom Christ has come to liberate. In Christ, God "not only takes color seriously, but takes [color] upon himself" (*GO*, 1975, p. 136; *Black Theology of Liberation [BTL]*, 1970, pp.

119-24). God is, in Christ incarnate, black. Christ *really* enters into the black life-world, accepts black people's affliction, and shoulders their pain and oppression in the struggle against the concrete sin and evil of white racist supremacy. Not surprisingly, some theologians disagree with Cone's insistence on the blackness of Jesus Christ. They do so on the grounds of the cultural particularity of the historical Jesus. To these objections Cone replies that his point has less to do with skin color, than with the transcendent affirmation that God has never abandoned the oppressed in the struggle for life (*GO*, 1975, p. 137).

On more than one occasion, Cone has stated that black theology as a theology of liberation can spare little, if any, attention to the christological concerns represented by the Nicene and Chalcedonian formulations. Black Catholic theologians, among others, find this disconcerting. Karl Rahner has maintained that these doctrinal statements are read more properly as points of departure in seeking understanding and ever greater Truth, than as conclusions. But even if this is the case, questions persist: Should black theology continue to sidestep the implications of metaphysics and ontology? How are trinitarian relations to be apprehended, understood, and thematized? And even if a black Christology shifts its hermeneutical foundation to pneumatology, how is the "Spirit" to be understood in relation to the "Father" and the "Son"? To put this issue baldly: Is black theology sufficiently attentive to its own cognitive foundations? Does black theology differentiate adequately between its own use of common sense and theory? To ignore these questions undermines the systematic or theoretical exigence of black theology and delimits its sources.

Human Nature

If black theology is primarily a theology of and for black people, then oppressed "black humanity" stands at its center. This is the case with James Cone's theology. In some of his most passionate theological language, Cone lays bare the poignant urgency of black human dignity to be realized in black self-determination. Yet this passion and urgency frequently dismay his readers, especially white readers who fail to discern that radical particularity is the only way into universality.

How does Cone understand the human person? During slavery, the institution of property nullified the moral and theological notion of personhood. The enslaved peoples were not perceived as human beings, persons, but rather as commodities, objects of property. The institutional and attitudinal tenacity of segregation, discrimination, and anti-black racism demands that black theology say something about what it means to be human, about what it means to be a person.

Cone offers two mutually deciphering paradoxes: "To be a human person is to be free, and to be free is to be human"; and "Freedom is the opposite of oppression, but only the oppressed are truly free" (*BTL*, 1970, pp. 86-87). Freedom, then, is a task; to be a free human person is to engage in a life-task. Cone outlines this life-task over against the typically market-culture values of individualism, self-sufficiency, acquisitiveness, and isolation as well as that culture's privatization of sin. Freedom is constituted by active discontent with the oppression of others and entails identification with an oppressed community. Identification obliges participation and personal engagement; it involves the commitment of one's life for the cause of the oppressed. Moreover, "Freedom means taking sides in a crisis situation"; freedom risks the possibility of suffering and death on behalf of the oppressed (*BTL*, 1970, p. 94).

From the perspective of a black theology of liberation, what does freedom mean in the social situation of the United States? In this situation, blackness is a symbol of oppression, freedom means an affirmation of blackness and resistance to whiteness (*BTL*, p. 101). To be free, blacks must embrace and affirm their blackness and reject whiteness; to do otherwise is to sin. Since most white men and women in the United States do not actively combat the racist decisions and behaviors directed at blacks, they benefit from and permit black oppression, even tacitly. To be free, whites must embrace and affirm blackness and reject their whiteness; to do otherwise is to sin.

Without a doubt, this is a provocative way of interpreting freedom, humanity, and sin. Cone analyzes Hegel's master-slave relationship in terms of oppressors (whites) and the oppressed (blacks) and uncovers its conditioning relation. The (white) oppressors use, manipulate, and "objectify" the (black) oppressed, but white self-assertion and will to power only enslave and dehumanize the (white) oppressors. The liberation of the oppressed and the liberation of the oppressors is linked inextricably. When the oppressed resist the oppressors, they affirm their freedom in God. In this way, the oppressed "not only liberate themselves from oppression, they also liberate the oppressors from an enslavement to their illusions" (*BTL*, pp. 185-86). In the United States social situation, this liberation will be expressed as authentic collaboration between blacks and whites, in response to the demands of the gospel, under the imperatives of black oppression and the leadership of oppressed blacks. To put this another way: In order to bring about that authentic way in which God intends for us to live, blacks and whites will work together, differently in solidarity, for the eradication of white racist supremacy and its effects in themselves, in political and economic arrangements, in culture, and in the church.

Jesus is the clearest example of what it means to identify with the oppressed, to take their side in the struggle for life—no matter the cost. *The Black Christ is freedom incarnate*. Jesus Christ is the norm for black theological anthropology. Jesus identifies with the black oppressed, commits his life to their cause, becomes one with them, and challenges whatever brings about their suffering, misery, and oppression. In realizing his life-task, Jesus signifies the possibility and power of God's image in black. Taking their bearings by the aims of the Black Jesus is a first step for blacks in realizing themselves as human persons. To follow the Black Jesus will mean "to rebel against every [white] infringement of black being" (*BTL*, p. 108). In realizing his life-task, Jesus stands as a contradicting sign to white men and women as well: He empties himself (kenosis) of all that would subvert or stifle authentic liberation. Taking their bearings by the aims of the Black Jesus is a first step for whites in realizing themselves as human persons. To follow the Black Jesus will mean to renounce the personal privileges of skin color, take sides with the black oppressed, and repudiate white racist supremacy in all its individual, social, and structural forms.

Conclusion

More than twenty-five years have passed since James Hal Cone first resisted the silence of Christian theology about the oppression and marginalization of black women and men in the United States. An economic and political analysis of the present situation would reveal that, for the vast majority of blacks, little has changed. Some analysts and critics suggest that the situation is far worse today. If Americans are to respond adequately to the gospel's simple, yet exacting imperative to love one another, we need Cone's passion, urgency, and example. Grappling with his theology is a necessary and demanding task if we are to forge a new and transformative future for ourselves and our country.

M. Shawn Copeland

Selected Primary Works

1969   *Black Theology and Black Power.*
1970   *A Black Theology of Liberation.*
1972   *The Spirituals and the Blues.*
1975   *God of the Oppressed.*
1979   *Black Theology: A Documentary History, 1966–1979,* ed. with Gayraud S. Wilmore.
1982   *My Soul Looks Back.*
1984   *For My People.*
1986   *Speaking the Truth.*
1991   *Martin & Malcolm & America: A Dream or a Nightmare?*
1993   *Black Theology: A Documentary History, 1980–1992,* ed. with Gayraud S. Wilmore.

Selected Secondary Sources

1987   Theo Witvliet. *The Way of the Black Messiah: The Hermeneutical Challenge of Black Theology as a Theology of Liberation.*
1994   Rufus Burrow, Jr., *James H. Cone and Black Liberation Theology.*

MARY DALY
1928–

There is no single more powerful influence upon the development of feminist theology than the work of Mary Daly. From her still courteously Christian challenge to the Roman Catholic patriarchy (*Church and the Second Sex*, 1968), to her exodus from patriarchal religion (*Beyond God the Father*, 1973), to her texts of postchristian feminist philosophy (especially *Gyn/Ecology*, 1978, and *Pure Lust*, 1984), each of her texts has become a classic in its own right. If the creative rage inscribing Daly's work mars the image of serene timelessness connoted by the "classical," nonetheless the conceptual density, the linguistic originality, and the sheer prophetic impact of her writing will place her among the great religious authors of Western civilization—truly, from her perspective, a case of the dubious honor. Her books mark the disruptive intersections of the women's movement with theology at the end of the millennium.

The question immediately arises, however, as to just whether and why Mary Daly is to be counted among "Christian theologians." For her this inclusion would be no compliment. She pointedly calls herself philosopher and *not* theologian. The Greek origins of these terms lend a clue: A feminist might well prefer *philo-sophia*, "love of Sophia," a female-identified wisdom, to the "word of God," in which both "logos" and "theos" designate masculine entities. Any honest answer to the question of Daly's disciplinary location will suck us into a *recapitulatio* of her own self-described "Labyrinthine Pathway," that is, into a condensation of her own intellectual autobiography (*Outercourse*, 1992) as it traces her development. Her lifework so far parses into four phases, or "Spiral Galaxies," themselves moving forward while recapitulating and anticipating one another. Each stage makes problematic, as we shall see, the relationship of theology and philosophy.

Rendering a just account of Daly's contribution must also echo her own stunningly original rhetorical style, daunting both to the prosaic and to the patriarchal. But as quotations will demonstrate, the unparalleled conjunction of poeto-sophic satire, spiritual ontology, and feminist metaethics can hardly be translated back into the "academented" discourse it was designed to subvert. Thus both in terms of style and subject, Daly resists assimilation into the present format, which nonetheless would remain glaringly incomplete without her. With these working paradoxes stated up front, we may proceed to unfurl the four movements of her intellectual journey in terms of their relationships to theology.

First Spiral Galaxy

Born in 1928 into a working-class Catholic milieu in Schenectady, New York, the only child of caring parents, Daly attended Catholic schools for her entire formal education. Although she holds two doctorates in theology, she accounts for them herself as roundabout ways to study philosophy. For a pre–Vatican II Roman Catholic woman, it took an indomitable will to study Catholic theology or philosophy. After completing one doctorate in the sole North American program open to women in the 1950s, she moved, unsatisfied, to Switzerland, where state-supported Catholic faculties could not exclude women. She delighted in this breakaway to the beauty of the medieval city of Fribourg, and supported herself teaching courses for North American students abroad. She first completed a dissertation with honors, entitled *The Problem of Speculative Theology: A Study in Saint Thomas* (1963). Even as she later confronted the angelic doctor's mysogyny, she would never forfeit the disciplined delight in systematic speculation that she gleaned from her early love of Aquinas. Thomistic tidbits would continue to cycle through every phase of her work (as with his doctrine of angels, lighting on the pages of *Pure Lust*). Finally she satisfied her hunger for a rigorous philosophical immersion by pursuing a second Fribourg doctorate (the resultant dissertation, published in 1966, was *Natural Knowledge of God in the Philosophy of Jacques Maritain.*) "Moving onward by degrees," she quips of this phase.

Before returning to the United States, she visited the Second Vatican Council then in progress in Rome, imbibing the atmosphere of high hope for a millennial transformation, and wrote *The Church and the Second Sex* (hereafter *CSS*).

Inspired by the lone feminist philosophical voice of Simone de Beauvoir's *The Second Sex*, Daly's meticulously researched text carefully analyzes the problems of sexism in the church, focused especially around the issues of women's ordination, the historical contribution of women religious, and birth control. Like so many Catholic thinkers, she speaks here as a philosophical theologian, or Christian philosopher; the distinction is insignificant. Publication of *The Church and the Second Sex* at the beginning of her teaching career at the Jesuit-run Boston College launched her into immediate national notoriety. By later standards, the book maintains an almost ladylike tone of polite faith in the capacity of the church to reform itself, to transcend its own history of "discrimination." Of this Vatican II–inspired optimism of her early self, Daly would write a decade later in the

"Feminist Postchristian Introduction" for the second edition of *The Church and the Second Sex:*

> So deceptive was this cloud of optimism that, despite the evidence that she herself amassed, Daly was unable to perceive that sexism was inherent in the symbol system of Christianity itself and that a primary function of Christianity in Western culture has been to legitimize sexism. (p. 17)

Her optimism quickly proved unwarranted. Boston College fired her immediately. The timing was right: It was 1969 and she became a *cause célèbre*. Students broke into mass demonstrations on her behalf, she became a symbol for academic freedom, the campus was overrun by reporters and cameras, the case hit the first page of the *New York Times,* and suddenly she was granted promotion and tenure. As she wrote later: "It was a strange victory. Apparently the book which had generated the hostility which led to my firing had generated the support which forced my rehiring." The experience revealed the connection between her own situation and the universal oppression of women. She now "understood more clearly the nature of the beast and the name of the demon: patriarchy" (*CSS,* 1968, p. 97). The bonds of misplaced hope began to fall away.

Second Spiral Galaxy

In the fall of 1971, Daly became the first woman to preach at a Sunday service in Harvard Memorial Church. It became a historic event, a translucent moment of public *practice* of theology. When the sermon declared the women's movement "an exodus community," and called the congregation to "affirm our faith in ourselves and our will to transcendence by rising and walking out together," hundreds of women and several men processed out with her. In 1973 the metaphoric exodus from patriarchal religion would find its theological consummation in *Beyond God the Father (BGF).* Its subtitle, *Toward a Philosophy of Women's Liberation,* indicates the shift to the boundaries of theology and its institutional context, the church. She departs from all Sunday school feminism in her response to the plausible claim that "Jesus was a feminist"—"so what?" The point is that women need no longer legitimate themselves by appeal to powerful males, however benign. Yet the text is very much a philosophy of God—a God now liberated from static anthropocentrism with the help of Tillichian ontology. Being Itself becomes her more dynamic "Be-ing, Who is the Verb from whom, in whom, and with whom all true movements move" (*BGF,* 1973, p. 198).

With Tillich she also situated her work "on the boundary" of philosophy and theology, and more politically, gave guidance to women in their locations on the boundaries of patriarchal religious institutions. Sparkling with its succinct, multifaceted vision, *Beyond God the Father* commits "methodicide" against the platitudes of "universal" or "human liberation," revealing the specificity of women's situation, while resisting any impulse to sociopolitical reductionism: The "Second Coming of Women"—as Anti-Christ—exposes the "Unholy Trinity" of Rape, Genocide, and War in order to bring to life a new language of transcendence. Here is enthroned the most glorious one-liner of feminist religious thought: *"If God is male, the male is God."*

Third Spiral Galaxy

In Daly's subsequent books, we witness a dramatic metamorphosis not so much of ideological standpoint as of rhetorical practice. "Anti-Christ" becomes "Nemesis," goddess of Justice, whose Rage now "a-mazes," that is, leads us out of the "man-made mazes" into the "Labyrinthine Passages" of a new mythography. The Labyrinth, like the popular lesbian symbol of the labrys, revives the imagery of ancient Crete, a goddess-worshiping and woman-centered civilization. The labrys, not a weapon but a tool, cuts two ways and so emblematizes Daly's method: the re-versing of reversals. If Adam is said to have birthed Eve, we re-member that as Hava, the Mother of Life, who represents the goddess-mythology that precedes all narratives of creation by males: thus the re-reversal. Likewise with Mary, already recognized in *Beyond God the Father* as an image of "stolen goddess power," here depicted in her reversed captivity as "dutifully dull and derivative, drained of divinity . . ." (p. 88). The return to mythological and etymological roots—the *radix*, or radical—accompanies the transition in North American feminism to a posttraditional goddess movement in spirituality. Although any literal goddess worship goes against Daly's philosophical grain, the labrys has cut her metaphors loose, into an ecstatic semantic rhythm in which prose breaks into poetry and through which women by the thousands broke into spiritual revolution. Thus her style, inspiring to as many as it infuriates—but then she rejoices in those ancient female Furies!—enabled and echoed the content of a new language. The rhetorical strategy of "Wild Words" seeks to free us from the "mindbindings" of the master myth of patriarchy.

The impact on its generation cannot be underestimated. We read with her that "patriarchy is itself the prevailing religion of the entire planet." From Buddhism to Hinduism through Judaism and Christianity and their secular heirs such as psychoanalysis and Marxism: All are "infrastructures of the edifice of patriarchy" (*BGF*, 1973, p. 39). And her arguments moved us into agonizingly concrete multicultural exposé. Chapters on footbinding, female genital mutilation, widow burning, and witch hunting detailed a global gynocidal impulse as not only historical ethnography but as metaphor for present sexism. We sought to "exorcise" ourselves of the patriarchal state of possession, which disfigures women as well as men.

She freed herself of some lingering conceptual bonds as well. Thus theologically she no longer evokes the name of "God," which even as a verb carries such powerful androcentric residues. The space of theology does not, however, reduce to anthropology, but re-reverses toward female identified metaphors. Likewise her anthropology now shifts from the *Beyond God the Father* ideal of "androgyny" (which she likened in the 1980s to Ronald and Nancy Reagan taped together) to a sheerly female-identified "Self" "dis-covered" and self-created by coming in touch with the Sister Self within, cleansing itself of traditional masculine-feminine admixtures (*BGF,* 1973, p. 338). What traditionally is called the kingdom of God becomes the "fire of female friendship" opening into the transcendent spaces of "Spiral Webs Converging." But rather than a supernatural heaven or an earth-despising salvation, Daly begins to work with animal and elemental imagery to spin out the cosmic implications of her metaphor of ecology. She now invokes the "Super Natural" "Otherworld" that will burst into full vision in subsequent work. Patriarchy according to Daly's doctrine of evil is understood as necrophilic, pitted not just against women but against life itself.

Rightly subtitled *The Metaethics of Radical Feminism,* suggestive of a philosophical ethic—passionately preoccupied with historical evil, with the holocausts of sacrificed women—*Gyn/Ecology* prepares the way for the unabashed cosmological exercise of her next work. As cosmology, *Pure Lust: Elemental Feminist Philosophy (PL)* performs her first full-scale philosophical opus. But of course, this is not the philosophy of pedants and patriarchs. It is a wildly, lustily personified vision, inhabited by a mythic cast of characters: the good gals are the Nags, the Brewsters, Dikes, Dragons, Fates, Phoenixes, Maenads, Muses, the Virgins, Vixens, Websters, and Weirds. The bad guys, populating the "Stag-nation," include snools, bores, cocks, danglers, disks, drones, fakes, fixers, jerks, jocks, pluguglies, pricks. . . . Interested readers may look them up in their Webster's or in Daly's own new edition, the *Webster's First New Intergalactic Wickedary of the English Language.*

The high tone of lustful humor cackles through this text, releasing into a constructive vision of unsurpassed imaginative complexity: especially her post-Thomist analysis of primary versus plastic and potted passions and virtues and her poetic evocation of tidal muses breaking free of the demons of tidiness ("As instrumental cooperators, women themselves become token tyrants of tidydom" [*PL,* 1984, p. 292].) have accompanied me through the years. Her hilarious revolutionary band of raging muses continues to accompany women in the process she names *metapatterning:* "the process of breaking through paternal patterns . . . real transcending of patriarchal patterns of thinking, speaking, acting. It is weaving our way through and out of these patterns. Erratic women weave our lives, our works, not as imitations of models, nor as models for others, but as unique diversified creations" (*PL,* p. 342). (It is important for readers, feeling the gravitational pull of her verbal power, to recognize she is not calling for clones who model themselves after *her* variety of correct feminism, either.) She, as philosophical wordmuse, will always be known as the supreme "Webster," the weaver of the web of words, of the feminist movement. The Wickedary, co-authored with Jane Caputi in 1987, mischievously assembles into parodic dictionary form her multitude of neologisms.

Fourth Spiral Galaxy

This is the phase marked by her most recent book, *Outercourse (O)*, which itself sets forth these stages of her intellectual autobiography. Here Daly self-critically and self-affirmingly re-collects the galaxies, envisioning them as a milky way of spiraling galaxies through which she sails as stellar pirate identifying with the cow who jumped over the moon. Lunacy—no doubt (from lune, moon). Utterly, burningly inspired lunacy, then, awakening us like Plato's divine madness, from our numbing illusions into philosophical ecstasy.

Not surprisingly, criticism of the radical Daly is incessant, from feminists as well as patriarchs, post-Christians as well as traditional theists. Other feminists have found her dualistic, oppositional, ahistorical, apolitical, separatist, essentialist, purist, naturalist, racist, eurocentric, elitist, universalist, apocalyptic. . . . The pounding waves of anti-Daly epithets embody the equal and opposite reaction to a very powerful force. Yet some recurrent questions may shed light on her project.

The main concern is with her dualism. Her quite Manichaean opposition between patriarchy, including its "fembot" women, and the "elemental" purity of radical feminism, scares many feminist sympathizers with its force of polarization. The doctrine of evil is apocalyptically clear: Patriarchy is the original sin, which sought, in its primal reversals, to render femininity itself as sinful. But for all the dualism of patriarchy versus feminism, she never identifies evil with "men"—only with patriarchal masculinity. And femaleness is not intrinsically good; only as liberated does it become the luminous, Super Natural force she prophesies into existence.

The force with which she summons up an integral feminist subject over against the patriarchal death-system continues, however, to elicit suspicions. Not just men, but many women, find themselves excluded from her discourse. The female-identified Self she proposes seems too global, too homogeneous, despite the claim of angelic diversity. Of these the most important criticism, and as it would seem in *Outercourse* the most painful for Daly, came from the Open Letter published by Audre Lorde in response to *Gyn/Ecology*. The great black lesbian poet charged Daly with failing to name black goddesses, yet while discussing the African atrocity of infibulation, and thus portraying black women as merely victims. Daly notes that she had intended to focus on those goddesses that were used—reversed—by Christian myth, but did not want to enter into public debate (*O*, 1992, p. 232). Yet the metanarrative of the integral Self that Daly constructs over against a universal and homogeneous force of patriarchy certainly complicates the reception of her work within the postmodern context of multiple discourses and pluralist sensibilities. Her Super Natural Self seems to presuppose a dualism sustainable only for a certain group of largely white, largely lesbian, largely educated North American women. Her unacknowledged apocalypticism, or rather, her apocalyptic denunciation of the patriarchal end-of-the-world dynamics, can certainly be read as driving her toward dualistic overgeneralizations. And those who find support for feminism within church-related institutions may concur: While recognizing their debt to Daly for their boundary spaces, they will resist the demonization of Judaism and Christianity in favor of more nuanced critique.

This returns us to the question of her place in this *Handbook*. All God-language dropped out after *Beyond God the Father*. Even her Goddess-language plays less a theistic than a kind of cosmo-psycho-social role. As ever, she says this best herself: "By assuming theology into my own Elemental Feminist Philosophy, decoding its symbols, reversing its reversals, I have challenged directly the authority of the male god in all of his guyses."

But interestingly, she herself admits that ultimately, however repugnant so many of the sexist answers, she does not want to abandon the questions explored by theology—which means not some abstract theism but the history of Christian theology from which she emerged. She now understands her "metapatterning" as "not only my overcoming of the dualism between abstract and mystical/poetic/mythic thought . . . but also transcending the dualism between theology and philosophy." She has not abandoned theology but rather "engulfed both" philosophy and theology in her elemental feminist philosophy. It represents thus a "transcendent third option."

We have thus included the postchristian Daly in good faith. Moreover, if the faith of theologians is to be any "good," it may require baptism by Daly. Christian theologians who recognize the primal idolatry involved in the exclusive personification of God as male will continue to appreciate, however uncomfortably, the power required to unmask so virulently sacralized an image. They will nod agreement to Krister Stendahl's early response to *Beyond God the Father*—that Daly, precisely in her onesided extremism, operates with the passion for justice, the exodus spirit, of the Hebrew prophets. This does not make her an "anonymous Christian"; it is not she who needs rebaptism. But Christians reading her must account in their own terms for their responses. We may recognize that the spirit goading the prophets was for all its radicalism held captive to a patriarchal form, and may in her voice be seeking this truly apocalyptic revelation. The *apocalypsis* of patriarchy—its revelation as a world-destructive construct rather than "the way things are"—threatens not only patriarchs, not only the patriarchal God, but the fabric of Christian world civilization. In a time of unraveling, the arachnid genius of Mary Daly, which both unweaves and weaves, offers a Webster inextricable from all coming theologies—all divine words.

Catherine Keller

Selected Bibliography

1968 *The Church and the Second Sex.*

1973 *Beyond God the Father: Toward a Philosophy of Women's Liberation.*

1975 "Feminist Postchristian Introduction," in *The Church and the Second Sex: With a New Feminist Postchristian Introduction by the Author.*

1978 *Gyn/Ecology: The Metaethics of Radical Feminism.*

1984 *Pure Lust: Elemental Feminist Philosophy* (repr. 1992).

1992 *Outercourse: The Be-Dazzling Voyage. Containing Recollections from My Logbook of a Radical Feminist Philosopher (Be-ing an Account of My Time/Space Travels and Ideas—Then, Again, Now, and How)* (contains a comprehensive list of Daly's publications).

AVERY DULLES

1918–

Life and Career

The Laurence J. McGinley Professor of Religion and Society at Fordham University, Avery Dulles has been an important and influential voice in Roman Catholic and ecumenical theology for more than thirty years. His contributions to theology have been mainly in the areas of apologetics, ecumenism, fundamental or foundational theology, and ecclesiology.

Born in Auburn, New York, on August 24, 1918, the son of John Foster Dulles, Secretary of State under Eisenhower, Avery Dulles came from a strict Presbyterian family background. He attended Choate and graduated from Harvard in 1940, in the same class as John F. Kennedy. After a year and a half at Harvard Law School, he entered the United States Navy and was discharged with the rank of lieutenant in 1946.

Significant for his subsequent theological development was his conversion to Roman Catholicism while a student at Harvard, an autobiographical account of which he published in 1946 as *A Testimonial to Grace*. That same year he entered the Society of Jesus, followed the usual course of studies in that Order, and was ordained to the priesthood in June 1956. After a year of ascetical and pastoral studies in Germany, he received the Doctorate of Sacred Theology from the Gregorian University in Rome, 1960.

Dulles taught fundamental theology and ecclesiology, first at Woodstock College, in Woodstock, Maryland, and subsequently in New York City, from 1960 to 1974, when Woodstock was closed. He then served on the faculty of the Catholic University of America until his retirement from there in 1988. He has been visiting professor at a number of institutions including the Gregorian University (Rome), Union Theological Seminary (New York), Princeton Theological Seminary, and Boston College.

He is past president of both the Catholic Theological Society of America and the American Theological Society, a member of the International Theological Commission, and for many years a member of the United States Lutheran-Catholic

Dialogue to which he has contributed a number of papers. Dulles is the author of sixteen books, most recently *The Craft of Theology: From Symbol to System* (1992) and *The Assurance of Things Hoped For: A Theology of Christian Faith* (1994), and more than five hundred articles.

When Dulles began teaching fundamental theology in 1960, the orientation of the course was basically toward apologetics, but an apologetics which placed unquestioning confidence in the powers of scientific historical method to defend the rational basis of the Christian faith—what Dulles called the "historicist apologetics" (*Apologetics and the Biblical Christ*, 1963, p. 6). In reaction to this, he began to devise a "softer" approach to apologetics by recognizing that the Gospels were confessional testimony and not strictly history in the modern sense of the word. Thus, the basis for the credibility of the Christian faith was "not in the force of the argumentation but in the power of the religious testimony" (ibid., p. 69). He produced *A History of Apologetics*, 1971, but subsequently turned his attention to more specific issues in fundamental theology and ecclesiology.

Avery Dulles' approach to theology is best characterized as honest, critical, and balanced. In his autobiographical memoir he admitted "that which I valued more than anything else [was] intellectual honesty" (*A Testimonial to Grace*, pp. 79-80). He is always critical of any dominant conventional wisdom or ideology, but he seeks to balance such a critical stance with an appreciation of the strengths and weaknesses of other positions. He is not unwilling to stake out and defend his own view, however. Given these intellectual qualities, it is not surprising that one of his main contributions to theology has been the use of models in theology, as exemplified in two of his most important and influential books, *Models of the Church* (1974) and *Models of Revelation* (1983).

Models in Theology

Confronting the pluralism in Christian theology, both Protestant and Catholic, and with ecumenism as a guiding aim, Dulles argued that

> the method of models or types, . . . can have great value in helping people to get beyond the limitations of their own particular outlook, and to enter into fruitful conversation with others having a fundamentally different mentality. Such conversation is obviously essential if ecumenism is to get beyond its present impasses.
>
> (*Models of the Church*, p. 12)

Furthering the ecumenical conversation, however, is not the only purpose of constructing typologies. In the Christian tradition (even in any one denominational variety), there is a multiplicity of images and symbols through which the basic religious experience is expressed and communicated. The church, for example, is imaged as the Body of Christ, the Flock of Christ, the Vineyard of God, the Temple of the Holy Spirit, or the People of God. "When an image is employed reflectively and critically to deepen one's theoretical understanding of a reality it becomes what is today called a 'model'" (*Models of the Church*, 1974, p. 27).

In the history of theology, some models have dominated over others for a period of time, and conflict and misunderstanding may result when there is a shift from one dominant model or paradigm to another. In the case of Roman Catholic theology, Vatican II was such an occasion. The dominant images of the church since the Reformation had been those of a juridical "perfect society" and the Mystical Body of Christ. In the documents of Vatican II, *Lumen gentium* and *Gaudium et spes*, the predominant image was that of the pilgrim People of God. By developing and comparing the various models built on these diverse images, Dulles enabled believers within his own tradition to become aware of the sometimes conflicting presuppositions involved in ecclesiological issues. He also made it clear that no one model by itself could suffice for a complete theology of the church. Hence, his goal was not just furthering ecumenism but also greater understanding of the theology of the church.

In the first edition of *Models of the Church*, Dulles listed five models: The Church as Institution, The Church as Mystical Communion, The Church as Sacrament, The Church as Herald, and The Church as Servant. In the later expanded edition (1987), he added The Church: Community of Disciples, which "can be seen as a variant of the communion model." It can include the best elements of the other five models and can provide the possibility of a more comprehensive ecclesiology.

Dulles employed the method of typological construction again in his approach to the theology of revelation in 1983, but he was more "concerned to surmount the conflicts" among the various models of revelation than he had been in *Models of the Church*. Here too, he lists five types of theologies of revelation: Revelation as Doctrine, Revelation as History, Revelation as Inner Experience, Revelation as Dialectical Presence, and Revelation as New Awareness. These models are constructed according to their central vision of how and where revelation occurs (*Models of Revelation*, 1983, p. 27). In this case, however, he attempted what he called "dialectical retrieval." "Using the concept of symbolic mediation as a dialectical tool," he later recalls, "I attempted to draw maximum value from each of the models and to harmonize them critically" (*Craft of Theology*, 1992, p. 50). This symbolic approach, which he calls "symbolic realism," can incorporate what is valid in each model and correct what is misleading.

Dulles has said that his use of models in theology was "partly in continuity with, and partly in reaction against, the neo-scholastic system" in which he had been trained, but it was also due to his study of the history of theology and the influence of Ernst Troeltsch, *The Social Teaching of the Christian Churches* (1911), H. Richard Niebuhr, *Christ and Culture* (1951), and Ian G. Barbour, *Myths, Models, and Paradigms* (1974). His use of models in theology exemplifies his honest and critical approach to theology: "Before refuting a theory," he wrote in *The Craft of Theology,* "one should make sure to have learned as much as one could from those who defended it." And in his use of models he also evinced his balanced, ecumenical bent "to illuminate and overcome the conflicts" in the pluralism of theologies that characterizes the situation of theology today (*Craft of Theology,* 1992, pp. 46-50).

Symbolic Realism

A second important contribution of Dulles to theology, especially Roman Catholic theology, has been his development of the symbolic approach to theology, what he calls "symbolic realism" or "symbolic communication." Reacting to a "historicist apologetics" and a rationalist and propositionalist approach to revelation in the neo-scholastic manuals that dominated Roman Catholic theology in the nineteenth and early twentieth centuries, Dulles began to recover the importance of symbol and myth as early as 1966 ("Symbol, Myth, and the Biblical Revelation," 1966). He brought this to its most thorough expression in *Models of Revelation,* especially chapter 9.

Theology is always about God's self-disclosure to humans, but this revelation "is always mediated through symbol" (p. 131). "A symbol, in this perspective, is a perceptible sign that evokes a realization of that which surpasses ordinary objective cognition. Symbolic knowledge is self-involving, for the symbol 'speaks to us only insofar as it lures us to situate ourselves mentally within the universe of meaning and value which it opens up to us'" (*Craft of Theology,* 1992, pp. 18-19; *Models of Revelation,* 1983, pp. 136-37). Symbols have a transforming effect on persons and exercise a powerful influence on commitments and behavior. They open up levels of reality otherwise closed to us. Because symbols are polyvalent, their meaning cannot be precisely limited; they are capable of bearing more than one meaning, but they are not "indefinitely pliable." Symbols always require interpretation, which must be done within the community for which they are the identifying symbols. Thus, Dulles describes the symbolic approach to theology as "ecclesial-transformative" (*Craft of Theology,* p. 18).

The symbolic approach allows Dulles to maintain a cognitive dimension of revelation and doctrine that is more, not less, than an objectivist form of knowledge. But neither is this a purely subjectivist approach, for symbolic knowledge has a basis in reality and in history—hence, "symbolic realism." In this, he has been influenced by Michael Polanyi's notion of "tacit knowledge," Newman's "illative sense," and Rahner's ontology of symbols. Symbols are "imbued with a plenitude or depth of meaning that surpasses the capacities of conceptual thinking and propositional speech" (ibid.). But they are still a form of communication, indeed, the only form of communication possible with a transcendent dimension of reality that can never be directly known but only mediated indirectly.

Although talk about symbolic knowledge still makes those with a propositionalist or fundamentalist view of revelation and theology uncomfortable, Dulles has done much to gain wider acceptance of this symbolic approach among Roman Catholic theologians.

Ecclesiology and Ecumenism

Dulles' ecumenical concern influenced his use of models in ecclesiology, and his contributions in ecclesiology and ecumenism are two areas that remain closely interrelated. In ecclesiology he has devoted considerable attention to teaching authority in the church—the relationship of the hierarchical magisterium and the magisterium of the theologians, the teaching authority of episcopal conferences, and the teaching authority of the pope. He has tried to restore some balance between these various organs of authoritative teaching, at least theologically if not structurally. For example, his treatment of papal infallibility in "Moderate Infallibilism: An Ecumenical Approach" (*A Church to Believe In,* 1982) was originally prepared as a paper of the United States Lutheran-Catholic Dialogue.

In that essay he tries to steer a middle course between George Lindbeck's two categories of "absolutistic infallibilism" and "fallibilism." His own position affirms that the pope, at least on certain occasions, has a charism "that may not too deceptively be called infallibility," but that this is "subject to inherent conditions which provide critical principles for assessing the force and meaning of allegedly infallible statements" (p. 134). Typically, he does not abandon an identifiably Roman Catholic position, but he does point out the limitations included in the Vatican I definition itself and in the general conditions presupposed for its exercise: agreement with Scripture and Tradition, agreement with the present faith of the church, agreement with the universal episcopate, and sufficient investigation. He then indicates some of the unarticulated presuppositions of the definition, its main target (Gallicanism), the juridical and metaphysical categories of thought, and the vocabulary available at the time. When all of these factors are considered, Dulles can offer a very moderate and contemporary interpretation of papal infallibility. Its importance for ecclesiology and ecumenism is obvious.

Equally balanced is Dulles' treatment of the hierarchical magisterium and the magisterium of the theologians. In recent years in Roman Catholicism, these two have seemed to be in frequent conflict, but Dulles sees them as having different functions that need to remain in dialectical relationship. He concludes that

one may say that the functional specialty of the ecclesiastical magisterium is judgment; that of the theologian is understanding. The hierarchy as judges publicly proclaim what is vital for the life and witness of the Christian community. Theologians as students and professors methodically pursue personal insight into the meaning and implications of faiths.

("The Two Magisteria: An Interim Reflection," *A Church to Believe In*, 1982, p. 125)

Both functions are needed in the process of handing on the gospel message with integrity. Dulles believes that his position "provides for a dialectical relationship of relative autonomy within mutual acceptance."

Taking up another disputed exercise of teaching authority—that of national or regional episcopal conferences—Dulles again is both critical and balanced. Vatican II encouraged the formation of such conferences where they did not already exist, and the 1983 Code of Canon Law gave them legal standing. But what authority they have to teach has been disputed. After reviewing the pertinent literature, Dulles concludes that national episcopal conferences are accorded the power to teach in canon law because of their parallel position with particular councils in the history of the church as they come together to serve the whole church. As usual, however, Dulles qualifies this conclusion with a number of conditions and limitations. The recovery of the synodal tradition within Roman Catholicism makes its structures more compatible with other Christian churches that have maintained a more conciliar structure.

Although his ecclesiological concerns have definite implications for ecumenism, Dulles has written explicitly about the need for an ecumenical approach to theology. He has argued that "for church unity one needs a certain measure of doctrinal accord but not absolute agreement on all points of doctrines" and that there is a hierarchy of importance in Christian doctrines (*Reshaping of Catholicism*, 1988, pp. 228-30). The church may have to learn to live with a certain amount of doctrinal pluralism in accord with Vatican II, which had said that some formulations may be seen to be complementary rather than conflicting.

Although substantive agreement may be reached in some areas, there are other doctrinal formulations that may have to be reexamined and can only be affirmed with modifications, explanations, or reservations, and there is no guarantee that Christians will reach full agreement short of the eschaton. Dulles is more hesitant than some other ecumenical theologians to call for immediate though imperfect communion on the basis of doctrinal agreement already achieved.

More recently, he has said that we may have reached a new moment in the ecumenical movement that requires new strategies. "After working for a generation to build up mutual confidence and friendship," he writes in *The Craft of Theology*, "the dialogues have matured to the point at which divisive issues may now be squarely faced. The theologians are today eager to explore the most neuralgic issues with a frank recognition that the prospects of full agreement are minimal" (1992, pp. 191-92). This new situation requires (1) that we maintain the primacy of truth and honest conviction rather than paper over real disagreements, (2) that we seek mutual enrichment from the dialogues rather than the minimum we need for agreement, (3) that the "time is ripe to welcome the more traditional and conservative churches into the dialogue," and (4) that we focus on spiritual renewal rather than on producing consensus statements or other activity with measurable results (ibid., pp. 191-94). His criticism of the current state of the ecumenical movement does not, however, imply a diminished commitment to it.

The entire theological career of Avery Dulles has been characterized by rigorous intellectual honesty, an ecumenical respect for all viewpoints, and a critical pursuit of an understanding of the Christian faith. He has consistently addressed some of the most crucial issues in post–Vatican II theology with an open and inquiring mind. Through his teaching and numerous writings he has been a model theologian and a faithful witness to the gospel.

T. Howland Sanks

Selected Bibliography

1963   *Apologetics and the Biblical Christ.*
1966   "Symbol, Myth, and the Biblical Revelation," *Theological Studies,* 27.
1967   *The Dimensions of the Church.*
1968   *Revelation and the Quest for Unity.*
1969   *Revelation Theology: A History.*
1971   *The History of Apologetics.*
1971   *The Survival of Dogma.*
1974   *Models of the Church* (expanded ed., 1987).
1977   *The Resilient Church.*
1982   *A Church to Believe In: Discipleship and the Dynamics of Freedom.*
1983   *Models of Revelation.*
1985   *The Catholicity of the Church.*
1988   *The Reshaping of Catholicism.*
1992   *The Craft of Theology: From Symbol to System.*
1994   *The Assurance of Things Hoped For: A Theology of Christian Faith.*

GERHARD EBELING

1912–

Life and Career

Gerhard Ebeling was born on July 6, 1912, in Berlin-Steglitz. His father, a teacher, undoubtedly instilled in him at an early age a deep respect for learning. In his later years Ebeling spoke with great fondness of his childhood in Berlin-Steglitz. In the house purchased by his grandfather, he grew up in the sheltered environment of the extended family and enjoyed the rich cultural setting that unfolded during the Weimar Republic. The period of the famous Weimar Republic was, however, an ambiguous one in German history, characterized on the one hand by flourishing cultural expression, but on the other hand by deep political divisions and economic distress. These inner tensions culminated ultimately in the downfall of the Weimar Republic, in economic and social catastrophe in Germany, and in the firm establishment of National Socialism. Significantly, the years of Ebeling's theological study in Marburg, Zürich, and Berlin (1930–35) fell precisely in this period of extreme crisis.

After completing his basic theological training, Ebeling was examined by the Council of the Confessing Church in Berlin-Brandenburg, and he entered the service of the church as vicar in Crossen and Fehrbellin. Shortly thereafter, he came in close contact with Dietrich Bonhoeffer, who urged him to take temporary leave of his service in the Confessing Church in order to complete a Doctor of Theology degree at the University of Zürich, Switzerland. Ebeling was awarded this degree after submitting his dissertation entitled *Evangelical Interpretation of the Gospels: An Investigation of Luther's Hermeneutic*. This early work by Ebeling investigated the hermeneutic of Luther and indicated already his unique interest in both *systematic* and *historical* questions, a twofold problematic that he pursued throughout his academic career. In fact, as his thought matured, Ebeling came to recognize the tension between systematic theology and historical investigation as an essential contrast in all theological work. This orientation finds lucid expression in his article "Theologie in den Gegensätzen des Lebens," 1985 (Theology in the Contrasts of Life), in which he renders a self-portrait of his theology.

In the turmoil of the late 1930s, Ebeling returned to Germany where he once again served as pastor in the Confessing Church. After the Second World War, in 1946 he both completed his habilitation at the University of Tübingen and assumed the chair for church history. In 1954 he changed his official area of academic specialty from church history to systematic theology; two years later he was called to the University of Zürich in the area of systematics. With the exception of the period from 1965–1968, when Ebeling was once again in Tübingen, his academic career unfolded in Zürich where he was the founder and, until his retirement in 1979, the director of the Institute for Hermeneutics.

From 1950 to 1977 Ebeling was the chief editor of the publication *Zeitschrift für Theologie und Kirche,* and since 1969 he has presided over the Commission for the Publication of the Works of Luther. Ebeling holds honorary doctorates from the universities of Bonn (1952), Uppsala (1970), St. Louis (1971), Edinburgh (1981), and Neuchâtel (1993). Over the years he has lectured at various academic institutions in the United States including Vanderbilt and Drew universities. In 1987 he received the Sigmund Freud Prize for açademic prose from the Germany Academy for Language and Poetry in Darmstadt, a testimony to the extremely high literary quality of his writings. His many essays and lectures on language, hermeneutics, the doctrine of God, Christology, ecclesiology, soteriology, faith, and ethics have been collected in four volumes under the title *Word and Faith (Wort und Glaube).* Ebeling's historical research, which has concentrated on the theology of Martin Luther, appears in a series of publications entitled *Studies in Luther (Lutherstudien).* The most extensive of these investigations is a three-volume work that presents a detailed analysis of Luther's understanding of human being in the *Disputatio de homine* (Disputation about Man, 1536) (*Lutherstudien,* vol. 2, pts. 1-3). Ebeling's systematic thought appears in its most concentrated form in his work *Dogmatic of Christian Faith (Dogmatik des christlichen Glaubens).*

The Subject Matter of Theology

The world as we know it is apparently made up of contrasting elements, sometimes in the form of harmonious configurations, sometimes as inhibiting dissonances. These contrasts are to be observed in the inorganic as well as the organic and point to the essential relatedness of all things. The theology of Gerhard Ebeling takes this essential relatedness of all things most seriously; it considers, however, the particular relation between God and humans as the key to understanding the whole. The concentration on the relation between God and humanity has great significance for the understanding both of the subject matter of theology and of the theological task. If God and humans belong essentially together, then one cannot speak adequately about humans apart from their relation to God. That is, a purely philosophical understanding of human being will remain necessarily abstract in the sense that it will, by its very nature, abstract humans from their fundamental, determinative relation to God. Likewise, talk about God apart from the relation to humans presupposes an independent being, perhaps metaphysically conceived, which upon deeper theological reflection proves to be chimerical. One should speak not about humans or God separately but rather of the *relation* between God and humans.

At this point Ebeling consciously departs from the substance ontology of the Western tradition stemming from René Descartes. Whereas Descartes in his *Meditations on First Philosophy* concentrated his first two meditations on an understanding of a human being as a conscious, independent being (*res cogitans* = a thinking substance or thing) and came only in the third meditation to a consideration of God, Ebeling takes as the starting point of theological reflection the relation between God and human beings. To be sure, one could describe this context of thought from a philosophical perspective as a relational ontology, but the deeper aspects of the relation between God and humanity become apparent only in light of the theological tradition. Here Ebeling appeals first and foremost to the creative thought of Martin Luther. At a time when Western culture was freeing itself from the bonds of medieval thought and in particular from the constraints of Aristotelian metaphysics, Luther was able, because of his dramatic personal experiences and his intense study of the biblical message, to bring the relation between God and humans into focus, as it were, through the lens of the Pauline doctrine of justification. The biblical language about the reality of sin and the necessity of justification introduces clearly an element of tension in the relation between God and humans. Every relation involves a contrast of sorts, but the Pauline message discloses the contrast between God and humans as an *opposition* that is provoked not from the side of God, but rather from humans. This opposition is, in fact, so extreme that the relation itself becomes hopelessly distorted, rendering a clear understanding of God and humans almost impossible. It is from this perspective that the subject matter of theology must be conceived.

Unlike other academic disciplines, theology has no well-defined subject matter to investigate objectively. At the onset of the theological task a theologian discovers himself or herself in the midst of a multitude of oppositions and contradictions that are apparently constitutive for human life, the most fundamental opposition being the relation to God. The distortion of this relation and the concomitant confusion that arises from it places the theologian not only as theologian but also as a person, before the task of making fundamental distinctions in order to bring clarity into his or her situation before God. For this reason, the word "distinguish" (German: *unterscheiden*) alongside the word "opposition" (German: *Gegensatz*) plays a decisive role in the thought of Ebeling. The fundamental opposition between God and humans gives rise to a host of other oppositions that are formulated in the theological tradition through expressions such as "law and gospel," "experience and tradition," "faith and reason," and so forth. These oppositions, being constitutive for human existence, are the subject matter of theology; and accordingly the theological task consists in making the necessary fundamental distinctions in order to clarify and rectify the relation between God and human beings. The inexhaustible character of this task excludes at the outset even a hint of arrogance with respect to the accomplishments of serious theological work. To use the metaphor of Ebeling, the work of theology is like a walk in the woods. At the end of the day, one realizes what one forgot to bring along, what one could have done differently, and out of this realization arises the desire to start over again from the beginning.

Hermeneutics and Proclamation

The modern tendency to think in clichés and to attach labels to cultural movements and modes of thought can have disastrous consequences for a serious endeavor such as theology, which is so tightly woven into the fabric of life itself. A prime example of this is the term "New Hermeneutic" that was attached to the work of Ebeling in the early 1960s. Under this title James M. Robinson and John B. Cobb, Jr., edited in 1964 a volume in the series New Frontiers in Theology. The very title of the series was, however, misleading as far as the theological thought of Ebeling was concerned. Ebeling never intended to devise a *new* hermeneutic, or for that matter anything else that was *new*. For a church historian and systematic theologian of Ebeling's caliber, educated in classical thought and steeped in the theological tradition, the word "new" smacks far too much of Enlightenment enthusiasm and of a break with the sources out of which Christian faith lives. Ebeling's goal was not to create something new, but rather through careful historical and systematic investigation to disclose hermeneutics as a way of thinking that is appropriate to the subject matter of theology and that has, in actual fact, been a thread of unity throughout the entire theological tradition from the time of the early church down to and beyond the Reformation. Only with the Enlightenment and its emphasis on "newness" was hermeneutic as a mode of thinking seriously questioned.

The appropriateness of hermeneutic to the subject matter of theology lies in the fact that hermeneutical thinking strives toward clarity in an initially confused and unintelligible situation. The beginnings of theological hermeneutics are to be observed in the Greek and Jewish traditions where it was initially limited to the interpretation of difficult texts. In the writings of the early Christian community, notably in the Pauline corpus, hermeneutics was expanded beyond a mere textual interpretation to an understanding of characteristic modes of existence: existence under the law and existence in faith.

In the theology of the Middle Ages, the existential dimension of the hermeneutic process was obscured by an often mechanical application of the fourfold scheme of interpretation including literal, allegorical, analogical, and moral senses. On the eve of the Reformation, Luther rediscovered in his first *Lectures on the Psalms* the existential dimension of the Pauline distinction between spirit and letter (later called "gospel and law"), and he developed a hermeneutic that pushed beyond a mere text-interpretation to an understanding of the ultimate subject matter of the text, namely to an interpretation of the relation between God and humans (see "The Beginnings of Luther's Hermeneutics," *Lutheran Quarterly,* 1993). As we have seen, the urgent need for an interpretation of this relation grows out of the fundamental opposition between God and humans, the ensuing distortion of this relation, and the resulting confusion of the individual's situation before God. In the tradition of Paul and Luther, Ebeling understands theological hermeneutics as a process of thinking directed toward a particular linguistic tradition (the writings of the Bible, the church fathers, the Reformers, etc.) that distinguishes between the demand-character (law) and the gift-character (gospel) of life, aiming ultimately at distinguishing between God and the individual in the immediacy of actual experience.

This movement in the hermeneutical process from text-interpretation to a relation-interpretation implies the linguistic character of human relationships, in particular of the relation between God and humans. The linguisticality of this relation manifests itself from both sides, from the side of God as the *Word of God,* from the side of humans as *faith.* Certainly faith does not mean in this context the assent to propositions of a creed; it refers instead to an act of trust at the very center of a person's being that is always directed toward word. This correlation between faith and word is the cornerstone of Ebeling's theology.

In the broadest sense, this word is not necessarily the Word of God; it can also be a deceiving and essentially meaningless word upon which faith projects itself. Be that as it may, the character of this word is determinative for the being of the person who trusts it. The centrality of language for human beings is reminiscent in the English philosophical tradition of Whitehead's statement in *Modes of Thought* "that the souls of men are the gift from language to mankind." Ebeling, however, sets the ontological role of language in strict correlation with the act of faith so that life in faith becomes the mirror image of the incarnation. Just as the Word became flesh in Christ, the individual becomes Word through faith.

By the phrase "Word of God" Ebeling does not, of course, understand merely the written texts of the Old and New Testaments, but rather precisely *that* word— wherever and however it occurs—which is at the same time disclosing and determining for the relation between God and individuals. Depending on the way in which this word occurs, either as law or as gospel, the relation takes on the fundamental character of demanding or giving. When the hermeneutic process comes to fruition, it ushers forth in proclamation which is nothing other than the actual expression of the Word of God at a particular place and time. This reference to proclamation brings to light another characteristic element of Ebeling's thought; namely, the inseparability of systematic theology and preaching. The two differ merely in their methodological approach. The formulation of a systematic theology can only be the penultimate goal of hermeneutic; its ultimate goal will always remain the proclamation of a word that transforms the debilitating *opposition* between humans and God into a viable *contrast.*

Sin and Reason

In the same way in which Ebeling has tried to recover the original sense of hermeneutic, he has also endeavored to rescue the notion of sin as a fundamental theological concept. Once again the theological task involved a combination of systematic and historical investigations. From a historical perspective, Ebeling has pointed to a characteristic development in the scholastic tradition. On the one hand, one observes among the scholastics a concentration of theological reflection on the doctrine of sin; on the other hand, sin is rendered basically harmless through a more or less thorough moralization of the concept. Especially in the late scholastic period (as in the writings of Gabriel Biel), humans are conceived as knowing the morally good and as being capable of performing it.

From a systematic point of view, Ebeling has registered concern about the troubling similarities between the scholastic theology and recent theological directions that concentrate the message of Christianity on ethical and political issues. Against all such attempts to transform Christianity into a form of ethics, one must maintain that sin is primarily a theological concept. The locus of sin is found in the relation between God and humans. Sin is not *this* or *that* deed that one performs, but rather a mode of being. Sin is hostility toward God, a refusal to *be* in relation to God as *God.* Sin distorts the relation between God and humans, and out of this fundamental distortion of life flows a history of wars, inhumane acts, and destruction. With Luther, Ebeling speaks of this one sin as the "root-sin" (German: *Wurzelsünde,* Latin: *peccatum radicale*). One might take the metaphor further: If theological sin is the root of the plant, the atrocities of humans against humans as well as their thoughtless abuse of the environment are the stems and buds. The recovery of sin as a theological concept is intended not to retard political and social action, but rather to show the boundaries within which such action is possible and to make clear where the root of the human problem ultimately lies.

So far we have been dealing with the concept of sin as though a theoretical knowledge would suffice. In actual fact, the true recognition of this root-sin is synonymous with self-knowledge and proves to be attainable only in faith. The relation between God and humans lies to a great extent hidden beneath the surface of consciousness and is thus not accessible to the faculty of reason. Following the language of Luther, Ebeling speaks here about the blindness of reason. The parallel between reason in the theology of Ebeling and the ego in the depth psychology of Sigmund Freud is very illuminating. Just as the ego conceals within itself defense mechanisms that continually suppress a knowledge of the unconscious, reason is infested with cunning schemes and treacherous designs that obscure the relation between God and the person, thus preventing this distorted relationship from coming clearly into view. And just as the ego is unaware of its own suppressing activities, so also the faculty of reason. Hence, reason is not only blind to sin; it is also blind to its own blindness. This double blindness leads inevitably to an inflation of reason beyond the boundaries appropriate to its nature. In particular, reason boasts a knowledge of essential human relations that are in truth understandable only in the midst of experience, not in the abstracted form in which reason grasps them. Reason's claim to understand the relation between God and humans is nothing else than an expression of arrogance and a testimony to its own blindness.

It is in this context of sin and blindness of reason that the opposition between *faith* and *reason* should be understood. The theological primacy of faith over reason does not entail the sacrifice of reason, but rather calls for a restriction of its range of application. Faith as a response to the Word of God brings with it a self-knowledge that unmasks reason for what it is, thus freeing reason from its own destructive tendencies and allowing it to function in a manner appropriate to human beings. Such self-knowledge cannot be obtained once and for all, as for example the knowledge of physics or mathematics. This self-knowledge occurs only in the midst of the oppositions of life as the *act* of distinguishing between God and the individual person. Knowledge and being are inseparably interwoven so that a lack of self-knowledge means a deficiency of being.

This correlation between knowledge and being leads Ebeling to the following consideration concerning a theological anthropology. In the theological tradition the image of God in human beings was identified with the faculty of reason. If, however, the faculty of reason is twisted through its own cunning and craftiness, then the image of God in the individual is no longer simply present, but rather in some way still outstanding. Furthermore, the impossibility of complete trust in the Word of God and the resulting lack of self-knowledge necessitates an eschatological understanding of the image of God. In short, human beings *are* not yet the image of God, they *will* become God's image when the opposition between God and them (i.e., sin) is fully transformed into a living contrast.

Jack Edmund Brush

Selected Bibliography

The following bibliography contains only those works of Gerhard Ebeling which have been translated into English.

1967   *The Problem of Historicity in the Church and Its Proclamation*, trans. Grover Foley (*Die Geschichtlichkeit der Kirche und ihrer Verkündigung als-theologisches Problem*, 1954).

1955   "The Meaning of 'Biblical Theology,'" *Journal of Theological Studies* 6: 210-25.

1961   *The Nature of Faith*, trans. Ronald Gregor Smith (*Das Wesen des christlichen Glaubens*, 1959).

1964   "Word of God and Hermeneutic," *New Frontiers in Theology*, ed. James Robinson and John Cobb, Jr. ("Wort Gottes und Hermeneutik," *Zeitschrift für Theologie und Kirche* 56 [1959]: 224-51).

1963   *Word and Faith*, trans. James W. Leitch (*Wort und Glaube*, 1960).

1965   "Theology and the Evidentness of the Ethical," *Journal of Theological Studies*, 2: 96-129 ("Die Evidenz des Ethischen und die Theologie," *Zeitschrift für Theologie und Kirche* 67 [1960]: 318-56).

1969   "The Ground of Christian Theology," *Journal for Theology and the Church* 6: 47-68 ("Der Grund christlicher Theologie: Zum Aufsatz Ernst Käsemanns über die Anfänge christlicher Theologie" *Wort und Glaube* 2:72-91).

1966   *Theology and Proclamation. A Discussion with Rudolf Bultmann*, trans. John Riches (*Theologie und Verkündigung. Ein Gespräch mit Rudolf Bultmann*, 1962).

1964   "The Message of God to the Age of Atheism," Graduate School of Theology Bulletin, Oberlin College 9/1:3-14 ("Die Botschaft von Gott an das Zeitalter des Atheismus," *Wort und Glaube*, 2:372-95).

1966   *On Prayer. Nine Sermons*, trans. James Leitch (*Vom Gebet. Predigten über das Unser-Vater*, 1963).

1964   "The New Hermeneutics and the Early Luther," *Theology Today* 21:34-46.

1970   *Luther. An Introduction to His Thought*, trans. R. A. Wilson (*Luther. Einführung in sein Denken*, 1964).

1967   "The Hermeneutical Locus of the Doctrine of God in Peter Lombard and Thomas Aquinas," *Journal for Theology and the Church* 3:70-111 ("Der hermeneutische Ort der Gotteslehre bei Petrus Lombardus und Thomas von Aquin," *Zeitschrift für Theologie und Kirche* 61 [1964] 283-326).

1968   *The Word of God and Tradition. Historical Studies Interpreting the Division of Christianity*, trans. S. H. Hooke (*Wort Gottes und Tradition. Studien zu einer Hermeneutik der Konfessionen*, 1964).

1968   "Existence Between God and God: A Contribution to the Question of the Existence of God, *Journal for Theology and the Church* 5:128-54 ("Existenz zwischen Gott und Gott. Ein Beitrag zur Frage nach der Existenz Gottes," *Zeitschrift für Theologie und Kirche* 62 [1965]: 86-113).

1966/1967 "What Remains If God Is Eliminated?" *The Drew Gateway* 37: 20-27 ("Angenommen: Gott gibt es nicht," *SBL* 18 [1965]).

1967   *God and Word*, trans. James Leitch (*Gott und Wort*, 1966).

1970 "Schleiermacher's Doctrine of the Divine Attributes," trans. James Leitch, *Journal for Theology and the Church*, 71:125-62 ("Schleiermachers Lehre von den göttlichen Eigenschaften" *Wort und Glaube* 2:305-42).

1974/1975 "Against the Confusion in Today's Christianity," *The Drew Gateway* 45:203-29 ("Memorandum zur Verständigung in Kirche und Theologie," *Zeitschrift für Theologie und Kirche* 66 [1969]: 493-521).

1973 Introduction to a *Theological Theory of Language*, trans. R. A. Wilson, (*Einführung in theologische Sprachlehre*, 1971).

1974 "Luther and the Beginning of the Modern Age," Papers for the Fourth International Congress for Luther Research, ed. H. A. Oberman, Leiden, 11-39 ("Luther und der Anbruch der Neuzeit," *Wort und Glaube* 3:29-59).

1978 *The Study of Theology*, trans. Duane Priebe (*Studium der Theologie. Eine enzyklopädische Orientierung*, 1975).

1985 The Truth of the Gospel. An Exposition of Galatians, trans. David Green (*Die Wahrheit des Evangeliums. Eine Lesehilfe zum Galaterbrief*, 1981).

1993 "The Beginnings of Luther's Hermeneutics," *Lutheran Quarterly* ("Die Anfänge von Luthers Hermeneutik," *Zeitschrift für Theologie und Kirche* 48 [1951]: 172-230).

HANS W. FREI
1922–1988

Hans Wilhelm Frei was born in Breslau, Germany, on April 29, 1922. His distinguished family was Jewish by ancestry, but thoroughly secular in outlook. As was the custom, Frei was baptized as a child in the Lutheran Church. When the Nazis came to power, however, the family's Jewish ancestry was inescapable. Faced with the Nazi threat, Frei's parents sent him as a teenager to a Quaker school in England in order to get him safely out of the country. In 1938 the entire family moved to the United States.

Frei's early secondary education gave little indication of his future as a theologian. Because of his family's financial problems in the United States, Frei accepted the only scholarship available to him and attended North Carolina State University in the field of textile engineering. While at North Carolina State, however, Frei became involved in a Christian student group and attended a guest lecture by H. Richard Niebuhr of Yale University. Impressed by Niebuhr, Frei began corresponding with him, and, upon Niebuhr's advice, enrolled for a B.D. at Yale Divinity School following his graduation from North Carolina State in 1942. For two years after his graduation from Yale in 1945, Frei served as the minister in a Baptist church in North Stratford, New Hampshire. During that time he became interested in the Episcopal Church because of its greater doctrinal freedom.

In 1947 Frei returned to Yale to pursue his doctoral studies under H. Richard Niebuhr. Nine years later, he completed his lengthy dissertation on Barth's break with liberalism and received his Ph.D. During those years, Frei was quite active: He was ordained an Episcopal priest in 1952 and taught at Wabash College (1950–53) and the Episcopal Seminary of the Southwest (1953–56). In 1956 Frei returned to the Yale faculty, where he would remain until his sudden and unexpected death on September 12, 1988.

Although he published only two books during his lifetime, *The Eclipse of Biblical Narrative* and *The Identity of Jesus Christ*, Frei has been one of the most influential North American theologians of his generation. His work singularly

151

influenced the development of the postliberal theology of the "Yale School." In addition, he provided significant intellectual and historical groundwork for a literary-theological approach to biblical interpretation, including a renewed appreciation for biblical narrative. Although Frei was critical of most forms of "narrative theology," his work contributed significantly to this development. Finally, Frei's distinctive appropriation of the work of Karl Barth contributed to the renewed appreciation for Barth's theology, including his approach to Scripture, as a creative voice in contemporary theological work in the United States.

Central to Frei's work is a concern for the purpose and method of theology. Throughout his career, Frei, like Barth, critiqued modern, liberal approaches to theology and sought to present an alternative to them.

According to Frei, liberal theology is fundamentally apologetics; its aim is to explain and defend the religious and moral meaningfulness of the Christian faith in relation to general human needs and common human experience. The method of liberal theology generally involves some form of correlation. The Christian message is correlated with dimensions of human existence discerned independently of Christian beliefs and practices. The result of liberal theology's aim and method, according to Frei, is that the primary content of theology becomes anthropology. Jesus Christ becomes little more than a cipher for an independent understanding of human existence, which sets the terms for his significance. Theologically, Christology becomes a function of an independently generated soteriology, with the result that Jesus gets absorbed into human experience and loses his unique, unsubstitutable identity.

Integrally related to this approach to theology, Frei contended, is a similar approach to biblical interpretation. Through most of the church's tradition, as Frei argued in *Eclipse*, the "world of the Bible" had been the one "real world" within which life was interpreted. However, during the eighteenth and nineteenth centuries, a great reversal took place. The "biblical world" ceased to provide the primary frame of reference, but rather came to be interpreted into a purportedly "wider" modern framework. More specifically, the Bible began to be read primarily as a source of historical information or philosophical ideas known independently of Scripture. Biblical interpretation became "a matter of fitting the biblical story into another world with another story rather than incorporating that world into the biblical story" (*Eclipse*, 1974, p. 130). Such an approach to Scripture was the natural counterpart to liberal, apologetic theology. Not surprisingly, contemporary hermeneutical theory, drawn on by "revisionist" theologians such as David Tracy, became the target of Frei's critique of liberal theology in his later work. For Frei, general hermeneutical theories, within which Scripture is subsumed, are the guise under which apologetic theology is pursued today.

In contrast to this liberal theological orientation, Frei defended a different theological aim, method, and content. For Frei, theology is a normative and critical task specific to the Christian religion; its aim is to describe the logic and content of

Christian beliefs as these are embodied in the language and practices of the Christian community, particularly, but not exclusively, in the Scripture that functions authoritatively within the church (*Identity,* 1975, p. xiii; *Types,* 1992, p. 2). The aim of theology is descriptive, not explanatory; it is dogmatics, rather than apologetics. As Frei argued in his later work, the task of theology is more closely related to the descriptive work of social sciences like cultural anthropology than to the explanatory work of philosophy.

The method for this kind of dogmatic theology is that of faith seeking understanding, which Frei appropriated from Anselm, through Barth. The theologian does not seek to correlate Christian beliefs with other independently validated theories or systems of truth. Rather, giving primacy to Christian language, beliefs, and practices, the theologian seeks to deepen the church's understanding of the faith, which has a cognitive as well as self-involving dimension. For Frei, Karl Barth was the best modern exemplar of this theological method. Indeed, Frei's appreciation for the Anselmian character of Barth's theology has been one of his important contributions to the newer interpretation of Barth.

This Anselmian method, however, does not rule out the use of philosophical concepts altogether. The theologian is not relegated to repeating verbatim the language of the Bible or the tradition. Rather, current concepts are essential; without them, Frei repeatedly noted, one cannot even begin to understand. Consequently, theology always involves conceptual *re*description. However, though necessary, philosophical concepts should always be employed in a subordinate role and in an eclectic, ad hoc fashion. They are not to be used to provide a general framework within which the Christian faith is explained, but rather should serve the purpose of describing and clarifying Christian beliefs. Again, Barth was Frei's model, despite the fact that Barth has often been incorrectly interpreted as antiphilosophical. Frei's own use of concepts of identity description in *The Identity of Jesus Christ* provides a good example of this use of philosophy within an Anselmian framework.

The primary content of theology, for Frei, is christological, not anthropological. Theology begins with Jesus Christ as he is rendered through the interplay of character and incident in the gospel narratives. Jesus is not a cipher for some independent analysis of the human predicament. Rather, Jesus is the unique, unsubstitutable person who defines and accomplishes the salvation of the world. For Frei, soteriology is a function of Christology. Thus, with regard to the aim, method, and content of theology, Frei offered a carefully developed alternative to liberalism.

In the North American context, the distinctiveness of Frei's work lies in his development of Barth's biblical, Anselmian, christocentric theology through categories of human identity taken from Gilbert Ryle (see *Concept of the Mind,* 1949) and through insights into biblical narrative appropriated from Erich Auerbach (see *Mimesis,* 1953). In his later work (during the 1980s), in which he was influenced by his colleague George Lindbeck, Frei further developed these insights within a cultural-linguistic framework that drew on the anthropological work of Clifford Geertz and the linguistic philosophy of the later Wittgenstein.

At a time when myth and symbol exercised a strong influence on biblical interpretation and theological reflection, Frei turned instead to Erich Auerbach's understanding of realistic narrative, which he appropriated from Auerbach's now classic work, *Mimesis*. Realistic narrative, Frei emphasized, is neither mythical nor symbolic, but rather "history-like" in its depiction of a common public world and in the close interplay of character and incident. The subject matter of realistic narrative is not separable from the story itself; character and circumstance are not shadows of something else more real or significant. Rather, the surface of the story itself renders its meaning (*Eclipse*, 1974, pp. 13-14).

In addition, with Auerbach, Frei stressed that the Bible does not claim simply to be one story among others. Rather, the biblical narrative claims to be the only real world and seeks to overcome the world of the reader (*Mimesis*, 1953, p. 15). According to Frei, Auerbach's insights captured the way in which the church had traditionally read Scripture prior to the "great reversal" of the previous two centuries. The concepts appropriated from Auerbach gave Frei a way to describe this traditional reading, which he thought Barth's interpretation of Scripture captured most faithfully.

This approach to the Bible and theology was further enriched by the work of Gilbert Ryle. At a time when existentialism was the dominant philosophy appropriated by Protestant theologians in the United States, Frei turned to the analytical philosophy of Ryle. In his important book, *The Concept of Mind*, Ryle critiqued the understanding of human identity inherent in the Cartesian mind-body dualism of modernity. The essence of human identity, Ryle argued, is not some hidden self—some "ghost in the machine"—indirectly manifested in a person's words and deeds. Rather, personal identity is best understood through a person's public, intentional acts.

Ryle's approach to human identity gave Frei the formal conceptuality for approaching Jesus' identity not in terms of his inner consciousness or experience, but in terms of the purposeful actions that one finds in the interplay of character and incident in the Gospel narratives. Rather than seeking Jesus' identity "behind" the text (a "ghost in the machine" approach), Frei located the identity of Jesus Christ in the interplay of character and incident in the Gospel narratives themselves. Indeed, for Frei the very purpose of the biblical narratives is to render the identity of God in Jesus Christ.

In his later work, Frei enriched his appropriation of Auerbach and Ryle with a cultural-linguistic model of Christianity. Just as he had interpreted Jesus in terms of his publicly enacted identity, so Frei came to interpret the Christian faith, not as some inner experience, but as the publicly enacted language and practices of the Christian community. He thus not only sought to avoid a "ghost in the machine" approach to Jesus, but also sought to avoid a similar approach to the Christian religion.

The most important consequence of Frei's cultural-linguistic model of Christianity was a shift of emphasis in his biblical hermeneutic. Whereas in his early work Frei had focused on the formal literary genre of realistic narrative, in his later work Frei came to stress the rules for reading scripture within a particular "community of interpretation," the church. A carefully delineated understanding of the "literal sense" of scripture, focused on the church's reading of the Gospel stories about Jesus, replaced Frei's earlier dependence on the genre of realistic narrative. Frei's actual reading of the Gospels was not significantly altered, but the rationale for this reading shifted significantly. Although Frei's main theological emphases remained the same throughout his work, they were placed in a broader framework in his later cultural-linguistic thought.

In light of his later work, the authority for Frei's theology can best be understood as scripture read within the Christian community. For Frei, the church's theology begins with scripture, which is read according to the logic of traditional doctrinal formulations (the "rule of faith") and the consensual rules for reading (the "literal sense"). Significantly, Frei never devised a theory of the authority of scripture. His approach to the Bible, enacted in *The Identity of Jesus Christ*, was not theoretical, but practical, based on the assumption that this text functions authoritatively within the community of faith.

Although Frei focused primarily on the formal development of a particular way of doing theology, he did engage in constructive theological work in the area of Christology. Central to Frei's Christology is the affirmation that the unique, unsubstitutable person, Jesus of Nazareth, enacts a salvation that is cosmic in scope. Frei seeks to hold together the universality of salvation with the particularity of the one who enacts it. As Frei repeatedly contends, the story of salvation is exclusively the story of Jesus of Nazareth (*Identity*, 1975, pp. 63-64).

The bond between the singularity of the savior and the cosmic scope of salvation lies in the "pattern of exchange" that characterizes the story of salvation enacted by Jesus (*Identity*, pp. 64-65). Drawing on Isaiah 53, Frei devises a vicarious theory of the atonement. In his perfect obedience to God, Jesus vicariously assumes the guilt and literally assumes the powerlessness of humanity on the cross. So thoroughly does Jesus identify with humanity that he himself must be redeemed in the resurrection. However, in his very powerlessness, Jesus is the power of salvation; through his identification with humanity, he exchanges his own moral purity for humanity's sinfulness. As the Savior, Jesus is simultaneously in need of redemption, redeemed, and redeeming (*Identity*, p. 122). Unfortunately, Frei never develops in detail the nature of human sin or the specific character of salvation, though his twofold emphasis on guilt and powerlessness is suggestive. Nor does Frei clarify exactly how Jesus' purity is transferred to humanity (*Theology and Narrative*, 1993, p. 248). Ultimately, Frei leaves this exchange a mystery (*Identity*, p. 65).

155

In Frei's thought, Jesus' salvific work is inseparable from his complex union with God. The Gospel narratives, Frei argues, depict the simultaneous distinction and union of Jesus and God (or Jesus and the First Person of the Trinity, though Frei does not use this language). Frei develops this complex unity not through the traditional categories of substance, nature, or being, but rather through the narrative logic of Jesus' intentionally enacted identity. In the Gospel narratives, Jesus obediently enacts the purposes of God for the good of humanity. In the course of the narrative, the agent of this enactment—Jesus and/or God—becomes increasingly complex. As Jesus undergoes a transition from power to powerlessness in his passion, God's activity increasingly supplants, but nevertheless remains identified with that of Jesus. In the resurrection this complex unity reaches its climax. At this point in the narrative God is the sole agent (Jesus cannot raise himself), but Jesus alone appears. At the very moment where God's supplantation of Jesus as agent is complete, Jesus alone is present. In the resurrection Jesus' unique identity is fully manifested; he alone marks the presence and action of God. Unquestionably for Frei, Jesus and God are one. However, that unity is narratively rendered and indissolubly complex (*Identity*, 1975, pp. 116-25).

Frei thus sought to develop a "high" understanding of the person and work of Jesus Christ, though he has been criticized as tending toward Nestorianism and adoptionism (*Theology and Narrative*, 1993, p. 250). Although the bulk of his work focused on formal, methodological matters, Frei nevertheless made an important contribution to constructive theological reflection. His attempt to reconstruct Christology not in terms of the classical categories of nature, substance, and being, but in terms of intentional action, offered a new way of construing the reality of Jesus and the First Person of the Trinity. Simultaneously, Frei demonstrated the logical connections between the biblical narratives and dogmatic theology, giving Scripture a central place in theological reflection.

Consistent with his critique of liberal theology, Frei does not seek to explain philosophically how the salvation accomplished by Jesus becomes meaningful today. For Frei, the salvific meaningfulness of Jesus Christ becomes a reality for us not by being correlated with some dimension of human experience, but rather through the work of the Holy Spirit, who is the indirect presence of God in Jesus Christ. Specifically, Christ's saving "presence" becomes real and effective through the practices of the church, particularly Word, sacrament, and discipleship. Jesus' meaningfulness depends not on an explanation of his relevance, but on the church's faithfulness as a community shaped by his identity.

Through this emphasis on the Spirit as Christ's presence for us today, Frei's Christology not only moves in a trinitarian direction, but also leads in circular fashion back to the church, with whose language and practices Frei begins. As the indirect, localized presence of Jesus Christ in the world, the church carries forward the story of Jesus by embodying and witnessing to God's providential ordering of history in its mysterious movement toward a final "summing up" (*Identity,* pp. 158-59, 164). The goal of Frei's descriptive, Anselmian, christocentric theology is finally the faithfulness of the church to Jesus Christ in and for the world.

Throughout his life, Frei sought to devise a way of doing theology that allowed for significant diversity. What is needed, he once stated, is a kind of "generous orthodoxy," a phrase that aptly characterizes his own project. Nevertheless, at the heart of Frei's theology, from beginning to end, was an emphasis on particularity. Consistently, he defended the particularity of the unique, unsubstitutable Savior, Jesus of Nazareth; the particularity of hermeneutics, which eschews general theories in favor of the Christian community's rules for reading; and the particularity of the church in and for the world. At a time when the "postmodern" church struggles to discern its distinctive identity, Frei's work represents both an important contribution and a significant challenge.

Charles Campbell

Selected Primary Works

1956   *The Doctrine of Revelation in the Thought of Karl Barth, 1909–1922: The Nature of Barth's Break with Liberalism.*

1974   *The Eclipse of Biblical Narrative: A Study in Eighteenth- and Nineteenth-Century Hermeneutics.*

1975   *The Identity of Jesus Christ: The Hermeneutical Bases of Dogmatic Theology.*

1992   *Types of Christian Theology,* ed. George Hunsinger and William C. Placher.

1993   *Theology and Narrative: Selected Essays,* ed. George Hunsinger and William C. Placher.

Selected Secondary Sources

1949   Gilbert Ryle, *The Concept of Mind,* repr. 1984.

1953/1974 Erich Auerbach, *Mimesis: The Representation of Reality in Western Literature,* trans. Willard R. Trask.

1987   Garrett Green, ed., *Scriptural Authority and Narrative Interpretation.*

1987   *Modern Theology* 3/3.

LANGDON GILKEY
1919–

L angdon Gilkey was born to parents who were deeply immersed in the life of the academy and the church to which he would later dedicate himself as a systematic theologian. His father, Charles W. Gilkey, was a minister to a church near the University of Chicago; his mother was prominent in the University community and the YWCA. The Gilkeys were of liberal religious and political persuasion. They understood their open and active commitment to the Christian faith and to social justice issues to be two sides of the same coin. Their insistence upon the intimate connection between faith and social action had a profound effect upon their son, whose career as a theologian has spanned five decades of cataclysmic social and political change from the 1940s through the 1990s. Langdon Gilkey found himself, as he himself has stated, a theologian living in a "time of troubles," determined to devise the most adequate theological responses to these troubled times throughout a dozen books and hundreds of articles and lectures.

From Skepticism to Neoorthodoxy

During Gilkey's college years at Harvard University, he was a self-proclaimed "ethical humanist," being skeptical of religion because he was convinced that humanity had moved beyond a need for it—until 1939. Then, the Nazi threat to overtake the free nations of Europe and to annihilate its Jewish citizens highlighted the implicit contradiction between his commitment to pacifism, on the one hand, and his commitment to justice and freedom, on the other. Just as his liberal, idealistic confidence in the progress of the world toward justice began to disintegrate, he discovered in the thought of Reinhold Niebuhr a way to reconcile his moral idealism with his growing sociopolitical realism. After his graduation from Harvard in 1940, he embarked on what he later acknowledged was "the most significant and formative period" of his life: an appointment to teach introductory English at

Yenching University in Peking, China. When the war began in 1941, the Japanese forcibly interned him, along with the other "enemy nationals," in a compound he described twenty-five years later in his book the *Shantung Compound*.

The compound's interns were forced to devise their own systems of governance for ordering community life among the vastly diverse groups of people constituting them. During his four years in the compound, Gilkey repeatedly witnessed the manifold ways in which human self-interest and pride could effectively foil God's creative purposes within their community life. This witness provoked him to reflect extensively on the dynamics and validity of the Christian faith in a moral and loving God—in particular, on how the dynamics of fully personal integrity manifest authentic faithfulness. Strength of moral integrity was important to preventing their fragile existence from descending into chaos, and yet, as Gilkey was shocked to observe, apparent commitments to Christian morality could also be used to excuse acts of flagrant self-interest and to obstruct the achievement of justice and the common good. Thus, from the beginning of Gilkey's career as a theologian, he was confronted with the difference between a self-righteous attempt to maintain some sort of "holiness" by adhering to certain narrowly defined rules of behavior, and the integrity whose reigning principle is concern to promote the welfare of the whole and to make personal sacrifices for it.

In retrospect, he realized that only by maintaining a commitment to something beyond one's own narrow self-interest, only by placing one's trust and center in God and not in oneself, is true integrity possible. Twin convictions inform his entire theological *corpus*. The first is that moral integrity both promotes fully personal integrity and is itself a result of it. For Gilkey, personal integrity refers to the wholeness that results from acting out of a fully reflective consciousness of all that one is and knows, in light of certain principles and goals. The second conviction is that fully personal integrity is the existential offspring of faith in the God of justice and love. To act with fully personal integrity is to act in such a way as to build up both oneself and the community, and this requires courage; retreat from such courageous action reduces the self to self-serving rationalizations and hypocrisy. These convictions inform the holism operative throughout his later theological vision and method, a holism that distinguishes it from the naively idealistic but ultimately reductionistic liberalism of his youth, on the one hand, and the conservative, Barthian mode of neoorthodoxy that cast a great divide between revelation and reason, on the other.

Gilkey later acknowledged that he learned the importance of integrity and wholeness from his "spiritual father," Reinhold Niebuhr, and from Paul Tillich, with whom he studied theology at Union Theological Seminary in New York upon his return from China in 1945. After completing his degree, Gilkey taught at Vassar College from 1951 to 1954, and at Vanderbilt Divinity School from 1954 to 1963, during a period of tremendous theological ferment. He became increasingly convinced of the necessity for revelation and grace to return modern society—riven with sin and meaninglessness, and threatening to self-destruct because of it—to a full expression of its true humanity. As he struggled to discern the historical implications of the Christian faith, he found himself as much at odds with the literalism of the conservative evangelicals as with the ultimately irrelevant optimism of the old-style liberalism. His own recognition of the necessity for interpreting the Christian traditions from the perspective of issues arising from within the current existential and historical situation to keep faith relevant (not to mention intellectually honest) distinguished him *as* liberal. Yet, his further recognition of the tragedy and sinfulness permeating the human situation, and consequently, of the need for the transcendent God to redeem humanity through the power of divine forgiveness and grace distinguished him *from* the old-style nineteenth-century liberalism that flourished until the 1920s, and moved him decisively into the neoorthodox camp dominated by Reinhold Niebuhr and Paul Tillich. This theological perspective marked his first three books, *Maker of Heaven and Earth* (1959, originally his doctoral dissertation), *How the Church Can Minister to the World Without Losing Itself* (1964), and *Shantung Compound* (1968).

In 1963, he took up residence in Chicago with a new appointment to the University of Chicago Divinity School and a new wife, Sonja (later, Ram Rattan), of Dutch descent and Sikh persuasion. To her influence he credited his increasing originality in thought and in personal appearance: His clean-shaven visage gave way to a beard and an earring in his left ear (as Dutch sailors wear them), his tweeds and flannels yielding to tie-dyed shirts and corduroys. Shortly thereafter, from 1965 to 1966, a sabbatical year in Italy introduced him to the leading theologians behind Vatican II (Karl Rahner, Bernard Lonergan, Hans Küng, and Edward Schillebeeckx), deepened his appreciation for the resources within the Roman Catholic tradition for responding to the crises of modernity, and prepared him for the growing ecumenism among his students and colleagues. His book *Catholicism Confronts Modernity* (1973) resulted.

The Role of Integrity in Gilkey's Public Theology

In subsequent decades at the University of Chicago, Gilkey (soon joined by David Tracy) helped to develop what has become known as the late-twentieth-century "Chicago School of Theology." The Chicago School was (and remains) renowned for its insistence that theology should be genuinely "public"—that is, the grounds for the validity of any theological claim should be apparent to anyone genuinely aware, intelligent, reflective, and responsible, regardless of whether that person is a believer or not. This perspective provoked heated debate among academic theologians during the 1970s. The "Yale School of Theology," represented by George Lindbeck, denied the possibility of public theology, while insisting on the necessity for theology to be confessional: theology understood and developed only from within a practicing faith community. This controversy highlights the ways in which theologians contended methodologically with the growing secularism of twentieth-century life, either by accepting the ability of human reason and experience to achieve genuine knowledge of the sacred through the exercise of its innate powers apart from faith (the Chicago School) or by insisting that that ability was dependent upon participating in a communal life of grace (the Yale School).

Gilkey's own approach to rendering theology public unfolded during the 1960s, when he became intrigued by the new radical or "death of God" theologies promulgated chiefly by William Hamilton, Thomas Altizer, and Paul van Buren. These theologians focused their work upon responding to secularity from within a Christian framework. In his next book, *Naming the Whirlwind* (1969), Gilkey distinguished for the first time his own distinctive theological perspective from traditional liberal and neoorthodox positions, as well as from the "a-theistic" theologies of the radical theologians, and he explored their adequacy in responding to the key issues of secularity.

Gilkey respected liberals for their integrity—for their commitment to integrating all that they knew and experienced into their theological visions. In particular, he commended their willingness to accept the validity of scientific and historical disciplines, and to integrate various facets of today's experience—rational and scientific inquiry, religious and moral experience—into the foundations of their visions, while jettisoning the claims of orthodoxy that contradicted them. Transforming the traditional emphases upon the supernatural as completely transcendent to humanity, liberalism conceived the divine as working immanently within the evolutionary processes of the natural, cultural, and historical worlds to create increasingly advanced, adaptive, and complex modes of science, technology, morality, and justice. Gilkey particularly admired the ways in which liberalism achieved creative accommodations to secularity by refusing to split reason and morality from belief and the "holy." He also recognized the ways in which it ran aground on the shoals of twentieth-century barbarism and cruelty during the First and Second World Wars. These experiences of the radicality of human evil created growing skepticism regarding both the ability of metaphysical or speculative reason to discern an ultimate harmony and order within reality, and the validity of its claims that evolutionary progress in nature, history, and the morality of humankind manifested the creative, salvific, and providential purposes of the divine. This, Gilkey argued, opened the way both for the radically antisecular perspective of the early neoorthodox and for the growing secularity of twentieth-century Western consciousness.

Neoorthodox theologians argued that the grounds for human creativity must lie in the revelation of the biblical Word that judged human confidence in humankind's own powers to be riddled with false pride and idolatry. Gilkey shared their fundamental conviction that biblical myths and symbols convey profound truths about humanity's lostness without the one sovereign and loving God, about the brokenness of its existence, and about its need for faith in God and God's Word in Jesus Christ to achieve truth and goodness in that existence. Science and historiography, he acknowledged, might inform one's understanding of those myths and symbols, but they offer scant foundation for the validity of Christian myth and symbol apart from the faith born out of difficult experiences of human brokenness and sin. But Gilkey sharply criticized neoorthodoxy in ways that implicitly recognized its fundamental lack of integrity. First, he uncovered its inability to specify the empirical or historical referents for its dubious claim that God acts in history. Second, he illumined its profound separation of religious experience and human rationality that created a chasm between human existence and thought, on the one hand, and faith, on the other. The neoorthodox, Gilkey argued, repeatedly interpreted Christianity's faith claims in terms of the existential meaningfulness and transformative power of its symbols and myths. By itself, this interpretation constituted a profoundly powerful and valid move, but one that required constant renewal through constant reinterpretation. Unfortunately, the neoorthodox failed at the latter, and so they lost their hold upon the faithful. The power of neoorthodoxy's vision inevitably weakened in the 1950s and 1960s, when its own proponents reduced it to dry doctrinal formulas, and when the historical memory of the radicality of human evil faded as secular confidence in human powers re-emerged.

Gilkey's constructive moves in *Naming the Whirlwind* disclosed his enduring talent as an analyst of secular culture and proponent of public theology. He argued that the heart of secularity lies in its presumption that human experience possesses no relation beyond itself to any ground or order; as a result, neither philosophy nor theology nor any other mode of rationality can achieve genuine knowledge of a transcendent ground or order (*Naming the Whirlwind*, 1969, p. 188). The radical theologies, which (to some extent at least) supplanted neoorthodoxy, appealed to this secular consciousness by radically doubting the existence of God and the validity of language about God, the eschaton, and any other suprahistorical entity, on the one hand, and by asserting the autonomous self-sufficiency of humanity in relation to any possible transcendent referent, on the other. Most radical theologies, however, insisted that the historical Jesus remained Lord to the extent that his life and teachings should serve to guide all ethical involvement in personal, social, and political realms. Life in the here and now was of utmost significance; concern about an afterlife, mere escapism.

Gilkey attacked the radical theologians for not living up to their own secular standards of rationality by not achieving intellectual consistency and coherence. He demonstrated how their attempts to assert the power and validity of human autonomy apart from a transcendent God, on the one hand, and to affirm Jesus as Lord, on the other, were incoherent and mutually contradictory. First, the attempts of radical theologians to establish the historical Jesus as Lord, apart from the transcendent Christ affirmed by traditional Christianity, ignored the sheer dearth of firm historical evidence about the life and teachings of the person Jesus of Nazareth. Moreover, their attempts ignored one incontestable feature of Jesus' teaching—his proclamation of the very sovereign and transcendent God whom the radical theologians were intent to deny. Second, they ignored the implicit contradiction between their insistence that one accept the authority of secular values, and that one also "become like Jesus." But worldly ways and values tend to be self-centered and self-aggrandizing—traits hardly consistent with the self-sacrificial love through which Jesus sought to serve the outcasts and downtrodden of the world. Third, if Jesus were Lord unto himself and as such served as the model for the secular believer's own autonomy, then the latter should also be lord unto himself or herself. Hence, affirming one's own autonomy and accepting another as lord seem to cancel each other. And if Jesus is to serve as model of this faithfulness, then on the conditions set by radical theology, he simply serves as a judge over against us, not as a forgiving and empowering presence within us, enabling us to achieve his ideals. In this way, radical theologies ended up, in effect, proposing a new heteronomous moralism—precisely that which they sought to avoid by denying a transcendent God. Such perspectives would be much more consistent if they simply lapsed into a humanism according to which each person defined his or her own standards from within. Finally, the radical theologies proposed that Jesus offers us the possibility of "authentic existence," but they offered no understanding of how Jesus helps us achieve this state. Indeed, Gilkey argued, one needs a conception of a transcendent power beyond the immediate sources that can effect the desired transformations—precisely that which the radical theologians were anxious to deny (*Naming the Whirlwind*, 1969, pp. 151-66).

Gilkey's subsequent analyses of the core experiences of secularity—its contingency, temporality, relativism, and autonomy—manifest the growing influence of Tillich's theological method and metaphysical vision upon his thought, and the inclusivistic holism of his method. Engaging in a hermeneutical phenomenology by which he elaborated the manifest meanings of these core experiences, Gilkey sought to establish the validity of key Christian symbols by disclosing within these experiences a hidden dimension of ultimacy, and with it, an ultimate presupposition behind typical ways of coping with them. This method disclosed not so much a new reality or presence—though Christians would surely interpret it as evidence for such—but a *final* or *ultimate* limit encountered through the threats and demands presented by the experiences of *being* limited. In accordance with Tillich's method of critical correlation, Gilkey analyzed each dimension of secular experience to demonstrate how it raises a question in the form of an experienced threat and, upon closer scrutiny, how it leads one to recognize as its limit intimations of an answer, an answer which is then thematized by the relevant religious symbol. In this way, he sought to validate the transcendent referent of the God-language that radical theologies were intent to reject.

The human experience of radical contingency, for instance, discloses a sense that some infinite, inexorable power is also at work through the indeterminacies of history. This power, commonly known as fate, is often experienced as an unconditional, unbearable threat to our ability to control our own destiny. Such secular experiences of radical insecurity raise the question of the existence of an unconditionally secure power that might rule over these fates that so threaten life with meaninglessness and insignificance. This question becomes a quest for God the Creator, the ruler over all those fates that threaten us, a quest which becomes manifest in our individual struggles to create a unified, coherent, meaningful whole out of our lives. When persons become convinced that, in spite of the apparent insignificance of lives, they attain some lasting validity, not as their own achievement but as an inexplicable gift, then they come to understand something of the Christian symbol of the providence of God (*Naming the Whirlwind,* 1969, pp. 320-54).

His further analyses of the hidden dimension of ultimacy experienced in personal and moral freedom disclose the ontological bases for his liberal convictions regarding the continuity between what human reason and morality can understand and require, on the one hand, and the Christian symbols of sin, atonement, and forgiveness, on the other. He argued that freedom in itself presupposes certain norms by which action is guided. In accord with this reason, then, he developed his anthropology by highlighting the ultimate significance of integrity, which includes the freedom to act in accordance with chosen personal and moral ideals, but argued that the tendency of autonomous freedom to pursue self-interest must be tempered with the ideals of self-sacrificial love and justice. To respond to these ideals enables persons to overcome any latent self-deception about their true motives and to achieve the fully personal integrity of true faithfulness. Failure to achieve personal goals leads persons to experience the call to do so not as a void but as personal judgment. The quest to overcome fragmentation, guilt, insecurity, and isolation leads persons to search for ultimates—in effect, to the point where the Christian symbols of the sovereignty and forgiveness of God make sense (ibid., pp. 373-95).

The development of theological anthropology in *Naming the Whirlwind* constituted Gilkey's prolegomenon to a systematic theology. Hesitating to invest the time and energy necessary to construct a full systematic, Gilkey published a "mini-systematic," *Message and Existence* (1979), which he developed as an introduction to the Christian theological task and vision. In it he explicated his basic understandings of the principal doctrines of the Christian faith: the nature of revelation (and with it, the theological task), God as Creator, human creatureliness, sin, Christ, and the Holy Spirit. Gilkey critically correlated these Christian symbols and their respective myths with his interpretation of humanity as tragically broken and estranged from itself, from others, and from God, and as reconciled only through the power of God's activity through Christ and the Holy Spirit.

Christian Philosophy of History

The full range and depth of Gilkey's theological vision comes most clearly to expression in his next prominent work, *Reaping the Whirlwind* (1976). In it, he systematically responds to the problem that has haunted him from the inception of his theological career, the problem of devising a Christian interpretation of history for these "troubled times." Today as never before, he argues, increasingly vast and rapid historical change confronts humanity with questions about the meaning and dynamics of history. In fact, the way in which humanity realizes itself is conditioned first and foremost by its temporality—by its realization of itself in and through historical contingency and change. As temporal, humanity finds itself both threatened by the unknown and yet challenged by the possibility of creating something new. It understands itself to be both fated—determined by social, economic, and historical conditions far beyond its control—and transcendent of such fatedness and free to create its own destiny in spite of fate. This polarity of destiny and freedom and the related polarity of actuality and possibility constitute the ontological structure of human temporality.

Gilkey worries that the postmodern loss of faith in progress has led to a deadly fatalism in some people and an equally deadly escapism in others. Still, he resists reverting to the naive optimism of nineteenth-century liberalism. Instead he draws on classic Christian doctrines: The true foundation of hope lies not in humanity's innate goodness but in the possibility of its discovering the way back to that goodness through the power of faith in a transcendent and beneficent deity. He elaborates a Christian interpretation of history that envisions God as a transcendent and unifying power reconciling the estranged and leading them to a deeper understanding of the meaning and ultimate validity of their historical lives. Such an interpretation understands fate not as dumb and blind, but as "the negative face of God, his left hand, his alien work" (*Reaping the Whirlwind,* p. 54). It understands the challenge of human existence to be the task of transforming fate into freely chosen personal destiny, and, overall, it understands that the most adequate answers to the question of what power ultimately rules history and gives it final validity lie in the Christian symbols regarding God's historical activity—providence and eschatology. In fact, the most adequate interpretation of history will accept that it can never be rendered fully intelligible, thus retaining a complex dialectic between clarity and opacity, intelligibility and mystery.

Actuality in history, Gilkey argues, is never fully reducible to clear meaning and order. First, the possibilities grounded in any particular actuality are never fully determined by or predictable because of it. Second, humanity, in actualizing its possibilities, also corrupts them. As a result, meaning fragments into meaningless-ness, true norms get obscured by false ones, and real goals get sidetracked into spurious ones. Thus, the structure of history itself becomes warped, and philosophical understandings of history based on its structure are never fully adequate. Only a theistic understanding informed by the categories of sin and grace, estrangement and reconciliation will be adequate to the task of understanding history. A third reason for the irreducible mystery of history is that human freedom is enacted, whether consciously or not, within a relationship to the ultimate, transcendent ground of the whole that forever eludes full comprehension (*Reaping the Whirlwind*, 1976, pp. 117-29).

In spite of the apparent dearth of meaning in the current era, Gilkey finds grounds for belief in the ultimate meaningfulness of history in experiences of the potential creativity of what initially appears to be undesirable and destructive, in experiences of the proximate intelligibility of what initially appears to be meaningless and destructive when they are grasped in light of past injustices and the need for change, and finally, in intimations that new creative possibilities will emerge out of revolutionary, even chaotic, events. Theological symbols present many levels of meaning. Their truth emerges out of their ability to bring order and coherence to a wide range of experiences and, in turn, to communicate a sense of the nature and dynamics of reality back to us. They also convey a sense of the transcendent mystery out of which the dynamics of reality emerge, most especially because they express the dynamics of the human relationship to God. When a group of symbols is used to describe how God acts in history, they take on a narrative or mythic form. Religious myths present this dialectic between meaning and mystery in narrative form. The task of the Christian theologian is to render these symbols and myths intelligible by explicating the theological doctrines of creation, anthropology, providence, revelation, incarnation, redemption, and eschatology (*Reaping the Whirlwind*, pp. 122-55).

Gilkey's rejection of the liberal, neoorthodox, and eschatological views on history again reflects the inclusivistic holism of his thought in his concern to bring all of human historical experience to bear upon the concepts of providence and eschatology. Liberals overemphasized the role of the divine in effecting progress toward realizing the kingdom of God in history, but they repressed the negative and cataclysmic reversals of such progress. The dialectical or *krisis* theologies took such negations as their points of departure, but they used them to support their denial that the Kingdom was relevant to the general course of history, thus subordinating secular to sacred history. The eschatological theologies of Wolfhart Pannenberg, Jürgen Moltmann, Johannes Metz, Rubem Alvez, and Gustavo Gutiérrez, which emerged in the 1960s, reasserted the conviction that the Kingdom would come in history, but that it would come solely as a result of God's future action in history. Unfortunately, while attempting to restore the significance of history, the eschatological theologies went only half-way, detaching contemporary human historical existence and action from the activity of God in space and time.

Devising a notion of divine providence that evades the pitfalls of the liberal, neoorthodox, and eschatological views, Gilkey responds to the modern consciousness that our lives are not determined by any transcendent being but remain inexorably contingent, relative to a variety of factors, and transient, while we act autonomously, without any transcendental determinant. The divine mode of causality does not deny contingency, transcience, and relativity, but sustains them. Nor does it negate human freedom; it establishes it and renders it creative and good. Gilkey's elaboration of these basic insights manifests his appropriation of the ontological modes of analyses common to the neo-Thomistic traditions of Roman Catholicism and the thought of Tillich, and to the biblical emphases upon sin, judgment, and reconciliation so common to the Protestant traditions.

The pattern of God's intervention in history follows the pattern of Israelite history: God established the structures of Israel's communal life, and then through the prophets called the nation back again and again when they went astray. In this, God discloses Godself as being, logos, and love: God establishes the structures of the world, sustains them through time, and restores them when they are broken. God as being mediates the transition of being from moment to moment, the movement from possibility to actuality. God as logos does not extrinsically determine all that happens, but instead serves as the condition and ground of its possibility, as the principle of order of the possibilities brought into actuality, as the ground of the meaning and creativity expressed within it. The concept of God as love emerges when taking the tragedy of history into account, when dealing with its sinfulness.

Unlike the early Greeks and certain Eastern religions, Christians see history not as an inexorable cycle of progress and decline, but as the emergence of new creative possibilities in spite of their distortion by humanity. The distortions of possibility that destroy by concupiscent desire and by demonic claims to ultimacy receive the judgment of God, the hidden, alien work of God that destroys the destructive and works to reconcile the broken and alienated, and to bring new life. The divine providential work, active in the love that judges and reconciles, is most clearly manifest in the historical person of Jesus of Nazareth. Jesus embraced not the powerful but the powerless, not the creative and distinguished but the outcast, guilty, and oppressed, not life at the price of integrity but suffering and death. In doing so, he revealed the alienation of the world from its true self. The problem of history, then, lies ultimately in the inner relation of each human being before God, and the concrete, external, historical lives of each person only find healing when that inner relation is made right again. In this way, Gilkey again asserts the ultimate relevance of all dimensions of human existence within the Christian conviction that God acts in history to create, sustain, and redeem.

As a result of these three dimensions of the Godhead, there are three dimensions to the divine providential action in history corresponding to the Trinity: (1) the divine action in preserving being through the transitions of each historical moment to the next, the ground of the preservation of the creature over time; (2) the divine action in creating new, unforeseen possibilities out of given actuality—in effect, as the fount of human creativity; (3) the divine action in loving the world by judging its sins that it might be returned to God in the eschaton. All of the divine providential activity is ultimately determined by this goal of reconciliation and return while creating the new and good. Christian faith in the providential action of God includes confidence that a world in which people will be determined not by fate but rather by freely chosen creative possibilities will indeed be realized in history, in the eschaton toward which history, often in spite of appearances, is moving. Eschatology forms a lure, a vision of creative possibilities for the future. Thus providence is the historical presupposition for eschatology; eschatology, the defining and controlling symbol for providence (*Reaping the Whirlwind*, 1976, p. 287).

Gilkey's complex interpretation of the fatedness of our times by violence and oppression, by industry and technology, and his equally complex interpretation of the nuances of the Christian faith in God's action in history for offering hope in the midst of it, form a magisterial summation of his entire vision. This vision is a holistic: It envisions the sacred as transcendent to the world but as working within it to be its healing, reconciling depth, so that together they form a differentiated unity, a unity encompassed by their irreconcilable difference. And it is born of the methodological conviction that theologians must take into account all fields of knowledge and all dimensions of experience in their deliberations, but still not lose sight of their goal—elaborating the distinctive claims to meaning and validity of the Christian faith in promoting the Kingdom of God on earth. This holism, then, avoids the reductionistic tendencies of liberalism, the ultimately splitting reactivity of early neoorthodoxy, and the inconsistencies of radical theologies to create a new synthesis responsive to our current scientific, technological, and pluralistic world, and informs his recent work elaborating the distinctive nature of the Christian faith in relation to two related areas of burgeoning human knowledge—science and world religions.

Christianity's Encounter with Science and World Religions

Gilkey affirms the necessity of integrating religious and scientific modes of understanding with one another by developing a complex model of their mutual interdependence. In *Religion and the Scientific Future* (1970) he argues that there are religious dimensions in science as well as mythic dimensions in scientific culture. Moreover, developments in science and technology since the Enlightenment have, often in ways left unacknowledged, transformed theological understandings of religious truth by clarifying their true nature. Religious narrative does not recount the world history. Grasped as myth, it expresses the ways in which ordinary experience opens itself up to its ultimate ground, a ground which serves as the basis for human meaning, creativity, security, and hope in the midst of all that threatens them. It is the task of theology to analyze these myths to explore and adjudicate their possible meanings and truth in relation to contemporary experience.

Gilkey testified as an expert witness for the American Civil Liberties Union in December 1981. The ACLU was concerned to contest the constitutionality of an article passed by the Arkansas State Legislature mandating that creationist views of the history and evolution of the universe be taught alongside evolutionary theory in high school science classes. Gilkey gave evidence supporting the ACLU's claim that creation science was not science at all, but religion cloaked in science. Although such evidence might not be surprising coming from a renowned scientist, it was so from a confessing Christian theologian. Gilkey argued that the concept of creation science was internally incoherent if it were not a specifically religious concept: While creation scientists maintained that the model of *creation ex nihilo* was independent of belief in God, their concept of creation actually lost its ability to explain the origins of the universe if it did not maintain such creation to be a divine act. The scientific character of any enterprise lay not in simply explaining certain facts, but in the nature of the theories developed to explain those facts and in the kinds of procedures developed to test their validity. But creation science offered no such theories or tests to render the divine act of creation intelligible to scientific understanding.

In effect, the fundamentalist Christians who insisted that creationism was scientific were falling prey to the modern mystique surrounding science and technology by believing that there could be only one kind of truth and that science and technology offered us that truth; hence, for their belief in divine creation to be true, it must be science. In actuality, Gilkey argued, the Christian belief in creation complemented, without competing with, scientific theories of the creation of the universe. Religious belief deals with different dimensions of reality, and so with different kinds of truth than science does. While the Christian belief in creation has served to inspire incalculable amounts of scientific inquiry to develop theories explaining various observable phenomena, it itself is a symbol that expresses the human desire to explain the source and ground of all such phenomena—in effect, the whole of existence—in order to clarify what had ultimate meaning and value. As a result, religion takes as its point of departure not the outer, objective realities of science, but the inner, subjective realities and experiences of individuals seeking meaning and fulfillment.

In response to the growing awareness of the validity of religions other than Christianity, Gilkey has joined other theologians in attempting to formulate a genuinely pluralist understanding of the relationship between Christianity and other religions, one that avoids the exclusivism which finds salvation only in Christ as well as the inclusivism which finds it elsewhere but understands these manifestations to be also, in some way, manifestations of Christ's redemptive work. Gilkey applauds the pluralist project for encouraging the love and understanding essential to ecumenical tolerance, but decries the radical relativity to which it leads religious claims to meaning and truth. Such radical relativity offers no grounds for rejecting clearly demonic forms of religion such as the absolutism of Khomeini and the Religious Right in America that would deny others' claims to meaning and truth and so crush all pluralism. Paradoxically, for the sake of the toleration of pluralism, Gilkey argues, we must assert without reservation certain values which themselves disclose a particular worldview and its attendant absolute commitments, a center on which to base the praxis that resists demonic and destructive expressions of the religious.

The pragmatics of contending with intolerance and oppression while affirming the validity of other faiths demands a praxis of relative absoluteness: One absolutely affirms one's particular faith stance as holding meaning and truth, and yet relativizes it by insisting that additional meaning and truth likewise remain with the other. Thus what might be seen as a contradiction in theory becomes acceptable in praxis. Such a praxis is born of the integrity that freely acts out of a fully reflective consciousness of the relativity of our absolute commitments. It finds the courage to assert itself in spite of recognizing the relativity of its perspective from the simultaneous consciousness that the sacred and absolute can nevertheless manifest itself in the profane and conditioned in unique and unpredictable ways. This praxis of relative absoluteness, Gilkey argues, must guide our responses to the radical pluralism of our time if we are to live out of the whole that nourishes true life in us all ("Plurality," 1988).

Jennifer L. Rike

Selected Bibliography

1959   *Maker of Heaven and Earth.*
1964   *How the Church Can Minister to the World Without Losing Itself.*
1968   *Shantung Compound.*
1969   *Naming the Whirlwind: The Renewal of God-Language.*
1970   *Religion and the Scientific Future.*
1975   *Catholicism Confronts Modernity.*
1976   *Reaping the Whirlwind: A Christian Interpretation of History.*
1979   *Message and Existence: An Introduction to Christian Theology.*
1981   *Society and the Sacred: Towards a Theology of Culture in Decline.*
1985   *Creationism on Trial: Evolution and God at Little Rock.*
1988   "Plurality and Its Theological Implications," in *The Myth of Christian Uniqueness.* Ed. John Hick and Paul F. Knitter.
1990   *Gilkey on Tillich.*
1993   *Nature, Reality, and the Sacred: The Nexus of Science and Religion.*

DAVID RAY GRIFFIN
1939–

Life and Career

Since 1973, David Ray Griffin has taught philosophy of religion and theology at the School of Theology at Claremont and at the Claremont Graduate School in Southern California. Best known for his scholarship in process philosophy and theology, forms of thought developing the implications of the philosophies of Alfred North Whitehead and Charles Hartshorne for theology and for a postmodern worldview, Griffin is also Co-Director of the Center for Process Studies, having served as its Executive Director throughout his tenure at Claremont.

In Griffin's telling of his own story in *Primordial Truth and Postmodern Theology*, his spiritual journey began in a small town in Oregon, where he was an active participant in a conservative church. Entering the University of Oregon in 1957 to major in music, Griffin transferred the following year to Northwest Christian College to prepare for the ministry; soon, however, he grew restless with its very conservative theology.

Returning to the University of Oregon, Griffin earned a master's degree in counseling in 1963. During that year, his theological world was opened to a number of new influences: Paul Tillich, who shaped Griffin's decision to concentrate on philosophical theology in seminary, Reinhold Niebuhr, and some process theologians. Although he was not particularly impressed with process theology at the time, Griffin visited the School of Theology at Claremont where he met John B. Cobb, Jr., who read his paper "A Personal Theology," which persuaded him to attend the school.

Process thinkers were not nearly as exciting to Griffin as other new influences at the University of Oregon. He was exposed briefly to parapsychological literature in a philosophy course, to altered forms of consciousness through peyote and the writing of Aldous Huxley, and to Edgar Cayce and reincarnation at the local Theosophy library. Griffin's personal theological world became a blend of Christianity and Hinduism. Consequently, Griffin decided to concentrate his graduate studies on Eastern religions.

This decision to focus on Eastern religions soon conflicted with Griffin's attraction to Cobb's course in Whitehead—Griffin found himself skipping his course in the history of religions to attend Cobb's seminar. Through Cobb's interpretation of Whitehead, Griffin recovered his interest in Christian philosophical theology, forsaking interest in parapsychological phenomena for about two decades. In 1970, Griffin completed his dissertation, which after extensive revision was published under the title *A Process Christology* in 1973.

After teaching at the University of Dayton from 1968 to 1973, Griffin accepted an invitation to return to Claremont to establish the Center for Process Studies with John Cobb. Since 1973, Griffin has organized and directed seminars, lectures, and conferences at the Center, thus advancing the discussion of process philosophy. Through the various meetings, participants have explored potential connections between process philosophy and other fields, such as Eastern religious philosophies and the natural sciences, especially physics and biology.

During the seventies, Griffin's scholarship made important contributions to process thought. With Cobb, Griffin cowrote *Process Theology: An Introductory Exposition,* and with Donald Sherburne, he edited a critical edition of Whitehead's *Process and Reality.* Griffin's most creative work during this period was his development of a process theodicy.

With an increasing sense that Whiteheadian philosophy could be articulated as a postmodern worldview, Griffin in 1983 founded the Center for a Postmodern World in Santa Barbara, California, as an affiliate of the Center for Process Studies. In the late 1980s, two chief successes of the Center for a Postmodern World were conferences bringing together an impressive array of scholars from a variety of disciplines: "Toward a Postmodern World" in 1987 and "Toward a Postmodern Presidency" in 1989. (Papers from these two conferences are contained in *The Reenchantment of Science* and *Spirituality and Society,* both published in the series "Constructive Postmodern Thought," which was edited by Griffin for S.U.N.Y. Press.)

Throughout Griffin's scholarly career, two themes recur. The first is God and the problem of evil, a theme that emerged early in his scholarship with the publication of *God, Power, and Evil: A Process Theodicy* in 1976. The second theme is the postmodern worldview. The critique of modernity and the language of postmodernity are evident in earlier works, but in 1988 Griffin published a collection of essays, *God and Religion in the Postmodern World,* his first book with a developed critique of modernity and a Whiteheadian postmodern alternative.

God and the Problem of Evil

In *God, Power, and Evil* and a 1981 essay entitled "Creation Out of Chaos and the Problem of Evil," Griffin established the fundamental framework of the process theodicy that continues to appear in his writing.

Griffin's interpretation of the problem of evil rests upon a particular understanding of God's relationship with the world. Simply and fundamentally, the presence of evil in the world brings into question either the goodness or the traditional view of the power of God. Griffin's solution to the problem depends on a revised understanding of divine power. Rejecting the view that God has a monopoly on power (the doctrine of divine omnipotence), Griffin follows Whitehead in describing God's power as persuasive or relational. This view of power recognizes that all existents have power (and, consequently, freedom) to determine themselves and to influence others. Because God does not determine what or who these existents will be, God cannot be the absolute controller. Instead, God is the one who influences all existents by envisioning their potentials and by offering a lure toward those possibilities.

The next important feature of God's relationship with the world is that God did not create the world out of nothingness, but that God created out of chaos a world of increasingly more complex entities. One of Griffin's distinctive ideas is his emphasis that any world that God could have created would have embodied four variables of power and value: (1) the capacity to enjoy intrinsic goodness (or value), (2) the capacity to suffer intrinsic evil (or dis-value), (3) the power of self-determination (freedom), and (4) the power to influence others (for good or ill). These variables are correlated in such a way that when one of the four increases, all four must increase. For example, if the capacity to enjoy intrinsic goodness increases (as it does for humans in comparison with other animals), then the capacity to suffer intrinsic evil increases, along with freedom and the power to influence others. The capacity for good and the capacity for suffering are necessarily correlated in the nature of things.

These variables apply to three general categories of existents in relation with God. The first category consists of low-grade enduring entities (such as electrons, atoms, molecules). If we take atoms as an example of the category, we observe that atoms have little capacity for self-determination and limited potential for a range of possibilities. Atoms cannot deviate significantly from the divine direction intended for them, nor can God present possibilities for the atom that deviate significantly from their present reality. So change comes very slowly in the behavior of atoms.

The second category consists of high-grade enduring individuals, such as humans, who have much greater capacity for self-determination and thus considerably more possibilities for choice. Change in humans can occur quickly in response to God's persuasion, but greater deviation from God's envisioned possibilities for good can also occur.

The third category consists of aggregate societies (such as rocks) of low-grade enduring individuals. Because these aggregate societies have no governing individual, God cannot directly influence them. At best, God can influence each of the low-grade individuals that form the aggregate societies.

These features of God's relationship to the world lead Griffin to draw some conclusions about God and evil. First, because God's power is persuasive rather than coercive, God is not directly the cause of either good or evil. God envisions that which is good in imaging real possibilities for existents, but God does not control existents. In their freedom and self-determination, existents determine themselves with either good or evil consequences and influences upon others. God is not the final determination of good or evil.

Second, because God created a world from chaos rather than from nothing and because God must abide by metaphysical principles, God at great risk created a world with more complex creatures capable of increasing intrinsic good and intrinsic evil. God could have chosen not to create humans and to eliminate the chance that greater evil would affect the world. The cost of that choice would have been the loss of the greater capacity for good. Because God chose to create humans, God is ultimately responsible for the presence of evil in the world, but God is not culpable. God chose for the good, but risked the introduction of greater evil. Because God is not an exception to the metaphysical principles applying to other actualities, God is also at risk of suffering from the introduction of evil into the world.

Griffin's process theodicy received significant attention. In 1991, Griffin formally responded to his critics in *Evil Revisited*, a collection of clarifications and responses in which he revised his theodicy in two important ways. He articulated a stronger doctrine of evil, adding the "demonic," and presented a stronger doctrine of divine power and hope, including a view of life after death and the triumph of the good. By 1991, Griffin's postmodern worldview had shaped his reflections on evil.

For Griffin, the demonic is not merely evil, but power that diametrically opposes divine power with the strength to threaten divine creation and purposes. In keeping with his previous descriptions of divine power, Griffin describes divine power as power that is used creatively and persuasively; it is based on responsive love, and it is characterized by active, creative love directed toward the good of those upon whom it is exercised. By contrast, demonic power is used coercively and destructively; it is based on hate or indifference, not being directed toward the good of all those upon whom it is exercised.

Griffin's conception of the demonic stands in contrast to the New Testament's mythic characterization of the demonic as a cosmic individual (such as Satan) and to traditional theism's view, which retains the image of Satan but assigns all power to God, thus confusing the mythic and the realistic. By understanding the demonic as an outgrowth of human creativity and freedom, Griffin retains the realistic character of evil while abandoning its mythic shroud personified as a cosmic figure. Restricted sympathies create possibilities for hatred and indifference. The rise of human beings with their enormous power and freedom created the possibility of the demonic. The demonic is not simply collective human disregard for others, but what Griffin calls a quasi-soul. Humans create a kingdom of evil through direct and indirect influences upon one another. The quasi-soul shapes humans for good or ill, and they in turn add their influences for good or ill to this shaping influence.

The other important change in Griffin's theodicy was the addition of an eschatology involving life beyond death. Griffin's naturalistic theism describes God as the one who influences all experience. All existents from atoms to Adam are persuaded by God's divine creative and loving power. The evidence of evolution is that God's power is persuasive, not coercive, and that persuasive power works slowly, but effectively, to accomplish God's purposes. Without implying an ontological dualism, Griffin argued from a numerical distinction between mind and brain and from parapsychological evidence that life after death is conceivable and probable. He recovers the notion of the spiritual journey in this life and extends it into the future beyond death. God's persuasive power is the ground of personal and cosmic hope that divine power and the good will have the last word over the demonic.

A Postmodern Worldview and a Postmodern Theism

Believing that a common and heightened antimodern sentiment is expressed in a variety of contemporary postmodern worldviews, Griffin categorizes his version of postmodernism as constructive or revisionary postmodernism, which promotes the building of a new worldview rather than merely eliminating the possibility of constructing worldviews, as in the case of deconstructive postmodernism.

Postmodern philosophy and theology begin with an intentional critique of modern thought. Griffin identifies a number of problems with modernism: a mechanistic view of nature that eliminates experience from nature's basic units, a sensationist view of perception that limits it to the physical senses, and an individualistic or atomistic view of human society as a collective of separate individuals. Early modern thought was characterized by dualisms that separated God from the world and the mind from the body. Late modern thought attempted to overcome these dualisms by denying both God and the soul while retaining early modernity's mechanistic, sensationistic, and even nihilistic worldview. Griffin's critique extends to both periods of modernism.

Griffin's constructive or revisionary postmodernism is not a return to a premodern worldview, but an appreciation of the advances made possible by modernism that moves beyond the destructive limitations of modernism to a new worldview.

To speak of God at all is a postmodern challenge to the atheistic materialism of late modern thought. Griffin's postmodernism understands God in terms of naturalistic theism, rejecting the supernaturalistic theism of early modernity. Although supernaturalism assumes that all creative power belongs to God in such a way that creaturely creativity is subject to God's will, naturalistic theism assumes that creativity is a power of every creature just as creativity is a power of God. Although supernaturalistic theism separated God from the world and defined God's relationship to the world as one of all-controlling power over essentially powerless creatures, naturalistic theism places God in the world and the world in God such that relations between God and the world are natural relations. God is the soul of the universe, not an independent individual who could exist apart from the world: God and world exist in relation to each other. Thus Griffin concludes that what exists is necessarily neither simply God nor simply a world, but God-and-a-world.

God's creative power in relationship to the world is persuasive rather than coercive or controlling. An evocative relational power, it is not unilateral and does not interrupt natural processes. God's creative power works within and with natural processes to inspire self-creativity in the world's creatures "by instilling new feelings of importance in them" (as Griffin says in *God and Religion in the Postmodern World*). God's creative power is the influence (the literal flowing in) of God's inspiration into creatures with the aim of heightening the self-creativity of the creatures.

God has no monopoly on creativity. Creativity is ultimate reality, while God is the ultimate, actual embodiment of creativity; but all existents experience creative power with respect to the influences that they receive from others' creativity, with respect to their self-creative response to creative influences, and with respect to the creative influences that they contribute to others. The creativity of existents is God's world, and it constitutes the actuality of God, who is, by nature, receptive and responsive to the creative influence of existents. As the world influences or enters God, God feels the joys and sorrows of the world (unlike the traditional concept of an impassive God who remains unaffected by the world). Postmodern theism in this sense is naturalistic panentheism: Mutually, the world is in God, just as God is in the world.

Like postmodern theism, postmodern spirituality requires a particular critique of modernist views of humanity, society, nature, and God. Besides defining society as a collection of individuals, early modern thought interpreted the relationship of humanity to nature in terms of domination and dualism: Nature is a mechanism and humanity in its freedom is completely different from nature. Early modernism understood God's relationship with humans as supernatural. In the shift to late modern thought, atheism replaced supernaturalism as a feature of modern spirituality, and materialism replaced dualism as an understanding of nature, which gave even greater license to the exploitation of nature and individualistic self-interest.

In contrast to this modern mode of spirituality, postmodern spirituality emphasizes internal relations and organicism. In other words, postmodern spirituality understands humanity as relational, so intimately connected socially that each individual is constituted by the experiences and influences of others and so connected by kinship with nature that humans and nature are one in their common purposive freedom or self-determination. Postmodern spirituality is communal, a direct rejection of individualism. Postmodernism replaces the exploitation and domination of nature with organicism as an alternative to mechanism and materialism. Postmodern spirituality is nondualistic.

The postmodern worldview understands spirituality as an essential feature of humanity. Although "spirituality" may be worldly or otherworldly in connotation, it suggests the ultimate values and meanings that shape life. Spirituality has religious connotations in the sense that ultimate values and meanings presuppose the holy, even when ultimate values are worldly values. Spirituality is not abstracted from social, political, economic, and ecological issues. Spirituality, in fact, suggests a noncoercive way of relating to society and nature that mirrors God's creative power in urging existents to create their optimal selves.

Griffin argues that postmodernism overcomes the liberal-conservative antithesis. By freeing conservatism from supernaturalism and authoritarianism and by freeing liberalism from the modern worldview, Griffin proposes concepts for a postmodern theism and spirituality that retain the best aspects of his youthful conservatism and the best spirit of his worldly liberalism as a postmodern Christian.

Nancy R. Howell

Selected Bibliography

1973   *A Process Christology.*
1976   *God, Power, and Evil: A Process Theodicy.*
1976   *Process Theology: An Introductory Exposition,* with John B. Cobb, Jr.
1981   "Creation Out of Chaos and the Problem of Evil," in *Encountering Evil: Live Options in Theodicy,* ed. Stephen T. Davis.
1988   *God and Religion in the Postmodern World.*
1988   "Introduction: Postmodern Spirituality and Society," in *Spirituality and Society,* ed. David R. Griffin.
1989   *Primordial Truth and Postmodern Theology,* with Huston Smith.
1991   *Evil Revisited: Responses and Reconsiderations.*
1993   "Liberal but Not Modern: Overcoming the Liberal-Conservative Antithesis," *Lexington Theological Quarterly* 28:3 (Fall).
1993   "Overcoming the Demonic: The Church's Mission," *Lexington Theological Quarterly* 28:3 (Fall).
1993   "Why Demonic Power Exists: Understanding the Church's Enemy," *Lexington Theological Quarterly* 28:3 (Fall).

JAMES M. GUSTAFSON
1925–

O ur century has posed stiff challenges to traditional Christian belief, even facing it with the alternatives of radical reinterpretation or ultimate irrelevance. Given the world wars, genocide, ethnic and racial hatreds, and the persistent ineradicability of disease and natural disaster, can we continue to claim that all things work to the good, or that God is present in all events that befall us? How are Christians to reply to scientific and secular construals of the natural environment and of history that make belief in a personal God, in a divine purpose guiding the world, in the resurrection and divinity of Jesus, and in the immortality of the soul, incredible to many people in modern societies?

James Gustafson grants the cogency of the hard questions now put to Christianity. But he absorbs their force in a theological response that affirms the transcendence of God, while holding every one of faith's expressions to the light of human experience and the natural and social sciences.

As a Protestant committed to the principle *semper reformanda,* and especially as a "Free Church" theologian, Gustafson is unwilling to be bound even by "historic creedal formulations" (*Theology and Ethics [TE]*, 1981, p. 163). Impatient with idolization of church forms and doctrinal orthodoxy over God, he reexamines the most tenaciously espoused elements of faith and practice. These include the privileged place of humanity in the universe, the providential guidance of history and of individual lives, the ultimacy of Jesus as the Christ, and life after death. But more than this, he offers a positive reinterpretation of Christian faith, in a context of religious community and pastoral concern. Gustafson's "theocentric" ethics reclaims certain central themes of the great Reformer John Calvin and his heirs: the sovereignty of God, the human response of "piety" and gratitude, and the interdependence of all things in relation to God.

Above all, Gustafson is critical of a self-serving Christianity that reduces God to human need-fulfillment, that projects an afterlife to avoid confronting real conflict and tragedy in this world, and that assumes arrogantly that God and all

God's creation exist to serve human well-being. For Gustafson, not only Christian faith, but the moral life as well, should be centered on worship of God, and response to God's purposes; to discern what *God* requires of us and enables us to do is the prerequisite of serving God rightly.

The relation between aspects of Gustafson's theology and his personal history are important, complex, and recognized by the theologian himself as foundational for the texture and shape of his cumulative project. James Moody Gustafson was born in 1925 and spent his boyhood in an iron-ore mining town of Michigan's Upper Peninsula. His father was a minister of the Swedish Covenant Church, an evangelical community with an immigrant membership. Inheriting from his father "a deep respect for the natural environment and an almost mystical relation to waterfalls, birch trees, and other of its aspects," the author recalls in a recent book about the environment, *A Sense of the Divine* (1994 *[SD]*), how he learned as a young boy to identify pine trees by bark and needles; to gather wintergreen leaves, wild raspberries, blueberries, strawberries, and hazelnuts; to care for elm trees and the endangered arbutus flower; to chop wood for the kitchen range; to love fishing on the Menominee River, canoeing on Spread Eagle Lake, and skiing, sledding, tobogganing, and ice-skating in winter. He knew early the dangers with which paper mill pollution, mining, and logging threatened nature.

The Upper Peninsula provided social as well as natural resources for Gustafson's theology. He describes himself as always at heart a "cultural relativist," recalling early immersion in the ethnic and social diversity of French-speaking Belgians, Italians, and Irish (all Catholic), and fellow Protestant Swedes ("Theocentric Interpretation," 1980, p. 86; "Tracing a Trajectory" [TT], 1995, p. 9). When the Gustafson family moved to a rural Kansas farming community in 1939, the dislocation was traumatic. Yet Midwestern farm life heightened Gustafson's appreciation of the dependency of human well-being on forces and factors that elude human control, and on a complex environment whose connections of interdependence and conflict do not always work out to human advantage. Kansas knew tornadoes and merciless, crop-withering droughts that could render human survival precarious. In the details and particularities of nature, Gustafson says, persons meet God; in responses to it, persons find clues to the divine purposes (*SD,* pp. 13, 14, 24). Nature teaches that, although everything exists interdependently, that interdependence is neither always harmonious nor in perfect equilibrium. God, one may infer, is the power that brings all things into being, sustains them, is the condition of their change and growth—but is also a power which bears down on, threatens, limits, and sometimes destroys them (*SD,* p. 14). In the terrible beauty of the natural world, one glimpses, if dimly, the majesty of God.

Gustafson began his undergraduate studies at North Park College in Chicago, where he studied with an acquaintance of his youth, Louise Roos. Her father was also a Swedish immigrant, and she had grown up on an Iowa farm. They married in 1947, and were to become the parents of two sons and two daughters. After a

179

tour of military duty with the United States Army Corps of Engineers in India and Burma (1944–46), Gustafson resumed his education at Northwestern University, delving into sociology and anthropology, and graduating with a B.S. in 1948. He pursued ministerial studies and ordination in the Congregational Church under the Federated Theological Faculty of the University of Chicago and Chicago Theological Seminary (B.D., 1951). Because of the merger of the Congregational and Evangelical Churches in the 1950s, Gustafson is today an ordained minister in the United Church of Christ.

In Chicago, Gustafson studied with Wilhelm Pauck, Daniel Day Williams, and James Luther Adams. Process theology was then dominant at Chicago; but particularly in the light of his and some of his classmates' recent war experiences, the logic with which its ontological claims were limned on chalkboards seemed too abstruse, too technical, and even too orderly to account for the human condition under God. With Adams' guidance, Gustafson read Ernst Troeltsch, whose historicization of Christian faith and identity seemed more experientially and theologically credible. World War II had brought Gustafson an excruciating sensitivity to human suffering and confirmed the depth of cultural differences. His conviction that religion is a dimension of human experience, that it is deeply affective and not wholly amenable to rationalistic explanation, found theological resonance in the Reformed tradition.

At Chicago, H. Richard Niebuhr's *Social Sources of Denominationalism* (1929) and *The Meaning of Revelation* (1941) made a special impact on James Gustafson's emergent theological sensibility. At the urging of Adams and other teachers, he left Chicago to begin doctoral studies with Niebuhr at the Divinity School of Yale University. He discovered immediately that he and his prospective mentor were much alike in religious imagination as well as theological outlook. Niebuhr, who proposed strongly historical readings of communal experiences of God in history, encouraged Gustafson in his study of social philosophy and the sociology of knowledge. Niebuhr's profound impact is reflected in Gustafson's rebuilding of the affective piety of Augustine, Calvin, Edwards, and Schleiermacher in light of the American pragmatic tradition in religion and philosophy (Dewey, James, Royce, and Mead).

These influences bore fruit in an early work that is still indicative of many of Gustafson's fundamental theological commitments. *Treasure in Earthen Vessels: The Church as a Human Community* (1961) faces the fact that particular forms of church are too often identified as the exclusive bearers of legitimate Christianity. On the other hand, only through its variant human functions, its political forms, its social organization, can the church survive over time and be effective in maintaining a community of "believers in God revealed in Jesus Christ" (ibid., p. x). Historical relativity is essential to the very mission of the church. But "cultural relativism" for Gustafson has never meant subjectivism or the complete relativity of truth to social perspective. As in his mentor's theology, the relativism of communal experience always has reference to an ultimate object: God ("Theocentric Interpretation," 1980, pp. 86-87).

The *objectivity* of that to which theological construals refer warrants the testing of religious traditions by external criteria, including evidence from human experience, and from the sciences. The *relativity* of human perceptions of God means that theology must be prepared to revise past formulations. This dynamic relationship between objectivity and relativity defines a key theological problem central to Gustafson's work: "How does a community working for good reasons within a historically particular tradition think about the object of its reverence, respect and gratitude in ways that can be honest with reference to its own culture and time?" ("Theocentric Interpretation," p. 87). Honesty requires incorporation into the theological enterprise of all the relevant disciplines of knowledge, and of the less formal, more inferential, and more inchoate senses of ultimacy and humanity that characterize one's cultural ethos. Gustafson has a tremendous respect and sympathy for what he calls the "natural piety" of nonreligious persons, who may respond to God's ordering of the world in ways that break the limits of standard conceptions of church, revelation, and faith (ibid., p. 90; TT, 1995, p. 22). What Gustafson refers to as his "common sense empiricism," as much as evidence from the natural and human sciences, has evoked many of his criticisms of classic theological doctrines (TT, p. 7).

After Gustafson received his doctorate in 1955, he was invited to join the Yale faculty, where he remained until 1972, when he moved to the University of Chicago Divinity School. A founding member in 1969 of the Hastings Center, an institute that has shaped the field of bioethics in the United States, Gustafson has commented on the moral ramifications of a wide variety of issues, including abortion, Down syndrome infants, genetic engineering, population control, and especially the methodological implications of exchanges among moral philosophers, theologians, and scientists. He is also conversant with business ethics, and has taken advantage of his university settings (Yale, Chicago, Emory) to participate in and initiate dialogue with colleagues in a variety of fields, such as clinical and research medicine, psychiatry, philosophy, law, social sciences, literature, and business. For Gustafson, theology is interdisciplinary. Its resources include not only Scripture and tradition, but also philosophy, the sciences, and human experience (*Ethics and Theology [ET]*, p. 143). Gustafson likes to use the metaphor of a raft balanced by way of its continuously shifting corners to describe the theological balance that keeps his approach afloat (*SD*, 1994, p. 46). Still, he once remarked, and frequently illustrates in practice, that "when the chips are down, it is adequacy to human experience—not just individual, but that of those whose experience is similar to one's own—that is decisive" ("Theocentric Interpretation," p. 92).

Pastoral work has always been important to Gustafson personally; it has been equally informative for his theology and for the manner of his moral analysis. He spent three years as pastor of a small Congregational church in Northford, Connecticut, while in residence in the Yale Ph.D. program, an experience that he recalls as "rich and formative."

> When one sat up most of a night with a family that was bearing the grief of a suicide, or when one was responsible to preach to a group of people in the village, all of whom one knew very well, theological studies had to be forged into an honest way of interpreting not only the experiences of human suffering, but the threats of McCarthyism and the cold war, and the proposals to rezone a rural village in the face of the coming suburbanization. Such coherence as my theological and ethical thinking had then, has ever had, and has now, has come in significant measure from trying to make sense of human life in the light of that measure of the knowledge of God that can be affirmed. ("Theocentric Interpretation," 1980, p. 92)

Yet Gustafson's relation to the institutional church has been far from simple and easy. Although Gustafson was a delegate to the General Council of Congregational Christian Churches in 1954, and was involved in the 1960s with the World Council of Churches Faith and Order Commission, he was then, as now, resistant to the conservative, ahistorical ecclesiologies under which organized religion often promotes its agenda (SD, 1994, p. 1). He has always been equally, if not more, impatient with faddish or trivial religion, and the instrumental use of piety even for morally worthy ends. Some Christian slogans of the late 1960s (such as "God is an unwed mother on the West Side of Chicago") went, in his view, beyond offensiveness to blasphemy, the irreproachability of their moral agenda notwithstanding (TE, 1981, p. 23).

Surely one of James Gustafson's main contributions to the theological guild has been his encouragement of a large number of doctoral students, both Protestant and Roman Catholic, who have themselves engaged in research and teaching in a number of denominations and from a wide variety of perspectives. In 1991 he was awarded an honorary degree by the Jesuit School of Theology at Berkeley (California) in gratitude for the number of Catholic students he has educated, many of them Jesuit priests. This remarkable and long-lasting mutual loyalty between teacher and students is one of Gustafson's most notable attributes, and a sign of the authenticity, generosity, high standards, and personal humility of a mentor who never insisted that students fit his own mold. In 1969, Gustafson served as elected President of the Society of Christian Ethics; in 1973, he was elected a fellow of the American Academy of Arts and Sciences. In 1988, he became the Henry Luce Professor of Humanities and Comparative Studies at Emory University, with the primary responsibility of organizing and leading interdisciplinary faculty seminars.

In the 1960s and 1970s, Gustafson was heavily invested in three aspects of Christian ethical debate to which he made interrelated contributions: situation ethics, Catholic-Protestant ecumenism, and bioethics. He shared with his Methodist colleague Paul Ramsey, also a former student of H. Richard Niebuhr, a vocal irritation with the looseness exhibited in Protestant moral analysis of the period. Both Ramsey and Gustafson decried (*Christian Ethics,* 1971, p. 114) Joseph Fletcher's book *Situation Ethics: The New Morality* (1966). Fletcher set a tone for the antilegalist mentality that was to pervade Christian ethics for at least a generation. Fletcher's unembarrassed and sanguine act-utilitarianism centered on "love," which, said Gustafson, "runs through Fletcher's book like a greased pig" ("Love Monism," 1967, p. 33). In a classic article ("Context Versus Principles: A Misplaced Debate in Christian Ethics," originally published in the *Harvard Theological Review* in 1965, and included in *Christian Ethics,* pp. 101-26), Gustafson wielded his characteristic talent for sorting out issues and rearranging them on a newly comprehensive paradigm. Arguing that the center of the whole debate had been misplaced, he maintained in the first place that the polarization of situation and rule was unnecessary, since most authors made some sort of move to accommodate both concerns. Moreover, the debate had been carried out entirely at the level of practical moral reasoning, without adequate attention to any one of the theological bases (social analysis, theological affirmations, moral principles, the Christian's life in Christ) that authors take as their points of departure, usually circling back to include the other three.

In the mid-1960s, the ecumenical impulse in Christianity had been given new energy by the Catholic church's Second Vatican Council (1962–65), which opened the doors to scriptural renewal, and to dialogue with the modern world and other religious communions. Gustafson undertook serious study of Roman Catholic moral theology, including Thomas Aquinas. An enduringly useful book, *Protestant and Roman Catholic Ethics: Prospects for Rapprochement* (1978), traced the divergence of the two traditions to historical factors such as the Catholic practice of private confession of sins (which required specific judgments and guidance from confessors); and Protestantism's contrast between law and gospel, as well as its preference for general, public confessions of sinfulness. Gustafson saw Protestants and Catholics as in general moving away from extreme rationalism and fideism, and toward more integral consideration on all sides of Bible and tradition, philosophy, scientific information, and human experience. Although Protestants and Catholics were not always able to agree on the way theological foundations and general principles should be organized, they had certainly become more successful in reaching consensus on practical moral issues. (Later, however, he was to lament the retreat from ecumenicity that the popularity of communitarian and narrative theology among both Protestants and Catholics might portend ["The Sectarian Temptation," 1985; "Roman Catholic and Protestant Interaction," 1989].)

Bioethics was one area in which the quest for greater analytic clarity, including the justification of principles and rules, and for interdenominational cooperation, was carried out. Gustafson has always wanted to keep the distinctively theological component visible in his contributions to public moral discourse, even as he has become increasingly convinced of the importance of being well-informed by contributory disciplines such as genetics, psychology, sociobiology, law, and economics. He has never endorsed a moral approach in which a mathematical model of knowledge governs the move from principles to action-guiding norms to the settling of concrete cases. Instead, on an issue like abortion or treating abnormal newborns, he sets out a finely tuned and balanced set of factual, theological, and moral considerations that move his readers through a process of discernment. In that process, religious experiences, theological commitments, personal history, and affective response can be engaged, as well as methods of formal, rational argument from either philosophical or theological premises.

The two-volume *Ethics from a Theocentric Perspective* (*Theology and Ethics [TE]*, 1981; *Ethics and Theology [ET]*, 1984) is James Gustafson's chief constructive work. Though exemplifying his ecumenical scope (Aquinas, Kant, Barth, Rahner, and Ramsey are "benchmarks" among the many figures woven into the argument), the two volumes center on the essentially Augustinian piety of the Reformed tradition, from Calvin to Jonathan Edwards, and from the Puritan roots of American Calvinism through the pragmatic tradition, including William James and H. Richard Niebuhr. For Gustafson as for Niebuhr, a key task of Christian theology is to account monotheistically for the varieties of religious emotion and affectivity (such as dependence, awe, gratitude, joy, consolation, obligation, fear, anger, remorse, repentance, hope, and trust) evoked by many different experiences, while denying neither the complexity of religious experience nor the sovereignty of a divinity who is both creative and destructive, merciful and wrathful, redeeming and judging. Gustafson concludes the work thus:

> God will not be manipulated.
> God will not be ignored or denied.
> God will be God. (p. 322)

The task of ethics is to discern, as far as finite intelligence is capable, how to participate in nature, history, and culture in ways that reflect the ordering of all things in relation to God. But Christianity historically has been more anthropocentric than theocentric. "Both individual pieties and social pieties become instrumental not to gratitude to God, the honor of God, or service of God, but to sustaining purposes to which the Deity is incidental, if not something of an encumbrance" (*TE*, 1981, p. 18).

In line with Augustine, Calvin, Edwards, and Niebuhr, there is a strong conversionist motif in Gustafson's theology and ethics. If persons and communities become rightly reoriented under God's purposes, their transformed theocentric focus will change their ways of being in the world (*TE*, p. 192). The church's role is to direct our consciousness toward God through prayer, worship, and the primary religious language of symbols, myths, and stories that preserve and enhance a "deeply felt relationship to God" (*ET*, 1984, p. 291; cf. *TE*, pp. 231-35, 318). *Ethics from a Theocentric Perspective* illustrates the theocentric vision and way of life with reference to bioethics, suicide, marriage, and family. *A Sense of the Divine (SD)* recasts the theological themes of the earlier book and directs them toward respect for humanity's place in the universe and the natural environment.

Gustafson's doctrine of God is itself integrally dependent on his experiential and inferential approach to the religious affections, and is the foundation on which to place a Christology that is minimalist by traditional standards. Insofar as God's will is displayed in the ordering of nature, the sciences are an important resource for discernment of the divine purposes, the proper human response to which is cooperation and consent (*TE,* 1981, p. 263; TT, 1995, p. 20). This does not mean that science or any other source can furnish persons with absolute and final certainty about God's purposes, God's ordering of creation, or about the specific responses required (*TE,* p. 244; *ET,* 1984, p. 293; *SD,* 1994, pp. 104-6). However, Christian theological affirmations and Christian moral exhortations must take into account not only past traditions of the community, but also information about the created world, including humanity, that changing conditions of knowledge can provide (*ET,* p. 144). As a consequence, even some traditionally "central" Christian tenets become objects of skepticism (*ET,* p. 84).

Gustafson says Jesus is "one who incarnates in his teachings, his manner, and his actions theocentric piety and fidelity" (*ET,* p. 292; cf. pp. 276-79, and Beckley and Swezey, *Theocentric Ethics,* 1988, p. 220). The moral dimension of Jesus' piety is his readiness, grounded in his openness to a transcendent source of courage and love, to be at the service of others, even at high cost to self. The cross is a central symbol of the self-denial that is required and enabled of persons who seek to glorify God in consent to dependence upon God, and in fidelity to God's purposes (*ET,* p. 22). Two decades earlier, Gustafson had written an entire volume, *Christ and the Moral Life* (1968), about the role of Christ in forming the vision, the dispositions, the goals and ends, and the norms of the Christian community, bound together by "a common object of loyalty, Jesus Christ," the one through whom "the ultimate powers and realities of life are known and understood" (ibid., pp. 240-41). Similarly, *Can Ethics Be Christian?* (1975) developed the proposal that Christian ethics infers values and principles from the biblical accounts centered on Jesus, always read and interpreted in the light of wider moral experiences and insights that Christians may share with other people (ibid., pp. 162-63). Yet Christian ethics is not translatable "without remainder" into secular or rational language, because of its integral origin in and coherence with a communal experience of God that is particular and historical (ibid., p. 175).

The Christology of *Ethics from a Theocentric Perspective* and later work is not discontinuous in substance with Gustafson's earlier portrayal of Jesus as a revelation of God and the continuing discernment of that revelation in a community of faith. The center of gravity of his theology has shifted more than its content, with relatively less priority explicitly given Christ as the cornerstone of Christian identity today. And as his work advances, Gustafson states more directly and strongly both that the redemptive or salvific significance of Christ should be very cautiously interpreted, and that a theocentric approach implies a profound critique of Christian doctrine (*ET*, p. 42). Yet, as early as 1951, Gustafson's ordination to the Chicago Association of Congregational Churches was almost blocked because he refused to affirm personal immortality (TT, 1995, p. 7).

Despite its retrospective consistency with fundamental elements in Gustafson's earlier theological and ecclesial positions, *Ethics from a Theocentric Perspective* came to many with a shock. Colleagues and students tended to contrast the later work's austere tone and severe claims with their personal impressions of the author—a lens through which they had interpreted, no doubt selectively, what he had written before. Now they wondered, in person and in print, whether their colleague had gone beyond the pale of Christianity to embrace any one of a number of alternatives, including scientific reductionism, naturalism, stoicism, Deism, and cultural accommodation (see secondary sources in the bibliography). A symposium on the book, held at Washington and Lee University, Virginia, in 1985, drew world-renowned scholars, and joined at least some of the issues between Gustafson and personally sympathetic but theologically bemused critics (see *Gustafson's Theocentric Ethics*, 1988).

Paul Ramsey addressed him with emotion: "I feel lonely at the drawing of a theological enterprise that does not center upon the things that we had thought we shared with you at the level of first-order discourse, namely, prayer, worship, liturgy, the confessions of the church, and going to the Lord's table." Gustafson, finding his old friend's disclosure "hard," responded that it was *as* a "faithful religious person" that he had come to realize that neither "profound religious sensibilities" nor "moral sensitivities" were limited to the churches. Indeed, the churches have repulsed many people's experience of God by failing to confront suffering, or to recognize and nurture piety outside institutional channels. Gustafson identified self-critical service to God rather than preservation of tradition as his own aim; that may require accountability to theocentric responsiveness that flourishes outside Christianity (*Theocentric Ethics*, pp. 238-39). Yet Gustafson has never criticized the inflated claims of Christian rhetoric as an alienated outsider, but as a committed participant who calls that church to greater honesty about human and Christian realities (TT, p. 9). His acquaintances know the satisfaction he takes in the fact that one of his two sons is an ordained minister and pastor, and one of his two daughters is a theologian and Presbyterian elder.

An overview of Gustafson's work attests that it is precisely uncompromising realism about God and the human condition that has enabled him to be personally empathetic and required him to be theologically stern; the critic of ecclesial triumphalism and of cheap grace is, as a pastor and teacher, capable of a radical intellectual honesty and an intense commitment to personal relationships which inspire tremendous respect. The intellectual companion and patron to whom *Ethics from a Theocentric Perspective* was dedicated, Elmer W. Johnson (an attorney who served as CEO of General Motors), sees Gustafson as at heart and perennially a pastor and counselor, one who offers no "magic tricks and sure-fire prescriptions." His way is to foster a process of discernment in which the complexities, ambiguities, and tragedies of life are confronted, in which evaluation proceeds in modesty and depends on careful listening, and in which the integrity of the decision-maker is always respected ("Style of James M. Gustafson," 1986, p. 2). Out of pastoral experience, Gustafson communicates the hope and mutual sustenance that humans give one another, not by judging and prescribing, but by keeping company—by "suffering with the suffering" and "being in pain with those who are in pain" (panel discussion in *Theocentric Ethics*, p. 239). Fidelity and forgiveness are components of authentic imitation of Christ, and part of genuine experience of God.

James Gustafson has made theology more broadly accountable to other disciplines, but without evacuating it of properly religious content, or reducing its criteria to theirs. The lasting effect of his theology will be to uphold the awesome reality of God as the center of theology and ethics. A prophetic theocentrism makes it very difficult for Christians to cling to comforting elements of received religion, even when their beliefs cannot meet generally recognized standards of validity, including experiential ones; and whether or not such beliefs are truly consistent with the ultimacy and magnificence of God as proclaimed by Christianity, especially in Reformed perspective.

Lisa Sowle Cahill

Selected Primary Works

1961   *Treasure in Earthen Vessels: The Church as Human Community.*
1963   "Introduction," in H. Richard Niebuhr, *The Responsible Self: An Essay in Christian Moral Philosophy.*
1967   "Love Monism: How Does Love Reign?" in John Bennett, et al., *Storm Over Ethics*, pp. 26-37.
1968   *Christ and the Moral Life.*
1968   *On Being Responsible: Issues in Personal Ethics*, ed. with James T. Laney.
1970   *The Church as Moral Decision-Maker.*
1970   "A Protestant Ethical Approach," in John T. Noonan, ed., *The Morality of Abortion: Legal and Historical Perspectives*, pp. 101-22.
1971   *Christian Ethics and the Community.*
1973   "Mongolism, Parental Desires, and the Right to Life," *Perspectives in Biology and Medicine* 16/4:529-57. (Reprinted in Thomas A. Shannon, ed., *Bioethics*, rev. ed., 1981.)
1974   *Theology and Christian Ethics.*
1975   *Can Ethics Be Christian?*

1975   *The Contributions of Theology to Medical Ethics.* The 1975 Pere Marquette
        Theology Lecture.
1978   *Protestant and Roman Catholic Ethics: Prospects for Rapprochement.*
1980   "A Theocentric Interpretation of Life," *Christian Century* 97:754-60. (Re-
        printed in James M. Wall, *Theologians in Transition: The Christian Cen-
        tury "How My Mind Has Changed"* Series, 1981. Page citations in the
        present essay are taken from the Wall edition.)
1981   *Ethics from a Theocentric Perspective,* vol. 1, *Theology and Ethics.*
1984   *Ethics from a Theocentric Perspective,* vol. 2, *Ethics and Theology.*
1985   "The Sectarian Temptation: Reflections on Theology, the Church, and the
        University," *Proceedings* 40:83-94.
1988   *Varieties of Moral Discourse: Prophetic, Narrative, Ethical and Policy,*
        The Stob Lectures of Calvin College and Seminary.
1988   *The U.S. Business Corporation: An Institution in Transition,* ed. with John
        R. Meyer.
1989   "Roman Catholic and Protestant Interaction in Ethics: An Interpretation,"
        Theological Studies 50:44-69.
1994   *A Sense of the Divine: The Natural Environment from a Theocentric Per-
        spective.*
1995   "Tracing a Trajectory," *Zygon,* in press. (Read and cited in manuscript.)

Selected Secondary Sources

1983   Gene Outka, "Remarks on a Theological Program Instructed by Science,"
        The Thomist 47:572-91.
1985   James F. Childress and Stanley Hauerwas, eds., Issue Focus on The Ethics
        of James M. Gustafson, *Journal of Religious Ethics* 13. (Essays by
        James F. Childress and Stanley Hauerwas, Stanley Hauerwas, Lisa Sowle
        Cahill, Stephen Toulmin, Richard A. McCormick, Paul Ramsey, and a
        bibliography by Charles Swezey.)
1986   Elmer W. Johnson, "The Style of James M. Gustafson and the Process of
        Moral Discernment," *Criterion* (Spring), p. 205.
1986   William Schweiker, "Theocentric Ethics: 'God Will Be God,'" *Christian
        Century* (January 15), pp. 36-38.
1988   Harlan R. Beckley and Charles M. Swezey, eds., *James M. Gustafson's
        Theocentric Ethics: Interpretations and Assessments.* (Essays by Beck-
        ley and Swezey, Gordon D. Kaufman, Edward Farley, John H. Yoder,
        Robert O. Johann, John P. Reeder, Jr., Robert N. Bellah, Robert Audi,
        Mary Midgley, James M. Gustafson, and panel discussion.)
1990   Julian N. Hartt, "Concerning God and Man and His Well-Being: A Com-
        mentary, Inspired by Spinoza, on Gustafson's *Ethics from a Theocentric
        Perspective,*" *Soundings* 73/4:667-87 (with a response by Gustafson,
        pp. 689-700).

GUSTAVO GUTIÉRREZ
1928–

Life and Career

A parish priest who labors among the poor of the Rimac district in Lima, Peru, Gustavo Gutiérrez is also founder and director of the Bartolomé de Las Casas Center. His pastoral work among the poor catalyzed his literary work and thereby set before the world his Latin American rendering of a "theology of liberation." An early formulator and most significant proponent of Latin American liberation theology, Gutiérrez repeatedly claims that theology is critical reflection on the Christian faith and on the struggle and hope of the poor. Gutiérrez strives to forge

> a theology which is open—in the protest against trampled human dignity, in the struggle against the plunder of the vast majority of humankind, in liberating love, and in the building of a new, just and comradely society—to the gift of the Kingdom of God. (*A Theology of Liberation*, p. 12)

More than twenty-five years after its appearance, his principal work, *A Theology of Liberation: History, Politics, and Salvation* (1973), remains the classic expression of Latin American liberation theology. It is the crucial synthesis of Gutiérrez's spiritual and theological vision, being at once political, economic, social, and pastoral. Different parts of this book's vision have been elaborated in scores of unpublished talks, mimeographed presentations, and informally distributed essays.

Biographical statements about an individual liberation theologian should not be mistaken for a description of liberation theology—even the liberation theology formulated by one of its first articulate spokespersons. This caveat is especially true of Gutiérrez, who reminded his hearers and readers that the often anonymous poor, especially as people "who die before their time" (Las Casas), are the real originators of his liberation theology. To be sure, Gutiérrez has made a salient contribution as an individual. Whether as ecclesial leader or as theologian, his role is to be viewed within the human solidarity that he shares with the poor and within the ministry he exercises among them.

Gutiérrez's life is best understood as occurring within the often conflictual pressures emanating from "First World" Europe and from "Third World" and oppressed Peruvian settings. This conflict, in fact, is etched into the most profound depths of his personal background.

Born Gustavo Gutiérrez Merino (June 8, 1928), in the nonprivileged sectors of Lima, he entered life among the oppressed of his land, part Hispanic and part Amerindian (i.e., Quechuan). The sociocultural oppression of his setting was compounded by personal disease (osteomyelitis) that confined him to bed and then to a wheelchair from age twelve to age eighteen, and left him lame. During this period he nurtured a voracious curiosity through extensive reading and academic study. His father was a poor urban worker and his mother was without formal schooling, but his own academic talents launched his formal education, beginning with preliminary studies in medicine at the University of San Marcos in Lima (1947–1950). He soon switched to philosophy and theological studies.

Watershed dates and periodizations are notoriously oversimplifying, but four periods can be distinguished in Gutiérrez's life and work. These periods might also be viewed as dimensions always present and in progress throughout Gutiérrez's life and writings. The crucial theological periods in Gutiérrez's work can be summarized through reference to the distinctive shape of his life.

Formal Theological Training (1950–1959)

Gutiérrez undertook formal theological work between 1951 and 1955 at the Catholic University in Louvain, Belgium, where he finished a master's degree in psychology and philosophy with the thesis, "Psychic Conflict in Freud." Beginning to drink deeply from general currents of European thought and to ponder particular new theological insights, Gutiérrez would maintain this psychological focus, integrating it in crucial ways into his understanding of social and political liberation. This psychological orientation, along with traditions of Christian spirituality, lent a dimension of profound interiority to the liberating action that he insisted was at the heart of Christian praxis.

While in Belgium, Gutiérrez did not neglect his ties to Latin America. In fact, many of his political interests were fueled by significant contact with seminar colleagues from around the world who also were studying at the Louvain. Among them were Juan Luis Segundo and Camilo Torres. Torres, who shared Gutiérrez's spirit of forceful critique of oppression, later departed from Gutiérrez's advice and practice by joining the guerrillas of Colombia, among whom he was shot in 1966.

In 1955, Gutiérrez moved to the University of Lyons in France where he completed work with the theological faculty on an M.A. thesis, "Religious Liberty"

(1959). Here he encountered *la nouvelle theologie,* which included new work on theologies of the laity (Yves Congar) and "social dogmatics" (Henri de Lubac).

This period culminates in Gutiérrez's ordination to the priesthood in the Roman Catholic Church on January 6, 1959. The ordination would serve as a marker, highlighting a transition to a new phase, not only of ministry but of an even more powerful education among the poor of Peru. As Gutiérrez returned to ministry in his native Peru, he did so in conversation with European thought, including Jacques Maritain's integral humanism, E. Mounier's personalism, and L. J. Lebret's theology of development. J. B. Metz's political theology, and also the Protestant theologies of Karl Barth and Dietrich Bonhoeffer were other European thinkers he read later. Although these European streams flowed into his emerging perspective, they never overwhelmed the mighty river of thought and cosmic vision flowing in Gutiérrez from the cultures of the oppressed, indigenous peoples of Peru.

Theological Realignment (1960–1967)

After additional studies at the Gregorian in Rome (1959–60), Gutiérrez began to teach at the Catholic Pontifical University in Lima. This part-time faculty appointment enabled him to spend time among the poor of his parish, among whom he worked and with whose need and vision he increasingly came to identify.

He began a period of "theological realignment" because his formal theological training did not easily fit with the courses being cut by the rivers of need, struggle, and hope flowing through the terrain of the Peruvian poor. Robert McAfee Brown, one of Gutiérrez's most sensitive theological interpreters in North America, characterizes this time as one of "unlearning much of his hard-won education." It was a period of comprehensive reinterpretation of theology and of renewed exposure to his own context's resources for theological work. These resources were both practical and intellectual.

Practically, he explored and experienced the resource of the poor's own community and life. The demands of ministry among the poor increasingly impressed upon him the need for Christians to "enter the world of the poor." This engagement is to be distinguished from merely standing alongside the poor, advocating their cause, or "speaking for" them. Gutiérrez's own ministry sought to be an entry into their world and to work from a vision from within, which might lead to a healing transformation of their world. Thus, his theology of pastoral action made urgent responses to poverty, class conditions, and conflict in Latin America. The development of this urgent pastoral focus is evident in two theological gatherings of this period: the 1964 conference in Petrópolis, Brazil, and a 1967 conference of student leaders in Montevideo, Uruguay. At both places, Gutiérrez presented the main lines of positions eventually published in his first book, *Lineas pastorales de la Iglesia en America Latina* (1968).

Intellectually, theological realignment also entailed exploring distinctive cognitive resources in his Peruvian context. Gutiérrez, at this time, for example, deepened his massive study of the sixteenth-century priest Las Casas, whom Gutiérrez interprets as one who saw Peru and its Incas as "the very touchstone" of the battle for justice in the Indies, even though Las Casas never visited Peru.

Gutiérrez also deepened his knowledge and feeling for Peruvian identity and freedom by dwelling in the rich literary heritages of three extraordinary Peruvian thinkers: José Carlos Mariategui (d. 1930), the author of *Seven Interpretive Essays on Peruvian Reality* (1971), who probed deeply for a true "socialism" and mythic vision consonant with Andean indigenous cultures; José Maria Arguedas (d. 1969), the passionate novelist who in works like *Deep Rivers* (1978) offered vivid portraits of the exploitation, pain, and beauty of Peru's indigenous poor; and Cesar Vallejo (d. 1938), a poet with unusual evocative power to render the common lives of the poor as revelatory of the sacred.

These thinkers not only offered occasional illustrative images for Gutiérrez's writings; they also provided a whole sensibility, feeling, and knowledge of the poor's world. Taken together, the three thinkers are emblematic of Gutiérrez's emerging theological work, as situated in the Peruvian poor's own world of knowledge—their suffering and unique joy. Although he does not jettison conversation with his European teachers and colleagues, Gutiérrez's rigorous inquiry and urgent feeling into the world of the Peruvian poor is what will leave a crucial mark. His position between the currents of First World and Third World is, therefore, given a new intensity.

Crafting the Theology of Liberation (1968–1979)

The crafting of his liberation theology with greater intentionality and formalization clusters around two formative events. First, there is the initial meeting with Arguedas, which began a brief but rich friendship between the two, but which ended a year and a half later with Arguedas's suicide in 1969. The two learned much from each other. Arguedas himself, perhaps in light of the friendship, wrote a novel in which a Catholic, activist priest "gave voice to the voiceless" instead of being, as Arguedas had long accused the Catholic Church in Latin America, a mere reinforcer of the poor's plight. Gutiérrez would eventually devote an extensive essay to Arguedas's literary contribution and solidarity with the Peruvian poor ("Entre las calandrias" ["Among the Larks"] in *Arguedas: mito, historia y religion* [1982]) and also place a quote from Arguedas as the frontispiece of his *Theology of Liberation*.

The first meeting with Arguedas coincided with a second important event inaugurating this period, a conference in 1968 at Chimbote, Peru, held by a group of priests advocating social change (ONIS, Oficina National de Investigation).

There he presented the basic lineaments of his theology of liberation. As Arguedas studied Gutiérrez's presentation in his last years, he wrote that Gutiérrez's words at Chimbote "strengthened my faith in a future which cannot fail me."

Gutiérrez's strengthening words at Chimbote would soon be further crafted toward his famous theology of liberation. Soon after Chimbote came the remarkable meeting of the Episcopal Council of Latin America, where Latin American bishops gathered in 1968 at Medellín, Colombia, to examine the topic "The Church in the Present-Day Transformation of Latin America in the Light of the [Second Vatican] Council." The discussions and decisions of the Medellín conference went beyond most of the dreams of even the most progressive post–Vatican II, Roman Catholic theologians and opened the door to a theology of liberation that would radically alter the theological landscape of Latin America. Gutiérrez was a "theological expert" who had relatively free access to the Medellín conference, and he played key roles in drafting its most radical documents, one entitled "Peace," another "Justice." He also wrote the theological paragraph for the document, "Poverty of the Church." Medellín affirmed and gave new voice to the Latin American poor, who grappled daily with a complex injustice that the "Peace" document termed "institutionalized violence."

After Medellín, Gutiérrez continued to clarify the contours of his liberation theology, crafting and presenting them in contexts as diverse as Cartigny, Switzerland, and Bogota, Colombia. The 1969 gathering in Switzerland involved presenting a general outline of A Theology of Liberation before a group more interested in reformist "development" than in "liberation," that is, the Pontifical Commission on Justice and Peace and the World Council of Churches. The 1970 gathering in Bogota, Colombia, enabled more precise tooling of his theological vision, before its release the next year as a Spanish publication, Teologia de la liberation: Perspectivas.

The publication of his classic book, though it invited worldwide debate and contestation, did not complete Gutiérrez's crafting of a liberation theology. Producing that text was crucial, but the struggle continued at the levels of historical and ecclesial practice. Soon after the book's publication, Gutiérrez participated in a conference in Santiago, Chile, at which he, along with Giulo Girardi, Hugo Assmann, and a few other Christian thinkers, set about the task of interpreting socialist resistance in order to "combat imperialism." The final document of the conference specified the need to break away from Latin American dependency on North American state powers.

Ecclesially, the struggle to craft a liberation theology at the heart of the church's ministry is evident in the many activities of Gutiérrez that culminated in the efforts to preserve the insights of Medellín at the 1979 bishops' conference at Puebla, Mexico. Gutiérrez and like-minded theologians, now coming under critique from the Vatican, were excluded from the conference center. Nevertheless, they and many other resource persons were nearby. Puebla did not rescind Medellín's revolutionary mandates. Moreover, the excluded liberationists influenced one-fourth of the final Puebla document, which asserted, for example, that "institutionalized violence" had worsened. Robert McAfee Brown reports that one of the outsiders later celebrated the document by saying, "There are fifty phrases we can use!" In the next and continuing period of his life, Gutiérrez would have occasion to use those fifty phrases—and many more. In fact, he would interpret the Puebla document as crucial for strengthening the church's understanding of "God's preferential option for the poor."

Contestation and Proclamation (1980–)

The fourth and continuing period is one of intense contestation, which yet also offered Gutiérrez fresh opportunities for what he termed the "proclamation" of the God of liberation and life.

In 1980, the Congregation for the Doctrine of the Faith under the personal supervision of Joseph Cardinal Ratzinger began a direct investigation of Gutiérrez's theology. This ecclesial contestation required Gutiérrez to debate long lists of charges coming from diverse sources. Most charges focused on Gutiérrez's alleged compromise with Marxist thought and with notions of class warfare. Liberation theology was always controversial for a number of reasons. (The best summary of this theological controversy is Arthur C. McGovern, *Liberation Theology and Its Critics: Toward an Assessment.*) For Gutiérrez, the continuing controversy sharpened into a direct ecclesial investigation that included the following: Gutiérrez's personal travel to Rome for examination and defense; Cardinal Ratzinger's travel to Lima in an attempt to pressure the Catholic hierarchy in Peru to repudiate Gutiérrez and his theology; a summons of the Peruvian bishops to Rome for yet another unsuccessful attempt to coax a repudiation of Gutiérrez's liberation theology; attacks on liberation theology by Ratzinger through his informal interviews with European mass-media; and finally, formal "Instructions" (issued in 1984 and 1986) from the Congregation for the Doctrine of the Faith about liberation theology, which offered severe warnings but seemed quite lenient and even supportive of key notions in liberation theology.

Gutiérrez's energy and schedule were severely taxed by this investigation, yet he remained a productive writer and parish priest throughout. Significant sections of books from this period (*The God of Life* in 1982 and 1989, *We Drink From Our Own Wells* in 1983, *On Job* in 1985) can be viewed as responses to the continuing ecclesial investigations. His most elaborate rebuttal of charges is contained in "The Truth Shall Make You Free," a long essay in his 1986 book that bears the same title. The essay was prepared as a response to an invitation in 1986 from the University of Lyons in France to have his writings and theology examined. The essay gives the substance of the lectures he provided at Lyons, where he also responded to a full battery of questions, before being awarded a doctorate in theology *(summa cum laude)* by unanimous consent of the Lyons faculty. This event, together with some waning in the Vatican's aggressive investigation of Gutiérrez, brought about an uneasy peace for Gutiérrez in the arena of ecclesial contestation.

At the same time, however, there had also been in progress a process of contestation in the arenas of historical practice and politics. Again, the year 1980 is significant, for then there occurred what Gutiérrez himself termed "a milestone" in the history of the Latin American church, the assassination of Archbishop Oscar Romero in El Salvador. Even though Romero was one of the "progressive" bishops with Gutiérrez at Medellín in 1968, he only slowly grew to embrace the cause of the poor and of liberation theology in El Salvador. In 1972, still on the way to his own liberationist voice, Romero took polite notes on lectures at Antigua, Guatemala, which Gutiérrez presented there at a conference for Central American bishops. By 1980, however, Romero found himself vigorously taking on the voice of the repressed poor, demanding that the U.S.-backed military stop its repression in his country, and calling upon President Jimmy Carter to halt aid to the military with its clandestine death squads and reign of terror. As a result, Romero himself was slain by a military-condoned death squad while he was saying Mass in March of 1980.

Romero's assassination drew worldwide attention. Gutiérrez journeyed to attend the funeral and was, in fact, among those in mourning when members of El Salvador's National Guard began firing into the crowd. Because of his slight stature, Gutiérrez, as Robert McAfee Brown reports, "expected to be knocked over and trampled to death" by the crowd, fleeing in panic. Instead, he somehow "made it safely to the cathedral and administered the last rites of the church to a woman who was bleeding to death." Gutiérrez's life and ministry, therefore, were taking place increasingly on the underside of a continent-wide struggle with militarism and violence directed at the Latin American poor.

Within months after Romero's assassination, U.S. President Reagan's new administration, through its Council for Inter-American Security, issued the "Santa Fe Report" to guide its policies in Latin America. It urged a low-intensity conflict against enemies to United States interests. Concerning liberation theology, the Santa Fe report stated that "U.S. foreign policy must begin to counter . . . liberation theology as it is utilized in Latin America by the liberation theology clergy. . . ." The United States, during Reagan's administration, would eventually provide almost $1.4 million per day to El Salvador's military. Reagan also began a decade of funding for a military intervention against Nicaragua, where experiments in a mixed economy (free-market capitalism with socialism) included contributions from liberation theologians and even their presence in Nicaragua's government (e.g., Miguel D'Escoto and Ernesto Cardenal).

Gutiérrez experienced contestation in historical practice and politics not only in Latin America generally, but very particularly in his native Peru. The sixteenth-century conquest of the Incas by the Spanish had already etched the ways of colonial domination deep into his country's past and present consciousness, leaving Peru's majority of indigenous poor mired in poverty and cycles of violence.

Beginning in 1980, Gutiérrez increasingly found himself and his people caught up in an especially agonizing vortex of violence. In 1980, the guerrilla movement known as *Sendero Luminoso* (Shining Path), under the leadership of a highly rationalistic, yet quasi-religious warrior caste, began to attack almost every other kind of organization (on the right, middle, or left) that might question *Sendero*'s own vanguard plans for revolutionizing Peru. Their vicious attacks provoked an increasingly repressive Peruvian government (which was receiving U.S. military assistance) to undertake widespread counterinsurgency campaigns, often equally vicious, on local communities, including torture and totalitarian control.

The systemic exchange of ruthlessness between the guerrillas and the militarized government evolved through the decade of the 1980s to yield nearly 18,000 dead, 3,000 missing, with two-thirds of the country under military rule. By the decade's end, Peru had already produced three consecutive years in which it led the entire world in numbers of people "forcibly disappeared." Although the *Sendero Luminoso* claimed allegiance to the indigenous poor of the Andes and to Peru's social theorist Mariategui, neither *Sendero* nor the military government in fact valued the agency and lives of indigenous Peruvians. *Sendero* never built a respect for the dynamics of ethnicity among Andean peoples, and while drawing on Amerindian ranks for their campaigns, the *Sendero* leadership had by the mid-1990s helped to leave the Peruvian left-wing in shambles before a relentless government and military machine.

The agony of Peru in the 1980s provided Gutiérrez perhaps the most vicious scene of contestation and challenge for his proclamation of a liberating gospel. In June of 1986, the same year that Gutiérrez was in Lyons for ecclesial debates, the government forces (by their own admission) executed rioting *Senderoso* men and women in various prisons. Gutiérrez was one of the first to respond to this national emergency. In a measured but passionate tone, he took to the leading newspaper's editorial page, decrying the government's action as one more example of the "institutionalized violence" he had helped to name at the bishops' conference in Medellín in 1968 and Puebla in 1979. But he refused to allow his editorial to become an apology for the *Sendero*. His fury at government violence did not lead to an embrace of the violence of *Sendero*'s revolutionary elite. Instead, he proclaimed his faith in the capacity of Peru's poorer classes to make their way toward economic and social healing, something denied them since the Spanish conquest. Amid the military *and* "Shining Path" contesters in violence, therefore, Gutiérrez protested and then proclaimed a gospel and practice of life on behalf of the Amerindian poor, those who were again being condemned to "die before their time."

Gutiérrez's practice in Peru was consonant not only with his own developed liberation theology, but also with the *indigenismo* of Mariategui's socialism and with the visions of the novelist of indigenous life, Arguedas. At a public forum in Lima, soon after his editorial against military violence, he affirmed his intentions to stay with Peruvian poor even under the conditions of military domination.

Given his commitment to the Amerindian poor, it was fitting that Gutiérrez worked throughout the 1980s in the southern Andes with church pastoral workers of the departments of Cuzco and Puno, where there live about two million Aymara- and Quechua-speaking peoples. Of utmost concern in those areas has been the struggle for land. Many of his positions, developed over years of workshops and courses for pastoral workers and campesinos in Puno and Cuzco, provided the warrants for a milestone document in the history of the Peruvian poor's land-struggle, *La tierra: Don de Dios, Derecho del pueblo* (The Land: God's Gift, The People's Right), which was published amid acute tensions in 1985 and 1986. In this pastoral-theological struggle, the emphasis was on restoring the people to their land. Land was central, not only to the people's economic health, but also to their religiocultural identity, built as it is around an Andean cosmovision that emphasizes the relationship of people to land. Gutiérrez insists, again, that their vibrant popular movements for life and land are the source of a true "evangelization"—one that the powerful cannot bring to the Amerindians, but that can only be carried out by the Amerindian poor themselves.

Precisely in this context of contestation, experiencing the Amerindian poor's proclamation to the worlds of warfare and institutionalized violence, can we best understand Gutiérrez's massive work, *Las Casas: In Search of the Poor of Jesus Christ* (1992). It is the magisterial restatement of his liberation theology, holding that the God of life, the Jesus Christ who brings integral liberation for all creation, is met above all among the scourged Amerindian poor of the New World. This was the insight hard-won by Las Casas in his own contestations with sixteenth-century officials, whether theological, ecclesial, or political. Five hundred years after the conquest that was witnessed by Las Casas, Gutiérrez proclaims a Christ of the poor amid a Latin American continent still dominated by Northern-based or Northern-supported elites, and amid seemingly abysmal agony in his native Peru. This proclamation puts his life and thought in a historical stream that includes not only Bartolome de Las Casas, but also the noted Peruvian witness who recorded the conquest of the Incas, Guaman Poma. About both witnesses, Gutiérrez concludes:

They both challenge us to hurry and write our names, in all haste and urgency, with purpose and determination, on the pages of long duration that is the coming of the Reign of life proclaimed by Jesus. (*Las Casas,* p. 460)

Mark McClain Taylor

197

Selected Primary Works

Several of Gutiérrez's principal essays are collected in two key volumes: *The Power of the Poor in History: Selected Writings* (1983), which develops important lines of his theological work in relation to more traditional theologies, and *The Truth Shall Make You Free* (1990), which ranges widely but has as its main focus his eloquent replies to ecclesial and other critics.

A Theology of Liberation was reissued in 1988 in a slightly revised edition that featured a new introduction entitled "Expanding the View." The expanded classic is complemented now by five other book-length studies in Gutiérrez's corpus.

Liberation and Change (1977), written with Richard Shaull, contains three probing chapters by Gutiérrez on freedom and salvation, exploring their relations as a political problem. *We Drink from Our Own Wells: The Spiritual Journey of a People* (1984), put the lie to all accusations that his liberation theology was a mere "reduction" of theology to social issues, solely a political "ideology," instead of what this book shows it to be, namely, a profound spirituality and mystical sense, the essence of which Dutch theologian Edward Schillebeeckx ably discerned as "evangelical militant compassion."

On Job: God-Talk and the Suffering of the Innocent (1987) not only offers key insights into his theological method, but gives the age-old theodicy question new, biting pertinence within the perspectives of the suffering of innocents among the Peruvian poor. It is, in fact, dedicated to the unjustly suffering ones of Ayacucho in his native Peru. *The God of Life* (1991) fills out Gutiérrez's vision of the liberating God as a God of "life," enabling his reinterpretations of divine justice, holiness, faithfulness, covenant-making, and action in history.

Finally, his most recent work, *Las Casas: In Search of the Poor of Jesus Christ* (1993), may be his most magisterial and passionate yet. It focuses on the life, theological debates, and present-day challenge posed by Bartolome de Las Casas, sixteenth-century priest and "defender of the Indians" in the New World. Across almost five hundred pages, Gutiérrez here reweaves his theology of liberation into a tapestry that stretches historically through the 500 years of European conquest and Amerindian resistance, and that reaches culturally and politically between the powerful European worlds and the sufferers of the New World. Appearing in the 501st year after Columbus's first exploits, Gutiérrez's *Las Casas* book came as a vigorous indictment of European thought and practice and as an urgent call, in the tradition of Las Casas, for embracing the Jesus Christ who is uniquely present in the scourged and yet joyous lives of the Amerindian poor.

Selected Secondary Sources

The best two secondary sources on Gutiérrez's life and theology are Robert McAfee Brown, *Gustavo Gutiérrez: An Introduction to Liberation Theology*

(1990); and Curt Cadorett, *From the Heart of the People: The Theology of Gustavo Gutiérrez* (1989), which includes the most extensive bibliography in English.

Theological discussion and evaluation of Gutiérrez's work can be found in the diverse collection edited by Marc H. Ellis and Otto Maduro, *The Future of Liberation Theology* (1989). For the most detailed discussion of the criticisms of liberation theologies of Gutiérrez and others, see Arthur F. McGovern, *Liberation Theology and Its Critics: Toward an Assessment* (1989).

CHARLES HARTSHORNE
1897–

Life and Career

Charles Hartshorne, along with Alfred North Whitehead, has been the chief influence on the movement known as "process theology." Although he has thereby had a strong impact on Christian theology, it might be asked whether Hartshorne himself belongs in a handbook of Christian theologians: Besides being a *philosopher*, he has not even portrayed himself as a specifically *Christian* philosopher. However, his thought has been devoted primarily to that branch of philosophy traditionally known as "natural theology." Also, it would not be inaccurate to call his position a "Christian natural theology."

Although Hartshorne's thought is to be judged entirely in terms of philosophical criteria, it has been decisively shaped by Christian intuitions, as he himself recognizes. For example, he says that the firmest residue from his pious upbringing is "summed up in the phrase *Deus est caritas* [God is love], together with the two 'Great Commandments': total love for God and love for neighbor comparable to love for self." To that, he adds: "If there are central intuitive convictions back of my acceptance or rejection of philosophical doctrines, these may be the ones" (*Creative Synthesis and Philosophic Method [CS]*, 1970, p. xviii).

As is appropriate for a philosopher who stresses the degree to which our experience, in spite of its own creative self-determination, is shaped by a multitude of influences, Hartshorne's autobiographical reflections are largely devoted to the experiences and people that shaped his attitudes and beliefs. In these reflections, he always stresses his "pious upbringing." His father was an Episcopalian priest; his mother was the daughter of an Episcopalian priest. Both of his parents not only believed that God is love and that love for God and fellow creatures sums up Christian ethics; they also lived out these beliefs, making a religion of love attractive. "From childhood," Hartshorne says, "I learned to worship divine love" (*Omnipotence and Other Theological Mistakes [OT]*,1984, p. 14). Regarding the central principle of his philosophy—that "the love that 'moves the sun and the other stars'" is "the abstract principle of the cosmos as besouled and cherishing of all sentient actualities"—Hartshorne says: "I have believed in this, with temporary hesitations, almost as long as I can remember. This came from my pious upbringing" (*Existence and Actuality [EA]*, 1984, ed. Cobb and Gamwell, p. 77).

Sometimes Hartshorne refers to his upbringing as "pious but liberal," emphasizing that his father accepted evolution and rejected biblical infallibility. An important ingredient in this pious but liberal upbringing was the decision to send Charles to a boarding school for his high school years. The headmaster, an Episcopalian clergyman, accepted and taught evolutionary theory. Hartshorne, accordingly, grew up seeing science and religion as fully compatible.

His parents were, however, orthodox with regard to Christology and beliefs about immortality, and in these areas differences arose. Reading Matthew Arnold's *Literature and Dogma* at about age seventeen led Hartshorne to reject the resurrection and the supernaturalistic interpretation of Jesus. More generally, Hartshorne says, reading this book broke his "dogmatic slumber": "Any religious belief I could henceforth accept would have to be a philosophical one, with reasons that I could grasp as convincing" (*The Philosophy of Charles Hartshorne [PCH]*, 1991, ed. Hahn, p. 14).

The loss of his Christian orthodoxy, however, did not leave young Hartshorne completely bereft of religion, because a religious sensibility of another type had been developing. Due in part to the fact that he grew up (first near Pittsburgh, then near Philadelphia) and went to high school in rural areas, he developed a Wordsworthian feeling for nature. Spending many hours in the woods by himself, Hartshorne focused on Kit Carson and Daniel Boone as two of his heroes. Hartshorne's first vocational plan resulted from this love of nature, in conjunction with a life-changing event in his second year of high school: Upon awakening from an appendectomy for which he had been given ether, he had vivid visual experiences of landscapes, which led to the desire to become a poet. He read as well as wrote much poetry for the next eight years, being especially influenced by Wordsworth and Shelley.

Another crucial event, at age fifteen or sixteen, was the discovery of *Emerson's Essays*. Besides listing Emerson as one of the "mystical poets" who reinforced his feeling for nature (*PCH*, p. 640), Hartshorne calls Emerson his "first philosophical hero" (*EA*, p. 12), saying that after reading his book he decided to "trust reason to the end" (*The Logic of Perfection and Other Essays in Neoclassical Metaphysics [LP]*, 1962, p. viii). Hartshorne's love for philosophical prose would eventually win out over his desire to become a poet, but it would never extinguish his love for nature. When in 1962 Hartshorne was invited to go birding all day by Edgar Kinkaid, the great field naturalist, Kinkaid's aunt suggested that Professor Hartshorne might not want to spend all day with birds. Hartshorne's response: "Philosophy all day long might well be too much, but not wild nature" (*The Darkness and the Light [DL]*,1990, p. 298). Hartshorne's study of ornithology, which began in high school after he discovered a book on birdsong, enabled his love of nature to become concrete and scientific and eventually resulted in his 1973 book, *Born to Sing.*

Hartshorne's first two years of college were at Haverford, where he began thinking about his religious ideas philosophically. The decisive influence on him was the Quaker philosophical mystic Rufus Jones, who started Hartshorne "on the consideration of the meaning of Christian or Judaeo-Christian love" (*OT*, 1984, p. 107). Under Jones, Hartshorne read *The Problem of Christianity,* by Josiah Royce, who became Hartshorne's "second philosophical hero" (*EA*, 1984, p. 12). His life was changed by Royce's chapter on "Community," which draws on Paul's statement that we are "members one of another," and which saved him from the doctrine of enlightened self-interest as our highest ethical motivation (*PCH*, 1991, p. 14). Also important was Jones' contention that mysticism is a matter of degree, so that all people are aware of God to some extent. Jones, furthermore, had his students read Tolstoy, whose writings persuaded Hartshorne to become a pacifist (*DL*, 1990, pp. 120-21). Although this stance did not long survive, it probably influenced his decision, once Wilson had announced America's entry into the World War, to volunteer as an orderly in an army medical corps in France. This decision, besides allowing Hartshorne to continue his studies and to avoid killing, also led to further decisive experiences.

One night while lying on deck under the stars during the Atlantic crossing, and after reading a novel by H. G. Wells that suggests a notion of a finite deity (*DL*, p. 126), Hartshorne had "close to a mystical experience" while thinking about God. Wells's view that God is the supermind of humanity, not the spirit of the cosmos as a whole, seemed to be based on a mind-matter dualism separating the human mind from the rest of nature. Hartshorne briefly accepted this view, until his next quasi-mystical experience, perhaps the most decisive one of his life.

One day during his stay in France, while looking at a beautiful landscape, he suddenly saw "into the life of things," gaining a sense of all of nature as alive and expressive of feelings (*EA*, p. 167). Recalling Santayana's definition of beauty as "objectified pleasure," he rejected the view that pleasure arises as a purely subjective feeling, which is then *projected* onto the experienced objects. Pleasure is, rather, "*given as in the object*. . . . Nature comes to us as constituted by feelings" (*PCH*, p. 17). Hartshorne would later describe his experience as a "phenomenological testing of the idea of mere *unfeeling yet directly given* objects of perception," resulting in the conclusion that no such objects are given (*PCH*, p. 691). He now had a basis in immediate experience for the view of nature suggested by the Romantic poets. With regard to God, this meant that, "if God is, as Wells says, the spirit or supermind of humanity, God may be the supermind of inanimate nature (so-called) as well" (*PCH*, p. 18). The rest of his career would involve developing this twofold idea of God as the soul of a universe constituted by feelings.

After his stint in the medical corps, Hartshorne transferred to Harvard, which was amply suited to help shape his developing philosophy. Hartshorne's rejection of materialism and dualism was reinforced by L. T. Troland, a psychologist who had adopted the panpsychism of the founder of psychophysics, Gustav Fechner. Under R. B. Perry, he studied William James, whose "Dilemma of Determinism" ended Hartshorne's flirtation with psychological determinism (*PCH,* p. 38). The implications of genuine freedom for theology were laid out by W. E. Hocking, who, rejecting divine immutability, portrayed the future as open even for God (*EA,* 1984, p. xv; *PCH,* 1991, p. 21). The two logicians, H. M. Sheffer and C. I. Lewis, from whom Hartshorne took the most courses, shaped his determination to bring logical precision into the philosophy of religion.

After four years at Harvard, the latter two as a doctoral student, Hartshorne received a fellowship to spend two years in Europe. Although still taking classes for credit, he wrote his dissertation in little more than a month, during which he experienced the "greatest rush of ideas" in his life (*DL,* 1990, pp. 174, 364). In this study, "An Outline and Defense of the Argument for the Unity of Being in the Absolute or Divine Good," he developed his panpsychist alternative to dualism and materialism, showing how this view allowed all things to be in God. Prominent are the two philosophers in whom Hartshorne had specialized, Plato and Spinoza, both of whom regarded the universe as the body of God.

In his stay in Europe, during which Hartshorne concentrated on the problem of sensation, he attended lectures primarily by Husserl and Heidegger. Given Hartshorne's experience in France, through which he had come to see sensation as a form of feeling, he was especially critical of Husserl's phenomenology, because of its dualism between feeling and sensation (*PCH,* p. 23).

The Influence of Whitehead

Upon returning to the States in 1925, Hartshorne became an instructor and research fellow at Harvard. His assignments, besides teaching, were to edit the papers of Charles Sanders Peirce and to serve as a teaching assistant for Alfred North Whitehead, who had just been appointed to the philosophy faculty. "By sheer luck," says Hartshorne, "I was to be intensively exposed, virtually simultaneously, to the thought of perhaps the two greatest philosophical geniuses who ever worked primarily in this country" (*PCH,* p. 24). They both reinforced Hartshorne's panpsychism, and from their combined influence he was led to think of "spontaneity" (Peirce) or "creativity" (Whitehead) as all-pervasive.

It was, however, primarily Whitehead's version of panpsychism that he adopted, thanks to its temporal atomicity and its revolutionary doctrine of "prehension," which Hartshorne considers "one of the greatest intellectual discoveries ever made" (*EA,* p. 124). The doctrine of temporal atomicity holds that enduring individuals, such as electrons, atoms, cells, and minds, are not the ultimate units of the world, but are composed of momentary events, each of which prehends its predecessor as well as other prior events. This prehension is a *sympathetic feeling of the feelings* of the prior experiences. Although the new experience, having its own creative power, is not completely determined by the influences it receives from these prior experiences, it is largely constituted out of these sympathetic feelings of prior feelings.

This doctrine has provided Hartshorne the basis for portraying love as the clue to existence. Fundamentally, Hartshorne has stressed, love is sympathy—feeling the feelings *of* the other *with* the other. The view that the enduring self is not simply a self-identical substance through time, being instead a temporal *society* of occasions of experience each of which is largely constituted by its sympathetic feelings of prior events, has given Hartshorne a philosophical basis for regarding his favorite Pauline statement, that we are "members one of another," as rather literally true (*OT*, 1984, p. 106).

This doctrine means that we are created out of our loves. We do not first have a self, which may then enter into loving relations. "It is our loves that make us anything worth mentioning" (*OT*, p. 108). Our strongest loves, at least initially, are for our bodily cells: Our sympathetic prehensions of their feelings result in pains and pleasures. We also identify deeply with the feelings of our own prior occasions of experience, so deeply that we tend to take this identification for sheer identity. But if our identity with our own past, as well as with our body, is only a relative identity rather than a strict one, then what we usually call "self-interest" is already a form of altruism, genuine sympathy for the welfare of others.

Recognition of this fact provides, in turn, the basis for making sense of the second Great Commandment. The usual view, according to which the self is an enduring substance, makes loving my neighbor *as* myself impossible in principle, because my relation to my self is one of sheer identity and my relation to my neighbor is one of sheer nonidentity. It thereby promotes a doctrine of egoism, according to which we can truly love only ourselves (*LP*, 1962, pp. 16-18). Accordingly, this "traditional interpretation of 'person' betrays the Gospel ideal" (*OT*, p. 107). The social view of the person, by contrast, explains self-love in terms of altruism, thereby showing that we really can, in principle, love other people in the same way that we love ourselves (*CS*, 1970, p. 191). The importance for Hartshorne of this ethical implication of the social view is revealed in his statement that, on this ground alone, he would not give it up "without the most rigorous proofs of its erroneousness" (*CS*, p. 198).

Besides explaining enduring individuality, the idea of prehension, as the feeling of prior feelings, accounts for causality (thereby overcoming Hume's problem), time, space, memory, perception, the subject-object relation, the mind-body relation, and the God-world relation. Nine apparently fundamental categories have been reduced to *one!* Hartshorne refers to this achievement as "the most powerful metaphysical generalization ever accomplished" and "a feat comparable to Einstein's" (*CS*, pp. 107, 92). Although Hartshorne correctly calls Whitehead the "greatest single creator" of this generalization, it is Hartshorne who has called attention to its importance. In any case, it is the power of the concept of prehension to make sense of all these categories, showing sympathy or love to be the clue to cosmology and epistemology as well as to religion and ethics (*CS*, 1970, p. xviii), that has enabled Hartshorne to flesh out his early intuition that love is the key to existence.

Science and Panpsychism

After three years as an instructor at Harvard, Hartshorne joined the philosophy department at the University of Chicago, where he would work out the distinctive emphases of his philosophy. At Chicago, Hartshorne also held a joint appointment with the Divinity School for more than a decade. Various encounters at the University, in conjunction with his prior ideas, shaped the direction his writing took. A most important encounter was that with Dorothy Cooper, a musician, who became his wife. Hartshorne attributes his first book, *The Philosophy and Psychology of Sensation,* to her influence, along with the fact that he had been asked to teach aesthetics (*DL*, 1990, p. 22). In this book he worked out, in relation to the science of psychology, his phenomenological argument that nature as directly intuited is given as feelings, along with his panpsychist argument that we can have a positive conception of "matter" only by conceiving it as consisting in lowly forms of feeling. Physics, accordingly, would be the most primitive branch of comparative psychology.

Hartshorne's panpsychism, which had already been supported by several eminent scientists (Fechner, Troland, Peirce, and Whitehead), received further reinforcement from the man who became his best friend at Chicago and whom he calls "the finest scientific mind I have ever known intimately," the evolutionary biologist Sewell Wright (*DL*, p. 327; *PCH*, 1991, p. 31). His friendship with Wright arose after he was included as the one philosopher in the scientific "X Club," to which Hartshorne belonged for twenty-five years and which gave him a firsthand acquaintance with scientific thinking. In his next book, *Beyond Humanism,* he argues that in various ways—for example, by showing that the inanimate objects of sensory perception are pseudo-unities, not genuine individuals; by showing that the objects of perception with which we do *not* sympathize are only indirectly, not directly, intuited; and by pointing to indeterminism in the elementary constituents of nature—science supports panpsychism and thereby "a companionable nature" (*Beyond Humanism [BH],* 1937, pp. 146, 196, 314, 316). We can now "see nature as the pervasively animate and sentient affair Wordsworth (also Shelley) and prescientific peoples saw it as being," Hartshorne says. "That science no longer stands in the way of so doing," he adds, "is a cultural fact the learned world has scarcely begun to take in" (*DL*, p. 378).

Panentheism and the Existence of God

This view of a nature that can be loved was articulated not in opposition to, but in support of, a theistic worldview. Hartshorne's argument is that humanism—the idea that the proper object of religious devotion is "humanity considered in its noblest aspirations and capacities" (*BH*, 1937, p. 2)—must give way to "the intellectual, aesthetic, and moral love of nature as the body of God, in all parts having some degree, however slight, of kinship with ourselves, and as a whole immeasurably superior to us, and hence worthy of our highest reverence" (*BH*, p. 5). In that book and his next, *Man's Vision of God*, Hartshorne calls his position *pantheism*, even while attributing freedom to both God and to creatures. In an epilogue to the latter book, however, Hartshorne points out that *panentheism* is a better term, because "it distinguishes God from the 'all' and yet makes him include all" (*Man's Vision of God [MVG]*, 1947, p. 348).

The key to Hartshorne's panentheism and thereby his theology as a whole, to which all his experience and thought had been leading, is the use of the mind-body relation, understood panpsychistically, as the basic analogue for thinking of the God-world relation. Unlike dualism and materialism, panpsychism makes the mind-body relation intelligible: "[C]ells can influence our human experiences because they have feelings that we can feel. To deal with the influences of human experience upon cells, one turns this around. *We* have feelings that *cells* can feel" (*LP*, 1962, p. 229). This relation can then be used as the analogue for the God-world relation: The universe is the body of God, and God is the mind or soul of the universe. Because all creatures have feelings, they can all feel God, who, as the "highest level of feeling" (*DL*, 1990, p. 375), feels their feelings in return. We can thereby understand how God can influence all creatures, including subatomic entities, so as to account for the basic laws of nature as well as human ideals, and how God can in turn know the world, and thereby include it—which is the meaning of panentheism.

The mind-body analogy, furthermore, is the only adequate one, Hartshorne insists, for understanding the idea that love constitutes the very nature of God. Although traditional Christian theologians have used the word "love" in describing the divine nature, "They emptied it of its most essential kernel, the element of sympathy, or the feeling of others' feelings" (*OT*, 1984, p. 29). A notable reason for this has been the tendency to understand perceptual knowledge in terms of sensory perception. The objects of such perception, being outside the body, are perceived only very indirectly. Using this type of perception as the analogue for divine perceptual knowledge of the world resulted in the idea that God could know the creatures without sympathizing with them. One consequence was the monstrous picture of God as enjoying, or at least indifferently observing, the sufferings of sinners in hell (*PCH*, 1991, p. 662; *CS*, 1970, p. 263).

As omnipresent, however, God is supposed to be immediately related to all creatures. We have this kind of immediate relation to our bodily members. In this relation, knowledge is sympathy, because in prehending our bodily members, we feel *their* feelings. This is most obvious in pain (or pleasure), in which we feel pain (or pleasure) because we are sympathetically feeling the pains (or enjoyments) of our bodily cells. (That this is also true in sensation, albeit less obviously, was the burden of Hartshorne's first book.) Our bodily members, however, are the only "others" with whom we necessarily sympathize. Accordingly, most of our knowledge of others can be devoid of love, because our bodies are very fragmentary portions of reality, so that most "others" are outside them and thereby beyond the range of our direct, sympathetic intuition. "But suppose all 'others' were within the body, as its members; then, since the need of the body is for the flourishing of its own parts or members, bodily desire and altruism would be coincident" (*Reality As Social Process [RSP]*, 1953, p. 141). If God is the soul of the universe, so that God directly prehends all creatures, the necessary goodness of God, meaning God's love for all creatures and desire to promote their welfare, follows naturally (*PCH*, 1991, p. 623).

The mind-body analogy also lies behind Hartshorne's two main reasons for believing in the existence of God: the twofold need for a cosmic source of order and for an everlasting recipient and preserver of value. That these are his two main reasons can be obscured by the fact that Hartshorne has developed several other arguments for God's existence, including the ontological argument, to which he has devoted two books, leading some interpreters to regard it as his main argument. He has clearly stated, however, that he has "not used this argument as *the* way, or even as, by itself, a very good way, to justify belief in God" (*EA*, 1984, p. 126), and that the arguments from order and value are the two primary ones (*PCH*, p. 665).

The argument from order to an Orderer depends in part on the fact that, in Hartshorne's panpsychism, the ultimate units of nature have an element of creativity or spontaneity: "Accepting creativity as ultimate category, how is cosmic order possible without a supreme form of creativity, a divine form, to persuade the lesser forms to conform to the minimal requirements of a viable universe?" (*PCH*, p. 665). We have some insight into how a soul of the universe could account for its order in our own experience:

> Why is it that my cells to a certain extent respond to my wishes or decisions? I am like a little deity in the mind-body system. . . . In this sense deity is the analogically ideal case of what we are as animals. Our conscious feeling or thought is superior to that of our cells; therefore they are somewhat obedient to our imperatives. We persuade them. In Whitehead's Platonic scheme this is what God does to all subjects.
> (*PCH*, p. 649; cf. *CS*, 1970, pp. 284-85)

The mind-brain analogy provides a basis for understanding not only divine ordering, but also divine creating, because "experiences exercise a creative influence upon the development of brain cells" (*OT*, 1984, p. 60). This analogy does not, to be sure, provide a basis for conceiving of creation *ex nihilo*. But Hartshorne has no interest in supporting that view, in part precisely because we have no analogies for it (*OT*, p. 58) and in part because it results in an insoluble problem of evil.

The problem of evil, of course, has been one of the main reasons for *denying* that the world's order points to a Divine Orderer. That problem resulted from the traditional concept of divine omnipotence, according to which God has "the power to determine every detail of what happens in the world" (*OT*, p. 11). Of this concept of omnipotence, which he also calls "the *tyrant* ideal of power," Hartshorne says: "No worse falsehood was ever perpetrated" (*OT*, pp. 11, 18). God has perfect power, in the sense of the *highest conceivable* form of power, but this cannot be the power completely to determine the actions of other individuals, because to be an "individual" is to have some power or freedom of one's own (*CS*, 1970, p. 30). Unlike many theologians, Hartshorne does not limit this explanation to evils caused by human beings: Not only human individuals but individuals as such necessarily have some degree of freedom or creativity. This view "enables us to get rid of the monstrous question, why would a loving God torture (punish or discipline) us with the ills from which we suffer?" (*PCH*, 1991, p. 676). This solution to the problem of evil, Hartshorne stresses, does not mean a "limitation" on God's power, because that way of putting it suggests that God's power, defined as not all-determining, "fails to measure up to some genuine ideal." His point, instead, is that "omnipotence as usually conceived is a false or indeed absurd ideal" (*OT*, p. 17). That is, the concept of an individual who could fully determine the actions of other individuals is a self-contradictory concept (*MVG*, 1947, p. 30; *Divine Relativity [DR]*, 1948, p. 138). The world's evils, accordingly, do not contradict the idea that the world's order points to a Divine Orderer.

Hartshorne's other main basis for believing in God is that, without God's everlasting experience to which we can contribute and from which we can derive a standard of value, there would be no supreme aim around which our lives could be rationally oriented (*CS*, p. 287; *PCH*, p. 665). In part the issue here is the need for an all-inclusive beneficiary: We presuppose that it is better to relieve the suffering of two or more persons than of only one, and yet, because good is always good *for* someone, this would be unintelligible apart from an all-inclusive Someone who experiences the greater good (*CS*, p. 289). The other part of the issue is that of immortality: Promoting my own good cannot provide an ultimate meaning for my life, given the fact that I will die. Even living for others is finally inadequate, because this "social immortality," assuming that it is limited to our influences upon other creatures, will also be limited in duration. The answer to these problems might seem to be personal immortality. But literal everlasting life, which would make us as infinite as God is in one respect, is not possible for creatures; existence forevermore, like omnipresence and necessary existence, can be predicated only of God (*OT*, 1984, pp. 35-36). The importance of this argument to Hartshorne has evidently contributed to his hostility to the idea of life after death, the distinction of which from everlasting life he generally blurs (*OT*, pp. 4, 47-49). In any case, serving God in the sense of contributing to the divine experience, primarily by contributing to the good of fellow creatures, is the only inclusive aim that can withstand examination.

Although it may sound like merely an argument for why we should *wish* that God exists, not for believing that God really does exist, Hartshorne's basic argument here seems to be that, because we all finally presuppose that life has meaning (*A Natural Theology [NT]*, p. 47), and because this presupposition can be true only if God as immortalizer of all our achievements really exists, we all, down deep, believe in God thus conceived. Just as the argument from order draws on the mind's ordering of its body as analogue, this argument from value draws upon the mind's inclusive experience of the multitude of bodily experiences. Both sides are reflected in Hartshorne's statement that "there must . . . be some highest level of feeling from which all the other forms receive directives by which their conflicts are kept within limits, also by which the others can add up to a significant totality" (*DL*, 1990, p. 375).

Contributionism and the Nature of God

This idea is of such overwhelming importance to Hartshorne that he speaks of his "religion of contributionism," according to which: "We contribute our feelings to others, and above all to the Universal Recipient of feeling, the One 'to Whom all hearts are open'" (*DL*, p. 379, quoting his favorite line from the Anglican prayerbook). This religion of contributionism is Hartshorne's way of explicating the Great Commandment, that we love God with all our being. Because of his panentheistic view of the God-world relation, this commandment is not in tension with that to love our neighbors as ourselves, because (Hartshorne says, with an allusion to Matthew 25) we should love all creatures, both ourselves and others, as valuable to God (*OT*, p. 107).

Most of Hartshorne's philosophical theology can, in fact, be understood as his attempt to overcome what he sees as the four main obstacles to this religion of contributionism. Three of these have already been discussed: atheism due to the idea that there are no valid arguments for God; atheism based on the problem of evil created by the conventional view of divine power; and the idea of our souls as immortal, which leads us to think in terms of God's everlasting contributions to us instead of ours to God (*Wisdom as Moderation*, 1987, pp. 85-86). The fourth obstacle to a religion of contributionism is the idea of divine independence or impassibility, according to which God *cannot* receive value from the world.

Hartshorne's rejection of this idea, which is implicit in the foregoing, has been at the center of his thought about the nature of God.

Early in his career at Chicago, Hartshorne was advised by his dean, fellow philosopher Richard McKeon, that he would be unwise to put his energy into philosophy of religion, because it was "less exact" than the other branches of philosophy. It was, however, "precisely this lack of precision" that Hartshorne saw a chance to correct (*PCH*, 1991, p. 34). The main form this concern has taken is that of trying to work out an exhaustive list of the logically possible ideas of perfection, or God. One way to argue for a position is to eliminate the other possible positions. But such arguments are usually invalid, because *all* the other possible views are seldom considered. Many discussions, for example, ask simply whether a "perfect" being exists, taking perfect to be equatable with "absolute." The choices are thereby reduced to two: atheism or classical theism. However, given the elementary distinction between *all* and *some*, the options are not limited to "absolute in all respects" and "absolute in no respects." There is also the possibility of being "absolute in some respects, relative in others." That this third, usually neglected, option is the truth about God is reflected in the title of Hartshorne's book *The Divine Relativity* and one of its chapter titles, "God as Absolute, Yet Related to All."

Hartshorne's doctrine of divine relativity involves a version of *dipolar theism*, according to which God has a relative as well as an absolute aspect or pole. Although several prior thinkers had implied such a distinction (as shown by *Philosophers Speak of God*, which Hartshorne co-wrote), Whitehead was the first leading thinker explicitly to enunciate such a position, while it was left to Hartshorne to work out this position more fully (*PCH*, p. 41). In Hartshorne's version, God is conceived by analogy with the mind as an enduring individual, meaning a personally ordered society of occasions of experience. The two poles, which Hartshorne calls God's "concrete states" and "abstract essence," are analogous, respectively, to the successive concrete experiences of a person and the abstract character that is exemplified in each such experience. Such a distinction means rejecting the traditional idea of divine "simplicity," according to which there is no difference between God's essence and actuality.

The rejection of that notion of simplicity involves, in turn, a rejection of the idea that God is nontemporal and thereby independent in all respects. On the one hand, the abstract essence of God is completely necessary, eternal, independent, absolute, impassible, and unchanging. Although it is analogous to a human being's abstract character, the divine essence is qualitatively different in the sense that it exists necessarily and eternally, cannot be affected by anything, and does not change in any sense. Because this aspect of God exemplifies the attributes that classical theism ascribed to God as a whole, Hartshorne calls his position "neoclassical theism." The difference implied by the prefix "neo," however, is radical, because those attributes apply to a mere abstraction.

The concrete states of God, which are God as fully actual at any moment, are contingent, temporal, dependent, relative, and changing. The distinction can be illustrated in terms of the distinction between God's *omniscience,* as an abstract characteristic that is exemplified by every divine state or experience, and God's concrete *knowledge* in any such state. God's omniscience, as the capacity to know everything that is knowable at any particular time, is an eternal, necessary, absolute, unchanging characteristic of God, which does not depend upon anything. But God's concrete knowledge of the world is contingent, insofar as it is knowledge of contingent events, which might not have happened. This point presupposes, of course, the idea that worldly events involve an element of spontaneity, so that they are not completely determinable by God or even fully knowable in advance. Omniscience, accordingly, as the capacity to know everything knowable, does not involve knowledge of the future, beyond whatever abstract aspects of the future are already determined by present forces.

Although some interpreters have thought that this divine dipolarity means that God is perfect in some respects, imperfect in others, that is emphatically not Hartshorne's meaning. He has come to speak of "dual transcendence" to stress that the two aspects of God involve two ways of being uniquely excellent (*PCH,* 1991, p. 643). These two types of perfection involve two kinds of value, those for which a maximal realization is conceivable and those for which it is not (*MVG,* 1947, p. 36). For example, a maximal realization is possible with regard to the capacity for knowledge, because a being could conceivably know everything (then) knowable. There can be no maximal realization of concrete knowledge, however, because there will always be new things to know. Likewise, there can be a maximal case of goodness: a being whose decisions would be based on sympathetic concern for *all* beings whatsoever. However, there cannot, the traditional language of "perfect bliss" notwithstanding, be a maximal case of happiness: Further joys, derived from subsequent events, can always enrich any given state of happiness; and, had there been more joy in the world, less agony, the divine happiness would be greater.

The two kinds of perfection are called "absolute" and "relative." God's perfection with regard to those values for which a maximal realization is possible is absolute, meaning "unsurpassable." To say that divine perfection with regard to the other kind of values is "relative" does not mean that God somehow responded less well than God might have; that would be imperfection. Rather, the perfection is relative to a subsequent state of the divine existence. These relative perfections involve surpassability, but *only by God in a subsequent state.* With this distinction between two kinds of perfection, the second of which allows the world to contribute value to God, Hartshorne has overcome his "sharpest objection to classical theism," which is "its making God the giver of everything and recipient of nothing" (*PCH,* p. 672). His revision means that Hartshorne, unlike classical theists, can use the cross as a symbol for divine perfection—that is, for divine love as perfectly responsive to the feelings of all creatures, including their sufferings (*OT*, 1984, p. 124).

The full development of Hartshorne's doctrine of dual transcendence involves his "logic of ultimate contrasts," which he regards as "the real center of the system" (*PCH*, 1991, p. 630). The idea is that the most general concepts express ultimate contrasts such as necessity and contingency, absoluteness and relativity, independence and dependence, simplicity and complexity, infinity and finitude, timelessness and temporality, being and becoming. The first member of each pair, which alone was attributed to God by classical theism, applies in neoclassical theism to God as merely abstract. It was the onesidedness of classical theism, involving the "fallacy of misplaced concreteness" (*RSP*, 1953, p. 124), that prevented the God of the philosophers from also being the God of religion. Hartshorne's contention is that, by *beginning* with the religious idea of God as love, we can have a doctrine of God that is philosophically intelligible as well (*DR*, 1948, p. 1). The attribution of these contrasting terms, such as absoluteness and relativity, or eternality and temporality, does not entail paradoxes, because the two attributes apply to different aspects of God, which are not on the same level.

Because the most general concepts come in pairs, the basic issues about reality can be stated in terms of a limited number of options. For example, taking the contrast of necessity and contingency and applying it to God and the world, we can see that there are only sixteen possibilities. Counterintuitive implications eliminate fifteen of these, Hartshorne argues, leaving as the truth the view that God is necessary in some respects and contingent in others, and that the world is contingent in some respects and necessary in others. The necessity of the world refers not to our particular world, but only to some world or other. The same sixteen options obtain for any of the other contrasts, such as absoluteness and relativity. Hartshorne considers this discovery, which is most thoroughly spelled out in his latest book, *Points of View and Other Essays in Neoclassical Philosophy*, to be his most important contribution (*PCH*, p. 656).

Conclusion

Hartshorne left Chicago for the philosophy department at Emory University in 1955, then in 1962 went to the University of Texas at Austin, where he became Professor Emeritus in 1978, after which he and Dorothy decided to remain in Austin. At this writing, although Dorothy has recently died, Charles, nearly one hundred, is still going strong, having published seven books and many articles since 1978. The connection between his extensive writing and his religion of contributionism is brought out in a gloss on the scriptural idea that one's life should be a "reasonable, holy, and living sacrifice" to deity: Hartshorne says, "If I can inspire multitudes who will never see me in the flesh, then the incense I send up to God will continue to rise anew for many generations" (*LP*, 1962, pp. 257-58). Hartshorne's recent writing includes his replies in a volume of the *Library of Living Philosophers*, through which he has been recognized as one of the great philosophers of the twentieth century. The fact that his is a profoundly Christian philosophy, in which love provides the key to existence, makes this recognition a matter of some importance in the history of Christian theology.

David Ray Griffin

Selected Primary Works

1934   *The Philosophy and Psychology of Sensation.*
1937   *Beyond Humanism: Essays in the New Philosophy of Nature.*
1947   *Man's Vision of God and the Logic of Theism.*
1948   *The Divine Relativity: A Social Conception of God.*
1953   *Philosophers Speak of God*, with William L. Reese.
1953   *Reality as Social Process: Studies in Metaphysics and Religion.*
1962   *The Logic of Perfection and Other Essays in Neoclassical Metaphysics.*
1967   *A Natural Theology for Our Time.*
1970   *Creative Synthesis and Philosophic Method.*
1973   *Born to Sing.*
1984   *Omnipotence and Other Theological Mistakes.*
1987   *Wisdom as Moderation: A Philosophy of the Middle Way.*
1990   *The Darkness and the Light: A Philosopher Reflects Upon His Fortunate Career and Those Who Made It Possible.*

Points of View and Other Essays in Neoclassical Philosophy, with Muhammed Valady. (Pending)

Selected Secondary Sources

1984   *Existence and Actuality: Conversations with Charles Hartshorne*, ed. John B. Cobb, Jr., and Franklin I. Gamwell.
1991   *The Philosophy of Charles Hartshorne*, Library of Living Philosophers, vol. 20, ed. Lewis Edwin Hahn.

CARL F. H. HENRY
1913–

Life and Career

One striking phenomenon of the American religious scene in the latter half of the twentieth century has been evangelicalism's surge to prominence, and Carl F. H. Henry is widely recognized as its prime theologian. Born January 22, 1913, in New York City to a Lutheran father, Karl Henry, and a Roman Catholic mother, Johanna, Carl was baptized and confirmed an Episcopalian as a teenager, but soon dropped out of the church. By the age of twenty, he was the editor of a weekly newspaper on Long Island. A series of influences culminated in a three-hour conversation with a Christian layman, at the conclusion of which Henry prayed to receive Christ for salvation.

Enrolling at Wheaton College in Illinois, Henry was influenced by the thought of evangelical philosopher Gordon Haddon Clark, and he adopted Clark's emphasis upon logical consistency as the primary test of truth. Upon completion of his B.A. degree at Wheaton, Henry began study for an M.A. degree in the graduate school of that same institution and also for a B.D. degree at Northern Baptist Theological Seminary, receiving both degrees in 1941. He also served a student pastorate in Chicago and was ordained in 1941.

Henry added the Th.D. degree from Northern in 1942, and thereupon was appointed to the faculty. He also undertook graduate studies in philosophy at Boston University with Edgar Sheffield Brightman, receiving the Ph.D. in 1949. In 1947 he became part of the founding faculty of Fuller Theological Seminary in Pasadena, California. He served as founding editor of *Christianity Today* from 1956 until 1968. After three years as professor of theology at Eastern Baptist Theological Seminary, he has served in a number of institutions as visiting professor and as lecturer-at-large for World Vision. Early in his teaching and writing career, Henry spanned the fields of philosophy of religion, ethics (particularly ethical theory), and systematic theology, but more recently he has concentrated on systematic theology.

In his philosophically oriented writings, Henry focused on apologetics. With the exception of *Giving a Reason for Our Hope*, a transcription of questions and answers, his main work has been in the analysis and refutation of secular and liberal views. An important contribution was *Remaking the Modern Mind,* conceived as something of a response to John Herman Randall's *Making of the Modern Mind.* Many of his writings, however, include extensive treatments of these competitive views, as for example, his *God, Revelation, and Authority.* The refutation frequently consists of showing the internal contradictions of these competitive systems.

Among his ethically oriented writings, Henry's chief contribution was his *Christian Personal Ethics,* which involved an analysis of naturalistic, idealistic, and existentialist ethics, as well as an extensive development of Christian ethical theory, based especially on belief in a biblical revelation. A briefer treatment was his *Aspects of Christian Social Ethics.* Most of his treatment of substantive issues of ethics has appeared in editorials and other writings in *Christianity Today.* Throughout them, he has shown a strong conviction for conservative positions, arguing for objectivism over against all forms of subjectivism.

Henry's theology can be fully understood only in its historical setting. By the late 1930s, fundamentalism had clearly lost the fundamentalist-modernist controversy, in many cases withdrawing from large denominations and ceasing to be an influence on the American intellectual and cultural scene. Together with others such as Harold John Ockenga and Edward Carnell, Henry saw the shortcomings of fundamentalism as its anti-intellectualism, its neglect of the social dimensions of Christianity, and its separatism. They resolved to go back to the roots of evangelicalism and reinstate it to its nobler tradition, as "the new evangelicalism."

Although Henry has never written a complete systematic theology, his *God, Revelation, and Authority* (1976–1983) is an exhaustive treatment of the doctrine of Scripture and related issues and the doctrine of God. Other doctrines have been discussed with varying degrees of thoroughness in his different writings.

In many ways Henry's theology is located in the middle of the evangelical theological road, enabling him to serve as a spokesperson for evangelical theology. He is Calvinistic, but moderately so. He is noncharismatic, but not militantly so. He is nondispensational but not antidispensational. He is a Baptist, but not polemical toward non-Baptists. His stance on doctrinal issues is firm, but not rancorous. He has reserved his strongest criticism for various non-Christian philosophies, and secondarily for nonevangelical theologies. Henry has concentrated most of his writing on the doctrines of revelation and Scripture and the doctrine of God.

Revelation and Scripture

Henry's view of revelation grows out of his apologetic stance as a presuppositionalist. All reasoning, including scientific thought, begins with certain unproved assumptions, or presuppositions, basic axioms that cannot be antecedently proved but that can be indirectly verified by tracing out their implications, thus evaluating the resulting system. The inadequacy of all non-Christian philosophies is seen in the internal contradictions that eventually issue from them. The Christian world-view, on the other hand, begins with the presupposition of God as revealed in the Bible, the source from which all of the rest of theology derives (*God, Revelation, and Authority,* 1:215; hereafter, citations are by volume and page numbers only).

Special revelation must be understood as propositional (3:455-81). God has revealed, at least in part, God's own mind, giving us clear, rational knowledge, which is univocal, not merely analogical (4:117-18). This contrasts with the neoorthodox view of revelation, with its understanding of truth as personal encounter derived from the underlying existentialist view of reality, and consequently leading to untold difficulties. The revelation, according to Henry, consists not simply of the person of God, but of actual information about God's own self, and that report is true and objective (3:248-54).

God is the ultimate authority. The authority of God is known to all persons through nature, history, and the image of God within; but humans reject divine authority (4:12-13). God's special revelation is contained in the Bible. Henry has no hesitation about terming biblical religion authoritarian religion. "God commands and has the right to be obeyed, and the power also to punish the disobedient and reward the faithful. Behind God's will stands omnipotent power" (4:15). The Bible reports throughout a recognition of God's authority or right to command belief and action, and it attributes this authority as well to the writings of prophets and apostles. Jesus himself acknowledged the authority of the scriptures of his day. They witnessed to him, and beyond that, the apostles were given to supply the interpretation of the things that he said and did (4:36).

Modern theology has done much to dilute the authority of the Bible, both by subjecting it to other norms, such as human experience or some formal principle, and by allowing the destructive effects of various types of biblical criticism (4:41-67). Henry believes that these critical methodologies rest upon naturalistic presuppositions and, in the case of persons like Bultmann, outdated scientific assumptions.

Also important is the inspiration of Scripture, which Henry defines as "a supernatural influence upon divinely chosen prophets and apostles whereby the Spirit of God assures the truth and trustworthiness of their oral and written proclamation" (4:129). Although he does not here link inspiration to the question of the origin of the content or the divine revelation, he does so in his twelfth thesis, which begins the chapter: "The Holy Spirit superintends the communication of divine revelation, first as the inspirer and then as the illuminator and interpreter of the scripturally given Word of God" (4:129). Although this definition emphasizes the relationship of the Spirit to the writer, Henry is quite clear that "inspiration is primarily a statement about God's relationship to the Scripture, and only secondarily about the relationship of God to the writers" (4:143).

Henry clarifies his view of inspiration by defining it both negatively and positively. Negatively, by inspiration, the biblical-evangelical view denies both mechanical dictation and an inspiration consisting primarily of God's heightening the psychic powers or the creative energies of prophets and apostles (4:138-49). Positively, the biblical-evangelical view of inspiration means that the Scripture is inspired as an objective deposit of language; that it is consistent with the full humanity of the writers; that it did not render them humanly infallible in ordinary affairs of life; that it is limited to a small group of chosen messengers, not given to all humanity; that it involved communication of information beyond the usual reach of humans; that the ultimate author is God but in a fashion not inconsistent with actual recording by human beings; that all Scripture is inspired; and that this view is the historical view of all denominations, not some innovation (4:148-61).

Related to the issue of inspiration is the idea of inerrancy, which has been subject to considerable debate in recent evangelicalism. Unlike some who hold that inerrancy is merely implied by Scripture and its teaching, or even that it is adduced, not deduced or induced from the doctrine of inspiration, Henry finds it taught in the very words of Scripture (4:169). Recognizing the difficulties caused by specific historical references of the biblical text, he points to numerous instances in which the supposed difficulty has been resolved, or at least alleviated, though warning that premature attempts at absolute harmonization have led to ludicrous results. Only Scripture can tell us in what sense the Scripture is or must be free from error (4:172-75).

Henry also clarifies his understanding of inerrancy with a series of denials and affirmations. Negatively, inerrancy does not require modern technological precision in reporting or discussing statistics, measurements, genealogies, or cosmology; it does not require only nonmetaphorical or nonsymbolic language to convey truth; it does not require verbal exactitude in New Testament use of Old Testament passages; it does not render personal faith in Jesus Christ dispensable or a guarantee that evangelical orthodoxy will necessarily follow from adopting this doctrine (4:201-4). Positively, it refers not only to theological and ethical teachings, but also to historical and scientific teachings, insofar as they are part of the express message of Scripture; it inheres in the very words, propositions, or sentences of the Bible, not merely the thoughts or concepts of the writers; it applies, in the strict sense, only to the original manuscripts, but not precluding the use of amanuenses; and finally it is not to be attached to any version or translation of the Bible (4:205-10).

The Spirit is involved not only in the inspiration of Scripture but also in its interpretation. Steering a course between post-Reformation Protestant scholasticism and neoorthodoxy, Henry insists that we must resist stifling the Holy Spirit (4:275), but that the work of the Spirit is not a continuing revelation. That has been done, once and for all (4:276). The work of the Spirit is described in a number of places in Scripture, such as 1 Corinthians 2:10, John 14:26, and Philippians 3:10. The Spirit's work to the first recipients is that of revelation, but to those who come much later it is illumination of that previously revealed truth which it presupposes (4:275-76).

God

The doctrine of God has occupied a significant place in Henry's theology, since it, like the doctrine of revelation, has been such a key doctrine for the twentieth century. In contrast to the panentheistic theology of Tillich (5:46-47) or process theology, which sees God as changing in some respects (5:62-63), Henry insists that the God revealed in the Bible is the only living God, the source of whose life is within Godself and who is clearly distinguished from his creatures (5:66-67).

Henry rejects three traditional ways of identifying the divine attributes—negation, eminence, and causation—as well as the ways of intuition and dialectical divine-human encounter (5:84-98). Instead, he insists upon the way of objective divine revelation: "Propositional revelation is a divine communication to man of objective knowledge of the nature of God as he is, both in his eternal glory and in his relations to man" (5:98).

Unlike many orthodox theologians of the nineteenth century, Henry rejects the idea that "being is a substratum in which attributes adhere, an underlying substance that supports its qualities or predicates" (5:119). Rather, all of the attributes of God revealed in nature are to be identified with God's essence, being, nature, or substance, and with what Scripture refers to as the deity or divinity of God (5:127). He also rejects any attempt to make one attribute more basic than the others, feeling that such privileging inevitably leads to the depreciation of some of these attributes. All God's attributes have an absolute divine character, each involved in every other (5:135).

One issue that has been subject to considerable debate in our time is the use of "inclusive" language with respect to God. While asserting that the gender-linked terminology of "Father" and masculine pronouns with respect to God are not based upon any ontological maleness or femaleness in his being, Henry insists that the gender-linked references are not to be lightly dismissed. The masculine imagery, Henry believes, more adequately conveys what was involved in God's act of creation, for example (5:157-64).

Undertaking the thorny problem of the Trinity, Henry insists that the Trinity is not a logical contradiction, as if it were saying $3x = 1x$. Rather, it must be logically understood as more like $3x = 1y$ (5:165). In fact, the doctrine of the Trinity contributes significantly to resolving the ancient philosophical problem of the one and the many (5:168). His discussion of the Trinity tends to follow the traditional or received orthodox position on specific points.

Henry also undertakes the difficult question of divine decrees. What is at stake here is God's freedom (6:76). God is not bound by any necessity to the universe, humanity, or the church. God's decrees are not simply enacted within time, but go back into eternity (6:78). Ironically, modern secularism's rejection of predestination has not really led to human freedom. It has instead substituted various forms of determinism for this benevolent and provident divine plan (6:80). God's plan is a comprehensive and cohesive one in which "God foreordains the entire course of world and human events" (6:84).

Henry clearly holds to creation *ex nihilo* (6:120): God is the origin of all that is. He discusses at length the several attempted coordinations of the Genesis creation account and the scientific data, without really opting for any one of them. He says,

> The Christian can be truly open-minded about biological evolution as simply an explanatory model and should be able to test its claims objectively in relation to both empirical and scientific data. But what is precluded to the Christian is a naturalistic philosophy and theistic dogmatism that postulates, when the Bible is silent, how God must have acted in various details. (6:193)

Henry does, however, point out at considerable length the "crisis of evolutionary theory" (6:156-96).

Henry acknowledges that the question of who and what humanity is constitutes the main underlying point of the tension between theological and scientific discussion of origins (6:197). He is willing to leave open some of the issues, such as the timespan of Adam (6:226) and the possibility of humanlike forms living prior to the creation of humans (6:222). Certain issues, however, are nonnegotiable; for example, "The First Adam or man is a creation supernaturally made in the image of God, an historical being divinely fashioned from the dust of earth and rationally, morally, spiritually, genetically, and culturally different from any prior species of life. Irrespective of their disagreement over the antiquity or recency of Adam, all evangelical scholars insist on the special divine creation, historicity, distinctiveness and fall of Adam" (6:227).

God not only creates; God also *stays*. That is, God exercises providential care over creation, preserving it and guiding it to good ends (6:455-58). Even the thorny problem of evil must fall within the purview of God's providence. This problem cannot, however, be discussed apart from the question of the foundation and basis of moral good, which is the will of God (6:291-93). Relief from the most severe dimensions of the problem of evil is found in the fact of Satan's rebellion and the human fall and universal sinfulness as the source of evil; the assumption of evil's effects and the victory over them by Christ's death; the use by God of evil to accomplish higher ends; and the coming eschatological removal of all evil (6:304).

Other Doctrines

Although writing much less extensively on topics other than revelation and God, Henry has marked out his positions on other significant doctrines, taking standard evangelical views on such matters as the full deity of Christ, substitutionary atonement, and salvation, and taking a noncharismatic approach to the work of the Holy Spirit (6:370-401).

Henry rejects any form of understanding of the future life that would remove the biblical distinction between the saved and the lost. He rebuts the idea that Christ may be found within other religions, and he even objects to the idea of implicit faith (6:360-69). He finds any idea of a universal reconciliation or a second chance after death incompatible with the biblical revelation, as is also true of annihilation (6:505-11).

Millard J. Erickson

Selected Primary Works

1947   *The Uneasy Conscience of Modern Fundamentalism.*
1948   *Notes on the Doctrine of God.*
1948   *Remaking the Modern Mind.*
1949   *Giving a Reason for Our Hope.*
1957   *Christian Personal Ethics.*
1964   *Aspects of Christian Social Ethics.*
1971   *A Plea for Evangelical Demonstration.*
1976–1983 *God, Revelation, and Authority,* 6 vols.
1986   *Confessions of a Theologian.*

Selected Secondary Sources

1983   Bob E. Patterson, *Carl F. H. Henry.*
1990   R. Albert Mohler, Jr., "Carl F. H. Henry," in *Baptist Theologians,* ed. Timothy George and David S. Dockery, pp. 518-38.
1993   Richard A. Purdy, "Carl F. H. Henry," in *Handbook of Evangelical Theologians,* ed. Walter A. Elwell, pp. 260-75.

JOHN HARWOOD HICK
1922–

Life and Career

The author or editor of more than twenty books and over a hundred scholarly articles during a period of forty years, John Hick has written about a wide range of topics. His academic career illustrates his dual foci of philosophy and theology, although he is formally a philosopher of religion.

Born January 20, 1922, in Scarborough, England, Hick began his university education by studying law at University College, Hull. After a conversion to evangelical Christianity—having previously been only nominally a Christian—he enrolled at Edinburgh University to study philosophy with the goal of becoming a Presbyterian minister. His education, however, was interrupted by World War II, during which, as a conscientious objector, he served in the Friends' Ambulance Unit from 1942 to 1945. After completing his M.A. at Edinburgh in 1948, he earned a D.Phil. at Oxford University in 1950, followed by theological study at Westminster Theological College, Cambridge, from 1950 to 1953.

In 1953 he married Hazel Bowers and served as a Presbyterian minister in Northumberland, England, until 1956, when he received an academic appointment as assistant professor of philosophy at Cornell University in Ithaca, New York. In 1959 he became the Stuart Professor of Christian Philosophy at Princeton Theological Seminary, and in 1964 he returned to his native country to assume a position as lecturer in Divinity at Cambridge University. In 1967 he became the H. G. Wood Professor of Theology at the University of Birmingham in England, where he remained until 1980 when he returned to the United States to become the Danforth Professor of the Philosophy of Religion at the Claremont Graduate School in Claremont, California. He was named Professor Emeritus from Claremont in 1992 and returned to Birmingham as Fellow of the Institute for Advanced Research in the Humanities. His philosophical and theological work reveals a radical reinterpretation of almost the entire corpus of Christian doctrine.

God as Necessary Being

Accepting the contemporary view among many analytical philosophers that the idea of a logically necessary being is meaningless, Hick argued in several articles in the 1960s that the "necessary" existence of God presupposed by the biblical writers, and explicitly formulated by Anselm, is not a logical necessity, but an ontological, or factual, necessity. That God has necessary existence means that God is "sheer, ultimate, unconditioned reality, without beginning or end." From this point of view Hick criticized the new versions of the ontological argument proposed by Hartshorne, Malcolm, and Plantinga. In the 1960s he developed the idea of eschatological verification, affirming that the total structure of the universe as envisaged by the religions differs from the way in which it is envisaged in naturalistic philosophies in ways that will begin to be evident to us after bodily death.

Religious Epistemology

Hick's philosophical defense of God's factual existence is a foundation for his religious epistemology. This in turn is tied to an anthropology that describes humanity as naturally religious. In archaic societies, "naturally religious" was understood as providing a determining cause; however, in more individualistic cultures it is understood only as an inclining cause. Although Hick acknowledges that there is no adequate definition of religion that has characterized individualistic cultures, his working definition is ". . . an understanding of the universe, together with an appropriate way of living within it, which involves reference beyond the natural world to God or gods or to the Absolute or to a transcendent order or process" *(God and the Universe of Faiths,* 1973). In his view, in its most funda-mental sense religious faith is not a matter of believing theological propositions, but it is the uncompelled interpretative element within religious experience. This understanding arises from the view (derived from Wittgenstein's concept of "seeing-as") that all conscious experience consists in experiencing-as in terms of concepts.

The religious mind may experience events *as* moments of encounter with God, or experience life *as* being lived in God's presence, or experience *samsara* (ordinary human life) *as* nirvana. In such ways the religious believer experiences the world differently from the nonbeliever. In response to the objection that claims about religious knowledge are subjective and gratuitous, Hick contends that all experi-encing is an experiencing-as that includes interpretation. Hick is a "religious empiricist" who relies upon religious experience as the foundation for theological claims about God. He argues that religious awareness, though it has a unique referent (God or the Transcendent), is structurally similar to all cognitive-experi-ential knowledge. Thus he argues that religious belief is reasonable and that by virtue of one's experience, the believer, in the absence of specific reasons to the contrary, is justified in his or her belief.

Theodicy

In *Evil and the God of Love* (1966), Hick chronicles the history of theological arguments that attempt to resolve the implicit contradiction between belief in an all-powerful and all-loving God and the experience of evil and suffering. He rejects the principal Western theodicy devised by Augustine, according to which, in God's perfect creation evil has no ontological status but is merely a privation of good, taking shape as sin in humans' exercising their free will. And the resultant Fall necessitated atonement by Christ the redeemer. In contrast to this Augustinian model, Hick grounds his theodicy historically in the writings of Irenaeus, who, on the basis of Genesis 1:26, distinguished between the "image" and the "likeness" of God in the creation of humanity. The "image" is the raw material that has the potential for further development into the "likeness," which, revealed in Christ, is the eventual goal of the process of maturation guided by the Holy Spirit. This two-stage process moves humans from creatures of God to children of God. The path to eternal life is one of continual moral development through personal effort and free choices in overcoming temptation whereby persons progress toward perfection.

In Irenaeus's schema, the Fall is not a past event but refers to our existence as imperfect and immature creatures. The world, with its moral challenges and natural obstructions, was never a paradise, but is an appropriate environment for the first stage of a process of development toward perfection. This teleological structure concentrates on an ultimate future union with God instead of longing for a past state of perfection now lost. Humans were created in a "fallen" state that is at an epistemic distance from God. In this situation humans do not know God in a coercive manner but have the cognitive freedom to become aware of God.

Expanding his theology beyond what is warranted in Irenaeus, Hick describes the experience of moving from raw material to the finished product as a soul-making process. This world—with its objective structure that includes contingency and unpredictability, the possibilities of pain and disaster, and the opportunity for experiencing beauty and joy—constitutes an appropriate environment for the soul-making process. Recognizing the unequal distribution of pain and suffering in the world and the varying life spans in which persons pursue the likeness of God, and recognizing the different degrees of success and failure that persons achieve in the soul-making process, Hick includes an eschatological dimension in his thought. Rejecting the theory of death and judgment according to which no new actions or further development of character can occur after death, he conjectures that there is continued soul-making after death during which moral and spiritual growth can continue. The nature of this postmortem existence is treated in his later book on death and immortality.

Death and Eternal Life

In 1976 Hick published *Death and Eternal Life*, a study on death and the question of immortality. Based in part on research in India and Sri Lanka, where Hick obtained a firsthand view of conceptions of afterlife in Indian religions (particularly Hinduism and Buddhism), this book examines the possibility of a global theology of death. The study investigates Eastern and Western eschatologies and "pareschatologies," a term that he introduces to identify the period between bodily death and the final eschatological state.

He explores the idea that religions, at their core, share a common conception of the ultimate human destiny. Religions conceive of the human as comprising a trinity of body-soul-spirit, in the Western view, and body-mind-*atman* in the Eastern. Recognizing the unsatisfactoriness of ordinary human existence as persons experience it, religions seek to help them overcome the ego through various methods of prayer, meditation, right thinking, right action, self-denial, and so forth, with the hope of achieving or receiving a transformed existence. This existence can begin in this life, and it can be seen in the saints of the different religions. Progress toward it continues beyond this life, Hick proposes, in a possible pareschatology, a series of lives in different "worlds" through which persons move toward the unknown ultimate eschatological state.

In chronicling this path from death to life, Hick documents anthropological, philosophical, psychological, and sociological evidence in addition to theological arguments for postmortem existence. The specific ways in which religions describe the afterlife differ significantly, as do the particulars of their understanding of the status of the "person," "soul," or "spirit" after death, ranging from reincarnation to a state of abeyance awaiting final judgment. Although each religion has its own pareschatological expectations, Hick holds that each teaches that the ultimate state lies beyond our present powers of imagination.

Christology

In his early work *Faith and Knowledge* (1957), Hick presupposes traditional Christology as proclaimed at the councils of Nicea and Chalcedon. In 1977 he published an essay outlining his emerging Christology in a controversial book that he also edited, *The Myth of God Incarnate*. By the time of the publication of his full-length treatise on the subject, *The Metaphor of God Incarnate* (1993), his Christology had changed radically. The change was from the orthodox understanding of Jesus Christ as literally God incarnate, to the understanding of him as a man who was so open and responsive to God that God was able to act through him and was thus "incarnate" in his life. Here "incarnate" is a metaphor, as in the declarations "Great men and women incarnate the spirit of their age" or "Washington incarnated the American spirit of independence." Hick holds that the historical Jesus did not lay claim to deity, and he rejects the dogma of Jesus' two natures and the concept of atonement that Jesus died for the sins of humankind. He argues that the doctrine of Jesus' two natures, divine and human, has never been given any intelligible meaning.

Hick suggests, however, that the metaphor of divine incarnation can be expanded in three ways. First, insofar as Jesus was doing God's will, God was acting through him on earth and was in this sense "incarnate" in Jesus' life. Second, insofar as Jesus was doing God's will he "incarnated" the ideal of human life lived in openness and response to God. Third, insofar as Jesus lived a life of self-giving love, he "incarnated" a love that is a finite reflection of the divine love. The truth of the metaphor of incarnation depends upon its being literally true that Jesus lived in obedient response to God and that he lived a life of unselfish love. In developing this view of "incarnation" as metaphor, Hick criticizes both the two-natures and the kenotic theories, including the two-minds conception. Instead he argues, not unlike Friedrich Schleiermacher in the nineteenth century, that Jesus had such a heightened consciousness of God that he lived to an extraordinary extent in the presence of God and that his will was in accord with God's will.

In suggesting that the language of incarnation is metaphorical rather than metaphysical, Hick opens the way to understanding other outstanding religious figures as also having "incarnated" the ideal of human life lived as a response to the divine Reality. Thus Jesus is not considered the sole historical intersection between God and humanity. No single figure can uniquely claim this. Rather, the Real has manifested itself in a number of historical figures who have been exemplars of the proper relationship to the Divine, some of whom (Gautama and Jesus being two examples) have become central to great religious traditions.

Hick reformulated his Christology partly in response to the dilemma he perceived in Christianity's relation to other religions. If only Christians are saved, and Christianity is the religion of less than one-fourth of the world's population, then it would appear that the vast majority of people are condemned. This seems unfair in a God who loves all creatures. If one argues that persons following other faith traditions are nevertheless saved by Christ, one sacrifices Christian uniqueness with regard to salvation. When one understands the incarnation in metaphysical rather than metaphorical ways, one implies that of all the religions on the earth God has personally founded only one. However, by viewing Christ as a genuine, but not the only, path to the Real, Hick suggests the salvific parity of other religious figures and traditions. The controversial implication of this theology is that it nullifies the claim of Christ's exclusivity and absoluteness.

Philosophy of Religious Pluralism

It is likely that in the twenty-first century Hick will best be remembered as the most significant advocate of a philosophy of religious pluralism that challenges the soteriological hegemony of Christianity. Since the time of the New Testament, Christianity has considered itself the exclusive mediator of salvation. The belief that Christ is the Savior and that Christianity represents Christ is found in many places in the New Testament, including Peter's claim that there is "no other name" by which persons may be saved than the name of Christ. And in the Gospel of John Jesus is portrayed as unique, saying, "I am the Way, and the Truth, and the Life. No one comes to the Father except through me." Reflecting on such passages, Christian theologians have supported this exclusive claim from the time of Cyprian's assertion that "outside the church there is no salvation" to today's evangelical pronouncements that insist on conversion to Christ in order to be saved.

As early as 1973, Hick published his vision of salvation-liberation-fulfillment among the world's religions in *God and the Universe of Faiths*, but his most sophisticated development of this idea is found in his 1986–87 Gifford Lectures, published as *An Interpretation of Religion* (1989). Hick describes a threefold typology in regard to the Christian understanding of salvation: *exclusivism*, which claims that only those who explicitly believe in Christ are eligible for salvation; *inclusivism*, which holds that all who are saved are saved by the merits of the death and resurrection Christ, whether they are Christians or not; and *pluralism*, which allows that persons may be brought to ultimate salvation-liberation-fulfillment within their own religious tradition, without reference (in the case of other religions) to Christ or Christianity.

In a way analogous to Ptolemaic astronomy, in which the earth was considered the center of the universe, the Christian theological tradition has insisted that Christ is the center of the soteriological process for all people. All salvation comes through Christ, whether men and women are conscious of the source or not. Hick proposes a "Copernican revolution" in theology, in which the center of the salvific process is not Christ, but God, or in more universal and less Western language, the Real. Like Copernicus' heliocentric theory, which changed cosmology thereafter, this change from a christocentric view of salvation to a schema that places the Real or Transcendent at the center is a paradigm shift that systemically affects Christian theology.

The Real is posited as the transcendent ground of all religious traditions. The Real was manifested to various prophets and peoples during the "Axial Period" (a term borrowed from Karl Jaspers), which coincided with the development of civilizations. These geographically and culturally separate revelations, or illuminations, were codified into religions. Thus religious awareness emanated from one source, the Real, but was pluriform in its manifestation. In itself, the Real remains beyond the range of our human conceptualities. Like Aquinas, Hick argues that things are known according to the mode of the knower. Following Kant, he distinguishes between the thing in itself (noumenon) and the thing as it appears to human consciousness (phenomenon). Thus the Real in itself is unknown to us, but the Real is known in its varying manifestations, as personal or impersonal, to prophets and seers in various places. The various conflicting "truth claims" of the different religions, such as the Real as triune or unitary, are claims about different manifestations, or appearances, of the Real to humanity.

The adherents of various religious traditions, Hick believes, are striving for the ultimate goal of a "transformation of human existence from self-centeredness to Reality-centeredness"—that is, they are seeking salvation-liberation-fulfillment. This transformation is named and described differently within different traditions, for example, as "moksha" in Hinduism, "salvation" in Christianity, or "nirvana" in Buddhism. Each tradition invites its disciples to follow a path that leads to ultimate fulfillment, absolute knowledge, or a state of perfection. The traditions are authentic representatives of the Real to the degree that each effectively brings about this transformation; and in Hick's view, the various "great world religions" have been more or less equally successful in achieving this transformation to salvation-liberation-fulfillment.

Chester Gillis

Selected Primary Works

1957   *Faith and Knowledge.*
1963   *Philosophy of Religion.*
1966   *Evil and the God of Love.*
1973   *God and the Universe of Faiths.*
1976   *Death and Eternal Life.*
1980   *God Has Many Names.*
1985   *Problems of Religious Pluralism.*
1989   *An Interpretation of Religion.*
1993   *The Metaphor of God Incarnate.*

Selected Secondary Sources

1987   Gavin D'Costa, *John Hick's Theology of Religions.*
1989   Chester Gillis, *A Question of Final Belief: John Hick's Pluralistic Theory of Salvation.*
1990   Gregory H. Carruthers, *The Uniqueness of Jesus Christ in the Theocentric Model of the Christian Theology of World Religions: An Elaboration and Evaluation of the Position of John Hick.*

1990   Paul Badham, ed., *A John Hick Reader.*
1991   Harold Hewitt, ed., *Problems in the Philosophy of Religion: Critical Studies of the Work of John Hick.*
1993   R. Douglas Geivett, *Evil and the Evidence for God: The Challenge of John Hick's Theodicy.*

PETER C. HODGSON
1934–

Peter Crafts Hodgson was born on February 26, 1934, in Oak Park, Illinois. He received his bachelor's degree in history from Princeton University in 1956 and went on to Yale Divinity School, receiving his Bachelor of Divinity in 1959, the M.A. a year later, and the Ph.D. in 1963 for work on the nineteenth-century German thinker, Ferdinand Christian Baur. In 1963 Hodgson began to teach at Trinity University in San Antonio, Texas, moving on to Vanderbilt University Divinity School in Nashville, Tennessee, in 1965, where he remains.

His first book, *The Formation of Historical Theology* (1966), a study of F. C. Baur's theological work, established the first of the two directions that Hodgson's work has taken ever since: attention to nineteenth-century historical and philosophical thought, later to flower in extensive and highly regarded Hegelian scholarship. His second lifelong interest has been in constructive theology. In the ten years following the publication of the Baur volume, Hodgson wrote three contributions to modern theology. His Christology, *Jesus—Word and Presence* (1971), was followed by a book on black liberation, *Children of Freedom* (1974), and shortly thereafter by a substantial foray into the then new field of liberation theology, *New Birth of Freedom: A Theology of Bondage and Liberation* (1976). During the same period Hodgson maintained his concern for historical studies by editing *Ferdinand Christian Baur: On the Writing of Church History* (1968) and the George Eliot translation of David Friedrich Strauss's massive work, *The Life of Jesus Critically Examined* (1972).

If the first ten years of Hodgson's tenure at Vanderbilt were largely marked by early attempts to come to terms with contemporary theological movements, the decade following was dramatically different. In the late 1970s and early 1980s he became deeply involved in an international venture to edit and publish Hegel's *Lectures on the Philosophy of Religion.* Working with Walter Jaeschke of the Hegel-Archiv in Bochum, in what was then West Germany, and with a team of English translators, Hodgson had primary responsibility for the English-language edition. The three volumes appeared between 1984 and 1987. The size and complexity of this project would have daunted many, since it required disentangling the confusion and conflation of the previous "editions" of the *Lectures,* based as they largely were on student notes of the four times the lectures were offered in Berlin. During this phase he also produced, in collaboration with Robert H. King, *Christian Theology: An Introduction to Its Traditions and Tasks* (1982), and *Readings in Christian Theology* (1985).

In the last decade, Hodgson has emerged as an important American theologian in our time. In 1988 he reappeared as a constructive theologian with a brief work on the church, *Revisioning the Church: Ecclesial Freedom in the New Paradigm.* The systematic complexity of his theological vision became clearer in *God in History: Shapes of Freedom* (1989), but was only fully presented to the public in *Winds of the Spirit: A Constructive Christian Theology* (1994). His forthcoming works include a cotranslation of another important Hegelian text and a volume on Hegel as a theologian. Never far from the historical concerns of nineteenth-century theology and Hegel in particular, and always aware of the complexities of life on what he has called "the bridge between modernity and postmodernity," Hodgson in his latest constructive work has shown the lasting value of his submersion in Hegel.

The smooth intellectual biography in the preceding paragraphs is only part of the story, of course. The different phases in this life of theological reflection have been occasioned, for Hodgson as for many others, by personal experiences and historical events and movements. So, for example, his theological education at Yale and the expectations of the Presbytery of Baltimore, into which he was ordained shortly thereafter, did not sit comfortably together. Although committed to the Reformed tradition, Hodgson wanted to carry Reformed theology in new directions. Later, at Vanderbilt, political engagements, coteaching a course with a black activist, and events on sabbatical leave in California, precipitated what he calls his "second theological education." But it may equally have been the mixed reception for *Children of Freedom* and *New Birth of Freedom,* two books written during that time, that led him into a kind of theological identity crisis. Whatever the reasons, Hodgson became aware of the importance of the themes of bondage and liberation, and his consequent need to write about them, while also being increasingly cognizant that as a middle-class white male his experiential credentials to do so were suspect.

Turning back to Hegel, Hodgson found "a holistic vision that is at once ontologically radical and socially transformative" (*Winds of the Spirit,* p. 336). Although this may not be how most of those who encounter Hegel in philosophy courses, or who attempt to read Hegel for themselves, would characterize his effect upon them, it was true for Hodgson. It had also to some degree been true, Hodgson claims, for Barth and Tillich before him. Looked at in this light, the return to Hegel led shortly thereafter to the chief theological works of his maturity. Here Hodgson consciously employs Hegel in a synthesis of the best of contemporary liberation and feminist perspectives with what would once have been called "ontotheology," but that he prefers to call a "theanthropocosmic" or, better, a "cosmotheandric" revisioning of theology.

With the benefit of hindsight, one can see even in Hodgson's earliest work some of the interests that have remained with him. For example, in his book on Baur, *The Formation of Historical Theology*, Hodgson responds approvingly to Baur's belief in the importance of "historical-critical theology" and in his insistence on the concomitant importance of the faith-stance of the theologian. A faithful commitment remains in the works of Hodgson's maturity as a distinctive characteristic, and one that for all his postmodern awareness allows us still to see him as something of a "church-theologian." In *Jesus—Word and Presence,* an extended dialogue with an almost exclusively German cohort of theologians, Hodgson offers hints of a later interest in Hegelian trinitarian thought that appear in a discussion of Jesus' death as the death of God (1971, pp. 212-14). He also provides a presciently programmatic utterance, "a theology of revolution requires a theology of freedom" (p. 190), that emerges with full force in *Children of Freedom* and *New Birth of Freedom,* and one that has continued to be a structural imperative for his thought. In these two works from the 1970s, Hodgson applies the commitment to freedom to the situation of black Americans and then utilizes it in the construction of a systematic theology. But the whole venture remained just a little too cerebral, for all the discussion of liberation and praxis. And so he turned back to Hegel.

Today, Peter Hodgson must be characterized as a "postmodern" theologian, despite the confusion that this term can create. To call him postmodern is not just to recognize that he stands beyond both a narrow confessionalism and a Christian imperialism, that he is deeply committed to the insights and advances of liberation theology and the contributions of feminist thought to theological thinking, or even that an awareness of contemporary science informs his thinking. More important than these commitments, central as they are, is a conviction that *because of* the new awareness of social and political oppression, human interrelatedness with the natural world, and the realities of religious pluralism, the idea of God must be thoroughly revisioned. Hodgson recognizes the problems of the anthropomorphic God in an anthropocentric universe, but unlike some other postmoderns, he is concerned to preserve the characteristic of personhood. "Person," of course, appears to be an anthropomorphic category. The challenge Hodgson accepts is to find a way to talk convincingly about God as person in a nonanthropomorphic way. "Our sense at the end of the twentieth century," says Hodgson in the opening chapter of *Winds of the Spirit,* "is that life is at risk and that God is involved in this risk" (1994, p. 8).

Hodgson is able to accomplish the task he has set himself, to retain a relational understanding of God in a postmodern world in which subjectivity has itself become suspect, because of his deep roots in the thought of Hegel that his earlier

231

editorial work nurtured. The complexity of the schema for history that he unfolds in *God in History* and the even more complex account of God, world, and spirit in *Winds of the Spirit* directly reflect Hegel's understanding of reality. Like Hegel, a simple idea behind the complexity draws together the divine, the natural, and the human. This vision of reality—from the idea of God "in self" to the fully realized notion of God as creator, redeemer, and sanctifier, and including the mental and physical structures of the human and the nonhuman, and indeed the social institutions of human history—displays the same internal triadic structure of self-relatedness.

We can obtain a clearer understanding of Hodgson and the nature of his project by looking more closely at the opening chapter of *God in History*. There, Hodgson distances himself from two types of postmodern religious thought. The first type is that of the "postliberal" thinkers of the so-called Yale school, whom Hodgson and many others see as motivated by an antipathy toward the heritage of modernity. The second type is its opposite, a celebration of modernity's demise not because it allows the reemergence of premodern religious sensibilities, but because it allows a preference for the aesthetic over the ethical, and a descent into "the nihilistic play of the elite" (1989, p. 41). In contrast to these approaches to theology, Hodgson wants to transcend both forms of postmodern anxiety by a pragmatic recourse to transformative, emancipatory praxis and the experience of empowerment that it occasions. But, and here Hodgson shows his own postmodern side, "A way of thinking must be found that is noninterventionist, nonmiraculous, and noncausal in its understanding of divine providence, nonlinear in its teleology, and nonsuprahistorical in its eschatology" (pp. 42-43).

Hodgson's proposal, first worked out fully in *God in History* and both modified and presented more digestibly in *Winds of the Spirit*, is that God and history are "coconstitutive categories." This phrase indicates a sense in which God is in history as "shapes of freedom," and in which history is in God, as the finite is always encompassed by the infinite. The more formal analysis of the earlier work is made tangible in *Winds of the Spirit* when Hodgson sees history as a bush, "not linear or unidirectional" but growing "into an incredible diversity." Moreover, this history is not merely human but also "the history of nature" (1994, p. 315). God's presence as spirit in this history is as "the transformer of futility into freedom," though God's presence is also a self-transformation through natural processes and through the emancipatory praxis of human beings.

Hodgson's Hegelian vision sees no opposition or separation between God and the world. Indeed, a mutual dependence exists, though the dependence of the world on God is more decisive. The world is the "other" of God (or, in the phrase that Hodgson borrows from his Vanderbilt colleague Sallie McFague, "God's body"), through which God passes in order to become more fully realized as spirit. God is trinitarian or triadic, expressed now not in the language of three "persons," but as three "figurations" or figures in relation to one another. Dismissing the traditional trinitarian formulation of Father, Son, and Spirit as "patriarchal and hierarchical,"

Hodgson sees God as the "ultimate and inclusive event of communication," which can be named and described in three complementary ways. "Cognitively and existentially," God is to be seen as "the relational process of identity, difference, and mediation that constitutes spiritual personal being as such and is intrinsic to the life process." This is balanced with a more personal and praxis-oriented model of God as "One," "love," and "freedom," or "the One who loves in freedom." Finally, in symbolic and figural terms, God is expressed as "God, World, and Spirit," (*Winds,* 1994, p. 153).

The Hegelian "dialectic of identity, difference, and mediation" from which Hodgson proceeds is enriched in the development of the "triune figuration," but it remains in the self-similarity of parts and whole. Both the human person and the figure of Christ are to be interpreted along the same dialectical, personal, and symbolic lines as the self of God. Within the world as the other of God, the human person exhibits personal, interpersonal, and transpersonal dimensions or structures of freedom, corresponding to the three spheres of the human: self, world, and God/Spirit (*Winds,* p. 201). Christ, or more correctly in Hodgson's language the "Christ-gestalt," is constituted by Jesus of Nazareth as the personification of the Wisdom of God, the *basileia* ("reign" of God) as the community of freedom, and the power of the cross as empowering love.

Hodgson, it will be remembered, utilizes a fundamentally Hegelian dialectic of the divine life as self-identity (subjective), othering of self (objective), and return to self (absolute). Although the same moments are present in a human life, however, the third moment cannot be a simple return to self, but must be an opening out to elements of the transcendent within the world. Personal freedom is the realm of bodily integrity and responsible action; interpersonal freedom divides into intersubjectivity and ethical life within the social world. And the transpersonal must go beyond the self-other polarity to what Hodgson calls, in language reminiscent of Karl Rahner, "a relationship to the eternal horizon of being, which discloses itself as God, as sacred presence and Holy Spirit, in and through specific communities of redemption" (*Winds,* p. 204). The human relationship to God is more one of "radical openness" than Schleiermacher's "radical dependence" (p. 208).

Human sinfulness begins in a tragic vulnerability, says Hodgson, manifested either in internal anxiety or external temptation, which leads through self-deceit to both personal and interpersonal structures of sin. Identified as idolatry, flight, and alienation, the structures of sin have the effect of putting human freedom into bondage of the will, which in turn "assumes certain cosmic and social objectifications that demonically intensify sin, converting it into structures of evil, which correspond to the structures of sin" (*Winds,* p. 215). In this thoroughly Pauline analysis, Hodgson enumerates the structures of sin: "law" as the psychological, political, and social structures through which we can rationalize our guilt; "death" as bondage to our own mortality; and subordination to the "heavenly powers" of ideology and the "earthly" powers of social injustice.

233

Redemption from this sinfulness must be offered; but how does it occur? Classically, the answer is through Christ's atoning death. Against the background both of postmodern challenges to the role of Jesus and also the classical christological dilemmas, Hodgson proposes to "loosen up" the connection between Jesus and Christ, to move "beyond the impasse of the two natures doctrine," and to show how the incarnation is redemptive while avoiding recourse to classical notions of atonement. The "assumption that it is primarily God who is injured by sin," says Hodgson, is not credible today (*Winds*, 1994, p. 249).

Hodgson's proposal is that God is present in the world as "specific shapes or patterns of praxis." God shapes human praxis by offering a normative shape or paradigm of transformative praxis, what Hodgson calls the "Christ-gestalt." This gestalt is incarnate in Jesus but not exhausted by Jesus, and it empowers the distinctive being of human being. Thus, the more human Jesus is, the more he is the incarnation of the Christ-gestalt. But the work of Jesus issues in the communal freedom of the *basileia*, "a new kind of communal existence," in which all "false provincialisms" are broken down, and it comes to its culmination in the death of Jesus, in which the power of nothingness is converted from "absolute negation" into "dialectical negation," that is, into being the possibility of the advent of the new. And the new emerges in the risen Christ, whose body we are. Indeed, Jesus' resurrection is "a specific instance of a universal human promise and possibility." Invoking the name of Karl Rahner, Hodgson argues that in death we become pancosmic rather than acosmic, coextensive with the world. And returning to Hegel he adds the twist: Since "God contains within the divine life both the individual self and the world in which the risen self is newly embodied," we can say that "in rising into the world, we also rise into God" (*Winds*, p. 274).

The Spirit of God for Hodgson is the presence of God in that which is not God, thus God embodied in the world, both the natural and the human world. Again challenging traditional trinitarian thinking, Hodgson argues that the Spirit of God is an "emergent person," an actualization of what can only have been a potentiality in God without the creation of the world. Spirit is thus a "social subject," emerging in nature as a cosmic eros and meeting its spiritual other in human spirit. Pursuing this highly original line of thought, Hodgson comes to the conclusion that the Spirit proceeds not from the Father and the Son, but from God and the world, but that the world from which the Spirit proceeds is "a world in process of being shaped and configured by Christ" (p. 291). At the same time, the world grows into Christ through the power of the Spirit. Finally, the Spirit proceeds not only from Christ, but from a plurality of "saving shapes of divine presence." And so the Spirit takes up its two tasks, the liberation of the world from alienation into freedom, and the perfection of God in the enfolding of the world back into the divine life.

Paul Lakeland

Selected Bibliography

Works Written

1966   *The Formation of Historical Theology: A Study of Ferdinand Christian Baur.*

1971   *Jesus—Word and Presence: An Essay in Christology.*

1974   *Children of Freedom: Black Liberation in Christian Perspective.*

1976   *New Birth of Freedom: A Theology of Bondage and Liberation.*

1988   *Revisioning the Church: Ecclesial Freedom in the New Paradigm.*

1989   *God in History: Shapes of Freedom.*

1994   *Winds of the Spirit: A Constructive Christian Theology.*

Works Edited

1968   *Ferdinand Christian Baur: On the Writing of Church History.*

1972   David Friedrich Strauss, *The Life of Jesus Critically Examined,* trans. George Eliot.

1982   *Christian Theology: An Introduction to Its Traditions and Tasks,* with Robert H. King.

1985   *Readings in Christian Theology,* with Robert H. King.

1984–1987 G. W. F. Hegel, *Lectures on the Philosophy of Religion,* 3 vols.

ADA MARIA ISASI-DIAZ
1943–

Life and Career

Although she has written extensively on solidarity, Hispanic women, and feminism, Ada Maria Isasi-Diaz has also made significant contributions in Mujerista theology by pursuing justice and peace particularly within the community of United States Hispanic women as they struggle for self-determination. The dynamic character of their lived experience prompts Hispanic women to conceive another theological reality, one that entails a liberative practice that Isasi-Diaz calls mujerista theology.

Born in Cuba in 1943, Isasi-Diaz graduated from a private American high school, Merici Academy in Havana, Cuba. She received her B.A. from the College of New Rochelle, New York, a master's degree in Medieval History from the New York State University at Brockport, and the M.Div., M.Phil., and Ph.D. from the Union Theological Seminary in New York City. For eight years, she lived as an Ursuline Sister, and in the 1990s she joined the faculty at Drew University as a professor of ethics.

Throughout her life, Isasi-Diaz has recognized several formative communities, events, and ideas. The greatest influence in her life has been her family, whose home was disrupted by the political climate of Cuba. Since 1960, she has lived in the United States, and yet she has always felt, in her own words, "politically exiled." She credits her family and religious affiliation as influencing her character development to include a commitment to service, honor, and the dignity of the person. Isasi-Diaz's theology has also been shaped by her experience of having worked with the poor in Lima, Peru. In three years there she underwent a profound conversion to an activist orientation. She credits the poor of Lima with teaching her what it means to be a Christian, learning from them the value of popular religion, and becoming involved, on their behalf, in action to promote justice. For her, solidarity with the poor entails living out one's beliefs and knowing that if the poor are not free, then no one is free.

A third formative influence in her life has been feminism. The oppression of women in the church and the oppression of women by the church made her a feminist. Yet as a mujerista theologian, Isasi-Diaz challenges Anglo feminist scholars. "*Feministas hispanas* have been consistently marginalized within the Anglo feminist community," she writes, "because of our critique of its ethnic/racial prejudice and its lack of class analysis" (*En la Lucha*, 1993, p. 3). Anglo feminists provide a critique from their own lived experiences, from their own priorities and values, and through their own class privilege. Thus Anglo feminists may fail to recognize the ways that they participate in the oppression of other women through their failure to include the voices and experiences of many, diverse women.

In her interaction with participants in the Anglo feminist scholarly community, Isasi-Diaz calls them to hear the voices of their mujerista sisters, as well as the voices and experiences of all other "different" women, and to allow these voices and experiences to *change* them.

> An analysis of gender oppression has to take into consideration the fact that sex-role socialization differs according to historical time and culture. This results in different conceptions of what is appropriate gender behavior and, therefore, in different experiences of gender oppression. This is precisely the reason why Hispanic women resist the conception of sexism as defined by Anglo women. Of course there are similarities, but there are also differences created by different understandings of gender behavior and by the role played by racist/ethnic prejudice.
>
> (*En la Lucha*, p. 24)

Because the maintenance of family life is deeply important to Hispanic women, Isasi-Diaz rejects the Anglo feminist critique of family as being a leading source of women's oppression.

Mujerista Theology in Context

Isasi-Diaz identifies her work as Hispanic women's liberation theology. She looks at the experience of the Hispanic woman through a liberative lens that she honed and focused during her time in Latin America. Reflecting upon the lived experience of Hispanic women within the dominant culture of North America, Isasi-Diaz searches for themes of liberation: as women, as women of a particular culture, and as women of faith within a patriarchal church. She develops her mujerista theology as one that focuses on the liberation and empowerment of Hispanic women, providing them with a platform for expressing their voices, which have not been easily heard, understood, or appreciated. Yet these voices of Hispanic women and their lived experience form the context of mujerista theology and its praxis (reflective action) that moves beyond equality to liberation.

One of Isasi-Diaz's distinct contributions is that she connects the academic and the Latina worlds. A professionally trained theologian whose experience includes university teaching, Isasi-Diaz insists on the validity and importance of Latinas' religious understanding and practices for the academic theological world and for churches themselves. In doing her theology, Isasi-Diaz searches for the life-giving elements of religious understanding that people carry in their hearts and minds in order to survive. When she asks persons what "God" means or who God is, she wants to hear not abstract answers but responses from people reflecting their daily struggle. Pointing to the long-standing tradition of the *sensus fidelium,* which acknowledges that persons composing the large body of the faithful are given credit for understanding God's action in their lives through their anointing by the Holy Spirit in baptism, Isasi-Diaz repeatedly urges theologians and the church in general to listen to the voices of those who are not usually heard within theological circles, and to gain from them a privileged and unique interpretative perspective on theology.

A proper understanding of the *sensus fidelium* must recognize the variety of meanings that the word "experience" can bear in the phrase "Christian experience." One must not confuse his or her own lived experience with that of another person or culture, for even the use of the word "experience" varies among different cultures. In Spanish, for example, the word *experiencia* is not equivalent to the English term *experience.* Rather, the Spanish word *la realidad* (translated as "reality") more nearly renders the English understanding of *experience.* One's experience is really a synthesis of experiences that are part and parcel of one's whole world in a given moment, entailing a psychosocial history that affects one whether one is conscious of it or not. Many factors in the lives of any two women may be the same, but their historical and cultural context and therefore their interpretative framework may be different. As a mujerista theologian, then, Isasi-Diaz presents *la realidad* of Hispanic women—a set of experiences that contrast with those of the dominant culture—in order to influence and inform that dominant culture.

Methodology

Isasi-Diaz begins the articulation of her theology with the task of naming herself. The act of naming oneself is the most powerful act that one can undertake. A name does not merely identify "the named" person, object, idea, or action, but it provides a conceptual framework, a point of reference. When others have named us "for us," we have been silenced and marginalized, becoming "invisibly invisible," a phrase that Isasi-Diaz frequently uses. To name oneself is to exercise a healthy power, to be an active agent in history and in the process of liberation. With mujerista theology, Hispanic women struggle to articulate who we are and to liberate ourselves, not merely as individuals but as members of a larger community.

The methodology that Isasi-Diaz highlights is twofold: doing ethnography, or gathering information by interviewing women about their lived-out experience; and providing meta-ethnography, or analyzing information and weaving together the common scenes that emerge. The process of listening to Hispanic women talk about their lived experience affords them respect and recognizes the dignity of their experience. Such a process of listening is, in fact, liberating, especially for members of a group who have suffered oppression from both within and outside their culture.

A key element of their experience is their ethnicity, which, in general, is the multiplicity and complexity of beliefs and traditions held in common by a group of people of a particular linguistic, historical, religious, racial, or cultural origin. Other significant issues and orientations related to ethnicity include *mestizaje*, survival, and socioeconomic reality.

The first of these related elements is *mestizaje*, a term that Virgil Elizondo uses to refer to the genetic mixing of sixteenth-century Spaniards and Amerindians that generated a new people, a new culture, and a new spirituality. For many in the United States the *mestizaje* continues, not just biologically, but psychologically. The *mestizaje* carry within them two distinct, sometimes conflicting worldviews that mingle differing religious practices.

The second element of ethnicity for these women is the struggle to survive. Isasi-Diaz indicates that survival for the Hispanic women whom she has interviewed is a matter of struggling for their very being. For Hispanic women, doing theology is a human activity rooted in the everyday experience of life and then reflecting upon it. Hispanic women are engaged in a quest for ultimate meaning that emerges out of their physical and cultural struggle for survival. Their quest for meaning pursues the power that they need in order to decide their destiny, and it is a constant struggle against oppression and "anthropological poverty," which results from threats to one's physical survival and to the achievement and expression of one's personhood. In other words, the quest for survival is a struggle to maintain self-identity and self-determination. It is a struggle for bread and celebration. And in the Hispanic culture survival is also intrinsically linked with the survival of the community, and the survival of the children in the community.

Isasi-Diaz pointedly discusses the fact that the survival of Hispanic women is directly related to the fate of the Hispanic culture, which includes the symbolic system for generating, expressing, and maintaining meaning and values. When one is preoccupied with the survival of the culture, one will be particularly concerned about anything that threatens families and communities. Consequently, maintaining family is an intrinsic part of the struggle.

A third element connected to the ethnicity of Hispanic women is their experience of socioeconomic oppression, which, Isasi-Diaz maintains, is the key to grounding mujerista theology in the daily lives of Hispanic women. Yet in the same breath she argues that this oppression does not define Hispanic women but that it provides the defining character or event in their struggle to overcome that oppression and to survive. Isasi-Diaz does not reduce survival to a socioeconomic function; she asserts, instead, that the struggle to survive is also cultural: "The cultural struggle is a struggle for life" (*En la Lucha*, 1993, p. 27). For Isasi-Diaz, culture, which guides relationships, provides social structures, and gives one a sense of rootedness in life, is a social reality involving thoughts, feelings, and religious understandings and practices formed in each member of the community since birth.

Ethics and Theology

Mujerista theology seeks to aid in the growth of the moral agency of Hispanic women. Isasi-Diaz begins her work as an ethicist in the lived experience of women, inviting them to reflect upon their experience in light of sacred scripture and the living tradition of the church—that is, living in faithful community with one another. She places heavy emphasis on women trusting their own life experiences. Isasi-Diaz sees women as their own moral agents motivated through the "primacy of conscience," which needs to be protected from those who would deny or deprive Hispanic women of their *consciencia*.

According to Isasi-Diaz, conscience is an intrinsic, inseparable part of being human. Using a holistic approach, she defines it not as a moral compass but as the ability of each person to be the

> agent of her own life, able to determine, and be responsible for, who she is and what she does. An important consequence of focusing on the person as agent instead of on conscience as an isolated part of the individual, is that ethical considerations are not confined just to decision making but rather focus on the self who continues from decision through decision and who actually affirms and creates one's moral self in and through those decisions.

Continuing her exploration of conscience, Isasi-Diaz reinforces its dynamic character and clarifies its connection to "moral consciousness."

> In *Mujerista* moral theology conscience is understood as the agent herself as morally conscious, and since consciousness is constitutive of the human person as agent, the formation of moral consciousness has to do with enabling the process of conscientization of the person. Conscientization is an integral part of the understanding of and the struggle for liberation and involves: (1) recognizing the distinction between nature in its inevitability and culture in its changeability; (2) unmasking the myths that allow oppressors to dominate society by blurring this distinction; and (3) exploring the alternatives available under the fundamental "generative theme" of our epoch, namely, liberation. (*En la Lucha*, p. 155)

Conscientization is rooted in action, in reflecting upon and learning from actions that guide further actions. Conscientization is rooted in the lived experience and growth of the individual person within community.

Isasi-Diaz rejects any attempt to separate systematic and dogmatic theology from moral theology and ethics, claiming that there is an intrinsic unity among them. Since the source of mujerista theology is the lived experience of Hispanic women, one of its central preoccupations is to enable personal moral agency. "In *Mujerista* theology ethics is always understood as social ethics. This follows from the centrality of community in our culture and from the fact that *mujeristas* denounce the split between the personal and the political as a false dichotomy used often to oppress Hispanic Women" (*En la Lucha*, 1993, p. 5). Because theology must necessarily be rooted in the concrete lives of believers, any separation of beliefs from practice provokes a false dichotomy.

Contributions to the Theological Community

Isasi-Diaz wants the work of mujerista theology to influence the larger theological community and the church as a whole. For such influence to be exercised, however, there must be an end to the "invisible invisibility" of Hispanic women that belittles the uniqueness of the Hispanic woman and that even questions the reality of her uniqueness. Isasi-Diaz rejects any attempt to assimilate Hispanic women into the church that excludes their diversity and specificity. Mujerista theology will allow the unique richness of the Hispanic woman's experience to enrich the faith journey of the larger community. Second, true engagement will need to occur. Hispanic women need to be taken seriously in theological conversation.

For engagement to happen, difference has to be recognized as an asset and not as a problem. Difference is truly an asset because those who are different are mirrors in which "you can see yourselves as no other mirror shows you. . . . Engagement requires that we enter into each other's worldview as much as possible and help others open up to new perspectives" (*En la Lucha*, p. 189).

Mujerista theology will affect the greater community when Hispanic women are willing to analyze power and to claim it. An important piece in the work of liberation, power can move women beyond oppression and manipulation, beyond "having to adapt to the way meetings are conducted, groups are run, businesses operate, U.S.A. society is organized, and the public interest is administered" (*En la Lucha*, p. 190), and toward equal participation and dynamic interaction within community. This power is transformative, working within the relationships of community and in solidarity.

As Isasi-Diaz points out throughout her writings, the work of mujerista theology is the total liberation of humanity, especially Hispanic women. This liberation is provoked by the oppressors identifying with the poor and oppressed in an expression of solidarity. For Isasi-Diaz, solidarity is the union of fellowship between classes, peoples, or groups that arises from common responsibilities and interests, that generates shared feelings, and that leads to joint action. According to her, two main interdependent elements characterize solidarity: mutuality and praxis. In solidarity, the mutuality between the oppressed and the oppressor must begin with a process of raising awareness. One must question one's own life in light of what has been truly heard from the other. And the praxis of solidarity is a kind of engagement involving conversation and dialogue. For Isasi-Diaz, true theology, which is liberating theology for the oppressed and the oppressor alike, builds on a dynamic relationship between action and theory (cf. "Solidarity: Love of Neighbor in the 1980s," 1990).

Conclusion

Isasi-Diaz has allowed the varied influences of her life to inform her theological thinking and doing. Through her willingness to reflect upon her own lived experience, she has been able to hear, think about, and then proclaim the message of her people: that liberation and justice are for *all* peoples. Not only is justice the message of her mujerista theology, its pursuit also identifies the Christian. "Justice is a Christian requirement," she declares. "One cannot call oneself a Christian and not struggle for justice" (*En la Lucha,* 1993, p. 41).

Her theology elevates the *sensus fidelium* back to its proper place in the doing of theology because her methodology draws in the voices and experiences of her people in a way that respects their ethnicity, culture, and socioeconomic reality. Seeking the synthesis of dogmatics and ethics, her mujerista theology drives to increase the moral empowerment of Hispanic women. Finally, in doing mujerista theology, Isasi-Diaz wants to engage the theologians and the church in a dialogue with the unique and challenging voice of Hispanic women.

Jeanette Rodriguez

Selected Primary Works

1985   "Toward an Understanding of *Feminismo Hispano* in the U.S.A.," in *Women's Consciousness, Women's Conscience,* ed. Barbara Hilkert Andolsen, Christine E. Gudorf, and Mary D. Pellauer.

1988   "A Hispanic Garden in a Foreign Land," in *Inheriting Our Mother's Gardens,* ed. Letty M. Russell, Kwok Pui Lan, Ada Maria Isasi-Diaz, and Katie Geneva Cannon.

1989   "*Mujeristas:* A Name of Our Own," in *The Future of Liberation Theology,* ed. Marc H. Ellis and Otto Maduro.

1990   "The Bible and *Mujerista* Theology" and "Solidarity: Love of Neighbor in the 1980s," in *Lift Every Voice: Constructing Christian Theologies from the Underside,* ed. Susan Brooks Thistlethwaite and Mary Potter Engel.

1992   *Hispanic Women: Prophetic Voice in the Church,* with Yolanda Tarango.

1992   "La mujer hispana: voz profetica en la iglesia de los Estados Unidos." *Informes de Pro Mundi Vita, America Latina,* 28.

1992   "!Viva La Diferencia!" *Journal of Feminist Studies in Religion* 8, no. 2.

1993   *En la Lucha/In the Struggle: Elaborating a Mujerista Theology.*

Selected Secondary Sources

1988   Virginia Fabella and Mercy Oduyoye, eds., *With Passion and Compassion: Third World Women Doing Theology.*

1989   Virgil P. Elizondo, "Mestizaje as Locus of Theological Reflection," in *The Future of Liberation Theology,* ed. Marc Ellis and Otto Maduro.

1989   Elsa Tamez, ed., *Through Her Eyes. Women's Theology from Latin America.*

1990   Ursula King, ed., "Hispanics and the Sacred," *Chicano Studies* 29 (August).

1990   Yolanda Tarango, "The Hispanic Woman and Her Role in the Church," *New Theology Review* 3:4 (November).

1993   Maria Pilar Aquino, *Our Cry for Life: Feminist Theology from Latin America.*

1993   Jeanette Rodriguez, "Experience as a Resource for Feminist Thought," in *Journal of Hispanic and Latino Theology,* 1:1.

1994   Ursula King, ed., *Feminist Theology from the Third World: A Reader.*

1994   ———, *Our Lady of Guadalupe: Faith and Empowerment Among Mexican-American Women* (August).

EBERHARD JÜNGEL
1934–

Life and Career

E berhard Jüngel is known as an able teacher who leads students beyond dependency on ready-made clichés and simplifications, making them stretch their own thinking and judgments. Whoever, therefore, merely asks about theological "positions" and is satisfied by superficial labels, will quickly find reading Jüngel burdensome. On the other hand, the person who wishes to gain or deepen the joy of theological reasoning will be truly enlightened by Jüngel's work. He instructs not by doling out what is fashionable or satisfying to a particular theological school of thought, but rather by thinking through the truth of Christian theology, "the truth that makes one free" (John 8:32).

Born in 1934 in Magdeburg, Germany, he grew up in a tradesman family. The question of truth acquired a personal dimension early in his life. After his secondary education, Jüngel studied philosophy and evangelical theology in Naumburg and Berlin. Before the building of the Berlin Wall and the border limitations within Germany, Jüngel spent several months of his studies illegally in Zürich and Basel. Participation in one of Karl Barth's seminars in Basel led to an intensive and intimate connection between the "grand old man" of Protestant theology and the young East German theology student, whose unusual talent Barth quickly recognized. The relationship lasted and deepened until Barth's death in 1968.

Jüngel's doctoral work was completed in 1961 under the supervision of his New Testament teacher Ernst Fuchs at the Kirchliche Hochschule in Berlin. His dissertation, *Paul and Jesus,* was an investigation of the relationship of Pauline teaching on justification and the proclamation of Jesus found primarily in the parables. A short six months later Jüngel produced his *Habilitationsschrift.* In two very concentrated studies he investigated the text fragments of pre-Socratic Parmenides and Heraclitus concerning the phenomenon of analogy. From 1961 until 1966, Jüngel taught New Testament and Dogmatics at the Kirchliche Hochschule, which, after the building of the Berlin Wall in August 1961, was cut off from the West. His uncompromising conflict with the ideology of the *Sozialistische Deutsche Einheit-*

spartei of the German Democratic Republic (GDR) brought him a series of unpleasant handicaps and disadvantages. Nevertheless, he courageously and successfully resisted the ideological prescriptions of the East German government. Until the collapse of the German Democratic Republic, most of his writings were banned, nor were his works cited.

During the Berlin years, the book that established Jüngel's reputation as an important systematic theologian and astute interpreter of the theology of Karl Barth originated, *Gottes Sein ist im Werden (The Doctrine of the Trinity: God's Being Is in Becoming*, 1976). It examines Barth's doctrine of the revelation of God with respect to the concept of the being of God, asking the question: How must God's eternal Being be thought of if it really is God who came into human history as Jesus of Nazareth?

In 1966 Jüngel was offered an appointment to an endowed Chair of Systematic Theology and History of Dogma in the theological faculty of the University of Zürich. To his own surprise the East German government allowed him to accept the position. After three years in Switzerland, Jüngel moved to the Evangelical theological faculty at the Eberhard Karls University in Tübingen, where (as of 1995) he holds the position of Professor of Systematic Theology and Philosophy of Religion. At the same time, he serves as Director of the Institute for Hermeneutics, founded by Gerhard Ebeling. It is at Tübingen that Jüngel has generated most of his writings.

Most of Jüngel's works have the form of highly concentrated shorter studies in which he studies a wide range of themes. Besides exegetical, linguistic, and ethical inquiries, they are primarily formal and foundational questions of dogmatics that often are debated in the form of interpretative discussions with important texts of the theological-philosophical tradition and modern thinkers. These studies show the uniqueness of Jüngel's thinking as well as the skill of his art of interpretation and his superior didactic talents. Most of these discussions are accessible in the three published collections, *Unterwegs zur Sache, Entsprechungen,* and *Wertlose Wahrheit.* The theology of Karl Barth warranted a separate set of essays with the title *Barthstudien.*

Among the numerous monographs from Jüngel's pen come his dissertation and the book, *The Doctrine of the Trinity: God's Being Is in Becoming.* Besides these, two other works are especially notable: The book *Tod* (Eng. *Death: The Riddle and the Mystery* [1971]) and the wide-ranging volume, *Gott als Geheimnis der Welt* (Eng. *God as Mystery of the World* [1977]). The latter, which must be regarded as Jüngel's most important work, examines in four large sections talk about the "death of God" as well as studies on the conceivability, speakability, and humanity of God. This volume serves as preparation for an unfolding doctrine of God. Indeed, the last part of the book already contains substantive material for the doctrine in its formative stage. *God as Mystery of the World* is an important theological publication that is a standard work for any contemporary doctrine of God.

In addition to his theoretical works, Jüngel has also published three volumes of sermons. Both inside and outside the church, they have found resonance, undergirding Jüngel's commitment that theology committed to reflection on the Word of God enhances positively the proclamation of the Word of God.

To be sure, Jüngel's theology is not fully contained in his published texts, but is completed in his academic teaching. Students are his first commitment. To them, he explains much material that is only implied in his published works. His thinking reflects a delightful freedom manifest in a continuing debate with such diverse teachers as Ernst Fuchs, Karl Barth, Heinrich Vogel, Gerhard Ebeling, and Martin Heidegger. Their influence descended into his theology in the form of a healthy skepticism—a skepticism regarding the enterprise of theology to pursue a programmatic course. Jüngel's work cannot be understood as a theological program, and as such, cannot be reduced to programmatic statements. Theology must be free, Jüngel contends, and it is free when it reflects on the liberating event of the Word of God. It is therefore appropriate to present the essential aspects of Jüngel's theology under the rubric of "freedom."

The Freedom of Theology

According to Jüngel's deepest conviction, theology is free because it has to do with liberating substance—the saving truth of God becoming human. This truth is liberating because it originates from the liberating God. Theology does not construct it, it only allows this truth to be spoken. Theology functions with the knowledge of faith that God is known only because God speaks from the divine essence. Permeating his work is the dictum: "God comes from speaking." The means by which God is known is in the person of Jesus of Nazareth. In the life and death of Christ God's loving essence is revealed, and in the power of the Holy Spirit God speaks to human beings in all times to the event of God's Love.

Jüngel designates the actual subject of theology as the Word of God, by which he means first of all the speaking God, divine revelation, or the *event* of the Word of God. It is this dynamic "Word" that theology must think about. For Jüngel, thinking "about" identifies the methodological assignment that Christian theologians must assume in reflecting on God, in contrast to any philosophical system as the paradigm of its thinking. Thinking about God *follows from* the event of the Word of God. The aim and purpose of theological reflection is to accept responsibility for human speech about God, since theological reflection occurs mainly in the proclamations of the Christian church—or, as Jüngel likes to say, this speech corresponds to the speaking God. For only where the speaking *of* God corresponds to the speaking God does the possibility exist that the Word of God can become an event anew and therefore awaken faith. (That this correspondence *actually* happens and people in fact come to faith is the concern not of theology but of the Holy Spirit.)

In order for theology to fulfill its task to measure the human speech about God, it must recognize a twofold tension: On the one hand, time is the product of the creative Word of God, *and,* on the other hand, time is contemporary with its consciousness of truth, its questions and challenges. Because theology is concerned with the *ever-present event* of the Word of God, it cannot ignore its contemporary context. Theology must, therefore, be concerned with the content of the Word of God as well as the contemporary situation. Because it accompanies church proclamation in such a critical way, theology has its concrete place in the Christian church, and should have it there. But theology must also be completely free from any ecclesiastical domination.

In order for theology to examine whether human speech about God can correspond to the speaking God himself, it needs criteria. Jüngel follows insights of the Reformation by emphasizing that the criteria for theology are given in the form of *biblical texts.* The Bible is the original and therefore normative witness of revelation. Of course, the Bible is also *human* speech about God and not simply identical with the speaking God. Because the texts of Holy Scripture are not identical with the speaking God, they must be interpreted—and thereby the Word of God can possibly become an actuality again. For Jüngel, theological work is essentially the task of interpreting the biblical texts, which exegetical theology explains as witnesses of history, and which systematic theology attempts to interpret and clarify as claims for relevant truth. Jüngel holds that this theological work of interpretation deserves to be called a *science* that corresponds to its special object, and that its scientific character must and can indeed be shown. Theology, he says, is *"the Science of the Word of God."* It formulates its sentences on the basis of its own special methodology, but with the claim of general validity and understanding. From this science no human being who is willing and able to think is excluded. The thoughtful responsibility of interpreting the truth of the revealing God can be done in principle by people who reject this truth for themselves. But what is possible "in principle," should not be the case in fact. Jüngel, as theologian, writes and thinks joyfully out of a commitment for the truth of faith.

The Freedom of the Trinitarian God

Jüngel's fundamental theological conviction is that, from God's viewpoint, what is called "freedom" can only be understood and determined where God's freedom becomes an event. Within Jüngel's doctrine of God, one finds again the central idea that Christian speech about God and its corresponding attempt to think about God are made possible only through a relationship with God. God is the one, who by speaking out of the divine essence, produces thinking on God. All so-called proofs of God therefore prove at most only something that has been *called* God, but they do not prove God's existence itself. According to Jüngel, the endeavor of "natural theology," which attempts to elevate the necessity of God out of the human experience of self and the world by bypassing faith in the revelation of God in Jesus Christ, is only correct in its goal: To show that God wants to address *all people* unconditionally (not only believers). But it is exactly this goal that so-called natural theology cannot achieve. "Natural theology" fails already on its internal contradictions of *logic,* as Jüngel has maintained in several of his studies.

The Christian faith therefore sticks exclusively to the self-revelation of God in the person of Jesus Christ as witnessed to in the biblical texts, in order to recognize and think of God's being and attributes. Even more exactly, faith holds tightly to the event of the death of Jesus of Nazareth, and it grasps this death as that event in which God is self-defined. God, as Jüngel's formulation suggests, identifies God's self with "the crucified Jesus," and this identification is revealed to the believer in the resurrection. God is revealed in this event as *the human* God. By participating in the abysses of a human existence unto death, God shows the divine being as a *being for humanity.* From this event of identification, the speech of the freedom of God receives its true meaning: The free God (without compulsion, that is, out of grace) makes the self-determination that the Eternal Being is vulnerable to death in order to overcome death, because the eternal being of God suffers death. According to Jüngel, God's being must be conceived in unity with mortality. God's being *is* the living event of the digestion of death, is "the unity of life and death in favor of life." This is what the New Testament means when it says that God is *Love.* For although love is materially considered to be the unity of life and death in favor of life, formally love is considered to be the unity of being focused on oneself and at the same time being selfless. In Jüngel's words: "In the midst of ever greater self-relatedness is an even greater selflessness."

Theology can think of this understanding of God only with the aid of the doctrine of the Trinity. Jüngel therefore never tires of emphasizing the meaning and origin of the doctrine of the Trinity in the cross of Christ. Only as God the Father, the Son, and the Holy Spirit can God be thought of as this relational being of love, who makes the divine essence vulnerable to death in order to overcome death. Only the doctrine of the triune nature of God explains the fact that and how the passion story of Jesus related in the Gospels can be a story of God with us and at the same time with Self, the fact that and how God's own being and God's being for us (in the traditional language of theology, the immanent and economic Trinity) form an original unity, and the fact that and how God's freedom is the freedom of love.

How the attribute of the freedom of God must be determined, however, is based on the event of God's coming to the world, and not on an already established concept of freedom independent from this event. From this basic starting point, other divine attributes are determined and given linguistic expression. The language of faith that expresses these attributes always uses words that are related to everyday existence (like power, justice, etc.). In order to safeguard against bypassing God with such "earthy" concepts, Jüngel contends that the language of faith must be grounded in God's revelation.

Jüngel tries, therefore, to show how God's coming to the world includes God's coming into language, and how human language has the power to make true statements about God. Although God's coming into the world is the basis for the fact that our language corresponds to God's being, Jüngel calls such correspondence that God makes possible an *Analogy of the Advent.*

The Freedom of Humanity and the Freedom of Faith

Jüngel's theological anthropology begins with the assumption that the revelation of God is able to provide the understanding of who and what God truly is and also who and what humanity truly is. In contrast to numerous modern anthropological studies, theological anthropology *defines* humanity. Anthropology has indeed brought enormous progress to detailed knowledge about human beings, but it has not been able to provide any answer to the question of what humanity itself is. According to Jüngel, theology gives a definition of humanness in the sense that it grasps *God's* definition of humanness in the *one* human being, Jesus of Nazareth, in whom God has shown definitively what the destiny of humanity is. Thus the essence of humanness is to allow oneself to be loved by God and to be justified by God. With Luther, Jüngel shares the opinion that the essence of the human being is to be justified by God. Likewise with Luther, this justification is understood as a distinction (not separation) of persons from their works. What the human being truly is, is decided not by human deed, but by God. The human being is recognized by God, and only on the basis of this divine recognition which a human being accepts is that person free—in faith.

This definition is controversial, especially because human beings want to define themselves through their own actions. They want to be the product of their good and bad deeds. Through this tendency of defining oneself in oneself and realizing oneself through oneself and being focused on oneself, the human being, who is designed to live in relationship, becomes a being who is defined void of any relationships. Jüngel interprets this lack of relationality as exactly what the Bible calls sin. From this prison or these bonds of fixation on oneself, sinners cannot liberate themselves through their own strengths. They must be able—as Jüngel calls it—to be "interrupted."

As one of the central categories of Jüngel's theology, such an elementary "interruption" enables human beings, who are focused on themselves, to leave themselves. That is what is meant by "faith." In faith, the liberation of the human being from a compulsive self-centeredness and focus on self-realization, occurs. In faith, God comes so close to the human that love of self is no longer the primary love.

Faith is therefore not a human achievement. Faith is the liberation of humanity, which is caused by God to say "yes" to divine justification. In the justification of humanity by faith, *God* is the one who really acts, and the human is on the receiving end of this encounter. Faith does not, however, *remain* passive. The passivity of faith is an extraordinarily creative passivity. Faith will always attempt to correspond to the activity of God through one's own human activity. Works of faith are works *out of* love, not *for love* (i.e., in order to cause or compel love). Because these works spring out of faith, they are not made for one's own person. They are selfless acts. They serve neighbor and the welfare of the world, and they deserve, according to Jüngel, to be called *good works.*

The Freedom to Complain to God: The Problem of Evil

Faith is an experience that cannot be derived from self or the world. It comes from an experience of God. Indeed, as an experience of God, faith is related to everyday human experiences. It is the possibility opened up by God to mold *new* experiences *with* everyday experiences. Faith is in this way an "experience with the experience." For from the event of revelation new possibilities grow for the reality of our world, a process that has decisively influenced Jüngel's thought about the relationship of reality and possibility of that which is. Of human experiences of self and the world, the experience of evil is the most frightening.

The question is asked whether faith can also make a new experience out of these terrible experiences. Jüngel's answer to this very difficult and often discussed problem is sobering, for it is determined from his insight into the impossibility of an *explanation* of evil and (therefore at the same time) the impossibility of a justification of God in the face of evil. The indisputable truth that God works in *everything*, even in evil, and the indisputable truth that God is not to be considered the originator of evil (i.e., as an evil God), offer for Jüngel no "solution." In the final analysis, this approach relates God and evil in such a way that either injures the deity of God or waters down the true terribleness of evil. And it is exactly this that is impossible in light of the event of God's revelation. Therefore, the only answer that Christian theology can give to the question of the fact of evil is not an explanation. Rather, it points to the God who on the cross of Jesus Christ *suffered and endured* evil. According to Jüngel, then, faith is related to the experience of evil in a way that does not allow this terrible evil experience to triumph over the experience of God, who proves on the cross to be Love. Faith dares to hold tight to the statement "God is Love," and therefore with respect to evil it does not speak of a "hidden God" *(deus absconditus)* but instead speaks of a hidden and inexplicable *work* of God *(opus dei absconditum).* The way this is done existentially, however, is by the human *complaint*. From the biblical texts one finds that human complaint is not only allowed, but indeed commanded. Faith claims the Christian freedom to say to God what for us is shockingly inexplicable about God's activity and remains for us revolting even until the last day.

The Freedom Toward the Future

In his 1971 book on death, Jüngel already deals with the question of for what and why we may hope. In more recent publications he again turns to eschatological themes. His theology of hope is guided by the insight that Christian hope is a *certain and comforting* hope, because it hopes for the new coming of God, who in Jesus Christ *has already come* to the world and to humanity. Therefore, Christians do not hope for something that is added to the event of the revelation of God. They hope rather for the *fulfillment* of revelation: the *visible* coming to the world of God. No longer is God's presence mediated through proclamation, but it is universally immediate, that is, for all the world the visible revelation of God. It is a revelation of the same God who in Jesus Christ definitively reveals the divine Reality as *Love*.

The resurrection of all people connected with the so-called *Last Judgment*, is also for Jüngel proof of this divine love. Here there would not be love if God treated all the work of human beings the same and without judgment allowed it to disappear into the darkness of history. An act of grace occurs when in the judgment of God enlightenment is given to human beings about what they have done and what they should have done. An act of grace happens when the sin of human beings is revealed in its deserved shame and is judged, and yet instead, God pronounces to them the undeserved honor and glory of Jesus Christ.

In the Last Judgment, which is the meaning of "Redemption," human beings are first and finally liberated to the freedom of deciding to believe in the merciful judgment of God, and therefore to living eternally, undeservedly with Jesus Christ, or bound to be dissolved with his sin in judgment. Eternal life for Jüngel means the definite success of the communion between God and humans, and among humans themselves. In this communion, the individuality of the human is maintained insofar as eternal life is the redemption of the *lived life* through participation in God's own life. The "eternalization of lived life" represents the transformation in which the human being becomes identified with one's "lived life" so that the *possibilities* which have not been realized in the "lived life" are laid open. Thereby the true being of every individual in his or her final depths is revealed. Such certainty of a decisive future in the kingdom of God has good consequences for the earthly present.

In numerous shorter writings, especially with respect to the doctrine of the state and to the problem of peace, Jüngel has tried to show how hope for the coming of God moves the believer to *act* for the welfare of this world. Activity based on hope *corresponds* to the activity of God. It does not bring about the kingdom of God on earth. It does, however, establish *parables* of God's kingdom in this world, and thus interrupts the reality of this world with that which God makes *possible* with human beings, namely, to become ever more human.

Volker Spangenberg
translated by D. Dixon Sutherland

Selected Primary Works

1962/1986 *Paulus und Jesus. Eine Untersuchung zur Präzisierung der Frage nach dem Ursprung dem Christologie.*

1975 Trans. Iain and Ute Nicol, *Death: The Riddle and the Mystery.*

1976 Trans. Horton Harris, *The Doctrine of the Trinity: God's Being Is in Becoming.*

1983 Trans. Darrell L. Guder, *God as the Mystery of the World: On the Foundation of the Theology of the Crucified One in the Dispute Between Theism and Atheism.*

1986 A selection of essays taken from Jüngel's *Barth-Studien* have appeared in English under the title *Karl Barth: A Theological Legacy,* trans. Garrett E. Paul.

1989 A selection of essays by Jüngel have appeared in English under the title *Theological Essays,* trans. J. B. Webster.

1995 A selection of essays taken from Jüngel's *Wertlose Wahrheit* appears under the title *Theological Essays II,* trans. Arnold Neufeldt-Fast and J.B. Webster.

Selected Secondary Sources

1986 J. B. Webster, *Eberhard Jüngel: An Introduction to His Theology.*

1994 John Webster, ed. *The Possibility of Theology: Studies in the Theology of Eberhard Jüngel in His Sixtieth Year.*

GORDON D. KAUFMAN
1925–

Born and brought up in the Mennonite Christian community in Kansas, Kaufman entered the Bachelor of Divinity program at Yale Divinity School, New Haven, Connecticut, in 1948, after completing his Bachelor of Arts degree at Bethel College (Kansas) and Master of Arts degree in Sociology at Northwestern University. Kaufman's keen interest in philosophical questions emerged very early. He read Immanuel Kant's *Critique of Pure Reason* for the first time at the age of eighteen when he was a conscientious objector during World War II. His interest in philosophy, combined with theology, led him to join the Ph.D. Program at Yale University in philosophical theology. He served as Assistant Professor of Religion at Pomona College (California) from 1953 to 1958, during which time he completed his Ph.D. at Yale University with the dissertation, "The Problem of Relativism and the Possibility of Metaphysics." A revised version of this dissertation was published under the title *Relativism, Knowledge, and Faith* in 1960. Kaufman served as Associate Professor of Theology at Vanderbilt University, Nashville, Tennessee, from 1963 to 1969, when he moved to teach theology at Harvard Divinity School, Cambridge, Massachusetts. He continues to teach there as Edward Mallinckrodt Professor of Divinity.

Kaufman's early theology was influenced largely by four factors. First, his Mennonite background provided him with a set of priorities, for example, the priority of right living over correct doctrine—a priority that has been important in the Mennonite community. Second, the influence of the neoorthodox theology of Karl Barth, Paul Tillich, and H. Richard Niebuhr can be detected in his early writings, especially in *Systematic Theology: A Historicist Perspective* (1968), where God as the "Wholly Other" who challenges and relativizes all that is human is a theme. Third, Immanuel Kant's philosophy and ethics have greatly influenced Kaufman's thinking as in his repeated emphasis on the "human" character of theological speech and the emphasis on praxis over doctrine. Fourth, through his study of Wilhelm Dilthey, R. G. Collingwood, and Paul Tillich, Kaufman came to see the "historical" nature of the human and began to be shaped increasingly by historicism.

In *God the Problem* (1972), Kaufman began to push his historicist perspective to its full potential and began to develop the idea of God as agent, as one who acts. This effort began to lay the groundwork for his developing the notion of theology as a work of human imaginative construction in *Essay on Theological Method* (1975 *[ETM]*). This book highlighted three continuing concerns. First, Kaufman spells out clearly the notion of theology as imaginative construction. Second, his refusal to appeal to either "revelation," "experience," "Scripture," or creeds as authorities, and his call to place theology in the public marketplace of ideas and concepts are elaborated. Theology, he explains, is our own work of construction and we need to take responsibility for it, not simply invoke authorities. Third, his preoccupation with praxis over against doctrine is given a clearer exposition by claiming experience as the last word in theology and not the first word. These ideas enabled Kaufman to see theology as a reflection that happens in a community larger than the church, and placed him in the midst of religious pluralism. This methodological approach to theology was reinforced by Kaufman's travels to teach and learn at United Theological College, Bangalore, India (1976 and 1988), Doshisha University in Kyoto, Japan, the University of South Africa, Pretoria, South Africa (1984), the University of Oxford, England (1986), the Chinese University of Hong Kong (1991), Beijing University, Fudan University (Shanghai), and Nanjing Theological Seminary in China (1991).

At the same time, Kaufman was also strongly influenced by the feminist, Latin American, and African American theologies of liberation. These influences can be detected in *The Theological Imagination: Constructing the Concept of God* (1981) and *Theology for a Nuclear Age* (1985).

His most recent work, *In Face of Mystery: A Constructive Theology* (1993), fleshes out a constructive theology on the basis of the methodological concerns he has discussed and provides a full-fledged theological work in which he elucidates clearly the themes of humanity, world, God, and Christ in one volume. Those who want to understand Kaufman's theological thought may do well to begin by reading his *Essay on Theological Method* and then proceed to *In Face of Mystery*.

Theological Task

The task of theology, according to Kaufman, is "to clarify our talking and thinking about God" (*ETM*, p. 21). The talk about God never happens in a vacuum; rather, it is done in relation to two other concepts, namely, humanity and the world. One can say that the task of theology is to clarify our talking and thinking about God, humanity, and world, while "God" functions as the "presiding" category among the three. Christian theology, in particular, adds a fourth category to this scheme—Christ. But Christ is not merely an additional category, it is the category that defines and measures the other three. Clarification of talking and thinking about God happens in two ways. First, we engage in a fundamental analysis and criticism of the views of God, humanity, world, and Christ, taking into account the way people in today's world—both secularists and religionists—articulate their views about these categories. Second, we attempt to construct a Christian understanding of these categories which will bring both clarity and relevance to our talk about God and help orient our lives in relation to the Christian worldview.

This perception of theology involves at least three implications. First, the context of theological reflection cannot be limited to the Christian church or churches. One needs to envision a wider context. Theology is not merely an intrachurch conversation; but it is a conversation and dialogue with people who are engaged in other disciplinary ways of thinking, and with people in other religions. Second, theology is a distinctly human activity. Though this appears to be obvious, Kaufman believes it has not been duly recognized by theologians. Such a recognition of the human character of the theological task frees theologians from enslaving authoritarianism, and it enables them to engage in the kind of constructive activity that is required. Third, such an understanding of the task of theology implies that theology is basically the work of imaginative construction. This imaginative and constructive character of theological reflection is in contrast to viewing theology either as interpretation of classical and scriptural texts, as an exposition of "experience"—individual or collective—or as correlating Christian "answers" to existential "questions." Instead, theology is imaginative construction.

Theological Method

The phrase "imaginative construction" not only describes the task of theology; it also suggests the method by which theology is to be done. In his *Essay on Theological Method,* Kaufman suggests three moments in theological reflection. The first moment involves a phenomenological description that puts "the varieties of contemporary experience together into a concept of the world as a whole" (*ETM,* 1975, p. 64), including both anthropological and cosmological perceptions that are relevant and meaningful to the people of today. One would bring the best efforts in the fields of the sciences (both natural and social) to bear on this perception of the world. The second moment introduces and locates the image/concept of God by highly imaginative and constructive thinking. This moment serves as the foundation for the third moment, in which the contemporary experience (anthropological and cosmological visions included) is grasped and interpreted in light of God, that is, theologically. Because these moments interlock with one another, one should always keep all in mind so that the interlocking is allowed full play. This also means that a sound theological method includes a full-fledged methodological consciousness at all times when one is constructing one's theology.

God

Kaufman's construction of the concept of God develops in two steps. The first one is to analyze how the concept of God has functioned in Christian thinking and praxis in the West. This would include examining the meaning and function of the word "God" in the English language and the development of the concept of God in the Christian tradition in the West. The second is to map out a contemporary picture of human existence and the world as it shapes the way people understand the reality and meaning of their lives. Such a map will help to locate and reconstruct the concept of God that is relevant and meaningful to contemporary humans, both in their thinking about God and in their attempt to orient their lives in relation to God.

The image/concept of God in the Christian tradition has its origins in metaphors such as creator, lord, and father. The purpose of these metaphors has been to place the motifs of God's transcendence and immanence in dialectical relationship. God as "father" is one who "fulfills all our deepest needs" and thus humanizes us; God as "lord" and "creator" stands apart from us and "relativizes all our values, ideas, and activities." To put it differently, God is one who "as a humanizing center of orientation" effects human salvation and fulfillment. On the other hand, God as "mystery" and "beyond all human knowing" relativizes everything that is human and finite. Both of these motifs need to be kept in tension because the overemphasis of one at the expense of the other distorts the understanding of God. For example, undue emphasis on the otherness or "radical transcendence" of God can lead to a tyrannical and oppressive picture of God, while a preoccupation with God's immanence may result in an idolatrous equating of God with our view of human fulfillment and happiness.

The current view of human existence and the world is shaped by evolutionary and historical perspectives. According to Kaufman, this view recognizes that in the long process of the evolution of this universe and particularly of the human species one can trace certain "trajectories" or "directional movements." These movements are not necessarily teleological in character. But in relation to these movements, humans need to understand themselves and their attempts to orient their lives under the presiding concepts of God and Christ. Such an evolutionary-historical view of the universe and our place within it recognizes that significant creativity occurs in the universe, what Kaufman calls "serendipitous creativity." In light of such a view of the cosmos, one needs to reconstruct the concept of God.

When one takes these two considerations (the twofold function of the concept of God, and the evolutionary-historical view of the cosmos) into account, "God" refers not to "a particular existent being within or beyond the world," but rather to "the creativity at work within the unfolding evolutionary ecosystem, giving reality a directional movement and interconnectedness to the great multiplicity of particular events and beings in the world." Talk about God always finds itself more at home with metaphors and images that come out of human experience (such as creator, father, etc.) precisely because of the humanizing function of God. These metaphors help to give concrete, devotional, and fleshly form to the kind of evolutionary-historical view of God seen in the light of "serendipitous creativity." Moreover, since the concept of God serves to relativize human values and ideas, each metaphor needs to be criticized, evaluated, and reconstructed. No single metaphor should be reified in order to avoid an idolatrous vision of God.

Thus, for Kaufman, to be devoted to God, or to have faith in God, means that persons commit themselves to a particular way of ordering their lives; that is, devote their lives to a humane and humanizing world within the ecosystem in which they find themselves. This faith acknowledges that God, as understood in terms of serendipitous creativity, is moving them toward such a humane mode of being in the universe.

Christ

Within the Christian categorical scheme, "Christ" is not simply the fourth category in addition to God, world, and humanity, but rather the paradigm for both God and humanity. The vision of God is normatively determined by the picture of Christ, and similarly the understanding of what it means to be human and humane is decisively shaped by the view of Christ. While acknowledging the normative role of the concept of Christ within Christian theological thought, Kaufman raises two cautionary points. The first is that the word "Christ" does not simply and straightforwardly refer to Jesus, but refers rather to a cluster of "events surrounding and including Jesus of Nazareth." This point is significant especially in relation to the feminist criticism of the oppressive possibilities embedded in the maleness of Jesus. This wider view of Christ symbolizes the new order of relationships that have come into being in the events surrounding and including and following upon the man Jesus, and gives meaning to the idea of God's incarnation in Christ as the new order of interpersonal relationships.

The second note of caution regards the kind of symbolic framework within which the idea of Christ has been understood and interpreted historically. For example, the idea of the cross as a symbol of self-sacrifice and the resurrection as the vindication and exaltation of Christ has often led to the exploitation of the weak and the downtrodden, and to the promotion of Christian triumphalism because of the dualistic and monarchical imagery within which Christ has been understood.

Taking these two notes of caution seriously, Kaufman suggests that we view Christ as offering a paradigm for understanding God and for orienting human living.

God comes to be seen as a social reality who grounds our interpersonal and ecological relationships toward a more humane and humanizing cosmos. The Christic images call people, not through the "violent use of power," but through the gradual transformation of individuals and societies, toward communities of reconciliation—communities that are governed by egalitarianism, mutual respect, and caring for one another.

Trinity

Kaufman offers a new interpretation of the doctrine of Trinity by placing the doctrine of God within the evolutionary-historical view of the cosmos. He prefers to use the word "intention" instead of "person" to explain the Trinity. Each of the three modes in Trinity is an intention—an intention of faith. The first intention (or "person") affirms the "ultimate mystery of things," namely, the transcendence and absoluteness of God. The second "person" or intention of faith, Christ, provides concrete orientation in the evolutionary-historical development of humanity and the world. The third component, the Holy Spirit, enables the transcendence of God to be related significantly to our experience. As "immanent," the third intention expresses the idea that God who is Mystery is also present as Spirit in the world so that God and world are not to be thought of as completely separated realities. God is "present to and 'within' every created being." Apart from these three motifs, God would not be God from a Christian viewpoint.

Humanity

A Christian understanding of humanity should be devised from two assumptions that are widely accepted by humans today. The first is that humans are "culture-creating beings" whose existence is created by humans themselves in history. The second assumption is that humans are part of a larger interconnected universe or ecosystem that is evolutionary in character. Thus humans are created and shaped by both historicity and biology. Kaufman calls this view a biohistorical conception of the human.

This perception of the human invites the human community to self-consciousness about its biohistoricity in order to work toward the "optimal realization of our historicity." Therefore questions of normativeness, morality, and ethics are very much a part of being human. Kaufman is aware that these have to be worked out in a sociohistorical and cultural setting rather than with an individualistic view of the human being. Using a Kantian framework as his base, Kaufman devises a scheme by which one can understand the character of human action in the world.

In this biohistorical setting, sin and evil can best be understood as the corruption of our historicity. As individuals, humans find themselves unable to act and to take responsibility for themselves, and thus are anxious on the one hand and feel responsible for this failure to act on the other. This produces anxiety and guilt. In society, human communities are corrupted, and one sees the evils of oppression and oppressive structures. When human predicament is seen this way, the question of salvation is perceived in terms of human flourishing or "humanization." For Christian theology, the view of the human predicament and human flourishing goes beyond the ideas of natural evil and moral evil. What one may call "theological evil" is at the root of the human problem. Sin is the failure to trust in the relativizing and humanizing power of God, both in one's individual life and in the life of societies, communities, and nations. So salvation, as imaged in the idea of "kingdom of God," is that trajectory that is leading us to "a more humane society in a well-ordered world." Salvation becomes possible as we give ourselves to this vision in full trust and engage in the struggle against sin and evil in confidence and hope.

Given such an understanding of human biohistoricity, the Christian perspective on human sin and salvation is one perspective among others which has developed over a long history of peoples and ideas. In the setting of the religious pluralism of today, Christians should acknowledge that neither Christians nor others possess the final or absolute truth necessary to orient human life to its fuller humaneness. This means that interreligious dialogue becomes essential to pooling our resources for finding an adequate orientation for life in today's world.

To summarize, Kaufman's theological ideas were shaped in the crucible of a neoorthodox theological framework while he was struggling with the demands of a thoroughly historicist view of the human and the world. This internal conversation led to his discovery and highlighting of the concept of theology as imaginative construction. Though his earlier writings held only dim and indirect hints at this view of theology, his writings since the publication of the essay on theological method have consistently worked with the imaginative and constructive view of theology. While some find his theology inspiring and enabling in the search for a theology which addresses the questions of liberation and interreligious relations, others find his view of God pantheistic, too conceptual, and not spiritually satisfying to a worshipful devotee of Christ.

M. Thomas Thangaraj

Selected Primary Works

1960   *Relativism, Knowledge, and Faith.*
1961   *The Context of Decision.*
1968/1978 *Systematic Theology: A Historicist Perspective.*

1972   *God the Problem.*

1975   *An Essay on Theological Method* (Rev. ed. forthcoming, 1996).

1979   *Nonresistance and Responsibility, and Other Mennonite Essays.*

1981   *The Theological Imagination: Constructing the Concept of God.*

1985   *Theology for a Nuclear Age.*

1993   *In Face of Mystery: A Constructive Theology.*

Selected Secondary Source

1991   A helpful companion volume is the Festschrift for Kaufman, *Theology at the End of Modernity: Essays in Honor of Gordon Kaufman,* ed. Sheila Davaney.

HANS KÜNG
1928–

Life and Career

Through four decades the Swiss-born Catholic theologian, Hans Küng, has been an outspoken proponent of church reform and of ecumenical and interfaith dialogue. During his periodic trips to the United States as a visiting professor or lecturer, the religious and secular media have often concentrated on his charismatic personality and controversial views. But over the years, Küng has been working steadily behind the scenes at his theological craft, producing a solid body of material with great implications for Christian unity and world peace.

Küng is an impressive theologian. Firmly committed to the Catholic heritage yet open to the thought of Luther and other Reformers, he consistently uses Scripture as a norm for judging developments in the churches; and he has passionately pursued the reconciliation of Catholics and Protestants, who have been divided for centuries.

Küng describes his theological development with the image of expanding concentric circles, like those produced when a pebble is dropped in a pond. For him the pebble is his decisive and enduring commitment to doing scientific theology as a committed Christian within the Catholic community. The concentric circles represent his theological interests, which have grown over the decades. In the 1960s the Second Vatican Council prompted him to reflect on ecclesiology and especially church reform. During the 1970s he turned to the more fundamental issues of Christology and the doctrine of God. Finally during the 1980s and into the 1990s, he devoted himself to interfaith dialogue among the world religions as a contribution to the cause of world peace.

Hans Küng was born March 19, 1928, in Sursee, near Lucerne, in a solidly Catholic part of Switzerland. He was the oldest of seven children in a happy and healthy family. At the age of fourteen he left his hometown to attend an interdenominational coed school in Lucerne. After deciding he wanted to be a priest for his home diocese of Basel, he went to Rome in 1948 to begin his studies. He was ordained in 1954 and eventually served for eighteen months at a large parish in

Lucerne. This pastoral experience, brief as it was, gave him an abiding sense of the concerns and needs of average Catholics.

Küng underwent his theological training during the 1950s before the Second Vatican Council. From 1951 to 1955, he studied the traditional scholastic theology in the strict atmosphere of the Pontifical Gregorian University in Rome, earning the licentiate for his thesis on Jean Paul Sartre's notion of atheistic humanism. His theological horizons expanded when he moved to Paris in 1955 to do his doctoral studies at the Sorbonne and the Institute Catholique. During this time he came to admire the work of the French Dominican Yves Congar, who gave him an abiding passion for Christian unity based on genuine church reform. At the urging of the Swiss Catholic theologian, Hans Urs von Balthasar, Küng wrote his doctoral dissertation on the notion of justification according to the great Protestant neoorthodox theologian Karl Barth. He concluded that there was fundamental agreement between Barth and the Catholic tradition on this issue which had divided Catholics and Protestants for more than four hundred years. Barth himself responded that Küng had indeed accurately understood his position, and the German Jesuit Karl Rahner attested that he had properly interpreted the Catholic tradition.

This dissertation was decisive for Küng's theological career. The affirmation generously given by these two giants of twentieth-century theology catapulted him into prominence within the theological community. Küng's success in solving a longstanding dispute between Catholics and Protestants gave him confidence that other disputed issues could also be solved. His studies of Barth gave him a methodological principle that he has used ever since: The scriptural witness to Jesus must serve as the supreme norm for judging all subsequent theological developments. This initial encounter with Barth flowered into a friendship that lasted until Barth died in 1968.

Ecclesiology

During the 1960s Küng responded to the challenges posed by the Second Vatican Council by addressing fundamental questions on the church. His book *The Council: Reform and Reunion*, originally published in 1960, two years before the Council began, alerted many Catholics to the need for reform in the church. Manifesting the boldness that has characterized his subsequent writing, he called for striking reforms such as rethinking mandatory celibacy and limiting the power of the Roman Curia. In the same year that he published this widely read book, he took a position as Professor of Ecumenical Theology at the University of Tübingen, which has remained his primary academic home. In 1962, Pope John XXIII designated him as an official theological consultant to the Council. For a time he worked with the commission drafting the document on the church, but conflicts with the conservative Cardinal Ottaviani prompted him to quit the commission and work on developing his own ecclesiology. The results of his studies appeared in his book *The Church*, published in 1967.

This large volume encourages readers to view the church as it really is, a graced but sinful community of faith that must always be reforming itself. The dark side of the church results from the sinfulness of the members and from contact with a society filled with distortions and contradictions. With great candor, Küng faced the history of anti-Semitism in the church as well as the abuse of power by leaders and the shameful treatment of women. For Küng, genuine reform must remain faithful to tradition while searching for creative ways to respond to the needs of the contemporary world. It requires personal conversion and structural changes so that the church can be a credible sign of the Kingdom. In reforming itself, the church must seek guidance from the example and teachings of the historical Jesus as reflected in the New Testament. Some developments in the church are in accord with the gospel; others are opposed and must be challenged so that the community of believers can better reflect Christ and the apostolic church.

Küng organized his thoughts on the nature of the church according to three fundamental models. Originally the church understood itself as the new people of God composed of Gentiles as well as Jews. Through God's call the baptized are equal members of this people so that there is no room for a clerical caste system. The "people of God" image reminds us that the church is not a perfect society and cannot simply be equated with the kingdom of God. It is rather a pilgrim community wending its way through history, always dependent on divine help to overcome its sinfulness and reach its ultimate destination.

Using the image promoted by the apostle Paul, Küng discussed a second model of the church as the Body of Christ. Those who are baptized are incorporated into Christ and partake of his life. By celebrating the Lord's Supper, the faithful encounter the risen Christ who is spiritually, personally, and really present. The Eucharist, which recalls the many meals Jesus celebrated with his disciples and anticipates the heavenly banquet, has the innate power to form believers into a local community of faith that is organically connected to the universal church.

Finally, Küng viewed the church as the creation of the Spirit which highlights the charismatic dimension of the community and the responsible freedom of its members. The risen Christ communicates his life-giving Spirit, which creates and sustains the church. Despite its limitations and sinfulness, the church is the temple of the Spirit. All the members possess charisms or free gifts given not for personal advantage but for the common good that demands both order and freedom. Thus the church has a charismatic structure that includes but always exceeds the charism of hierarchical leadership.

Küng believes that these three models, which focus attention on local Christian communities living under the judgment of the New Testament, provide a comprehensive view of the nature and structure of the church.

In subsequent reflections on his beloved Catholic church, Küng has maintained his passion for genuine reform based on truthfulness. Drawing courage from the gospel teaching that the truth given by Jesus sets believers free (John 8:32), he has attacked various forms of falsehood and hypocrisy that he detects in the church, including the authoritarianism of the Roman Curia, the official ideological teaching on birth control, the unwillingness of the hierarchy to admit errors in church teaching, and papal opposition to full rights for women in the church. Küng has suffered for his candor. His book *Infallible? An Inquiry* (1971) initiated a long dispute with the Congregation for the Doctrine of the Faith, which challenged his reinterpretation of papal infallibility, a dogma proclaimed by the First Vatican Council in 1870. Eventually, in 1979 the Congregation revoked his canonical mission to teach in the Catholic faculty at Tübingen. This ruling came as a complete shock to Küng because it was done without benefit of a hearing and without prior notification of the German bishops. A few thousand students at Tübingen demonstrated on his behalf, and theologians from around the world signed petitions protesting this action. The University worked out an arrangement so that he could continue to function as Professor and Director of the Institute for Ecumenical Research, a position he still holds today. This disciplinary action against Küng has not diminished his passion for reform, nor has it kept him from speaking forthrightly on church issues.

Christology

During the decade of the 1970s, Küng turned from questions of ecclesiology to the more fundamental issues of Christology and the doctrine of God. In response to the challenge of contemporary atheism, secularism, and historical criticism he produced three important books: *On Being a Christian* (1974); *Does God Exist?* (1978); and *Eternal Life?* (1982).

The Christology of *On Being a Christian* is the key to understanding his fundamental defense of Christian existence. Therein Küng presents Jesus as the definitive model for human beings in our relationship to God, others, and society. Christianity keeps alive the memory of Jesus as ultimately decisive for human existence.

Classical theology used a "top-down" approach to understanding Christ that begins with his divine sonship. Küng prefers a "from-below" method that begins with the man Jesus and later examines his relationship to God. Rejecting the extreme skepticism about the historical Jesus adopted by scholars such as Rudolf Bultmann and Paul Tillich, Küng insists that we have "a relatively reliable" knowledge of the proclamation, behavior, and fate of Jesus of Nazareth.

On Being a Christian is especially helpful in demonstrating the uniqueness of Jesus in the context of his own Jewish society. Jesus was not a Sadducee who collaborated with the Roman occupying power; not a Zealot who opted for violent revolutionary tactics; not an Essene who withdrew from the world into a monastery; and not a Pharisee who concentrated on strict observance of the Law. As Küng puts it, Jesus was closer to God than the priests, more revolutionary than the revolutionaries, freer of the world than the ascetics, and more moral than the moralists. His uniqueness also appears when he is compared with other great religious leaders: He was not a lawgiver like Moses, not an ascetic like the Buddha, not a scholar like Confucius, and not a political ruler like Muhammad.

He was an itinerant preacher, a public storyteller, a charismatic healer who went about doing good. He was wholly dedicated to the cause of God and thus to the cause of humanity. His chief metaphor for this cause was the kingdom or reign of God, which indicates an absolute and unsurpassable righteousness, freedom, love, reconciliation, and peace. As suggested by the urgent tone of his parables and sayings, Jesus expected God to establish this reign in the "immediate future." Decisions for the Kingdom should not be delayed indefinitely.

As even his enemies admitted, Jesus was a miracle worker who cured the sick and those possessed by demons. According to Küng the miracles should not be seen as divine interventions that broke the laws of nature, but rather as astonishing deeds that were signs of the Kingdom and "advance portrayals" of human salvation. Our faith today is not in the miracles but in Jesus, who demonstrated the presence and power of the reign of God.

For Jesus, the supreme norm guiding human conduct is not a law that gives security, but rather the will of God that invites an ever more generous response. Following God's will with childlike abandon brings us a richer life of freedom and joy on this earth and ultimate happiness in heaven.

Analyzing the ethical teaching of Jesus, Küng stresses that the command to love God and neighbor is not a universal theoretical law, but a concrete practical demand to help actual neighbors who are in need. The two laws cannot be separated. Furthermore, we are to love others as much as we love ourselves. The uniqueness of the teaching of Jesus appears most starkly in his insistence that we love even our enemies because they are already encompassed by God's love. Jesus not only taught the law of love but lived it out by curing the sick, supporting the weak, challenging sinners, and eating with outcasts.

Jesus did not speculate about the nature of God, but did address God in a familiar and respectful way as his Father. This metaphor suggests that God loves us and is absolutely reliable. The true God is not silent, apathetic, and aloof, but a living "Thou" who calls us by name. Küng often refers to God as our partner, variously described as compassionate, approachable, and caring. Our divine partner, however, always remains mysterious and beyond our control.

Küng likes to contrast the apparent insignificance of Jesus' life with his unparalleled claims to being the supreme public advocate for the cause of God and humanity. This man from an insignificant family in Nazareth who was without education, money, office, or property, proclaimed the reign of God and placed himself above the Law and even above the great prophet Moses.

Such extraordinary claims brought Jesus into conflict with the religious and political authorities. Despite the evident danger, he went to the capital city of Jerusalem as part of his strategy to convert all of Israel. There he celebrated a final meal with his disciples and then was caught up in a fast-moving series of events: betrayed by Judas, arrested by the Jewish authorities, condemned by the Jewish high priests and elders, handed over to Pilate, convicted as King of the Jews, and crucified by Roman soldiers. Küng sees the death of Jesus as the logical conclusion of his provocative life. In contrast to Moses, Buddha, Confucius, and Muhammad, he died young and unsuccessful. His friends and disciples abandoned him in his hour of need. The religious authorities branded him as a heretical teacher, a false prophet, a blasphemer, and a seducer of the people. The Romans feared him as a political revolutionary. In Jesus' time of crisis, God did not intervene to save him from an especially degrading and painful death.

And yet, as Küng puts it, we are faced with the "historical enigma" that the early Christian church grew in explosive fashion precisely in the name of the crucified leader. The explanation offered by the primitive community was that the crucified one lives on. God raised Jesus to life and he continues to be life-giving Spirit for us. Küng insists that the resurrection signifies neither a return to life in space and time nor a mere continuation of the cause of Jesus fueled by the subjective faith of the disciples. Rather, the resurrection means that God has taken up Jesus into a new relationship. The disciples proclaimed Jesus as Lord because he truly lives and reigns forever with God his Father. Through the resurrection God validated the life of Jesus and vindicated his cause. Despite appearances, his faithful behavior and his courageous proclamation of the Kingdom were both wise and fruitful. He was who he claimed to be: the final prophet and the true advocate of the cause of God and humanity. Exalted by God, Jesus became for his followers the personification of the Kingdom. A decision for Christ is a decision for the rule of God. Christianity is not an abstract philosophy or a political ideology. At its core it calls for a commitment to Jesus Christ crucified and raised to life. When Christians affirm Jesus as true God and true man, they mean that he is the definitive advocate and delegate of God as well as the ultimate norm for human existence.

Critics have attacked Küng's Christology as being merely functional and neglecting the ontological questions about the essential nature of Jesus and his resurrection. Küng's general response is that his approach is faithful to the New Testament, which narrates the death of Jesus from the perspective of his resurrection without attempting any theoretical explanations.

Pluralism and Ecumenism

During the 1980s and into the next decade, Küng's expanding theological horizons brought him into dialogue with the world religions. He prepared himself for this culminating phase of his theological career through extensive travel and religious dialogue. He was, for example, the first Western theologian to visit Iran after the Islamic revolution and the first foreign theologian to address the Chinese Social Science Academy.

In 1982 he convened a conference at Tübingen with Islamic, Hindu, and Buddhist scholars; the conference papers were later published as *Christianity and World Religions* (1986). Küng set up a similar dialogue with an outstanding Chinese scholar, Julia Ching, later published as *Christianity and Chinese Religions* (1989). Following these dialogues he turned his attention to the monotheistic prophetic religions of Judaism, Christianity, and Islam. He published *Judaism* in 1992 and *Christianity* in 1994 and is working on a volume dealing with Islam. Throughout this whole project his goal has been to write a complete systematic theology in the context of the world's religions.

Küng's deep involvement with interfaith dialogue prompted him to reflect more explicitly on the question of theological method. In *Theology for the Third Millennium: An Ecumenical View* (1988), he pulls together his thoughts on how theology can best respond to the challenges of the postmodern world, including the tensions among the world religions. Küng employs a method of correlation that creates a dialogue between the Christian message and the contemporary world. The norm for judging all developments in church and society, however, remains the crucified and living Christ depicted in the New Testament and proclaimed by the church. In response to significant crises in culture and society, theology has periodically made crucial paradigm shifts—a term that was made popular by Thomas Kuhn in a scientific context and that suggests a fundamental change in the constellation of beliefs and values held by the faith community. Thus, in the thirteenth century Thomas Aquinas produced a new theological synthesis that incorporated the recently rediscovered philosophy of Aristotle.

Today we are living through a great crisis caused by the breakup of the modern world with its optimistic belief in progress through reason and science. We are moving toward a new world that Küng describes with the vague phrase "postmodern." To respond adequately to this age of transition we need, according to Küng, a "critical ecumenical theology." This theology should seek a relatively adequate foundation based on a basic act of trust in reality as a whole despite its broken, complex, and ambiguous character. Given the postmodern distrust of reason, it must defend belief in God not as a logical deduction or a blind leap, but as a reasonable act of trust in the ultimate source of reality. Christian theology today should adopt a global perspective that takes seriously the truth, goodness, and beauty found in the other world religions. For Christians this openness is rooted in the conviction that Jesus Christ is the definitive advocate for the cause of God and humanity.

For Küng interfaith dialogue is absolutely crucial to the well-being of the human family. During the past decade he has constantly repeated his fundamental conviction: "No peace among the nations without peace among the religions. No peace among the religions without dialogue between the religions. No dialogue between the religions without investigation of the foundations of the religions." At the 1993 Parliament of the World's Religions in Chicago, Küng wrote "The Declaration of a Global Ethic," which was signed by about 250 religious leaders from around the world. The document marks a new stage in interfaith relationships by stressing the need for collaborative efforts on behalf of peace and justice. In the declaration Küng recognizes that religions have at times been misused to promote disharmony, violence, and wars. But he also insists that they possess spiritual resources and common ethical principles that can help bring peace to our troubled world. The great religious traditions hold in common that all human beings possess an inalienable dignity that demands respect. This general principle leads to other commonly held ethical imperatives: One shall not kill, but should respect life; one shall not steal, but should respect property; one shall not lie, but should speak truthfully; one shall not commit sexual immorality, but should love another. Küng concludes by calling on believers all over the world to commit themselves to a common global ethic rooted in their respective traditions in order to further the cause of universal justice and peace.

In the meantime Küng continues to labor mightily on his grand project of analyzing the foundations of the world's great religious traditions. He often speaks about "the three great religious river systems" that flow into the one religious history of humankind: the prophetic traditions of Semitic origin, today often referred to as the three Abrahamic religions of Judaism, Christianity, and Islam; the mystical traditions begun in India, especially Hinduism and Buddhism, which stress the experience of ultimate unity through meditation; and the Chinese wisdom traditions of Confucianism and Taoism, which treasure social harmony rooted in traditional ethical principles. Although the three systems intermingle and overlap to some degree, they do maintain a primary orientation and distinctive spirit that interfaith dialogue must respect. For Küng the goal of the dialogue is not a superficial harmonization leading to one universal religion, but rather an open exchange of information leading to mutual transformation and effective collaboration for the good of the human family. The task for Christians is to deepen their commitment to Christ while maintaining the greatest possible openness to the cultural, ethical, and religious values of the other traditions. Christians serve the cause of humanity by making the spirit of Jesus visible throughout the world in ever new cultural forms.

After his initial exploratory dialogues with the mystical and wisdom traditions, Küng began his systematic treatment of the religious situation today by examining

Judaism, the first of the great prophetic religions. In *Judaism: Between Yesterday and Tomorrow* (1992), he argues that the "permanently valid and constantly obligatory" center of Judaism is a belief in Yahweh, the one God who freed his people from slavery and gave them the promised land. This core belief enunciated by the great prophet Moses has given continuity to the Jewish people through the paradigm changes in their history: from the early tribal period in the twelfth century B.C.E. to the current efforts of the Jewish community to maintain its identity in the postmodern world. Küng believes that genuine dialogue demands resolute self-criticism. Jews, for instance, remind Christians that the doctrine of the Trinity should not undercut belief in one God. On the other hand, the Gospel portrayal of Jesus invites Jews to a generous forgiveness of others.

In his books on Christianity and Islam, Küng follows the same general approach of concentrating on the fundamental convictions at the core of each tradition. Thus Jews, Christians, and Muslims are joined together in their belief in the one God who is active in human history. They are divided, however, on the way this God is definitively revealed: for Jews through the covenant establishing Israel as the chosen people; for Christians through a person, Jesus, crucified and risen; and for Muslims through their sacred book the Koran.

Conclusion

In April of 1967 Küng visited the beautiful and peaceful city of Beirut for a religious conference that included speakers representing Christianity and Islam. When he asked why the Christian and Muslim scholars did not participate in direct dialogue with one another he was told it was too soon. In retrospect, he is convinced that interfaith dialogue properly fostered in the 1960s could have warded off the bloody civil war that later inflicted so much suffering on the people of Beirut. This story helps explain the passion Küng brings to the ambitious project that has absorbed his time and energy since the early 1980s. For him, world peace is essentially linked to interfaith dialogue rooted in solid scholarship. Like the pebble cast into the pond, his plunge into the world of theology has produced a ripple effect that embraces the world's great religious traditions. Hans Küng has made important contributions to ecclesiology and Christology that have advanced the cause of Christian unity; but his even greater legacy will be the interfaith dialogue he has inspired.

James J. Bacik

Selected Primary Works

1967   *The Church.*
1971   *Infallible? An Inquiry.*

1976   *On Being a Christian.*
1988   *Theology for the Third Millennium: An Ecumenical View.*
1989   *Christianity and Chinese Religions*, with Julie Ching.
1990   *Reforming the Church Today: Keeping Hope Alive.*
1991   *Global Responsibility: In Search of a New World Ethic.*
1992   *Judaism.*
1994   *Christianity.*

Selected Secondary Sources

1981   Robert Nowell, *A Passion for Truth: Hans Küng and His Theology.*
1985   John Kiwiet, *Hans Küng.*

GEORGE LINDBECK
1923–

Life and Career

Geeorge A. Lindbeck was born in China in 1923, the son of Lutheran missionaries who were Americans of Swedish descent. He lived and went to school in China and Korea until he came to the United States to attend Gustavus Adolphus College in Minnesota. Having completed his B.A. there in 1943, Lindbeck received the B.D. from Yale Divinity School in 1946, and the Ph.D. from Yale in 1955. His doctoral dissertation, completed after study in Toronto and Paris with Étienne Gilson and Paul Vignaux, two of the century's leading scholars of medieval thought, was on essence and existence in the philosophical theology of John Duns Scotus. Appointed to the Yale faculty in 1952—where he remained until his retirement in 1993—Lindbeck's early teaching and writing focused on later medieval philosophy and theology.

Lindbeck might be known today primarily as a medievalist were it not for Pope John XXIII's decision to convene the Second Vatican Council. Largely because of his work on medieval Roman Catholic thought, Lindbeck was invited to be one of the sixty or so delegated observers to the Council from outside the Roman Catholic Church. He represented the Lutheran World Federation at all four sessions of the Council (1962–65). This experience turned his theological career in a new direction: Following the Council, Lindbeck devoted himself primarily to ecumenical theology, and in particular to Lutheran–Roman Catholic dialogue. Much of Lindbeck's extensive bibliography is concerned with doctrinal, conceptual, and practical problems of ecumenical dialogue, as is the work for which he is best known, *The Nature of Doctrine: Religion and Theology in a Postliberal Age* (1984; hereafter *ND*).

Together with some of his more recent articles, this book has had an influence far beyond the circle of those who share Lindbeck's motivating interest in the doctrinal reconciliation of historically divided Christian confessions. In relatively brief compass, Lindbeck maps a wide-ranging vision of the nature of religion, Christian doctrine, and Christian theology, challenging the views that have tended to dominate American academic theology over the last generation. In the course of articulating this vision of religion, doctrine, and theology, Lindbeck makes a number of suggestions about the central topics of Christian theology, such as God, Christ, church, and salvation. But his overall outlook is perhaps most readily approached by attending to the way he conceives of theology's tasks and commitments.

Theology's Tasks

In order to arrive at a clear conception of its nature and tasks, Christian theology should, according to Lindbeck, be distinguished from and related to both first-order Christian practice and church doctrines.

Theology presupposes continuing practices of liturgy, sacraments, preaching, prayer, service, and the like, which are indispensable to the identity and continuity of the Christian community. Theology, in other words, presupposes the Christian *religion*. Religions, including Christianity, are for Lindbeck most plausibly understood as "cultural-linguistic" systems, structured networks of belief and practice which shape the primary truth claims their adherents make and the deepest experiences they have. Lindbeck draws on recent social science (especially Clifford Geertz) and philosophy of language (especially Ludwig Wittgenstein) to support this way of understanding the nature of religion, and he contrasts it with two other approaches that have held sway in Christian theology: traditional "propositionalism," for which religions are chiefly competing sets of truth claims, and modern "experiential-expressivism," for which religions are chiefly ways of giving outward utterance to prior inward experiences.

Church doctrines are "communally authoritative rules of discourse, attitude, and action"; these may be (and in Christianity often are) expressly articulated, but any coherent community that exists over time will necessarily have at least implicit doctrines in this sense (*ND*, 1984, p. 18). What church doctrines regulate is precisely the continuing practices of the Christian community, and so they specify the community's sense of its own identity on matters of central importance to it; belief and practice inconsistent with these rules cannot endure in the community without producing either division or a decisive loss of identity. Conceiving church doctrines primarily as rules for speech about God and Christ (and many other matters of great importance to the Christian community), rather than as first-order speech directly about God and Christ, best captures the function that these doctrines have actually had in Christian history. It also allows for significant differences of belief among people who nonetheless share the same doctrinal commitments—that is, who belong to the same community. Lindbeck strives to support his argument for a "rule theory of doctrine" through an analysis of the trinitarian and christological doctrines of the ancient church, and of the more recently contested doctrines about Mary and papal infallibility (see *ND*, 1984, pp. 73-111). Here lies the heart of Lindbeck's ecumenical proposal.

Theology itself neither generates nor recaptures adequately the communal practices upon which it reflects, and so it is essentially a second-order task distinct from those practices. But it is one that the Christian community through most of its history has had difficulty doing without; theology has been invaluable in the church's understanding and correction of its own continuous belief and practice. In contrast to church doctrines, theology typically examines "everything that it is desirable to teach rather than only with that which functions as communally essential" (*ND*, p. 76). This distinction suggests that theological diversity (limited by the rules essential for communal identity) within the Christian community is not only possible but desirable. The theological differences which regularly occur need not be divisive; they need not, in other words, constitute disagreements about what is communally essential. Lindbeck's position also suggests that what is best to teach cannot simply be derived from what is communally essential, so that identification of what is communally essential—of Christian "doctrine" in his precise sense of the term—leaves most of the theological task still to be done.

As Lindbeck sees it, the theological task has three basic aspects: the dogmatic, the practical, and the foundational (to use the established labels). Although distinguishable for purposes of analysis, these three projects always shape one another in practice.

Dogmatic theology attempts to give "a normative explication of the meaning a religion has for its adherents," or, we could say, to unfold as thoroughly as possible the community's vision of the world and of how we should live in it (*ND*, p. 113). This task inevitably involves a mix of normative and descriptive elements; the theologian makes a broad range of judgments about what constitutes, in a specific time and place, a faithful articulation of the worldview and ethos of the community, and the theological outcome is then tested for the adequacy with which it recaptures reflectively the deep commitments of the community displayed in its actual historical practice. This is accomplished most directly, perhaps, by seeing whether competent speakers of the community's language who are able to understand a theology recognize the practice it describes as their own.

Practical theology aims to apply the community's overarching vision of reality to specific problems in the church and the world in ways that are both faithful to the community's vision and relevant to the problems at hand. In his own account of the task of practical theology, and even more in his massive ecumenical labors, Lindbeck attends especially to ways in which this aspect of the theological task may enable us "to shape present action to fit the anticipated and hoped-for future" (*ND*, p. 125).

What is usually called *foundational theology* (or apologetic theology) aims to show how the worldview and ethos of the community is intelligible and credible—how they depict what Lindbeck calls a "followable" or "habitable" world and not an ultimately mythical or primarily imaginary one. Lindbeck's own way of handling the issue of credibility precludes labeling this task "foundational" theology, since he rejects the apologetic appeals to epistemic foundations which characterize much of modern theology. He does not, however, reject the question of credibility; rather, as the next section explains, he suggests a different way of answering it.

In undertaking its various tasks, theology should engage in a conversation that is expansive and critical, and it should undertake its engagement with others in a generosity of spirit that is unsatisfied with criticizing an apparently opposing position until the theologian can make a better argument for the opposing position than its critic can make against it. These theological *desiderata* are seldom mentioned explicitly by Lindbeck, but are rather displayed in the way he attempts to go about doing theology. Theology should aim to construct a comprehensive vision of the world, which does not ignore but rather tries to make Christian sense out of apparently alien beliefs and practices. Conceptual tools for this task may be found in both explicitly theological sources and secular disciplines. Lindbeck, for example, engages the social sciences not only in his theory of religion and doctrine but also in his handling of disputed ecumenical questions like infallibility. In a phrase from Kenneth Burke (to which David Tracy also appeals in characterizing the demeanor of theology), theology as Lindbeck conceives it should "use all that can be used." To be sure, not everything can be used (or more precisely not everything with which one is acquainted, which will always be very far short indeed of "everything"); theology must have a critical edge the sharpness of which matches its breadth of vision. Deciding what cannot be used especially requires a willingness and ability to see an issue and its supporting arguments from an opponent's point of view. Lindbeck's primary model for this quest to see each theological question from every available angle is Thomas Aquinas, but the very effort to do so is simply the theological application of Luther's injunction always to put the best construction on things.

Theology's Commitments

Lindbeck's definition of theology aims to permit considerable diversity. Lindbeck proposes, however, that in the present circumstances of church and academy theology needs a definite shape; it will best fulfill its tasks if it is guided by at least the following specific commitments.

Theology should ascribe consistent primacy to the scriptural story of Israel and Jesus Christ in articulating both the meaning and the truth of a Christian vision of reality. Lindbeck relies on his longtime colleague Hans Frei for the notion that the Bible is unified by a complex but coherent narrative which centers on the personal agent Jesus of Nazareth, whose unique identity emerges in the Gospel stories of his path from Bethlehem to Golgotha and the Emmaus road. This overarching narrative holds together the diverse materials of the Bible: "poetic, prophetic, legal, liturgical, sapiential, mythical, legendary, and historical" (*ND*, 1984, p. 120). Here Lindbeck clearly thinks that the exegetical labors of theologians like Karl Barth and Hans Urs von Balthasar provide considerable support for reading the Bible this way.

This narratively centered text, Lindbeck argues, "evokes" its own "domain of meaning" (*ND*, p. 116). It may and should be interpreted theologically by extended attention to its own linguistic details, and especially to the interconnections of action, character, and circumstance that constitute its unique narrative shape. By contrast, the Bible should not be read theologically by trying to find another, independent "domain of meaning" or interpretative framework into which the theologian attempts to translate the language of the biblical text and determine its sense. Lindbeck is especially concerned to avoid theological interpretation that takes descriptions of putatively universal human experience to constitute just such a quasi-independent interpretative framework.

To read the Bible by ascribing interpretative primacy to the narrative that identifies Israel and Jesus Christ does not, on Lindbeck's account, allow for complete interpretative neutrality, but is tied up with some basic claims about the content of that narrative and of scripture as a whole. The story of Israel and Jesus Christ unfolds so that it identifies as its primary agent the God of Israel, who fully shares the divine life with the world by sending both the Son and the Spirit into the world. So the central narrative, and with it the whole of Scripture, should be read in a deeply trinitarian and christological way. The sort of theological reading for which Lindbeck argues interprets the text, in what he characterizes as the classical Christian manner, "as a canonically and narrationally unified and internally glossed (that is, self-referential and self-interpreting) whole centered on Jesus Christ, [which tells] the story of the dealings of the Triune God with his people and his world in ways which are typologically . . . applicable to the present" ("Scripture, Consensus, and Community," 1989, p. 75).

The aim of reading the Bible in this "internally glossed" and "self-referential" way is not to isolate the Bible from the rest of human belief and practice, but the opposite: to construct a comprehensive vision of life and reality. Or as Lindbeck puts it, this sort of interpretation aims at "imaginatively incorporating all being into a Christ-centered world" (*ND*, p. 118). The narratively centered biblical text ought to have primacy in shaping a Christian vision of all life and reality; thus Lindbeck concludes that the Bible may and should be handled theologically so that it not only evokes its own domain of meaning but generates its own criteria of truth. Judgments about truth and falsity are ultimately, though not solely, judgments about the coherence of beliefs and practices with the Christ-centered world depicted in Scripture, rather than judgments about how this Christ-centered world fits with some other criterion. And Christian visions of the world constructed by ascribing primacy in the order of meaning and of truth to the biblical narrative of creation, fall, redemption, and consummation will display their truth, and anticipate their eschatological confirmation and fulfillment, precisely by their ability to make sense of, and to hold true on their own terms, the ever-varied claims to truth that the Christian community encounters on its way from Pentecost to the parousia.

This way of reading the Bible is at bottom the historical practice of a particular human community, the church, rather than a product of the individual theological imagination. This community's identity, and so its own continuing reality, are decisively shaped by this practice. Therefore the natural home for a theology that ascribes interpretative and epistemic primacy to scripture read as a trinitarian and christological narrative is the continuing life of the church and the decisions that this community continually must make about its own identity—about how to be faithful to the God depicted in this narrative. As Hans Frei observes, precisely in order to do justice to *both* the churchly and academic vocations of the theologian, this sort of theology calls on one "to order one's priorities. . . . Both vocations are best served when theology is seen to be in service to the church first, to the academy second" (Frei, "Lindbeck," 1990).

The church, moreover, finds not only its God in the story of Israel and Jesus Christ, but finds itself as well. On Lindbeck's account, "The church is fundamentally identified and characterized by its story" (*Scriptural Authority and Narrative Interpretation,* 1988, p. 165); attributing specific characteristics to the church, however distinctive (such as unity, holiness, catholicity, and apostolicity), depends on the identification of the church as a particular community that takes place by means of the scriptural narrative. And this story, Lindbeck stresses, binds the church irrevocably to Israel, past and present. Since the publication of *The Nature of Doctrine,* Lindbeck has concentrated particularly on the articulation of an ecclesiology for which the church is primarily the pilgrim people of God in unity with and dependence upon Israel, despite the division, perhaps to endure until the eschaton, between the church and the Jewish people. This ecclesiology, which Lindbeck suggests could also be viewed as an "Israelology," comes not at the sacrifice of the church's distinctive belief in the triune God and the incarnation, but as required by the same narrative which supports those very beliefs.

Conclusion

Lindbeck's recommendation of a theology centered on the scriptural word that creates and sustains a community in which that word is continually interpreted anew clearly displays its Lutheran provenance, although Lindbeck does not rely on distinctively Lutheran theological arguments to justify it. He labels this approach to theology "postliberal," but only in order to distinguish it from what he takes to be the dominant trend in nineteenth- and twentieth-century academic theology, and not in order to suggest its distinctiveness or novelty on some larger scale. Earlier theologians like Luther and Aquinas are Lindbeck's favorite examples of skilled practitioners of this way of doing theology, which he finds massively embodied in recent theologians like Barth and von Balthasar, who share relatively little of Lindbeck's conceptual idiom for articulating what he takes to be the classically Christian sense of theology's tasks and commitments. Thus on Lindbeck's own account any attempt to articulate those tasks and commitments best serves not as a topic of interest in its own right, but as a modest aid toward what really matters, which is to do theology well.

Bruce D. Marshall

Selected Bibliography

1984   George A. Lindbeck, *The Nature of Doctrine: Religion and Theology in a Postliberal Age.*

1988   George A. Lindbeck, "The Story-shaped Church," in Garrett Green, ed., *Scriptural Authority and Narrative Interpretation.*

1989   George A. Lindbeck, "Scripture, Consensus, and Community," in R. J. Neuhaus, ed., *Biblical Interpretation in Crisis.*

1990   Bruce D. Marshall, ed., *Theology in Dialogue: Essays in Conversation with George Lindbeck.*

1990   Hans W. Frei, "George Lindbeck and *The Nature of Doctrine,*" in Marshall, ed., *Theology and Dialogue.*

SALLIE McFAGUE
1934–

Sallie McFague is the E. Rhodes and Leona B. Carpenter Professor of Theology at Vanderbilt University. After graduating *magna cum laude* from Smith College in 1955, McFague became one of a very few women of her generation to seek graduate training in theology. She earned the B.D., M.A., and Ph.D. degrees from Yale University (awarded in 1959, 1960, and 1964, respectively). She assumed a teaching post at Vanderbilt in 1970, serving as the Divinity School's dean from 1975 to 1979. McFague firmly established her place at the forefront of current Christian theology with the publication of her fourth book, *Models of God: Theology for an Ecological, Nuclear Age* (1987), which received the American Academy of Religion's Award for Excellence of Books in the Field in 1988.

To fully appreciate this work, one needs some familiarity with the issues and interests that fund McFague's theological vision and method as both emerge from the books that preceded *Models* and shape the work that has grown out of it. As a working theologian, McFague is concerned with promoting theological reflection that speaks to the issues of our day. She names the nuclear and ecological crises as particularly crucial issues facing today's world. However, these crises are not separable from issues of gender oppression, racial prejudice, or economic injustice. Like other feminist theologians, McFague sees that issues of ecological exploitation and the oppression of women are intertwined, but McFague also reminds her readers that the impact of ecological problems differs with socioeconomic location. Attempts to solve ecological problems have to take issues of economic justice into account. McFague is certainly keenly aware that she writes from a particular socioeconomic location; that of a white, middle-class, feminist, first-world theologian. She addresses her work specifically to other first-worlders, calling them to acknowledge a special responsibility for the ecological crisis because the first world's pattern of consumption created the crisis.

McFague also acknowledges that, to call itself Christian, constructive theology must hold itself accountable to what is essential about the Christian tradition. Her normative vision of Christianity centers on the claim that there is a personal power in the universe that is on the side of life in all its forms and against whatever impedes life's flourishing. Therefore, rather than supporting relationships of domination, Christianity should be destabilizing, inclusive, and nonhierarchical. This vision of Christianity is, she argues, coherent with the portrayal of God's activity in the Hebrew Scriptures and in the New Testament, especially in the life of Jesus. However, McFague is not a narrow biblicist. She rejects any strong division between the three traditional sources of Christian theology: scripture, tradition, and experience. Scripture is the earliest layer of tradition, she argues, and both scripture and tradition are codified experience. McFague prefers to think of scripture (and tradition) as a Christian classic—that is, a collection of paradigmatic experiences with the divine that serves as a model for subsequent generations of believers. She takes the *form* rather than the content of scripture to be normative. All theology should be "risky, adventurous interpretation of the salvific love of God for our time" (*Models*, 1987, p. 44). This way of construing theology's traditional sources allows her the freedom to broaden the stream of what counts as "tradition." Although maintaining her grounding in biblical and theological texts, McFague also mines poetry, novels, and religious autobiographies as resources for theological reflection.

The most distinctive feature of McFague's concerns is the level at which she engages in theological construction. McFague aims to affect the religious imagination. She is far more concerned with how Christianity *imagines* the relationship of God and the world than with working out a coherent *conceptual* account of that relationship. McFague's work mediates between second-order theological reflection (abstract conceptual argumentation) and first-order religious language (symbols, images, and stories). From her early interests in literature and story as a resource for Christian life and thought (see her dissertation, published in 1966 as *Literature and the Christian Life*) to her more recent work, which she describes as "remythologizing" Christianity (*Models*, p. xi), McFague has tried to stay close to the stories, symbols, and images that fund theological reflection while keeping clearly in view the issues that motivate theology—how to construe the relationship between God and the world, how to conceive the problem of the existence of evil, and how to comprehend what salvation means.

McFague has found a rich methodological resource in Paul Ricoeur's theory of metaphor. The theory of religious language she devises using his account of metaphor initially appears in her second book, *Speaking in Parables: A Study in Metaphor and Theology* (1975), and it lays the groundwork for her subsequent work. According to Ricoeur, metaphors produce meaning in a unique way. Where analogies work on the basis of a presumed similarity between the referent and its analogue, metaphors exploit the *difference* between the referent and what figures it. Metaphors produce meaning through a "twist"; metaphorical meaning appears through the rupture of literal meaning. The metaphor, "War is a chess game," creates the similarity between "war" and "chess game" through the difference between them. War involves people (who risk and sometimes lose their lives) and weapons rather than game pieces, for example. However, viewing war through this metaphorical twist highlights the aspect of strategy in war.

In McFague's view, Ricoeur's theory provides the best account of how religious language works. All language for the divine is metaphorical, she argues. Images for God do not work on the basis of a presupposed similarity between the divine and the mundane, but create a resemblance through a twist produced when the image is transposed from its appropriate context to an unexpected one. Language for God does not describe God's being, but attempts to articulate human beings' *experience* of God in terms that, by definition, do not fit.

Speaking in Parables reads the parables of Jesus through the lens of Ricoeur's theory. The parables are not allegories reducible to straightforward moral messages, McFague argues; rather, they are radical redescriptions of reality. The conventional setting of the parable draws its readers into the narrative only to turn their world upside down. In the parable of the prodigal son, for example, the father subverts ordinary expectations by rewarding the profligate son rather than the dutiful son. This re-vision of God's love occurs in and through the details of the parable, through its "twist" on conventional expectations. God's love both "is" and "is not" like that of a father's love for his children.

Speaking in Parables focuses on the quality and character of primary religious language. The projects that come after it carry the tensive, dynamic quality of parabolic language toward the generally "cooler" realm of theological abstraction. In her next three books, McFague turns her attention to what she argues mediates between first-order and second-order religious language. *Metaphorical Theology: Models of God in Religious Language* (1982) uncovers the bridge between the two kinds of religious discourse, models of God. Models are extended metaphors that, because of their explanatory power and fit, have become paradigms within which Christianity lives. Models are drawn from primary religious language but shape and fund second-order theological reflection. For example, the parable of the prodigal son makes use of a central metaphor for God in Christianity, that of God as father. McFague argues that this metaphor has combined with other central metaphors (lord and king) to become *the* model within which Christianity thinks. It has become the paradigm within which Christian theology reflects on the meaning of Christian faith.

Metaphors become models because they are able to provide a coherent framework for fleshing out theological concepts. The Christian tradition has derived an entire theology from the paternal-monarchical model. Imaging God as Father-King organizes Christianity's conception of the divine-human relationship. If God is Father, then human beings are his children. Within that model, sin comes to be conceived as the rebellion of the child against the father. Redemption requires the sacrifice of an elder sibling who pays for the wrongdoing of the other children.

McFague acknowledges the structuring power of the monarchical model, but she recommends that Christianity seek out other models because the monarchical model has become idolatrous and irrelevant. Christianity has come to assume that "Father" is literally God's name; thus, the model has lost its metaphorical character. Christians seem to have forgotten what Christian theology has always claimed— that no language about God can adequately describe God's being. McFague also argues that the paternal-monarchical model is irrelevant to today's concerns. As she notes, human beings choose those things that are most valuable to them to image the divine. Given that Christianity developed in a patriarchal culture, it is no coincidence that male metaphors for God dominate the Christian landscape. However, imaging God as Father-King legitimates the domination of men over women and the powerful over the powerless. McFague joins with other feminist theologians in arguing that language for the divine needs to reflect the broad spectrum of human experience, including the experiences of women. McFague further argues that this paternal, monarchical model is dangerous in a nuclear, ecological age. Imaging God as Father-King allows human beings to abdicate responsibility for the created order. It encourages them to assume a childlike position before God in which they simply trust that God, as Lord of Creation, will take care of his own.

The problems with the monarchical model lead McFague to the next stage of her work. At the close of *Metaphorical Theology,* she proposes a "thought experiment": What if Christianity were to think within *different* models for God? She takes preliminary steps toward working out one such model, God as friend, in the last pages of *Metaphorical Theology;* her next book, *Models of God,* takes up this "thought experiment" as its primary task. All models run the risk of losing their metaphorical character, especially when one model is allowed to dominate the scene, as has been the case with the monarchical model. For that reason, McFague advocates developing a plurality of models for God. In *Models of God,* McFague offers three fully articulated models of God (mother, lover, and friend) as alternatives to the dominant paternal-monarchical model. The text explores distinctive aspects of the God-world relationship opened up by each model. Her portraits of these models include careful assessments of each model's claim to being Christian and of its ability to accommodate critical issues in Christian theology. McFague's assessment focuses on the concept of divine love and the mode of divine activity that each model articulates as well as the ethic for human activity the model promotes. Her primary aim is to develop models that will support Christian *involvement* in caring for the world. All three models stress the radical dependence of all life, including the divine life, on other forms of life.

To function as good models, these metaphors must be rich in symbolic resources and must speak to human experience at its deepest level. The three models McFague develops are drawn from the most basic relationships in human life. They are rich in symbolic connotations because they also deal with the basic "stuff" of life. Yet no matter how rich the resources for theological reflection that a model offers, it will always exhibit limitations. McFague's account of each model's merits not only takes note of their limits, but calls the reader's attention to them. As she argues, metaphorical theology, rather than reducing the divine to the mundane, underscores the gap between them. Metaphorical theology thus draws attention to the tentativeness of all naming of the divine.

McFague turns first to the model of God as mother. She grounds this model in Christianity's claim that God is the ground of being and source of all that is. Indeed, she argues, God as mother models the creative love of God particularly well because of the model's associations with birth and gestation. She acknowledges that some Christians will resist this model because it seems explicitly sexual. However, she notes, the model of God as father also has sexual connotations, although they have receded from view. McFague argues that imaging God as mother *seems* more sexual only because our culture associates women more closely with sexuality. She also reminds her readers that God as mother is a model, not a description. To image God as mother is not to claim that God *literally* gave birth to the cosmos, but that God "bod[ies] forth" the world (*Models,* 1987, p. 110). God's creative activity is continuous. The world, rather than being separate from God, is part of God's very being.

McFague refuses to limit divine activity as seen through this model to stereo-typically feminine attributes such as nurturing. This process advances her claim that the Christian tradition needs *female* (rather than *feminine*) models for the divine to counter the dominance of male models. God as mother is concerned with promoting the just treatment of her creation. McFague notes that this model's association with justice has precedence in scripture and tradition. Divine wisdom has been personified as female and described as the source of order and justice in the created order (see, e.g., Proverbs 9). Justice is also the ethic for human activity that this model promotes. If the world is "bodied forth" by God, human beings cannot love God without loving the rest of the world. Loving the world involves working for a just order that will balance the needs of different forms of life for the good of the whole. This ethic, McFague argues, is particularly appropriate for an ecological, nuclear age.

McFague's second model of God as lover envisions the love of God as "a passionate attraction to the valuable and a desire to be united with it" (*Models,* p. 131). This model has strong and deep roots in the Christian tradition from the Song of Songs in the Hebrew Bible, to various theologians' portrayal of God as attracting believers to Godself, to the rich development of the metaphor in the writings of Christian mystics. The ethic supported by this model is one of healing whatever afflicts the flourishing of the beloved. McFague points out that modeling God as lover offers an important corrective to the traditional concept of God as loving God's creation in spite of its flaws. By emphasizing the unworthiness of creation, the traditional concept of God's love gives creation a low value. A lover, on the other hand, continues to hold the beloved in high esteem even when recognizing the lover's faults. Thus, viewing God's love through the lens of this model emphasizes the high value God continues to place on the created order.

The model of God as friend forms the final piece of McFague's thought experiment. At first glance, this model faces a significant set of problems. How appropriate is it to describe the relationship between obviously unequal parties as "friendship"? McFague proposes conceiving friendship as mutual commitment to a common project. This definition allows her to argue that the covenant between Yahweh and Israel supports this model. Jesus' table fellowship, which includes outcasts, also fits with this model of God as friend. The ethic promoted by this model is one of solidarity and mutual commitment to a common project, the work of salvation as healing.

The three models come together to form a trinity. Where the model of God as mother images the divine in its role as creator and the model of lover images the divine as redeemer, the model of God as friend images the divine as sustainer. This trinitarian structure is more than fortuitous. The three models reinforce one another in many ways. While each speaks to a different dimension of the relationship between God and the world, together they promote a common ethic (solidarity and justice) and common understanding of salvation as working to overcome alienation and suffering. Taken together, the three models also offer resources to address the problem of evil. Modeling God as mother means that God is intimately involved with the created order, including the suffering experienced within it. Modeling God as lover and friend suggests a way of conceiving of God's place within a cosmos that includes so much suffering. God as lover suffers with creation as a lover suffers with his or her beloved. Moreover, God as lover and friend works to alleviate suffering and to overcome the conditions that produced it in whatever ways are possible. McFague acknowledges that such a view cannot offer a defense of God that keeps God's hands clean of involvement with evil and suffering. However, conceiving divine presence as suffering with those who suffer offers comfort. In addition, it offers a model for how God's followers should position themselves in relation to persons who suffer.

McFague's most recent book, *The Body of God: An Ecological Theology* (1993), grows directly out of *Metaphorical Theology* and *Models of God*. *Models of God* broaches the model of the world as God's body as a way of conceiving the underlying relationship between God and the world evoked by the models of God as mother, lover, and friend. *The Body of God* turns to developing that model in its full scope. *Body of God* also pursues another valuable aspect of McFague's work. Beginning with *Metaphorical Theology*, McFague takes on the task of bridging theology and science. Religion and science are often assumed to have radically different foundations and, therefore, truth claims. Where religion is understood to be grounded in the human being's desire for meaning, science is understood to be grounded in objective fact. However, McFague's reading of recent literature in the philosophy of science (most notably, Thomas Kuhn's research on paradigm shifts in science) leads her to suggest that religion and science share a common foundation. In *Metaphorical Theology*, McFague argues that both science and theology are dependent on models that provide the paradigm within which their thinking is done. For example, wave-particle theory in physics uses what is known (the behavior of waves and particles) to explain the unknown (the behavior of electrons).

In *Body*, McFague brings science and theology into even closer proximity. Her reading in contemporary science leads her to argue *not* just that theology can and should be coherent with scientific accounts of the cosmos, but that science can enrich the religious imagination as it thinks through the implications of imaging the world as God's body. McFague's own work in *Body* illustrates this claim. First, she argues that Christian theology has reason to take embodiment seriously. After all, Christianity's central claim is that God became incarnate in the person of Jesus. However, as she notes, Christianity has historically shied away from positively valuing bodies. Moreover, when and where it has spoken positively about embodiment, the bodies included in that evaluation have tended to be only human—and paradigmatically white male bodies. Contemporary scientific research encourages Christianity to expand its notion of embodiment to encompass the enormous variety of physical life in the cosmos. McFague describes looking at a tidal pool through the lens of biological science in order to share with her readers her sense of amazement at the sheer diversity of bodies in this microcosm of the cosmos.

McFague continues to be concerned with promoting a way of imagining the relationship between God and the cosmos that stresses the interdependence of all life. Early in *Body of God*, she pulls what she has gleaned from her study of scientific accounts of the origin of the universe into what she calls the common creation story. That story enriches the religious imagination by refiguring the relationship between unity and diversity. According to the common creation story, all life is literally unified by the fact that it is all made of matter-energy derived from one source. Physics also says that matter-energy-life tends toward ever greater diversity, dispersion, and variety. In other words, unity in the sense of organic, physical connectedness lies in the cosmos' past, not in its future. On the other hand, science also makes it clear that all elements of the ecosystem are linked together in interdependent relationships. Thus, science tells us that diversity stretches farther than we have imagined and encourages us to think differently about what unites the created order.

McFague distinguishes the bridge she is building between theology and science from more traditional projects. She is not, for example, attempting to devise a natural theology; that is, she is not turning to the natural world in order to discern God's activity in initiating and directing its emergence and maintenance. The classical account of God's relationship to the world is no longer possible, she thinks.

Science will not support classical claims that God constitutes the *telos* (end, goal, origin) of the created order. McFague is instead interested in exploring the "loose fit" between the scientific picture of the origin, growth, and function of the cosmos and theological claims. She is not bothered by the fact that contemporary science does not support claims for divine direction of creation. Rather, she proposes that we start with what we know: a sense of wonder at the complexity and diversity of creation. Regardless of *how* creation happened, it did happen—and in a most marvelous way. Christianity claims that God was and is involved in that marvelous process. McFague willingly leaves behind "how" and "why" questions about God's involvement in favor of the more pragmatic question of what Christians should do in light of the claim about God's involvement.

McFague's focus on what lies between primary religious language and abstract conceptual language—that is, her focus on the religious imagination—is the source both of the strength of her work, and of its limitations, according to some critics. Even critics most sympathetic to her work (Gordon Kaufman and Maurice Wiles, for example) continue to call McFague to a more careful consideration of the relationship between metaphorical theology and conceptual theology. Other critics have argued that bringing God and the world into such proximity requires more rigorous attention to the "how" questions McFague leaves behind. McFague is clearly well aware of the limits of the kind of theology she writes. As she repeatedly asserts, the claims that metaphorical theology makes are small and limited. On the other hand, if conceptual theology were to ground itself anew in these redescriptions of the relationship between God and the cosmos that McFague has provided, it would surely be enriched and reshaped.

Ellen T. Armour

Selected Primary Works

1966   *Literature and the Christian Life.*
1975   *Speaking in Parables: A Study in Metaphor and Theology.*
1982   *Metaphorical Theology: Models of God in Religious Language.*
1987   *Models of God: Theology for an Ecological, Nuclear Age.*
1993   *The Body of God: An Ecological Theology.*

Selected Secondary Sources

1988   Gordon D. Kaufman, Review of *Models of God: Theology for an Ecological, Nuclear Age, Theology Today* 45, no. 1 (April): 95-101.
1991   B. Jill Carroll, "Models of God or Models of Us? On the Theology of Sallie McFague," *Encounter* 52, no. 2 (Spring): 183-95.

1993   David J. Bromell, "Sallie McFague's 'Metaphorical Theology,'" *Journal of the American Academy of Religion* 61, no. 3 (Fall): 485-503.

1994   Maurice Wiles, Review of *The Body of God: An Ecological Theology, Journal of Theological Studies* 45, part 1 (April): 429.

THOMAS MERTON
1915–1968

Life and Career

Thomas Merton cannot be classified as a theologian in the strict sense of the term, but his writings have exerted sufficient impact on religious thought, especially in spirituality, to merit him a place in this volume. Born in Prades, France, on January 31, 1915, he experienced a great deal of tragedy during his early years. His mother died when he was six, his father when he was fifteen. In the interim his father, a landscape painter named Owen, carted Tom around Europe and placed him in boarding schools in France and in England. After he was "sent down" from Cambridge, his guardian brought him to the United States, where he enrolled at Columbia University and majored in English literature. At Columbia he came under the tutelage of Mark Van Doren, a professor of English literature, and Daniel Walsh, a professor at Manhattanville College who taught as an adjunct at Columbia. A serious religious search resulted in Merton's conversion to the Roman Catholic Church and a decision to join the Order of Cistercians of the Strict Observance (Trappists), after being turned down by the Franciscans. He entered the Abbey of Gethsemani on December 10, 1941, and remained there until his death on December 10, 1968, during a trip to Bangkok to participate in a gathering of monks.

Shaped by the training required in the novitiate and, even more, by his dramatic personal experience, Merton's theology, while remaining in most points faithful to Catholic tradition, underwent some unusually telling changes following a sort of "second conversion" in 1950. In 1941 Merton had entered Gethsemani clanging the doors shut and pronouncing a not very polite curse on the "world," understood as everything and everyone outside the monastery. He found, however, that the "world" that had scarred him so badly and that he loathed so fiercely, had come in with him. It resided in his false self, a self overlaid by hypocrisy and conceit. Undergoing a "submarine earthquake" in 1949 to 1950, he came out a "new Merton" capable of accepting responsibility for the world, now viewed in a very different light.

By the 1960s Merton addressed with prophetic insight and compassion a United States society wracked by a bitter and divisive war in Vietnam, strife and violence in its cities, racism, autonomous technology, and many other problems. The message that he spoke so eloquently, however, came from the contemplative tradition that he embraced when he hearkened to the calling of a monk at Gethsemani over that of a social worker in Catherine de Hueck Dougherty's Friendship House in Harlem. As he extended his pipeline farther and farther outward to a world hungry for the contemplative message, he sought more and deeper solitude, on the one hand, and looked to the religions of the Orient, especially Zen Buddhism, on the other, to find solutions to problems endemic to Western civilization. Sadly, a defective fan switch cut off his quest at the age of fifty-three.

The Purpose and Authority of Theology

Merton did not think of himself self-consciously as doing theology, certainly not as a theologian. He was, first of all and above all, a contemplative. In early writings he confessed his lack of qualifications. He did not have the "sharpness, definiteness, precision in theology" of a Dominican (*Sign of Jonas*, 1953, p. 208). As time passed, he grew more and more impatient with scholastic subtleties that did not ring true to his experience or allow him to speak with clarity to modern problems. Already in *The Seven Storey Mountain* (1948), he identified himself as "essentially Augustinian" and concluded that he leaned "not so much towards the intellectual, dialectical, speculative character of Thomas, as towards the spiritual, mystical, voluntaristic and practical way of St. Augustine and his followers" (p. 199). Others, failing to take into account his contemplative bent and personality, frequently faulted him for sloppy theological writing. But Merton tried scholasticism and found it wanting; though he confessed early on, maybe for his censors, that it kept him on the right road, near the end of his life he dared to express surprise that Thomism had come out of the "dangerous" Thomas Aquinas and rued the fact that to embrace Thomism one had to renounce everything else (*Conjectures of a Guilty Bystander,* 1966, p. 205).

As a contemplative, once past the period of hostility to everything outside the monastery, Merton conceived his task, whether self-consciously or not, as one of feeding the experience of the whole contemplative tradition through his own fertile mind and heart and piping it outward toward other contemplatives and toward a world whose eagerness and hunger for that message had not occurred to him until publication of *The Seven Storey Mountain* made him a world celebrity. Merton turned especially to the Eastern Fathers to find justification for theology as essentially mystical and to explain the task of theologians as one of awakening people to the presence of the Universal Christ at the heart of the universe.

Until the Second Vatican Council, which he watched closely, defined more clearly the "One Source Theory" of authority, Merton kept on a path close to the contemplative tradition to which he thought he belonged. In the early and popular *Seeds of Contemplation* (1948), Merton listed as his basic sources the gospel of Christ, the Rule of Benedict, Catholic ascetic writings, Cistercian writings of the twelfth century, especially Bernard of Clairvaux, and John of the Cross's thoughts on contemplative prayer. This book also cited Augustine, Pseudo-Dionysius, Ignatius Loyola, and Teresa of Avilá. His notes for the choir novitiate of 1959 and 1961 extended the list to include the desert monks, Evagrius Ponticus, Gregory the Great, John Cassian, William of St. Thierry, Aelred of Rivaulx, Guigo the Carthusian, Richard Rolle, John Nicholas Grou, Louis Lallement, Charles de Foucauld, and Charles Péguy. Merton's *Bread in the Wilderness*, a study of the Psalms in contemplation, suggests that the Psalms also played a significant role in shaping his theology. By the sixties Merton was expending quite a bit of time in study of the scriptures.

The early Merton, prior to the fifties, went out of his way to affirm his desire to speak in new and fresh ways without inserting "a line that is new to Catholic tradition or a single word that would perplex an orthodox theologian" (*Seeds of Contemplation*, 1948, p. xv). He later loosened up on his understanding of "Catholic," expressing regret that he once exhibited a "ghetto" Catholic mentality. In his more mature phase he had developed a good grasp of the contemplative "tradition," sharply distinguished from "convention," and let this serve as the measuring rod for other ideas and experiences and activities. He did not "proof text" either from scriptures or tradition. A highly literary person himself, he spiraled ever outward from this center to incorporate insights from numerous sources. He discovered "grace" in all sorts of things. He thought his love for William Blake had "something in it of God's grace" (*Seven Storey Mountain*, 1948, p. 85). In the sixties he delved more and more deeply into Zen Buddhist literature and ranged far and wide among modern literary figures such as Jean-Paul Sartre, Albert Camus, Ernest Hemingway, James Baldwin, and Flannery O'Connor. Experience taught him that "books and ideas and poems and stories, pictures and music, buildings, cities, places, philosophies were to be the materials on which grace would work" (ibid., p. 178). As Aelred Graham remarked in reviewing *No Man Is an Island*, Merton possessed "an instinctive sense of the orthodox blended with the originality, not of one who must think differently from other people, but of one who thinks for himself" ("Mysticism of Thomas Merton," 1965, pp. 155-59).

God and Christ

For Merton God is, above all, the "I AM" who spoke to Moses. God is mystery. "God is not a *what*," not a "thing." God is a pure *"Who."* God is "the 'Thou' before whom our inmost 'I' springs into awareness" (*New Seeds of Contemplation*, 1962, p. 13).

Merton moved increasingly toward the apophatic tradition of the Christian East—Gregory of Nyssa, Pseudo-Dionysius—which emphasized God's unknowability. "The living God, the God Who is God and not a philosopher's abstraction," he wrote in *New Seeds of Contemplation,* "lies infinitely beyond the reach of anything our eyes can see or our minds can understand" (1962, p. 131). God so surpasses human ability to conceive that we see God only as darkness. Since we cannot hear God, we must enter into silence. Only God can understand God. We cannot really understand the mystery of the Trinity. Contemplatives may run aground trying to understand the subtleties of dogma.

Despite his leanings in this direction, however, Merton evidently accepted the solution that the anonymous author of *The Cloud of Unknowing* gave to the problem posed by the mystics of the East. We cannot know God by cognition, but we can know by love. God is pure Love. God is the initiator of the search. God utters Godself in us, speaks the Divine Name in us; otherwise, we would never know God. "The only One Who can teach me to find God is God, Himself, Alone" (*New Seeds of Contemplation,* p. 36).

Although Merton did not attempt anything like a Christology, Christology held the same central place in his contemplative theology as it did in Bernard of Clairvaux's. Contemplation occurs only in Christ. "The soul of the monk," he said in his best-selling autobiography *The Seven Storey Mountain,*

> is a Bethlehem where Christ comes to be born—in the sense that Christ is born where His likeness is reformed by grace, and where his Divinity lives, in a special manner, with His Father and His Holy Spirit, by charity, in this "new incarnation," this "other Christ." (1948, p. 372)

The centrality of Christology, as a matter of fact, was one of the magnets pulling him toward Karl Barth. In this area, too, however, Merton's thinking underwent a significant shift as his thought matured during the fifties and sixties.

Prior to his "second conversion," Merton was at pains to square what he wrote about Christ with accepted Catholic teachings. In *The Ascent to Truth,* the most theological of all his writings, he pointed out that John of the Cross and Gregory of Nyssa both centered their mysticism on Christ as true God and true man, the minimum "required to make a mystical doctrine Christian" (1951, p. 244). "Saint John of the Cross," he judged, "would be the last man in the world to dispense the mystic from subjection to the *Magisterium*" (ibid., p. 248). John agreed fully with the schoolmen. Merton definitely tended toward Christology "from above" in this period. His Christ was the triumphant figure of the great churches of Rome.

The "new" and "reborn" Merton of the fifties and sixties bore witness to a kenotic Christ, as he wrote more boldly out of experience and plunged more deeply into scriptures. He spoke increasingly about Christ "from below." Though not contesting anything found in Catholic tradition, he confessed in his postconversion anthem

No Man Is an Island that he no longer intended "to accept points of that tradition blindly, and without understanding, and without making them really my own" (1955, p. 11). He had to live what he believed.

As he made more room for what he lived, his Christ grew. In "A Tribute to Gandhi" (*Seeds of Destruction*, 1964, pp. 221-34), he decided it was irrelevant whether Gandhi "believed in" Jesus in the Christian sense or not. Gandhi not only understood the ethic of the gospel as well as or better than most Christians, he was one of a very few who applied it. In a letter to a rabbi, Merton concluded: "The suffering Servant is One: Christ, Israel" (*Seeds of Destruction*, p. 189). In *Mystics and Zen Masters* (1967), he was groping for a way to link Zen Buddhists to Christ and thought it might be found in a convergence around "the transcendent and personal center" that is "the Risen and Deathless Christ in whom all is fulfilled in One" (p. 42). He did not share the optimism of Teilhard de Chardin based on an evolutionary model, but he grasped something of Teilhard's universal Christ at the heart of the universe and thus in everyone. To effect the reunion of divided Christians, indeed of all humankind, "We must contain all divided worlds in ourselves and transcend them in Christ" (*Conjectures of a Guilty Bystander,* 1966, p. 21). Reflecting on the unitive character of love in "The Power and Meaning of Love" (*Disputed Questions*, 1960, pp. 97-126), he seized the promise of Matthew 25 that the other person "is Christ." To this he added: "Our faith is given us not to see *whether or not* our neighbor is Christ, but to recognize Christ in him and to help our love make both him and ourselves more fully Christ" (*Disputed Questions*, p. 100).

Human Nature and Evil

As in most other areas of his thought, Merton had to revise the estimate of human nature that he carried with him to Gethsemani. Terribly scarred by his early experience of life—the deaths of both parents, loneliness, the Depression, the onset of World War II—he entered the monastery to slam the doors shut on the decadent "world" outside. After a while, however, he discovered both that the "world" existed in the monastery as it did outside and that the "world" outside, that is, other human beings, was not as bad as he imagined when he entered Gethsemani. By the 1950s, therefore, Thomas Merton reached the point in his transformation where he could accept some responsibility for the "world," which he now learned to view in a more complex and friendly fashion.

Already in *The Sign of Jonas* (1953) Merton expressed embarrassment at his "very supernatural solution" to the problems of the world expressed in his *Journal of My Escape from the Nazis*. "The false solution went like this: the whole world, of which the war is a characteristic expression, is evil. It has therefore to be first ridiculed, then spat upon, and at last formally rejected with a curse" (*Sign of Jonas,* p. 314). What nine years as a contemplative had taught him was to distinguish people from their wars. Wars are evil, but people are good. He could not withdraw from them, therefore, and wash his hands of their problems. Coming to the monastery had given him perspective and enabled him to see how he could share the life of people in the world.

This dramatic shift notwithstanding, Merton remained a realist in the Augustinian tradition in his assessment of human nature. His own experience confirmed the reality of "the Fall" and "Original Sin." Consequently he could use either traditional language and imagery or those borrowed from existentialism to express his understanding.

We human beings are "born in sin"; that is, our real self is overlaid by a "false self." Our true self is distorted by a selfishness or egocentrism that skews everything we do. Until we recognize that our "I" is not our self, we will remain captives of our false selves. Fortunately, God takes the initiative. Out of love God entreats us to pray, as Augustine did at Cassiciacum, "Teach me to know myself. Teach me to know Thee" (*Soliloquies*, 1.6). Contemplation is the road to our recovery, "the highest expression of man's intellectual and spiritual life" (*New Seeds of Contemplation*, 1962, p. 1).

Perhaps in part because of his mother's early death, Merton struggled personally with the issue of sexuality. At Cambridge he got a woman pregnant and carried with him some guilt exacerbated by both her and their child's death during World War II. During a lengthy stay in a Louisville hospital a short time before his own death, he fell in love with a nurse and carried on a clandestine love affair for a time until the Abbot discovered and put a stop to it. He did not express his opinion about homosexuality, but his conviction that the other person, whoever it is, *is* Christ mandated an acceptance of persons whose outlooks and lifestyles differed from his own.

The early Merton held a somewhat superficial view of evil that he himself, in retrospect, labeled "Manichaean." Like Augustine, however, he found Neoplatonic interpretation—evil not an entity in itself but the absence of good—inadequate to explain why he did what he did not want to do. The vividness of his own battle with evil ensured the persistence of a certain degree of pessimism throughout his life. In 1961 he defended this stance to a priest who criticized him for the latter trait. He was optimistic about the Christian hope, he insisted, for it was "hope in the Cross and Victory of Christ" (*Seeds of Destruction*, 1964, p. 221). He could not agree fully with Teilhard de Chardin, however. He felt a greater attraction to the realism of Kierkegaard, Romano Guardini, Bonhoeffer, Rahner, and others of their persuasion.

Where Merton shifted gears was in his decision to address the contemplative message to persons outside the monastery. An experience of "awakening" at a downtown Louisville street corner in 1958 gave impetus to the new direction his thought had taken in the early fifties. He "was suddenly overwhelmed," as he put it, "with the realization that I loved all those people, that they were mine and I was theirs, that we could not be alien to one another even though we were total strangers." He felt as if he had awakened from "a dream of separateness, of spurious self-isolation in a special world, the world of renunciation and supposed holiness." He "almost laughed out loud" at the sense of liberation he felt. He now knew that "it is a glorious destiny to be a member of the human race, though it is a race dedicated to many absurdities and one which makes many terrible mistakes; yet, with all that God Himself gloried in becoming a member of the human race!" (*Conjectures of a Guilty Bystander*, 1966, pp. 56-57).

In *Conjectures of a Guilty Bystander*, Merton took vigorous swipes at a wide array of social dilemmas in Western society—racism, autonomous technology, selfish autonomism, collective irrationality, nuclear weaponry, the war in Vietnam. He decided by this time (1968) that

> true Christian "openness to the world" proceeds from a genuine respect for being and for man, and for man's natural and historical setting in the world. But to "respect" man in his historical situation today without taking account of his need, his anguish, his limitations, and his peril, above all without consenting to share in his guilt, ends only in a cruel mockery of man. (Ibid., p. 223)

He sharply questioned John A. T. Robinson's proposal that we "accept life on their terms." Would that mean to "accept the affluent society of the West on *its* own terms?" (ibid., p. 323). If so, he would not go along. The Christian mission is to free people from the world's myths, idolatries, and confusion.

Salvation and Hope

By his own confession, the Merton who entered the Abbey of Gethsemani in 1941 was too preoccupied with his own salvation and envisioned hope too narrowly. Our true joy on earth, he wrote in *Seeds of Contemplation* (1948), is to escape our self-prison and enter by love into union with God. Until we love God fully, our world will be full of contradictions. He later criticized his quest for a self-serving solitude that took no thought for others.

It is important to recognize that Merton did theology as a contemplative. This means that, while he mentioned traditional symbols such as resurrection, heaven, and the kingdom of God in passing, he thought more in contemplative categories. The goal of humankind is union with God. Human hope rests in the initiative God has taken and continues to take to restore the relationship ruptured by human egocentrism. Contemplation is central here, for through it we awaken to the Real, God, who is at the center of our lives. Contrary to what the Protestant Reformers may have believed, contemplation is not "works righteousness"; it is dependent on grace. God, the Living Christ, the Holy Spirit alone awakens us to our true selves and transforms us. We must realize that Christianity "is not merely a doctrine or a system of beliefs, it is Christ living in us and uniting men to one another in His own Life and unity" (*New Seeds of Contemplation*, 1962, p. 79). Union with Christ means union with humankind. Anyone who thinks that contemplation implies withdrawal to escape the miseries of human life does not understand what it is and will never find God in contemplation.

Religious Pluralism

In *The Seven Storey Mountain* the new convert to Roman Catholicism had little room for other faiths. He panned the Quakerism of his mother and the Anglicanism of his father. Despite some early fascination with Eastern religions, he relegated them to "the natural order" and judged them "more or less useless" if not evil (p. 185). Once again, he underwent a drastic shift as his horizons enlarged in the fifties and sixties. The accession of Pope John XXIII in 1958 and the Council he called to effect a "New Pentecost" opened a wide door through which Merton eagerly stepped. The mature Merton envisioned for contemplatives like himself a mission of unifying humankind.

In the mid-fifties Merton grew rapidly in his appreciation for other Christians. In *No Man Is an Island* (1955), he echoed John Donne:

> Every other man is a piece of myself, for I am a part and a member of mankind. Every Christian is part of my own body, because we are members of Christ. What I do is also done for them and with them and by them. What they do is done in me and by me and for me. But each one of us remains responsible for his share in the life of the whole body. (p. 16)

Several years later, he confessed his preference for and confidence in the Catholic church but was ready to urge Protestants as well as Catholics to seek the light. "I will be a better Catholic," he contended, "not if I can *refute* every shade of Protestantism, but if I can affirm the truth in it and still go further" (*Conjectures of a Guilty Bystander*, 1966, p. 144).

Merton's appreciation for other faiths also mushroomed as he sought wisdom to address Western social crises. By the sixties he was insisting that the West needed Eastern wisdom and looked especially to Zen Buddhism, in which he found much similarity to his own contemplative tradition. He would return to the Pauline formula—becoming a Jew to the Jew, a Buddhist to the Buddhist, a Hindu to the Hindu—rather than try to persuade them to become Catholics.

> If I affirm myself as a Catholic merely by denying all that is Muslim, Jewish, Protestant, Hindu, Buddhist, etc., in the end I will find that there is not much left for

me to affirm as a Catholic: and certainly no breath of the Spirit with which to affirm it. (*Conjectures of a Guilty Bystander,* 1966, p. 144)

He felt a special link to Israel. "One has either got to be a Jew or stop reading the Bible" (ibid., p. 23). His attraction to Zen took him to the conference in Bangkok, where he met his death on December 10, 1968.

Merton's literary endeavors forced him to spiral outward in an ever-expanding circle. Christ in every person gave him a license for linking up with a professed agnostic such as Albert Camus and an avowed "anti-Christian" writer such as James Baldwin. He insisted on the right of other nations, races, and societies "to be different from us and to stay different" (ibid., p. 88).

Merton believed contemplatives such as he could unite in themselves the most diverse elements of human culture—Eastern and Western Christendom, the Greek and the Latin Fathers, the Russians with the Spanish mystics. They could foster a communion that went beyond words and thoughts as they sought to grow "toward the full maturity of the universal man."

E. Glenn Hinson

Selected Primary Works

1948   *Seeds of Contemplation.*
1948   *The Seven Storey Mountain.*
1951   *The Ascent to Truth.*
1953   *The Sign of Jonas.*
1955   *No Man Is an Island.*
1960   *Disputed Questions.*
1962   *New Seeds of Contemplation.*
1964   *Seeds of Destruction.*
1966   *Conjectures of a Guilty Bystander.*
1967   *Mystics and Zen Masters.*
1968   *Faith and Violence.*
1969   *Contemplative Prayer.*

Selected Secondary Sources

1965   Aelred Graham, "The Mysticism of Thomas Merton," *Commonweal* 62 (May).
1971   James T. Baker, *Thomas Merton: Social Critic.*
1974   Frederic Joseph Kelly, *Thomas Merton on Social Responsibility.*

1975   Raymond Bailey, *Thomas Merton on Mysticism.*
1981   Brother Patrick Hart, ed., *The Message of Thomas Merton.*
1981   William H. Shannon, *Thomas Merton's Dark Path: The Inner Experience of a Contemplative.*
1982   Anthony T. Padovano, *The Human Journey: Thomas Merton: Symbol of a Century.*
1985   Donald Grayston, *Thomas Merton: The Development of a Spiritual Theologian.*
1989   David D. Cooper, *Thomas Merton's Art of Denial: The Evolution of a Radical Humanist.*
1992   Lawrence S. Cunningham, ed., *Thomas Merton: Spiritual Master.*
1993   George Kilcourse, *Ace of Freedoms: Thomas Merton's Christ.*

JOHN MEYENDORFF
1926–1992

Life and Career

John Meyendorff was born in 1926 in Neuilly-sur-Seine, France, of Russian emigré parents of Baltic German aristocratic origin. He went to French schools and completed his theological education at the Orthodox Theological Institute of St. Sergius in Paris in 1949. In 1958 he was awarded the Doctorat-et-Lettres by the Sorbonne for his critical edition, translation, and commentary of the *Defense of the Holy Hesychasts*, generally known as the *Triads*, by the Byzantine monastic theologian and bishop of Thessaloniki, St. Gregory Palamas (c. 1296–1359).

In 1959, after being ordained a priest in the Russian Orthodox Church in France, the year which saw the publication of his doctoral work and his book *A Study of Gregory Palamas*, Meyendorff came to the United States with his wife and four children to join the faculty of St. Vladimir's Orthodox Theological Seminary in New York. He was Professor of Patristics and Church History at St. Vladimir's until his death from pancreatic cancer on July 22, 1992. He served as seminary dean and rector of the seminary chapel from 1984 until his retirement from these positions a month before his unexpected death.

In America, Meyendorff also joined the faculty of Harvard University's Byzantine Research Center, Dumbarton Oaks, in Washington, D.C., where he taught until 1967 and then became a Senior Fellow. He served Dumbarton Oaks as Acting Director in 1978. Beginning in 1967, Meyendorff was also Professor of Byzantine History at Fordham University. He lectured occasionally at Columbia University and Union Theological Seminary in New York. He served as president of the Orthodox Theological Society in America, president of the American Patristics Association, and as a member of the Executive Committee of the U.S. Committee for Byzantine Studies. He was a Fellow of the National Endowment for the Humanities (1976–77), a Guggenheim Fellow (1981), and a Corresponding Fellow of the British Academy.

From youth onward, John Meyendorff was an active member of the Orthodox Church. In France, he served as sub-deacon for the famous Metropolitan Evlogy at the Russian Orthodox cathedral in Paris, and he was a founding member and first General Secretary of Syndesmos, an international organization of Orthodox youth movements. After coming to America, he served as a pastor, spiritual guide, and popular church teacher during his tenure as a priest and professor at St. Vladimir's. He was a leader in the movement to transform the Russian Orthodox Missionary Metropolia, begun in North America in 1794 in Alaska, into the self-governing Orthodox Church in America comprising Orthodox believers of various nationalities and ethnic origins in the United States, Canada, and Mexico. For many years, he edited this church's newspaper, *The Orthodox Church*, as well as the *St. Vladimir's Theological Quarterly.*

In the last years of his life, Meyendorff was deeply involved in the restoration and renewal of Orthodox Church life in the Balkans, Eastern Europe, and the former U.S.S.R. He traveled to Russia where he had previously been denigrated, slandered, and declared an "enemy of the people" by the Marxist regime. He lectured on various themes in universities, theological academies, and scholarly institutes. He appeared on television, gave interviews, and received academic and ecclesiastical honors, including the Order of St. Vladimir from Russian Orthodox Patriarch Aleksy II.

Meyendorff was a devoted ecumenist. He participated in countless ecumenical dialogues and conferences, and contributed articles, reports, and reviews to many ecumenical publications. He was a member of the World Council of Churches' Faith and Order Commission, serving as Moderator from 1967 to 1975. He also represented the Orthodox Church in America on the World Council's Central Committee.

The Task of Theology

As a scholar and theologian, Meyendorff was a Byzantinist, church historian, and patristic theologian in the line of Georges Florovsky and Vladimir Lossky. He supported, promoted, and elaborated a critique of "school theology" through a creative "return to the church fathers" rooted in Orthodox liturgical worship and spiritual life. He enthusiastically engaged contemporary issues and questions. He welcomed conversation and dialogue on all theological, philosophical, cultural, and ecclesial issues. He rejoiced in scholarly, spiritual, and cultural achievements wherever they were to be found. He despised closed and narrow-minded sectarian attitudes and actions, and harshly judged pettiness and provincialism in all its forms. He also strongly criticized relativism, indifference, and irresponsibility masquerading as openness and toleration.

Meyendorff was a person, to use Lossky's expression, of "catholic consciousness" who welcomed for the modern Orthodox East what Florovsky called a "free encounter with the West." He did not believe that Orthodox theology was particularly "oriental" or "Eastern." He considered it rather to be an articulation and defense of "the faith once for all delivered to the saints" of the universal catholic Christian church expressed in, but not enslaved to or bound by, its particular historical and cultural forms.

For Meyendorff, theology's task is to articulate Christian faith and spiritual experience in contemporary language and categories for the edification of the church, the enlightenment of minds, the salvation of souls, and the transformation of human society. He believed that this task could only be accomplished by believers who participate in the church's sacramental and liturgical life rooted in the biblical Word of God and who struggle to actualize the faith in daily living through personal ascetical and spiritual discipline. Meyendorff contended that this is what "following the church fathers" means. This spiritual discipline is not simply the mechanical repetition of the fathers' words and arguments, but rather the personal and communal gaining of their mind and vision, accompanied by its application within contemporary conditions. In this approach Meyendorff agreed with his friend Jaroslav Pelikan in affirming that "tradition is the living faith of the dead" (though for Meyendorff the saints were hardly "dead" in the church's experience), as opposed to "traditionalism" defined as the "dead faith of the living." In one of his essays collected in *Living Tradition,* Meyendorff identified five "fundamental affirmations of patristic and Orthodox theology" that he considered to be most crucial and relevant to our time: (1) The world is not divine and it needs salvation; (2) human being is a theocentric being; (3) Christian theology is christocentric; (4) true ecclesiology is personalistic; (5) the true conception of God is trinitarian. (These rubrics organize the remainder of this essay.)

The World and Humanity

Meyendorff taught that the world, meaning the physical universe and a spiritual realm *(cosmos noetos)* of "bodiless powers," is God's good creation that is made by and for God's divine Son and Word incarnate as Jesus Christ, through the effective power of God's Holy Spirit. Following the Bible and church fathers, he saw the world as the created epiphany of God's uncreated fullness, the created expression of the divine words *(logoi)* of the divine Word *(Logos)* who became flesh as Jesus. He saw heaven and earth filled with the splendor and glory of God's uncreated "divine energies" that, in the patristic expression, "reach even unto us."

Viewing creation as the free and voluntary act of God, Meyendorff criticized the Hellenistic teaching that the world is the result of a movement in the Godhead that results in a becoming of things that will necessarily, even somehow "automatically," return to an unmoving, undifferentiated monadic stability in the Godhead, only perhaps to "fall apart" again and again. He countered this view of stability *(stasis)* and movement *(kenesis)* and beginning *(genesis)* by an exactly opposite view that was clearly, but hardly exclusively, articulated by one of his favorite church fathers, Maximus the Confessor. The world begins by God's divine fiat *(genesis)*, which starts the movement *(kenesis)*, which results in a stability *(stasis)* in God that is "evermoving." The goal of creation brought into being from nothing by God's will is "dynamic stability" or "stable dynamism" in unending communion with God.

Humanity is the center of creation. All persons, both male and female, are made in God's image and likeness for everlasting life in communion with God through God's Son and Word, who creates and redeems the world by the power of God's Holy Spirit. As "kat'eikona theou," human beings are made, following the fathers, "to become god by grace"; to be, and ever more perfectly to become, by God's good pleasure and power "everything that God is by nature."

Both men and women, personally and in their communion with one another, embody and integrate every aspect of created being and life: spirit and flesh, soul and body, intellect and will, understanding and feeling. They are made to be prophets who know and proclaim God's word, priests who mediate and consecrate all things by God's grace, and pastors who care for creation, transforming chaos into cosmos by participation in divine being and life.

The tragedy is that human beings sin. They reject their divine calling. They bring disorder, distortion, and destruction to the world. By their own choice, under demonic delusion, they are directed to death and not to life, to the nothingness out of which they are made, rather than to God their creator. They, with their world, are in need of salvation.

Meyendorff's view is not only the classical patristic critique of pantheistic and deterministic Hellenism, particularly Origenism; it is also a critique of modern views of the world and humanity as self-enclosed and self-defined entities whose meaning is found not outside and beyond them in God but, if there is meaning at all, solely and exclusively within themselves. Like his well-known colleague and coworker, Fr. Alexander Schmemann, Meyendorff was a radical critic of naturalism and secularism in all its forms.

Christ and Redemption

As a strictly Chalcedonian and Byzantine Orthodox theologian, Meyendorff conceived Christ in terms of classical Christianity. Jesus is the divine Logos who takes flesh. Son of God from eternity, as Nicea affirms, "light from light, true God from true God, begotten not created," this same Son becomes a real human being in his temporal, fleshly birth through Mary, who is confessed as *theotokos:* the one who gives birth to God. Jesus is a real human being, Meyendorff affirms, but he is not a "mere" human being; nor is he a human person. He is a divine person, "one of the holy trinity," who becomes human in every respect without sin; and for Meyendorff sin is not an essential element of being human. On the contrary, sin is an alien intruder in human being and life brought in by human freedom and passed on through mortality from generation to generation in various degrees of intensity and power.

In Meyendorff's Christology, which is that of the Eastern Church, Jesus Christ is the Godman *(theanthropos)* who is divine with the same divinity as God the Father and the Holy Spirit, and human with the identical humanity of all men and women. He takes on the weaknesses and wounds of fallen humanity, embracing human sickness and sin, in order to heal and save the human race, and indeed the whole of creation, through his blood on the cross. As prophet, high priest, and pastor-king, God's incarnate Son assumes and saves everything by recapitulating in himself the entirety of human experience, including its abandonment by God in death, in order to bring everyone and everything into communion with God through his renewed, resurrected, and deified humanity.

One Catholic Church

Meyendorff taught that the Orthodox Church is Christ's one, holy, catholic, and apostolic church, which alone among Christian churches truly and fully preserves Christian doctrine, worship, and spiritual life. Following the fathers, he affirmed that Christ's church is neither a sect nor a denomination, nor a federation of denominations, nor a merely human organization, nor an invisible assembly of those being saved. The church is the community of sinful believers, visible and traceable in history, identical in each place, which in its liturgical and sacramental being, its apostolic doctrine and worship, and the catholic fullness of its spiritual and mystical life is indeed Christ's very body and bride, "the fullness of him who fills all in all" (Eph. 1:23) and "the pillar and bulwark of the truth" (1 Tim. 3:15).

Meyendorff criticized contemporary structures, attitudes, and actions in all Orthodox churches for largely betraying the faith and life expressed in the church's scriptures, liturgy, dogma, canons, and saints. He called the Orthodox churches to repentance on the basis of their own authoritative teachings and witnesses. He also criticized the Roman and Reformed churches for deviating from Christian orthodoxy in teaching and practice. He rejoiced to recognize grace and truth in these churches, however, and gladly affirmed what he saw in them of the church's catholic and apostolic tradition. His ecumenical efforts for the restoration of visible unity among Christian churches was rooted in his conviction that "vestigia ecclesiae" remain in divided churches in varying degrees, and that ecclesial unity, however incomplete and impaired, exists among the churches confessing, baptizing, and worshiping in the name of the Father, Son, and Holy Spirit.

Following the fathers once again, Meyendorff saw the activity of God's grace outside the bounds of God's covenanted community in Christ. He confessed that every man, woman, and child is made in God's image, which can never be wholly denied or destroyed. He affirmed that all logical and spiritual beings act in, with, and by God's own Logos and Spirit whenever they act according to their God-given nature in goodness, beauty, and truth. His teaching about Christian witness in the world, as well as his views on political, ethnic, racial, and gender issues, is rooted in this fundamental perception and conviction.

Trinitarian Divinity

Meyendorff's view of the created world, humanity, Christ, the church, and human society in all its aspects, is rooted in his vision of trinitarian divinity. For Meyendorff the one true God is the God of Israel, the Father of Jesus the Messiah. Jesus Christ is the human being God's divine Word has become. He is the eternal Son of God, "born of the Father before all ages" (Nicea) in a timeless generation inconceivable to created minds. Together with the Holy Spirit, who "proceeds from the Father and rests in the Son" (a patristic expression now used in Orthodox liturgy), God the Father and the Son Jesus constitute the Holy Trinity; in patristic theology and Orthodox worship they are confessed as consubstantial: "one in essence and undivided."

The "essence" of the tri-hypostatic Godhead, which is one and the same for each of the divine persons, is "beyond essence" in nature and content. What God is in God's inner being and life cannot be seen, known, comprehended, or participated in by creatures. But human beings can and indeed must come to know and share God's divine being and life through participation in God's divine operations and energies, which "reach even unto us" by the personal activity of the one God and Father through his divine Son and Word incarnate as Jesus the Messiah, in and by the one Holy Spirit.

Meyendorff's vision of the trinitarian Godhead in which cataphatic affirmations about God's uncreated divine nature are combined with apophatic declarations about God's incomprehensible divine essence is that of the Palamite synthesis of patristic theology with which he began his scholarly career. It remained the ground and framework of his comprehensive worldview throughout his entire life.

Thomas Hopko

Selected Bibliography

1959   *A Study of Gregory Palamas (English trans. 1964).*
1963   *The Orthodox Church: Yesterday and Today.*
1966   *Orthodoxy and Catholicity.*
1969   *Christ in Eastern Christian Thought.*

1973   *Byzantine Theology.*
1975   *Marriage: An Orthodox Perspective.*
1978   *Living Tradition.*
1980   *Byzantium and the Rise of Russia.*
1981   *The Byzantine Legacy in the Orthodox Church.*
1983   *Catholicity and the Church.*
1987   *Vision of Unity.*
1987   *Witness to the World.*
1989   *Imperial Unity and Christian Divisions: The Church 450–680 A.D.*

JÜRGEN MOLTMANN

1926–

Life and Career

Jürgen Moltmann (born in Hamburg, Germany, in 1926) is one of the most read, most productive, and most relevant Christian theologians at work today. Next to Karl Barth he is internationally the best-known Reformed theologian in our century. His works have been translated into seventeen languages. He is read by theologians and interested laypeople alike. He has influenced the life of the church and its witness in the world not only in his home country, Germany, but also throughout the world.

Moltmann is a *German* theologian. At the age of seventeen during the Second World War, he was drafted into the German armed forces. At the delicate age of nineteen he had not only witnessed the atrocities of war, the destruction of his hometown, and the senseless waste of human life, but he had also experienced the humiliation associated with the injustice that his country had brought on the rest of the world, and had shared in the guilt of being part of a nation that had set out to commit genocide against the Jewish people. In this existential crisis, he experienced the dawning of meaning and hope through faith in Jesus Christ.

This faith, however, was immediately confronted with demanding questions: How can one believe in God "after Auschwitz"? Why had so many German churches and German Christians refused to join the confessing church in its opposition to the Hitler regime and the Nazi ideology? Why was the German church so reluctant to confess its guilt and to reform itself after the war? Attempting to find theological meaning in this existential dilemma, Moltmann was attracted to the theologies of Karl Barth and Dietrich Bonhoeffer. Barth sought to protect the identity of Christian faith against a fascist state and against churches that either actively or passively supported that state, and Bonhoeffer risked his life to oppose Hitler and, from a prison cell in a concentration camp, began to formulate theological thoughts that dealt with the question of how one can believe in God in a secular and unjust world. Moltmann tuned into that tradition by arguing that Christian faith by its very nature needs to assume responsibility for the world in which it lives. At the same time he criticized churches that used the word "God" to justify political and economic structures. Rather, he encouraged them to be true to their confession of Jesus Christ as Lord by being therapeutically and critically involved in the conflicts of our world.

Moltmann is a theologian of the *Protestant* and *Reformed* tradition. Returning home from prisoner-of-war camps in Belgium and Scotland (1948), he studied theology in Göttingen, a university that in addition to its Lutheran faculty also had a chair of Reformed theology (occupied by Reformed theologians such as Barth, Otto Weber, Hans Joachim Kraus, and Eberhard Busch). Through the teachings of Otto Weber, Ernst Wolf, and Hans-Joachim Iwand, he was exposed to the best that German Protestant theology had to offer. Beyond these immediate mentors Moltmann seriously studied the great shapers of the Reformed tradition: John Calvin and Barth and also the Dutch Reformed theologians Hendrikus Berkhof, Arnold van Ruler, and J. C. Hoekendijk. Also formative for his theology were the New Testament studies of Ernst Käsemann and the Old Testament studies of Gerhard von Rad, Walter Zimmerli, and Victor Maag.

Initially a pastor in Bremen-Wasserhost, Moltmann became Professor of Theology in Wuppertal in 1958, then at Bonn in 1963, before joining the Protestant faculty of theology at the University of Tübingen in 1967, where he taught until his retirement in 1994. There he built his theology in constant dialogue not only with the work of Barth, Rudolf Bultmann, and Paul Tillich, but also with Bonhoeffer, Eberhard Jüngel, Wolfhart Pannenberg, Karl Rahner, and Johannes Baptist Metz. He neither forgot that theology is the servant of the church, nor that the church should be the servant of life in a world that is too often shaped by the servants of death. Moltmann's theology has an inherent thrust toward the *praxis* of Christian discipleship in a needy world.

Important for understanding his theology is the *ecumenical* context from which he profited and to which he significantly contributed. Intentionally an *ecumenical* theologian, Moltmann understands his theology as *one* contribution to the theological task that belongs to the whole people of God. From the Orthodox tradition he gathered an emphasis on pneumatology, cosmic Christology, and worship; he contributed significantly to the "Faith and Order" discussions of the World Council of Churches on the new understanding of the *filioque* in the Nicene-Constantinopolitan Creed of 381. In his ecclesiology he gained important insights from the "free church" tradition. In his constant dialogue with Lutherans he not only insisted on the togetherness of justification and justice, but he also pointed to the dangers of the "Zwei Reiche Lehre," the problem of infant baptism, and the need for a mission-oriented rather than an "institutional" church. In the ecumenical context Moltmann became aware of the plight of the poor and the oppressed and realized that Christian theology cannot bypass the "wretched of the earth," but must be their friend and lend them its voice. He is among the few European theologians who have given positive recognition to the contributions of liberation and feminist theologies. In Barth's tradition he maintains that Christian ethics must be part of theology and cannot be separated from it. Both within his own tradition (the World Alliance of Reformed Churches) and within the context of the ecumenical movement, he has made a significant contribution toward developing a Christian approach to human rights and the rights of nature.

Essentially, Moltmann is both a *modern* and a *postmodern* theologian. As a *modern* theologian, he realized that theology must not only respond to the needs of the situation (ecological crisis, denial of human rights, nuclear danger, militarism, and consumerism), but that theology must also acknowledge the modern "turn to the subject" and thereby change from a metaphysical to an anthropological and historical understanding of reality. But theology must go further and move from the *modern* paradigm of history to the *postmodern* paradigm of nature. In both cases, however, theology must remain aware of its own identity and ask in which way the resources of the Christian faith can be related therapeutically and critically to the modern situation.

While not surrendering to the postmodern insistence on relativism and pluralism, Moltmann seeks a transition from a traditional metaphysics of substance to a relational understanding of reality. His theological career is therefore marked by an openness and readiness for dialogue. In the 1960s he participated in Christian-Marxist dialogues. He was fascinated by the eschatological vision of Ernst Bloch. He learned to appreciate the Frankfurt School (Habermas, Horkheimer, Adorno), and he saw how neo-Marxists and Christians can unmask each other's weaknesses and profit from each other's strengths. Beginning in the 1970s he entered an ever-deepening dialogue with Judaism. He learned from Franz Rosenzweig, Gershom Scholem, Abraham Heschel, and Martin Buber; he entered into public dialogues with Pinchas Lapide; and he designated his Christology "Christology in *Messianic* Dimensions," subtitling his ecclesiology "A Contribution to *Messianic* Ecclesiology." Nevertheless, the dialogue with Judaism needs to be widened into dialogue with all religions, and therefore Moltmann has contributed to the theological task of devising a Christian theology of religions. In recent years he has been showing an increasing interest in modern natural science as a source for unmasking the anthropological captivity of science and theology, and for devising an ecological theology.

Theological Content

The Theological Task. "Christian Theology has the task of relating the Christian tradition and message *critically* and *therapeutically* to this modern situation" (*Theology Today,* 1988, p. 94). This means, first of all, that theology must be relevant. It must enable the church to address the problems of its time and situation. It must cast the traditional content of faith in forms that can be meaningfully communicated to the modern situation. It must accept responsibility for the world and its future. Theology today, for instance, cannot bypass the ecological crisis, the crisis of justice and human rights, and the anti-Semitism, sexism, and racism that are rampant in many parts of the world. The pain and joy of faith must be celebrated in the arena of everyday life.

But if faith is to make a constructive contribution to the world and to addressing its problems, it must not simply repeat the solutions of the past. The church must make its own contribution. It must say something new, and it can say something new, because it believes in a God who raised the crucified Jesus from the dead. Before church and theology can be relevant they must therefore, second, be conscious of their identity. For Moltmann this identity is found in the cross of the risen Christ.

This means, third, that "the path of theological knowledge leads irreversibly from the particular to the general, from the historic to the eschatological and universal" (*Theology of Hope*, 1964, p. 141). The concrete starting point for the theological reflection is the story of Jesus viewed from the perspective of the cross as the intensification of Jesus' life. God raised this particular Jesus from the dead and thereby opened up a new future, the future of the crucified Christ.

And this means, fourth, that the present must be interpreted in light of the future of the crucified Christ. Theology must therefore not only be therapeutical, ministering to the needs of people, but it must also be critical and prophetic, unmasking and denouncing those aspects of life that are not in harmony with the *shalom* of God. "The theologian is not concerned merely to supply a different *interpretation* of the world, of history and of human nature, but to *transform* them in expectation of a divine transformation" (*Theology of Hope*, p. 84).

A fifth emphasis is that the knowledge and verification of God's truth must be understood in terms of *orthopraxy* rather than orthodoxy. To believe in a God who does not simply validate the status quo, but who impinges on the present and wants to change things, means that believers must allow this God to determine their *whole* life. Moltmann reshapes the famous theological dictum *fides quaerens intellectum—credo, ut intelligam* into *spes quaerens intellectum—spero, ut intelligam* (*Theology of Hope*, p. 33). This shift implies a new way of living. Reason is no longer used to justify what is. Rather, being aware of its own "estrangement" and "fallenness," reason becomes a servant of the Christian hope that is fueled by faith in the ultimate triumph of the crucified Christ, and out of that conviction it informs and motivates the believer to anticipate that triumph by following Jesus here and now.

> The *promissio* of the universal future leads of necessity to the universal *missio* of the Church to all nations. The promise of divine righteousness in the event of the justification of the godless leads immediately to the hunger for divine right in the godless world, and thus to the struggle for public, bodily obedience. The promise of

> the resurrection of the dead leads at once to love for the true life of the whole imperilled and impaired creation. (*Theology of Hope*, 1964, p. 225)

The believer is motivated by the conviction that God will be faithful to God's promises, that God will bring about the triumph of the crucified Christ, and that ultimately, therefore, the oppressor will not triumph over this innocent victim.

However, in order that the praxis of discipleship not be reduced to a sterile moralism or issue into a dreary activism, Moltmann emphasizes the importance of joy, praise, and worship. He is one of the few theologians who ascribe theological importance to the Sabbath as the crown of creation. By celebrating the Sabbath we interrupt the busyness of life and ask about its meaning, we celebrate life as God's creation, and we anticipate the ultimate fulfillment of God's *shalom*.

Authority. As a *Christian* theologian, the basic source and authority for Moltmann's theology are the Christian scriptures, and he ascribes special importance to those motifs and narratives that emphasize God's passionate interest in saving and liberating his creation. As an *ecumenical* theologian Moltmann develops his thinking in constant dialogue with theologians from various Christian and Jewish traditions. He retrieves, when relevant, the voices of the formative theologians of the church (e.g., Augustine, Thomas Aquinas, Luther, and Calvin), and shows a special interest and respect for great thinkers of the Jewish tradition (e.g., Heschel, Rosenzweig, and Buber).

He accepts the modern *philosophical* shift from a metaphysical worldview to a historical understanding of reality, but at the same time he goes beyond it with his insistence that history can only be understood in the context of nature, urging theologians to develop an ecological theology. Such a theology must unmask the forces that destroy nature, and it must seek to provide resources for a responsible partnership with nature.

Knowledge. In his attempt to build a theory of knowledge that corresponds to the Christian vision of God, Moltmann develops alternative ways of knowing. First of all, he observes that knowledge can only add something to what we know already if we retrieve the dimension of *wonder*, and thereby appreciate the *difference* in the object of knowing. Then we will learn to appreciate the "otherness" in people, in God and nature, and not try to define them according to our own needs and interests. This retrieval of wonder then implies a new "soft" way of knowing. No longer do we use our powers of reason to define in order to rule over the object of inquiry. Rather, we must learn to listen and, thereby, enter into a creative and participatory relation with the object of inquiry. The knowledge of the mind is complemented by the knowledge of the heart. Intellect and intuition in their togetherness lead to a holistic way of knowing.

God as Trinity. The philosophical presupposition for Moltmann's doctrine of God is the shift from a metaphysics of substance ("God" as one substance, but three persons) and a metaphysics of subject ("God" as one subject with three modes of existence) to a relational ontology, a metaphysics of community. On that basis he devises an understanding of God as a trinitarian community of equals. At the same time this new approach allows him to retrieve the biblical emphasis that God can change, love, suffer, and die, without losing divine self-identity. Nevertheless, neither philosophical nor theological speculations, but rather the Christian experience of God in Christ, and its confession and celebration in baptism, lead with an inherent necessity to the doctrine of the Trinity.

To appreciate Moltmann's contribution to the doctrine of God, we have to understand what he rejects on biblical and experiential grounds. He rejects an understanding of God as one who lives in splendid isolation, who cannot change, who cannot suffer, and who cannot really be affected by the pain and agony that exist in history and nature. Such a God could not experience the agony of enslaved people which the Exodus story relates; and such a God could not be involved in the passion of the Son.

Moltmann also rejects a *monotheism* that describes God in terms of a single subject who relates to the world in three "modes of existence" or three "ways of being"—as Father, Son, and Holy Spirit. Since human beings in their own lives tend, consciously or unconsciously, to reflect their understanding of God, a monotheistic view of God encourages individualism and competition and discourages community, partnership, and solidarity. Historically monotheism has justified hierarchical structures of domination and submission in church (one God—one Christ—one Peter—one bishop—one church) and in society (one God—one emperor—one church—one empire). This kind of monotheism has hindered the process of democratization that is so important to people's claiming and experiencing freedom and responsibility in community.

Moltmann aims to solve this dilemma by taking seriously that the *cross* of Christ is the foundation and criticism of Christian theology, because the cross best expresses that "God *is* love." "Love," however, must not be romanticized, and the "cross" must not be reduced to an ecclesiastical symbol or an abstract theory of atonement. The cross is an event *in* God. The Father expresses love by giving the Son for the sins of the world, and the Son manifests his solidarity with all that is godless in the world, thereby experiencing the forsakenness of the Father. God is therefore affected by the suffering and death of the Son, and since the Son represents the suffering and estrangement of all of nature and history, God has made God's very being vulnerable to the pain and injustice in creation.

This emphasis leads to a *trinitarian* understanding of God. God the Father is self-constituting and at the same time is the origin of the Son and of the Spirit; God the Son is the unique and eternal Son who was begotten from the being (not the will) of the Father, and God the Holy Spirit proceeds from the Father, rests on the Son, and receives form from the Son. Adopting the ancient concept of *perichoresis,* Moltmann speaks of the communion and dynamic interrelationship of Father, Son, and Holy Spirit. They live in a mutual relationship with one another without being dissolved into one another. This Trinity is a dynamic process that is "open" toward the world and nature; it will achieve fulfillment in the eschaton when God will be all in all.

This trinitarian understanding of God as a dynamic "community of equals" provides the theological basis for the structuring of church and society. The glory and power of God are revealed in the cross of the risen Christ. The Godhood of God—the otherness of God—does not consist of being separated from the world, but of being involved with creation as the One who can and does change things. Adopting this understanding of God, church, and society would be characterized by fellowship, service, partiality for the poor and oppressed, and solidarity with the outsider.

The understanding of God as Trinity also provides the basis for recognizing the theological dignity of *creation*. Apart from the Spirit of God nothing can exist (Ps. 104:29-30). The God who is love has created the world (by the Father), has reconciled the world with God (through the Son), is present in creation, and will lead creation to its promised future in the glory of God (with the Holy Spirit).

Moltmann's doctrine of God also has a *prophetic* and a *priestly* dimension. It is *prophetic* because it is suspicious of any attempt to use the word "God" to validate political, economic, or ecclesiastical structures. At the same time it is *priestly* because it makes clear that God identifies with creation, that in Christ God has begun to heal, liberate, and save creation, and that God, as evidenced in the resurrection of the crucified Christ, will be faithful to the divine promises.

Jesus Christ. In developing his Christology, Moltmann is aware of the traditional christological categories—Jesus as "truly divine" and "truly human," and the threefold office of Christ as prophet, priest, and king—which he transfigures into a *relational*, a *narrative*, a *dynamic*, a *Spirit* Christology. Following the form of biblical narratives rather than theological speculation, Moltmann tells the story of Jesus from the perspective of his resurrection and his presence in the Spirit.

Jesus Christ is not primarily a private person whose identity could be captured by assigning attributes or characteristics to him. Jesus Christ lives in *relationships*, and these relationships are essential to understanding his being. His relational existence is developed in two directions, his *"being-in-history"* and *"being-in-relationships."*

His *"being-in-history"* is part of the eschatological history of the trinitarian God that leads to the redemption of the world and the fulfillment of his creation. The acting subject in this process is the Spirit, who raised Jesus from the dead and thereby made him universally accessible. The "way of Jesus" in the power of the Spirit includes the following stages: the messianic expectations in the history of Israel; the empowering of Jesus by the Spirit in his birth, baptism, and temptations; the mission of Jesus as the messianic prophet of the poor; the suffering of Jesus by which he reveals the partiality of God for those who exist on the underside of history; Jesus' death, by which he anticipates the apocalyptic end of this world, and at the same time makes the new creation of all things possible; his resurrection as the beginning of the new creation; his continuing presence in the power of the Spirit in the church, and his hidden presence in the poor and downtrodden; his universal mission to all nations; his reconciliation of the cosmos; his final judgment to establish justice and make sure that ultimately the murderer will not triumph over his innocent victim; and the fulfillment of the promise of universal salvation in the glory of God.

The Spirit also constitutes Jesus as a *being-in-relationships*. His relational existence includes his relationship to God (the "Father" and the "Spirit") and to Israel (as the "Messiah"). But it also includes his relationships to the poor, the sick, and the outcasts, to whom he is ontologically related and who, therefore, profit from his saving and liberating activity. Through his body Christ is, finally, woven into nature and the cosmos so that through his bodily resurrection from the dead, nature and the cosmos participate in the process of salvation.

Although traditional cosmic Christologies have proclaimed Christ as the "Lord" over and redeemer from spiritual powers, today a cosmic Christology must be an ecological Christology, a Christology of nature. It must help to bridle the destructive powers of humanity and lead to an ethic of partnership with nature. Moltmann recognizes that history is only possible within the context of nature, just as the soul cannot be separated from the body. With their bodies human beings relate equally to nature (eating the fruits of the earth, breathing air, and drinking water) and history (acting and shaping the historical process). Moltmann therefore insists on the bodily resurrection of Christ as the presupposition for the redemption of nature and the cosmos.

In the final analysis, however, Christology is primarily concerned not with true doctrine and its theoretical acceptance, but with following Jesus. For Moltmann faith in Christ and the ethics of Christian discipleship cannot be separated. A responsible Christology implies a corresponding praxis of Christian discipleship.

Holy Spirit. Moltmann emphasizes that the Spirit, as one person of the Trinity, has a unique identity. The Spirit is interrelated with, but also distinct from, the Father and the Son: "The personhood of God the Holy Spirit is the loving, self-communicating, out-fanning and out-pouring presence of the eternal divine life of the triune God" (*Spirit of Life*, 1991, p. 289).

Welcoming insights from the charismatic movement, Eastern Orthodoxy, and Pietism, Moltmann retrieves a healthy expectation for the *experience* of the Holy Spirit in the formation and celebration of life. The Spirit relates the riches of God's kingdom to the present and invites people to share in it. "Following Jesus" is interpreted as "life in the Spirit," and consequently the unity of praxis and celebration is affirmed.

At the same time Moltmann wants to free the Spirit from any ecclesiastical domination and portray the Spirit as the Spirit *of life*. The experience of God and the experience of life are the same. In human experience the Spirit brings liberation for those who are hungry for life, justification for the sinner, justice for the oppressed, a meaningful spirituality, and a new awareness of our ontological interrelationship with nature. Experiencing the Spirit of God means being freed from the chains of sin, law, and death, and being liberated to life, justice, and hope.

Human Nature. Traditional Christian anthropology has described human beings as the *crown and center of creation* and then has undergirded this by showing the *differences* between humanity and nature. Drawing on the discoveries of modern science (biology, astronomy, and psychology) and a rereading of the biblical creation accounts, Moltmann emphasizes that humanity is part of and interwoven with history, society, nature, and the cosmos. Although nature can survive without human beings, humanity cannot live apart from nature. Like animals, human beings cannot survive without air to breathe, water to drink, food to eat, and fertility to procreate. The human being reflects the world and the cosmos *(imago mundi)*, and as such it represents the world before God. The distinctive *humanum,* however, derives from the privilege that humanity is called, at the same time, to represent God in the midst of creation *(imago Dei).*

The *imago Dei* is not understood in terms of a given substance (the soul, or human reason, or the upright walk), but as a *relational* reality. This relational existence is grounded in God's relationship to humanity, and manifests itself in humanity's relationship to God, to nature, to history, and to fellow human beings.

Since the *imago Dei* is grounded in God's activity, it cannot be destroyed. However, it can be, and indeed has been, distorted by human sin. Faith then turns to superstition, love turns to hate, and a life of openness toward the "other" turns to self-centeredness. Human beings focus life upon themselves and thereby cut themselves off from the true sources of life that lie outside themselves. By raising Jesus from the dead, God has renewed the *imago Dei,* and through faith in Christ people can regain what they have lost by their rebellion. They are then destined for a life of glory in the eternal Sabbath of the kingdom of God. This openness toward the future is essential for understanding human nature. Against a theological vision that insists that the human being finds its authentic identity in the event of faith, Moltmann emphasizes the interrelationship of faith and hope: "Faith binds man to Christ. Hope sets this faith open to the comprehensive future of Christ. Hope is therefore the 'inseparable companion' of faith" (*Theology of Hope,* 1964, p. 20).

Moltmann's anthropology also has important social and ethical consequences. He resists the devaluation of the body and affirms the God-given dignity of all human life, including the life of the unborn and disabled. A consequence is his engagement in the shaping and implementation of human rights and the rights of nature.

Eschatology. For Moltmann all of theology has an eschatological thrust. The God who is self-revealed in the resurrection of the crucified Christ draws the process of history into God's own future. Revelation has the character of *promise.* It promises the fulfillment of what God has begun in and with the resurrection of the crucified

Christ. This promise creates hope that makes believers restless in the present because they become dissatisfied with the status quo. The community of faith is the exodus community, participating in God's passion for justice and liberation, in the assurance of faith that God can and will be faithful to God's promises. Indeed, when the kingdom of God comes, then God will become who God is—the economic Trinity will arrive at its destiny in the immanent Trinity.

Theodicy, Evil, and Sin. How can one believe in God in the face of evil and injustice? Moltmann answers this challenging question in response to the tragedies of Auschwitz and Hiroshima, to the ecological crisis, to the nuclear threat, to the abject poverty in the "two-thirds world," and to the worldwide denial of human rights.

The *theodicy* problem—how can a God who is almighty and good or loving allow the existence of evil and suffering?—escapes rational explanation. Nevertheless, on the basis of the Old Testament narratives about God's passionate "indwelling" *(shekinah)* with the fate of the chosen people, and on the basis of the New Testament insistence that God was involved in the passion and death of Christ, Moltmann relates the being of God to suffering and injustice in a fourfold manner. First, for the Judeo-Christian tradition it is impossible that God causes suffering, or that suffering is always the result of divine punishment. The only alternative is that God also suffers. Indeed, in the godforsakenness of Jesus, God made God's own self vulnerable to the godforsakenness of all people. God suffers in and with them. Second, by raising the crucified Jesus from the dead, God has established the promise of the triumph of justice, so that ultimately the murderer will not triumph over his innocent victim, and those on the underside of history and the victims of evolution will not be forgotten. This implies, third, that the theodicy problem can only be answered with respect to an eschatological perspective. In the eschaton God will transform humanity and nature and create a "new" heaven and "new" earth. God will establish ultimate justice before coming to "his rest in the Sabbath of his new creation" (*Way of Jesus Christ,* 1989, p. 182). In the meantime, and fourth, the God who raised Jesus from the dead in the power of the Spirit makes believers restless in the face of injustice, and empowers them to struggle for justice.

Evil has no ontological dignity. In that sense it is "nothing." It is real, but it is not caused by God and therefore has no eternal status. Although its manifestations are evident, the origin of evil escapes our understanding. All we can say is that God accepts and maintains responsibility for creation. In Christ God has reconciled the world to God, and by raising Jesus from the dead God has begun the "new" creation that ultimately will also mean the concrete negation of evil so that God will be all in all.

Sin is the perversion of the human relationship with the source of all life, God. Although humanity cannot undo God's commitment to creation, humans can distort the relationship with God. This distortion has cosmic dimensions and manifests itself not only in personal immorality but also in structural evil and cosmic conflicts because humanity is, as we have seen, intimately interwoven with society, nature, and the cosmos. Therefore humanity, the world, nature, and the cosmos are in need of salvation.

Salvation. Salvation is the *process* by which God claims back the creation that has become estranged from God. Grounded in the election of Israel and in the life, death, and resurrection of Jesus the Messiah, this process leads to the fulfillment of the reign of Christ when death and its messengers will finally be defeated, when the kingdom of God (the new creation) is ushered in, when the cosmos is redeemed, when God will be all in all; and when those who belong to God will experience eternal life. The process climaxes in the glorification and justification of God when the theodicy question gives way to the eternal praise of God.

Salvation is a *holistic* reality *(shalom)*, and Moltmann safeguards his understanding against popular distortions. Salvation must neither be spiritualized nor postponed to the future. It must correspond to creation, including therefore the salvation of humankind, the world, nature, and the cosmos. It is a future and a present reality. It includes healing and forgiveness, liberation from oppression, as well as faith in God and love for one's neighbor. It justifies the sinner and provides justice for the poor and oppressed. Salvation implies responsibility for future generations, and as part of the kingdom of God it entails the ultimate triumph of justice for the victims of evolution and those who were relegated to the underside of history.

The Church. Moltmann recognizes that the *corpus christianum*—that great marriage between Christianity and culture which has lasted from the fourth century to the present day in countries with large *Volkskirchen* ("state churches")—is coming to an end. Hierarchically structured and doctrinally oriented churches lose members, while charismatic churches and churches where people can participate in shaping their religious life seem to grow.

The shape of the church of the future, Moltmann suggests, should be *ecumenical,* rather than *denominational.* It should be *congregational,* rather than *hierarchical.* It should be an "open" church, accepting responsibility for the world rather than a church that is *closed* in on its own dogma and tradition. The church of the future must affirm the achievements of modernity (human rights, freedom of conscience, and freedom of religion) without losing its identity in the cross of the risen Christ. It will not be the social glue of any given society, not provide the divine validation for cultural institutions and values. Rather, it will insist on the separation of church and state, and it will attempt to provide a viable alternative to the present society that is marked by consumerism and competition. In doing this the church will be more concerned with creative worship and relevant praxis than with doctrinal integrity and denominational identity.

Drawing on the free church tradition, Moltmann sees the church of the future as a voluntary community of the friends of Jesus who live by the messianic torah (the Sermon on the Mount), who celebrate in anticipation of the future of Christ, and who reflect the creative restlessness and the passion for justice that is implied in faith in the resurrection of the crucified Christ. The voluntary nature of Christian discipleship implies a critique of the practice of indiscriminate infant baptism. The Christ-centeredness of discipleship calls for an open eucharist because Christ shared his life with all people. Following its Lord, the church seeks fellowship with the poor and oppressed because Jesus was the messianic prophet of the poor. All this will be done in the power of the Spirit who inspires the church actively to anticipate the future of Christ.

Religious Pluralism. Moltmann realizes that the time of monolithic societies with one dominant and all-encompassing regional or national religion is past. Religious pluralism is a fact of life. This challenge must be accepted and must lead to constructive dialogues with other religions. There will be no peace and justice in the world until there is peace and justice among religions. Today the ecological crisis, the nuclear threat, the crisis of human rights, and the unjust world economic order make a dialogue among the world religions necessary. World religions must relate to one another and together accept responsibility for the world and its future. This does not mean that all religions are equal or equally true. Moltmann is critical of a pluralistic theology of religions that does not give adequate attention to the questions of truth and justice. Rather, each religion should be true to its own convictions, but at the same time enter into dialogue with other religions in the common struggle to preserve the earth on which we all live together.

Thorwald Lorenzen

Selected Primary Works

1964   *Theology of Hope: On the Ground and the Implications of a Christian Eschatology,* trans. James W. Leitch.

1972   *The Crucified God. The Cross of Christ as the Foundation and Criticism of Christian Theology,* trans. R. A. Wilson and John Bowden.

1975   *The Church in the Power of the Spirit. A Contribution to Messianic Ecclesiology,* trans. Margaret Kohl.

1977   *The Open Church: Invitation to a Messianic Lifestyle.*

1977   *The Passion for Life. A Messianic Lifestyle,* trans. M. Douglas Meeks.

1980   *The Trinity and the Kingdom of God. The Doctrine of God,* trans. Margaret Kohl.

1985   *God in Creation. An Ecological Doctrine of Creation,* The Gifford Lectures 1984–1985, trans. Margaret Kohl.

1988   *Theology Today. Two Contributions Towards Making Theology Present,* trans. John Bowden.

1989   *The Way of Jesus Christ: Christology in Messianic Dimensions*, trans. Margaret Kohl.
1991   *History and the Triune God: Contributions to Trinitarian Theology*, trans. John Bowden.
1991   *The Spirit of Life. A Universal Affirmation*, trans. Margaret Kohl.

Selected Secondary Sources

1974   Douglas M. Meeks, *Origins of the Theology of Hope.*
1979   Christopher Morse, *The Logic of Promise in Moltmann's Theology.*
1986   Herrmann Deuser et al., eds., *Gottes Zukunft—Zukunft der Welt. Festschrift für Jürgen Moltmann zum 60. Geburtstag.*
1987   Dieter Ising et al., eds., *Bibliographie Jürgen Moltmann.*
1987   Richard Bauckham, *Moltmann: Messianic Theology in the Making.*

ROBERT CUMMINGS NEVILLE
1939–

Life and Career

One of the most creative and productive scholars in religion, theology, and philosophy in North America is Robert Cummings Neville, Dean of the School of Theology and Professor in the departments of philosophy and religion at Boston University. Author of fourteen books and a number of essays in a wide array of publications, he has served as president of a number of professional organizations, notably and recently the Metaphysical Society of America (1989), the American Academy of Religion (1992), and the International Society of Chinese Philosophy (1992).

Born in 1939 in St. Louis, Missouri, Neville attended public schools there and received his undergraduate education at Yale University. Since he was interested in God as a philosophical problem, he was encouraged not to attend seminary—an ironic bit of advice in light of his current position and professional identification. He continued with graduate studies in philosophy at Yale, writing a doctoral dissertation in 1963 entitled "A Theory of Divine Creation." Neville has since taught philosophy, theology, and religion at Yale, Wesleyan, Fordham, State University of New York at Purchase and at Stony Brook, as well as at Boston University.

Neville has exercised his Christian ministerial vocation as pastor and preacher as an ordained United Methodist elder. His greatest contribution, however, has been as teacher, scholar, editor, and academic leader and spokesperson. He has focused his inquiries on the problem of God such that religious traditions of the world can find access to one another and that philosophers and theologians can raise seriously the question of truth of any and all religious claims.

Theological Emphases

Simply, theology is the intellectual discipline for pursuing the truth in religious matters. The first job of a theologian, therefore, is not to provide an identity for a

317

religious community (that is, "This is what we Christians believe"); rather, it is to develop, classify, understand, explain, and critically assess interpretations of divine things. Ultimately, the theologian is interested in what anybody ought to believe about divine matters. If issues of truth are neglected, then all other legitimate theological concerns—guidance, identity, and worship—are made questionable.

Because knowing and telling the truth are difficult, theology is first of all a matter of inquiry—asking, searching, probing, hypothesizing, and testing. No single discipline (biblical studies, for example) nor single method (textual interpretation of scriptures, creeds, or official pronouncements), nor single tradition (Lutheranism or Catholicism, for example), nor even a single religion (such as Christianity) ought to direct the theologian's inquiry. Any proposed answer emerging from inquiry is a possible interpretation of a subject matter, or hypothesis. Before a hypothesis can be judged to be true, it has to be set in the context of alternative trial explanations (collectively, the claims of world religions as well as feasible secular options is now the new base of survey), and the refining give-and-take of analysis and critique has to be engaged. The theological enterprise is therefore fully public and objective (one has to make one's case to others relative to other possible interpretations), and any claim by its very nature is vulnerable.

Authority. Can one make a case simply by citing a source and thereby settling an issue? No, Neville answers, abandoning any single authority in favor of a plurality of sources, especially preferring the Wesleyan quadrilateral of Scripture, tradition, reason, and experience. Each of these four "authorities" serves as a critical check on the other three; and when there is a genuine conflict among the sources, which is not at all unlikely, the issue must be decided by the merits of the case made. Interestingly, the case, not the source, decides; yet the case is no authority. Furthermore, authorities can only establish themselves at the end of the interpretative process, not at the beginning: Scriptures have to be interpreted, not simply cited; the multiple and often contradictory layers of tradition have to be sorted out; the range of rational methods and strategies has to be considered, assessed, and appropriately employed; the varieties of experience—individual and communal, culturally dominant and culturally repressed, parochial and universal, sacred and secular—have to be sensitively factored in.

The notion of revelation as a special kind of authority cannot be upheld; rather, revelation is a special kind of learning, a cognitive transformation brought about through engagement with the divine. There are at least four kinds of revelatory learning: (1) religious symbols that have continuing power to evoke the divine presence; (2) persons, events, and situations that, when interpreted, engage transformatively the community with the divine; (3) traditional symbols and events that can be effectively employed to illumine present experience; (4) spiritually disciplined lives in and through which the divine appears, and not simply to them (saints, for example).

God. God must be discussed in two distinct but related ways: theoretical and religious. With regard to the theoretical, the first question must consider whether or not there is any reality to which the welter of divine symbols points. To speak of theory is necessarily to acknowledge a multiplicity needing a unifying grasp, that is, an explanation. An enormous range and depth of divine representations has to be sorted out, studied, and assessed: sky fathers, earth mothers, savior deities and cosmic heroes, sacred principles, illuminations, saints, skeptics, shamans, warriors, sages, fools, angels, and demons—all of which make up the empirical base for theory about the divine. But symbols, themes, and experiences *by themselves* do not represent the divine—or anything else, for that matter. Thus, there is needed a theory which takes the symbol or event as representing the divine reality in some respect.

The second theoretical question must address whether or not the array of divine symbols points to something within or outside the universe. Since the European Renaissance the issue of closure has been paramount: Everything that exists must be measurable according to some relevant standard. Everything is determinate and the universe is understood as the sum of all determinate things. But determinate things cannot generate themselves as determinate or as positively real. An indeterminate yet productive ground is needed to explain why anything is this way rather than that, why there is any order at all and not simply chaos, why things hang together to the degree that they do, and in fact, why anything *is* at all and not nothing. This ground cannot be essentially determinate, for then it would need something else to account for it, suggesting the ancient notion of creation out of nothing *(creatio ex nihilo).* To create out of nothing is not obtuse theological talk about a supposed Big Bang; rather, the expression means that the universe, in part and in whole, is entirely dependent on some indeterminate ground, a source essentially independent of all determinate things. This view expresses the asymmetrical logic of creation, which is unique and not to be confused with the logic of relations, which we find applicable within the universe and on which everyday logic and our ordinary imaginations thrive.

In line with various world traditions, the indeterminate source of all can be called, vaguely, divine or God. Divine creation thus issues in a product, a determinate world, a definite something apparently made up of a variety of things, processes, patterns, events, and qualities. The normative measure of that world, what we might call the collective transcendental properties of all things whatsoever, is the Logos. Neville sees the Logos comprising four fundamental dimensions, suggested by Plato: form, components, actuality, and value. Everything in the world, whatever other properties it might possess, has in some way the four fundamental features or dimensions. Under certain circumstances these features or dimensions are experienced powerfully and imaginatively, and they are expressed as the masculine, feminine, existential (grounding), and soteriological (saving) deities of world religions. One can say that the Logos is experienced through various religious images and symbols.

Statements about the indeterminate creator-the divine-God are abstractly true and have important theoretical value, so Neville believes, but such teaching hardly suffices for religious purposes. What kind of religious imagery allows people to *engage* the divine, to be vitally shaped by, to interact with, and to be transformed by it? Vital religious imagery emerges in the profound historical experience of persons and communities. The early Christian community steeped in the Jewish cultural milieu and religious tradition was transformed by the experience of Jesus and his continuing presence. Images of warrior, king, lover, messiah, healer, shepherd, breath of life, teacher, father, son, and so forth, were constellated, sorted, extended, prioritized, and employed—largely unconsciously—in the turbulent life of the community as it emerged in the Greco-Roman, Eastern-Mediterranean world. The issue was how to connect the experience of Jesus' life, death, and continuing felt presence with the strict monotheism of classical Jewish culture. The imagery of a loving father transcended the older warrior-king symbolism, and the obedient son's path of life reflected the purification of the imagery of wonder-worker, wandering rabbi, and social revolutionary whom death ultimately could not defeat and whose spirit continued to energize his followers. This historical experience lies behind the classical doctrine of the Trinity—that God is best understood as Father, Son, and Spirit.

Sensitive to the patriarchal structures and values of the time, Neville nonetheless thinks that the problem of the "persons" of the Trinity is not primarily about concerns over gender or bad metaphysics. There are profound religious sensibilities underlying the traditional doctrine, and the necessarily imaginative expression does not allow full translation into concepts such as creator, redeemer, and transformer. Nevertheless, full understanding does require the religious spirit to weave onto an appropriate metaphysical frame the powerful strands of imagery and experience. Neville believes that the abstract doctrine of creation out of nothing best allows for the unfolding of the Christian understanding of God as triune.

Human Nature. The most profound theological statement about human beings is that they have been created to be in covenant with their creator, with persons and social institutions, and with the natural world. The covenant motif is fundamental to both Hebraic and Christian scriptures and history. As the creation story in Genesis 2 and 3 suggests, covenant is crucial for people's identity, stipulating how everybody is to get along with God, one another, and the environment. A more systematic statement is needed, however, for reflective understanding; consequently, Neville identifies four ideals of the covenant: righteousness, oriented toward the Logos element of form; piety, toward the components; faith, toward the actuality of existence; and hope, toward the values achieved in existence, specifically in the path of fulfillment of both individuals and groups. Love is the conjunction of these four ideals and the capstone of the covenant (the Great Commandment). Thus, humans have been created to work for justice in whatever neighborhoods they inhabit; to respect the natural world, and all the diversity of orientations, talents, and energies of persons; to be courageous in accepting the actualities of existence, including their own limitations and failures; to maintain hope and avoid despair on their journeys; and, above all, to show love in all dealings with the creator and all creatures.

Sin and Evil. But inevitably, profoundly, and, as far as we can tell, universally, people fail to fulfill their covenant obligations. The Christian term for the covenant failure is sin, and its dimensions are both personal and social. At one level, sin is the refusal of one's covenant status as God's finite but beloved creature; at another, it is the unrighteousness, impiety, faithlessness, despair, and the perversion of love that so characterize life as we know and live it. Moreover, sin produces evil consequences of often large-scale and tragic proportions. People are often very naive about what results from their actions; recent history and a befouled environment witness to the enormity of both the acts and the ignorance.

Salvation. Salvation is none other than the restoration of the broken covenant, and it works on both personal and social levels. It begins with justification, a making right with God, and it continues in sanctification, a making holy of both persons and institutions. Salvation starts with divine action (grace), making people want to be restored and setting them on a path of giving up a past (repentance), helping people to accept a present as being loved (faith), and enabling them to embark on a new life of commitment to the creator and creation (freedom); this is justification, as seen from the side of the subject. Salvation as a process continues as individuals and communities struggle to bring ever-widening harmony to both persons and groups; this is sanctification, at least in the human, effortful dimension. Furthermore, it is the great truth of Christianity that God has made Christ our "wisdom, [our] righteousness and sanctification and redemption" (1 Cor. 1:30). Both the making righteous and the making holy are the objective work of God in human history and community. This work is the restoration of the covenant, the embodiment (incarnation) of the Logos—Christ present in rabbi Jesus and continued in the church (the Body of Christ) past and present.

Christ. The threads already described can be gathered up to speak of Jesus Christ, the focal point of Christian life and thought, as both human and divine. As human, Jesus was a complete flesh-and-blood person rooted in the historical Jewish community with its religious and cultural traditions and its geographical and political situatedness. At the same time, he embodied the Divine Logos, the covenant ideals of righteousness, piety, faith, and hope, all united in love (Col. 3:14), in a unique way that can transform people and communities beyond what could be thought humanly possible. He was and continues to be Im-manu-el ("God with us"). Encounter with, and living in, Christ mediated by his Body the Church is salvation here and now.

Persons are saved in the repairing of broken relations and structures in the time in which they live, aligning the temporal with the eternal. The religious significance of death and resurrection is temporal, dying and being raised with Christ now. Immortality as simply having more time is an inadequate symbol of the deepest hunger of the human spirit: eternity. Better by far, Neville believes, is Resurrection as the symbol of conscious and corporate participation in eternity here and now. It is the reversal of the fragmentation and finitude of our lives and the conquest of spiritual death in the modes of sin, ignorance, and disharmony. Having more time, having a fulfillment after death denied in one's history, being free of physical limitations or possessing special psychic or spiritual powers are not religiously important; being raised with, and living in, Christ here and now is religiously important.

Religious Pluralism. The creator is present in the creation everywhere and always. In addition to this general presence in the world, God is focally or specifically present, at least for the Christian church, in Jesus Christ. Is God also present specifically in other traditions, perhaps in other ways? For Neville, the only reasonable answer is Yes. The exclusiveness of some Christian claims—and claimants!—presupposes a view of history no longer tenable. Neville affirms a number of historical streams and manifestations of God. To view all specific manifestations as expressions of the Christian revelation, as in "anonymous Christianity," is offensive and imperialistic. This claim, however, does not entail that all manifestations of God are of equal historic moment or possess the same salvific significance. Manifestations of God are always relative to the particular historical circumstances. Some manifestations seem to have a capacity for transcending the immediate situation and appear as a live option for women and men far and wide. Christians believe the Good News of the gospel transcends the originating cultural circumstances and is to be shared with all who will listen. Christian salvation should be seen as specific to the Christian revelation and community, and in this sense "outside the Church there is no salvation" *(extra ecclesiam nulla salus)*. However, God can and does work in other transformative ways in other traditions, or so it seems to open-minded participants, like Neville, who engage in dialogue with members of other religious traditions. Among other things, Christians interested in the truth of their assertions will welcome the challenge of seeing their claims in the light of the claims of other traditions.

Conclusion

Neville's thought is a significant option on the current theological scene because of (1) his clear understanding of the importance of truth to the extent that it is objective, public, and hypothetical; (2) his abstract interpretation of, yet unremitting theological focus on, the ancient notion of creation out of nothing; (3) his treatment of the covenant, as rooted in the Logos elements and ideals, as the metaphor of profound depth and extension to illumine the normativity, brokenness, and restoration witnessed in human life and centered in the figure of Jesus and the church; and (4) his understanding of interreligious dialogue as crucial to current theological efforts to provide identity for religious communities and to enhance the possibilities of arriving at truth.

J. Harley Chapman

Selected Bibliography

For students of Christian theology, the best place to begin the exploration of Neville's thought is in Robert Cummings Neville, *A Theology Primer* (1991). Those fascinated with his central notion of *creatio ex nihilo* should consult his groundbreaking *God the Creator* (1992; orig. ed., 1968). For those with interests in comparative religion and philosophy of religion, two of his other texts are important: *The Tao and the Daimon* (1982) and *Behind the Masks of God* (1991). Neville's most recent systematic theological treatment of time and eternity is to be found in his *Eternity and Time's Flow* (1993).

H. RICHARD NIEBUHR
1894–1962

Born in Wright City, Missouri, in 1894, H. Richard Niebuhr was the son of a minister in the German Evangelical Synod of North America who had immigrated to the United States in 1878. The family proved theologically exceptional. Richard's older brother, Reinhold, became Professor of Applied Christianity at Union Theological Seminary in New York City and perhaps the most acclaimed theologian in America. Their sister, Hulda, was Professor of Christian Education at McCormick Seminary in Chicago.

Richard attended Elmhurst College in Illinois and graduated from Eden Seminary in St. Louis in 1915. He became pastor of the Walnut Park Evangelical Church in St. Louis in 1916, and while ministering there he completed a master's degree in history at Washington University. He joined the faculty of Eden Seminary in 1919 as a teacher of theology and ethics. In 1922, he began graduate training at Yale Divinity School, where he completed his B.D. and Ph.D. degrees in 1924 and wrote his doctoral dissertation, "Ernst Troeltsch's Philosophy of Religion." Niebuhr then became president of Elmhurst College until 1927, when he returned to Eden as academic dean. In 1931, he became associate professor of Christian ethics at Yale Divinity School, and he taught there, training many of the leading theologians and theological ethicists in the United States, until his death in 1962.

Niebuhr's writings exhibit an enduring concern with the relationship between faith in God and other human commitments. Indeed, he found his constructive voice during the 1930s as he labored to distinguish Christian faith and the Christian ethic from the dominant interests of Western culture. Years later, he remained convinced that the relationship between loyalty to God in Christ and the many loyalties of culture constitutes the recurrent problem of Christianity. He remained convinced, too, that "questions about *faith* arise in every area of human existence" (*Faith on Earth*, 1989, p. 1).

Faith and Ethics

An initial step in Niebuhr's effort to interpret the web of human confidences was to formulate an understanding of the connection between faith and ethics. Essentially, Niebuhr held that humans are creatures of faith in the sense that we center our lives on objects of devotion. Human life, he claimed, is always ordered, oriented, and directed in relation to objects of devotion that constitute centers of meaning and value. Thus, our practical stances in life depend upon our faiths in valued realities, and the business of theological ethics is to probe human faiths and their objects of devotion as well as the patterns of practical life that they support.

Niebuhr's early prophetic judgment—one bolstered by economic depression and the rise of totalitarian fascism—was that modern Western culture is caught up in idolatrous faiths that bring with them a train of bad consequences. The idolatries are variant forms of "anthropocentrism" that place human beings at the center of things, so that a human community, activity, or desire becomes a limiting, distorting, and even dangerous center of value (*The Church Against the World*, 1935, p. 136). Thus, nationalism teaches people that their own country is the most valuable reality, while capitalism insists that their own economic production is the prime power and source of meaning. Racism takes a particular ethnic group as the center of meaning and value.

Now, in this situation, Niebuhr believed that Christians and their churches are tempted to substitute one or another social religion for faith in God. They are tempted to equate faith in God with loyalty to the nation, confidence in a capitalist economy, commitment to their own racial group, or other alternative mistakes. That is why, in his contributions to the book *Church Against the World*, Niebuhr concluded that any true emancipation of the church from cultural bondage can only begin with clarity about the basic devotion to God that comprises the precondition for Christian integrity. Genuine faith in God is fundamental because it displaces inappropriate centers and leads to the criticism and reconstruction of our practical lives.

Faith and Revelation

This frame of reference provides one way to understand Niebuhr's book *The Meaning of Revelation*. For Niebuhr, the revelatory event discloses God, a valued reality who forms a new foundation for our practical reasoning about other realities. Revelation offers a new and dynamic suggestion for our further reasoning and interpretation. A true disclosure and apprehension of God presents us with a new center of value in terms of which we are impelled to reinterpret all other things that we value, for example, the nation, economic production, the race. Revelation moves us to reconstruct our vision of the world and our place in it.

According to Niebuhr, the revelatory event enables a radical reinterpretation of self and world because it displaces our inordinately self-invested points of reference with a sense for the divine associated with the image of Jesus Christ as self-emptying servant. The christological image is a gift to the imagination that enables us to reinterpret our experiences in light of a new dramatic pattern. When we reason about our experiences in connection with Jesus Christ, we begin to understand ourselves and our world in accord with a new point of reference.

We might describe Niebuhr's understanding of the relationship between faith and revelation as follows. Humans are always devoted to something. Moreover, when persons become involved in explicit religious practices, their tendency is to equate faith in God with their loyalties to other objects, such as the nation or the race. The disclosure of God in Jesus Christ precipitates a transformation in their typically contracted and inordinately self-invested faiths or pieties because it challenges their corrupted preconceptions of divine unity, power, and goodness.

The God that humans anticipate, said Niebuhr, is one who will bind together our cherished unities of self, nation, race, and so on. But the God who comes to persons in Jesus Christ is not just the transcendent source of these lesser unities; this God is also their immanent enemy whenever they are elevated to false gods and idols. Again, persons expect an omnipotence that is like the powers of the world, only raised to the ultimate degree. But in Jesus Christ, God's power is made perfect in weakness, so that "revelation is the beginning of a revolution in our power thinking and our power politics" (*Meaning of Revelation*, 1941, p. 136). Again, persons seek a good to protect their own goods, but here is the true good emptying itself. Here is "a goodness that is all outgoing, reserving nothing for itself," and so it convicts us "of having corrupted our religious life through our unquenchable desire to keep ourselves with our love of our good in the center of the picture" (ibid., p. 138). In sum, Niebuhr maintained that revelation means the "conversion and permanent revolution of our human religion through Jesus Christ" (ibid., p. 139).

Faith and Culture (1)

But how, then, shall faithful Christians be disposed toward the many other things their cultures respect, such as philosophy, education, science, political community, and the arts? What is or should be the relationship between faith in God and the many ends of culture that attempt to advance human well-being? In *Christ and Culture*, Niebuhr distinguished five ways that Christians have typically resolved this problem.

Tertullian, medieval monks, Mennonites, and Leo Tolstoy, said Niebuhr, take up a "Christ against culture" stance, which affirms Christ's sole authority and rejects culture's claims. For them, the key question becomes whether one remains loyal to God-in-Christ or else falls away from this loyalty by compromising with cultural commitments. By contrast, Thomas Jefferson, Immanuel Kant, Albrecht Ritschl, and others adopt a "Christ of culture" stance, which regards Christ as the fulfiller of their society's finest ideals. Here, the question becomes, "With which cultural impulses and achievements shall we align Christian faith in the struggle for an ethical commonwealth?"

Three further stances, which Niebuhr identified as "the church of the center," share the convictions that sin's corruption infects all dimensions of human life but that God's grace also is at work in both nature and culture (*Christ and Culture*, 1975, pp. 116-20). For centrists, the enduring problem is not essentially one of resisting compromise, since at least some elements in human nature and culture mediate God's grace. Nor is it basically a matter of aligning Christian faith with the best that culture has to offer, since every human achievement suffers sin's corruption. The problem is to understand how sinners are enabled to live faithfully.

Clement of Alexandria, Thomas Aquinas, and others, said Niebuhr, adopt a "Christ above culture" stance, which attempts a synthesis between faith in God and culture's many ends. For synthesists, faith in God is compatible with the best impulses of human nature and culture, although it also transcends them. Thus, Aquinas believed that the faithful employ reason in order to identify valid principles for ordering society. At the same time, the faithful must consult revealed law because their understanding of moral principles often remains unclear and because revealed law goes beyond the standards of right reason to direct humans toward their salvific end.

Others, such as Martin Luther, take up a stance of "Christ and culture in paradox," which points toward an unrelieved tension between Christian faith and culture. So, Luther believed that in the realm of society and culture's many ends, the faithful employ reason and justice in order to restrain evil. By contrast, their spiritual lives are governed by the gospel, love, and free forgiveness.

. Augustine, John Calvin, John Wesley, Jonathan Edwards, and F. D. Maurice, said Niebuhr, adopt a "conversionist" or "Christ the transformer of culture" stance. They believe that faithful Christians make use of principles of right reason and justice, but that the faith in God that comes to us by grace through Jesus Christ converts our understanding of these principles as well as our understandings of all other cherished loyalties and commitments. This transformative faith encourages us to reorient and reorder our many cultural ends so that, however imperfectly, it then becomes possible for persons and institutions to both restrain evil and pursue good.

Niebuhr's typology in *Christ and Culture* offers an illuminating analysis of different strands in Christian moral theology. At the same time, it is clear that the transformationist stance accords with his own reflections about faith, ethics, and revelation. For Niebuhr, faith in God converts our confidences in and loyalties to the many cultural ends that promise to advance human flourishing. That is how it transforms practical self-understandings as well as the wellspring for human actions.

Faith and Culture (2)

Much of what Niebuhr's view of faith and culture means can be seen in *Radical Monotheism and Western Culture*. Niebuhr claimed that human faiths have taken three basic forms during the course of Western history. Henotheism regards the social group as the center of value or most cherished reality. Persons, things, and activities are valued to the extent that they serve the society's ends. Nationalism is an example. Here, the nation is the supreme end of life, and respect for the national welfare becomes the orienting disposition for morality. Polytheism means commitment to different causes in different contexts. Now the family, now economic success, now artistic creativity, now scientific knowledge, now increase in religion furnish the causes for which people labor and live. Human faith and morality become radically pluralistic; persons and things are valued differently to the extent that they further the ends authorized by different objects of devotion.

Niebuhr called the third form of faith radical monotheism. Here, the power by which all things are, becomes the center of value. The community of moral concern is no closed society, but extends to the entire community of being, and so there is no privileged or "in" group. Whatever participates in the community of being has value. To promote the well-being of this community is good; to injure or repress it is bad.

Niebuhr believed that radical faith emerges in both Israel and Jesus Christ. For Israel, trust in the one creator goes together with a moral concern that breaks narrow bounds. This is what lies behind being just to the poor as well as to foreigners whose contributions to the national community may be slight. Relations between God and people and also among people become matters of covenantal responsibility. Again, Jesus Christ's fidelity to the God of Israel radicalizes love of neighbor, so that neighbor now is defined as "any member of that community of which the universal God is the head" (*Christian Ethics*, 1955, pp. 34-35). Radical faith also comes to expression in the first sentence of the Apostles' Creed, wherein Jesus Christ, the principle of redemption or of value, is identified with God the Father Almighty, the maker of heaven and earth, or the principle of being. Here again, being and the universal community of being become the center of value.

Radical monotheism constantly comes into conflict with the other forms of faith. In Western religion, conflict arises wherever we encounter efforts to ascribe sacredness exclusively to some special, narrow community in contrast to others. Thus, radical prophets rail when a sacred cult is juxtaposed with an unhallowed economic and political world, or when the sacredness of human personality is maintained along with a purely utilitarian appreciation for animal life and for inanimate being.

Or consider Western politics. Niebuhr argued that radical faith supports a commitment to equality. People are said to have equal worth because they are equally related to the common source of existence. When narrower loyalties infect politics, egalitarian dogma comes under attack. Polytheists point out that people are unequal with reference to their contributions to knowledge, or to economic production, or to excellence in the arts. Other attacks express henotheistic loyalties. Thus, racists reject the doctrine of equality in light of their faith in the supremacy of a particular race or ethnic group. Nationalists qualify egalitarian dogma by setting it within the context of their constricted loyalty, recognizing the right of loyal citizens to equal treatment but denying it to foreigners.

It makes a difference whether political life is ordered by polytheistic, henotheistic, or radically monotheistic patterns of devotion. Polytheism threatens the integrity of the *polis,* and the civil commonwealth is differently understood depending on whether one is oriented by henotheistic or monotheistic loyalties. From a radically monotheistic perspective, wherever politics capitulates to lesser devotions, justifications for gross manipulation, injustice, and oppression follow close behind.

In short, radical faith places the cherished loyalties and practices associated with the many dimensions of Western culture into an expanded context. It represents the transformative enlargement of human faith beyond its typically corrupted and inordinately constricted polytheistic and henotheistic bounds. That is why radical faith means the transformation of our ethics.

Faith and Responsibility

At the time of his death in 1962, Niebuhr was at work on a "Christian moral philosophy" that interprets human beings in light of the metaphor of responsibility. Moral agents, he noted, may be pictured as makers who purposively pursue goals, ends, and ideals, or as citizens who adhere to laws, commandments, and rules. By contrast, the image of responsibility portrays human agents as answerers who respond to actions that impinge upon them. Responsibility points to the fitting action, to "the one that fits into a total interaction as response and as anticipation of further response" (*The Responsible Self,* 1963, p. 61).

Faith enters in because different faiths encourage different visions of the "total interaction" or context for our responses. They suggest different horizons within which persons are responsible. Thus, where a nationalistic commitment predominates, people understand themselves in the midst of interactions with other loyalists to the nation. This community and its well-being become the primary point of reference for our reflections about fitting actions and replies, and the world beyond is envisioned as one of powers that threaten the nation, its causes, and its continuing viability. The story of the nation, its memories, and its anticipations defines the historical context within which persons understand actions to be fitting or not. This story, in turn, may be placed into a wider history of nations and empires in which the future holds out inevitable decline. The result, Niebuhr believed, is a defensive nationalistic ethics of survival or of national self-maintenance against the threatening powers present in the nation's interactions with all things.

In Jesus Christ, however, Christians confront a radical faith that leads them to envision as their companions all those who participate in the entire community of being. This universal society becomes the spatial horizon for their reflections about responsibility. Again, in Jesus Christ, they are enabled to reinterpret the ultimate historical context for their actions as the story of creation and redemption, or the universal history of an all-encompassing divine activity that destroys only to reestablish and renew. This context becomes the temporal horizon for our reflections about responsibility. Christians therefore are delivered from the defensive ethics of self-maintenance and survival. They are both encouraged in and set at liberty for an ethic of universal responsibility.

Conclusion

Throughout his career Niebuhr was concerned with faith as a morally relevant and even determinative dimension of human existence. He believed that different ethics are founded on faiths in different objects. His Christian moral philosophy draws on the radical faith incarnate in Israel and in Jesus Christ. Its analytical task is to probe human faiths and the patterns of practical life that they support. Its prophetic task is to criticize narrow faiths and their disastrous practical consequences. Its constructive task is to reorder and reinterpret all of life in relation to the universal God as the cherished center of meaning and value.

Douglas F. Ottati

Selected Primary Works

1935   *The Church Against the World,* with Wilhelm Pauck and Francis P. Miller.
1941   *The Meaning of Revelation.*
1955   *Christian Ethics: Sources of the Living Tradition,* with Waldo Beach.
1963   *The Responsible Self: An Essay in Christian Moral Philosophy.*
1975   *Christ and Culture.*
1989   *Faith on Earth: An Inquiry into the Structure of Human Faith.*
1993   *Radical Monotheism and Western Culture with Supplementary Essays.*

Selected Secondary Sources

1982   Douglas F. Ottati, *Meaning and Method in H. Richard Niebuhr's Theology.*
1986   Jon Diefenthaler, *H. Richard Niebuhr: A Lifetime of Reflections on the Church and the World.*

REINHOLD NIEBUHR
1892–1971

Life and Career

In the years between his birth in Wright City, Missouri, June 21, 1892, and his death at home in Stockbridge, Massachusetts, June 1, 1971, Reinhold Niebuhr was to become the single most influential American interpreter of Protestant theology in the crises marked by World Wars I and II, the Great Depression, and the mercifully stalemated Cold War that led to the collapse of the Soviet Union. His theological perspective—Christian realism—helped Americans to cope with the global responsibilities unexpectedly thrust upon them as a result of these crises. Indeed, Christian realism's identification with the defining moments of the twentieth century is so great that the enduring significance of Niebuhr's work is in doubt, now that many of the main social and political issues that provoked much of his thought have changed.

Niebuhr grew up in an immigrant's home, the third of four children born to pastor Gustav Niebuhr and his wife, Lydia Hosto, herself the daughter of a missionary in the same denomination, the German Evangelical Synod of North America. Reinhold, along with his elder sister, Hulda, and his younger brother, Helmut Richard, were to place the Niebuhrs among the most celebrated clergy families in mainline Protestantism, with outstanding contributions to the fields of Christian education, theological ethics, religious journalism, and religious social thought. Reinhold's father may have been the single most important influence on his early intellectual development, for he made good use of his father's personal library, and was conversant with the works of Adolf von Harnack and other leading German liberal Protestants well before he graduated from Eden Seminary in 1913, or from Yale University after obtaining the B.D. and M.A. degrees in 1915. While at Yale, Niebuhr came under the tutelage of Douglas Clyde Macintosh, who helped him integrate his Midwestern German piety into a larger vision of Social Gospel idealism, tempered by the philosophical discipline of American pragmatism.

Despite, or perhaps because of, this early brush with the mainstream of American Christianity, Niebuhr cut short his studies at Yale and accepted his denomination's call to a pastorate in Detroit in 1915. His thirteen-year service at Bethel Evangelical Church was decisive in his personal development as a theologian, for, as his minor classic *Leaves from the Notebook of a Tamed Cynic* (1929) eloquently testifies, his theological reflections were shaped by the twin challenges of building and maintaining a community of faith while collaborating in an ecumenical coalition bent on implementing the Social Gospel in the workers' utopia that Henry Ford claimed to have created in Detroit. His talents as a preacher and publicist soon found him a national audience, whose dreams of a postwar return to normalcy were to be disturbed by Niebuhr's penchant for unmasking the injustices of an urban industrial society. From early on in his pastorate, he kept a typically exhausting schedule that combined active involvement in a range of public policy issues, both foreign and domestic, with pastoral service, and with increasingly heavy responsibilities as a religious journalist and "circuit rider" in the nation's colleges and universities. By 1928 his efforts had captured the attention of Henry Sloan Coffin, who appointed him the Dodge Professor of Applied Christianity at Union Theological Seminary in New York, which was to remain his intellectual home base until his death in 1971. During his long and illustrious career at Union, Niebuhr wrote the many books and essays upon which rests his reputation as a theologian.

Scholars examining Niebuhr's works conventionally divide them into three parts: an early period of Marxist militancy (1927–35), called *religious socialism;* a middle period of Augustinian reflection on the grim necessities of World War II and the Cold War (1935–52), typified as *Christian realism;* and a later period (1952–71) in which a physically impaired Niebuhr became an icon for the post–New Deal liberal establishment, often characterized as *Christian pragmatism.* Recent studies, like Ronald H. Stone's *Professor Reinhold Niebuhr* (1992) and Robin W. Lovin's *Reinhold Niebuhr and Christian Realism* (1995), provide sufficient reason to be suspicious of this reading of Niebuhr's works on both practical and theoretical grounds. Stone documents the elder Niebuhr's firm support for the Civil Rights movement and his increasingly pointed criticism of United States involvement in the Vietnamese civil war, and he shows how both of these commitments reflect deep continuities in Niebuhr's thought throughout his career. Consistent with Stone's historical analysis, Lovin argues that Niebuhr's overall contribution to Christian theology and ethics is best understood as a response to and variant within the philosophy of American pragmatism. One advantage of the revisionist theses of Stone and Lovin is that the internal logic of Niebuhr's theological development can now be better appreciated; in their view, Niebuhr's theology is not simply a reflection of the twentieth-century *Zeitgeist,* or spirit of the times.

Christian Realism

When one rereads Niebuhr's principal works in order to test the hypothesis that Christian realism is a theological expression of American pragmatism, one may get the impression that throughout his career Niebuhr was simply rewriting his first book, revising its substantive arguments in light of new insights provoked by the political crises and ideological struggles of the twentieth century. *Does Civilization Need Religion?* (1927) contains all the elements of a pragmatic approach to Christian apologetics, or, if you will, a model for practical theology focused less on Christian ministry and more on effective Christian witness in the world. Although this work is couched in the assumptions of an idealized Social Gospel, Niebuhr commends Christian faith as a practical resource for solving the problems of a modern industrial society. Echoing certain themes in the liberal Protestantism then still reigning in Germany, Niebuhr sees "the concept of personality" as defining the essence of Christianity, and he tries to show how this idea can make a practical difference in the struggle for social justice. Nevertheless, his apology already contains a critical challenge for the churches: Given the "social complexity" of modernity, the churches run the risk of "ethical impotence" unless they are able to wed an "astute intelligence" to their religious idealism. What he had in mind was a critical appropriation of the social sciences that would restore a degree of political realism to the Social Gospel.

On the basis of his own experience as a pastor and ecumenical activist in Detroit, Niebuhr meant to hold Christian theology to a pragmatic test: Can the "personal religion" that it commends actually contribute to solving the problems of an "impersonal civilization"? Niebuhr's initial call for the creation of an effective "social imagination" is somewhat ironic in the way that *Does Civilization Need Religion?*, as Stone first pointed out, is almost devoid of sociological content. Niebuhr's next important work, *Moral Man and Immoral Society* (1932), returned to this same pragmatic challenge in light of a significant change in perspective. The essence of Christianity is no longer described in idealistic terms, nor is it the only religious alternative under consideration. Marxism now enters the picture not simply as a social science, but as a social movement capable of generating the kind of fanatical "religious passion" that can mobilize the masses to struggle for social justice. With the onset of the Great Depression shortly after his appointment to the faculty at Union Seminary, Niebuhr found himself confronted with an intensification of social conflict well beyond anything he had experienced in Detroit, and the ready availability of a "millenarian" ideology that could make sense of the impending class struggle better than what he now discounted as the "sentimentality" of the Social Gospel.

So began Niebuhr's historic struggle with the legacy of Karl Marx. Initially, he was deeply impressed by Marxism's religious roots and what seemed to be its political and ideological superiority. But his conversion to the new faith was, at best, half-hearted. *Moral Man and Immoral Society* thus advocates a "frank dualism in morals," according to which the social struggle will be governed by the mille-narian "illusions" of Marxism, while personal morality should still be guided by the eschatological virtues of faith, hope, and charity. A few years later, as the political convulsions of the 1930s were at their peak, Niebuhr would become disenchanted with Marxism, again, primarily on religious grounds. Confronted with Marxism's failure to check totalitarianism, either as an internal development (Stalinism) or as a rival ideology (Nazism), Niebuhr came to reject millenarianism in any form as a basis for radical politics.

The consequences of idolatry turned out to be no less pernicious in politics than they were in personal morality. *Reflections on the End of an Era* (1934) thus dramatizes the decisive turn in Niebuhr's theological reflections, toward a synthesis of "a more radical political orientation and more conservative religious convictions than are comprehended in the culture of our era." Within this program, Niebuhr began to wrestle with the practical significance of traditional Christian claims for the "experience of grace," the need for careful attention to "the aesthetic motif in religion" in order to discover a language appropriate to the experience of grace, and the political efficacy of the mythologies of history—especially those of traditional Christianity—disclosed within this aesthetic dimension. This was the nucleus of Christian realism, both substantively and methodologically: The analysis remained pragmatic, and the focus was emphatically public. But from this point on, as Niebuhr's theology reflected more conservative religious convictions, the question would be in what sense the policies that it supported could actually be considered a radical politics.

Niebuhr's next book, published only a year later, demonstrated remarkable progress in fleshing out the theological program announced in *Reflections on the End of an Era*. The nature of Christian realism's opposition to both liberal and orthodox forms of theology, Niebuhr spelled out in *An Interpretation of Christian Ethics* (1935). Although he faulted Social Gospel liberalism for promoting a false optimism about politics, Niebuhr was equally critical of the all-too-fashionable political pessimism that the newly imported dialectical theology seemed to be sponsoring. Though Karl Barth's and Emil Brunner's theologies were closer to the conservative religious convictions that Niebuhr now affirmed, he deliberately sought to undercut their perspectives by insisting, like the liberals, upon the ethical significance of the teachings of the historical Jesus. But unlike liberals who regarded the ethic of Jesus as a blueprint for transforming the social order, Niebuhr insisted that Jesus' ideal of sacrificial love represented an "impossible possibility" that still must be used to benchmark the efficacy of Christian social action. Given the intractable nature of so many social conflicts, Niebuhr saw the relevance of "the law of love" precisely in its superior ability to sustain political engagement in the struggle for justice and equality, while also promoting a degree of spiritual disin-terestedness that, he hoped, would curb the partisans' inevitable tendency to demonize their opponents. In the highly polarized atmosphere of the mid-1930s, such a proposal could plausibly claim to be the basis for a radical politics.

The next important step in Niebuhr's development of Christian realism was prompted by an invitation to deliver the 1939 Gifford Lectures in Edinburgh. As he was preparing himself for these by reading more deeply in the works of Augustine and several leading figures in the history of Protestant theology, he was also—despite his own warnings against demonizing one's political adversaries—rallying American Christians to support the Allies against the Axis. As anything other than an act of personal witness to the absolute demands of Jesus, pacifism was an evasion of Christian social responsibility. Niebuhr's vision of radical politics was meant to honor the "impossible possibility" of sacrificial love, but it also had to empower Christians to make difficult choices among political alternatives, the most promising of which were only relatively good. Forced to choose between the moral ambiguities of war and a religious perfectionism that made the triumph of Nazi totalitarianism just that much easier, Niebuhr chose war, mournfully, but forthrightly. Nevertheless, when the Gifford Lectures were later published as the two volumes of *The Nature and Destiny of Man* (1941, 1943), they represented less the sentinel's call to arms than a blueprint for the postwar reconstruction of Western civilization.

Christian realism was meant to see beyond the daily headlines of tragedy and triumph on the battlefields of Europe and the Pacific to the underlying religious and moral disasters that had brought the West to the brink of self-destruction. It was also an exercise in pragmatic apologetics, for in Niebuhr's analysis, World War II was the result of deep ideological conflicts, themselves rooted in a range of post-Christian heresies. Western modernity had become captive to the errors of rationalism, romanticism, individualism, and naturalism. Niebuhr attempted to show that all four were rooted in a basic error about human nature, namely, a willful refusal to acknowledge our common human identity as God's creatures, and hence the unwitting participation of persons in the pervasive reality of sin. Lacking a theological self-understanding, persons are apt to misinterpret the signs of God's grace, without which our faltering efforts to better ourselves can only lead to further difficulty. Niebuhr's view of human nature thus grows out of the more conservative religious convictions of classical or Augustinian Christianity, but in the course of being interpreted these conservative religious convictions are transformed into practical hypotheses that can be confirmed or discounted through experience. Basing his argument as much on extensive reading in the social sciences, particularly psychology and the sociology of knowledge, as on the writings of the church fathers, Niebuhr argued that Christian faith offers a useful political perspective, because it is based on an appreciation, deeper than that of any other ideology, of the truth about persons in society.

If the first volume of *The Nature and Destiny of Man* can be construed as a theological anthropology, the second volume is its complement, a practical theology of history. Success in reconstructing the postwar social order would depend on a proper understanding of what is, and is not, possible for humans to achieve in history. The work is emphatically christocentric, as Niebuhr deploys the mythic structure of Christian eschatology, to show the pragmatic consequences of religious hope. With eventual Allied victory now foreseeable, Niebuhr was not about to repeat the youthful mistakes of Social Gospel idealists who thought World War I would finally make the world safe for democracy. He offers here no hope of a linear progression in history toward the kingdom of God. Nevertheless, the kingdom of God continues to beckon as an eschatological fulfillment beyond history that must serve as the norm for judging all our struggles in history. How this norm must be understood as both an inspirational resource for Christian social action, and as an eternal reproach against our noblest achievements, is worked out symbolically by Niebuhr in a theological reflection on the meaning of Renaissance and Reformation.

If Western civilization is to resolve the political obstacles standing in the way of its future development, it will have to reaffirm the truths embedded in the Renaissance and Reformation. A politics organized on the basis of a creative synthesis of the two will exhibit a chastened attitude of self-criticism even in the throes of ideological conflict, and a commitment to continually adjusting the balances of power in order to achieve incrementally whatever social justice can be achieved within history. In thinking ahead to the postwar world, Niebuhr envisioned moving toward some sort of international community of nations, but consistent with his general observations on the need for an organizing center in any political order, he insisted that the process of forming this community would inevitably involve some sort of hegemony, preferably one that was constitutionally accountable. The political program implicit in *The Nature and Destiny of Man* is more succinctly presented in *The Children of Light and the Children of Darkness* (1944), a brief work that occasioned one of Niebuhr's most memorable aphorisms: "Man's capacity for justice makes democracy possible, but man's inclination to injustice makes democracy necessary." By the end of the war, Niebuhr's theological convictions were both a reflection of and an argument for the policies, both foreign and domestic, of Franklin Delano Roosevelt.

In his later years, Niebuhr was to write a number of works that would return to the themes of *The Nature and Destiny of Man*. Each of these stands not as a fundamentally new departure, but as a partial reassessment of Christian realism provoked by further learning from more recent experience, or by more leisurely reflection. *Faith and History* (1949), for example, on technical grounds is a more careful statement of Niebuhr's theology of history than that offered in the second volume of *The Nature and Destiny of Man*. But what it gains in coherence it may have lost in dramatic immediacy. *The Self and the Dramas of History* (1955) replicates the organization of the Gifford Lectures with their twin foci on theological anthropology and theology of history, and it does correct Niebuhr's earlier readings of the social sciences by being more appreciative of the "organic" dimensions of human community; but it does not substantially alter the basic tenets of Christian realism. As Ronald Stone, and more recently, Henry Clark, have argued, the real test of Christian realism in the postwar period turns not on what Niebuhr may or may not have written, but on what kind of leadership he embodied as an elder statesman among Christian social activists.

Christian realism's chief merit is that, fortified by such a lofty perspective, one is not likely to be taken by surprise by any historical event, except, perhaps, the Second Coming of Christ! The transmutation of World War II into the Cold War may have unleashed from Niebuhr a torrent of rhetoric in which Soviet communism was characterized as a menace more threatening than Hitler's Germany, but it did not cause him to advocate any crusade to roll back the Red Army from Eastern Europe. In Niebuhr's hands, Christian realism dovetailed readily with George F. Kennan's policy of containment; it firmed up Christian support for a protracted political struggle conducted globally under the umbrella of nuclear deterrence; above all, it counseled prudent diplomacy and military restraint abroad and resisted efforts, like those of the McCarthyite reactionaries, to curtail American civil liberties because of the alleged necessities of anticommunist resistance.

Niebuhr's acceptance of the moral logic of the Cold War, of course, can be assigned as one of the factors contributing to the United States' disastrous involvement in the Vietnamese civil war after the French withdrawal in 1954. But with the dramatic escalation of the conflict after the assassination of John F. Kennedy, Niebuhr became increasingly sharp in his protests against the conduct of the war, showing how it failed the just war test of proportionality. Christian realism, Niebuhr once again insisted, ought to enable its adherents to make discriminating judgments, "the nicely calculated less and more," among a variety of complex public policy options. His own conduct showed how it was possible in principle to support the basic aims of the Cold War while criticizing, as occasion warranted, the execution of those aims in Vietnam. The collapse of the Soviet Union under the weight of its own spiritual and moral decay, arguably, confirms the wisdom and humanity of Niebuhr's nuanced response to the dilemmas of the postwar world.

Conclusion

The world has changed dramatically in the quarter of a century since Niebuhr's death in 1971. Twenty-first-century theologians are not likely to assess the merits of Christian realism on the basis of its answers to questions that no longer make any practical difference to them. Less concerned with the clear and present danger of totalitarianism, they may want to know whether Christian realism can empower oppressed groups for effective political participation, or does it, instead, reinforce the waning white male, Eurocentric hegemonies that are identified with the World War II generation. They will want to know, for example, whether Niebuhr's understanding of human nature—with its emphasis on the pervasiveness of sin, particularly, the sin of pride—reflects the experience of anyone other than successful white males. They will question whether Niebuhr's ideal of sacrificial love might not be disastrous when preached to the victims of oppression, domestic as well as political. They will suspect that Christian realism's limited view of the prospects for establishing the kingdom of God on earth may actually immobilize Christian social activists, rather than sustain their commitment to social justice. Some may conclude, because Niebuhr succeeded so well in providing an honest brokerage among competing political interests, that Christian realism can never be more than an elitist ideology designed to manage, and hence defuse, social conflict. Finally, those who assume that the center of gravity in world affairs has shifted to the Pacific Rim will fear that Niebuhr's lack of insight into the spiritual and ethical resources of non-monotheistic religions renders Christian realism all but irrelevant to the strategic concerns of the twenty-first century.

Those who continue to defend Christian realism, despite these criticisms, seem to have three options. First, they can categorically reject these criticisms by disputing their premises. This seems to be the road traveled by Niebuhr's neoconservative admirers. Second, while admitting that these criticisms do identify certain existential risks in Christian realism, they can show—as Henry Clark has tried to do recently—how these risks can be curtailed for the sake of preserving the broadest possible coalition among Christian social activists. This is the strategy of neoliberals who believe that Niebuhr's own development demonstrated sufficient openness to emerging perspectives to warrant accommodating the concerns of a new generation of Christian radicals. Finally, however, if the neoliberal response is to be regarded as credible, Christian realism will have to submit to a theoretical overhaul.

If the methodology of American pragmatism, properly understood, is operative throughout Niebuhr's development, then it ought to be deployed to show how Christian realism can address the challenges of public life in the twenty-first century. As Robin Lovin has argued, Christian realism's underlying pragmatism about religion and public life already constitutes a common ground shared and sharable with Niebuhr's most effective critics.

Dennis P. McCann

Selected Primary Works

1927   *Does Civilization Need Religion?*
1929   *Leaves from the Notebook of a Tamed Cynic.*
1932   *Moral Man and Immoral Society.*
1934   *Reflections on the End of an Era.*

1935   *An Interpretation of Christian Ethics.*
1937   *Beyond Tragedy.*
1940   *Christianity and Power Politics.*
1941   *The Nature and Destiny of Man: Volume One.*
1943   *The Nature and Destiny of Man: Volume Two.*
1949   *Faith and History.*
1952   *The Irony of American History.*
1955   *The Self and the Dramas of History.*
1965   *Man's Nature and His Communities.*
1986   *The Essential Reinhold Niebuhr,* ed. Robert McAfee Brown.

Selected Secondary Sources

1956   Charles W. Kegley and Robert W. Bretall, eds., *Reinhold Niebuhr: His Religious, Social, and Political Thought.*
1972   Ronald H. Stone, *Reinhold Niebuhr: Prophet to Politicians.*
1980   Judith Plaskow, *Sex, Sin, and Grace.*
1981   Dennis P. McCann, *Christian Realism and Liberation Theology.*
1981   Robert Benne, *The Ethic of Democratic Capitalism.*
1985   Richard Fox, *Reinhold Niebuhr: A Biography.*
1986   Karen Lebacqz, *Six Theories of Justice.*
1988   Cornel West, *The American Evasion of Philosophy: A Genealogy of Pragmatism.*
1992   Charles C. Brown, *Niebuhr and His Age: Reinhold Niebuhr's Prophetic Role in the Twentieth Century.*
1992   Harlan Beckley, *Passion for Justice: Retrieving the Legacies of Walter Rauschenbusch, John A. Ryan, and Reinhold Niebuhr.*
1992   Ronald H. Stone, *Professor Reinhold Niebuhr.*
1994   Gabriel Fackre, *The Promise of Reinhold Niebuhr* (rev. ed.).
1994   Henry B. Clark, *Serenity, Courage, and Wisdom: The Enduring Legacy of Reinhold Niebuhr.*
1995   Robin W. Lovin, *Reinhold Niebuhr and Christian Realism.*

THOMAS C. ODEN
1931–

An ordained United Methodist minister presently serving as the Henry Anson Buttz Professor of Theology and Ethics at Drew University, Oden is one of the more surprising figures in theology today. Educated at the University of Oklahoma (B.A.), Perkins School of Theology (B.D.), and Yale University (M.A. and Ph.D.), he has written numerous books and articles covering a wide range of theological and psychological topics, especially in the area of pastoral theology. His early career closely reflected the theological training he received. A self-professed "movement theologian," he published early works on both Rudolf Bultmann and Karl Barth.

In these early works some of Oden's concern with issues of human identity and definition emerge as reflections on humankind's authentic existence in the world. In the work on Barth, Oden writes that Barth's ethics has promise for theology because it is an ethic of freedom to be human before God in response to the freedom of God for humanity. In an echo of Bultmann and Heidegger's philosophy, Oden states that people are called to "authentic" humanness, an authenticity that calls them to actualize their own humanity, whose basis is in the truly authentic person Jesus Christ. This humanity entails a covenantal relationship with God in the form of God's initiating grace. Humanity is called to what it is meant to be by being the recipient of God's reconciling action.

From the beginning, Oden's concerns are mostly anthropological in nature as he seeks to analyze humankind from a theological basis to discern the essence of humanity as creation of God. He draws on a number of different disciplines in this effort as he tries to speak to the age in which he is writing. In *Structures of Awareness* he writes to the "spiritually serious" readers whom he identifies with the seekers of the age. In this work Oden sets up a phenomenology of the human subject, what he refers to as "field theory of authenticity," where he seeks to find the authentic and inauthentic ways that human beings interact in the world.

340

Employing categories of time and being, he explores the human orientation of awareness in past, present, and future with the interaction of God, self, neighbor, and the world. He uncovers the distorted ways that we live and, using therapeutic categories, tries to set up how we can move from negating, inauthentic, and dysfunctional ways of living, to self-actualizing awareness (which he distinguishes using such dynamics as forgiveness, trust, faith, love, and self-discovery).

As early as *Structures of Awareness,* Oden was using the term "post-modern" to describe the cultural context in which he wrote and his dissatisfaction with the failure of theologians in the late 1960s to explore systematically the dimensions of Christian faith. As one reads this work, one can see the uneasiness Oden feels with his culture. He seems to search for a center to hold the foundations of Christian faith together amidst a culture that is crumbling. But Oden also put his faith in the cutting-edge theologies that he felt would lead the way to new insights concerning Christianity and its place in the world. As his theological path continued, he would turn from this hope to one rooted in a deeper sense of the tradition of the early church.

During the next decade Oden began the shift to the positions with which he is most identified. His continual concern for pastoral care would lead him to write still more books that explore the intersection of human existence and theological concerns. Involved in the client-centered movement, he published books and articles on transactional analysis, behavioral psychology, and even parapsychological phenomena. Even these works were theologically oriented, seeking to explicate from human experience some notion of God and God's revelation to humankind in Christ.

During the mid-1970s, however, Oden again reoriented his theology with the publication of the book *Agenda for Theology: Recovering Christian Roots.* In an autobiographical tone, he speaks of a fundamental hermeneutical reversal. As he explained later in an article in *The Christian Century,* he had been asking questions on the hidden premise of four key value assumptions of modern consciousness: "hedonic self-actualization, autonomous individualism, reductive naturalism, and moral relativism." Now in the light of his reading in the patristic texts, Oden pronounced that the questions of modernity should be formed and shaped by ancient, consensual, classical Christian exegesis of the Holy Scripture.

This work would launch the public change of attitude that had been taking shape in Oden for some time as he moved away from Freudian and Rogerian psychology, away from absorption in "individualistic self-actualization and narcissistic self-expression and toward durable habits of moral excellence and covenant community."

From this point on, all of his works would show his critique of how modernity has led to reductionistic accounts of Christian belief, and how the integration of ancient Christian wisdom can overcome the chauvinism of a modern theology that seeks to arrogate to itself a position of privilege by claiming that the present offers a superior position from which to critique the past. This relativism is, he argues, the chief distinguishing (and disintegrative) influence in theological education today. For Oden, ancient wisdom allows for a critique of modernity and its attendant corruptions, and it would thereafter provide order for his systematic and pastoral theology.

Oden believes that what has gone awry in today's context can be set right by returning to the theological methods that prevailed in Christianity's first millennium. Close adherence to the apostolic faith and a more representative ecumenical consensus, affirmed by subsequent traditions, allows for a more accurate transmission of the faith. The gravity of the tradition causes him to eschew innovation or how scholars "feel" about theological perspectives.

Although theologians probably cannot directly adopt a method of ancient ecumenical orthodoxy, Oden believes that the patristic age can stand as an important corrective for the distortions of our age, in the same way that Kierkegaard, one of his favorite theologians, served as a corrective for his time. Turning away from the liberalism that defined so much of his career, Oden says that classical Christianity is wiser and better than its modern interpreters and alternatives.

After spending the first part of his career on building bridges between psychology and religion, Oden felt that the conversation had become a one-way street with far too much acquiescence by theology to the present moment. In his words, "It is the winter season for rigorous Christian teaching. . . . Modernity is a winter season for classical Christianity. Spring will come, but only to those who have survived the winter." With *Agenda for Theology* Oden announced that the thaw in his world was beginning.

Consequently, Oden rigorously pursued the wisdom of the patristic era and has published volumes dedicated to the recovery of patristic writing (see especially the series *Pastoral Care in the Classic Tradition* and such books as *Pastoral Theology*). In these works he endeavors to show how Gregory, Chrysostom, or Cyril of Jerusalem, just to name a few, possess insight into the care of souls that should be integrated into today's pastoral care concerns.

In *Pastoral Theology,* Oden works out a systematic pastoral theology that encompasses a host of issues with which those who consider the vocation of Christian ministry struggle . Concerns about ordination, sacraments, preaching, and the care of souls, prompt Oden to return to the earliest strata of Christian tradition to guide ministry. By incorporating the quadrilateral of Scripture, tradition, experience, and reason, he lays out a perspective that employs his postmodern orthodoxy in the service of ministry. In a section on a theodicy for pastoral practice one can see clearly the direction Oden takes theologically. With pastoral intent more than philosophical speculation, Oden approaches theology with heavy appeal to the Bible and the patristic authors, particularly Augustine, to affirm God's holiness and power in the face of suffering.

The centering of Oden's theology also shows up in his recently published systematic theology in three volumes, *The Living God, The Word of Life,* and *Life in the Spirit.* In the first volume he targets his audience as the working pastor, the candidate preparing for ordination, and the intelligent layperson preparing for baptism. The book is essentially a compendium recollecting classical thought about God.

Self-consciously attempting to devise a postmodern orthodoxy and to instill a "paleo-orthodox" consciousness in the present generation of the community of faith, Oden consistently uses the methodology that he adopted in the mid-seventies. He works with a pyramidic structure wherein scripture and the earliest patristic witnesses form the largest foundation. Those who keep closest faith with the classical consensus, such as Thomas Aquinas and the Reformers, occupy the middle tiers; and at the very top, with the fewest references, appear the theologians of modernity.

In *The Living God* (1987), Oden exemplifies his method by incorporating numerous quotations from the ancient writers (indeed, Oden jokes that he has written a book where the quotations are more important than the text, and Oden's own remarks merely point to the meat of the work). His main concern is to show that the tradition shows God as both personal and living, and as he moves through the work he treats such issues as the names of God, the attributes, and the arguments for God's existence with copious notes from the church's earliest tradition. The classical positions are presented and accompanied by a defense of the orthodox understandings of the nature of God, the Trinity, and the divine attributes of omnipotence, omniscience, and immutability.

The Word of Life (1992) contains a detailed account of two millennia of Christian attempts to answer the question, Who is Jesus of Nazareth? Once again Oden seeks a "core of consensual belief." He goes through the ancient writers and ecumenical councils to those who continue to clarify the creeds and confessions of these sources. He supports a detailed defense of the Chalcedonian position that resists modernity's attempt at reductionism. The understanding of the two-natures doctrine is affirmed without any apologies to the sensibilities of modernity. All the christological issues that the church has struggled with are treated similarly, thus rendering this work a thorough resource about how the church developed its understanding of the person and work of Christ.

In the third work of this trilogy, *Life in the Spirit* (1994), Oden returns to the ancient touchstones. The Holy Spirit's work in soteriology, ecclesiology, and eschatology is covered from an understanding of the third person in the context of the immanent Trinity. Most of the work is dedicated to the work of the Holy Spirit in "the administration of Redemption after the Incarnation." A strong emphasis on the application of Christ's work as both pardon and power leads to interesting sections on sanctification and perfecting grace. Once again proposing a "paleo-orthodox" perspective, Oden provides a compendium of the wisdom of the writers of the early church, scripture, and those who closely follow this perspective.

These three works and the subsequent works on pastoral care reflect the dream that Oden recounts in *Agenda for Theology* (1979), where he saw his own epitaph: "He made no new contributions to theology." Indeed, Oden seeks to adhere to this dream because he sees the present age as so corrupt and disintegrative that Christian faith has been debased by the hermeneutical and methodological tools of modernity, reducing Christianity to a reflection of modernity's narcissistic self-image.

Oden's commitment to recover the witness of historical sources has led him to become embraced by the evangelical community, having served as senior editor of the fortnightly *Christianity Today*. Oden himself recounts that through "grace enabled stages" he found himself in the middle of a flourishing evangelical ecumenism in which the evangelical community is recovering the ancient Christian tradition. Some theologians welcome Oden's work and passion not to capitulate to the lure of empty relevance, not to be carried about by every wind of doctrine, and of believing that one's particular social location does not automatically grant epistemological privilege. Oden's call for recovery of ancient wisdom provides a necessary correction to the peculiarities and partialities of the current age.

Yet the weaknesses of Oden's approach can be found within the strengths. Oden calls attention to the characteristics of the so-called postmodern situation. An emphasis on embodiment, contextuality, and construals of the subject are very much in the forefront of the current quest for understanding. In the midst of the voices of modernity that argue that understanding domesticates difference, Oden's work will not have much appeal. But these perspectives cannot be ignored, and the problematics they point to cannot be looked beyond to construct a simple view of the past.

Oden, to his credit, points his critics to the bulk of his work, which is an in-depth treatment of the understandings of modernity. He did not make his turn toward tradition without a careful examination of what the present has to offer, he argues. Those who ponder the necessity of overcoming the present tensions for the future of the culture and church may be engaged by Oden's work; however, they may also ask whether Oden has given adequate consideration to some pressing concerns.

Perhaps the most important concern is whether Oden has sought recovery in a too simplistic manner. Is there a too easy juxtaposition between a corrupt present and an honored past in Oden? When the recovery of the sources was emerging in the Reformation era, the ancient sources led to the formation of different communities. The Anabaptists in their historiography of the "golden age" of the Scripture and the early church came up with far more radical perspectives than did the magisterial Reformers (whom Oden seems to quote more than Menno Simons). Is it the case that a return to the consensus Oden sees in the early church will issue in a consensus for our age? It did not provide such for the sixteenth century, and it is doubtful if it will for ours.

The context that gave rise to the very texts Oden seeks to recover held enormous tensions and was not as unified as one might gather from Oden's treatment. In the classical tradition, doctrine develops within new contexts, replete with philosophical assumptions borrowed from sources other than scripture. Can we incorporate without further examination the way the early church understood terms like *hypostasis, persona,* or *substantia* without extending the discussion?

Likewise, are Hellenistic categories the primary ones with which to interpret the attributes of God? One of the questions that is still open for debate is to what extent ancient texts can be used without an understanding of the context in which they emerged. The previously mentioned community of the Anabaptists saw all doctrine after Constantine as suspect, given that the empire had too great a stake in maintaining peace, even if it meant the emperor influenced doctrine. The recovery of these sources must be accomplished with historical and textual criticism for a comprehensive and reflective understanding. Citing Anselm needs to be accompanied with an understanding of why *satisfaction* was so central to Anselm's *Cur Deus Homo?* (or for that matter why Gregory the Great had entirely different perspectives in mind when he formulated his theories of atonement). Going even further, we should be able to discuss whether these perspectives need new language to communicate to our age the saving action of God in Christ. There are cultural constructs to be considered when seeking to explore the multiplicities inherent in the tradition.

If doctrine does develop within new contexts, should not today's context have useful and necessary wisdom to add to the discussion? In Oden's pyramidic structure these voices occupy the narrowest position because they are of least importance, being farthest removed from the purer past.

Is our world one that must be fought against as an age of accommodation, in which there is a reduction of Christian faith to the spirit of the age (and in fairness to Oden's position, in which Freudian projections of God created in our image are rife in theology)? Or maybe these same voices are also God's way of raising questions that theologians need to hear. Oden does theology a good service by reminding us of the need to listen to the wisdom of the past, especially in the area of pastoral care. His treatment of those voices shows the continuity of human existence and struggle through the ages. But in the same sense the theologies of the current age may offer not so much an accommodation to the spirit of the age as prophetic perspective to extend the tradition in order that the church may yet have something of importance to say to the world.

Jeffrey C. Pugh

Selected Bibliography

1969   *The Structures of Awareness.*
1979   *Agenda for Theology.*
1983   *Pastoral Theology.*
1987   *The Living God.*
1992   *The Word of Life.*
1993   *The Transforming Power of Grace.*
1994   *Life in the Spirit.*
1995   *Requiem: A Lament in Three Movements.*

SCHUBERT M. OGDEN
1928–

Life and Career

Schubert M. Ogden is University Distinguished Professor of Theology Emeritus at Southern Methodist University. For thirty-four years—between 1956 and 1969 and again between 1972 and 1993—he taught at S.M.U., and for the three years between 1969 and 1972 he was University Professor of Theology at the University of Chicago. An ordained United Methodist minister, he also served as Director of S.M.U.'s Graduate Program in Religious Studies from 1974 to 1990.

He earned his A.B. degree from Ohio Wesleyan University (1950) and his B.D. and Ph.D. degrees from the University of Chicago (1954, 1958). He is also the recipient of honorary degrees from both universities as well as from Southern Methodist University.

At various times in his career he has been a Fulbright Research Scholar, a John Simon Guggenheim Memorial Fellow at Philipps University in Marburg, Germany, and a visiting fellow both of the Council of the Humanities at Princeton University and of the Institute for the Advanced Study of Religion at the University of Chicago. He has taught and lectured in many other schools and universities both in Europe and in the United States, and was appointed Sarum Lecturer in Oxford University and Ferguson Lecturer in the University of Manchester. A past president of the American Academy of Religion, he was elected in 1985 as a Fellow of the American Academy of Arts and Sciences.

The author of seven books, he has also contributed chapters or essays to some fifty other books, and he has published articles and reviews in a wide range of scholarly journals. In addition, he is the editor and translator of *Existence and Faith: Shorter Writings of Rudolf Bultmann* (1960) and *New Testament and Mythology and Other Basic Writings* (of Rudolf Bultmann) (1984). A Festschrift in his honor, *Witness and Existence,* published in 1989, contains a complete bibliography of his published writings through 1988.

Ogden's most recent work reflects a wide range of involvements and interests— from participation since 1984 in the International Buddhist-Christian Theological

Encounter Group to service on special committees of the American Association of University Professors concerned with both general policy and particular problems pertaining to the place of theology in the university. Since his retirement he has continued to work primarily on a one-volume systematic theology.

Overview

The content of Schubert Ogden's theology may be summarized as a sustained commentary on the following proposition: Christian faith represents the decisive answer to a universal human question. His work joins a powerful metaphysical expression of the Christian claim that God is love with a vigorous Christian anthropology that finds its roots in Rudolf Bultmann, John Wesley, Martin Luther, and Paul the apostle. An appropriate interpretation of the christological witness of the New Testament confronts us with the correct understanding of human existence; alternatively, a comprehensive analysis of human experience uncovers our implicit awareness of God. The New Testament thus makes manifest what is already disclosed in human existence; Christianity represents the true and authentic expression of what it means to be a human being.

Because of its consistent focus on the center of Christian faith, Ogden's theology is entirely of a piece, and one may successfully enter it through any of several doors: concepts of God, Christ, human experience, or authentic human life. The present essay organizes Ogden's theology "from the bottom up." Beginning with a discussion of the human question of meaning, it examines the Christian answer as it is disclosed in the implicit human awareness of deity, and as it is made fully manifest through Jesus the Christ.

The Existential Question

Human beings, according to Ogden, may be defined as the creatures who ask and answer the question of what it means to be a human being. Each person unavoidably confronts and, by the way he or she chooses to live, answers such questions as: How ought I to understand myself? What is really true about the world? How should I live in the world? Taken together, such inquiries constitute the existential or religious question of the meaning and purpose of life.

Underlying the existential question is the presupposition that there is in fact some form of self-understanding that is uniquely "authorized" as an appropriate or authentic response to reality. We could not even seriously raise the existential question unless we were already convinced that one or another understanding was warranted by the way things are. Ogden refers to this conviction as "existential faith," the faith that human life is worth living according to the appropriate interpretation of its significance.

Existential faith, although inevitable, is not unchallenged in human life. Especially in the face of such "boundary situations" as dealing with profound guilt, trying to understand the meaning of random violence, facing one's own death, or grieving the death of a loved one, persons are driven to seek reassurance that their basic faith is indeed true. Thus, although the implicit conviction *that* there is an authentic way to understand ourselves is a universal feature of human experience, just *how* we are to construe that understanding explicitly through concepts and symbols is a matter of human freedom.

Human culture generally addresses the existential question through art, architecture, literature, and so forth; but religion is the primary form of culture in which the existential question is explicitly posed and answered. Characteristic of the various religious answers is the claim to decisive authority: *This* is the true understanding of reality! *Thus,* therefore, ought you to understand yourself and live in the world! In this broad sense, Ogden's notion of religion includes not only the various world religions, but also Stoicism, Marxism, or atheistic humanism—in fact, any answer to the existential question that carries authority for some group of people.

Is there a "right" religious answer to the existential question? Because each specific answer makes claims about what reality ultimately *is* as well as claims about how we therefore *ought* to live, the validity of any religious answer can be determined only according to the—admittedly controversial, but necessary—procedures for validating metaphysical and ethical claims. A "right" answer to the existential question, in short, will be both *true* and *authentic*.

The Nature and Task of Christian Theology

Christianity claims that its answer to the existential question is the right one. Even before examining the material content of that answer, we may pause to consider the methodological implications of this claim.

Ogden conceives Christian theology as "the fully reflective understanding of the Christian witness of faith as decisive for human existence" (*On Theology,* 1986, p. 1). The phrase "fully reflective understanding" acknowledges that Christian faith makes cognitive claims, and so theology reflects upon their meaning and truth. And the phrase "as decisive for human existence" acknowledges Christianity's own claim to being "the full and adequate objectification of human existence in its authentic possibility" (ibid., p. 41).

It follows, in terms of method, that the theologian is responsible both for accurately retrieving the Christian answer and for expressing that answer in terms of human experience. Theology must be *appropriate* to the Christian faith and *credible* to human experience.

Because the Christian answer has been expressed historically through many and varied witnesses, the criterion of appropriateness needs to be tied specifically to the center of Christian faith. Which of the multiple expressions of Christianity represents the essence of Christianity? What is the norm that provides the norm for the tradition? Where do we locate the canon of theological appropriateness? Ogden rejects two usual answers to these questions.

It is not possible, he maintains, for Christian theologians to locate the canon in "Jesus himself," because the New Testament writings are expressions of faith in the significance of Jesus, rather than historical reports about Jesus. The historical Jesus is not recoverable. Nor can Christian theologians simply locate the canon in the New Testament, because the New Testament writings are themselves faithful to witnesses that precede them, namely, the apostles. In this sense, the New Testament is already tradition. Ogden concludes that the norm that provides the norm for all theological statements is the apostolic witness as it can be reconstructed from the New Testament documents: "That alone is canonical which is also apostolic" (*The Point of Christology,* 1982, p. 112).

The apostolic witness cannot be the sole, or even the ultimate, theological authority, however. Given the Christian claim to be decisively true for all human existence, the final court of appeal must be human experience itself. This should be construed not as the invasion of an "alien rationalism" into Ogden's theology, but rather as the straightforward recognition that a claim to universal truth must be supported by universally accessible evidence. There can be no special pleading on behalf of, or special status afforded to, Christian truth claims. If Christian faith cannot be validated in terms of human experience, then either it is not universally true or our understanding of human experience is truncated.

Ogden thus advocates a "postliberal" model for doing theology, one that seeks, without compromising essential Christian truth, to make good on liberal theology's conviction that "Christian faith is not utterly alien to people, whatever their historical situation, but rather is their own most proper possibility of existence, which can and should be understandable to them, provided it is so expressed as to take their situation into account" (*The Reality of God,* 1966, p. 6).

The Original Revelation of God

"For the secular person of today, as surely as for any other person, faith in God cannot but be real because it is in the final analysis unavoidable" (*The Reality of God,* p. 21). We have already seen how this seemingly remarkable claim is entirely appropriate to Christian faith. But is the theistic claim credible? Ogden's affirmative answer involves two important philosophical moves: broadening the notion of human experience and revising the classical conception of God.

Christian theology must be credible in terms of human experience, *properly understood*. With Alfred North Whitehead, Ogden rejects as inadequate any empiricist doctrine that interprets human experience in terms of sensations and what can be derived from them. Instead, recognizing in Whitehead's doctrine of nonsensory awareness a philosophical contribution of the first magnitude, Ogden argues that logically prior to sensory experience is the vague and elementary awareness of self and others as included in an encompassing whole. Also given in this primitive layer of human experience is the dim awareness of worth: Our lives derive value from, because they are significant to, the inclusive whole.

Ogden contends that this primal awareness of self and others as making a difference to the whole—what is identified above as "existential faith"—drives all human praxis; indeed, even the act of consciously denying that life has meaning presupposes that the denial is meaningful. In this sense, existential faith is not a matter of human choice (although how one conceives it and how one lives it are), but is an unavoidable response to reality. "I experience the meaning of life not as something which I project on life but as something which claims me and demands that I acknowledge it" (*Theology in Crisis*, 1967. p. 52). The question, then, is not *whether* life has abiding meaning, but rather *how* we are to construe that meaning.

Among the many candidates proffered as explanations of existential faith, the only true answer—the only answer that can support the full weight of existential faith—Ogden argues, is the reality of God. All other answers are "false gods." The fundamental intuition underlying a theistic interpretation of the world is that it *matters* and it matters *finally* that we are here. To say that reality evokes from us a sense of abiding worth is to say that reality is theistic, where "God" means "the ground of basic trust."

Because significance or worth is a relational idea (something is significant to someone), Ogden argues that the ground of existential faith must be personal, and it should be conceived in terms of two defining characteristics. In one respect God is, as Whitehead expressed it, "the infinite register of our experience," entirely sensitive to and affected by us; in another respect, God is—again in Whitehead's words—"the great anchor which cannot drag," and so God's relatedness to us is itself related to nothing, but is absolute.

The most adequate conceptuality for respecting this two-sided or dipolar insight regarding deity Ogden finds fully developed in the neoclassical metaphysics of Charles Hartshorne. Hartshorne's work stands as the leading alternative today to the Greek philosophical conception of deity, an alternative that avoids the antinomies of classical theism and more faithfully articulates the Christian proclamation that God is love. Ogden thus appropriates Hartshorne's philosophical theism, with its social understanding of deity, its reconception of "perfect being" as "the self-surpassing surpasser of all," and its crucial distinction between *what* God is and *how* God is. This distinction explains, for example, the difference between the formal truth that God loves everyone perfectly and the powerful religious realization that God loves *me* unconditionally.

Of particular importance is the neoclassical understanding of divine omnipotence. Because human beings really have some freedom of choice, divine power is conceived on a social rather than a monopolistic model. God acts in the world persuasively rather than coercively. God determines the cosmic order (for example, the natural laws) within which human history is played out, and God inspires and reacts to humans' choices. But humans set the local orders, and they are free to accept or reject divine guidance. The result is that moral evil is unequivocally human responsibility, and not God's. The Holocaust, for example, was not part of any divine plan; it was the result of a human plan that tragically ran afoul of the will of God.

The Special Revelation of Jesus

For Ogden, the study of Christology is not another chapter in the book of Christian theology, alongside the chapter on the doctrine of God. Properly understood, the content of Christology simply *is* Christian theology, just as, properly understood, the complete doctrine of God *is* Christian theology. The full content of the Christian answer to the existential question is the divine love disclosed in God's original self-presentation to the world and made fully manifest through Jesus.

Since the writing of his doctoral dissertation, Ogden has consistently argued that Christian theology must clarify what the point of Christology is and what it is not: "Unless the *theocentric* basis and sanction of 'christocentrism' is explicitly acknowledged, emphasis on Jesus Christ can be a snare and a delusion and a mere travesty of authentic apostolic faith" (*Christ Without Myth,* 1962, p. 143). For the most part, he concludes, Christian thinking about Jesus has headed down the wrong road.

On one level, Ogden contends that uninterpreted mythological language and outmoded metaphysical categories make traditional Christologies incredible in the minds of many people today. But this is a comparatively small issue that can be resolved by grasping the New Testament's own clue about the provisional nature of mythology and then acting on it through the use of appropriate categories of self-understanding.

The real problem is deeper:

> The far more serious difficulty with traditional christology, as well as with the usual efforts to revise it, is not its conceptual tools but . . . the wrong question it asks and tries to answer by means of its conceptuality. Instead of asking, rightly, about the meaning of Christ for us, for our own self-understanding as human beings, it asks

about the person of Christ in himself, in abstraction from our existence. ("The Point of Christology," 1975, p. 390)

The point of Christology has to do not with the person of Jesus, but with the God whom Jesus reveals. So, for example, such questions—all too common in the Christian tradition—as "What was Jesus like?" or "What was Jesus' self-understanding?" are not only historically unrecoverable, they are theologically, and dangerously, beside the point. The question Christology answers is not, Ogden contends, "Who was Jesus?" but rather, "Who is God if Jesus is the revealer of God?"

Ogden thus advocates a fundamental reorientation in the direction of Christology, away from the historical person of Jesus to what we may call the existential significance of Jesus proclaimed in the apostolic witness. This is a truly revisionary and "radical" Christology just in the sense that it adheres rigorously to radical monotheism. Jesus is indeed the "word" of God, because the function of a word is precisely not to draw attention to itself but to reveal a thought. In this sense also, one may say that Jesus is a window on deity; the more one looks just at the window itself, the more one misses what the window reveals.

Another way Ogden expresses the point of Christology is to say that Jesus re-presents, but does not constitute, salvation. The universal possibility of authentic human existence is given with human existence itself: This is God's original self-presentation to all people. The Christian claim that "Jesus is the Christ" means, not that authentic existence first becomes possible with Jesus, but rather that what was always possible now becomes evident or manifest to us. In this regard, Ogden quotes favorably John Knox's statement that "Jesus did not bring a new idea; rather, in him an old idea ceased being an idea at all and became a living reality" (*Christ Without Myth*, 1962, pp. 162-63).

This point also explains why, although the content of Jesus' special revelation is no different from the content of God's general revelation to all people, Jesus is not simply a dispensable midwife of true self-understanding. For the Jesus of the apostolic witness "is the occurrence *in our history* of the transcendent event of God's love" (*On Theology*, 1986, p. 43; italics added). Jesus, we may say, is not necessary for the truth about our lives, *but that truth is necessary for our lives and Jesus is its decisive manifestation*. It is *in Jesus* that the Christian community has explicitly been confronted by the gift and demand of God's love. Jesus thus re-presents God's universal love, and, in so doing, he constitutes the Christian tradition (*Is There Only One True Religion*, 1992, p. 98).

Can there be true religions other than Christianity? In principle, yes; for if God's forgiving love is poured out upon all human beings alike, then the manifestation of that love cannot be artificially restricted. Whether there are, in fact, other true religions is a question whose answer is difficult to determine. After a decade of dialogue with Buddhism, Ogden is prepared to say as a Christian theologian that if there are other true religions, they will also make manifest the God disclosed by Jesus. "The only God who is to be found anywhere—*though God is to be found everywhere*—is the God who is made known in the word that Jesus speaks and is" (*Christ Without Myth*, 1962, p. 144).

What Jesus discloses, what genuine Christian faith attests, and what any true religion will represent, is the all-encompassing, all-embracing reality of God as the final truth about reality. The universal gift of God's love is the origin and the end of all that is or ever could be. This is the meaning of strict monotheism—that the only source of all meaning is God's gratuitous and unconditional acceptance of us, and that therefore the only abiding significance of human lives lies in their contribution to the glory of God.

The unearned gift of divine love confronts us also as moral demand. Just as we are accepted unconditionally by God, and so are finally free from the destructive preoccupation with our destiny, so are we now free for others, to be of service to all those who are accepted by God, which is to say, everybody. God is the center of value. Precious to God; therefore, precious to me: This is the logic of theocentrism.

Significantly, Ogden concludes both of his books on Christology with a brief discussion of the parable of the last judgment (Matt. 25:31-46).

> The utterly striking—in fact, mind-blowing—thing about this witness is that the criterion by which the nations are finally judged is in no way a christological, or even a theological, criterion. Not a word is said about believing in Christ, or even in God, but only about acting to meet the most ordinary of human needs.
>
> (*The Point of Christology, 1982*, p. 167)

What finally matters, what matters more even than true belief, is that we live authentically. Being loved by God, we are to love others. Because of the gift of divine love, we take up thankfully the demand of divine love to feed the hungry, clothe the naked, visit the sick and the imprisoned, and act to change the structures of society that contribute to injustice. In this regard Ogden now argues that any fully believable interpretation of Christianity must be "deideologized" as well as demythologized. Authentic Christianity cannot ever support social or political positions that dehumanize persons; and in this sense, "Christian theology today *must* be conceived as a theology of liberation" (*The Point of Christology*, p. 150).

Summary

At the beginning of his latest book, *Is There One True Religion or Are There Many?* Ogden draws attention to John Wesley's statement: "True religion as right tempers towards God and man. It is, in two words, gratitude and benevolence:

gratitude to our Creator and supreme Benefactor, and benevolence to our fellow-creatures. In other words, it is the loving of God with all our heart, and our neighbour as ourselves." This is the Christian answer to the existential question. Perhaps the simplest description of Ogden's theological project is that it is the rigorous defense of basic Christian piety.

George L. Goodwin

Selected Primary Works

1962/1979 *Christ Without Myth: A Study Based on the Theology of Rudolf Bult-mann.*
1966/1977/1992 *The Reality of God and Other Essays.*
1967 *Theology in Crisis: A Colloquium on the Credibility of "God,"* with Charles Hartshorne.
1975 "The Point of Christology," *Journal of Religion* 55/4 (October).
1979/1989 Faith and Freedom: Toward a Theology of Liberation.
1982/1992 *The Point of Christology.*
1986/1992 *On Theology.*
1992 *Is There Only One True Religion or Are There Many?*

Selected Secondary Source

1989 *Witness and Existence: Essays in Honor of Schubert M. Ogden,* ed. Philip E. Devenish and George L. Goodwin.

RAYMOND (RAIMUNDO) PANIKKAR

1918–

Life and Career

Born 1918 in Barcelona, Spain, to a Hindu Indian father and a Roman Catholic Spanish mother, Raimundo Panikkar earned doctorates in philosophy (1946, Madrid), chemical science (1958, Madrid), and theology (1961, Rome). He was ordained in 1946 to the Roman Catholic priesthood. In addition to a variety of special appointments and lectureships, as well as service on the editorial boards of journals, his principal teaching positions have been in Madrid (1943–51), several schools in India (1947–73), the Center for the Study of World Religions at Harvard University (1967–71), and finally the University of California, Santa Barbara (1971 until retirement).

Panikkar has claimed that key formative experiences for him were the Spanish Civil War and its brutality, some years spent beside the Ganges River where he "experienced the human condition in its barest form," and a time of commuting between the affluent West and the less affluent East now joined in the embrace of "technocratic man" (*Dwelling Place for Wisdom*, 1992, p. 83). Particularly notable, and consistent with much of his theology, has been his wide participation in international, interdisciplinary, and interreligious colloquia, seminars, and dialogue-study groups. His principal interests have been the dialogue between religion and secularity (modernity), between Christianity and Hinduism, and between Christianity and Buddhism. Panikkar's goal has been to devise, in his words, a critically grounded *cosmotheandric* spirituality that helps persons to embrace the reality of God within the diversity and pluralism of the late twentieth century. The primary means to such an end is the cultivation of *dialogue* between persons and groups, the fruit of which is the concrete experiencing of the richness and truth of the faith-journey of the other and the recovery of an authentic *contemplation* for modern persons.

Theological Method

In terms of method, Panikkar is a comparative religionist who attempts to relate different religious and ideological traditions at the level of their internal philosophical structure. He strives to discern the mythic foundation and inner ordering of a tradition as they come to light in the tradition's own philosophical self-understanding. After this critical sifting, he elucidates the structural analogues between traditions in order to set them in mutual dialogue; the result is actually a trialogue: between Christianity and Hinduism or Buddhism, and between them and the contemporary socio-political-religious ideology of pluralism.

In accordance with his philosophical interest, he compares these traditions by means of their most philosophically articulate exponents: for Christianity, patristic and Catholic (primarily Thomistic) theology; for Hinduism, the Vedantic writings and their expositors; for Buddhism, a body of precanonical concepts as these emerge in various expositors; and for modern secularism, the voices of atheistic materialism beginning with Marx. For Panikkar such a discussion is mandated by the social, political, and ideological pluralism of the postcolonial world, as well as by the clashing of cultures and creeds that historically have tended to make absolute truth claims for their own construal of reality. In the here-and-now experience of dialogue among these parties, there emerges for Panikkar the One who is the "ground" of the dialogue (*The Unknown Christ of Hinduism*, 1981, pp. 57-61), the divine source whose presence can be known under the conditions of modernity only within such encounters.

Panikkar thus constructs his own way of thinking about theological method, both in terms of hermeneutics and in terms of "fundamental theology." He insists that theology is in every way a hermeneutic enterprise—that it is an interpretative process in which interlocutors learn to speak and to listen in ways that make their experience and insight intelligible to the other. Such a process suggests that experience and its meaning are inseparable from specific historical, social, and cultural contexts that must be taken into account. Panikkar rejects basic theology in its classical sense—as an endeavor built on agreed-upon assumptions about universal human nature ("The Invisible Harmony," 1987, pp. 120-24). Instead he calls for a "metatheology," which he defines as "the religious endeavor to understand that primordial human relatedness we perceive in dealing with ultimate problems." Such relatedness is derived not from a view of human nature, but it is "the fruit of pluri-theological investigations" (*Myth, Faith, and Hermeneutics*, 1979, p. 331).

God

Revealing his neo-Thomist roots, Panikkar speaks of God as the Absolute that is revealed at the term or limit of all human aspiration and striving. All thought and action, if critically interpreted, manifest a search for this Absolute, as well as an implicit reliance on such an Absolute, in the way that their truth claims are stated. Human activity, specifically human experiencing, shows itself to be not only unique for each individual, group, or culture, but also relative in its significance to larger constructs of meaning that are carried in various ways by an individual, group, or culture. These constructs are the myths that receive concrete embodiment in mythologies and then gain rational exposition in philosophies. For Panikkar the critical analysis of these philosophies in the situation of dialogical encounter reveals progressively deeper layers of truth in such a way that the critical process itself becomes revelatory in direct experience of the Truth. God is seen as the powerful engine, so to speak, as well as the goal, of the search—as Truth creating the conditions of its own apprehension. Consequently, not only is the analysis of the mythic structure of human experiencing central for Panikkar, but the outcome of the analysis is itself experiential, resulting in an apophatic vision of God, who dwells in deep silence.

Statements about God are, therefore, onto-theological in nature: They are statements about the God-manifesting nature of reality as well as the God-limited capacities of human thought and conceiving. Panikkar thus argues for the radically transcendent nature of God as well as for radical divine immanence: God is utterly "beyond" and simultaneously completely "within." Panikkar's Thomism is perhaps most evident in his assumption that the human capacity for knowing, purified and fulfilled through critical dialogue with others, will finally rest secure in that love where "heart speaks to heart," where firsthand and mutual experiential awareness of God brings human beings to the compassionate and just community to which all faith traditions, religious or secular, aspire.

Panikkar's statements about divine being should be kept in close relation not only to his understanding of "critical method" itself, but also to his views about the sapiential and mystical core of religious experience. Critical method for Panikkar follows the techniques of transcendental and phenomenological reduction. That is, he attempts to "reduce" the activities of the human subject to its innate structures— structures of thinking or of consciousness—such that the invisible grounding or foundations of subjectivity are brought to light. For Panikkar, however, unlike Kant or Husserl with whom these methods originate, it is the *experience* of living, a certain way of being-in-the-world (here appears the influence of Martin Heidegger's philosophy), that is foremost in analysis. The analysis of experience, moreover, suggests to Panikkar that the essentially rational-logical approach of Western philosophy cannot contain the richness that is manifest. Consequently, he turns to the spiritualities of the East, where he finds a respect for the trans-rational, supra-temporal, and essentially mysterious dimensions of truth in a way matched in the West only in certain monastic and mystical traditions.

In the East God is conceived as beyond all categories of thought with a radicalness mostly unparalleled in the West. Panikkar's characteristic assertion, however, is that the true essence of Western thought can be interpreted with the help of Eastern thought and thus brought into line with the deeper spiritual intent of the Catholic tradition. Thus Panikkar makes a central assertion when he claims that

God is found in silence, at the still point where a true apophaticism would lead us, indeed beyond even that apophaticism. Such an approach to God, deeply mystical though it is, results in a practical wisdom wherein all human culture is simultaneously embraced and relativized, for an aniconic dynamic, which rejects all representations in order to worship the true God, is established along with a deep reverence for the icon, which appreciates that God can be known only in the representation.

Christ

For Panikkar, Christology is primarily a function of the trinitarian structure that is the expression of God's relation to humankind and the cosmos. All of reality reveals the trinitarian God, of whom the Logos-Son, the outpouring in incarnation, is an essential dimension. Incarnation is the means by which God becomes concrete and particular within the transitoriness of human existence. Analysis of the radical relatedness of human existence reveals that the very being of God is to be internally and eternally relative. Panikkar's interpretation of the classical and technical trinitarian terminology suggests to him that Father, Son, and Spirit describe the poles of God-human-world relatedness within God's own being and thus are about the "cosmotheandric" center of all being. Panikkar concludes that formulations homologous to that of the Christian Trinity exist in Hinduism and Buddhism in the sense that these traditions also proclaim the radical relativity of finite existence. From such a perspective Panikkar shows little interest in the "historical Jesus" or the positivism that he would associate with such a concept. Indeed for him, thinking of Jesus in such nakedly historical terms would be a symptom of the very obsession with historical time that is the disease of Western culture, and that leads to imperialistic claims to universal truth: Instead, we must think of the Christian Jesus as a "christic moment" with its own unique properties (cf. "The Jordan, the Tiber, and the Ganges," 1987, p. 90).

Humanity

Panikkar's view of human nature is summed up in his term *theandric,* which refers to the way in which God is revealed in human nature, at the same time that human nature is understood to have its existence within God. Concretely Panikkar speaks of a unity and simplicity at the heart of human existence, which are manifest in the integration and wholeness defining the center of a person. In contrast, he speaks of the complexity, diversity, and polar opposites that characterize any single person, particularly a person living amid the pluralism of the modern world. The synthesis into a working harmony, an inner equilibrium, a practical balance of elements, of the unity and the complexity of a person manifests the God-human unity of Christ and the nature of God. In this way a unity of the human and the transhuman in each individual defines a humanness incandescent and luminous with divinity. Body and soul, spirit and matter, masculine and feminine, action and contemplation, sacred and profane, vertical and horizontal: All are joined in a human being. Such a synthesis excludes nihilism, humanism, and angelism in speaking of human potential, for it is simultaneously realistic in its appreciation of the human dilemma as well as idealistic in its view of human destiny.

Evil

For Panikkar evil is reducible to all that would disrupt or distort the rich complexity, depth, and fullness of the self-revealing trinitarian God and theandric human nature. Even more, evil spoils the richness of the cosmotheandric universe in which God, humankind, and the whole natural order are at once in a harmonious unity-in-diversity and diversity-in-unity. The outward manifestation of such evil is the relentlessly despoiling, depersonalizing, instrumentalizing, and homogenizing movement of worldwide technology and scientism. Such a phenomenon reveals the atheistic soul of secularity while such secularism contains an implicit yearning for God. The biblical Tower of Babel represents for Panikkar the divine judgment on all premature uniformity, all selfish individualism, and self-aggrandizing power-seeking for the purpose of subjugating others. God has created confusion now so that all persons must learn the hard lessons of coming to understand the neighbor through the indirectness of poetry and myth and symbol, not in the univocality of a single language and culture. As Panikkar understands the symbol, "Babel" is less a curse than God's ratification of pluralism and a punishment of all that would idolatrously and faithlessly stand in its way (cf. "The Myth of Pluralism," 1979, pp. 226-30).

Salvation

Salvation for Panikkar is equivalent to what Paul Ricoeur calls a "second naiveté." In Panikkar's term, it is a "New Innocence" that is comparable to "contemplation" in monastic tradition or "ecstasy" in mysticism. It is the very opposite of modernity with its perpetually restless, disquieted, acquisitive, and obsessive spirit. Modernity for Panikkar is built on a consciousness in which time itself has been corrupted into linear historical consciousness with its evolutionism and progressivism, resulting in the enslavement of human beings to historically justified ideologies of the right and the left. Instead, Panikkar calls for a transformation of consciousness in which the eternal is not perceived as future and remote, but as fully and immediately present within the conditions of living and relating. "Every day is a life and each day is enough in itself" ("The Contemplative Mood," 1981, p. 264).

In salvation, every moment is lived in the fullness of time, such that each activity is done for its own sake and finds its meaning in the very moment of its happening. Being and doing become identical within each person and between them and the universe itself. Political activism has its place and value, but Panikkar tends to be critical of political expressions of Western cultural consciousness, for which the notion of reality, of the cosmos itself, has been corrupted through a historicistic and materialistic philosophy. In fact, political action can have real meaning only when it is kept in careful subordination to a properly religious vision of order in which political efforts are relativized. In short, salvation is the living of a wisdom about the nature of reality, a wisdom in which true freedom and true love are experienced. A person who has experienced salvation is finally, irreducibly, unpredictably his or her own true self.

Religious Pluralism

From the start of his career the issue of religious pluralism pervades Panikkar's work. He has never wavered in his conviction that social, cultural, ideological, and religious pluralism is a gift from God and particularly critical at this juncture in world history. Each faith tradition needs the stimulus and challenge provided by the others in response to the challenge of secularism. Each tradition can be rejuvenated with regard to its own richness by engaging in dialogue with the others. The central truths of each tradition are stated in a way that makes sense to those who share that specific heritage and experience, and thus possess the character of absoluteness. In dialogue with other traditions, these truths, and the practical wisdom enshrined in them, are enabled to shine more clearly, with greater existential brilliance.

Through interreligious dialogue one is enabled to experience a truth that is central for Panikkar and that runs through his work from early on until the present. This concept, the "advaitic" or nondualistic nature of reality, is one that he learned from vedantic tradition, and he uses it as a kind of master key to unlock the spiritual truth of Christianity, Hinduism, Buddhism, and the pluralism of modern culture. According to this concept, separate experiences cannot be viewed as existing with an impassable gulf between them (this would be dualism); nor can they be viewed as ultimately the same (this would be monism). Rather, they must be seen as fundamentally different, yet sharing a common ground in the light of which they can become intelligible both to ourselves and to one another. Panikkar says that perceiving cross-cultural or cross-religious dialogue in this way frees us from being "monochromatically obsessed" with only one of the colors in nature; it allows us to become "loving gardeners of all that grows on valleys, slopes, and peaks of that reality of which we are the human partners" ("Religious Pluralism," 1984, p. 115). In this way Panikkar contends that his theology is finally a spirituality for life, and thus he exhibits how Eastern religions have helped him to understand Western culture's own Christian soul.

For Panikkar, a special problem, often addressed, is the question of how believers can remain loyal to the truth claims of their own tradition, while engaging with complete openness in dialogue with another tradition. Here Panikkar emphasizes experience to keep the encounter from becoming a deadlocked clash of absolutes. A tradition, he believes, can be known only by way of experience—from the inside; thus it can be interpreted only with its own chosen language. The recognition of this last fact can then lead to a certain kind of relativizing of claims in which, to use the example of the classical Christian statement "outside the Church there is no salvation," one dialogue-partner can genuinely learn from the truth maintained by the other without giving up one's own stance. In fact, a Christian has not lived the faith of another; therefore, a Christian cannot judge its truth, but can only try to understand it as it understands itself. With the help of another's experience, the eyes of Christians, who remain within the confines of their experience, can be opened to the deeper truth of what they already believe. More simply stated, to the Christian who believes that "God is Love," an Eastern believer with the notion of *bhakti* has much to say from which the Christian will benefit. In Panikkar's words, "There is no reason for Christians to abandon the conviction that they have the true religion, if they well understand that they must find all their truth in a Christianity that is open and dynamic. This will lead to an authentic religious dialogue" ("In Christ There Is Neither Hindu nor Christian," 1989, p. 486).

Peter J. Gorday

Selected Primary Works

1973   *The Trinity and the Religious Experience of Man: Icon—Person—Mystery.*

1973   *Worship and Secular Man.*

1975   "The Contribution of Christian Monasticism in Asia to the Universal Church," *Cistercian Studies* 10:73-84.

1978   *The Intra-Religious Dialogue.*

1979   *Myth, Faith, and Hermeneutics: Cross-Cultural Studies.*

1979   "The Myth of Pluralism: The Tower of Babel—A Meditation on Non-Violence," *Cross Currents* 29:197-230.

1980   "Hermeneutics of Comparative Religion: Paradigms and Models," *Journal of Dharma* 5:38-51.

1981   "The Contemplative Mood: A Challenge to Modernity," *Cross Currents* 31:261-72.
1981   *The Unknown Christ of Hinduism: Towards an Ecumenical Christophany, rev. and enlarged ed.*
1982   *Blessed Simplicity: The Monk as Universal Archetype.* ·
1983   "The End of History: The Threefold Structure of Human Time-Consciousness," in *Teilhard and the Unity of Knowledge,* ed. Thomas M. King and James F. Salmon, pp. 83-141.
1983   "Religion or Politics: The Western Dilemma," in *Religion and Politics in the Modern World,* ed. Peter H. Merkel and Ninian Smart, pp. 44-60.
1984   "Religious Pluralism: The Metaphysical Challenge," in *Religious Pluralism,* ed. Leroy S. Rouner, pp. 97-115.
1987   "The Invisible Harmony: A Universal Theory of Religion or a Cosmic Confidence in Reality?" in *Toward a Universal Theology of Religion,* ed. Leonard Swidler, pp. 118-53.
1987   "The Jordan, the Tiber, and the Ganges: Three Kairological Moments of Christic Self-Consciousness," in *The Myth of Christian Uniqueness: Toward a Pluralistic Theology of Religions,* ed. John Hick and Paul F. Knitter, pp. 89-116.
1989   "In Christ There Is Neither Hindu nor Christian: Perspectives on Hindu-Christian Dialogue," in *Religious Issues and Interreligious Dialogues,* ed. C. Wei-hsun Fu and G. E. Spiegler, 475-90.
1989   *The Silence of God: The Answer of the Buddha.*
1992   *A Dwelling Place for Wisdom.*

Selected Secondary Sources

1979   *Cross Currents* 29. Symposium in Honor of Raimundo Panikkar, intro. Ewert Cousins.
1980   Kana Mitra, *Catholicism-Hinduism: A Vedantic Investigation of Raimundo Panikkar's Attempt at Bridgebuilding.* Dissertation, Temple University.
1989   Peter J. Gorday, "Raimundo Panikkar: Pluralism Without Relativism," *Christian Century* 106:1147-50.
1990   Rowan Williams, "Trinity and Pluralism," in *Christian Uniqueness Reconsidered: The Myth of a Pluralistic Theology of Religions,* ed. Gavin D' Costa, pp. 3-15.

WOLFHART PANNENBERG
1928–

O ne of the most sophisticated and complex theological visions of the last half of the twentieth century has emerged in the systematic theology of Wolfhart Pannenberg. The vision announces a gospel of God's future healing of all that is broken in creation, and it seeks to inspire transformation and renewal within present reality.

Life and Career

Born in 1928 in Stettin, then Germany and now Poland, Wolfhart Pannenberg grew up in a secular, nonreligious home. The Second World War broke out before he became a teenager; and he fled for cover during the British bombing and firestorm that engulfed his hometown of Aachen in 1940. The family moved to Berlin, and then in March 1944 he watched his Berlin home become rubble during an American bombing raid. A member of the *Hitlerjugend*—an inescapable destiny for boys during the Nazi period—he joined the army in January 1945, still sixteen years old. Being confined to the hospital with a case of scabies prevented his being sent to the Russian front to fight. While in the hospital he was imprisoned by the British.

Pannenberg's path to his deeply held Christian faith began like that of Paul on the Damascus road: While walking home from the train station near a wood, he found himself engulfed in light and was assured that God was present. Also important was the continuing care of a high school literature teacher who regularly invited young people to his home to discuss matters of philosophical significance. Pannenberg refers to these events as a set of experiences that brought him to the realization that Jesus Christ had claimed him and his life. This nascent faith grew to express itself in the pursuit of truth through theology.

He began his university study at Humboldt University in then East Berlin, focusing on Marxist philosophy. His knowledge of Marxist literature combined with a nonideological interest in Marxism gave him a particular perspective with which to interpret the student revolutions of the late 1960s and the liberation theology of the 1970s. He studied in Göttingen in 1948 and then moved to Basel in 1949, where he studied primarily with philosopher Karl Jaspers. He also read all of Karl Barth's works, which so significantly influenced him that he describes himself as a disciple of Barth, even if he is a peculiar kind of Barthian.

Finally, in 1950 he studied at Heidelberg where he wrote his doctoral dissertation on John Duns Scotus and his *Habilitionsschrift* on the principle of analogy in medieval thought. In Heidelberg he came under the influence of Gerhard von Rad in Old Testament, Hans von Campenhausen in patristics, Karl Löwith in philosophy of history, and Edmund Schlink, his primary adviser, in systematic theology. Although Pannenberg, a Lutheran, could not conceive of the theological task in the narrowly confessional Lutheran way that Schlink did, it was Schlink who pressed the young scholar to engage in interdisciplinary research with the natural sciences and with ecumenics.

From 1958 to 1961 Pannenberg taught in the Theologische Hochschule in Wuppertal, where Jürgen Moltmann was a faculty colleague. In 1961 he moved to the University of Mainz and then in 1968 to the University of Munich, where he taught until his retirement in 1993. He was introduced to America early in his career by a *Time* magazine article on his work and with guest lectureships at Harvard, Chicago, and Claremont in the 1960s and numerous return visits in subsequent decades.

The Theological Task

Pannenberg begins his theological enterprise with the hermeneutical question, the question that defines all modern theology as modern: How can the Christian faith, first experienced and symbolically articulated in an ancient culture now long out-of-date, speak meaningfully to human existence today amid a modern world-view that is dominated by natural science, secular self-understanding, and the worldwide cry for freedom? Pannenberg's answer has been fairly consistent throughout nearly four decades. He answers in six parts: First, the modern secular self-understanding is misguided when it fails to recognize what is true; namely, God is everywhere present. Second, Christian theology should pursue the truth, and it should do so in conversation with the secular world surrounding the church. Third, a historical examination of the biblical claim that Jesus Christ rose from the dead on the first Easter will show that he in fact did rise from the dead. Fourth, the Easter resurrection of Jesus is the prolepsis—that is, a concrete anticipation—of a larger reality yet to come in the future, namely, the eschatological kingdom of God in which all the dead will rise. Fifth, the still outstanding future of God reaches back into the present moment with the power to free us from our past and open us toward a new future. Sixth, the future arrival of the consummate kingdom of God will finish what has been in progress all along, namely, God's continuous creating of the world out of an inexhaustible supply of divine love.

Revelation as History

Beginning during his student years and lasting into the early years of teaching, some of Pannenberg's colleagues from differing theological disciplines, enamored with von Rad's exegetical vision, formed the "Heidelberg Circle," sometimes called the "Pannenberg Circle." The circle eventually published the groundbreaking book, *Revelation As History* (1961). This work was revolutionary in its day, even if the issues that prompted it have been forgotten near the end of the century. It marked a move from a radically transcendent Word of God theology (associated primarily with Karl Barth and Rudolf Bultmann) to a theology invested in the historical, the immanent, and the particular.

Existentialist and neoorthodox theology had been reigning in the post–World War II era, a theology that had dug a wide ditch between the Jesus of history and the Christ of faith. Rudolf Bultmann, for example, had opened his two-volume *Theology of the New Testament* by announcing in the very first line that the message of the historical Jesus was only a presupposition for the theology of the New Testament, not a part of that theology itself. According to the Bultmannian school, Christian faith could not exist until there was a kerygma—a kerygma proclaiming the eschatological event of salvation in Jesus Christ the crucified and risen one—and this kerygma had to come from the Word of God breaking into history from the transcendent beyond. Or, to say it Karl Barth's way, Christian faith could not exist but for the self-revelation or self-disclosure of God that was delivered directly to human faith. Eliminated from the divine-human equation according to the existentialist and neoorthodox calculus was any medium of revelation distinct from God in Godself. Eliminated was human history as a medium of divine presence and action.

Pannenberg and his Heidelberg Circle, in contrast, argued that history—especially the history of Israel that included Jesus, but also history in its broad scope—provides the medium and even the content of God's indirect, not direct, revelation. Pannenberg opens the second of his two essays in *Revelation As History* with the thesis: The self-revelation of God in the biblical witnesses is not of a direct type in the sense of a theophany, but indirect and brought about by means of the historical acts of God.

This shift was important in two ways. First, the Heidelberg Circle was asserting ontologically that God could be present within history and that history could serve as a medium for divine action. Second, epistemologically, God could be revealed in the course of historical events and, in addition, faith should be understood as a response to historical revelation. The existentialist and neoorthodox theologians of the previous generation had operated within Schleiermacher's legacy and proffered that the subjective faith of the believer serves as a hermeneutical lens necessary to look through if one wants to see God acting. Without the eyes of faith, it was presumed, history would be nothing more than a jumble of secular facts without inherent or transcendent meaning. In short, for the prevailing midcentury view, faith comes before revelation in history; whereas for the Pannenberg school revelation as history precedes faith and elicits faith as a response. This new position aroused violent and malign reactions from Bultmannians and Barthians alike.

One of the most influential theological books of the 1960s was *Jesus—God and Man,* Pannenberg's Christology that demonstrated how once again the Jesus of history could be seen as constitutive to the Christ of faith. Even more revolutionary for the time was Pannenberg's rational argument for affirming the historicity of Jesus' Easter resurrection, arguing that the eschatological meaning of the resurrection is built into the interpretation of the historical event. This giant step turned away from the existentialist theologians who had locked faith into a subjectivized and psychologized and privatized closet toward a more objective and public arena for theological discourse.

Somewhat unpredictably, this historical and rational emphasis drew initial interest to Pannenberg on the part of many post–Vatican II Roman Catholics and American evangelicals. To Roman Catholics, just then willing to open church windows to let the breezes of modernity blow through *(aggiornamento),* Pannenberg appeared as a "safe" Protestant, one who could affirm philosophically as well as exegetically the classical foundations of the faith. Also attractive to Roman Catholics was Pannenberg's high regard for tradition. Whereas the Reformation churches in general and Bultmannian existentialism in particular interpreted the hermeneutical question so as to jump from the biblical text to the twentieth century—jumping what was known as the "hermeneutical gap" and leaving out two thousand years of church history—Pannenberg cultivated philosopher Hans-Georg Gadamer's notion of effective history *(Wirkungsgeschichte),* which traces the historical development of ideas as a means for pursuing truth. Rather than being a hermeneutical gap, the two millennia of church history belong to the history of divine revelation, according to Pannenberg.

American evangelicals also found themselves attracted to Pannenberg's rational defense of the historical resurrection. The historicity of Jesus' resurrection was one of the Five Fundamentals of Fundamentalism, something conservative Christians believed the liberal establishment had lost to modern naturalism. In Pannenberg they thought they had found a first-rate German critical scholar who affirmed what they affirmed. They were right on both counts. Pannenberg did affirm the Easter resurrection, to be sure; but he was also a *critical* scholar. This means he worked in partnership with the biblical critics of his own era such as Bultmann, critics whom American evangelicals judged to be anathema. Pannenberg's method pressed for historical knowledge that went behind the biblical text; he did not appeal in any naive, let alone literal, way to the authority of scripture. So, American conservatives welcomed into their citadel Pannenberg's theory of the resurrection but later discovered that their guest brought along some disturbing ideas. The Pannenberg agenda was tacitly abandoned by American evangelicals for two decades until the 1990s when Stanley Grenz published his *Reason for Hope,* an appreciative study of Pannenberg.

Hope, Revolution, and Liberation

Although the phrase "Theology of Hope" is usually identified with Reformed theologian Jürgen Moltmann, Lutheran Wolfhart Pannenberg and Roman Catholic Johannes B. Metz also championed this dynamic school of thought during the 1960s. The eschatological vision of a divinely transformed future designated the content of Christian hope; and this vision of the future provided leverage against the conservative weight of the status quo. Hope could spring Christian ethics free to embrace the revolutionary spirit then sweeping the globe. Future-oriented theology soon became political theology. Eschatology quickly became the guide to social transformation. The transcendent vision rapidly became translated into immanent ethics.

In North America the hope school took the name "Theology of Revolution." Carl Braaten's counter-cultural systematic theology of 1969, *The Future of God,* expanded the Pannenberg program into a "politics of hope." Against the skeptical Marxist dictum that the Christian faith with its hope for resurrection beyond death is an opium that drugs the proletariat into acquiescing to economic domination by the bourgeoisie, Braaten asserted boldly that Christian faith—especially Christian eschatology—is not a sedative but rather a stimulus to vigorous social action.

In Central and South America, the legacy of the Theology of Hope became "liberation theology." Latin American students studying in Europe adapted this revolutionary thinking to their home situation, putting Marxist class theory together with the vitality of Christian eschatology and egalitarian politics. In addition to the ethical stimulus provided by applied eschatology, the retrieval of the historical Jesus for systematic theology by Pannenberg led to an emphasis on solidarity with the human Jesus, the Jesus who is God present among the humble and the oppressed and who brings the message of hope for liberation. Pannenberg's direct influence is most visible in the work of El Salvadoran Jesuit Jon Sobrino.

Although the revolution and liberation trajectory of the 1960s continued into the next decade for Pannenberg's disciples, it did not for Pannenberg himself. Pannenberg turned increasingly toward ecumenical matters and away from political theology because he became disenchanted with the student revolution of 1968 and its ideological aftermath. The student excesses made him more keenly aware of the unpredictability of irrational factors still shaping the course of history. Although Pannenberg sees himself as a theological champion of the Enlightenment and its democratic values, his stand on issues during the 1970s and 1980s moved him more and more into the conservative social camp. Pannenberg and colleagues such as Braaten became increasingly critical of liberation theology, suggesting that this school prematurely makes eschatology immanent so that the transcendent kingdom of God is collapsed into a political program. To the contrary, I would argue that the best liberation theologians have cautiously guarded against such a collapse into immanence, and Pannenberg's partners in ethics should be Latin Americans such as Gustavo Gutiérrez.

Retroactive Ontology

Theologians have often interpreted Christian faith within a philosophical framework. Which philosophical horse should a theologian ride? Bultmannians ride Heidegger's existentialism. Process theologians are riding the neoclassical metaphysics of Alfred North Whitehead. Karl Barth rides on no philosophy, preferring to see theology walk on its own. Pannenberg, like Barth, looks through the stable of philosophical horses and decides to ride none. Yet, theology does not walk alone for Pannenberg. It drafts philosophical reasoning for plowing the ground of faith. Human reason, especially as the philosophers of the classical Greek tradition have cultivated it, aids faith in asking about the truth value of its own claim and in interpreting the wide meaning of faith's content. Faith and reason walk the road together, according to Pannenberg.

Although Pannenberg identifies with no particular philosophical system, a consistent and coherent structure of underlying reality can be discerned throughout his work. He proposes what I call a "retroactive ontology"—that is, a dynamic view of reality as an open historical process in which the present and past take their final shape and meaning from the yet-to-be-determined divine future. A key article, "Theology and the Kingdom of God" (1967), provides an outline of the ontology that underlies his entire constructive project down to the publication of his *Systematic Theology* in the 1980s and 1990s.

This retroactive ontology is based on the central motif of Jesus' message—the imminent kingdom of God. The starting point of a theological vision, Pannenberg believes, should be the kingdom of God understood as the eschatological future brought about by God. Jesus was not a metaphysical philosopher, so the Nazarene did not spell out the ontological implications of his teachings. But today's systematic theologians should spell out these implications.

This leads to Pannenberg's startling proposal to reverse the commonsense understanding of cause and effect. Instead of viewing the present as determining the future, we ought to view the present as an effect of the future. The future, not the present or even the past, is the source and power of being.

The power of being issues from God, and God is future. Pannenberg's doctrine of God asserts, first, that God is the power of the future and that all historical reality is—or, perhaps better, will be—determined by the God of the future. He asserts, second, that God is in the process of becoming God through the trinitarian involvement in the historical process that is creation. Looked at from the perspective of the present, God is not yet. Looked at from the perspective of the future, all that will have been will be taken up into the divine eternity. The meaning, the reality, of what is now is open for transformation; its present definition is subject to revision until finally determined by its place in the eschatological kingdom of God.

The result is that creation and eschatology are brought together into a single ontology. In addition to Jesus' message regarding the coming Kingdom, Pannenberg appeals to the commonsense observation that things with a future exhibit power. To have no future is to be powerless. To speak of God as all-powerful would imply that God—the very being of God—is the future of the world. This is the central point: God's eschatological future is the source and destiny of all that is.

This future orientation applies to God as well as to creation. The symbol of the kingdom of God is a political symbol that includes the notion of kingly rule or lordship. Pannenberg expands this political metaphor into an ontological principle: God's rule and God's being are inextricably tied, so that God does not become fully God until the entire creation functions according to the divine will.

To be truly God, Pannenberg believes, God must be the Lord of creation; and the creation must live according to God's will. Once the creation has come into existence and has become a reality distinct from God—and, as fallen, the creation stands in rebellion against God—the very deity of God is threatened. God will be "all in all" (1 Cor. 15:28) only when the whole of creation is reconciled and God receives full lordship. This will occur eschatologically with the advent of the kingdom of God, with the arrival of the eternal new creation.

Christology and Creation

Pannenberg's Christology—a trinitarian Christology—enters at this point. He operates with a dialectic of self-differentiation and unity between the Son and the Father. The Son as the Logos differentiates himself from the abyss of the Father, thereby permitting the coming into existence of a creation that is similarly differentiated from the Father. This differentiation can become a separation, of course, when the creatures cease to acknowledge that they have a God and cease to live daily according to the divine will. The Father is no longer God, so to speak, if his

Godness is dependent upon his now lost rule. The obedience or loyalty on the part of the Son, who is differentiated from the Father, is key to reconciling the world to God. Reconciliation happens within creation history when the Son cedes lordship to the Father. Because Christ the Logos is a representative of all creation, all creation through Christ cedes lordship to the Father who then becomes God "all in all."

Pannenberg's God, however, is not a becoming God in quite the same sense as the dipolar deity of process theism. Pannenberg's God is eternal. Yet, a distinguishing mark of this position is that God's eternity is eschatologically dependent. The eschatological consummation of the entire history of creation constitutes creation itself; and this creation history also contributes to the everlasting content of God's eternal life. Viewed from our present situation within time, the God who is not-yet will yet become God in the fullest sense. Viewed from eternity, God as the final future has always been the God of every present and every past.

As with God, so also with the creation, including the human creature. The creation is not finished yet. Nor are we. Who we are is yet to be determined by our eschatological future. All essences are anticipatory, awaiting their place in the nexus of relationships which will constitute the kingdom of God. Who we are today will be retroactively determined by our resurrection from the dead and our place in the eternal new creation. The secret of spirituality is this: The dynamic power of God's eternal being can be released into the daily life of faith if we orient ourselves wholly toward God's reconciling and saving will for the final future of creation—that is, if we live proleptically.

Christology and Prolepsis

Essential to Pannenberg's Christology is the element of prolepsis. Prolepsis means the concrete pre-actualization of a still outstanding future reality. It is the eschatological reality appearing within history ahead of time. The focal prolepsis is the Easter resurrection of Jesus, which constitutes the still outstanding eschatological future for the whole of creation appearing ahead of time in the person of Jesus. As Jesus' resurrection overcame his death and fulfilled his life, so also will the coming of the kingdom of God and the advent of the new creation transcend while fulfilling the history of all creation to that point.

The concept of prolepsis acknowledges the ontological priority of the future and its retroactive power. Just as the future kingdom or rule of God will determine for all previous time the deity of God, so also did the resurrection of Jesus determine for his entire life earlier that he was the incarnate Son of God. Only in light of the resurrection is he the preexistent Son.

God as Trinity

Pannenberg continues the conversation about the Trinity begun by Karl Barth and Karl Rahner at midcentury, a discussion that is being continued today by Eberhard Jüngel, Jürgen Moltmann, Catherine Mowry LaCugna, and Robert Jenson. Two points distinguish this train of thought. First, the Christian faith is not one member of an inclusive club of monotheists that might include Jews, Muslims, and others affirming a single transcendent deity. Christians believe in one God, to be sure; but as revealed in Jesus Christ this one God has a trinitarian life. Trinitarians constitute an exclusive club, the Christian church. Second, they affirm to a greater or lesser degree of commitment that the immanent Trinity is the economic Trinity and the economic Trinity is the immanent Trinity. One important implication is that any hiatus between a transcendent or eternal set of internal trinitarian relations, on the one hand, and a set of external relations involving creation and redemption of the temporal world, on the other hand, is overcome. The internal relations experienced by Father, Son, and Spirit are activities that take place in and through the history of the created world.

For example, the obedience to the Father on the part of Jesus when suffering on the cross does not mimic the Son-Father relation that exists elsewhere in eternity. Rather, this historical event of obedience is in fact that eternal relationship taking place within time. Through his complete obedience the Son cedes lordship to the Father, thereby granting the Father appropriate deity. The result is dependent divinity—that is, divinity in relationship. Pannenberg, following Athanasius, holds a relational rather than an autocratic understanding of divinity.

Each of the three persons is a person only in relationship. The Father is the Father only in relation to the Son, in the generation of the Son. The Son is the Son only in obedience to the Father, which includes recognition of the Father's lordship. The Spirit exists hypostatically as Spirit only as the Spirit glorifies the Father in the Son and the Son as sent by the Father. The intratrinitarian relations are constitutive of their personhood.

With regard to the Holy Spirit, Pannenberg follows Augustine for whom the Spirit is the love that unites the Father and the Son. For Pannenberg the third person of the Trinity is the relationship enjoyed by the first two and, as such, is a distinct person. All three divine persons are not divine in exactly the same way; yet in their relationship to one another they find their respective divinity.

In the case of the Holy Spirit, Pannenberg makes an unprecedented move in the dialogue between theology and the natural sciences. He incorporates the concept of the force field from physics and applies it to the power that the Holy Spirit exerts in maintaining unity in distinction. The idea of the divine life as a dynamic field sees the divine Spirit who unites the three persons as proceeding from the Father, received by the Son, and common to both, so that precisely in this way he is the force field of their fellowship that is distinct from them both. But the Spirit is not

371

just the divine life that is common to both the Father and the Son. The Spirit also stands over against the Father and the Son as a personal center of action.

In order to affirm only a Trinity and avoid a quaternity—a quaternity would include Father, Son, Holy Spirit, along with a divine nature they hold in common—Pannenberg emphasizes that the eternal essence of God is not itself a subject alongside the three persons; rather, only the three persons are subjects of divine action.

When the economy of salvation becomes internal to the divine life in this fashion, it raises the question of patripassianism—that is: Did God suffer and die when Jesus suffered and died? The orthodox theological tradition says: No, the Father did not suffer or die, because the divine nature is immutable; only Jesus suffered and he did so according to his human nature. Martin Luther, in contrast, was willing to say that "God died for us." Jürgen Moltmann came perilously close to patripassianism in his book *The Crucified God,* but stopped short by speaking of Jesus' death *"in"* God rather than offering a version of "the death of God." Where does Pannenberg stand? On the one hand, he upholds the classical distinction between the suffering of the temporal human nature of Jesus versus the eternal unaffected divine nature. Yet, on the other hand, empathetically feeling the pain of another, which is indicative of the Father's love for the Son, places suffering under the ills of the world squarely within the divine life. The Father, out of empathetic love, suffers with the Son on the cross.

Eternity and Time

Finally, the trinitarian understanding of the God-world relationship requires that eternity not be divorced completely from time. Eternity and time are not separate and distinct entities. Rather, what happens temporally becomes an eternal reality. In virtue of trinitarian differentiation, God's eternity includes the time of creatures in its full range, from the beginning of creation to its eschatological consummation.

The transition from temporality to an eternity that comprehends time takes place at the eschatological advent of God's kingdom. What we human beings experience in the present is the separation of times—the separation of past and future from a present that is constantly sinking into the past—and we mistakenly think that this separation of times belongs inherently to our finitude. Now Pannenberg believes that eternity will maintain a distinction between past, present, and future; but it will be a distinction without a separation. Finitude in the sense of distinction—distinction between God and creatures or distinction between one creature and another—can be eternal. Therefore, the end of the temporal aeon and the beginning of the eternal is more than just one more epochal turning point in the flux of time. It is the eternalizing of finite history.

For Pannenberg, eternity is not simply a timeless realm that generates its own reality and remains aloof from the sequence of historical events within the temporal flux. Rather, eternity, at the point of eschatological transition, takes the temporal creation up into itself, unites it while maintaining its distinct history, and grants it everlasting perdurance. This is by no means an everlasting preservation of what has been divisive and evil. It is salvation, because the transition from time to eternity is also the reconciliation of the world to God.

Conclusion

At the close of the twentieth century when competing visions of what might become postmodernity draw the attention of theologians, Pannenberg may appear to be stuck with a strictly modern agenda. Of the two types of postmodernism—the radical pluralism of deconstructionist postmodernists versus the (w)holist postmodernists who envision global integration and a unity of the human race with nature—Pannenberg comes closer to the latter and is clearly out of sync with the former. He believes that God, the author of all things, is one and, further, that the love of this one God for the creation is both universal and unitary. Pannenberg's theology begins with particular events within history but then stretches out to embrace the most universal and uniting concepts possible. All of reality, he believes, is imbued with the grace of a loving God who through the Easter resurrection of Jesus Christ has promised a future reconciliation of all creatures with one another and with the divine life itself.

Ted Peters

Selected Primary Works

1968   *Revelation As History,* with Rolf Rendtorff, Trutz Rendtorff, and Ulrich Wilkins.
1969   *Theology and the Kingdom of God.*
1970–1971 *Basic Questions in Theology,* 2 vols.
1973   *The Idea of God and Human Freedom.*
1976   *Theology and the Philosophy of Science.*
1977   *Jesus—God and Man,* 2nd ed.
1981   "God's Presence in History," *The Christian Century* 98 (March): 260-63.
1985   *Anthropology in Theological Perspective.*
1987   "Problems of a Trinitarian Doctrine of God," *Dialog* 26 (Fall): 250-57.
1989   "The Doctrine of Creation and Modern Science," in *Cosmos as Creation,* ed. Ted Peters.
1990   *Metaphysics and the Idea of God.*

1991–1996 *Systematic Theology,* 3 vols.
1993 *Toward a Theology of Nature,* ed. Ted Peters.

Selected Secondary Sources

1966 Carl E. Braaten, *History and Hermeneutics.*
1967 Jürgen Moltmann, *Theology of Hope.*
1969 Carl E. Braaten, *The Future of God.*
1969 Johannes B. Metz, *Theology of the World.*
1973 Don H. Olive, *Wolfhart Pannenberg* in Makers of the Modern Theological Mind series.
1973 E. Frank Tupper, *The Theology of Wolfhart Pannenberg.*
1974 John Cobb, "Pannenberg's Resurrection Christology: A Critique," *Theological Studies* 35:711-21.
1974 Jürgen Moltmann, *The Crucified God.*
1976 Daniel L. Migliore, "How Historical Is the Resurrection: A Dialogue," *Theology Today* 33:5-14.
1976 Jon Sobrino, *Christology at the Crossroads.*
1976 William C. Placher, "Pannenberg on History and Revelation," *Reformed Review* 30:39-47.
1977 Eugene B. Borowitz, "Anti-Semitism and the Christologies of Barth, Berkouwer, and Pannenberg," *Dialog* 16/1 (Winter): 38-41.
1977 "A Retraction About Pannenberg," *Dialog* 16/2 (Spring): 81.
1981 Anne Carr, "The God Who Is Involved," *Theology Today* 38:314-28.
1982 Brian J. Walsh, "Pannenberg's Eschatological Ontology," *Christian Scholars Review* 11/3:229-49.
1983 Elizabeth A. Johnson, "Resurrection and Reality in the Thought of Wolfhart Pannenberg," *Heythrop Journal* 24:1-18.
1983 Roger E. Olson, "Trinity and Eschatology," *Scottish Journal of Theology* 36:213-27.
1986 Roger E. Olson, "Pannenberg's Theological Anthropology," *Perspectives in Religious Studies* 13/2 (Summer):161-69.
1987 Gary M. Simpson, "Whither Wolfhart Pannenberg: Reciprocity and Political Theology," *Journal of Religion* 67:33-49.
1988 Carl E. Braaten and Philip Clayton, eds., *The Theology of Wolfhart Pannenberg.*
1989 David Polk, *On the Way to God: An Exploration into the Theology of Wolfhart Pannenberg.*
1990 Stanley J. Grenz, *Reason for Hope: The Systematic Theology of Wolfhart Pannenberg.*
1992 Ted Peters, *GOD—The World's Future: Systematic Theology for a Postmodern Era.*
1993 ———, *GOD as Trinity.*

KARL RAHNER
1904–1984

Life and Career

Karl Rahner, born in Freiburg, Germany, entered the Society of Jesus in 1922 and studied in Jesuit schools in Austria, Germany, and Holland. Planning to teach philosophy, he enrolled in the University of Freiburg where, in addition to Thomist studies in the Catholic faculty, he attended Martin Heidegger's seminars. At Freiburg he wrote his first philosophical-theological work, *Spirit in the World*, a study of Aquinas's metaphysics of knowledge in the context of German philosophy from Kant to Heidegger. After this effort was rejected by his Thomist adviser, Rahner completed a degree in theology with a dissertation on patristic exegesis at the University of Innsbruck, where he taught from 1937 until the Nazis closed the faculty in 1939.

During World War II, he did pastoral work in Vienna; after the war he resumed teaching. In 1948 he returned to Innsbruck where his lectures and writing drew wide attention. He was *peritus* at the Second Vatican Council for Cardinal F. König (Vienna). In 1964 Rahner succeeded R. Guardini in the chair of Christian Worldview and Philosophy of Religion at the University of München (Munich). He moved to the University of Münster in 1967 as professor of dogmatic theology and stayed until retiring in 1971 and returning to München. In 1981 he was at Innsbruck, where he worked in retirement, bringing the number of his publications to more than four thousand. He died there at eighty, ending a life he described as "monotonous" in regularity but which, in theological creativity, was extraordinary. His archives are at Innsbruck.

Rahner wrote several books; his many essays are collected in *Theological Investigations* (in English, twenty-three volumes; in the German *Schriften zur Theologie*, sixteen volumes). Although his work did not derive from a methodological plan, he was a systematic thinker, casting each question within the framework of a theological vision. This vision, contained in his early philosophical-theological *Hearers of the Word* (1941) and synthesized in *Foundations of Christian Faith: An Introduction to the Idea of Christianity* (1976), captured the minds and hearts of both theologians and laypeople, making Rahner a kind of twentieth-century Aquinas in Catholic universities and seminaries and spokesperson for Catholic thought in the ecumenical community. It is also apparent in his spiritual writings, such as *Encounters with Silence* (1938) or *Spiritual Exercises* (1965), and in his encyclopedia articles. Despite Rahner's disclaimers of concern with method, he devised a distinctive approach to theology.

Rahner's Theology

Rahner's vision is one of unity in diversity: sacred and secular, essence and existence, divine and human, theology and philosophy, grace and nature, transcendence and history. He advocated an approach to theology that accounts for both the a priori, "transcendental" conditions of possibility for Christian revelation, and the a posteriori, "categorical" historical data. Christianity, for Rahner, is the message and reality of God's self-communication in the incarnation, grace, and beatific vision. His theology explicates the unity in which God is personally related to humankind and the world, so that they are related to God and set free in their own autonomy. This dynamic unity-in-difference is the pattern for the systematic coherence of Rahner's thought. Its center is in ordinary existence reflected upon from both philosophical and theological, transcendental and historical perspectives. Each leads to the other because they are one in the unity of the person, existence and reflection, being and knowing.

There are two starting points in Rahner's theology. One is the *philosophical analysis* he early proposed for the possibility of theology after Kant. He began with the (Heideggerian) phenomenon of questioning. That persons ask the question of the nature of being indicates both knowing and unknowing. There cannot be inquiry about the utterly unknown; yet inquiry asks after the unknown. Following Aquinas and Kant, Rahner insisted that all human knowledge is grounded in sensible experience. His reflection on the sensing "performance" of the questioner showed transcendence in the knowledge and freedom of ordinary life. This transcendence is a pre-reflective, original knowledge that persons are in their actual existence. He described persons as subjects in the world who are transcendent of it in knowledge. Similarly, his analysis of freedom, responsibility, and love showed freedom not merely as the ability to choose but as the capacity to create an identity by choosing the self one becomes in world-transcendent fashion. This experience of transcendence is not limited to a privileged few but is a part of ordinary experience for everyone.

In his first philosophical work, *Spirit in the World* (published in 1939), Rahner joined the "turn to the subject" of modern philosophy to Thomism, mediated by the work of the Louvain Jesuit philosopher Joseph Maréchal. Rahner argued that the scope of human transcendence in knowledge is unbounded, using the term "horizon" to show that in human performance, being itself is revealed in dim, unreflexive knowledge *(Vorgriff)* of God. Yet God is never the direct object of knowledge but remains concealed, the horizon only glimpsed in ordinary knowledge. In *Hearers of the Word* (1941), his other philosophical work, Rahner showed that in freedom and love, persons transcend experience within the horizon of freedom. The form of finite freedom in space and time is historicity, in which transcendence of the world is realized. Consequently, persons must look for possible revelation on this basis. The *Vorgriff* is only "known" as the horizon of temporal experience. If God is further revealed, it must be through a word, a human symbol, a spatiotemporal event, commensurate with the historical structures of knowledge and freedom. If God were not to speak, the message of history would be God's silence, the silence of the infinite horizon of human spirit.

Yet, even in these early works, Rahner was a philosopher-theologian whose philosophy served theology. Because his early works proposed the transcendental conditions for the possibility of revelation, Rahner is a "transcendental Thomist" who unites the transcendental questioning of Kant with the theology of Aquinas, showing human transcendence of the world toward the infinite horizon, God. Rahner's approach to theology is a transcendental method, asking about the conditions for the possibility of Christian faith. Indeed, he suggested an analogy between the structures of Christianity and of human subjectivity as uncovered in transcendental and existential thought. His theology was a "turn to the subject" of Christian revelation. His transcendental method is a theological anthropology.

That transcendence is always *in history* implies examination of *both* the human structures implied in Christian revelation *and* the historical data of revelation itself. Essence *and* existence, transcendence *and* history are concomitant. "Knowledge" of the infinite horizon of being is simultaneously known in the judgment of the being of the object of knowledge; the transcendental structures of the subject of revelation are simultaneously known in knowledge of revelation's history. Thus Rahner's program called for a theological anthropology that analyzed the historical data of Christian faith and for inquiry about the structures of subjectivity implied in this history.

A second starting point for Rahner is the *theological approach* proposed in his early work on grace and Christology. In writings on nature and grace, he developed his idea of the "supernatural existential," humankind's existential orientation toward grace. In contrast to the previous "extrinsicist" Catholic theory of nature and grace as being distinct, grace is the dynamic, personal self-communication of God for which humans are created. This self-communication, he argued, presupposes an open readiness ("obediential potency") for its unexacted gift. There is no pure nature, only graced nature, always oriented toward grace. This existential reality pervades experience, even if implicitly. The idea of pure nature, devoid of persons and meaning, is a "remainder concept" *(Restbegriff)*.

Just as grace envelops the nature it presupposes and alters, so theology supersedes philosophy while presupposing its autonomy. Grace, the supernatural existential, is an expansion of the a priori horizon of which persons are conscious in being self-conscious. Hence, every philosophy contains elements that are "anonymously" theological. From the perspective of theology, pure philosophy is also a remainder concept, what would have been had revelation not occurred.

A similar pattern of unity-in-difference emerges in Rahner's early christological reflections, his work to retrieve the essence of the dogma of Chalcedon. His effort was a "seeking for the question" that inspired the ancient formula, in order to both preserve and overcome the past; Chalcedon's formula was a beginning for reflection, not an end. Although he did not develop a systematic synthesis, certain themes characterize his Christology.

An important theme is the unity and diversity of the doctrines of creation and Christ. Rahner described the union of the divine and human natures in Christ (their "unconfused" distinction and "inseparable" unity) as a dialectical, "unifying" unity. This unity-in-diversity is similar to that between philosophy and theology, creation and redemption, secular and salvation history, nature and grace, and symbol and reality. Rahner devised a method that moved reciprocally from ontological or anthropological presuppositions to and from the doctrine of Christ. This method is apparent in his discussion of the relationship between the theory of human evolution and the incarnation. Creation is the evolutionary movement intended by God to reach its finality in Christ. In the incarnation, God prepares for self-communication. Because the self-communication of God is first in God's plan, creation and incarnation are not separate acts but two phases in God's single self-gift to humankind. Thus "hominization,"—the emergence of spirit from matter—occurs under God's work in moving toward the incarnation. The human person emerges when God's self-gift occurs *ad extra.*

Rahner's Christology culminates in a theology of symbol: Christ is both the *Realsymbol* of God and the unique expression of the human. His discussion of symbol exemplifies his method, which involves the retrieval of tradition into a new christological formula. Substantively, the mystery of divine self-communication is given in the doctrine of Christ. That doctrine points backward to the dialectical ontology of the doctrine of God (the "immanent" Trinity) and forward to that of the human (creation, grace, the beatific vision, the "economic" Trinity) as a single unity in diverse moments. It portrays an ontology of symbolic reality within God and an anthropology in which human persons are in continuity with the ontology of symbol. Humankind is, in Christ, the symbol that emerges when God is expressed in the world. The human person is the evolutionary achievement of consciousness, history, and freedom in matter, and is the embodiment of God in matter and history.

Rahner's Christology bears a similar conceptual structure to his early studies of human knowledge, freedom, and historicity. Christology is both the beginning and the end of anthropology. Christ's humanity is the *ek*-sistence of God into the world and provides the clue to the central mystery of human existence. Christology cannot form the only point of departure for ontology and anthropology, since statements about Christ are made through the doctrine of creation and its implied ontology and anthropology. But Christology is used retrospectively in assertions about persons and the world to indicate dimensions of ontology and anthropology that might have remained hidden had not the incarnation in Jesus Christ revealed them. Rahner's Christocentrism, therefore, defines human persons with reference to Christ. In contrast to Karl Barth's however, Rahner adds a philosophical point of departure in which human subjectivity entails implicit knowledge of God, the horizon and goal of human transcendence. Philosophical theology is therefore transcendental anthropology. Natural theology explores the unlimited horizon of the human spirit and is an inner moment in revelation theology. Rahner maintained that anthropocentrism and theocentrism are not opposing positions but the same reality understood from two perspectives.

He elaborated his dual approach in the discussion of revelation. The universal salvific will of God in the order of grace or salvation is the goal of history; salvation history coincides but is not identical with world history. Following the principle of the unity of being and knowledge, Rahner argued that the order of grace implies the elevation of the human spirit to new knowledge (not in a temporal sense), perhaps unthematized, correlative to the new being of grace. He called this a priori, unthematic knowledge constituted by God's self-communication "transcendental revelation." It is the supernatural existential in its integral knowledge. "The history of revelation and what is usually called revelation . . . is the historical self-unfolding in predicamental terms, or the history of that transcendental relation between God and man constituted by God's communication of a supernatural kind, made to every mind by grace, but inescapably and always . . ." (Rahner and Ratzinger, *Revelation and Tradition,* p. 13). Revelation is twofold—the transcendental, always given, and the objective as explicitly accepted or rejected. The transcendental is made conscious through its mediation in history in language, thought, and action. Transcendental revelation is not merely new conceptual content but a change in the human condition, meaning that, whether or not one objectively knows it, one lives under the horizon of grace. Although mediated through the Christ-event, grace is prior to it because of God's original christological, salvific plan.

Rahner's theory of the supernatural existential, similar to Bonhoeffer's "religionless" Christianity, enabled him to argue that life and action in grace are not limited to Christians. Grace is universal, prior to justification and outside the church; God's self-gift is neither intermittent nor rare:

Theology has been too long . . . bedevilled by the unavowed supposition that grace would be no longer grace if it were too generously distributed by the love of God! Our whole spiritual life is lived in the realm of the salvific will of God, of . . . prevenient grace, . . . an element within . . . consciousness . . . which remains anonymous as long as it is not interpreted from without by the message of faith. Even when [one] does not "know" it, . . . [one] always lives consciously in the presence of the God of eternal life. (*Theo. Inv.* IV, pp. 180-81)

This does not mean that every individual is justified, but that in moral action, for example, one is open to the God who is offered, whether this offer is accepted or refused. In every choice, one takes a stance toward a particular object or person, toward the totality of one's existence and ultimately toward God. Since human existence is pervaded by grace, every decision and action is salvific (or sinful) in relation to grace. Even when it is "anonymous," grace is manifest in individual and social life in the history of religions, for the religious aspirations of humankind are enveloped by grace. Hence the preaching of the church does not bring utterly unheard of news; it makes explicit who the person is, an anonymous Christian called by God and who, even as a sinner, is enfolded in grace.

Rahner held that theology must recognize that its content symbolizes an experience of mystery that it never completely grasps. Transcendental experience is consciously operative even when unrecognized. Anonymous theism exists wherever one is open to the infinite mystery of human existence. Because human nature is touched by God's self-gift in Christ, anonymous Christianity exists wherever in the depths of experience one accepts one's own ultimate mystery, even if one denies its institutional expression. The church remains the sacrament of salvation, "the historical manifestation" of the grace of God's self-communication, even though today's church is a "little flock" in a world where institutional Christianity has waned as a historical power. Theology can reconcile the principles of the universal salvific will of God and the necessity of Christian faith in recognizing that wherever the grace of Christ is at work, individuals are anonymously but really related to Christianity.

Sin appears wherever humanity's transcendent freedom in the world is closed to God. The redeeming power over sin is in the grace of the incarnation that embraces sin from the outset in the will to forgive. Freedom, guilt, and sin are not merely an inevitable part of development. Far from reducing sin to insignificance, Rahner believed that persons were never so convinced of their own evil and fallibility than in the twentieth-century experience of doubt and insecurity.

Rahner discussed sin and redemption under the rubric *simul justus et peccator* (simultaneously just and sinful). Freed from the polemics of the sixteenth century, Catholic theology may retrieve Reformation recognition of the self as sinner even in knowledge of divine forgiveness. This paradox can be integrated with the Roman Catholic position on the "new creation" of grace, a state in which there is no certitude of salvation in this life. Even in grace, one can sin in ways that threaten orientation toward God. One never grasps the depths of one's own being; one must always live in hope. Grace destroys neither the ambiguity of freedom nor of history. Sin and evil remain in a christocentrically evolving world. At the same time, within these ambiguities, authentic Christianity, explicit or anonymous, will appear in the church and in those who never explicitly accept Christian faith.

Hence theology looks to the world to discern its relationships to grace, the "connections by correspondence" between Christianity and experience, presupposing their common ground so to formulate theological statements appropriate to experience. Such connections are possible because personal, transcendent "nature" is an inner moment in the dynamism of grace. If grace transforms experience, its presence can be discovered in experience. Because of the inherent relationship of nature and grace, theology stresses the "fundamental and formal" structures of the human spirit in its worldly context that are the implicit conditions for the possibility of revelation. Such an approach to theology is needed for several reasons. Chief among these is the structure of Christian revelation itself, *for* human persons, *for* salvation. Because God's self-gift is given both transcendentally in personal self-communication and categorically in Jesus Christ and explicit "word" revelation, this self-gift is conscious. It may be unthematized, but it calls for conceptual articulation.

Prior to Vatican Council II, Rahner is concerned with the subjective dimensions of Christian faith and the human person primarily as knower. He clarifies the dogmas of Christianity within the "hierarchy of truths" of faith and their implications for human understanding. Convinced that the "turn to the subject" of modern philosophy must be integrated within Catholic theology, his writings on the supernatural existential, the experience of grace, and Christology and evolution exemplify his working out the relationship between transcendence and historicity, particularly with regard to the implicit dimensions of pre-reflective knowledge.

Rahner argued, for example, that one can thematize the experience of grace (and revelation) that pervades conscious human life in conscientious decisions, in generous love, in silent sacrifice, and in facing death in faith. He compared Jesus' developing consciousness of his identity and mission to the experience of all persons as they come to know themselves in relation to the dimly known source and horizon of their own existence. In Jesus, this developing awareness need not contradict his unobjectified awareness of his identity and task. Or when the theory of evolution is understood in relation to Christian doctrines of creation and Christ, it indicates the way that God's creative action occurs through natural causes to reach its goal in Christ. Thus, Rahner brought ancient dogma into contact with questions posed by philosophy, science, exegesis, and history to demonstrate their relevance for humankind.

After Vatican Council II, Rahner shifted his focus onto the context of Christian faith because he held that the cultural and spiritual changes of a pluralistic, secularized, technological culture created a new situation for theology. Signs of this broadened focus are found in dialogues with Marxist themes—hope, the future, ideology. He suggested that theology may find its most significant dialogical partner not in philosophy but in the natural and social sciences that shape human self-understanding. Further, the difficulties of this context led him to consider that religious experience is possible in a world where God seems silent and distant. He called for a new "mystagogy" to explore religious experience in secular culture.

He suggested that the power of human freedom toward the future that points to "self-creation" reveals unknown and uncontrollable consequences. In the unprecedented and seemingly infinite capacity to master and manipulate, persons also experience themselves as "disposed into freedom" and come to the mystery of God through the limits of freedom. In the new responsibility that persons know in freedom, Rahner pointed to the anonymous experience of God: the source of human honesty, objectivity, humility, and integrity. Christian "mystagogy" concentrates on openings into the mystery of existence, an access that in the past was often taken for granted.

Rahner's later focus included a changed understanding of the church's teaching function. He wrote that the church is in a new position in relation to theology, as listener and discerner, and should seldom exercise judgment. Pluralism in theology, philosophy, and other disciplines meant the impossibility of a common theology or new dogmatic formulations. Rahner demonstrated the historical conditioning of theological and dogmatic statements, including the possibility of error in theology. Further, in pluralistic context, no one is in a position to understand the many theological languages or to mediate between them or to judge their adequacy. Nevertheless, Rahner insisted on the universality of grace and revelation: The mystery of existence is the Christian mystery, present wherever human life is lived authentically, whatever words define it.

The church's purpose is to proclaim and serve the mystery of God's self-communication to the world in Jesus of Nazareth. Rahner's early reflections on ecclesiology stress the church as the fundamental sacrament, the visible sign of God's offer and gift in Christ. As Jesus Christ is the *Realsymbol* of God's self-communication, the church is the symbol of Christ's grace. As sacrament, the church is sign and cause of grace, signifying and making effective God's irrevocable gift in Christ. Rahner's essays on the faith of the recipient of the sacraments, the charismatic element in the church, freedom in the church, the church of sinners, and the sinful church are important contributions to Roman Catholic ecclesiology. He argued that the church of the future will be a "diaspora church" to which members will belong by choice, not birth, and urged the importance of personal conviction in the small "pockets" of Christians who will constitute the future church.

Rahner's post–Vatican II writings argued for a declericalized church of service that preaches morality without moralizing, that affirms the equality of women, and that offers a depth-spirituality in relation to the incomprehensible mystery of God. He wrote of a church of "open doors" that recognizes its own "marginal settlers" who are not fully members, yet not entirely outside. He called for a church "from below," "from the roots," that is, open, ecumenical, democratic, taking social and political stands and criticizing sinful institutions. This "shape of the church to come" matched Rahner's interpretation of Vatican Council II as the church's self-discovery as a pluralistic, undogmatic, non-Western, world church. The full meaning of this "theological caesura in church history" will only appear in the future.

The future is an abiding theme for Rahner. In contrast to Rudolf Bultmann, he maintained the importance of a real future that is hidden, mysterious, and uncontrollable. At the same time, present experience is related to past and future; the future grows from the present. Eschatological statements are extrapolations from presently received grace to its definitive fulfillment. This fulfillment is both individual and collective, corporeal and spiritual—as the resurrection of Christ is the beginning and symbol of the resurrection of Christians. The mystery of eternity is already known to Christians in unconditioned faith, love, and hope. Eternity is not the prolongation of time after death but time's definitive fulfillment. In an early essay Rahner suggested that death, the event "from the outside" that is the final human diminishment and passivity may also be the definitive act of freedom. The Christian who dies in Christ recapitulates Christ's acceptance of death. Rahner's later writings on collective hope extended this theme of active receptivity: The Christian's attitude toward the future combines work to bring about the "utopian" future for which human beings plan *and* the awareness that God's future is a gift beyond human hopes. This openness of Christianity toward the future distinguishes it from "ideology" that, for Rahner, identifies the mystery of the future—God's future—with a particular human scheme.

Although Rahner was not a moral theologian, his theology has significance for moral thought. He held that the possibility of freedom rooted in the subject's capacity to shape the self finally before God is basic freedom, one's "fundamental option," an inner, immediate self-direction that is never fully objectified. This unifying commitment, modified by grace, is expressed in the self's relations with others. Thus he affirmed that the love of God is one with love of neighbor. As the deepest experience of the self is one with the experience of God, human love for another is achieved within the dynamism of the self toward God. God is truly loved in the concrete love of neighbor.

A person may freely express the self in "works" toward the neighbor. Through choice and activity, this fundamental option shapes the self in a world of other selves in the ambiguity of history. For Rahner, the moral significance of human action is measured according to freedom's loving or sinful orientation. He was critical of moral theology that emphasized mere conformity or coerced obedience to law. A pretheoretical moral knowledge, a "global moral instinct," guides decisions that must be made before a theory is conceived to justify them. All moral theology is the product of this graced moral knowledge. Within certain "essential" boundaries derived from the nature of the person (as self-conscious and free), freedom is open, "existential," and creative. This constitutes Rahner's distinction between essential and existential ethics: Although there are many licit courses of action (discernible through essential ethics), it may be, in the immediacy of grace, there is *one* decision to which God calls one (discernible through existential ethics).

According to Rahner, earlier versions of natural law viewed human nature as static. He noted that the definition "rational animal" compared human beings with animal natures rather than emphasizing their openness to God. When the conditions of the thinking, deciding, creative subject are accounted for, the "person" who shapes the self in time and history must be seen in dialectical relationship with "nature." Human nature thus includes both mutable and immutable aspects. Rahner claimed that what often passed for "nature" in traditional scholasticism were really factual continuities in human societies, elements that may be changeable human creations. The normative content of natural law can be discerned only through critical reflection. To act rationally is to preserve and enhance human freedom; moral theology translates the structures of the human as self-conscious and free— what "is"—into moral "oughts" in new historical situations. This translation is accomplished through disciplined reflection on experience and on the conditions for the possibility of freedom. For Rahner, moral theory is rooted in practice, in the experience that particular action conforms or conflicts with the limiting and empowering conditions of freedom itself.

Rahner's theology met with wide approval but also criticism. Hans Urs von Balthasar argued that Rahner's focus on the human subject and theory of anonymous Christianity reduces God's Word to a merely human word and diminishes the objective, supernatural character of revelation, rendering the missionary task of the church superfluous. Rahner's response to this criticism was that the divine and the human, the theocentric and anthropocentric, are indissolubly united in knowledge, the incarnation, and grace. Another criticism, which Rahner took very seriously, came from his former student Johannes B. Metz, a proponent of political theology who found Rahner's theological anthropology too privatized and individualistic. Metz wrote that Rahner failed to account for actual societal situations, the crucial importance of historical praxis rather than "historicity" in its emphasis on the "already and always" fulfillment of a world of grace. Rahner agreed with Metz that the social and political context of human freedom must be concretely developed. However, he pointed out that he always held that transcendental experience (of God and of grace) is mediated in history, in interpersonal relationships, and in society. A political *theo*logy truly concerned with God must also reflect on the essential characteristics that transcendental theology uncovers.

Thus Rahner concluded that transcendental and political theology are complementary; a concrete "mystagogy" is mystical *and* political. Rahner's responses to liberation and political theologies and to the women's movement would suggest that he would have affirmed recent black, Third World, feminist, and womanist theologies. Their advocates might question Rahner's affirmation of a common human experience of knowledge and freedom in all humankind, holding that historical and geographical context, race, class, and gender so shape experience that differences rather than commonalities must be stressed. Although Rahner affirmed these perspectives, he would probably still insist that, while attending to the data of history, theology must speak of God and the openness of all human beings to God's triune self-communication and revelation.

Rahner's thought exhibits two special elements: (1) his conviction about the self-gift of God in Jesus Christ, the source of graced experience; and (2) his openness to new questions that emerge in history. The latter is apparent in the discussions of Christology in later volumes of *Theological Investigations.* In several essays and in a book he coauthored with a New Testament scholar, Rahner considered findings of biblical exegesis about the historical Jesus and concluded that his incarnational, "descending Christology" should be supplemented by "Christology from below" or "ascending Christology." He maintained that the two methods require each other and that recent approaches to the history and humanity of Jesus are not only helpful for preaching but are new expressions of the faith of the Council of Chalcedon.

Rahner's confidence in graced experience within the ambiguity of history was echoed throughout his theology and in his spiritual writings, which reflect the tradition of the mystics. Theology, for Rahner, springs from and is directed toward worship and adoration. The Ignatian spirituality of "finding God in all things" was translated in his "mystagogy" as the "mysticism of everyday life," as was the Thomistic theme of the hidden God adored in the symbols of earthly and sacramental life. Rahner's theology and his spiritual writings both center on the self-communication of God and the graced freedom of human response in the struggle of prayer, intelligent thought, and loving commitment to the neighbor in the earthly task. This connection between theology and spirituality may account for his wide influence.

Rahner believed that the integration of Catholic theology with the modern focus on the subject would enable it to be responsive to the intellectual life and pastoral needs of the modern church. His theological anthropology realized these goals. Rahner's effect on Catholic thought has been enormous. He wrote with insight on a range of questions, exploring each to discover its relation to the Holy Mystery, the triune God given to humans in unfathomable closeness in Jesus Christ and the Spirit, and the free response of persons to that gift as the single mystery of human life in time.

Anne Carr

Selected Bibliography

1978   *Foundations of Christian Faith: An Introduction to the Idea of Christianity.*

1980   Leo J. O'Donovan, ed., *A World of Grace: An Introduction to the Themes and Foundations of Karl Rahner's Theology.*

1986   *The Practice of Faith: A Handbook of Contemporary Spirituality,* ed. Karl Lehmann and Albert Raffelt.

1992   *The Content of Faith: The Best of Karl Rahner's Theological Writings,* ed. Karl Lehmann and Albert Raffelt.

PAUL RICOEUR
1913–

Paul Ricoeur has never claimed to be a theologian; as a philosopher he maintains that his work is marked by no deliberate apologetic purpose or intent. He is, however, someone who listens to the Christian message. He is also astute in theological matters, and he is conversant with developments in twentieth-century theology and biblical exegesis. He is, in fact, quite capable of discussing and interpreting scripture and the Christian tradition in ways that speak clearly to both active parishioners and theological scholars. So it is not surprising that his work has received a respectful hearing from theologians and biblical scholars. Indeed, his philosophical work, complemented by his occasional forays into exegesis and areas where theology and philosophy overlap, has had a profound and growing influence on theological reflection and biblical scholarship, for both theory and practice.

Life and Career

Ricoeur was born to a Protestant family in 1913 in Valence, France. His mother died shortly thereafter, and his father, who was an English teacher, was killed in combat early in World War I. With his sister, he was reared by his paternal grandparents and an aunt in Rennes in Brittany. He received his first university degree from the University of Rennes, where his early studies focused on the French neo-Kantian tradition that was then dominant in French philosophy. Combined with the classical French emphasis on Descartes, his interests in the French neo-Kantian tradition form the basis for his commitment to a reflective philosophy whose goal is an increased self-understanding that is always linked to the question of a meaningful life and action.

During his first years of university study when he began to think through his religious upbringing in light of neo-Kantianism, Ricoeur found Bergson's *Two*

Sources of Morality and Religion and Karl Barth's theology of the word of God, especially his *Commentary on Romans,* particularly influential. In 1934 he moved from Rennes to Paris and the Sorbonne where he continued his studies, participating in weekly discussion groups hosted by the French philosopher and Roman Catholic convert, Gabriel Marcel, who subsequently developed a manner of thinking called "Christian existentialism." At these open houses, Marcel invited participants to take up well-known philosophical issues, by relating them to their own experience, rather than by appealing to established authoritative doctrine or thinkers. Out of these Socratic conversations came the idea of a second-order reflection that Ricoeur would later call a "second naiveté." And from Marcel's discussions Ricoeur developed the aspect of his thought that some have called "existentialist." Because of Marcel's influence Ricoeur read the work of Karl Jaspers, who talked of boundary experiences and ciphers of transcendence, but who failed to acknowledge God. Jaspers' thought, too, subsequently influenced Ricoeur's thinking in two of his early books and in an influential, critical essay on Jaspers' philosophy of religion.

During his early period in Paris Ricoeur also became better acquainted with the work of the lay Catholic philosopher and social reformer, Emmanuel Mounier, the founder of the influential journal *Esprit* and a leading advocate of the philosophy called personalism. In later years, when he returned to Paris to teach at the Sorbonne, Ricoeur joined the residential community located in a suburb to the south of Paris that had been founded by Mounier in 1939. He continues to live there today, except for long periods in the summer which he spends at a summer home in Préfailles on the Atlantic coast west of Nantes.

At the Sorbonne, Ricoeur pursued his study of the two German philosophers who were most to influence his early thinking, Jaspers and Edmund Husserl, the rigorously methodical German phenomenologist whose work stands in sharp contrast to the more open-ended approach of Marcel. Following the usual path of French academic philosophers, Ricoeur began his teaching career at the level of the lycée, at the same time beginning to work toward the two doctoral dissertations that were required of anyone who expected to move on to a university level position. In the late summer of 1939, he was in Munich to improve his German when he was called back to France and mobilized into the army. Captured by the Germans, he remained a prisoner until the war ended. During this time in the prison camp he and a future university colleague, Mikel Dufrenne, organized classes on the history of philosophy—taught from memory—that were later recognized by the French academic authorities as counting toward degree credit. Allowed only German books, Ricoeur undertook a translation—in the margins!—of an important book by Husserl. With its commentary this translation was to become one of his dissertations after the war, and its publication immediately established him as one of the leading Husserl scholars in France.

When the war ended, Ricoeur returned to his studies and his own philosophical work. He taught for three years in the secondary school in Chambon-sur-Lignon, a Protestant village in southern France that had become famous for hiding many Jewish refugees during the war. From there, having completed his doctorate, he moved to his first university position at Strasbourg, where he began to select one prominent figure from the history of philosophy each year and to work through the primary and important secondary material in depth. This practice accounts for his impressive knowledge of the history of philosophy and his later concern to situate his own work in relation to that history.

Ricoeur returned to Paris in 1957 to take a position at the Sorbonne, and he taught there until 1967, when he accepted a position at the new university in Nanterre, a suburb of Paris. At Nanterre the first student demonstrations began that led to the great uprising in Paris itself in 1968. Following them, Ricoeur was asked to become Dean at Nanterre, a position he held for barely a year before he resigned, having found himself trapped between radical students, political agitators, conservatives within the faculty, and the police and education ministry, all of whom contributed to making the situation unworkable. In response to these difficulties, Ricoeur decided to accept part-time teaching positions at the University of Louvain in Belgium and at the University of Chicago, where he was appointed to the chair previously held by Paul Tillich. He continued to move between these positions, also teaching part of the year in France and serving as the director of the Husserl archives in Paris. In retirement, he continues to write and lecture widely, delivering the 1986 Gifford Lectures, now published as *Oneself as Another.*

Freedom

Ricoeur's original philosophical project was to be a three-volume study (follow-ing the model of Jaspers' three-volume *Philosophy*) on a philosophy of the will. His initial concern was for the problem of freedom, its nature, limits, and possible misuse. The first volume, which was presented as his main doctoral dissertation, is entitled *Freedom and Nature: The Voluntary and the Involuntary.* Reflecting the influence of his study of Husserl, this book is a phenomenological description of the will in terms of the interaction of the voluntary and the involuntary dimensions of the human condition, subject to two abstractions or phenomenological bracket-ings: (1) the fault, or the misuse of human freedom by doing wrong and by denying freedom, and (2) transcendence, which he initially conceived as the answer to the fault. The second and third volumes of the projected original project were expected respectively to reintroduce the fault and transcendence into his overall account of a philosophy (or "poetics") of the will.

In *The Voluntary and the Involuntary* Ricoeur describes how a voluntary act involves a movement from decision, itself involving a shift from hesitation to choice, to making an effort that may lead to action, and necessarily involves and depends upon aspects of reality that are not subject to human control. Ultimately freedom always requires an aspect of consent to that which is beyond and prior to freedom. With the second volume of his project, however, Ricoeur begins to reveal the importance of his work for theology and biblical exegesis. He considers the question about why humans misuse their freedom, even if it is a merely human, limited freedom, if there is nothing in the fundamental structures of such freedom that calls for such misuse. As he saw, the problem was how to introduce reflection on the fault, which is irrational, into the rational reflection and discourse that is philosophy. His response split the second projected volume into two parts: *Fallible Man*, a transcendental reflection in a Kantian mode on the fault's rational conditions of possibility, and *The Symbolism of Evil*, an attempt to take seriously—philosophically seriously—the reality of the fault as it is conveyed through its confession in symbolic and mythic language.

Fallible Man begins from what Ricoeur terms the "pathos" that marks the human condition: As human beings we find ourselves pulled between the concrete and the universal, the actual and the possible, the here and now, and an unsituated perspective that seems to transcend time and place. Within this setting of the human condition between being and nothingness, Ricoeur examines how we are capable of working out a synthesis that unites these opposite poles, and he shows how the various forms of this synthesis point to our "affective fragility." This "fragility" indicates the underlying condition of fallibility that makes the fault rationally possible, but not necessary; for nothing within the concept of fallibility requires that we act wrongly or misuse our freedom. That we do is a fact, but not a fact that can be predicted or deduced from what rational reflection reveals about the human condition. Because the actual existence of the fault leads to evil and paradoxically seems to presuppose it, Ricoeur argues that evil is indicated by the way in which humans have acknowledged the existence of the fault and have tried to make sense of the origin of evil, not by using rational, philosophical arguments, but by using a confessional language marked by myth and symbols. To make sense of this fact, philosophy must attempt to reenact this confession and learn to think from what it finds there.

Evil

In the *Symbolism of Evil*, Ricoeur begins from a phenomenology of confession that leads to the identification of the primary symbols of the fault: defilement, sin, and guilt. Finding a polar structure here, Ricoeur moves from the more external, objective pole (defilement) to the more internal, subjective one (guilty conscience). Defilement, or stain, is the outward mark of evil from which one must be cleansed; sin is the breaking of a rule or law that must be compensated for in some way; and guilt refers to the experience of a guilty conscience, the Pauline sense that I cannot fail to sin, yet I am also responsible for this inevitable fault. Ricoeur argues that these primary symbols—defilement, sin, and guilt—depend on and overlap with one another, leading to increased self-understanding. Once again, attempting to discover a unifying concept that accounts for this dynamic structure, Ricoeur suggests the concept of the "servile will," or what Christian theologians know as the bondage of the will.

Ricoeur considers how these symbols and this concept are conveyed through myths that recount the beginning and end of evil, a move that anticipates his later extensive work on narrative. He discerns four basic types of such myths: (1) those that see evil as tied up with the very creation of the world, requiring periodic renewal through ritual; (2) those that speak of a wicked god and of human existence as necessarily tragic, requiring that persons learn what it means to suffer; (3) "Adamic" myths that lead to the notion of an eschatological end of history; and (4) those of the exiled or fallen soul that can return to its origin through some hidden or secret knowledge or *gnosis*. Again, Ricoeur sees a cyclic structure that binds these different types to one another, so that one cannot be accepted and the others rejected. At the same time, he also argues for the priority of the Adamic myth as best expressing what all these myths together mean to convey, even if it remains in constant tension with the other forms, particularly the myth of the exiled soul.

On this basis, Ricoeur returns to his original problem: How is philosophy to make sense of the fault if the fault is irrational? His response is that philosophy must learn to think by beginning with the symbol and continuing through a creative interpretation of the surplus of meaning that is to be found there. Through interpretation we can hope to hear again and perhaps approach a second naiveté, one that has passed through the critical moment introduced by philosophy's asking, "Is it really so? How do we know that? Are those good reasons for saying that we know?" Something like a wager is required, one that may lead to increased self-understanding and to increased understanding of the bond between human existence and the being of all beings. The wager can be confirmed only on the basis of an increase in intelligibility, which at its limit might point to something like a transcendental deduction of the symbols of evil and the reality of the fault. To put it another way, philosophy must make sense of the fact that "the symbol gives rise to thought," as Ricoeur says, even if this process is always open-ended, and even if thought can never completely exhaust the meaning of the symbol or its expression in myth.

With the *Symbolism of Evil* Ricoeur reaches the hermeneutical turn in his thinking, which means that there is a requirement in philosophy to interpret myth and symbol and to analyze concepts and logical deduction. With this turn, owing to the emphasis on the language of confession, comes another important development and commitment in his thought. Philosophy must learn to attend to the fullness of language, including its symbolic, mythic, poetic, and narrative forms.

The theory of symbols presented in the *Symbolism of Evil* was neither a complete theory of interpretation nor intended to be generally applicable. It was a methodological development that allowed Ricoeur to advance his projected philosophy of the will. The importance of this hermeneutical turn combined with other developments in French philosophy, however, forced him to postpone indefinitely his initial project in order to explore the consequences of the turn that his thinking had taken, what he himself has since characterized as an extended series of detours. The first directions of these detours may be mapped out in two ways: first, the development of hermeneutics as a general theory of interpretation, as opposed to an ad hoc solution to a particular set of materials; and, second, a response to an alternative model of reflection that denies the very existence of the subject. These two developments or "detours" may in turn be understood as Ricoeur's response to structuralism and to "the hermeneutics of suspicion."

Hermeneutics

Ricoeur's contributions to a general theory of hermeneutics not only expand upon the theory of the symbol as a double-meaning expression that he introduced in the *Symbolism of Evil;* his contributions extend to the challenge of interpretation theories identified with Marx, Nietzsche, and Freud, who held that interpretation is necessary only to show that things do not mean what they first seem to mean. For these theorists the real significance of things lies elsewhere, beneath the surface, whether in the economic conditions of production, the will to power, or the unconscious. For such theories the self, if it can be said to exist at all, is at best a product of what really counts, what is really real, the underlying deep structure. In this sense, structuralism too is a form of the hermeneutics of suspicion in the sense that it tries to claim objectivity apart from all subjectivity. But Ricoeur saw structuralism's real importance as lying elsewhere, in its claim to having an objective model of explanation that can claim to be a new science.

Ricoeur's response to the hermeneutics of suspicion, most comprehensively developed in *Freud and Philosophy,* argued that both the hermeneutics of suspicion and that of trust or hope can be shown to be part of a larger whole, the hermeneutical field. Ricoeur's critique of structuralism emphasizes the necessary relation between explanation and understanding. As he was later to phrase it, we need to explain more in order to understand better. Therefore, he is willing to agree that all hermeneutics has to incorporate a critical and explanatory moment. Such an explanatory moment, however, does not exhaust all that there is to know or, in light of this, to do. This understanding can lead to meaning and action that is once again the desired goal.

Structuralism, which dominated French thought for a brief period, had a particular impact on Ricoeur's thought for two reasons connected to this tie between explanation and understanding. First, it offered a new model of explanation in terms of "structures," where the idea of structure was taken from developments in the theory of linguistics. It was then applied by Claude Lévi-Strauss to the problem in anthropology of kinship patterns, and then extended to the study of mythology, the very area Ricoeur had come to from another direction. A structure is a finite system of elements, all of which depend upon one another and whose significance in fact is determined by the differences among the elements of the structure rather than by the elements themselves. For structuralism, these elements in fact do not exist apart from the encompassing structure.

Although the structural model is a powerful analytic tool when it is applied to literary texts, including the Bible, Ricoeur's critical insight was that it can also take an ideological turn when it ignores its presupposition that there is nothing beyond the structures it describes. As long as this presupposition is recognized as a methodological *assumption,* Ricoeur stands ready to learn from structural methods and to try to incorporate them into what he sees is the need for a critical, explanatory moment in interpretation. At the same time, he is able to demonstrate, however, that every attempt to formulate a complete structuralist theory always presupposes in some way the understanding of what it claims to model, and in so doing it leaves out of its allegedly exhaustive and objective theoretical account this prior knowledge upon which it in fact depends.

Metaphor

According to Ricoeur another problem with structuralism was its emphasis on discovering objective structures that are atemporal. In this attempt, change is at best a variation of an underlying deep structure that itself is finally unaffected by such variations. Indeed, in its most extreme formulations this deep structure is held somehow to bring about any such variation in the surface structure, which then is at best a reflection of the deep structure, bringing us back again to a form of the hermeneutics of suspicion. Ricoeur, however, argues that no form of structuralism has ever been able to demonstrate this convincingly, and he points to the steps where something is left out or where an addition from one level to another is introduced but not really accounted for. This argument is important, for if structuralism is actually able to reduce everything to an underlying deep structure, then there is no possibility of truly new meaning; at best it must simply be a new variant of what was already there.

Ricoeur refuses to accept this restrictive understanding of metaphorical meaning, and he attempts to justify the possibility of new meaning through innovative uses of language. Metaphor, in Ricoeur's eyes, is not, as traditional rhetoric claimed, the substitution of one word for another, either because a word is lacking or just for decorative effect. Such theories presuppose that all metaphor can be translated directly into a literal statement. Ricoeur's point is that this is not true for live metaphors, which may eventually "die" and enter the lexicon—for example, "leg of the chair." Then, however, they are no longer metaphorical. But, Ricoeur argues, "live" metaphors are not in fact single words, like "leg" in "leg of the chair." The sentence, which involves an act of predication, is where the semantic innovation that characterizes a live metaphor occurs, because a live metaphor says "is" and "is not" at the same time. And in so doing, it "re-describes reality," thus issuing in both epistemological and ontological import. A live metaphor can tell us something that we didn't know before, and it can show us a new reality insofar as it gives us something like an image of what it says, an image that philosophy will rightly try to build into a concept.

When Ricoeur applies this account of metaphor to religious language—especially to the parables and eschatological sayings of Jesus—he shows that such language is best understood as a peculiar kind of poetic language rather than as a weak form of scientific discourse. The poetic language here constitutes a discourse (meaning the actual use of the underlying structural basis of language to say something about something to someone) that "names God." Through metaphorical power the poetic language of the parables and eschatological sayings conveys the sense of the kingdom of God by redescribing everyday experience in terms of a proclaimed reality beyond all expectation, a reality that *is* and *is not* like things that we already know. If the kingdom of God can be characterized at all, we should speak of it in terms of "how much more" and what Ricoeur has called a logic of superabundance.

Combining his reflections on hermeneutics and metaphor, Ricoeur concludes that, because the parables and eschatological sayings are embedded in a larger extended discourse (the Gospels), they also involve the one who is presented as speaking them, thus adding a christological aspect to their redescriptive power. An ability to convey new meaning, which is found in the originary discourse of faith, made possible subsequent theological reflection on the meaning of this discourse, especially when early Christianity encountered the already existing Greek philosophical tradition. Insofar as symbols and metaphors share common functions in redescribing reality, the language of faith, like the symbol, can give rise to thought. Such thought, however, will always depend on the originary forms of the discourse of faith and can never exhaust them or completely translate them into the language of univocal concepts that defines the ideal model of theological discourse.

Extending this kind of analysis to other aspects of the Bible, Ricoeur recognizes a variety of different biblical genres of such originary forms of the discourse of faith: legislative writings, wisdom texts, hymns, prophecy, narratives. Each genre names God in its own way, and together they contribute to a polyphonic effect that unites them in their naming of one God. Ricoeur's work had an immediate impact on biblical studies because it appeared at the time when the theological significance of the historical-critical method seemed to have run its course. The historical-critical method had assumed that the way to make sense of scripture is to identify its component parts, to discover what they meant in their original setting, and then to translate that meaning into current, demythologized language. Ricoeur's biblical hermeneutics, by contrast, suggests that biblical theology is not a question of replacing what scripture says by what it actually means, or by what, at least, makes sense to us today. Not only is it important to attend to the different literary genres in the Bible and how they express faith, it is also necessary to consider how the text uniting all these genres is in its final redaction an originary expression of faith whose meaning is not reducible to how it was understood by its original audience in its original setting.

According to Ricoeur's hermeneutics, discourse inscribed in texts outlives its original author, audience, and setting without losing its capacity for meaningfulness. Ricoeur attempts to make sense of this fact and to incorporate it into his theory and practice. Drawing on and extending the hermeneutical theory of Hans-Georg Gadamer, Ricoeur argues that understanding always involves an element of the interpreter's self-understanding that is brought about by an imaginative fusion of horizons with what is at issue in the text in question, even when that text seems far removed from readers because of its historical distance. The "world of the text" is a world that interpreters appropriate through the process of interpretation and through their ability to imagine such a world as one that they might inhabit. Through this fusion of horizons the meaning of the text finds a new audience in a new setting, and possibly an innovation in meaning since meaning always involves both sense and reference, which includes the new audience and its life world.

In his most recent writing about biblical texts Ricoeur has begun to emphasize the contemporary reception of such texts. To cite just one example, biblical hermeneutics must learn that a text can be used in a variety of settings. In one, the erotic love poetry of the Song of Songs may be used in worship and directed to God as the lover of the beloved congregation. In a very different setting it can be used by individual mystics who recognize God still as the lover and the mystic's soul as the beloved. Neither use rules out studying these texts for what they teach us about ancient Israel or its relation to the wisdom or prophetic traditions.

Narrative

Based on his theory of metaphor and his developments in hermeneutical theory, Ricoeur's work on the specificity of religious language unfolds into an extended concern for narrative. A live metaphor is something like a poem in miniature, and a poetic text, as an extended work of discourse, has something of the redescriptive power of metaphor. Ricoeur examines extended narrative in *Time and Narrative,* claiming that through narrative we make sense of time, not through a philosophical theory of time but through a practical solution that in the best of cases refigures our understanding of our own temporal existence and experience. In the move from metaphor to narrative, redescription gives way to refiguration. To make this case, Ricoeur does three things. First, he defines narrative as an extended form of discourse about human action. All narrative has a complex internal temporality because plot configures the episodes of a well-wrought narrative into a meaningful whole that cannot be reduced to an atemporal point or a timeless understanding. When narrative is so understood, Ricoeur argues, both histories and fiction belong together because they draw upon each other: Historians learn from the innovations of literary fiction new ways of emploting their accounts, and novelists draw upon history in order to make sense of what the world has been and to appropriate the idea of historical time and historical existence. Therefore, history and fiction can be said to interweave in narrative. Ricoeur's essay on the passion narrative in the Gospel of Mark in *Figuring the Sacred* provides an example of how this understanding of narrative applies to a New Testament text.

The idea of historical time is central to the second point in Ricoeur's argument. The problem in making sense of time and narrative is that philosophy has not been able to account fully for both physical or cosmological time and for our lived experience of a present with a finite past and future. In the opening section of volume 3 of *Time and Narrative,* Ricoeur shows that all attempts to devise a phenomenology of time have failed and must fail. A narrative solution is necessary if human beings are to make sense of their temporality and its impact on human action. Historical time unites the cosmological and human dimensions through its use of devices such as the calendar, the succession of generations, and the notion of the trace of the past that can serve as evidence for its continuing presence. Literature's ability to explore the possibilities of such historical time gives rise to innovations in the rhetoric of historiography.

Ricoeur's third point is that narrative is appropriated through hearing and reading such "histories." This process leads to the imaginative exploration of the world of texts that we might inhabit, which again has implications for our subsequent action, even in the case where we reject the options we thereby discover. Such action, in either case, calls for new recounting and the process recurs. In effect, we are part of a tradition of interpreting human action that goes forward by a process that Ricoeur calls "rule-governed deformation." Ricoeur claims that what is at stake is our historical consciousness and its implications for who we are. To put it another way, narrative not only is a way of making sense of time and action, it is also a means to what Ricoeur calls narrative identity at both an individual and a communal level. Who we are is significantly related to our stories that are meant to answer the question, Who?

Selfhood

The notion of narrative identity brings us to Ricoeur's most recent work, arising out of his Gifford Lectures, *Oneself as Another,* where the central issue is selfhood and its relation to self-understanding and right action. Ricoeur argues three points. First is the question of selfhood as the question of personal identity. Working his way through the immense current literature on this topic, he asserts that this issue involves his notion of narrative identity and an answer to the question, Who? Ricoeur's notion of narrative identity suggests that the self is not just someone who can be identified, but that a self is also an agent who can be held responsible for its actions. Following that understanding of selfhood, Ricoeur discusses the need for both a teleological and a deontological aspect to any adequate theory of moral agency and selfhood, an ethics that can address the problems of our living a good life with and for others in just institutions.

The question concerning moral aim and its manifestations relates to the theme of "testimony" mentioned earlier, for Ricoeur's points are that moral selves as agents finally bear witness to who they are, and that such testimony needs to be appreciated and interpreted where the meaningfulness of *a* life and of life itself are in question. Furthermore, testimony calls for a decision about whether it is to be believed or not. Applied to the testimonies of faith, the testimony does not simply bear witness to the testifier but to something that comes from somewhere else to which the witness testifies. If a philosophy of such testimony is possible, it must be a hermeneutics, for in such cases absolute knowledge is impossible. Interpretation and judgment are required, moreover, because we also recognize the possibility of false testimony. What is finally at issue in such a hermeneutics is the mutual promotion of faith and reason. It is in the direction of such a hermeneutics that Ricoeur's thought points us.

David Pellauer

Selected Primary Works

1966   *Freedom and Nature: The Voluntary and the Involuntary,* trans. Erazim V. Kohák.

1967   *The Symbolism of Evil,* trans. Emerson Buchanan.

1970   *Freud and Philosophy: An Essay on Interpretation,* trans. Denis Savage.

1974   *The Conflict of Interpretations: Essays in Hermeneutics.*

1977   *The Rule of Metaphor: Multidisciplinary Studies of the Creation of Meaning in Language,* trans. Robert Czerny et al.

1980   *Essays on Biblical Interpretation,* ed. Lewis S. Mudge.

1981   *Hermeneutics and the Human Sciences,* ed. and trans. John B. Thompson.

1984/1988 *Time and Narrative*, 3 vols., trans. Kathleen Blamey and David Pellauer.
1986   *Fallible Man*, trans. Charles A. Kelbley.
1991   *From Text to Action: Essays in Hermeneutics, II*, trans. Kathleen Blamey and John B. Thompson.
1992   *Oneself as Another*, trans. Kathleen Blamey.
1995   *Figuring the Sacred: Religion, Narrative, and Imagination*, ed. Mark I. Wallace, trans. David Pellauer.

Selected Secondary Source

1995   Lewis Edwin Hahn, ed., *The Philosophy of Paul Ricoeur*.

ROSEMARY RADFORD RUETHER
1936–

If one is inimical to contradiction, commitment, and compassion, one will not be open to the message and vision of Catholic feminist theologian Rosemary Radford Ruether. "Openness to" does not demand "agreement with," but it does require one to have the capacity to listen deeply. To listen deeply to the voice of Ruether one needs to realize she is a radical Catholic Christian. In her own words she is "a conservative in depth whose rebellion grasps the authentic roots of the tradition which have been distorted to false uses" ("An Unexpected Tribute," 1970, p. 339).

Life and Career

Ruether was reared in an economically comfortable, patriotic, and pious family. Her father died when she was twelve years old, and her mother, Rebecca Cresap Ord Radford, became the most influential person in her development. From her mother, Ruether learned that Catholicism was a religious tradition with depth and breadth. Exposed as a young girl to the intellectual richness of Jesuit preaching at Georgetown, to Carmelite contemplatives who ministered to the elderly, as well as to a private Catholic school education, Ruether had no experience of Catholicism as myopic, imperialistic, or parochial. Her mother, a devoted Catholic and avid ecumenist, taught her to recognize the intellectual and spiritual depths of Catholicism, to challenge its clerical hegemony, and to realize that there are other, equally valid religious paths. Finally, her mother and her mother's women friends were influenced by the feminist movement of the late nineteenth and early twentieth centuries. These women of spiritual breadth, intellectual vigor, and great social concern had a strong impact on Ruether's growing understanding of what it meant to be a religious woman. Consequently, they bequeathed to Ruether a deep understanding of God as the matriarchal ground of being. This realization and experience of divinity continues to shape her theology to this day.

Among the other significant persons who influenced Ruether were her Uncle David and her teacher Robert Palmer. David was an uncle by marriage who seems to have communicated to her, indirectly, the pathos of being Jewish in a predominantly Christian world. Here, perhaps, lay the seeds of her later theological critique of Christian anti-Judaism that has become a hallmark of both her Christology and her approach to religious pluralism. Palmer, on the other hand, was a classics scholar who taught Ruether when she was an undergraduate fine arts major at Scripps College. Contemptuous of Christianity, Palmer enabled Ruether to recognize that "religion begins and ends in theophany" (*Disputed Questions,* 1982, p. 26), in the existential experience of divine revelation. From Palmer she also learned that divinity may be one fundamentally, but its manifestations are many and varied. He galvanized her deepest religious sensibilities, which already ripened under her mother's spiritual guidance. As a result, she changed majors: the aspiring young artist became the aspiring young theologian who earned a Ph.D. in the social and intellectual history of Christian thought at the School of Theology at Claremont.

Besides these key people, several formative circumstances influenced Ruether's development as a woman, U. S. citizen, and theologian. She married Herman Ruether toward the end of her undergraduate years at Scripps. He was studying political science and he deeply respected her intellectual gifts. From this creative partnership came, among other things, a countercultural commitment to mutuality in male-female relationships, a poignant critique of the clerical domination of Catholic laypeople's lives in the area of reproductive rights, and her social activism, spawned by being married to a political scientist! These activities and commitments energized her for the ensuing challenges provided by the Second Vatican Council (1962–65), and the civil rights and women's movements of the late sixties. The social contradictions she experienced in these movements—racism, sexism, militarism, imperialism—she identified as "social sins." Denouncing such contradictions, she has called all people of goodwill to create life-giving alternatives in commitments to community, justice, and compassion. This is the heart of the challenging theological work being done by Rosemary Radford Ruether.

Purpose of Theology

If one were to ask Ruether what the purpose of theology is, specifically Christian feminist theology, she would probably respond by saying that its purpose is to engage human beings, through critical dialogue, prayer, and reflective social action, in a continuing compassionate commitment to the healing and liberation of all human beings and the earth. Theological activity must involve, given the patriarchal character of all traditional theology, three "moments": (1) a critique of the sexism, androcentrism, and misogyny of patriarchal theology; (2) a recovery of alternative traditions that affirm the autonomy and full personhood of women, and other groups of people dehumanized by patriarchal ideologies; and, (3) a reconstruction of the whole edifice of Christian theology—its symbols, doctrines, ethics, and so forth, with the full personhood of women at the center of its self-understanding ("Future of Feminist Theology," 1985). Such a theology will also be consciously pluralistic and ecological; that is, its center will include not only acknowledgment of the full humanity of women, but also constant awareness that voices of insight and wisdom can be found in other religious traditions. Further, this ecological impulse includes the realization that Christian theology must reconfigure its teachings about the relationship between humans and the earth in ways that will promote personal and global commitment to what Ruether calls "earth healing" (*Gaia and God,* 1992).

Theological Methodology

The purpose of theology, as Ruether conceives it, must be understood in the context of her theological methodology, which achieves integrity through the sources and norms that she employs. The fundamental sinew of her theological methodology ties together both tradition and reality in a dialectical, rather than a dualistic way. Dualistic thinking is two-dimensional thinking in contrast to dialectical, or multidimensional thinking. The former reduces any reality or issue to "either/or." Further, dualistic thinking is predicated on a hierarchy of domination in which one of its two dimensions is upheld as superior to the other. For example, men are superior to women, whites to blacks, rich to poor, and so on, in this worldview. Dualistic thinking thus fosters the ideological deformation of reality that culminates in such evils as racism, sexism, heterosexism, classism, militarism, and so forth.

Dialectical thinking, on the other hand, demands ". . . an exploration of the repressed 'other side,' in order to move beyond both poles to a new synthesis that could include them both" ("Beginnings," 1975, p. 44). Dialectical thinking for Ruether provides a way to discover deeper truths about persons, communities, and ideas that may appear on the surface to be oppositional or negative, but that after their polarities are explored in a mutually critical way, reveal new insights and syntheses heretofore unrealized. The "moments" mentioned above exemplify this. One critiques, for example, the evils of patriarchy such as sexism; one then recovers the repressed "other side" these evils have tried to destroy or render invisible; finally, one attempts to reconstruct reality from within the new synthesis to which this critique and recovery have given birth.

A further example of Ruether's dialectical methodology is obvious in the Introduction to her book *Gaia and God: An Ecofeminist Theology of Earth Healing* (1992). Always her methodology includes (1) denouncing evil or a critique of injustice; (2) affirming what has been negated or recovering positive elements within the tradition or the issue under discussion; and finally, (3) forging a new synthesis that results from having examined both the positive and negative dimensions being considered. Ruether states at the outset of this book that she intends to examine the cultural and social foundations of the destructive relationships between men and women, oppressors and oppressed, human and nonhuman being, found historically in Western classical cultural traditions. Second, she intends to cull these same traditions, particularly Christianity, to discover positive and useful ideas that can be retrieved and that may prove helpful in our efforts to create right relationships with one another and the earth. Finally, she seeks to articulate a new transformative vision that arises out of the destructive and constructive contributions found in these cultures. The resulting synthesis will call us to "... a new consciousness, a new symbolic culture and spirituality" (*Gaia and God*, 1992, p. 4). Her methodology is a hopeful tribute to the human potential for creating well-being. By constantly employing her dialectical approach to reality, she pays humble homage to the ineffability of the Divine and the complexity of human beings within the dialectics of nature and history.

Ruether acknowledges the five sources and norms in this dialectical methodology: (1) the Hebrew and Christian scriptures; (2) the largely delegitimated texts from "heretical" traditions like Gnosticism, Quakerism, and others; (3) the principal theological themes of the Protestant, Catholic, and Orthodox traditions; (4) religious and philosophical ideas from the non-Christian, Near Eastern, and Greco-Roman worlds; and, (5) critical post-Christian perspectives, particularly those of liberalism, romanticism, and Marxism (*Sexism and God-Talk*, 1983, pp. 21-33).

Ruether finds in the prophetic tradition of the Hebrew and Christian scriptures the most salient critique and transforming alternatives to ideological deformation and domination. She believes that these traditions reveal, through their dialectic of promise and judgment, that the sin and apostasy that create social injustice are to be negated, while peace, harmony, and mutual relations are to be affirmed. Religious feminists can appropriate this paradigm only if they radically recontextualize it, since the biblical authors did not address their prophetic critique to the patriarchal oppression of women. What Ruether calls "feminist midrash," or retelling the stories in a new way by applying the prophetic critique to the experiences of oppression women suffer today, is a key way to critique, recover, and reconstruct faith communities corrupted by ideological distortion. Ruether's dialectical methodology, as complex as it remains, lays the foundation for her continuing articulation of her theo-political project.

God/ess

Ruether's earliest ideas of the divine as "the empowering matrix" and as a Singular Reality manifested in a multiplicity of ways and historical contexts, developed over the years as a result of myriad personal, sociopolitical, and theological experiences. If one listens to her descriptions of the Divine, one cannot help recognizing therein a profoundly open, fluid, and transpatriarchal understanding of the ineffability of the Holy One. Her own written symbol, "God/ess," testifies to this, as does a more personal statement she made in this regard:

> My own assumption is that the Divine Being that generates, upholds and renews the world is truly universal, and is the father and mother of all peoples without discrimination. This means that true revelation and true relationship to the divine is to be found in all religions. God/ess is the ground of all beings, and not just human beings.
> ("Feminism and Jewish-Christian Dialogue," 1987, p. 141)

This implosive concept of Ultimate Reality connects all in the community of creation. At the same time, Ruether's continuing search for God/ess transcends not only male gender exclusivity and superiority, but also obsessive reliance on parental imagery. In this matter she has proposed that

> overreliance on parental imagery for God suggests that we should relate to God primarily in the mode of childlike dependency. When this mode of relationship is made the primary language for God, it promotes spiritual infantilism and cuts off moral maturity and responsibility. God becomes the neurotic parent who wishes us to remain always dependent children and is angry with us when we want to grow up. Thus we must balance the language of God as parent with other images, such as teacher, guide, liberator. We need to see the dynamic relationship between God as the source of our being and God as the empowerer of our aspiration and growth toward new being, toward redeemed and fulfilled humanity.
> ("Feminist Theology and Spirituality," 1984, p. 17)

Here she vigorously affirms women's impulses to trust the God/ess we come to know and experience precisely as women in the unique particularities of our lives.

Although Ruether speaks of God/ess within the parameters of the Hebrew and Christian traditions as "the God of history, the God of Exodus who liberates us from slavery and leads us to the promised land of future wholeness and goodness" ("Feminist Theology and Spirituality"), she does not sanction the patriarchal and dualism-breeding images of God these traditions have upheld. For her, the God of the Exodus is the God/ess of both creation and redemption, the God/ess of the whole of life, rather than a God who sides only with spiritual, rational, and otherworldly concerns vis-à-vis natural, bodily, and temporal matters. Thus, Ruether's idea of God/ess, in true dialectical fashion, provides us a holistic understanding of Ultimate Reality as that which is present in the experiences of both women and men, human and nonhuman being, the personal and the political, as well as in all religious traditions.

Christology

Ruether's Christology denounces (1) ahistorical and apolitical claims about Jesus; (2) exclusivistic Christologies that have caused incredible suffering for Jews and other "non-Christian" peoples; (3) misogynistic Christologies that have been used to justify the denigration of women; and (4) humanocentric Christologies that have ignored the integrity and goodness of creation.

Ruether has critiqued traditional christological teaching, especially on the nature and person of Jesus as articulated by the Council of Chalcedon in 451 C.E. She argues that this understanding of Christology is not faithful to the words and deeds of the historical Jesus as presented in the Synoptic Gospels. Although she admits that Chalcedon's use of Greek philosophical concepts was a brilliant way to present Christ the Logos in fifth-century Hellenistic culture, she also insists that its language, imagery, and symbolism are obstacles to people trying to answer the question "Who do you say I am?" today. Men and women of faith are less concerned with the ontology of Jesus, who he was in his very being, and more concerned with his soteriology—his salvific significance in an abused and brokenhearted world.

Traditional Christologies have been used to justify oppression because they are not grounded in the message and praxis of the historical Jesus. As Ruether has poignantly stated, "If the paradigms of Christology perpetuate political detachment, religious bigotry, sexism and the negation of nature, then we have to ask serious questions about the saving content of Christology" (*To Change the World,* 1981, p. 4). Consequently, she makes several suggestions for transforming oppressive christological perspectives. Initially, she challenges Christians to transcend the patristic portrayal of the historical Jesus as the only model of Christ. Coupled with her reaffirmation of traditional Christian teaching regarding God's ultimate incomprehensibility, as well as with her urgent plea to Christians to be open to discovering the divine in unexplored places (women's experience, non-Christian religious traditions, etc.), she encourages Christians to be open to new models of Christ, what she calls "other paradigms" of redeemed humanity.

Second, Ruether denounces any christological perspective that identifies the maleness of Jesus with normative human being and the "maleness" of God. This is misogyny and heresy. Such christological teaching underscores the subordination and inferiority of women in creation, redemption, and church ministry. Thus for her the Jesus of the Synoptic Gospels who was the "iconoclastic prophet" and liberator of the oppressed, especially poor women, is the foundation of her Christology. The mythologies that portray him as Messiah or divine Logos and emphasize his masculinity rather than his humanity she rejects.

Third, like many liberation theologians, her starting point for Christology is the historical Jesus, particularly his praxis—his efforts to transform the unjust world in which he lived. She argues that his praxis was rooted in his vision of the reign of God, which begins in this world where injustice and oppression are being transformed. The challenge to Christians today, then, is to work for this reign of God as a social and historical event, not a spiritual, otherworldly enterprise. This commitment will mean embodying personal and social relationships characterized by integrity, mutuality, justice, and freedom. Such relationships constitute our only hope for a peaceful, just world.

Finally, Ruether's christological vision denounces the "humanocentrism" that has justified the rape of the earth. She seeks to recover the messianic vision of redemption Jesus announced when he began his public ministry. This redemptive vision is rooted in the Hebrew scriptures and includes a harmonious covenantal relationship between nature and society. The Hebrew idea of the Jubilee, which centers in righting relationships among human beings and between humans and the land, expresses this well. Debts are canceled, slaves and their children are freed, and the earth is allowed to lie fallow (*Gaia and God,* 1992, pp. 212-13).

Ruether maintains that even though Jesus proclaimed this vision when he began his public ministry, Western Christianity distorted it by appropriating a dualistic view of the relationship between human beings and nature from Greek philosophy. Like women and other oppressed groups, nature was subjugated, in dualistic fashion, to male domination and control and perceived to be distinct from and inferior to "spiritual" men. The same dualism has been incorporated into religious language that also opposes nature and grace, earth and heaven, world and church, and so forth.

Consequently, there have been two primary models of nature that have shaped the Western Christian imagination. One perceives nature as a great hierarchical chain of being in which God rules all, the angels rule the universe, and humans rule creation. The other understands nature in a linear, evolutionary fashion. Such a view is predicated on unlimited expansion and development, that are expected to culminate in a period of final perfection. Using the lordship of Christ in this context, Ruether denounces both of these models of nature and the humankind-nature relationship that they envision. Her alternative ecological model is none other than the embrace of continuing conversion, rooted in Jesus' own example of lordship as servanthood. According to her, he models in his message and praxis the end of hierarchy in all relationships, including the relationship between human beings and nature. Jesus, then, is our example for right relationships with one another and the earth. Such relationships must be based on respect and promote justice and harmony for all God has created.

Anthropology

Anthropological questions play a significant role in Ruether's theology. Traditionally, she would argue, Christian anthropology has been patriarchal. Augustine, Aquinas, Luther, Calvin, and Barth, in sequence, have denied that women represent the image of God as fully as men. She has denounced any dualistic anthropology that claims women represent a "lower" form of physical and sexual humanity while men represent a "higher" more spiritual and rational human nature. Further, she rejects any androcentric anthropology that asserts that women are inferior to men by nature and thus more inclined to sin, responsible for the Fall, and consequently in need of being ruled by men. Equally, she has opposed the concept of "androgyny" because to her it continues the kind of thinking that splits the human psyche into masculine and feminine sides with corresponding unequally valued traits. In her own words,

> There is no valid biological basis for labeling certain psychic capacities, such as reason, "masculine" and others, such as intuition, "feminine." To put it bluntly, there is no biological connection between male gonads and the capacity to reason. Likewise, there is no biological connection between female sexual organs and the capacity to be intuitive, caring, or nurturing. Thus the labeling of these capacities as masculine and feminine simply perpetuates gender role stereotypes. . . . We need to affirm . . . that all humans possess a full and equivalent human nature and personhood, as male and female. (*Sexism and God-Talk*, 1983, p. 111)

Ruether is adamant that maleness and femaleness exist foremost as specialized roles in the process of human reproduction. Such biological complementarity does not necessarily result in either psychological or social role differentiation. Enculturation and socialization, not "nature," create these insidious patriarchal perspectives about what constitutes human nature.

Ruether's egalitarian anthropology emerges particularly from her Christology. Using Jesus as the paradigm for liberated human being, she argues that in him there appears a new kind of humanity, one best expressed, not in his being "male," but in the way he related to other human beings: compassionately, mutually, justly. Her christological perspective maintains that the incarnation is inclusive of both genders, all races and historical circumstances. She challenges Christians to cultivate an interreligious and intercultural hospitality toward the growing body of current anthropological insights, for she insists that no one religious tradition can have the definitive word on the richness of being human (*Sexism and God-Talk*, 109-15; *Gaia and God*, 1992, 165-72).

Flowing out of her anthropological position is her perspective on human sexuality. She maintains that all persons are probably bisexual and polymorphously sexual originally, as Freud theorized. This means to her that as human beings "we all have the capacity for sexual attraction and response to people of the same sex. We are not born heterosexual. We are taught to become heterosexual" ("Homophobia," 1989, p. 30). Patriarchal heterosexuality, which ensures white, male-ruling class and race domination, enforces this. Therefore, most people accept their heterosexual socialization and channel sexual attraction not only to persons of the "other gender," but also to their same race, socioeconomic class, and religion. Some people resist this conditioning; others obviously do not ("Homophobia").

For Ruether then, the key moral question with regard to the issue of sexual preference is not whether it can lead to "natural" reproductive sex or "complementarity" of the sexes. To her these are specious arguments. Rather, sexual relationships are moral (no matter one's sexual preference) if they are mutual, faithful, committed, and seek the wholeness of each partner. They are immoral if they embody abuse, violence, lying, deceit, betrayal, and fail to nurture the personal development of each involved. Thus, for her, "The morality of homosexual or heterosexual relations is judged by the same standards, rather than different standards" ("Homophobia," 1989, p. 27).

Sin and Evil

For Ruether, sin is primarily a distorted view of what it means to be in relationship to another, whether that "other" is oneself, God, mother earth, or human beings. The distortion has its roots in the alienated perspective of dualistic thinking where men are seen as superior to women, whites to blacks, Christians to non-Christians, rich to poor, heterosexuals to homosexuals, humans to the earth. Further, Ruether argues that sin is never just a personal matter; "there is no evil that is not relational" (*Sexism and God-Talk*, 1983, p. 181). All evil and sin are both personal and social. And, Ruether explains, social sin is something we inherit historically. It arose and continues because individuals were and are socialized into roles predicated on domination and oppression and taught that these roles are right ("Social Sin," 1981, p. 46). Consequently, social sin is embodied in societies and institutions where distorted relationship is encouraged as "normal." Here social sin takes on a life of its own, although it begins with personal sin. When individuals come together believing Jews, blacks, women, homosexuals, and the poor, for example, are subhuman, the conditions for evil prevail. A commitment to conversion—to changing our hearts and social systems so that they model mutuality, justice, and compassion, along with solidarity toward the most vulnerable among us—is Ruether's answer to overcoming distorted relationality. For Christians this will require a change of heart so deep that the values and vision of Jesus become the center of one's life and community.

Salvation and Hope

Ruether is extremely modest when she speculates about "the Last Things," that is, about death, heaven, immortality, and so on. Yet she rejects traditional Christian teaching about salvation as the escape of one's soul from one's body to heaven. She is also critical of the teaching that holds that there is a final, futuristic event beyond history that will make right what is wrong with the world, because she is committed to the belief that Jesus' vision of the kingdom or reign of God was not eschatological but a reality that began on this earth. It is manifest in personal efforts and social movements that promote just, mutual relationships among human beings, and between humans and the earth. Thus for her, hope for salvation must be rooted in active participation in the struggles to bridge the gap between what is and what could be. For Christians, Jesus is the model in this struggle, for he is the messianic prophet who embodied this hope in an exemplary way. Ruether therefore spends little time theologizing about heaven or the afterlife, claiming that a certain "agnosticism" is the only responsible stance (*Sexism and God-Talk*, 1983, p. 257).

Providing an alternative, she is more concerned that Christian commitment to the work of continuing conversion be hope for salvation and a symbol of the reign of God, rather than some useless and irresponsible preoccupation with an "endless flight into an unrealized future" (*Sexism and God-Talk*, p. 254). According to her, persons must be committed to *metanoia*—to a ceaseless willingness to enter into right relationships with themselves, one another, the earth, and God/ess. Questions concerning the Last Things should not distract Christians from more concrete concerns. As she has stated:

> Our responsibility is to use our temporal life span to create a just and good community for our generation and for our children. It is in the hands of Holy Wisdom to forge out of our final struggle truth and being for everlasting life. Our agnosticism about what this means is then the expression of our faith, our trust that Holy Wisdom will give transcendent meaning to our work, which is bounded by space and time.
> (*Sexism and God-Talk*, p. 258; *Gaia and God*, 1992, pp. 247-53)

Religious Pluralism

For several reasons, Ruether's theology encourages ecumenism and interreligious dialogue. Unlike most Roman Catholics who grew up prior to the Second Vatican Council, Ruether was nourished in an ecumenical environment. Specifically, from her mother she learned, at an early age, to view religious diversity as something positive rather than as an obstacle that could threaten her religious faith and tradition. Years before Vatican II, then, she had already "moved beyond dialogue into something which might be called 'intentional unity,' into a catholicity which takes its 'tradition' as the whole Christian experience, perhaps even the whole human experience" ("Catholicism and Catholicity," 1965, pp. 191-92).

Second, Ruether's christological perspective requires her to be supportive of religious pluralism. For her, Christology must be understood as a model or paradigm relative to Christians—people who claim a particular history and religious experience. Christians cannot insist that belief in Jesus is the only way, or a superior way, to God. Jesus may be the Christian's way, but other religious people may have equally graced ways to God. She urges Christians to refuse to use belief in Jesus to deny the validity of non-Christian religious experience. Honoring other religious ways can lead to increased solidarity among religious people as they work together to heal an anguished earth and world.

Ruether has cultivated a third critical respect for feminist interreligious dialogue in particular. Long committed to deepening and clarifying her admittedly limited perceptions of truth, she has urged Christian feminists to enter dialogue not only with representatives of traditional Christianity, but also with Jewish and Muslim feminists as well. This dialogue must include the feminist adherents of nonbiblical religions who are engaged in recovering the memories of the ancient goddesses and the visions held by those women burned as witches, both of which are denounced by patriarchy ("Feminism and Jewish-Christian Dialogue," 1987, p. 147).

Ultimately, as a longtime proponent of religious pluralism, Ruether challenges all feminists, women and men, to avoid any form of "feminist fundamentalism" in their common search for truth. Women and men have much to learn from one another, and they cannot afford to let differences divide them so deeply that they refuse, in the final analysis, to "live the questions" that exist among and between them. Too much is at stake for all who seek to live justly with one another and the earth.

Conclusion

Rosemary Radford Ruether's theology is complex and in process. It is an outstanding and substantive contribution to the whole enterprise of Christian feminist theology in the latter half of the twentieth century. When one listens carefully to her voice, one hears the words of a woman who has immersed herself in the largest issues of her time: racism, sexism, classism, militarism, heterosexism, neocolonialism, and ecofeminism.

Rooted deeply in the Christian tradition, this ecumenical Catholic theologian has challenged all women and men of goodwill to face both the sin and grace, despair and hope, darkness and light that have confronted and continue to confront them as they move to the edge of the twentieth century. Her passion for truth, justice, and right relationship; her belief in the capacity of human beings to grow, repent, and change; her indefatigable resistance toward all in church and nation that undermines Jesus' vision of the reign of God; her monumental intellectual contribution to feminism and Christian theology; her patient and tenacious immersion in the concrete struggles of women, blacks, Latinos, Jews, Palestinians, homosexuals, children, and our threatened earth—all of these testify to her pervasive sense of kinship with all, especially those most vulnerable, in God's community of creation.

And what, most basically, is the key to her radical, iconoclastic vision? She herself suggests that "what we need is neither optimism or pessimism ... but committed love. This means that we remain committed to a vision and to concrete communities of life no matter what the 'trends' may be" (*Gaia and God,* 1992, p. 273). "Committed love"—no two words more aptly describe, in sum, the theological contribution of Rosemary Radford Ruether.

Mary Hembrow Snyder

Selected Primary Works

1965   "Catholicism and Catholicity," in *The Generation of the Third Eye,* ed. Daniel Callahan.

1970   "An Unexpected Tribute to the Theologian," *Theology Today* 27 (October): 332-39.

1975   "Beginnings: An Intellectual Autobiography," in *Journeys: The Impact of Personal Experience on Religious Thought,* ed. Gregory Baum.

1981   "Social Sin," *Commonweal* 108 (January): 46-48.

1981   *To Change the World: Christology and Cultural Criticism.*

1982   *Disputed Questions: On Being a Christian.*

1983   *Sexism and God-Talk: Toward a Feminist Theology.*

1984   "Feminist Theology and Spirituality," in *Christian Feminism: Vision of a New Humanity.*

1985   "The Future of Feminist Theology in the Academy," *Journal of the American Academy of Religion* 53 (December): 703-13.

1987   "Feminism and Jewish-Christian Dialogue," in *The Myth of Christian Uniqueness: Toward a Pluralistic Theology of Religions,* ed. John Hick and Paul F. Knitter.

1987   "Spirit and Matter, Public and Private: The Challenge of Feminism to Traditional Dualisms," in *Embodied Love: Sensuality and Relationship as Feminist Values,* ed. Paula M. Cooey, Sharon A. Farmer, and Mary Ellen Ross.

1989   "The Development of My Theology," *Religious Studies Review* 15/1 (January):1-4.

1989   "Homophobia, Heterosexism, and Pastoral Practice," in *Homosexuality in the Priesthood and the Religious Life,* ed. Jeannine Gramick.

1992   *Gaia and God: An Ecofeminist Theology of Earth Healing.*

1993   "Can Christology Be Liberated from Patriarchy?" in *Reconstructing the Christ Symbol: Essays in Feminist Christology,* ed. Maryanne Stevens.

Selected Secondary Source

1988   Mary Hembrow Snyder, *The Christology of Rosemary Radford Ruether.*

EDWARD SCHILLEBEECKX
1914–

Life and Career

In the final decades of the twentieth century the question at the heart of Edward
Schillebeeckx's theological reflection has become: How can Christians continue to proclaim hope in the God of Jesus in the face of a world of radical
secularization and senseless suffering? Concerns about God's relation to history
and creation and the church's relation to the world are not new to Schillebeeckx's
theological agenda, however; they have engaged him for more than fifty years.

Edward Cornelius Florentius Alfons Schillebeeckx was born into a middle-class
Flemish Catholic family in Antwerp on November 12, 1914, shortly after the
German occupation of Belgium. The sixth of fourteen children, he received his
primary education in Kortenberg (between Louvain and Brussels) and his secondary education at the Jesuit boarding school in Turnhout. In 1934 he joined the
Dominican Order (the Order of Preachers) in Ghent, where he pursued studies in
philosophy under the mentorship of Dominic De Petter from 1935 to 1938.
Schillebeeckx was an avid student of philosophy, reading even thinkers officially
banned to seminary students at the time, including Kant, Hegel, and Freud. He
was particularly interested in phenomenology, specifically the work of Maurice
Merleau-Ponty. Influenced by De Petter's own original work, Schillebeeckx espoused a Thomistic theory of human knowing that included an implicit intuitive or
experiential element that goes beyond conceptual knowledge. Although he later
disavowed that position, Schillebeeckx has consistently argued that theology as a
system of concepts holds only a relative value.

A brief period of compulsory military service in the summer of 1938 surprisingly
afforded Schillebeeckx time to read philosophy, psychology, and sociology and to
converse with pastors from other Christian churches, thus marking early signs of
his characteristic interdisciplinary and ecumenical commitments. He next moved
to Louvain to study theology at the Dominican House of Studies in preparation for
his ordination as a Roman Catholic priest in 1941. Schillebeeckx found his courses
there far less engaging than his philosophical studies had been, however, since the

medieval texts of Thomas Aquinas and neo-Scholastic commentaries on Aquinas's writings were presented without reference to their historical context or to a developing theological tradition.

In 1945 Schillebeeckx began his postgraduate studies at Le Saulchoir, the Dominican faculty of theology in Paris, one of the centers of the *nouvelle theologie* ("new theology"), a renewal movement in Catholic theology that advocated a "return to the sources" of the patristic and medieval periods as the grounding for all later theological development. From professors such as Yves Congar and Marie-Dominique Chenu, Schillebeeckx learned the importance of locating theological sources within their historical context and of the theologian's active engagement with the political and social movements of the day.

Although Schillebeeckx originally intended to write his doctoral dissertation on nature and grace under Chenu's direction, he shifted the focus of his research to sacramental theology when he was assigned to teach a course on sacraments at the Dominican House of Studies in Louvain in 1947. He completed his dissertation, *De Sacramentele Heilseconomie* (The Sacramental Economy of Salvation), in 1951. During his ten years of teaching dogmatic theology at Louvain, Schillebeeckx also served as student master for the Dominican students, chaplain in a local prison, editor of the spirituality journal *Tijdschrift voor Geestelijk Leven,* and professor at Louvain's Higher Institute for Religious Studies. In 1957 he was invited to join the faculty of the Catholic University of Nijmegen in the Netherlands as Chair of Dogmatics and the History of Theology, a position he held until his retirement in 1982.

Although he was not an official theological adviser *(peritus)* at the Second Vatican Council (the progressive Dutch church was viewed with suspicion), Schillebeeckx served as personal theologian to Cardinal Alfrink and adviser to the Dutch bishops, and became a strong influence on the Council through his theological lectures to large gatherings of bishops. In 1961 he founded the Dutch journal of academic theology *Tijdschrift voor Theologie,* and in 1965, he became a founding editor of the international journal *Concilium.*

Schillebeeckx's constant efforts to relate theology and culture were publicly celebrated with the award of the Quinquennial prize for promoting Flemish language and culture in 1969 and the Dutch government's award of the Erasmus prize for contributions to European culture in 1982 (the first time the award had been given to a theologian). Since his retirement from Nijmegen in 1982, Schillebeeckx has continued to be active in the Dutch Catholic Church (particularly the critical base communities), to publish, and to serve as editor of *Concilium.* His theological writings were critically investigated by Vatican officials in 1968, 1976, and 1982. Although Schillebeeckx's theological positions were judged consistently to be within the bounds of Catholic belief, questions were repeatedly raised about his theological method as it became less dogmatic, and more historical, hermeneutical, and critical.

Theological Task and Method

Throughout his early writings on revelation and theology, the sacraments (specifically eucharist and marriage), nature and grace, and the church and its mission in the world, Schillebeeckx endeavored to express in contemporary terms the mystery of revelation that had been handed on in the Christian tradition. Although Schillebeeckx never identified revelation with its conceptual formulation in doctrinal terms, his task as a dogmatic theologian did include historical analysis and reinterpretation of classical Christian doctrines. In the early 1960s, his volume *Christ, the Sacrament of the Encounter with God* (1960, Eng. trans. 1963) provided a breakthrough in Catholic sacramental theology. Concerned that many Catholics viewed the sacraments as impersonal rituals that "gave grace" as if it were a thing, Schillebeeckx described grace as the relationship between God and humankind. Broadening the notion of sacramentality, he explained that Jesus Christ is the primordial Christian sacrament because in Jesus the presence of God has become visible, tangible, and historical. In a similar way, the church itself can be described as a sacrament since its mission, as the Body of Christ in the world, is to make tangible and concrete God's love for humanity. Only in that context, Schillebeeckx maintained, can one speak of the seven sacraments of the Catholic Church as visible signs of the community's encounter in faith with the risen Christ and therefore with the living God.

In the mid-1960s, Schillebeeckx's tour of the United States during the height of the Death of God movement, his contact with French University chaplains, and his dialogue with Dutch humanists deepened his growing concern about the alienation of secularized society, particularly intellectuals and the young, from Christian faith. Convinced that Christian theologians had to address a fundamental skepticism regarding the very possibility of revelation, Schillebeeckx shifted his approach to theology. Rather than beginning with scripture or the doctrine of the church, he turned to concrete human experience as the starting point for his theology. His goal was to listen to the questions and struggles of ordinary people and to probe the depths of their experience, always trying to discover amid the "signs of the times" an "echo of the gospel."

Western culture's emphasis on technology, secularization, and progress toward the future in the 1960s with its implicit claim that human beings could control nature and determine the future of history challenged Schillebeeckx to search for a new way to speak of God. Explicitly rejecting the "turn to the subject" taken by Karl Rahner and other leading Catholic theologians of his day, Schillebeeckx turned to history as the arena for God's presence and activity. Granting that the "God of the gaps" was no longer necessary, justifiable, or credible, Schillebeeckx argued that God is "Wholly New, the One who is our future" (*God the Future of Man [GFM]*, 1968, p. 181). Devising his own version of the "theology of hope" associated with political theologians in the 1960s, Schillebeeckx reworked his basic convictions on nature and grace in terms of history and the future. With a strong accent on God as creator, Schillebeeckx argued that the same "living God" who empowered creation from the beginning and entrusted history to humankind remains the source of creative energy and future possibility for human history and all of creation.

Even in the mid-1960s, Schillebeeckx remarked, however, that the experience of human hope was born most frequently in the midst of negative experiences of life in which human beings protest and resist injustice and oppression. These "negative contrast experiences" make us realize the absence of what "ought to be" and move us to protest and action on behalf of the well-being of humanity and all of creation (*GFM*, 1968, p. 136). In the decades that followed, this notion of negative contrast experience was to become even more central to Schillebeeckx's theological project in the context of global suffering.

His conviction that the crisis of faith was primarily a crisis of culture (and more practically, his assignment to teach a course on hermeneutics at Nijmegen in 1966) led Schillebeeckx to investigate a variety of hermeneutical theories. In dialogue with the writings of Martin Heidegger, Rudolf Bultmann, the post-Bultmannians, Hans-Georg Gadamer, Paul Ricoeur, Wolfhart Pannenberg, and Jürgen Moltmann, Schillebeeckx wrestled with the radically historical character of human existence and hence the necessity of plural cultural expressions of the one Christian faith. He began to develop his own hermeneutical stance with an emphasis on tradition as the necessary context for all interpretation, the primacy of the future in interpreting history, and the continuing critical question of how to preserve the identity of faith in plural cultural contexts (see *GFM*, pp. 1-49). Schillebeeckx also explored structuralist, phenomenological, and logical linguistic analysis for criteria for the meaningful use of language, searching always for language that was connected with everyday lived experience and was intelligible to all human beings, not only to Christians (see *Understanding of Faith*, 1974). Granting that Christian faith is not empirically verifiable and that the reappropriation of the Christian faith could not remain a purely theoretical task, Schillebeeckx asserted that only ethics (orthopraxis or "right action") can provide a historical verification of the credibility of the Christian faith. A living tradition of faith is preserved not by theoretical identification of some unchangeable essence within historically and culturally conditioned formulations, but by the practical and concrete actualization of the gospel.

Schillebeeckx's hermeneutical approach to theology took a decidedly more critical turn in the 1970s. Drawing on the work of critical theorists from the Frankfurt School, particularly Jürgen Habermas, Schillebeeckx stressed that power struggles and manipulation are inevitable in the transmission of any human tradition, including the living Christian tradition. Thus retrieval of the authentic Christian tradition must include ideology critique as well as creative appropriation of the tradition in a new moment, a theme that Schillebeeckx expounded in his farewell address at Nijmegen in 1983. Theology's task of correlation between the Christian tradition and current experience and culture must be a *mutually critical* correlation.

This critical appropriation of the tradition is perhaps most evident in Schillebeeckx's two volumes on ordained ministry, *Ministry: Leadership in the Community of Jesus Christ* (1980, Eng. trans. 1981) and *The Church with a Human Face* (1985). Beginning with "negative contrast experiences," Schillebeeckx highlights the growing numbers of Catholic communities in the world that are deprived of official leadership and even the eucharistic celebration because of the lack of male, celibate ordained clergy. From that perspective he analyzes the history of ordained ministry in the Catholic tradition with attention to "whose interests were being served" and which moments in the history of the tradition were forgotten or suppressed. The entire study raises the question of whether distortion in the authentic Christian tradition is to be found in the growing forms of alternative practice among critical base communities or rather in the restrictions and practices of a Roman clerical system that is resisting new movements of the Holy Spirit. In *Church: The Human Story of God* (1989, Eng. trans. 1990), the third volume of his christological trilogy, Schillebeeckx reiterates his critique of institutional efforts to preserve hierarchical church structures that no longer serve the common good of the community and argues instead for a democratic form of church government that includes genuine participation by all the baptized.

Christology and Soteriology

Although Schillebeeckx is convinced that questions of ministry and ecclesiology need to be addressed since they can be a source of scandal and block the church's effective mission in the world, the primary focus of his theological work in recent decades has been the question of salvation—the future of humanity and the earth amidst a world of radical evil and senseless suffering. In the early 1970s, Schillebeeckx began an ambitious project of rethinking the Christian claim that Jesus is universal savior in the face of radical human suffering, structural injustice, and the devastation of the earth. At the heart of the project is his conviction that to say that evil, in the proportions that we have known it in the twentieth century, is somehow part of God's redemptive plan is to undermine the very possibility of Christian faith. Christians finally have no theoretical answer to radical evil. Instead, Schillebeeckx suggests, we have God's response to evil and suffering in the human story of Jesus. Thus he proposes a "narrative-practical," rather than a purely theoretical, approach to Christology.

In *Jesus: An Experiment in Christology* (1974, Eng. trans., 1979), more accurately translated from the Dutch as "Jesus: The Story of a Living One," Schillebeeckx retells the story of Jesus based on a historical-critical analysis of the Synoptic Gospels, searching for the basis for the first disciples' faith in Jesus. He emphasizes the liberating lifestyle and parabolic preaching of Jesus, highlights Jesus' profound experience of God ("Abba experience") as the secret and source of his identity and mission, and accents the negativity of the cross as the climax of human injustice and evil, an event in which "the God of Jesus" remained silent. Schillebeeckx concludes, however, that in remaining faithful to Abba, to his mission, and to solidarity with all who suffer, Jesus filled an absurd and meaningless event with love and meaning. Although he discusses the Easter event primarily in terms of the disciples' experience of conversion, Schillebeeckx ultimately interprets the resurrection in terms of God's fidelity to Jesus, the radical defeat of death and evil, and the definitive opening up of the future to those who appear to have no future. The emphasis throughout the book is on the disciples' experience of Jesus as salvation coming from God and their search for language and titles to identify Jesus in light of that experience (eschatological prophet being the core of all later developments).

Foundational to all of Schillebeeckx's work is his understanding of the relationship between revelation and human experience. Revelation or the disclosure of the mystery of God in human history occurs within, but cannot be identified with, human experience. Schillebeeckx begins with the conviction that all human experience has a revelatory structure. We learn through a process of discovery in which our traditional framework for the understanding that is derived from our culture and the history of our previous experiences is called into question by new experiences that don't fit our categories or expectations. These experiences of failure are at the same time opportunities for discovery of something new. Our previous framework of interpretation needs to be radically revised in view of "resistant reality." The religious experience of revelation follows a similar dynamic. The religious tradition of the past constitutes a necessary framework for understanding our present "new moment" in that tradition. At the same time new impulses of the Spirit constitute real developments within the tradition precisely so that the tradition can remain vital in new cultural contexts.

In the second volume of his christological trilogy, *Christ the Experience of Jesus as Lord* (1977, Eng. trans. 1980), Schillebeeckx explores the need for new language and structures to mediate the experience of salvation in the twentieth century. In sketching the necessary elements for a theology of salvation for our day, Schillebeeckx again turns to human experience—both the experience of the absence of salvation in negative contrast experiences and the "fragments of salvation" or positive experiences of meaning that give an experiential basis for the hope that the future can be different from the past and present. Searching for new language for the experience of salvation in our day (note the translation of the Dutch title of this volume: *Justice and Love, Grace and Liberation*), Schillebeeckx underscores the social and political dimensions of grace that have so often been missing from earlier Christian anthropologies and soteriologies.

While salvation remains an eschatological reality, Schillebeeckx emphasizes that since God acts in human history, "there is no salvation outside the world." Identifying a series of "anthropological constants" or constitutive dimensions of the salvation that we hope for ("livable humanity"), Schillebeeckx includes human corporeality and relationship with all of nature, our essential relatedness to others, and the redemption and conversion of social structures and institutions, as well as of history and culture. Salvation needs to be concretely realized through praxis on behalf of humanity and action against evil, as well as reflected on theoretically. Finally, but not divorced from the prior elements, salvation encompasses the religious dimension of human existence: salvation from sin, union with God.

In the four structural elements that, as Schillebeeckx maintains, will be found in any Christian theology of salvation, it is possible to identify a brief summary of the main emphases in his theology:

1. *God's cause is the human cause.* In Jesus the mystery at the center of all of reality has been revealed to be a "God bent toward humanity." The Creator God who is the source of all that is, the power of all liberation, takes delight in the flourishing of creation. God who is absolute goodness, pure positivity, remains the power over against all evil. The living God who is in solidarity with creation continues to hold open future possibilities in the most desperate circumstances. The living God is concerned with humankind; salvation is concerned with human wholeness and happiness.

2. *Salvation, the meaning of life, has been disclosed in and through Jesus the Christ.* The God who remains hidden has been disclosed most comprehensively in history in and through Jesus. The story of Jesus is both the "parable of God" and the "paradigm of humanity." In his life, ministry, and death, Jesus reveals God's affirmation of life and God's "no" to human suffering. The omnipotent and free God has chosen to become vulnerable, taking on the pain, suffering, and injustice of human history in solidarity with all those who suffer in order to defeat the power of evil from within. Schillebeeckx's understanding of the Christian claim is that Jesus is universal savior, but not the absolute savior. Although the power of God has been revealed definitively in the history of Jesus, salvation is a matter of action ("telling the fifth gospel with our lives") rather than explicit belief in Jesus. God's gracious presence is found wherever "a glass of water is given to those who thirst," wherever good is done and evil resisted.

3. *Human communities mediate salvation.* The living Christ and his Spirit are encountered today in and through communities of faith who continue to speak, act, and live as Jesus did in solidarity with the human cause. The mission of the church is to be sacrament of salvation in the world, in the vanguard of this life of active discipleship, political holiness. But the mediation of grace occurs beyond the boundaries of Christian churches, and the Christian churches can fail to mediate salvation. Hence, this principle moves beyond a narrowly ecclesiological principle to a broadly anthropological principle of salvation. The story of God—a promise

417

of well-being and happiness for human beings and all of God's beloved creation—is narrated with the words of human lives. In a world of global suffering, the story of God among us is told most clearly in the stories of hope and resistance of those whose human dignity is in any way diminished or denied and those who remain in solidarity with them.

4. *History is without historical end.* Although Schillebeeckx stresses the importance of human mediation of God's grace, an eschatological proviso is key to his understanding of salvation. The living God who is "the future of humanity" transcends our limited human efforts and can redeem even our sinful failures. The experience of reality as ultimately compassionate is made credible to others only if human communities continue to make present in concrete ways the experience of salvation—justice and love, grace and liberation. The fulfillment of that hope, final salvation, however, lies beyond the bounds of human history and exceeds all human expectations.

These four principles describe not only Schillebeeckx's abiding theological interests, but also the basis for Christian hope amid a world of suffering as it approaches the third millennium.

Mary Catherine Hilkert

Selected Primary Works

1968   *God the Future of Man.*
1974   *The Understanding of Faith.*
1979   *Jesus: An Experiment in Christology.*
1980   *Christ: The Experience of Jesus as Lord.*
1983   *God Is New Each Moment: Edward Schillebeeckx in Conversation with Huub Oosterhuis and Piet Hoogeveen.*
1984   *The Schillebeeckx Reader,* ed. Robert J. Schreiter.
1987   *On Christian Faith: The Spiritual, Ethical, and Political Dimensions.*
1990   *Church: The Human Story of God.*

Selected Secondary Sources

1989   Robert J. Schreiter and Mary Catherine Hilkert, eds., *The Praxis of Christian Experience: An Introduction to the Theology of Edward Schillebeeckx.*
1993   Philip Kennedy, *Schillebeeckx.*

JUAN LUIS SEGUNDO
1925–1996

Life and Career

Born in Montevideo, Uruguay, in 1925, Juan Luis Segundo was one of the most prolific and influential Latin American theologians of the twentieth century. He was a leading exponent of liberation theology, the Latin American movement that has developed a theological reflection rooted in the experience of the poor. In 1955 Segundo was ordained a priest of the Society of Jesus (Jesuits). A year later, he received a licentiate in theology from the University of Louvain and, in 1963, a doctorate of letters from the University of Paris.

Segundo's book *Función de la Iglesia en la realidad rioplatense* (1962) was one of the earliest attempts to articulate a theology from the perspective of the Latin American poor. Also among his most influential works are *A Theology for Artisans of a New Humanity* (5 vols., 1973–74); *The Liberation of Theology* (1976); *Jesus of Nazareth, Yesterday and Today* (5 vols., 1984–89); and *The Liberation of Dogma* (1992).

Theological Method

Like many liberation theologians, Segundo understands the theological enterprise as fundamentally a collaborative task rooted in the lived faith of the ecclesial community rather than an individual endeavor whose primary context and audience are academic. This pastoral concern led him to found the Peter Faber Pastoral Center in Montevideo in 1965, which, for political reasons, was forced to close ten years later. This pastoral interest is also reflected in his five-volume *A Theology for Artisans of a New Humanity*, whose Spanish subtitle is translated "open theology for an adult laity."

Segundo's many writings on the themes of systematic theology reveal a consistent concern for theological method. Like other liberation theologians, Segundo insists that the *way* one does theology greatly influences the *results* of one's theological reflection and scholarship. Consequently, an attentiveness to theological method and to the process of doing theology is essential in the work of the theologian and in the theological reflection of every Christian.

Segundo's greatest contributions to Christian theology in general, and Latin American liberation theology in particular, have been in the area of theological method. His most influential works on the subject have been *The Liberation of Theology* (1976) and *Faith and Ideologies*, volume 1 of *Jesus of Nazareth Yesterday and Today* (1984). In these books, Segundo addresses the central methodological issue of the relationship between the theologian's social context and his or her interpretation of theological doctrines and texts. The continuing, circular relationship between one's social context and one's theological reflection is what Segundo calls the hermeneutical circle, the cyclical process through which theologians interpret God's word.

Segundo's hermeneutical circle has four steps: (1) the particular individual and communal experience of reality (i.e., the social context), which leads one to suspect, or question received theological truths that conflict with one's experience; (2) the application of these questions to one's communal and personal understanding and interpretation of the Christian faith in general; (3) the application of this general theological suspicion to more specifically received interpretation of Scripture; which yields (4) a new interpretation of Scripture, one now in accord with our communal and personal experience and, thus, capable of incarnating God's word in the contemporary world. As experience is ever changing, moreover, so too is the interpretation of Scripture—at least if Scripture is to continue to speak to contemporary experience.

Implicit in this hermeneutical circle is an important methodological presupposition: As all ideas are always encountered in and within a social context, one cannot know God's self-revelation except as that revelation is embodied in a social context, or lived experience. To presume, conversely, that the truth of the Christian faith can be known in some "pure" ahistorical form is to presume that we can jump out of our historical skins.

Faith, Ideology, and Revelation

Segundo elaborates this methodological point in his extensive analysis of the relationship between faith and ideology. He defines ideology in a neutral sense, as any system of goals through which persons structure their lives, and as the means which persons use to realize those goals. Everyone, in Segundo's view, lives according to implicit and explicit ideologies that give meaning to life and that provide the symbolic, religious, cultural, political, and linguistic instruments through which to express and realize that meaning. Examples of these are doctrinal concepts, creeds, symbols such as the cross; political beliefs such as "one person one vote" or "liberty, equality, fraternity"; political systems, economic systems, assumptions concerning gender roles, culture-bound presuppositions; and so forth.

Faith becomes present—and, therefore, knowable—only as embodied in the particular "system of goals and means" available to persons in a given place and time. Persons have no access to revelation except as that revelation is, by definition, "revealed," or made present to them in history—not just any history, but *their* history, with its implicit and explicit ideological structures (e.g., cultural, economic, racial, gender, linguistic) that both limit and, more important, *make possible* their encounter with God's word. If divine revelation were merely "ideological," only disembodied angels would have access to it—and only they would be able to put it into practice.

In setting forth his theological method, Segundo proffers a critique of European theologies that fail to take into account the essentially historical character of the Christian faith and, therefore, the historical character of the theological enterprise. Instead of recognizing the intrinsic and necessary relationship between the Christian faith and historical ideologies, too often Christian theologies have viewed these as mutually incompatible: *All* ideologies (e.g., Jewish culture, Greek culture, Aristotelian philosophy, Marxist social analysis, sociological analyses of racism) have been viewed, precisely as ideologies, as external corrupting influences on the Christian faith. According to Segundo, this methodological mistake inevitably condemns the Christian faith to irrelevance and meaninglessness by denying it the historical instruments necessary for being known in and having an impact on the lived experience of human persons and communities of today. Since persons are embodied historical beings, their social context, lived experience, and ideologies provide both the limits to *and* the necessary condition for any knowledge of God, which knowledge will thus be necessarily embodied, historical, and ideological.

If there is no faith without ideology, however, how can one know the "true" God of the Scriptures? If faith is always limited by social context, how can one know the "real" Jesus Christ? According to Segundo, the faith that one encounters in Scripture is as bound by the demands of its historicity as is our own faith; the faith of Abraham, of Jesus, or of Paul is also necessarily mediated by, or embodied in, the culture, language, and other ideological structures of their time and place. In order for the reader of the biblical texts to encounter the God of whom these texts speak, the reader must, thus, "translate" the language, or ideology, of the biblical texts (appropriate to their time and place) into an ideological language appropriate to today. Merely to repeat, literally, the words of the text in our social context would thus be to *distort* their message, since the ideological structures (e.g., language) through which that message was mediated in biblical times and cultures do not carry the same meaning today. Hence, for example, the word "flesh" for Paul meant something very different from what that same word means for us today; in a modern context, the term "flesh" refers to a physical part of the person, whereas Paul used the term as a metaphor for the whole person and his or her way of life (see *The*

421

Humanist Christology of Paul [1986], volume 3 of *Jesus of Nazareth Yesterday and Today,* and *Grace and the Human Condition* [1973], volume 2 of *A Theology for Artisans of a New Humanity,* pp. 77-81). Merely to repeat the words would thus be to lose the message or truth expressed through those words.

Consequently, argues Segundo, the Scriptures are not so much texts that teach us information about God as texts that teach us *how* to learn about God. The Uruguayan theologian distinguishes between proto-learning, the simple acquisition of information, and deutero-learning, the continuing process of learning how to learn, so that we can discern God's presence in the new, unforeseen situations that we will encounter. In school every student acquires information (proto-learning) and learns means and methods for learning from future experiences which he or she cannot presently foresee and for which the present acquired information may, indeed, be irrelevant (deutero-learning). In the Scripture, persons learn the many different ways, or ideologies, in which God is revealed throughout Jewish and Christian history. By learning how God has become manifest in past cultures, religious practices, theologies, and politics, persons learn guidelines or clues for discerning the ways, or ideologies, in which this same God is manifest today, and they learn how to create new ideologies (e.g., concepts, symbols, religious practices) that will more truthfully and effectively make God present today and in the future. Although one can theoretically distinguish God's revelation (the content of faith) from the different cultural, religious, political, and linguistic forms in which that revelation is manifest (ideologies), in practice the content and form are inseparable. One never encounters the Christian faith except in the form of ideologies.

According to Segundo, only such an understanding of revelation can account for the many apparent contradictions in the Bible, especially those between the Hebrew Scriptures and the New Testament. For example, the difference between a God who is revealed in Israel's political struggle for liberation and a God who is revealed in the apolitical "turning the other cheek" is not a difference in gods, or faiths, or truths, but a difference in ideologies: The God who, in a particular sociohistorical context, condones violence in defense of justice may, in a different sociohistorical context (where, perhaps, such resistance may be ineffective, counterproductive, or unnecessary), call for nonviolent resistance. To suggest, as Christians often do, that Jesus' nonviolent ethic supersedes that of the Hebrew Scriptures would be to deny the equal authority, or canonicity, of the Hebrew Scriptures. Segundo argues that only by taking seriously both the historical unity of and the theoretical distinction between faith and ideologies can we avoid such an error.

Furthermore, the relation between faith and ideologies is what allows one to "translate" the biblical revelation into ideologies that will reveal how and where God is present today. For example, Christians are commanded to love and serve the poor. In the relatively simple society of Jesus' time, with its strict economic stratification, one loved the poor primarily by giving alms. Today, in a much more complex society, the influence of political and economic structures of power is much more pervasive and profound. Moreover, through participation in this complex, global network of structures (whether, for instance, as voters or consumers), persons have an impact on the lives of many people around the world, people whom one may never encounter face-to-face. Given this social complexity, one's participation in structures that promote or permit the unjust treatment of the poor necessarily implicates all participants in that injustice. Consequently, in today's situation, the Christian command to love and serve the poor must involve not only almsgiving but political action as well, so that these structures may be made more just.

Ironically, to limit one's love of the poor to almsgiving in our complex context may actually do more harm to the poor, in the long run, insofar as almsgiving, or philanthropy, serves merely to uphold, make more viable, and thus perpetuate the unjust political and economic structures, without bringing about any substantial change in those structures. Almsgivers, then, would be *literally* doing what Jesus may have meant, in his time, when he commanded persons to love and serve the poor, but *actually* perpetuating injustice and, therefore, disobeying Jesus' command. Christian faith, then, is fundamentally a practical encounter *today* with the living God, who is incarnate in everyday life, an encounter guided by this same God's revelation in the Scriptures. The biblical texts do not provide us with blueprints to be copied, or information to be memorized and repeated, but norms and guidelines to assist in discerning God's presence today.

The teachings of Scripture have authority for the Christian community because, and only because, that community has first experienced the concrete reality of Jesus Christ in its life; the encounter with Jesus Christ in the present is what lends authority to Scripture, not vice versa. In *Faith and Ideologies,* Segundo explains that, as human beings, all persons are attracted, first, not to abstract values or principles, but to specific persons whom we come to admire. Only then can one come to "believe" in certain values and principles, because one sees these embodied in some person's life and one thus chooses to become like that person. One takes on the values of specific persons whom one admires and seeks to emulate—often beginning with one's parents. One places trust in, or has "faith" in, these persons.

What is often called "religious" faith as expressed in the form of creeds, is grounded in this more fundamental "anthropological" faith, which is the faith placed in certain persons and on which lives are structured. Christian faith, then, is not *fundamentally* an intellectual assent to conceptual beliefs (orthodoxy), but primarily, though not exclusively, a practical response to the Jesus Christ who is revealed here and now in personal and social lives and in relationships with other persons.

This highly incarnational understanding of faith yields, for Segundo, an equally incarnational understanding of God and Jesus Christ. Segundo emphasizes in his interpretation of trinitarian doctrine the social and historical character of the God in whom Christians believe—over against Christian theologies influenced by Aristotelian philosophical categories that have emphasized the impassibility and immutability of God. Reflecting overly individualistic and rationalistic views of the human person, which are then projected onto God, these latter theologies result in a sacralization of the confessing *individual* and the rational *concept* as the fundamental context of God's self-revelation. But for Segundo, the fundamental context of God's self-revelation is the *community's historical* encounter with the God who has chosen to be revealed in society and in history. The doctrine of the Trinity is a community's attempt to express in conceptual categories its historical encounter with God in the person of Jesus Christ. Like all Christian doctrines, therefore, the doctrine of the Trinity is founded in Christians' experience of God. The Trinity is the Christian community's acknowledgment of that God as an essentially and intrinsically relational God, a God who is, in Godself, social, communal, historical, and personal. And to believe that persons are created in God's image and likeness is to believe that persons, too, are intrinsically social, historical, and personal beings.

For Segundo, then, what gives rise to the Christian doctrine of the Trinity is the experience of the incarnation: The former presupposes the latter. One's response to God is always, first, a practical response and only secondarily an intellectual, explicitly theological response. The disciples of Jesus were not drawn to him because they had, first, believed his teachings; rather, they came to believe his teachings only after they had been personally drawn to him—by his life, death, and resurrection. Anthropological faith precedes religious faith. This implies, further, that one cannot truly know Christ theologically, and thus "believe" in Christ, unless one lives a Christlike life through which one comes to know Christ concretely and practically, in one's relationships with one's brothers and sisters. This is the point of the well-known story of the Last Judgment in Matthew 25:31-46, where the knowledge that saves the "sheep" in the story is not religious knowledge but the practical knowledge of Jesus they had attained as they fed the hungry, gave drink to the thirsty, welcomed the stranger, and such. Indeed, the story does not even mention whether the saved had religious faith or were atheists, a question that is apparently irrelevant for the evangelist; what they did have, and what saved them, was an anthropological faith, a practical faith and trust in these hungry and poor persons whom they encountered and through whom they implicitly encountered Jesus Christ—a fact that was only retroactively revealed to them. Their religious faith was dependent on their practical lives of charity and justice, not vice versa. In our own context, it is possible to say that religious faith is dependent on one's willingness to feed the hungry and welcome the stranger, not only through charity, but also through political involvement that will help change those social structures which perpetuate hunger and homelessness.

Authentic religious belief in Jesus as the Christ is predicated upon a thoroughly human—and not explicitly religious or theological—response to one's neighbor.

Thus, in teaching his disciples what it means to be his followers, Jesus directs their attention away from himself and toward their neighbor, especially the poor. Moreover, as has been noted, the disciples' own attraction to Jesus was not dependent on some prior religious belief concerning Jesus' identity. The opposite is the case: Their religious questions concerning his identity were the consequence of their attraction to his humanity. Jesus' uniqueness was recognizable and credible only to those who were attracted to his humanity; to everyone else he was, at best, merely the carpenter's son and, at worst, a subversive and a charlatan. For this reason, Segundo suggests the possibility of an "antichristology," an understanding of Jesus that does not begin with the assumption that Jesus is God, or the Christ, but that begins, instead, with the assumption that what makes Jesus theologically significant is that he is humanly significant to us (*The Historical Jesus of the Synoptics,* 1985, p. 17).

Segundo's theological method thus yields a thoroughly incarnational theology. He in no way reduces Christian faith to ethical and political (i.e., ideological) commitments alone. (See Segundo's defense, in *Theology and the Church* [1985], against the Vatican's charge that some liberation theologians reduce Christian faith to political action, thereby secularizing the faith.) Yet Segundo's theology represents an important attempt to remind Christians that the God in whom they believe is always revealed and known in history and society, in the midst of communal and personal lives, especially in loving of the poor. That love, made historically concrete not only in interpersonal relations but also in sociopolitical commitment, is the foundation of all religious belief and theological reflection. Christians know a loving, just, and liberating God because they have experienced love, justice, and liberation, and in turn, they know this God only insofar as they love their neighbors, work for justice, and struggle for liberation.

Roberto S. Goizueta

Selected Primary Works

1962   *Función de la Iglesia en la realidad rioplatense.*

1973   *The Community Called Church.* Vol. 1 of *A Theology for Artisans of a New Humanity.*

1973   *Grace and the Human Condition.* Vol. 2 of *A Theology for Artisans of a New Humanity.*

1973   *Our Idea of God.* Vol. 3 of *A Theology for Artisans of a New Humanity.*

1974   *Evolution and Guilt.* Vol. 5 of *A Theology for Artisans of a New Humanity.*

1974   *The Sacraments Today.* Vol. 4 of *A Theology for Artisans of a New Humanity.*

1976   *The Liberation of Theology.*
1978   *The Hidden Motives of Pastoral Action: Latin American Reflections.*
1984   *Faith and Ideologies.* Vol. 1 of *Jesus of Nazareth Yesterday and Today.*
1985   *The Historical Jesus of the Synoptics.* Vol. 2 of *Jesus of Nazareth Yesterday and Today.*
1985   *Theology and the Church: A Response to Cardinal Ratzinger and A Warning to the Whole Church.*
1986   *The Humanist Christology of Paul.* Vol. 3 of *Jesus of Nazareth Yesterday and Today.*
1987   *The Christ of the Ignatian Exercises.* Vol. 4 of *Jesus of Nazareth Yesterday and Today.*
1988   *An Evolutionary Approach to Jesus of Nazareth.* Vol. 5 of *Jesus of Nazareth Yesterday and Today.*
1992   *The Liberation of Dogma: Faith, Revelation, and Dogmatic Teaching Authority.*

Selected Secondary Source

1979   Alfred T. Hennelly, *Theologies in Conflict: The Challenge of Juan Luis Segundo.*

JON SOBRINO
1938–

Life and Career

Jon Sobrino, who was born in Barcelona during the Spanish Civil War, entered the Society of Jesus when he was eighteen. After earning a master's degree in engineering mechanics at St. Louis University (1965) and a doctorate in theology at the Hochschule Sankt Georgen in Frankfurt (1975), he has taught at the Universidad José Simeón Cañas in El Salvador (Central America). Both his doctoral studies in Germany and his years of teaching in Latin America are reflected in his numerous writings, many of which have been translated into English.

One prominent characteristic of Sobrino's theology is his indebtedness to European theologians, especially Karl Rahner, Jürgen Moltmann, and Wolfhart Pannenberg. Yet in contrast to European theology, which has customarily sought a better understanding of Christian revelation in light of current philosophical questions, Sobrino has taken a praxis approach: Instead of simply engaging the contemporary world in dialogue, theology should help transform that world.

Sobrino's insistence on the transformative role of theology reflects his experience in Latin America, where poverty and injustice are pervasive, and where the cry of the poor and oppressed for liberation grows ever louder. Unfortunately, the attempt of liberation theologians and progressive church leaders to address these problems has frequently produced serious conflicts between the church and those in power in business and government. Such has certainly been the case in El Salvador, where thousands have been assassinated, including Archbishop Oscar Romero (1917–80), whom Sobrino served as an adviser. In 1989, a death squad machine-gunned six of Sobrino's Jesuit colleagues at the Universidad José Simeón Cañas; had Sobrino not been absent that night, he undoubtedly would have been killed.

Like many theologians of his generation, Sobrino has been influenced by the call of the Second Vatican Council (1962–65) for *aggiornamento* ("bringing up to date"), which means that the gospel needs to be preached in ways that the modern world can understand. And like many other theologians in Latin America, he has responded to the postconciliar opportunities and challenges provided by the meetings of CELAM (Latin American Episcopal Conference) at Medellín, Colombia (1968), and Puebla, Mexico (1979), both of which emphasized the need for justice and peace in tandem with an advocacy for human rights and human development.

By fostering *aggiornamento* within the church and espousing economic, social, and political reforms within their respective countries, liberation theologians like Sobrino have found themselves under attack not only by government officials and power elites, but also by various bishops and Vatican officials who have preferred to rely on traditional theological approaches and on long-standing diplomatic agreements between church and state. Such ecclesiastical officials have questioned not only the political and economic aspects of liberation theology, but the doctrinal orthodoxy of its proponents.

In response, Sobrino, like other liberation theologians, has defended his orthodoxy but insisted that the Latin American church must chart a new course and not simply repeat formulas that are often irrelevant and sometimes even conducive to maintaining injustice and oppression. In his quest for a theology that would truly foster the liberation of the poor and oppressed, Sobrino has made a distinctive contribution by asking the simple, yet provocative question: What does it mean to be a Christian today?

Sobrino's reply identifies the follower of Christ as a disciple who faithfully follows the historical Jesus by seeking to further the kingdom of God through serving the poor and oppressed. This response has three important facets: (1) a Christology of liberation, (2) the church of the poor, and (3) following Jesus.

A Christology of Liberation

For Sobrino, the starting point of Christology must be the historical Jesus, not the Christ of doctrinal confessions. Sobrino feels that this option is justified by the actual social and political situation in Latin America, which is similar to the one in which Jesus personally lived and worked. In other words, the history of Jesus and the historical situation of Latin Americans are mutually illumined: In his preaching, Jesus, the Servant of God, defended the fundamental rights of the poor and oppressed; similarly, persons preaching the gospel in Latin America must seek the betterment of the poor and the liberation of the oppressed.

Sobrino's decision to focus on the historical Jesus admittedly contrasts with more traditional Christologies that concentrate on the heavenly figure of the Son of God. Sobrino does not reject such Christologies; in fact, he has repeatedly acknowledged the binding character of the classical dogmatic formulas that proclaim the divinity of Christ. Yet, Sobrino has insisted that such Christologies are inadequate when they come to answering questions about what it means to follow Jesus in today's world.

For Sobrino, a Christology that concentrates on the divinity of Christ may easily forget that the resurrected Christ is none other than the historical Jesus who made a preferential option for the poor and oppressed of this world. By focusing on the Christ of the next world, one may ignore the faceless people whom the Jesus of history served. Thus, Christology should begin with the historical Jesus, in order to actualize his deeds and his attitudes in the present.

Looking at the historical Jesus, one can see that his basic practice was twofold: challenging the power of the privileged and defending the marginalized and disadvantaged. This practice brought Jesus into conflict with the religious and political leaders of his time. Simultaneously, the fundamental attitude of the historical Jesus was a gratuitous love that extended to all, including his enemies and ultimately even his executioners. Although the God preached by Jesus is a God who desires the salvation of all, nonetheless, this God is a God who has a special predilection, a special love, for the poor.

The preaching and practice of Jesus soon led to conflict with the groups in Palestine that then possessed religious, economic, and sociopolitical power. At the center of this conflict was his solidarity with the poor and his proclamation of God as a defender of the oppressed and persecuted. In effect, Sobrino's focus on the historical Jesus is not merely an exercise in speculative theology. Like the historical Jesus, his followers today cannot accept, much less justify, the presence of poverty, injustice, and hatred in the world. Indeed, one of the reasons why Sobrino and other liberation theologians have aroused the opposition of the wealthy and the powerful is their denunciation of nominal Christians who profit from situations of injustice and oppression.

The fact that situations of injustice and oppression exist in Latin America today provides Sobrino with an interpretative key for presenting the message of Jesus. The poor and oppressed can identify with the mysterious experience of a Jesus who was abandoned by the Father, with a Jesus who, in spite of this abandonment, maintained his radical fidelity to the will of God and a radical hope in the God whom he obeyed. Latin Americans can envision the crucified Jesus in the kidnapped, the tortured, the assassinated: all those who suffer for the sake of justice at the hands of the forces of "national security" and the modern idolaters of riches.

In this context, the resurrection of Jesus assumes a striking significance: The historical Jesus, who expended himself in the service of the poor, only to be abandoned by God on the cross, was vindicated by the resurrection. The risen Lord is the historical Jesus who inaugurated the kingdom of God, who manifested a preferential option for the poor, and who sought to transform the entire social and political situation of his day. Thus, the resurrection of Jesus introduces believers into the historical process by which he came to be Lord: His followers are called to share in the liberation of the world from the forces of oppression and to work for the transformation of humanity.

In other words, the paschal mystery is the summit of the personal history of Jesus and thus the fundamental fact of Christian discipleship. Jesus, who lived, not for himself but for the mission received from the Father, died for the salvation of all and has been exalted by the Father. This exaltation confirms the ultimate truth of the life and person of Jesus as Lord. Simultaneously, the resurrection is the universalization of Jesus' existence for humanity: His followers are called to actualize his lordship in the particular situations in which they live.

The Church of the Poor

The church is brought into existence by the crucified Lord. Nonetheless, if the church were to focus on the Lord of Glory without identifying him as the crucified Jesus, the church would be triumphalistic: a church that would claim to save people merely by informing them of divine truths, a church that would claim to be a depository of divine power. The church must resist such temptations by recalling that its Lord ministered to the poor, confronted the powerful, and was put to death for his unwavering commitment to the poor and oppressed.

Accordingly, just as the historical Jesus committed his life and his ministry to working on behalf of the poor, the church must concentrate its mission on the lives of the least fortunate, because God is the Father of all, because human beings are brothers and sisters. Thus, the church, which was brought into existence by the crucified and risen Jesus, must be the "church of the poor": a church that is concerned about the poor and oppressed and finds in them the basis of its structure and mission.

The church then does not exist for itself, but only in view of accomplishing its mission, the mission of Jesus: To prepare for the coming of the kingdom of God. To carry out this mission, the church should promote new ministries, not only on the basis of exigencies (such as the lack of clergy), but in order to be enriched by new ministers and new ministries among workers, campesinos, indigenous peoples, among others. Yet the mission of the church should not be merely intramural. The church should simultaneously seek to bring about Christian love in history by fostering basic structural changes and by expressing solidarity with popular movements organized to defend the legitimate rights of the poor.

Ideally, the church in Latin America should manifest the four marks or characteristics traditionally ascribed to the church: The church should be *one* by breaking down the barriers between hierarchy and faithful, between priests and workers, between campesinos and intellectuals; the church should be *holy* by promoting justice and fostering solidarity among all people, as Jesus did; the church should be *catholic*, both locally and universally, through providing mutual help, mutual inspiration, and mutual enrichment; the church should be *apostolic*, both in its reliance on the witness of the apostles and by its dedication to mission and evangelization.

Finally, the church should be the voice of the voiceless. The way in which the church is to live the reality of God in history, is through a fundamental option for the poor. Yet, such a commitment to, and such a mission for, the poor involves action as well as proclamation; and action leads to conflict, which was also the experience of Jesus.

Following Jesus

Discipleship has a prominent place in Sobrino's theology. For example, Christology does not simply tell us about Jesus; Christology presents us with the historical Jesus who summoned his followers to serve the kingdom of God; discipleship is a fundamental way of having access to Jesus and to knowledge of his person. Similarly, ecclesiology should not be merely a speculative study of the origins and structure of the church; ecclesiology calls upon Christians to constitute a "church of the poor," for in the poor, Christians meet the hidden face of Christ.

Sobrino has emphasized that the following of Jesus does not consist in imitation. Rather, the following of Jesus is a commitment to reproduce here and now the fundamental stance of Jesus. In other words, Christians are challenged to follow Jesus in the service of the Kingdom, to mediate his love through concrete praxis. For Christians, the ultimate question is: What must be done in order to establish the kingdom of God?

To be a follower of Jesus, one must discern the "signs of the times"; aided by the grace of the Holy Spirit, the disciple of Jesus is challenged to lead a genuinely Christian life. Following Jesus is then the process of transforming oneself into a new human being by serving the poor and oppressed. Like Jesus, who emptied himself in the service of others, his disciples must expend themselves in solidarity with the poor. Accordingly, followers of Jesus must draw near to the poor in order to meet Christ in them, and from them to learn what the gospel means by presenting Jesus as "the way, the truth, and the life."

In solidarity with the poor, Christians must clearly condemn all types of oppression and take those actions necessary to eradicate oppression and to promote human rights. In other words, it is not sufficient for Christians simply to proclaim the divinely given dignity of every human person; it is necessary for them to eliminate the historical degradation that prevents people from living with human dignity; it is necessary for them to change the social, economic, and political structures that are conducive to oppression.

Accordingly, disciples of Jesus must engage in the struggle for justice, which, although difficult, must be carried out with the demeanor of the Beatitudes. Followers of Jesus are to be merciful in the conflicts that are necessary for justice;

they should always search for justice with eyes fixed on the truth of God; they should be agents of peace in the struggle for justice, even when—in exceptional cases—the struggle for justice includes some form of violence. For Sobrino, disciples seeking to bring about peace in a situation of violence need to be persons committed to peace, but not necessarily pacifists.

Truly to be followers of Jesus, persons must seek liberation from every type of oppression, must foster the dignity of all the children of God, must have the courage to tell the truth, and must have strength in conflict and persecution. In following Jesus, his disciples will realize their own conversion from oppressors to servants. If his disciples have the spirit of Jesus, they will act with mercy and compassion; in working for justice, they will seek peace, and in seeking peace, they will act justly; moreover, they will do all this because Jesus did it.

And like Jesus, his followers will be ready to give their lives so that others might live. Following Jesus may lead persons to the cross, as has been the case with Archbishop Romero and thousands of others in El Salvador and many countries in Latin America.

Critique

Sobrino's theology has received considerable attention in the English-speaking world, sometimes favorable, at other times not. One of the anomalies about Sobrino's theology is that, although it is presented as a Latin American theology, much of his thought is influenced by European theologians; there is little reference to popular movements such as *comunidades de base* or *religiosidad popular.* Where the Latin American influence is prominent, it is usually in reference to the social and political situations that have long entailed the oppression of the poor. Some have felt that this has led Sobrino to overemphasize social and political issues, or even to promote a secular humanism. For example, some have claimed that Sobrino's view of the lordship of Christ seems to have relevance only in advocacy for a transformation of social systems.

From a more theological perspective, Sobrino's focus on the "historical Jesus" also seems somewhat anomalous because of his disregard for a chronological biography of Jesus, which many theologians would consider an impossibility insofar as the New Testament is "historical" only in a kerygmatic sense. Others have felt that in presenting the historical figure of Jesus, Sobrino has emphasized practice, at the expense of the message of the gospel. Similarly, although Sobrino has emphasized that discipleship means that the followers of Jesus must live by the Beatitudes, some feel that Sobrino's description of discipleship overstresses the need to work for justice, at the expense of personal holiness: In other words, his activist advocacy seems to leave little place for prayer and contemplation. One evident point of contention is Sobrino's view that a follower of Jesus may in exceptional cases participate in armed struggles for liberation.

Yet, as Sobrino has remarked, the theology of liberation has not always been read, much less understood, by some of its harshest critics. In any case, Sobrino's theology has had considerable appeal far beyond Latin America.

First of all, Sobrino's Christology presents the historical Jesus as a dynamic and challenging religious leader at a time when religion has lost much of its appeal; one can hardly read Sobrino's description of Jesus and his ministry to the poor without being deeply moved. In addition, the parallels that Sobrino has drawn between the situation of the poor in Israel at the time of Jesus and the poor today is very thought-provoking, particularly in light of the involvement of the United States in El Salvador. Finally, Sobrino's call to follow Jesus in the service of the Kingdom appeals to the highest ideals of Christian ministry to the poor and the disadvantaged, the oppressed and the marginalized.

In sum, Sobrino's presentation of Jesus and the gospel not only resonates well with the Latin American context, but speaks provocatively to the English-speaking world.

John T. Ford

Selected Primary Works

1978　*Christology at the Crossroads: A Latin American Approach.*
1984　*The True Church and the Poor.*
1987　*Jesus in Latin America.*
1988　*Spirituality of Liberation: Toward Political Holiness.*
1993　*Jesus the Liberator: A Historical-Theological Reading of Jesus of Nazareth.*
1994　*The Principle of Mercy: Taking the Crucified People from the Cross.*

Selected Secondary Sources

1984　Juan Alfaro, "Análisis del Libro 'Jesús en América Latina' de Jon Sobrino (San Salvador, 1982)," *Estudios Eclesiásticos* 59:237-54.
1988　Frederick Herzog, "New Christology: Core of New Ecclesiology?" *Religious Studies Review* 14/3 (July): 214-16.

MARK C. TAYLOR
1945–

The work of Mark C. Taylor may be considered the meridian point of late-twentieth-century theology. As a key architect of, and motivating force behind, what has come to be known as "postmodernist theology," Taylor has employed contemporary and avant-garde themes in the general culture to redraw the map of religious thought in ways not seen since the demise of the existentialist movement a generation ago.

Inspired first by the nineteenth-century Danish writer Søren Kierkegaard (who ironically is also regarded as the founder of existentialism), then by the German "speculative" philosopher G. W. F. Hegel, and finally by the present-day French thinker Jacques Derrida, the genius behind so-called deconstructionism, Taylor has helped resuscitate academic theology at a time when the enterprise lies ravaged by the neoorthodoxy of the 1960s and the anti-intellectual social activism of the 1960s and 1970s.

But Taylor's venture can also be viewed as a kind of theological "endgame." At least since the early 1980s, the gray eminence behind Taylor's probings and reflections has been Thomas J. J. Altizer, best known in popular circles as the prophet of the "death of God" during the tempestuous 1960s. The death of God has culminated with the "end of theology" itself—an idea that Taylor did not invent, but one that he has persistently and scrupulously pursued with the insight that what remains of the "divine" in a post-Christian, and even postreligious, world is the interminable task of writing.

The notion of theology as a sort of sacral writing that paradoxically does not reveal the sacred, but inscribes the anguish of God's absence, is of course Talmudic in origin, as many recent commentators have observed about deconstructionism as a whole. It is also a worldview well-suited for a generation of "religious studies" scholars who, more than a quarter century ago, left the comfortable cloisters of the theological seminary for the relatively recondite and anticonfessional environment of the secular university with its emphasis on the purity of scholarly production, and who probably along the way were obliged to efface any pretense of "faith" as well.

Taylor has spent his entire career as such a scholar, moving directly from the study of religion as an undergraduate major at Wesleyan University to earning a doctorate in the philosophy of religion at Harvard University and then finding a professorate at Williams College in Massachusetts. But it was less his personal mise-en-scène than the impact of Altizer that transformed Taylor in the late 1970s and early 1980s from a careful exegete of nineteenth-century religious thought to a most original author propounding what in his groundbreaking book *Erring* he dubs "a/theology"—a theological discourse that is strangely characterized by God's absence.

The fundamental and consistent theme that runs throughout Taylor's later and most influential writing, the theme of "total presence," which paradoxically signifies the evacuation of any sign of divine transcendence, derives from Altizer. For Altizer, the "death" of God on the cross is the founding event of the Christian tradition, which in turn comes gradually to be disclosed as the most holy "absence."

Whereas Altizer reads the doctrine of the Incarnation as implying the radical immanence, or "total presence," of deity within the world and by extension secular culture, Taylor turns this insight into a linguistic principle. As far as Taylor is concerned, "crucifixion" means that the divine referent is now contained thoroughly within the materiality of the text itself. No such thing as the "Word of God" metaphysically overarches and fulfills the purpose of Scripture.

The "death of God," for Taylor and for Altizer, consists in the actualization of the divine logos. But this moment of actualization is no longer an abstract subject for dogmatics. It amounts to the inauguration of the "word" as the process of writing, of an endless differentiation and production of meaning associated with texts, discussions, and commentaries.

Although the term "deconstruction" has a variety of obscure technical connotations within the philosophy of Derrida that cannot be explicated here, it connects closely with Taylor's intuition that written discourse does not congeal, but "disseminates" the meaning of words over time. Thus all writing is "deconstructive" in the sense that whatever seems to be signified by singular instances of speech is torn apart and dismembered through the movement of language on the page.

For Derrida, writing effaces forever the "presence" that allegedly lurks behind the word, even the Word of God. In Taylor's view writing is a kind of finality, or ending in silence, of what was once "revealed." Although it has the form, as Altizer would say, of "total presence," it is in fact the revelation of absence, the apocalypse of all utterances and sentences.

If deconstruction is the death of God put into writing, theology is the monumentalizing of divine absence. In *Erring*, Taylor explores this notion with wordplays and double entendres that are the signature of his style as an author. The theological mission is an "erring" in the sense of mistaking the act of transcendental signification for what is signified as well as of becoming an expository nomad and a wanderer—in the way that Don Quixote was a "knight errant." The theologian, like the Son of Man, has nowhere to rest, or to lay his head. The theologian trudges beside a caravan of rhetorical tropes and mobile phrasings across a wilderness of infinite textuality. Writing, according to Taylor, "presupposes an other that cannot be mastered." Taylor dubs this "otherness" that pertains exclusively to textuality its "altarity," a mode of sacrality that stems ultimately from the nonpresence, or emptiness, of what is implied in the inscription itself. Errancy drives both the author and interpreter, or translator, to "the edge of the abyss," to silence and even "madness."

All theology is *au fond* an "a/theology" in Taylor's vision, because the theological event of "writing down" annihilates the essential reality of what is transcribed. To speak about God is the same as for God not to speak. To delimit the divine presence as "theologoumenon," or as the core language of a theological legacy, is equivalent to an unmasking of the divine absence, of the greatness of space beyond the clouds, of an immense void in which the myriad stars of discourse twinkle remotely and enigmatically.

The no-thingness of the theological object, therefore, lays bare the root condition of theological language, which is negativity, the "not." In his book *Nots*, Taylor ventures into an arena that has not been seriously essayed since the late Middle Ages—negative theology. The "question of the not" is the primordial possibility of thinking itself, the "oldest" of subject matters for recollection, and reflection. Negative theology, the thinking of "not," defines the character of theology once the facade of divine reference has been stripped clean.

If the death of God is really an "eschatology" of signs, which is what we truly mean by "the end of theology," then the "deconstruction" of theological syntax elapses from the "that which is not" that is exposed in the writing down of God's word and purpose.

In his most recent work Taylor expands on such a negative eschatology through an examination of twentieth-century art and architecture. Out of this study of aesthetic forms and modes of experience he brings to fruition the deeper implications of what he means by a theology of the "not," or an "a/theology."

One should note that the very notion of "postmodernism" springs from certain strategic shifts that have taken place over the past several decades in twentieth-century art and architecture. Although the precise moment of conception for talk about the "postmodernist" style in the arts remains obscure, the expression has generally come to designate the change from the strictly formalist, material, or "painterly" preoccupation of such modernists as Picasso or Jackson Pollock to the pure representationalism of pop art, or the sensuality of performance art.

In his interpretation of the arts entitled *Disfiguring*, Taylor translates these sorts of trends into a theological idiom. Through the method of uncompromising abstraction, he says, modernism creates a sense of the "Kingdom" as wholly other, as "elsewhere." The theological correlate to modernism would be neoorthodoxy, for which eschatology is always a glance toward the "impossible possibility," as Reinhold Neibuhr would have expressed it, of the Kingdom.

The postmodernist analogue, says Taylor, is the writings of Altizer, who declares that the Kingdom is wholly immanent, that it is "everywhere." Just as postmodernist art finds an aesthetic opportunity in every kind of image or random site from a soup can to the saline pools of the Great Salt Lake, so postmodernist religious thought— if such a concept connotes a genuine movement instead of a cultural metaphor— means that the divine presence is "everywhere."

Taylor, however, claims that such a vision of postmodernism is puissant, but incomplete. The principle of "altarity" challenges contemporary religious reflection to think the absolute negativity that crouches behind both the modernist reverie before the abstract otherness of the holy and the postmodernist enchantment with living presence.

In *Disfiguring,* Taylor accuses both modernism and postmodernism of posturing for the sake of "utopia." The radical truth, according to Taylor, is that the prospects for utopianism have evaporated in these "apocalyptic" times. But neither is there any chance for "salvation," Taylor declares. "The door is closed, closed tightly; there is no upper room."

Just as theology terminates in an "a/theology," so art and the theory of art resolve themselves into an "a/theoestetics," a kingdom that is not a kingdom of anything, the pretense of presence that is utter absence, a religion that becomes cultural form without content, a system of "structures" that cannot save. Although Taylor would vehemently deny it, he remains, however, through and through a modernist. Indeed, the comprehensive project Taylor has undertaken since approximately 1980 can be described as a carrying forth of the modernist hermeneutic of historical experience through structural, as opposed to content, analysis. In the same way that the lushness of anthropological data flattens in the massive studies of Claude Lévi-Strauss into contrapuntal structures and binary patterns of cross-referencing, so in Taylor's hands the sweep of religious thought since the Enlightenment, as well as twentieth-century art history, unrolls as an irresoluble dialectics of presence and absence. In modern art the subject, or artist, grows irrelevant along with the nature of the "picture." The properties of the work of art, as contrasted with its object, are disclosed as its essential makeup. Art becomes increasingly self-referential as it turns abstract. The vocabulary of aesthetic experience is reduced to those "meta-structures" that reveal the "discipline" of art rather than what art actually bespeaks.

Similarly, Taylor becomes caught up, albeit self-consciously, in his own knot of "nots." The logic of self-reference always leads to insurmountable paradoxes, and Taylor repeatedly discovers himself in double-binds, and double-blinds, that he mistakes for the order of the world, when in fact they are but semantic mirages glimpsed when the mind has been wandering too long in what the philosopher Frederick Jameson calls the "prison house of language." "How can one communicate nothing?" Taylor asks in *Tears.* But that, in fact, is what Taylor has set out to do with his "a/theological" initiative. Taylor fails to realize that the problem of nothingness is generated in modernist thought by the view that there is nothing speakable, or intelligible, outside the endless chains of discursive innovation. Whether the starting point is the philosopher Ludwig Wittgenstein's dictum that "the limits of language are the limits of my world," or Barth's emphasis on the "infinite difference" between the temporality of religious forms of expression and God's eternity, the modernist theme recurs in Taylor's repeated attempts to make absolute the paradoxes of speech as they arise in the play of communicative action.

Taylor's constant juxtaposition, in both his early scholarly writings and his mature theological core, of Hegel and Kierkegaard may be construed as a long, Hamlet-like pondering of which of the two to choose. "Speculative" Hegelianism with its epochal insight into the complementary character of "Being" and "nothingness" remains the framework for so many of Taylor's meditations. Yet, in the end Taylor comes down on the side of Kierkegaard, on whom he wrote his doctoral dissertation and his first writings in the early 1970s.

The central figure in Kierkegaard's literary and theological musings is Abraham. Abraham is both a wanderer and an enigma. Although he is a "friend" of God, the deity remains opaque. Just as God rains brimstone down on Sodom and Gomorrah for crimes largely kept secret, so God calls upon Abraham to ascend Mount Moriah and sacrifice Isaac by his own hand. Although Isaac is the child of the promise, and the divine summons to filiocide contradicts the very moral law of the Hebrews supposedly pronounced from on high, Abraham responds to what Taylor calls the "call of the Other."

In the same manner that the founder of faith goes forth on hearing a "voice" that is conceivably malign and defies the standards of religious and moral reasoning, the "a/theologian" answers to the "not" that is all we can infer from the experience of "otherness." The sense of "altarity" now becomes Taylor's altarity. The epiphany of the holy is encountered not in a burning bush, but in a pun.

The pun of "altarity," of course, is Taylor's theological adaptation of Derrida's famous theme of "differance." Deconstruction, according to Derrida, starts with the realization that if one simply changes the "e" in the word "difference" to an "a," it is still pronounced the same. The argument works virtually the same in English as well as French. The "difference" of differance resides in the instant of its inscription, neither in its phonetic attributes nor in its "logical" relation to other terms. Thus it is writing, not language in the abstract, that reveals what lies behind language. What lies behind language is a "space" or "rupture" or "lesion" in the exact codings of the game of language. Through writing we find that language discloses nothing.

The same is true for theological writing, Taylor discovered in his earliest books and essays on deconstruction. But Taylor goes well beyond Derrida in seeking to craft what might be dubbed a "holy calling" in the nomadism of open-ended theological writing. Taylor's academic and literary productivity in itself has been remarkable over the years. But this productivity mirrors Taylor's perception that writing is comparable to Abraham's own vagrancy. Abraham's "sanctity" depends on his looseness, his uprootedness, his virtual status as an "outlaw," which is the English translation of the original Semitic word "habiru," or "Hebrew."

By the same token, Taylor persists as a self-conscious outlaw, or transgressor, in the settled land of long-standing, polite, academic theology. He is Abraham with the knife in his hand, raised above the "altar" of a twentieth-century theological idiom that seems to make sense to the multitude of its communicants, but remains hollow at the core.

In that respect Taylor is Nietzsche's "madman" in the marketplace, the stranger at the door, the evangel of what Nietzsche in declaring the death of God also proclaimed would be the unspeakable secret of liberal theology and dogmatic philosophy in the modern era—its underlying and inextricable "nihilism." Nihilism, said Nietzsche, is the meaning of the twentieth century. It is something we must stare in the face and embrace before it can be exorcised.

Perhaps twenty-first-century historical theologians will remember Taylor primarily as such an exorcist. Perhaps they will recall him as the one who finally convinced them that the emperor had no clothes, or that the end of theology was something more profoundly wrenching than what Barth identified as a crisis of the church.

Taylor's theology is incapable of assimilation into an ecclesial format under any circumstances. It is both "hermetic" to the extent that it remains, for most readers, alluring and cryptic and "eremetic" inasmuch as it counsels a flight to the desert. At the same time, it is self-consciously "nihilistic" insofar as it denies there is "anything" beyond the sign, any substance underlying appearance. "Behind every veil," Taylor writes in *Erring,* one discovers "but another veil."

Theology begins and ends in the desert, in the wilderness of words that have been untethered from their primordial acts of inscription, in the Sinai of a history that seems closed to all interpretation. Yet the "theologian" again and again climbs the mountain. As Taylor remarks—cryptically—in *Altarity:* "The 'text' of Abraham is finally indecipherable."

Carl Raschke

Selected Bibliography

1975   *Kierkegaard's Pseudonymous Authorship: A Study of Time and Self.*
1984   *Erring: A Postmodern A/theology.*
1987   *Altarity.*
1990   *Tears.*
1992   *Disfiguring Art, Architecture, Religion.*
1993   *Nots.*

HOWARD THURMAN
1900–1981

Life and Career

Howard Thurman was recognized by *Life* magazine in 1953 as one of the twelve great preachers of the century. Others have acclaimed him "one of the greatest spiritual resources of this nation" (Harding, unpublished MSS., 1992). Today Thurman is increasingly acknowledged to be the foremost African American religious philosopher in American history. A Baptist minister, he was also a university professor and chapel dean at several institutions, and he wrote more than twenty books on the spirituality of self-discovery, social struggle, and the convergence between them. His life spanned the black experience in the United States from the Jim Crow era of legalized discrimination in the segregated South to the current era of retrenchment following the gains of the 1960s black freedom movement.

Thurman's stature as a leader and mentor may be compared to that of W. E. B. Du Bois (1868–1963), black America's premier activist-scholar. Even before Du Bois's death during the inaugural years of the freedom movement, Thurman had emerged as another singular figure: as a religious leader and social prophet on issues of ethnic and interfaith reconciliation. He became a mentor to a new generation of African Americans seeking a nonviolent activism and a cross-cultural ethic. Among his students were the civil rights leaders Martin Luther King, Jr., Jesse Jackson, and Whitney Young, Jr. (Makechnie, *Howard Thurman*, 1988, p. 81).

Thurman's relative obscurity may be attributed to a contemplative style of leadership and mentoring that distinguished him from his more celebrated predecessors and more familiar followers. He was by no means the typical activist, and indeed, he was vigorously criticized by one commentator for exhibiting during the sixties "so little impulse to join" those other "American clergymen [who] moved down from their pulpits and into the trenches of social protest and reform" (Benita Eisler quoted in Smith, *Howard Thurman*, 1991, p. 198). Yet a thorough comparison of Thurman with his more radical contemporaries increases rather than diminishes his stature, for their vision and fortitude in many ways drew upon the pervading, culture-wide power of this one man's mentoring presence.

What most distinguished Thurman from his contemporaries, and from African American religious thinkers before and after him? Thurman scholars concur in acknowledging the distinguishing feature of the man's persona in terms like: "a 20th century holy man" (Bennett, 1978), "the mystic as prophet" (Smith, 1981), a "shaman and prophet" (Mitchell, 1985), a prophetic communitarian (Fluker, 1989), and a mystic-activist (Pollard, 1992). Mozella Mitchell especially, in her "Spiritual Dynamics of Howard Thurman's Theology" (1985), highlights the shamanic dimension of Thurman's genius. A singular feature of that genius was his ability to integrate the shaman's role with his professional identity as a university professor and chapel dean. Moreover he was much acclaimed by observers for the harmony and efficacy with which he achieved that integration. What accounts for the phenomenal coherence of Thurman's vocational identities, spanning the roles of minister, scholar, and theologian on the one hand, and mystic, shaman, and social prophet on the other? The answer begins in the African American folk religious tradition that gave him nurture; that gave him models of transcendence, and gave him a vocational mandate.

Biography

Howard Thurman was born in Daytona Beach, Florida, on November 18, 1900. Saul Solomon Thurman, his father, worked for the Florida East Coast Railroad, and his mother, Alice Ambrose, was a domestic worker serving both local white households and wealthy white vacationers wintering at Daytona Beach. The young Howard and his two sisters, Henrietta and Madeline, were reared primarily by their maternal grandmother, Nancy Ambrose, following their father's death when Howard was seven years old. He attended a private black high school, the Florida Baptist Academy, in Jacksonville, Florida, graduating as class valedictorian in 1919. Entering Morehouse College in Atlanta that fall, he was eventually be-friended by its future president, Benjamin E. Mays, and by "Daddy King," the father of Martin Luther King, Jr. Again, as class valedictorian, Thurman graduated from Morehouse in 1923.

Despite his evident academic merits, religious character, and leadership poten-tial, Thurman was denied admission in spring of the same year to Newton Theo-logical Seminary in Massachusetts on the basis of race. Undeterred, he went to Colgate-Rochester Divinity School where, due to the unexpected severity of the cold winters, he learned to keep warm by wearing newspapers under his clothes. In the summers he held pastoral internships at a black Baptist church in Roanoke, Virginia, where he was ordained in 1925, thereafter taking his first pastorate in 1926 at Mt. Zion Baptist Church in Oberlin, Ohio. Mt. Zion provided him with his first and only experience of pastoring a conventional Christian congregation. Also in 1926, Thurman married Kate Kelley, a native of LaGrange, Georgia, and an alumna of Spelman College. In 1929, following the birth of their daughter, Olive Katherine, Thurman began an intensive reading of Rufus Jones, the renowned Quaker mystic, philosopher, historian, and social reformer. He spent most of that year in private study with Jones at Haverford College, near Philadelphia, while Kate and Olive remained in Oberlin. That apprenticeship in the theory and practice of mysticism provided the foundation for Thurman's own spiritual practices and also his spiritual direction of others, as highlighted particularly in *The Disciplines of the Spirit* (1963). The young family was reunited in autumn 1929 when Thurman began his first teaching position at Morehouse and Spelman colleges.

Unfortunately, Kate Thurman succumbed to tuberculosis at the end of 1930. The following year Thurman took a leave of absence from Morehouse, entrusting the young Olive to the care of his elder sister, Madeline. Until the end of the summer, he traveled in England and Scotland and experienced a much needed recovery from months of exhaustion and despondency. His domestic fortunes took a brighter turn in 1932 when he married Sue Bailey, a friend and coworker in the Christian Student Movement (CSM). A national YWCA staff member, Sue Bailey was a native Arkansan and an alumna of the Oberlin Conservatory of Music, and she brought to their collaborative ministry a gifted role as a musical performer. In the same year Thurman began to teach at the Howard University School of Religion. In his seminary teaching and chapel preaching at Howard, Thurman perfected his characteristic meditative worship style. In 1935 the Thurmans traveled to India where they met with Rabindranath Tagore, the great Indian poet and spiritual leader. The trip became a seminal moment in the African American "pilgrimage to nonviolence," for it concluded with the Thurmans' encounter with Mohandas K. Gandhi, India's celebrated philosopher and practitioner of nonviolent civil disobedience. Gandhi effectively prophesied at that meeting that "it could be through the Afro-American that the unadulterated message of non-violence would be delivered to all men everywhere" (Thurman, *With Head and Heart*, 1979, p. 132). (The fermenting role of this event in black cultural history, as background to the emergence of Martin Luther King, Jr. and the movement of nonviolent direct action that he spearheaded, has been insightfully retold by Sudarshan Kapur in *Raising Up a Prophet: The African American Encounter with Gandhi*.)

Another dimension of the India trip had important consequences for Thurman. Among the South Asians he met was one interlocutor who challenged his African American commitment to a Euro-American Christianity that oppressed his own people and other dark-skinned peoples the world over. Pressured to account for the integrity of his faith, Thurman crystallized his characteristic distinction between "the religion of Jesus" and the religion of Christianity. That critical distinction was subsequently featured in his groundbreaking work, *Jesus and the Disinherited* (1949), and in his pioneering interfaith relations with Jews and Muslims, Hindus and Buddhists, Quakers and Unitarians, and many others. Upon his return to Howard University he became the first Dean of Rankin Chapel and began to devise innovative worship experiences that included the arts, meditation, experimental liturgies, and attention to social concerns. Eventually that emphasis issued in two commitments that framed the remainder of his life's work: a prolific publishing career, and the cofounding of the Church for the Fellowship of All Peoples in 1943. That year Thurman was invited to establish in San Francisco "a religious fellowship worthy of transcending racial, cultural, and social distinctions" (Thurman, *With Head and Heart*, p. 142). In order to build the first interracial religious congregation in the United States, he took a leave of absence without pay from Howard and, in fact, never returned. Among his other pastoral and prophetic emphases, Thurman developed the church as "a resource for activists . . . who were in the thick of struggle for social change [and needing] to find renewal and fresh courage in the spiritual resources of the church" (ibid., p. 160). Such a resource remains significant even today.

In 1953 Thurman embarked on yet another new challenge. He was invited by President Harold Case of Boston University to become Dean of Marsh Chapel and, coincidentally, the first African American appointed to such a position at a predominantly white university. In addition to his chaplaincy he served as Professor of Spiritual Disciplines and Resources and, in that dual capacity, influenced a generation of students in the latter half of the century—notably Martin Luther King, Jr., who was then pursuing graduate studies at the university. Other features of Thurman's tenure at Boston University included his use of radio and television media, and more extensive outreach to international students. Upon retirement in the early 1960s, he embarked upon international travel again, including a longed-for trip to Africa in 1963. In 1965 he returned to San Francisco and founded the Howard Thurman Educational Trust. The Trust, still operating today, was originally started to support Thurman's lecturing and preaching in the United States and abroad, to provide resources (books and audio recordings) for searching students, and to sponsor informal seminars in his home for a younger generation of religious and activist leaders. His autobiography, *With Head and Heart* (1979), was published prior to his death in 1981.

Biography as Theology

In his lifetime Thurman resisted applying the term "theologian" to himself. For that reason Luther Smith, in the first and still definitive introduction to Thurman's thought, *Howard Thurman: The Mystic as Prophet* (1981; revised 1991), begins by distinguishing Thurman from more conventional theologians. Thurman himself regarded theology as a systematizing discipline that, in its efforts to organize and

443

explain the divine nature and activity, violates the dynamic, creative, and varied manifestations of the divine.

> Thurman was not concerned that his beliefs about God, Jesus, the Church, humanity, and nature be compiled in a systematic theology. He had a bias against such an approach for he felt that once the system is formed, it is not able to speak to life in all its fluid manifestations. Life is so dynamic that it requires religious insights which are equally dynamic, equally prepared to change with the new demands or revelations which life brings.

Despite this disclaimer, Smith proceeds to "extract" from Thurman's writings and speeches "a core of ideas which constitute his theological foundation" (Smith, *Howard Thurman*, 1991, pp. 47-48). Smith inventories these ideas under the following categories, beginning with a kind of origin and goal of Thurman's theology, namely the self-in-community. On the one hand (1) his "theology begins with the individual," while on the other hand, (2) "defining community is the end purpose of his theology." The intervening categories provided by Smith are: (3) freedom and responsibility; (4) the transformation of evil; (5) the meaning of Jesus; (6) the nature of God; (7) religious experience; and (8) the inclusive church (ibid, pp. 53-88).

The unconventional nature of these categories as a theological "foundation" becomes evident after an initial scrutiny. Thurman's emphasis on individuality and human personality as theology's starting point, combined with the trajectory of his theology toward inclusive community, can easily be understood as displacing traditional theological priorities of emphasis: God, God in Christ, the gospel of salvation, or the church as the bearer of divine revelation. In traditional theology the formation of self and community follows from the doctrines of divine creation or revelation, redemption, or salvation. But Thurman inverts the traditional priorities. Not so obvious, however, is his motivation for such an inversion. It is convenient to attribute it to a mystical insistence on the importance of religious experience, a turn that is characteristic of mystical thinkers like Thurman. Mystical experience serves as one source for theological reflection for Thurman, along with his Baptist heritage and his use of narrative themes (Mitchell quoting Luther Smith in her *Spiritual Dynamics*, p. 2).

Mysticism, however, is often suspect to conventional theology. For experience is notoriously ambiguous, requiring interpretation by external criteria and, if not subordinated to these thoughtful, deliberated criteria, readily able to exceed its capacity as a medium of understanding and wisdom. Indeed, Thurman himself was suspected of mystical commitments that exceeded the boundaries of Christian identity. Thus Mozella Mitchell reviews the charges of "syncretism" leveled at Thurman, in another early assessment of his theological significance, *Spiritual Dynamics of Howard Thurman's Theology* (1985). Mitchell cites the observation by Deotis Roberts, for example, that Thurman was "inspired by the Quakers (especially Rufus Jones) and blends Hindu Mysticism (Advaita) with the Platonic concept of immortality of soul . . . [bringing] East and West together." However, Mitchell rightly denies that the mere inclusion of extra-Christian and quasi-Christian mystical sources in Thurman's theology constitutes syncretism. She claims instead that the inclusiveness of such sources serves the purpose of reconfiguring Christian identity and community with "a sense of interrelatedness and interdependence" (Mitchell, *Spiritual Dynamics*, 1985, p. 2).

A second way to analyze Thurman's theology focuses on his early religious training. Thurman was raised a Baptist, and though he served only briefly as minister of a traditional Baptist church before pursuing more exotic domains in his spiritual quest, we should hesitate to discount those influences. If one construes the "baptist" vision broadly as does, for example, James William McClendon, Jr., one can see Thurman's indebtedness to his baptist heritage. According to McClendon, the baptist vision includes: (1) *biblicism,* or the recovery of the genuine theology of the Bible; (2) *mission,* not as an imperialism but as responsible witnessing or evangelism; (3) *liberty* or freedom—freedom of the church vis-à-vis both the state and church hierarchy, and freedom of the individual conscience; (4) *discipleship,* not as vocation for the few or disciplines for an elite but as the service to Christ expected of all believers; and (5) *community,* formed by present-day believers and linking them to the primitive (apostolic) Christian church on the one hand and to the coming (eschatological) reign of God on the other (McClendon, *Ethics,* 1986, pp. 28-31).

These characteristics of the baptist vision dominate Thurman's theology. His insistence on distinguishing Christianity from "the religion of Jesus," his post-Constantinian critique of Christianity as "an imperial and world religion . . . [marching] under banners other than that of the teacher and prophet of Galilee," his free church style of eschewing hierarchical and ecclesiastical limitations, his modeling and mentoring of disciples in the "disciplines of the Spirit," and his lifelong quest for inclusive community across ethnic, religious, and political divisions, and as the most evident manifestation of the presence of God—all these highlights in his theological repertory connect him to, rather than separate him from, his baptist heritage (Thurman, *With Head and Heart,* 1979, p. 114).

Unlike many of his fellow baptist intellectuals, however, Thurman insisted on rendering his own experience—particularly his storied experience as an African American—as a valid source for theological-ethical reflection and discourse (cf. McClendon, *Biography,* 1974). Historically, most baptists, including black baptists, have

> failed to see in their own heritage, their own way of using Scripture, their own communal practices and patterns, *their own guiding vision,* a resource for theology unlike the prevailing scholasticism round about them . . . [They have distrusted] their

445

> own vision, their common life, their very gospel; whereas it might have been the
> resource for their theology, and theology in turn the means of exploring that gospel,
> revitalizing that life, focusing that vision. (McClendon, *Ethics*, p. 26)

Despite baptists' frequent failure to account personal experience as a theological resource, Thurman consistently grounded theological reflection in black religious experience. As early as *The Negro Spiritual Speaks of Life and Death* (1947) and *Jesus and the Disinherited* (1949), he anticipated the particular appeal of black theology, which was to emerge more than a decade later as a formal academic discipline.

Another way to analyze and interpret Thurman's celebrated storytelling style of preaching and lecturing, with his dynamic, nonsystematizing approach to theology, is to view him in the light of recent approaches to narrative theology and ethics. In this regard, Thurman's theology can be understood as a narrative theological imperative to live out or substantiate "the practice of doctrine" over against the mere analysis and explication of doctrine. (McClendon, *Doctrine*, 1994, p. 29). For, on the one hand Thurman "was not interested in persuading people to believe certain doctrines, dogma, theological systems, creeds or way of doing biblical interpretation" (Smith, *Howard Thurman*, 1991, p. 189). Yet on the other hand his "prophetic mysticism" (Smith), in its focus on the disinherited and the oppressed, and in its inclusive and reconciling love-ethic in relation to oppressors, generated practices that exemplified precisely such doctrines, dogmas, theologies, creeds, and biblical interpretations. Just here, however, a critique of Thurman emerges that has been applied to his most celebrated protegé and that other practitioner of "the beloved community," Martin Luther King, Jr. (See Walter Fluker, *They Looked for a City* [1989], for a comparison of these two related leaders.) Like Thurman, King sought for the beloved community, seeing

> no adequate account of the disciplined community, the church, that must be the
> kingdom's forerunner and sign. . . . Did the beloved community remain unrealized
> exactly because it sought only to be a disembodied church (or a church whose only
> body was the movement or the nation)? The issue remains with us. (McClendon,
> *Doctrine*, 1994, p. 54)

The issue of disembodied communities of practice is especially critical for disciples of Thurman, for successive leadership of his Fellowship Church in San Francisco has had difficulty in crafting the practices that would enable its members to replicate his seemingly idiosyncratic blend of inclusive Christian mysticism and prophetic social change. Of course, as has been indicated, Thurman deliberately avoided the fixity and authoritarian excesses of conventional church communities. But disciples today as well as the generations to come rightly demand structures and practices that preserve the wisdom and resources displayed in his vocation.

Although Thurman's legacy is universal in its power and promise, it is especially appropriate and urgent for African Americans to make demands on that legacy. Black America's need for racial and economic justice, for practices of civility, for humane and inclusive community, and for the spiritual discipline and moral character to achieve those goals, has not diminished but has rather increased despite the gains of the 1960s civil rights era and the activist legacy of King and others.

In this connection, Mozella Mitchell has affectionately chided Thurman on behalf of "those who admire his style and character of religious development and leadership but lack the stamina for the kind of rigorous personal discipline Thurman himself undergoes to reach spiritual maturity." Indeed, on our behalf as well, Mitchell voices the need for "a little more direction and methodology from Thurman" while also recognizing that it was "not within his character and intentions to offer such" (Mitchell, *Spiritual Dynamics*, 1985, p. 89). The Thurman legacy awaits a next generation of theological and ethical, shamanic and prophetic practitioners, who can fulfill in enduring communities the integrity that this master modeled in his own embodied person.

Theophus (Thee) Smith

Selected Primary Works*

1945/1975 *Deep River.*
1947/1975 *The Negro Spiritual Speaks of Life and Death.*
1947   *Meditations for Apostles of Sensitiveness.*
1949   *Jesus and the Disinherited.*
1954   *The Creative Encounter: An Interpretation of Religion and the Social Witness.*
1959   *Footprints of a Dream: The Story of the Church for the Fellowship of All Peoples.*
1963   *Disciplines of the Spirit.*
1965   *The Luminous Darkness: A Personal Interpretation of the Anatomy of Segregation and the Ground of Hope.*
1971   *The Search for Common Ground: An Inquiry into the Basis of Man's Experience of Community.*
1979   *With Head and Heart: The Autobiography of Howard Thurman.*
1984   *For the Inward Journey: The Writings of Howard Thurman.* Selections by Ann Spencer Thurman.

Selected Secondary Sources

1953   Jean Burden, "Howard Thurman," *Atlantic Monthly* (October).

1974   James Wm. McClendon, Jr., *Biography as Theology.*

1978   Leron Bennett, Jr., "Howard Thurman: 20th Century Holy Man." *Ebony* (February), pp. 68-85.

1982   "Simmering on the Calm Presence and Profound Wisdom of Howard Thurman," special edition, *Debate and Understanding* (Spring).

1983   Henry J. Young, ed., *God and Human Freedom.*

1985   Mozella G. Mitchell, *Spiritual Dynamics of Howard Thurman's Theology.*

1986   James Wm. McClendon, Jr., *Ethics: Systematic Theology,* vol. 1.

1987   Alton B. Pollard, III. "Howard Thurman and the Challenge of Social Regeneration: Transformed, Always Transforming," Ph.D. Dissertation, Duke University.

1988   George K. Makechnie, *Howard Thurman: His Enduring Dream.*

1989   Walter Fluker, *They Looked for a City: A Comparative Analysis of the Ideal of Community in the Thought of Howard Thurman and Martin Luther King, Jr.*

1991   Luther E. Smith, Jr., *Howard Thurman: The Mystic as Prophet,* rev. ed.

1992   Alton B. Pollard, III, *Mysticism and Social Change: The Social Witness of Howard Thurman.*

1992   Mozella G. Mitchell, *The Human Search: Howard Thurman and the Quest for Freedom. Proceedings of the Second Annual Thurman Convocation.*

1994   James Wm. McClendon, Jr., *Doctrine: Systematic Theology,* vol. 2.

* Many Thurman works have been reissued by Friends United Press (Richmond, Indiana). Also, a five-volume collection of unpublished Thurman writings and correspondence is forthcoming from the Thurman Papers Project, ed. Walter Fluker, the Divinity School, Rochester, New York.

PAUL TILLICH
1886–1965

There is a traditional distinction in academic circles between theology characterized by *synthesis* and theology characterized by *diastasis*. The word *diastasis* means "to stand apart," and so a theology of diastasis attempts to formulate its concepts apart from the philosophy and culture of society. A theology of synthesis, on the other hand, brings together theology and the prevailing thought forms. Since the earliest days of Christian theology, examples of both ways of doing theology have occurred. In the twentieth century, Karl Barth is most commonly associated with diastasis, and Paul Tillich produced what is unquestionably the best example of synthesis theology. For Tillich, theology should perform two functions, namely, "the statement of the truth of the Christian message and the interpretation of this truth for every new generation" (*Systematic Theology* 1, 1951, p. 3; hereafter *ST*). To this end Tillich made use of philosophy, psychology, natural science, art, and other cultural expressions to create a theological system that he felt best communicated to his generation. Consequently, Tillich's theology is most adequately described as a theology of culture or a philosophical theology.

Life and Career

Paul Tillich was born on August 21, 1886, in the small German town of Starzeddel in the province of Brandenburg. Since 1945 this town has been part of Poland and is called Starosiedle. In 1900 Tillich's father, a Lutheran pastor, accepted a call to a post in Berlin where Tillich attended Friedrich Wilhelm Gymnasium (an advanced "high school" for university preparation), graduating in 1904. He attended several universities (as was the German custom) and received the doctorate in philosophy from the University of Breslau in 1910 and the licentiate in theology from the University of Halle in 1912. That same year Tillich was ordained as a pastor of the Evangelical Church of the Prussian Union.

Philosophical and theological influences on Tillich's work were to come from several sources. Tillich studied philosophy on his own and at universities, acquiring an excellent knowledge of the history of philosophy. He became most interested in the philosophy of Schelling and wrote two theses on this Romantic philosopher. Tillich also gained knowledge of the work of Søren Kierkegaard, whose work was at that time being revived. Tillich was also very strongly influenced by the thought of Martin Heidegger, especially since both were teaching at the University of Marburg in the 1920s. The influence of these three philosophers was to have a great effect on the subsequent work of Tillich. Martin Kähler was one of the theologians who made the most profound impact on him. Kähler influenced Tillich's way of viewing the historical criticism of the Bible, particularly his view of the relationship between the historical Jesus and the Christ of faith.

At the outbreak of World War I, Tillich enlisted as a military chaplain. From 1914 to 1918, he witnessed the horror and brutality of war (particularly at the Battle of Champagne in 1915), and as he later said, much of his German classical philosophy proved to be conceptually inadequate. Consequently, after the war Tillich became involved with the movement of Religious Socialism as one of its founders. He and the other members of this group felt that they were entering a new period of history. Unfortunately their hopes were not realized.

Tillich's academic career began in 1919 at the University of Berlin, where he cultivated his interest in art that had begun during the war as a means of escape from the horrors of the carnage around him. Expressionism was the style of art that particularly attracted Tillich, and it remained his favorite for the rest of his life.

In 1924 Tillich was called to the University of Marburg, but soon moved to Dresden, Leipzig, and finally Frankfurt, where he remained until 1933. During this period he came into contact with the popular neoorthodox movement in theology, a movement generally associated with the name of Karl Barth. But Tillich remained highly suspicious of the neoorthodox position, feeling that it excludes all cultural problems from theological discussion. In addition to discarding such theologians as Schleiermacher, Harnack, and Otto, this new movement seemed to exclude all social and political ideas from its theological agenda.

As a result of his complaints against a group of Nazi Brownshirts who had beaten up some students during the winter semester of 1931–32, as well as for the publication of his book *The Socialist Decision* in 1933, Tillich was removed from his post at the university, later saying that he "had the honor to be the first non-Jewish professor dismissed from a German University" (*New York Times,* October 23, 1965, p. 1). While on a trip to Germany, the American theologian Reinhold Niebuhr saw the announcement of Tillich's dismissal in a newspaper and arranged to have Tillich invited to teach at Union Theological Seminary and Columbia University in New York City.

After considerable hesitation, Tillich moved to the United States and began what amounted to a second career. He taught at Union Seminary from 1933 to 1945, at which time he took a post as University Professor at Harvard University. In 1962 he became the Nuveen Professor of Theology at the University of Chicago, where he remained until his death on October 22, 1965. Tillich's body was cremated and his ashes were interred finally in a park named after him in New Harmony, Indiana.

Philosophy and Theology

As a theologian of synthesis, Tillich emphasized the importance and interrelation of theology *and* philosophy. For Tillich, philosophy first of all tries to understand being itself and the structures common to all the different kinds of entities. Only then can philosophy attempt to describe the unity of the world in common human experience, both scientific and nonscientific. In this sense, the distinction between philosophy and theology is difficult if not impossible to make, for, according to Tillich, "whatever the relation of God, world, and man may be, it lies in the frame of being; and any interpretation of the meaning and structure of being as being, unavoidably has consequences for the interpretation of God, man, and the world in their interrelations" (*The Protestant Era*, 1948, p. 86).

The language of being is common to both theology and philosophy, as is concern for being itself. But for Tillich the language of theology and philosophy is ultimately symbolic, although the symbols are different, and the concern that each has can express itself only through symbols.

Symbols

In *The Dynamics of Faith* (1957), Tillich summarizes his theory of symbols. Both symbols and signs point beyond themselves to something else, but unlike signs, which are arbitrary and interchangeable, symbols participate in the power of that to which they point. In so doing, symbols open up levels of reality that would otherwise be hidden. Recognizing that symbols are generated in a particular situation in response to certain needs, Tillich also avers that symbols arise out of the individual or collective unconscious. Symbols, he concludes, cannot be produced deliberately or arbitrarily. A final characteristic of symbols that Tillich identifies is that they grow when the time is right and that they die when they no longer elicit a response in the group where they originally found expression. Religious symbols express the ultimate reaches of being itself, but particular religious symbols address the specific questions of people in particular cultural contexts.

Related to Tillich's concept of symbols is his understanding of myth, which is a symbolic story or a story made up of symbols. We must use symbols and myths, because they express what cannot be expressed without them, but we must also see that they are not supposed to be taken literally as historical fact. A myth which is understood in this way is called in Tillich's terminology a broken myth.

Theological Method

For Tillich, the right method is as important in doing theology as the right tools are important to building a house. For doing theology Tillich devised the method of correlation, which explains the contents of the Christian faith through existential questions and theological answers in mutual interdependence (*ST,* 1, 1951, p. 60). The questions shape the answers, and in the light of the answers the questions are asked.

In the method of correlation, first, the human situation is analyzed in order to determine the existential questions which arise from it. Second, the Christian message is presented in a way that provides answers to those questions. The questions are existential, which means that they express humanity's deepest or ultimate concern. The analysis out of which the questions arise is also existential. In existential analysis "[man] has become aware of the fact that he himself is the door to the deeper levels of reality, that in his own existence he has the only possible approach to existence itself" (*ST,* 1, p. 62).

The analysis of the human situation yields the question that theology must answer, and this analysis poses a philosophical task. If in this analysis the theologian "sees something he did not expect to see in the light of his theological answer, he holds fast to what he has seen and reformulates the theological answer" (*ST,* 1, p. 64). Existential analysis and the resulting questions generate one side of the correlation. The other side is composed of the theological answers that emerge from revelation. Philosophy must provide the concepts and categories and the problems implied in them, while theology gives the answers drawn from the substance of the Christian message.

Source and Norms

There are three sources of theology for Tillich: the Bible, church history, and the history of religion and culture. The Bible is the primary source for theology because it contains the original witness to the events upon which Christianity is based. But the Bible is not the only source, because it could not have been either written or received without preparation in human religion and culture. The theologian must investigate the Bible using historical-critical methods while also reflecting concern with and devotion to what is being studied.

Church history must be included as a source of systematic theology because the formation of the biblical canon is an event that took place in the history of the church. Tillich's position is between the extremes of what he calls radical biblicism and the position of the Roman Catholic Church. In his reaction to biblicism, Tillich says that one cannot "jump over" two thousand years of church history and become contemporaneous with the writers of the New Testament. At the opposite extreme, some theologians limited their task to the interpretation of their own dogmatic tradition. Using a principle that he calls "the Protestant principle," Tillich opposes "the identification of our ultimate concern with any creation of the church, including the biblical writing insofar as their witness to what is really ultimate concern is also a conditioned expression of their own spirituality" (ST, 1, 1951, p. 37). The theologian, then, is free to use church history and critically examine it, without being actually bound to it.

The third source for systematic theology is the history of religion and culture. Theologians must use the material provided by these sources since the language they use, the culture in which they live and are educated, and the political and social context in which they work influence every theological expression that they make. Culture is primarily the source of the existential questions that theology attempts to answer, thereby determining the form of every theological answer derived from the Bible and church history.

Because the method of correlation requires that there be a connection between the two sides of existential question and theological answer, human experience, which establishes the connections between them, also becomes important for Tillich's theological method.

The sources for systematic theology and the experiences that mediate them are judged by what Tillich calls the "norm of theology." It is necessary because all sources and all experiences do not have equal value. Unless there is some principle against which sources and experiences can be judged, the Christian faith can have no definite content and theology can have no organization. In his own generation Tillich felt that a new expression of the norm of theology was necessary, one that expressed the peculiar situation of his time, which he described "in terms of disruption, conflict, self-destruction, meaninglessness, and despair in all realms of life" (ST, 1, p. 49). The question arising from this situation is "the question of a reality in which the self-estrangement of our existence is overcome, a reality of reconciliation and reunion, of creativity, meaning, and hope" (ST, 1, p. 49). This reality of reconciliation is the New Being, based on what Paul calls the "new creation" (2 Cor. 5:17). The New Being is manifest in Jesus as the Christ, answering the question implied in human existence, and it becomes Tillich's norm for theology. If this norm is combined with the critical and protective principle of theology, which Tillich describes as "ultimate concern," then "one can say that the . . . norm of systematic theology today is the New Being in Jesus as the Christ as our ultimate concern. This norm is the criterion for the use of all the sources of systematic theology" (ST, 1, p. 50).

Reason and Revelation

The concept of reason holds an important place in Tillich's theology. Tillich is concerned here not with what he calls "technical reason," that is, reason that uses logic and works to accomplish goals. For Tillich, the basic concept of reason is ontological reason, or "the structure of the mind that enables the mind to grasp and to transform reality" (*ST*, 1, 1951, p. 72). *Logos* is the term that Tillich uses for the rational structure of everything and in which mind and reality participate. Consequently, for Tillich the logos *is* ontological reason. Ontological reason has an objective side, which is the rational structure of reality, and a subjective side, which is the quality of the mind by which it grasps reality. There is also what Tillich calls the "depth of reason," which lies behind reason in both its subjective and objective structures and points to "truth itself," "beauty itself," and so forth. Existential reason experiences finiteness, conflicts, and the other ambiguities that are always present in actual existence. The resolution of such conflict and anxiety can be provided only by that which is itself not subject to the structures and ambiguities of finitude. The resolution, then, must come through revelation. Through the actual and final revelation of Jesus as the Christ the reintegration of reason is achieved. In spite of his participation in all of the ambiguities of existence, Jesus remained in union with God, who is the ground of all being, and this unity with God makes him the Christ. This revelation of Jesus as the Christ is universally valid for Tillich, and serves as the criterion of all revelation, all religions, and all cultures.

Being and God

The first question of philosophy—one that Tillich calls the ontological question—is the question of being. "The question of being is not the question of any special being, its existence and nature, but it is the question of what it means to *be*. It is the simplest, most profound, and absolutely inexhaustible question—the question of what it means to say something *is*" (*Biblical Religion and the Search for Ultimate Reality*, 1955, p. 6). Moreover, this question itself implies some understanding of what being is since being as such provides the possibility for asking the question. For Tillich, as for other existentialists, the basic issues are of being and nonbeing. Since the questions of being and nonbeing are ultimate questions, answers to them will necessarily be symbolic and incomplete.

Another ontological concept of importance to Tillich is that of finitude. Humans are unlike animals because humans have imagination and can thus transcend the finitude that is part of being human. One can know finitude by looking beyond finite being to infinity. Of course no one can envision infinity, but one's mind can be pointed in the direction of infinity by imagination so that one becomes aware of infinity. Humans, then, become aware of finitude through imagination. To be aware of finitude is also to be aware of death as inevitable. Human being is always threatened by nonbeing, which generates anxiety. For Tillich anxiety is an "ontological quality" that is as basic to human existence as finitude. Extensively analyzing human finitude and anxiety in *The Courage to Be* (1952), Tillich proposes that the question about what can save persons from the threat of nonbeing is the question of God.

Humans can ask the question of God because, being aware of their finitude, they are aware of infinity. Therefore Tillich defends the ontological argument of Anselm of Canterbury (1033–1109 C.E.), not as a proof, but as an analysis, because it shows that "the question of God is possible because an awareness of God is present in the question of God. This awareness precedes the question" (*ST,* 1, 1951, p. 206).

The question of the ground and power of being can be the basis of humanity's courage to be. This question can only be answered by the second half of Tillich's method: the exposition of the answer of God.

Before answering the question of being in the doctrine of God, Tillich offers a description of what people mean by the word "god" (here Tillich uses a lowercase "g"). The main theme found throughout this discussion is the necessity of concreteness over against ultimacy and transcendence in the idea of god. Whatever people hold as their ultimate concern they call "god." But they can be concerned only with that which they encounter concretely, and they can only be concerned ultimately with that which transcends every concrete and finite concern.

Tillich considers this conflict between the concrete and the ultimate in the concept of god to be the key to the whole history of religion. In a brief analysis, he argues that polytheism arises from the need for concreteness in religion; that the need for ultimacy, or the absolute, causes a move toward monotheism; and that one's "need for a balance between the concrete and the absolute drives him toward trinitarian structures" (*ST,* 1, p. 221).

The mark of monotheism is not that it allows only one god, but that the principle of ultimacy prevails over the concrete. Trinitarian monotheism affirms the quality of God that allows humans to speak of God as living; it is the concept that unites the ultimate and the concrete in God.

The question of God, based on the knowledge and experience of finitude, requires an answer in the form of a god who is both concrete and absolute. The fundamental proposition of Tillich's theological system is that God is being itself. God has being, God is being, but God is not *a* being. God does not exist as *a* being. God is the ground and power of being, and as such God is the answer to the question of being generally. Everything that is has both its origin and its power to be in God, in being itself.

Humanity can escape from finitude and its hold on knowledge, Tillich concludes, only by using the depth of reason, by imagining the infinite. Yet all descriptions of the infinite are expressed through that which we really know, the categories of finitude. Thus the question arises: How can humanity "know" God? How can one legitimately apply segments of finite knowledge to the infinite? Tillich answers with the *analogia entis* (analogy of being): Because "that which is infinite is being-itself and because everything participates in being-itself" (*ST,* 1, p. 239). He insists that, although it does not give us knowledge of God, the *analogia entis* does explain the possibility of knowing and saying anything about God. If humanity can only approach God through the categories of finitude, then everything said about God is necessarily symbolic except "the statement that God is being-itself" (*ST*, 1, 1951, p. 238). Later, Tillich modified this conclusion by allowing that the statement "God is being-itself" is the most nearly nonsymbolic statement that one can make about God.

Existence and the Christ

Tillich points out that the word "exist" means "to stand out" of something (from the Latin *existere*). But the word can also mean, somewhat paradoxically, to be included in something. For an athlete to be a "stand out" (or "outstanding"), he or she must also be a part of the group of athletes with whom he or she is being compared. Existence is a finite mixture of being and nonbeing—being that stands out of nonbeing. Consequently, humans experience conflicts and estrangement because, through finitude, they are estranged from their essential nature, from being.

For Tillich, the biblical story of "the Fall" (Genesis 3) is not a historical account of what happened a long time ago but is a profound expression of the human awareness of existential estrangement. Human beings possess a freedom to contradict their essential nature. But this freedom contains the anxiety of finitude. The essence of humanity is to be without sin; but this essence is not the actualized state of humans in existence. The essence of humanity without sin (or in the story from Genesis, the state of Adam and Eve before the Fall) Tillich describes as the psychological state of "dreaming innocence." The term "dreaming" describes the state of essential being, and "innocence" indicates unactualized potentiality. In the very act of actualizing freedom, the state of dreaming innocence comes to an end. Hence it should not be taken as a state of perfection. The act of disobedience in the Genesis account is symbolic of the estrangement that accompanies the actualization of freedom. Along with the realization of freedom comes self-awareness. Once again, the story in Genesis includes this self-awareness as the realization by Adam and Eve of their nakedness. The very positive elements of experiencing freedom and self-awareness are unfortunately countered by feelings of guilt and the fear of death. Estrangement from God is inescapable if human freedom is to be realized. Sin, then, is separation from God, from one's true self, and from others. Salvation is the overcoming of that separation.

Human beings are constantly trying to overcome the situation of alienation by themselves, but inevitably and necessarily they fail because all of their attempts emerge from existence, from the limits of finitude, and from structures of imperfection. Humans cannot save themselves. In their failure to save themselves, they see the need for New Being. The only way salvation (or reconciliation) can take place is for the divine reality to enter into estranged existence. This is precisely what Christianity claims happened in the life of Jesus. Jesus as the Christ is the manifestation of the New Being in that he establishes undistorted essential being within the conditions of human existence. The biblical picture of Jesus as the Christ contains no indications of estrangement between him and God, between him and the world, or even within himself. As a human he possessed finite freedom under the conditions of time and space, but he was not separated at all from the ground of his being. Since the council of Chalcedon (451 C.E.), Christians have discussed this issue in a way that describes Jesus as the unity of two natures in one being. In Jesus there was the divine nature and the human nature, each complete and uncompromised, yet both united. Tillich rejects this view if it implies a literal statement that God has become human in the sense of a mythological metamorphosis. But if what is being communicated is that the God who transcends the universe now appears in it under its conditions, then Tillich can agree. The traditional doctrine seems to indicate that within the one human are contained two static entities. Tillich prefers a more dynamic picture of Jesus as the Christ.

Within Christianity two central symbols indicate the way in which Jesus as the Christ is to be understood as savior: the Cross and the Resurrection. Tillich observes that these two symbols are by their very nature related and should not be separated. The Cross is the symbol of Jesus' subjection to the conditions of existence. The Resurrection is the symbol of how through Jesus the finality of estrangement—death—was conquered. For Tillich, then, salvation is understood as healing—the healing of human estrangement from God, the world, and oneself. There are three aspects of this saving, healing event. The first aspect is regeneration, which is the power of the New Being to grasp and draw those in bondage to existence. In being grasped by the New Being one experiences the opposite of the marks of estrangement (faith and love, among other things). Salvation is also experienced as justification, in that God accepts as not estranged those who really are estranged. Finally, sanctification is the process in which the power of the New Being transforms persons, not only as individuals but as communities.

Christianity and World Religions

Tillich discussed issues in the history of religions and world religions, but it is a safe generalization to say that he believed it was wrong to view the world religions as if only one was true and all the others false. In his most extended discussion of religious pluralism, *Christianity and the Encounter of the World Religions* (1962), Tillich rejects the traditional approach of comparative religions in which such concepts of God, humanity, and salvation are compared. Instead he proposes that interreligious discussion should start by examining how each religion discusses the "intrinsic aim of existence," which he also calls the "*telos* of all existing things"

457

(p. 63). In this work he considers three alternatives about the future of religions. The first possibility—that all religions will ultimately blend together—is not desirable since it would destroy the concreteness of each religion that provides each its dynamic power. The ultimate victory of one religion over all others—a second possibility—is also not a good option since this would mean imposing one particular set of religious answers on all other particular questions and answers. Finally, Tillich rejects the idea that the religious quest will (or even has) come to an end, because as long as there are human beings, they will always raise the question of the ultimate meaning of life. Tillich concludes that the reality to which each religion points breaks through the particularities of the religion, bringing individuals to spiritual freedom accompanied by the realization of the spiritual presence in other religions.

Conclusions

Paul Tillich has had a profound impact on theology, particularly in the United States, and he has left his mark on many contemporary theologians. Langdon Gilkey, John Macquarrie, and Robert Scharlemann are just a few of the prominent theologians whose work reflects Tillich's influence. Particularly influential have been Tillich's method of correlation and his theory of symbols, although neither is without serious problems. Terms such as "ultimate concern" as a definition for faith and the identification of God as "being-itself" or "the ground of being" have worked their way into the vocabulary of many nontheologians. Whatever future generations may say of him, Paul Tillich was probably the most widely known theologian in the United States while he was alive, and he remains one of the most influential of theologians even today.

Warren A. Kay

Selected Primary Works

1948 *The Protestant Era*, ed. James Luther Adams.
1951 *Systematic Theology*, vol. 1.
1957 *Systematic Theology*, vol. 2.
1963 *Systematic Theology*, vol. 3.
1955 *Biblical Religion and the Search for Ultimate Reality*.
1957 *The Dynamics of Faith*.
1963 *Christianity and the Encounter of the World Religions*.
1967 *A History of Christian Thought. From Its Judaic and Hellenistic Origins to Existentialism*, ed. Carl E. Braaten.

1987/1994 The best edition of Paul Tillich's most important books and articles is Paul Tillich, *Main Works/Hauptwerke*, 6 vols., ed. Carl Heinz Ratschow.
1987   *On Art and Architecture*, ed. John Dillenberger and Jane Dillenberger.
1990   *Theology of Peace*, ed. Ronald H. Stone.

Selected Secondary Sources

1976   Wilhelm Pauck and Marion Pauck, *Paul Tillich: His Life and Thought*, vol. 1: *Life*.
1980   Carl Heinz Ratschow, *Paul Tillich*, trans. Robert P. Scharlemann.
1982   Charles W. Kegley, ed., *The Theology of Paul Tillich*, 2nd ed.
1984   John P. Newport, *Paul Tillich*, Makers of the Modern Theological Mind.
1985   James Luther Adams, Wilhelm Pauck, Roger Lincoln Shinn, eds., *The Thought of Paul Tillich*.

THOMAS F. TORRANCE
1913–

Thomas Forsyth Torrance is one of the leading Reformed theologians in the Anglo-Saxon world. In 1978 he was awarded the Templeton Foundation Prize for Progress in Religion for his contributions in theology and its relation to natural science.

Life and Career

Torrance was born in China in 1913 and lived there for the first fourteen years of his life. His parents were missionaries of spiritual depth (his father was from the Church of Scotland, his mother was Anglican). They provided Tom with a decidedly missionary and evangelical outlook that has been passed on to his children, who are, variously, engaged in ministry or theological work.

In 1927 the Torrance family left China for Scotland. However, Torrance's father returned to the mission field for another seven years while the rest of the family remained in Scotland where Torrance pursued his education.

Torrance entered Edinburgh University in 1931 where he studied classics (Latin and Greek) and philosophy. Two of his teachers were Norman Kemp Smith, an authority on Kant and Hume, and A. E. Taylor, who was an expert in Platonic thought. Three years later Torrance moved to New College, the Divinity faculty, where he studied systematic theology with H. R. Mackintosh, who introduced Torrance to the theology of Karl Barth.

At this early stage in his theological development, Torrance became convinced that any rigorous scientific approach to Christian theology must begin with actual knowledge of God reached through God's self-revelation in Christ and the Holy Spirit. Theology's task is to inquire into the essential connections embodied in the knowledge of God as it arises out of God's relation to humanity in creation and redemption. This basic orientation, combined with his interest in physical science, reappears throughout Torrance's subsequent work.

In 1937 Torrance won a scholarship that enabled him to pursue postgraduate studies with Karl Barth in Basel, Switzerland. There Torrance proposed to work out a scientific account of Christian theology from its christological and soteriological center and in the light of its constitutive trinitarian structure. Barth suggested a less ambitious project, which resulted in his dissertation, *The Doctrine of Grace in the Apostolic Fathers*. Torrance acknowledges that his two semesters spent with Barth had a tremendous impact on him.

Torrance's studies in Basel were interrupted when John Baillie persuaded him to take a position at Auburn Seminary in New York City. After a year at Auburn, Torrance (then twenty-six years old) was offered a position at Princeton University in the new Department of Religion. But it was June 1939. The situation in Europe was tense, and Torrance decided to return to Scotland with the intent of becoming an army chaplain.

However, since there was a two-year waiting list, Torrance spent a year at Oriel College, Oxford, working on his thesis. He then accepted a call to serve the parish of Alyth, a small country town in Scotland a few miles northwest of Dundee where he was pastor from 1940 to 1943. Toward the end of World War II, Torrance did serve as an army chaplain, first in the Middle East, and then in Italy as a Church of Scotland Chaplain to a battalion, the King's Own Rifles.

After the war, Torrance completed his thesis. With his studies behind him, he returned to the church he had served in Alyth. There he married Margaret Spear, an Anglican from Bath, Somerset. The following year (1947) they moved to Aberdeen, and Torrance became the minister of the large Beechgrove Church where H. R. Mackintosh, A. J. Gossip, and J. S. Stewart had all served. During this time Torrance published a book on Calvin's doctrine of man (1949), an attempt to untangle the debate between Barth and Brunner on the relation between nature and grace. He also founded the Scottish Church Theological Society and started the *Scottish Journal of Theology*, which he edited for more than thirty years. In 1950 Torrance was called to the Church History Chair at New College, University of Edinburgh. He switched to the Chair of Christian Dogmatics in 1952, where he taught until his retirement in 1979.

Also in 1952 Torrance began the monumental task of overseeing the English translation of Karl Barth's *Church Dogmatics*, a project that continued for twenty-five years and kept Torrance in intense and sustained interaction with Barth's theology throughout most of his career. Despite a number of significant disagreements with Barth, this interaction unquestionably influenced Torrance's theological development.

Torrance was also heavily involved in the ecumenical movement under the auspices of the World Council of Churches. He served on the Faith and Order Commission from 1952 to 1962. He was one of the key figures in the dialogue between the Reformed churches and the Eastern Orthodox Church. Always deeply involved in the life of the church, Torrance served as Moderator of the Church of Scotland from 1976 to 1977.

Torrance is a member of the International Academy of Religious Sciences (having served as its president from 1972 to 1981) and the International Academy of the Philosophy of Sciences. He is also a Fellow of the Royal Society of Edinburgh and the British Academy. He has published more than twenty-five books and several hundred articles dealing with all the principal themes in theology and has lectured throughout the world. His special focus has been on theological method, what he calls "Philosophy of the Science of Theology," and the dialogue between theology and natural science. He has also contributed to patristic and Reformation studies, as evident in his recent books, *The Trinitarian Faith* (1988), on the theology of the Nicene-Constantinopolitan Creed, and *The Hermeneutics of John Calvin*. His earlier work, *Theological Science* (1969), received the first Collins Award.

Under the aegis of the Templeton Foundation, Torrance recently edited a series of books on theology and scientific culture, Theology and Science at the Frontiers of Knowledge, which envisages nothing less than "a reconstruction of the very foundations of modern thought and culture." This indicates Torrance's conviction that Western civilization is in the midst of a tremendous intellectual and cultural upheaval in which older patterns of thought have broken down. His concern is that science and theology work together to reground Western culture intellectually in a time of unprecedented fragmentation.

Theological Themes

When asked about what constituted the heart of his theology, Torrance once remarked that "it is deeply Nicene and doxological (theology and worship going inextricably together), with its immediate focus on Jesus Christ as Mediator, and its ultimate focus on the Holy Trinity" (See "Tom Torrance," 1976, p. 14). From early in his career, Torrance has sought a rigorous scientific approach to theology that would allow actual knowledge of God, attained through careful attention to God's self-revelation in Christ, to determine the structure and material content of theology.

While reading the second chapter of the half-volume on the revelation of the Triune God in Barth's *Church Dogmatics,* Torrance uncovered what he was looking for in the doctrines of the hypostatic union between the two natures of Jesus Christ and the consubstantial communion between the persons of the Trinity. Here Torrance believed that he was probing the "essential connections" embodied in our knowledge of God upon which he could build a coherent account of Christian theology in a rigorously scientific mode. Torrance has pursued this theological goal throughout his career in the hope that it would lead to a core of basic theological concepts and relations that could serve to clarify and simplify the corpus of accumulated doctrines in theology.

Theological Method

For Torrance, theology is always faith seeking understanding. It is one aspect of the church's response to God in worship, obedience, and mission. Furthermore, theology can never be more than a refinement and extension of our ordinary knowledge of God that arises out of the evangelical experience and worshiping life of the church as it meditates on the message of Scripture.

Theology returns to the biblical witness, with the aid of the church's theological reflection throughout its history, to refine, extend, correct, and unify the church's knowledge of God. A rigorous scientific theology pursues this end by allowing the *nature* of its object or subject matter (God in God's self-revelation) to determine its methods and ways of expressing its results.

Torrance sees theology as unfolding and presenting the content of the Word of God within the life of the church on the basis of the incarnation in Jesus Christ and the apostolic witness. Such a theology finds itself immediately focused upon Jesus Christ as Mediator.

Jesus Christ

At the center of Torrance's theology is the whole incarnate life, death, and resurrection of Jesus Christ, who is none other than God the Son, the second Person of the Triune God, present to persons in astonishing closeness as a human being, Jesus of Nazareth.

This orientation makes Christology pivotal in all our knowledge of God, for the incarnation of the Word or Son of God provides not only a revelation of God, but the actualization of knowledge of God *within* the human condition. Here, Torrance speaks of the vicarious humanity of Jesus Christ. In Jesus Christ, the eternal Word of God graciously condescended to participate in the human condition, fulfilling God's revealing and redeeming purposes. Yet this same Jesus Christ is a truly human being who provides a true and faithful human response to the revelation Christ incarnated. Thus in Jesus Christ, real knowledge of God is realized within the undiminished reality of our humanity, which Jesus Christ assumed vicariously on our behalf. This means that Christ is not only God's exclusive language to humanity, but also the embodiment of humanity's knowledge of God and response to God.

Furthermore, following the Greek fathers, Torrance argues that Christ assumed our fallen and diseased humanity. However, far from sinning or being contaminated by the alienated human condition, Christ overcame the destructive evil entrenched in the human situation. From his birth to his resurrection, Christ condemned sin, reconciled humans to God, and re-created humanity for new life in union with God through Christ and in the Holy Spirit.

Thus there is a deep interrelation in Torrance's theology between the incarnation and the atonement, and between revelation, reconciliation, and redemption, all on the basis of the vicarious humanity of Christ. In Jesus Christ, revelation and knowledge of that revelation are actualized within our human existence.

The Triune God

However, as the early church reflected on its experience of the revelation of God in Jesus Christ, the church discovered that its knowledge of God was *trinitarian* from the outset, though in an implicit manner. Torrance argues that in Jesus Christ, the church found itself in touch not just with a mode or aspect of God, but with God's very self. Thus the early church felt compelled to affirm a oneness in being *(homoousion)* between the Son of God in Jesus Christ and the One God Jesus called "Father." Yet the church knew that this incarnate form of God's self-revelation and self-communication in Jesus Christ is only understandable to us and realized with us through God's self-giving in the Holy Spirit poured out at Pentecost. Thus the church again felt compelled to affirm a oneness in being not only between God the Father and God the Son, but also with reference to God the Holy Spirit.

In distinguishing between God's self-giving in Jesus Christ and God's self-giving in the Holy Spirit, the church found that it had to recognize ineffable differentiations within God. What God is for humans in God's revealing and redemptive activity as Father, Son, and Holy Spirit, God is antecedently and eternally in God's own Being.

Utterly inexpressible though the Holy Trinity is, the early Christians were convinced that they had to affirm the Trinity, not simply in their exegesis of Scripture, but because the Trinity is already there in the church's most basic evangelical knowledge, experience, and worship of God the Father through Jesus Christ in the Holy Spirit.

Thus the Trinity is the ultimate focus of Torrance's theology, for in the Trinity we find the ultimate ground of all knowledge and experience of God. Theology investigates and brings to coherent articulation the essential connections embodied in this knowledge of God.

Philosophy of the Science of Theology

In Torrance's mind rigorous reflection upon the content of God's self-revelation is not enough. The theologian must go a step farther and reflect upon the *process* of scientific activity in theology. The theologian must attempt to clarify *how* theology has arrived at its basic concepts, like the doctrine of the Trinity.

Torrance calls this activity of clarifying how theology proceeds, "Philosophy of the Science of Theology." It is analogous to Philosophy of Science in the natural sciences. Torrance has devoted a significant portion of his theological career to this task of clarifying how theology goes about its scientific activity.

Realism as an Alternative to Dualism

Dualism might be defined as the division of reality into two independent or incompatible domains. Torrance sees dualism (cosmological and epistemological) as an enemy of Christian faith.

In cosmological dualism a gap is posited between God and the world. Whether in the Greco-Roman philosophy in the cultural and philosophical milieu of the early church or the Newtonian or Deistic versions of the modern period, a deep gulf between God and the world makes it impossible for any real Word to pass from God to the world of space and time.

In epistemological dualism the gap is between the human subject as a knower and the realm of objects that the human subject seeks to know. This form of dualism maintains that one cannot really know reality in itself, because all knowing is colored by the cultural milieu in which we are immersed. Torrance rejects both forms of dualism and affirms realism in their place.

Rather than view God in separation from the universe (or as the inner identity of the universe, the "Ground of Being," as in many forms of theology today), Torrance offers a "realist" or "interactionist" theology as an alternative. Here God is viewed as interacting closely with the world of nature and history, while remaining distinct from it.

This enables Torrance to develop a realist interpretation of God's self-revelation. Torrance views God as interacting with the nation of Israel, as reflected in the Hebrew Scriptures, and even as entering human history in the incarnation in Jesus Christ and in the outpouring of the Holy Spirit at Pentecost. Revelation is not a series of symbols created by human imagination, but rather the living God entering into history, providing real divine self-communication and knowledge not of human invention.

Torrance also argues for a realist epistemology that sees reality as disclosing itself to human knowing in such a way that human beings are capable of real understanding of the created reality of the natural world and also of God. Torrance views this as a basic affirmation of trust (ultimate belief) in reality that is operative everywhere in our everyday experience and confirmed by the success of scientific endeavor. Persons go about the daily business of life believing that they are really able to know their world. Thus, Torrance sees a remarkable continuity between the human subject and object of knowledge, rather than a disjunction that makes real knowledge impossible, as in the case of dualism.

Yet for Torrance, knowledge is not automatic. There is *not* a necessary correlation between reality and thought, but only an actual correlation *if* the human knower actively responds to the self-presentation of reality in the appropriate manner. This means that Torrance is a critical realist rather than a naive one.

It is fairly easy to see that Torrance's entire theological project depends on this clear rejection of dualism and his staunch affirmation of realism. However, in Torrance's mind, it is God's self-revelation in the incarnation in Jesus Christ that is at the root of his rejection of dualism and affirmation of realism.

Conclusion

Throughout his career Torrance's intent has been to prepare the way for a restatement of Christian theology, especially the kind of theology found in Calvin and Barth, in the rigorous scientific context of the present day. In addition, Torrance wants to evangelize the foundations of scientific culture so that Christian faith can take root there. In fact, Torrance views his work in theology as an attempt to do today what Athanasius (his favorite theologian) and the other Greek fathers did in theirs. Rather than let the dualisms latent in the cultural milieu deform theological reflection, theology should allow the realism of the gospel to transform the surrounding cultural mind-set. It is not enough for the church to evangelize individuals. Christian faith must evangelize the entire culture, including the controlling ideas of modern scientific civilization. Only then will the gospel deeply take root and grow within the modern world.

Elmer M. Colyer

Selected Primary Works

1969   *Space, Time, and Incarnation.*
1969   *Theological Science.*
1971   *God and Rationality.*
1976   *Space, Time, and Resurrection.*
1980   *The Ground and Grammar of Theology.*
1982   *Reality and Evangelical Theology.*
1983   *The Mediation of Christ.*
1984   *Transformation and Convergence in the Frame of Knowledge.*
1985   *Reality and Scientific Theology.*
1988   *The Trinitarian Faith.*

1989   *The Christian Frame of Mind.*

1990   *Karl Barth: Biblical and Evangelical Theologian.*

Selected Secondary Sources

1976   R. D. Kernoha, "Tom Torrance: The Man and the Reputation," *Life and Work* 32, no. 5 (May): 14.

1984   John Hesselink, "A Pilgrimage in the School of Faith—An Interview with T. F. Torrance," in *Reformed Review* 38/1 (Autumn): 49-64.

1984   Robert J. Palma, "Thomas F. Torrance's Reformed Theology," *Reformed Review* 38/1 (Autumn):1-46.

1988   A. Walker, ed., "Interview with Professor Thomas F. Torrance," in *Different Gospels*, pp. 42-54.

1989   Daniel Hardy, "Thomas F. Torrance," in David F. Ford, ed., *The Modern Theologians: An Introduction to Christian Theology in the Twentieth Century,* vol. 1, pp. 71-90.

DAVID TRACY

1939–

Life and Career

David Tracy, the Andrew Thomas Greeley and Grace McNichols Greeley Distinguished Service Professor of Roman Catholic Studies at the University of Chicago Divinity School since 1987, was born on January 6, 1939, in Yonkers, New York. Tracy's theological education consisted of initial seminary training at St. Joseph's Seminary, Yonkers, New York, followed by studies leading to a licentiate in 1964 and a doctorate in 1969 from the Gregorian University in Rome. He was ordained a priest for the Diocese of Bridgeport, Connecticut, in 1963. In 1967 Tracy assumed the position of Instructor in Theology at the Catholic University of America in Washington, D.C. Two years later he became Professor of Theology at the University of Chicago, where he has taught for more than a quarter century. In 1977 Professor Tracy was elected President of the Catholic Theological Society of America. He is a member of the American Academy of Arts and Sciences, he has written or cowritten eight books and more than one hundred and thirty articles, and he has served on half a dozen prominent theological editorial boards.

This impressive list of appointments and accomplishments includes only the most easily named contributions to the field of theology that David Tracy has made. All of his scholarship has been stamped by the transcendental imperatives rooted in his early study with Bernard Lonergan: "Be attentive, be intelligent, be rational, be responsible, develop and, if necessary, change." From his earliest work on an analysis of Lonergan's work, through his texts on fundamental theology, systematics, hermeneutics, church history, the dialogue with non-Christian religions, and currently, on the naming of God, Tracy has displayed a careful scholarship, judicious evaluation, and bold planning that few scholars have been able to accomplish.

In constant conversation with fellow scholars in many fields, he has kept his readers abreast of the trends of postmodern scholarship in a unique way. Schleiermacher and Barth, Rahner and von Balthasar, Hegel and Nietzsche, Ricoeur and

Derrida, Eliade and Abe, Booth and Kristeva, and so many more—all seem to sit at Tracy's table engaged in conversation about the knowing and valuing that most enrich the complex life of the late-twentieth-century Christian. Because of the array of conversations in which Tracy is involved, his theological scholarship is not easily characterized by standard categories, such as fundamental, systematic, historical, or mystical theology. Throughout his work Tracy stretches and revises both the conventional categories of the theological conversation as well as the expectations that the nontheologian has about the religious dimensions of human existence and the Christian faith in particular.

The Hermeneutical Character of Tracy's Theology

The task of the theologian in Tracy's view is, in a word, interpretation. Much of what Tracy writes is an explanation of the conditions, methods, possibilities, and problems that any theologian faces in the continuing project of understanding the meaning and truth of the Christian tradition in the contemporary world. Because of this focus on interpretation, Tracy's work can be appropriately described as *hermeneutical*—that is, a mode of theological reflection which explicitly raises the question of how human understanding and its objects, often described as "texts," shape and are shaped by the cultures, economies, social structures, traditions, sciences, languages, and symbols of the times. Interpretation is "thickly" described throughout the corpus of Tracy's work. Thus, one way to understand the task of the theologian in Tracy's perspective is to understand what is entailed by "interpretation."

For Tracy interpretation is an activity encompassed by the larger notion of *participatory understanding.* As human beings we exist in our worlds by the ways we understand. We find ourselves already in a history, language, culture, and society, prior to any choice on our part. Human being does not start with a clean slate historically, linguistically, or genetically. Rather, human existence already finds itself participating—on the way. Human existence works, so to speak, transparently: We speak the sentences of our natural language without constant consultation of grammar books; we share the symbols of our cultures and histories without constant recourse to cultural dictionaries. In short, we already understand much by our very participation in existence. This understanding may often be nonreflective, fragmented, partial, even destructive, but understanding, nevertheless, names the way in which human beings exist.

Interpretation is the activity of human understanding characterized by relating a word, idea, or symbol of action to another. Interpretation is some form of judgment in which something is understood as something else, or something that was not understood is related to a larger whole, the result being "a better understanding." As an activity of understanding, interpretation can range from the near reflex response of habitual associations to the highly reflective and self-critical approaches encouraged by, for example, a scholarly community. Tracy writes:

> Interpretation seems a minor matter, but it is not. Every time we act, deliberate, judge, understand, or even experience, we are interpreting. To understand at all is to interpret. To act well is to interpret a situation demanding some action and to interpret a correct strategy for that action. To experience in other than a purely passive sense (a sense less than human) is to interpret; and to be "experienced" is to have become a good interpreter. Interpretation is thus as unavoidable, finally, as experience, understanding, deliberation, judgment, decision and action. To be human is to act reflectively, to decide deliberately, to understand intelligently, to experience fully. Whether we know it or not, to be human is to be a skilled interpreter.
>
> (*Plurality and Ambiguity*, 1987, p. 9)

This relation between interpretation and participatory understanding is important in Tracy's work for at least two reasons. First, all interpreters, including those who identify themselves as religious or theological, partake in the process of becoming more thoroughly human by becoming those who better understand precisely through interpretation. Second, interpretation is not the restricted activity of any particular elite, but rather the activity of all human understanding that has the possibility of being more or less informed, responsible, or creative. For Tracy, interpretation, including theological interpretation, neither alienates from participatory understanding nor generates a privileged and controlling elite.

In the fundamental analysis of interpretation, Tracy holds that interpretation is an interaction of three realities: "some phenomenon to be interpreted, someone interpreting that phenomenon, and some interaction between these two rarities" (*Plurality and Ambiguity*, p. 10). The interaction between the two rarities results in a form of understanding that relates parts to wholes or imaginatively relates one thing to another, often through some process of analogy. What makes the interpretation theological comes largely from the phenomenon to be interpreted, variously named: religion, the religious classic, the other, the power of the whole, the self-disclosure of God in the person and event of Jesus, or revelation. The phenomenon provokes interpretation, specifically theological interpretation, insofar as it touches on the *limit experiences* of human existence and can be correlated, in the case of Christian theology, with the central Christian symbol of God.

Limit experiences are understood by Tracy to be part of human experience, its moments of *intensification*, when events and times become particularly acute, when crucial issues become particularly clear and demanding, and when the big questions of life pierce through routines: What can I know? Why have these people suffered? What is the good thing to do? How can I respond to others out of the riches of my own life? What should our society hope for? These sorts of questions and concerns typify the limit experience, which is thus understood not as super-nature, the bizarre, or the essentially life-threatening, but as the ordinary in those moments and instances when the everyday conventions are shaken, when the ordinary discloses the mysteriousness of human existence that calls for hope, faith, love, and further interpretative understanding.

For the Christian theologian this provocation to interpretative understanding will find in the symbols of the Christian tradition, particularly in the event and person of Jesus, a source from which to understand the ordinary and its intensifications in ways that can be called "more authentic." Theological interpretation is not then for Tracy a philosophy of religion (which interprets conceptually what the phenomenon of human religiousness might mean, or how it might be explained), nor is it the conceptualization of an individual's faith position. Rather it is the interpretation of the encounter with "the other" in all its dimensions that takes the form of *mutually critical correlation* involving both the interpretation of our common human situation in all of its dimensions and the interpretations of the Christian tradition in all of its dimensions.

A thoroughly hermeneutical task, theological interpretation will find in the Christian symbols of a trinitarian understanding of God, of salvation, of incarnation and creation, of Jesus, ways in which participatory understanding is made more authentic. Likewise theological interpretation will find ways in which the Christian tradition—its symbols, texts, and practices—is understood differently, is corrected or chastened when necessary, and is appreciated anew, precisely because it is correlated with the disciplined understanding of human existence.

Characteristics of Tracy's Theological Interpretations

Several characteristics consistently emerge for theological interpretation from the hermeneutical context in Tracy's work, among which five are particularly important.

First, all theological interpretation is *situated. "Postmodern"* is the term that Tracy uses most frequently to describe the situation in which theological interpretation today must occur. "Postmodern" names for Tracy an interdependent complex of position and reactions marked by the suspicion of comprehensive and coherent schemes of reason and social order, the chastening of the subject understood as autonomous individual, the recognition of both the plurality and the ambiguity of all interpretative understanding, the demise of the assumption of the superiority of Western culture, and an ethics of resistance to the seductive and outright oppressive powers that continue to subject race, gender, speech, and, most important, human imagination.

Not antimodern—indeed Tracy is consistently appreciative of the contribution of both the Enlightenment and modernity as well as much in Western culture— Tracy recognizes that the theological interpreter must indeed be critically faithful both to the preunderstandings of today's often largely secular world, and to the traditions of Christianity broadly understood. The theological interpreter's situation is the postmodern world, and the claim of such an interpreter is that the proper understanding of the Christian tradition is a "correct reflective inventory" of this world (*Blessed Rage*, 1975, p. 9).

Second, the most appropriate model for theological interpretation is *dialogue* or *conversation*, which names the back-and-forth interaction that occurs in any authentic interpretation. Whether the subject is a classic text or individual, a historic event, or a current situation of oppression, interpretation as conversation allows the rhythms of questions to take over. Thus theological interpretation is not marked primarily by certainty, assertion, thesis, or even argument. Like true dialogue and conversation, truth as the disclosure of what is, and may be, is the goal, which seldom has the assurance of certainty or final assertion when limit experiences are at issue. Dialogue is much more than convivial exchange. In *Plurality and Ambiguity* Tracy identifies its sometimes stringent demands:

> Conversation is a game with some hard rules: say only what you mean; say it as accurately as you can; listen to and respect what the other says, however different or other; be willing to correct or defend your opinions if challenged by the conversation partner; be willing to argue if necessary, to confront if demanded, to endure necessary conflict, and to change your mind if the evidence suggests it. (1987, p. 19)

Third, theological interpretation is authentically *public*, which Tracy explains by describing two clusters of topics: the social realities that each theologian addresses, in short, the *publics;* and the notion of the *classic*.

Regarding the "publics" Tracy identifies three distinct but not separate social realities that the theologian addresses: the wider society, the academy, and the church. To be sure, the nature of theological questions is often deeply personal, yet theological interpretation can never confuse the deeply personal with privacy of individuality. The theological interpreter speaks to and from a social location that shares a certain consensus about what counts as informed discourse, what needs to be addressed, how convictions are to be supported and questioned. The patterns of consensus are not identical over time, nor are they the same even in the multiple social locations in which each theological interpreter exists. Indeed the very pattern of consensus may be so distorted in any particular social location that authentic dialogue is severely hampered or completely impeded. Whatever the patterns and whatever the distortions, theological interpretation must take part in, and be conversant with, the publics for which the theological interpretation is primarily offered. Usually, the theologian must address all three social realities, although one is often primary. Concretely for the theological interpreter this means that a variable mix of loyalties and responsibilities in the dialogue is always at work: The theologian is simultaneously part of a technoeconomic culture; the theologian is informed by the disciplines and methods of public intellectual inquiry; and the theologian in various ways is part of the institutional, interpersonal, and traditional life of the religious community.

Theological interpretation thus takes many forms depending upon the mix of expectations and loyalties that make up the public to be addressed. The academy tends to work through the structure of disciplines, each of which operates with a shared sense of what counts as information, reliable method, modes of discourse and exchange, as well as the boundaries and vocabulary for the investigation of issues. *Fundamental theologies* are most often directed to this particular "public." The "public" of the church describes a sociological and theological reality that understands itself as a community responding to the disclosure of God in Jesus Christ maintained however tentatively in the history of Christianity. The theologian's role is to make explicit, to order, to recall, sometimes to correct, the faithful understanding that the community shares. Such theological interpretation is often described as *systematic.* The "public" of society "encompasses the technoeconomic structures, the polity and the culture which make up contemporary human communities" (*Analogical Imagination,* 1981, pp. 6-7). For the public of society the theologian will generally utilize all the skills of analysis and transformation available to explain better the meaning, value, and effect of the vast symbol systems inherent within any society. The form such theological interpretation takes is often labeled *practical theology.*

The "publics" and the forms of theology are not distinct entities; much overlaps in the questions posed, the positions taken, the warrants accepted. For Tracy, however, this rhetorical map of the "publics" suggests better the plurality of the contexts in which theological interpretation currently occurs, as well as the consequent expectations and demands upon the theologian to address the issues of meaning and truth within these communities.

Tracy uses the notion of classics to explain the authentically public character of theological interpretation. The *classic* names the texts, events, or persons that "bear an excess of permanence of meaning, yet always resist definitive interpretation" (*Plurality and Ambiguity,* 1987, p. 12). They are the particular cultural items that historically have helped found and direct the ideas and actions of succeeding generations. In Tracy's terms, borrowing from Hans-Georg Gadamer, the classic claims attention, not by some extrinsic authority, but because of the intensification of meaning and value that occurs in this work. The classic is inherently public on several counts: Historically it is that phenomenon to which people return to be informed again; hermeneutically, it calls repeatedly for reinterpretation, further dialogue, better argument; socially, it is recognized by its sustained claim for interpretation on multiple readers over time, thus being distinguished from "the period piece." If it is a "religious classic," like the person and event of Jesus, or the Gospel of John, then the classic is no less public than any other cultural classic: the

Lotus Sutra, the *Bhagavad Gita, Hamlet,* the *Odyssey,* the French Revolution. The religious classic thus attracts analysis and interpretation as does any other classic.

What distinguishes the religious classic is the intensification of the limit experience, its disclosures and questions, all of which take place in the work. Like any classic, the religious classic invites multiple interpretations. It is augmented by careful readings, argued about, shared, and ultimately informs our social and personal imagination. The person and event of Jesus, like that of Gautama Buddha, Moses, or Muhammad, constitutes on all accounts a religious classic; so also are certain texts, rituals, art works, lives, and practices to which communities and cultures consistently return. From such classics and their interpretation, appreciative or critical, communities better understand the relations between their members, their histories, their worlds, and their future possibilities. The encounter with the classic is what calls and recalls the interpreter to that which in each age is most authentic and thus most worthy to be engaged.

A fourth characteristic of theological interpretation is its *plural* nature. In "Christianity in the Wider Context," Tracy avers that "plurality is a fact. Pluralism is one of many possible evaluations of that fact" (1987, p. 8). On all accounts, Tracy maintains, the buzz and hum of everyday reality is diverse and multifaceted, with little sense that this "reality" can be explained by one language, one history, or one set of concepts. *Pluralism* in its many forms is a recognition of this diversity. At a hermeneutical level, the discussion to be engaged for Tracy is not that between pluralism and metaphysical monism, but rather that between pluralism and "mono-theorism," a position which holds that a single theory, method, or system, fully developed, better explains apparent diversity than does any form of pluralism.

Tracy identifies pluralism as a *strategy for possibility,* an approach that appreciates the variety of possibilities open to human transformation, and that opens these possibilities in a noncoercive way. Consistent with the hermeneutical character of Tracy's thought, the plurality of interpretation accounts for the recurringly disclosive nature of all classics. Rather than calling for mere repetition, the interpretation of the classic, including the religious classic, invites challenge, change, and transformation. Monotheorism tends to occlude such an approach by positing an implicit or explicit normativity to a set of concepts or a particular systematic ordering. Thus while rejecting "monotheoretic" structures of interpretation because they tend to limit interpretative possibilities prematurely, Tracy is not unaware of the inauthentic tendencies within pluralist positions. "The key to appropriation of cultural pluralism," he writes,

> remains the recognitions which occur in conversation and the judgments which occur in conversation and argument. The keys to pluralism remain both. Without an appreciation of different possibilities through a focusing on possible disclosures of truth, pluralism slides into repressive tolerance. Without an appropriation of those possibilities *as* possibilities by means of conversation and argument and their atten-

dant criteria, pluralism collapses into eclecticism and its unwelcome partner, "indifferentism." Without conversation and argument it remains true that if pluralism comes, can relativism be far behind?

("Christianity in the Wider Context," 1987, pp. 13-14)

If a responsible, authentically dialogical pluralism is a strategy for possibility, then the *analogical imagination* is its technique. The title of Tracy's most sustained systematic theological work to date, "analogical imagination" describes the stance in understanding that simultaneously grants the otherness of the other (difference) while recognizing the possibilities that the other presents for the tradition in which one finds oneself (similarity). Tracy often invokes the phrase "similarities-in-difference" to describe the technique of analogy in the context of possibilities open to imagination. Conversation or dialogue is the tool of this technique. Conversation at once respects the position of the other and demands self-respect, namely the recognition of being critically rooted in a particular tradition.

The critical pluralism characteristic of Tracy's thought is clear in several of his theological positions. While recognizing the contributions that Deism, theism, atheism, and pantheism have made to interpretation of God, Tracy's position of *panentheism,* understood in process categories, interprets the notion of God by recognizing the adequacy of language that emphasizes transcendence and radical relationality. Tracy understands panentheism in its process categories to be a "poetics" of God that remains faithful to the biblical traditions by emphasizing the suffering and change of God while at the same time distancing the discussion of God from the projections of anthropomorphism. Such a position best interprets metaphysically for Tracy the claims for transcendence and incarnation in the Christian tradition, and thus it is "appropriate" to the tradition. Likewise, process categories best account for the metaphysics of change and interdependence in a contemporary world, and thus are most "relatively adequate" to the current, critically informed interpretation of human existence.

Christologically, the critical pluralism of Tracy's thought encourages the appreciation of a wide variety of interpretations of the person and event of Jesus. Tracy is acutely aware that the Jesus of the Christian tradition is the Jesus witnessed to by an apostolic tradition, which resulted not in a single written Gospel, but in a variety of perspectives contained in the mixed genres of the Gospels. The traditions of presentations of Jesus are no less varied, grouped largely as traditions of manifestation and traditions of proclamation. Traditions of manifestation tend to emphasize the relation of the event and person of Jesus to creation, incarnation, sacramentality, and the comprehensible-incomprehensible God; traditions of proclamation tend to emphasize redemption, the cross, the word, and the hidden-revealed God. Both of these traditions are subject to their excesses, but both are present in Christianity and need each other.

Theologically, Tracy's position is *christomorphic*—a position that interprets the person and event of Jesus as the primary, shaping disclosure of God for the Christian tradition and tends to be more at home in the tradition of manifestation. But this christomorphic theology does not issue in a single or exclusive set of categories. Traditions of manifestation issuing from John's Gospel and its almost mystical disclosure of love are ones that Tracy finds most compelling. Yet these are always tensively balanced with historical, apocalyptic, and prophetic strains within the same tradition. Consequently, the orthodoxy of Tracy's position encourages interpretations of the classic event and person of Jesus that can make justifiable claims both appropriate to the tradition and relatively adequate to a timely understanding.

Critical pluralism is also characteristic of Tracy's emphasis on the importance of dialogue with non-Christian religions. Over and over Tracy has recognized that a consistent danger of any Christian approach that valorizes "the tradition" in an uncritical way is the production of "more of the same," the same language, the same possibilities, the same oppression. The recognition of religious pluralism and its honest challenge to the Christian tradition is increasingly important to Tracy's work. The analogical imagination and the tools of dialogue find some of their most challenging uses here, for it is in this recognition of religious pluralism that the Christian tradition is forced to understand anew its prophetic and mystical namings of God, to reappropriate its own forgotten histories, and to chasten some of its own petrified theological positions.

A fifth characteristic of theological interpretation is its *ambiguity*. One of the strongest marks of the postmodern mentality for Tracy is the recognition that the large cultural narratives of progress, development, and social evolution are spent. In the aftermath of two world wars, the Holocaust, the atomic bomb, world environmental threat, and the reiterated instances of national and tribal genocides of this century, the dreams of calculative and instrumental reason have been "interrupted." Such radical *interruptions* for the postmodern mind have not simply generated malaise or theoretically generated relativism; they have also spawned a variety of critical theories that bring to light the oppressive, destructive, and frightening underside of these dreams and projects. The Christian tradition has been a part of this history of ambiguity.

While "plurality" names the recognition of possibility, "ambiguity" names the recognition of the odd, often unsuspected, mixtures of good and evil in all phenomena including Christianity. For Tracy this recognition of ambiguity recasts the discussion of evil in typically postmodern terms. Where for the modern period evil and sin could largely be interpreted through the category of error, the postmodern period more acutely recognizes the issues of *systematic distortion*. Systematic distortion describes the very infections of reasoning, dialogue, understanding, interpretation, and action that make us blind or insensitive to oppressive distortions in what we understand to be normal and everyday. The discussion of evil, theologically carried out for Tracy, is not primarily one resembling classical theodicy, seeking a balance between a good and powerful God theistically interpreted, and the presence of suffering. For Tracy the discussion of evil shipwrecks if it is theoretical alone; evil calls for redemption, salvation, release. Requiring interpretation, evil and oppression must be adequately understood in order to curb their repetition in our best, but often self-deceptive, responses.

Evil surely requires release, emancipation; yet Christian salvation is more than freedom from oppression. Here ambiguity meets the strategy of critical pluralism, for salvation demands also a freedom "for," a set of imaginative possibilities for existence opened in the classics of hope and life. For the Christian, the freedom "for" is found most specifically in the person and event of Jesus. "All the victims of our discourses and our history," Tracy realizes,

> have begun to discover their own discourses in ways that our discourse finds difficult to hear, much less listen to. Their voices can seem strident and uncivil—in a word, other. And they are. We have all just begun to sense the terror of that otherness. But only by beginning to listen to those other voices may we also begin to hear the otherness within our own discourse and within ourselves. What we might then begin to hear, above our own clatter, are possibilities we have never dared to dream.
> (*Plurality and Ambiguity*, 1987, p. 79)

Conclusion

Tracy's theological work is marked by breadth of knowledge, fairness, and a critical love for the Christian tradition. He is firmly convinced that theological interpretation is a necessity for our world and not a sectarian luxury. When such interpretation is carried out authentically, it allows for the disciplined dialogue with all forms of otherness. Such dialogue discloses what is at work in the everyday, its mysterious depths as well as its oppressive distortions. The price of not engaging in such theological interpretation exceeds all measures of church attendance, all debates about orthodoxy, and all the worried concerns about religion in a secular world. The price for not engaging in theological interpretation is the foreshortening of the possibilities of human existence, sometimes to such an extent that self-destruction in all its forms or the pain of the other in all its forms seems to be commonplace. The price of doing theological reflection in our world is likewise high. For Tracy, it demands broad scholarship, honest engagement, and the risk of change. The dimensions of human existence to which theological interpretation speaks, however, are not idiosyncratic or sectarian. They are the demands of faith, hope, and love that seek forms for today's world. Tracy speaks for the disclosures that the Christian tradition can contribute to these forms, which themselves finally compose the heart of theological interpretation.

John P. McCarthy

477

Selected Primary Works

1970   *The Achievement of Bernard Lonergan.*
1975   *Blessed Rage for Order: The New Pluralism in Theology.*
1981   *The Analogical Imagination: Christian Theology and the Culture of Pluralism.*
1983   *Talking About God: Doing Theology in the Context of Modern Pluralism,* with John Cobb.
1984   *A Short History of the Interpretation of the Bible,* with Robert Grant, 2nd ed.
1987   *A Catholic Vision,* with Stephen Happel.
1987   "Christianity in the Wider Context: Demands and Transformations," in *Religion and Intellectual Life* (Summer).
1987   *Plurality and Ambiguity.*
1989   "The Uneasy Alliance Reconceived: Catholic Theological Method, Modernity and Postmodernity," in *Theological Studies.*
1990   *Dialogue with the Other: The Inter-Religious Dialogue.*
1990   "On Naming the Present," in *On the Threshold of the Third Millennium, Concilium.*
1991   "The Hermeneutics of Naming," in *Irish Theological Quarterly* (December).
1994   "Theology and the Many Faces of Postmodernity," in *Theology Today* (April).

Selected Secondary Sources

1991   Werner Jeanrond and Jennifer L. Rike, *Radical Pluralism and Truth: David Tracy and the Hermeneutics of Religion.*
1993   T. Howland Sanks, "David Tracy's Theological Project: An Overview and Some Implications," *Theological Studies* (December).

DESMOND TUTU
1931–

I f it weren't for faith, I would have given up long ago. I am certain lots of us would have been hate-filled and bitter. For me the Scriptures have become more and more thoroughly relevant to our situation. They speak of a God who, when you worship him, turns you around to be concerned for your neighbor. He does not tolerate a relationship with himself that excludes your neighbor.

. . . In the middle of our faith is the death and resurrection. Nothing could have been more hopeless than Good Friday—but then Easter happened and forever we have been prisoners of hope. ("Into a Glorious Future," 1985)

Life and Career

Born in 1931, Desmond Tutu grew up in a very religious Christian family in Transvaal Province, South Africa, and attended mission schools, a factor that exerted a strong influence in his decision to enter the ministry. Like his father, he worked as a schoolteacher in his younger days within the notorious Bantu Educational system, enforced under apartheid.

Tutu became politically responsive about the reality of black oppression in South Africa during his time at Federal Theological Seminary in Alice, Cape Province, in the 1960s. While working as a chaplain at the University of Fort Hare, he encountered political leaders such as Mangaliso Sobukwe and Oliver Tambo who espoused black consciousness and African nationalism and who influenced Tutu in both regards.

In 1972, Tutu assumed the position of the Associate Director of the Theological Education Fund of the World Council of Churches in Kent, England. His work catapulted him into the domain of global theological education, with special emphasis on theological educational development in Africa, whose churches and theological institutions he assisted in assuming a more indigenous character.

In 1975 Tutu was appointed Dean of Johannesburg, becoming the first black Dean of the Anglican Church in South Africa. It was yet another challenge for Tutu, who ministered to a white congregation that generally refused to accept black leadership. Further, many members found Tutu's style of administration and practices of embracing and kissing during the Kiss of Peace in worship unconventional and embarrassing. While he served as Dean of Johannesburg, Tutu became more familiar with the activists of the Black Consciousness Movement, like Mamphele Ramphele, a medical doctor, and other noted black leaders such as Nthatho Motlana, leader of the Soweto Civic Association. Tutu's prominence as a black theologian struggling against apartheid became evident when he was elected the General Secretary of the South African Council of Churches (SACC). Under Tutu's leadership, the SACC was able to withstand constant attacks by the apartheid state.

Tutu visited resettlement camps housing people forcibly relocated from their homes under apartheid's Bantustan policy. He often recounts a visit to the village of Zweledinga, where he spoke to a small girl who told him that she drank water when she felt hungry, an excruciating reminder of the toll that apartheid takes on the bellies of children (see *Crying in the Wilderness*, 1982, p. 108). He also demonstrated his solidarity with the dispossessed people of Mogopa in Transvaal province in 1983, undertaking a vigil with the community in their forced uprooting.

Tutu was consequently ushered into a role as one of the most outspoken critics against apartheid and a leading Christian prophet in South Africa. The agony and pain of black people and the gravity of their suffering under the scourge of apartheid compelled him to be willing to sacrifice everything, including his life, to be rid of so evil and repugnant a system. With ecumenical reach he raised the consciousness of South African clergy about the need for relating the gospel directly to the situation of apartheid. His compassion and heartfelt concern for the colonized black underclasses of South Africa were vividly captured in his powerful sermons and moving addresses, originating from the depths of his being and rooted in the God of the Exodus.

Tutu was also instrumental in making the SACC relevant to the experiences of black workers. In 1981, he opened the doors of the SACC to meetings of the burgeoning trade union movement. He was adamant in his position that the Christian church be in the forefront of defending the rights of black workers, most vulnerable and unconscionably exploited by apartheid's system of racial capitalism. The ruling white regime threatened the SACC and its leaders with arrest in the event that the SACC infringed South African laws by encouraging resistance to apartheid. Unmoved by the threats, Tutu challenged the unjust South African rulers to retaliate against the church in its proclamation of justice and equality for all people.

During his tenure as General Secretary of SACC, Tutu was drawn into the international arena as he vehemently denounced apartheid abroad. He advocated the exercise of economic pressure by Western capitalist countries involved in South Africa, and he subsequently urged the imposition of global economic sanctions as a means toward weakening the intransigent posture of the white minority regime. On one occasion, in 1979, his passport was withdrawn, after he criticized Denmark for purchasing South African coal during a visit to that country. Throughout the 1970s and 1980s, he called repeatedly for the release of Nelson Mandela, leader of the African National Congress (ANC) of South Africa, and the unbanning of the ANC and other liberation organizations. In his defiant struggle against racism and oppression in South Africa, Tutu was condemned as a "communist agitator" and an "unworthy cleric" by the racist regime that ruled South Africa.

In 1984, Tutu was awarded the Nobel Peace Prize for his involvement in the South African liberation struggle. In 1985, he was elected Bishop of Johannesburg, making him the most powerful Anglican clergyperson in the industrial capital of Johannesburg. His elevation into the uppermost echelons of the Anglican ecclesial hierarchy did not end there, however, for in August 1986 he was consecrated as Archbishop of Cape Town, which established him as the leader of the entire Anglican communion in Southern Africa. As democratic rule began in South Africa in the 1990s, Tutu became increasingly supportive of the ruling African National Congress party.

Theological Method

In a very practical sense, Desmond Tutu is a black liberation theologian. Consistently through his sermons, addresses, protests, and marches, he has demonstrated a model of theological resistance to the evil of racism. His consciousness of social factors in theology makes him an important figure in the global liberation movement of the oppressed.

For Tutu, theology is provisional and temporally conditioned. It is never static; instead it responds to the existential needs of a particular people during a specific generation. There are no universally valid norms or criteria that authenticate theological reflection. Theological validity becomes assessed in terms of theology's relevance to the immediacy of the situation, a principle that he finds in biblical accounts about the experiences and events of the Hebrew people ("The Theology of Liberation in Africa," 1979, p. 165).

Black theology is one such contextual theology, Tutu contends, that is relevant to the predicament of racism and repression faced by black people. It is concerned with humanization, liberation, forgiveness, and justice ("Black Theology/African Theology: Soul Mates or Antagonists?" 1979, p. 77). Holistic and organic, black theology effects the liberation of white oppressors just as much as the black

481

oppressed. It is, as with all other theologies of liberation, directed toward the obliteration of suffering as it seeks to maintain black sanity in a racist world that fosters the absurdity of black suffering. It is, Tutu suggests, a reflection on the facticity of God's purposely creating people black, and it explores the optimal development of the potential of the black self.

Tutu is a black liberation theologian who also prides himself on being an African theologian, coming from the southernmost tip of Africa. In contrast to other leading African theologians like John Mbiti from Kenya, Tutu asserts that black theology in fact has much in common with theologies emerging from independent Africa. Ontologically, through the umbilical tie to Mother Africa and through religious baptism, Africans are one. Tutu holds that the African cultural heritage is the paradigmatic framework that informs the perceptions, cosmologies, and social practices of Africans on the continent and those throughout the African diaspora, however variegated. Although black and African theologies are allies in a fundamental theological sense, Tutu postulates that African theologies often lack the dimensions of political involvement and social criticism, which they need to adopt from black theology.

God and Christ

Black theology essentially asserts that God is on the side of the oppressed, an idea derived from the Exodus motif in the Bible. According to Tutu, God is aligned with the weak ones of history; as omnipotent, dynamic, and forceful, God is able to break the shackles of racist repression and economic exploitation. Tutu maintains that God is never neutral, but sides with the victims of oppression. Consequently, Christians are called to identify themselves with the marginalized and exploited peoples of the world.

Jesus, who is central to the Christian revelation, through his life of ministry and consequent death exemplified for us unwavering dedication to the liberation of the oppressed. This was the subversive quality of Jesus' religious role in the society of his day, Tutu declares. Jesus did not spend much time with the religious teachers and theologians of his time, but spent it instead with the outcasts, the poor, the lepers, and the prostitutes—the "social pariahs"; and he empowered these folks to overcome their exploitation.

The work of the Christian community ought to be Christ's work of compassion and love: feeding the hungry, caring for the aged, furnishing health education for the needy, supporting struggling students with scholarships, and providing clean drinking water to the thirsty. Tutu underscores the point that the motivation for his liberatory actions is not political, but essentially theological.

Social Analysis

Even though Tutu has not written extensively on the issues of social analysis in black theology, he nevertheless has addressed these questions within the maze of his writings, sermons, and addresses. Conscious and critical of the evils of monopoly capitalism, Tutu is aware of the role that socioeconomic factors play in oppression and the vast disparities that prevail between the industrialized northern countries and the impoverished nations of the South. He has excoriated the voracious practices of the mammoth transnational corporations that accumulate inordinate profits at the expense of the hungry peoples of the underdeveloped South. He repudiates industrial capitalism for its accent on profit and belittlement of the worth of the human person (cf. "Dollars More Important Than People," 1989). He contends that the Western capitalist rhetoric of free enterprise is mythic, essentially providing a license to exploit others and hoard unregulated wealth. Tutu's denunciation of the acquisitive nature of capitalism and his vision of an alternative society are predicated on his theological conviction that all socioeconomic and political orders must preserve the dignity of human beings, since humans are created in God's image.

In the same vein Tutu takes the Western cultural precept of rugged individualism to task for its abrogation of the African practice of communal ownership and corporate individuality. Tutu argues that African cultures stress organic interaction and collective responsibility, principles that a liberated South African society ought to practice. Conscious of the manner in which the apartheid system has portrayed itself as benign, Tutu is cognizant of the internal dynamics of capitalism playing themselves out in creating institutionalized hierarchical class structures that breed inequality. The apartheid system has executed this facade by providing increments in social opportunities and economic benefits for a minuscule sector of the colonized black majority while keeping the bulk of the population struggling in poverty-stricken conditions. The obscene maldistribution of wealth and resources between blacks and whites in South Africa, for instance, Tutu asserts, is one of the results of this system of injustice. Following South Africa's first black-white elections in April 1994, Tutu described the act of voting for the first time as akin to "being in love." He views the current post-apartheid situation as one of liberation, even though many actual conditions that obtain in South Africa today hardly warrant such a description.

The Role of Culture

Tutu contends that Christianity in Africa must be wrapped in African garb and speak the language of African people. As a black theologian he insists on African cultural identity being an integral component of the praxis of black theologies of liberation, Africa being the wellspring of black ontology.

In this connection Tutu views the ancient Near Eastern world (as described in the Hebrew Scriptures) as having much more in common with the experiences of African culture than Western European culture. He avers that traditional religious concepts must be reclaimed and the richness of the African cultural past must be tapped in the evolution of black theology of the present. He cites the African notions of corporate individuality and the sacralization of the human person, for instance *ubuntu* in the Zulu language and *botho* in the Sotho language, as one area where the wellspring of culture serves to inform paradigms of liberation for blacks, a people fragmented by racism.

For this reason Tutu held the founder of the Black Consciousness Movement in South Africa, Steve Biko, in such high esteem. At his funeral, Tutu identified Biko's involvement in the liberation struggle for which he was killed as the epitome of Christian faith and praxis. Black Consciousness represents the sociopolitical concomitant of black theology and is an imperative of the deliberation on behalf of black liberation.

The relational or communal understanding of the self that is employed across the African continent is fundamentally a theological concept, Tutu maintains. It serves to meld the individual women, children, and men of the oppressed black community into an indivisible bond of social solidarity to confront the divisive obstacles of racist repression. In the African cosmology, the universe is seen as part of a composite entity in which all elements are interrelated and interdependent. Individuality is perceived in terms of communal integration. Such insights serve to unify black people, discarding the self-seeking objectives of individuals in the collaborative effort to realize liberation from racism and exploitation.

The Question of Gender

Tutu demonstrates increasing awareness of the need for black theology to address the question of domination and inequality of women under patriarchy, although he has not elaborated on the connection between gender and the system of racist oppression and economic exploitation. He has not been as vociferous on this issue as one would expect of a liberation theologian. He has not raised it as a primary concern within his Anglican ecclesial community where there are so few women clergy.

Tutu has made occasional pronouncements on the subject of women's rights, however. In an article entitled "South African Insights and the Old Testament" (1972), he notes that patriarchal domination has been a stumbling block to women in society, as it was historically in the ancient Near Eastern world. Since the publication of the essay, his sensitivity to the swelling movement demanding full participation of women in the theological arena has grown incrementally. He recognizes the necessity for a holistic concept of God that will be inclusive of both sexes created by the Creator. He argues that women and men were meant to work alongside one another as opposed to men ruling over women. The Genesis story of creation in the second chapter describes this complementarity (cf. *Hope and Suffering*, 1983, pp. 120, 150).

Tutu recognizes that the liberation of society is seriously incomplete without the integral liberation of women. He believes that women are the persons whose lives and experiences can restore the optimism and confidence of the world in human nature, since women demonstrate a distinctive ability to endure and persevere in the struggle for realizing our greatest human potential. In the context of apartheid society in South Africa, in particular, black women have had to contend with the stigma of being both black and female. Nevertheless, they have exhibited exemplary courage in resisting the draconian laws of apartheid that have consistently undermined and fragmented the cohesion of black social life. Tutu lauds this deep resilience, determination, and valiance on the part of black women, whose Christian praxis is a witness to the dynamism of black womanist faith. In the impoverished community of Crossroads and the neighboring black areas of Langa, Nyanga, and K.T.C., the courage of black women was particularly evident during the siege of these communities when the police attempted to evict residents and demolish their humble dwellings. Tutu was passionately moved by this level of determination among the women to resist these intimidation tactics of the white state, giving him hope that the struggle for liberation from racism and sexism would see fruition by way of the central role of women in this effort (cf. "Persecution of Christians Under Apartheid," 1983).

Nonviolent Struggle

Tutu is committed to the principle of peace with justice in the world, the struggle for which he was awarded the Nobel Peace Prize. He is particularly prominent for his advocacy of peaceful change in South Africa, in response to the brutality of apartheid and imposition of white minority rule, while maintaining that the primary expression of violence in South Africa is that represented by the apartheid system. In light of the events of 1990 and 1991, when previously banned organizations were legalized in South Africa and the white minority regime claimed that it was serious about negotiating a peaceful transition to majority rule, Tutu's hopes for change through relatively peaceful means appear to have been fulfilled.

In May 1983, when he was General Secretary of the South African Council of Churches, he condemned the guerrilla bombing of the South African Defense Force headquarters in Pretoria by the African National Congress, one of the chief liberation movements battling against apartheid, in which nineteen people were killed. Consistent with his philosophy of "nonviolence," Tutu made public his disapprobation of the resistance movement's guerrilla action. The subsequent retaliatory strike by the South African Air Force on the capital of neighboring Mozambique, accused for allegedly harboring ANC military cadres, was equally excoriated by Tutu.

Tutu is an advocate of peaceful change in situations of oppression, while comprehending the need for armed resistance to overthrow certain evil systems such as the Nazi regime in Germany during the Second World War. For this reason Tutu describes himself as a peacemaker and not a pacifist, since he does not make an ideological or philosophical dogma of "nonviolence" in response to oppressive violence. Nevertheless, he considers any form of violence evil regardless of its ends. "Revolutionary violence" as used by people fighting against Hitler, Tutu concludes, would be considered the lesser evil—a view similar to that held by Dietrich Bonhoeffer, the German theologian who was executed for participation in an abortive attempt to assassinate Hitler.

Tutu is well aware of the fact that increasing numbers of black South Africans, particularly the youth, are still disillusioned with the use of "nonviolence." Few positive changes have resulted for the black masses, even after a negotiated settlement of the apartheid conflict, for South African whites still appear obstinate in their determination to retain many of the privileges and comforts that accrued from an apartheid society. They are too snugly ensconced in their sofas of affluence and residences of opulence to volunteer to participate in a transformation of the status quo, especially one in which their monopoly of wealth will be threatened.

Certainly, some changes have occurred peacefully since the demise of formal apartheid, yet substantive structural changes involving redistribution of South Africa's wealth and return of lands to the black dispossessed appear to be distant ideals under the new "democratic" dispensation. Tutu has not made any critical pronouncements on these vital issues recently, one indication that he may have overlooked the real reason for apartheid's existence in the first place: expropriation of the country's vast mineral wealth and natural resources by ·large capitalist corporations. Bold and outspoken though he was against apartheid, Tutu does not view recent political developments in South Africa critically. His position may reflect a lack of deepened social analysis and a sense of naivete in assessing political and economic situations.

Conclusion

Desmond Tutu has distinguished himself as one of the most engaged Christian theologians of our time. His courage and perseverance, resolve and boldness, even in the face of violent and seemingly insurmountable odds in South Africa, serve as an inspiration to oppressed peoples everywhere. As a black theologian working in the South African context, he has much to offer for the empowerment and expansion of theological movements emerging in the rest of Africa. His theological contributions will greatly assist in the continuing struggle for the continent's independence and liberation.

Julian Kunnie

Selected Primary Works

1972   "Some African Insights and the Old Testament," *Journal of Theology for Southern Africa* 1 (December).

1977   "God Intervening in Human Affairs" in *Missionalia* 5/1.

1979   "Black Theology/African Theology: Soul Mates or Antagonists?" in *Black Theology: A Documentary History, 1966–1979,* ed. G. Wilmore and J. Cone.

1979   "The Theology of Liberation in Africa" in *African Theology En Route,* ed. Kofi Appiah-Kubi and Sergio Torres.

1980   "Tearing People Apart" in *South African Outlook* (October).

1982   *Crying in the Wilderness.*

1983   *Hope and Suffering.*

1983   "Persecution of Christians Under Apartheid," in *Martyrdom Today,* ed. Johannes-Baptist Metz and Edward Schillebeeckx.

1984   "Barmen and Apartheid," in *Journal of Theology for Southern Africa,* no. 47 (June).

1985   "Into a Glorious Future," in *Sojourners* (February).

1989   "Dollars More Important Than People," in "The Bias of God," in *The Month: A Review of Christian Thought and World Affairs* (November).

Selected Secondary Sources

1975   Kenneth Best, ed., *African Challenge.*

1979   Gayraud Wilmore and James Cone, eds., *Black Theology: A Documentary History, 1966–1979.*

1979   Kofi Appiah-Kubi and Sergio Torres, *African Theology En Route.*

1983   Johannes Baptist Metz and Edward Schillebeeckx, eds., *Martyrdom Today.*

1984   Rafael Suarez, "The Bishop and South Africa: An Interview with Desmond Tutu" in *Worldview* (December).

1987   Buti Thlagale and Itumeleng Mosala, eds., *Hammering Swords into Ploughshares: Essays in Honor of Desmond Tutu.*
1987   David Mermelstein, ed., *The Anti Apartheid Reader.*
1988   Shirley Du Boulay, *Tutu: Voice of the Voiceless.*
1989   Noami Tutu (selector), *The Words of Desmond Tutu.*

PAUL M. VAN BUREN
1924–

Paul M. van Buren studied at Harvard College, at the Episcopal Theological School in Cambridge, Massachussetts, and at the University of Basel, where he studied with Karl Barth and received his Doctor of Theology degree in 1957. He has served as a priest in the Episcopal Church, as a teacher of theology at the Episcopal Theological Seminary of the Southwest (1957–64) and at Temple University (1964–86), and as Honorary Professor of systematic theology at Ruprecht-Karls University in Heidelberg (1987–) and with the Shalom Hartman Institute for Judaic Studies in Jerusalem (1982–92). He has been a visiting professor at Union Theological Seminary, Harvard Divinity School, Andover Newton Theological Seminary, Princeton Theological Seminary, Oxford University, and Austin Presbyterian Theological Seminary.

Throughout his career, van Buren has sought to be a theological sense-maker. His pursuit of this task has mainly taken the form of inquiring into the nature of theological language. In the successive steps of his theological development, he has pursued the project of making sense of the Christian faith by attending to its grammar, to how its language works. Van Buren's initial theological forays were made in conversation with Karl Barth, and his first book, *Christ in Our Place* (1958), reflects the systematic turn of mind of one deeply involved in conversation with Barth. Barth was not alone among his early conversation partners; among them were Ludwig Wittgenstein, Anthony Flew, R. M. Hare, Ronald Hepburn, Schubert Ogden, and Ian Ramsey, along with William James and Søren Kierkegaard. The later, overwhelmingly important, conversation partner for van Buren is the Jewish tradition.

Van Buren burst upon the theological scene in 1963 with *The Secular Meaning of the Gospel,* which led to his being associated with the "death of God" movement in theology. But the careful reader will discern that whatever "death" van Buren was talking about was not God's. The question van Buren pursued in this book was: How can one who is both Christian and secular understand the gospel in a secular way? The answer is attainable only by analyzing what a person means when using "the language of faith" and repeating the earliest Christian confession: "Jesus is Lord" (p. 1). Citing the work of Anthony Flew, van Buren contended that traditional supernatural language about God had "died the death of a thousand qualifications" (p. 2). At this time, some theologians talked much about "the mighty acts of God." But when pressed as to what they meant with such language, they were only clear that they did not mean what a biblical movie from Hollywood would suggest. As to what in our commonly available experience would count as a "mighty act of God," they were much less clear.

Van Buren wanted to find a way of speaking as a Christian that made sense in this-worldly terms. He pursued this aim with the help of Wittgenstein's concept of a "language game," and with that of the principle of verification of analytic philosophy. This principle stipulates that whenever one uses an empirical term one must be able to state the experiences relevant to verifying or falsifying the claims made on its behalf. If one cannot, one has a "nonsense" term. The concept of a "language game" postulates that various kinds of "language" (e.g., the language of biology and that of theology) are like different games that people play. Every game, whether chess or checkers, has its own rules, and those who play one game may not make all other games conform to its set of rules. Hence, theology is a language game of its own, played by its own rules. Our difficulty resides "in the character of the language of faith, . . . the problem is not so much one of bad religion as it is one of bad, or at least unworkable, language" (p. 81).

Working with Ian Ramsey's concept of "disclosure models," R. M. Hare's "blik" (our basic but unverifiable assumptions about the world), and Braithwaite's argument that what a person means by a religious statement (such as "God is love") is the moral plan of action one understands it to entail ("God is love" means "I intend to love my neighbor as myself"), van Buren argued that both an objectified and a nonobjectified theism is meaningless (p. 86). Hence, theological statements that would be meaningless when taken as "straightforward empirical assertions about the world, nevertheless prove to have a use and meaning as the expressions of a historical perspective [blik] with far-reaching empirical consequences in a man's life" (p. 199). The result is van Buren's Christology, which claimed that in the event of Jesus Christ Christians are caught up in the contagious freedom and contagious love of Jesus; there is no God "'above' or 'beyond' that which is 'revealed' in Jesus" (pp. 160-61).

One can see both why van Buren became identified with the "death of God" movement and why that identification was a mistake. What died for van Buren, for a while, was not God but the ability to use the word "God" in the manner to which believers had become accustomed—either in its simple literal use or in the non-objectified use that had died the death of a thousand qualifications. Perhaps the term, he hinted, should be retired until Christians learned again how to speak it. Reaction to *The Secular Meaning of the Gospel* ranged from denunciation to celebration. Some welcomed it as a voice of candor in theology; others deplored what they saw as its reduction of Christian faith to what the terms of a secularist discourse would allow.

For van Buren himself, the book was merely the beginning of a search for credible ways to speak of God. In conversation with two thinkers in particular (William James and Ludwig Wittgenstein), he continued to wrestle with the task of theological sense-making. In "William James and Metaphysical Risk" (Theological Explorations, 1968), van Buren deals with five matters. First, James's style of writing was in "ordinary language. Rough and ready, popular and down to earth as is our ordinary language, there and for that reason is where James wanted to do his work, using just those concrete, robust tools with which in practice we do get about 'from next to next' in our ordinary experienced world" (pp. 89-90). Second, James stressed that we have a "*right* to believe, that there is a justification for beliefs in certain sorts of matters, although we have only partial evidence for any definite conclusion" (p. 90). In some cases, we not only have a right to choose one belief over another, but must do so. When neither empirical verification nor logical demonstration will settle an issue, when the issue is live, momentous, and forced, we have a right to take a metaphysical risk. Belief in the God of Christian faith is such an issue: live, forced (either we choose not to believe or we choose to believe), and momentous—so to choose is to commit oneself to a way of living, of viewing the neighbor and acting in regard to the neighbor. Faith as radical trust points up the fact that choosing is part of what in any case is meant by believing. Third, there is a plurality of ways in which the world is one, of points of view in terms of which we slice up experience. For any of these "language games," what is "real" is what must be taken into account for the purpose of this way of seeing the world. Fourth, metaphysics is "human metaphysics," "a view of things which is our view." An idea can be said to be true "if it leads me on from next to next in my experience" (p. 97). Wittgenstein would say: "To understand is to know what to do next." There is risk in language: "The world we experience (speak of) is the world we experience (speak of)" (p. 99). James was more comfortable than Wittgenstein with the insecurity that characterizes all language; his pragmatism "was a rough anticipation of the use theory of words: find the cash value of a word, see how the word is used, its 'particular go,' and many a problem can be dissolved, James argued" (p. 100).

With this understanding of language we have moved into the world of the later Wittgenstein. The constraints imposed by the principle of verification that haunted both the early Wittgenstein and the early van Buren have been left behind, as have the understandings of theological language that would reduce it to moral assertions. Van Buren makes a quantum leap from his earlier stance while still exploring the task of theological sense-making.

Evidence for this quantum leap from his earlier position is provided in *The Edges of Language* (1972), near the end of which he comments: "I once argued that the word 'God' was meaningless, that it was dead—an example of the same mistake about language that we are discussing here" (p. 144). We have seen how van Buren gets part way to this assertion. Now we must see how he gets the rest of the way and where it lands him. We should not let pass unnoticed the courage to follow one's thought where it leads; not many theologians admit their mistakes in print.

The thesis of *The Edges of Language* is that talk about God "takes place along the edges of language, at the farthest reaches of our rules for, or agreements in, the use of words" (p. 4). Van Buren rejects all attempts at meeting the challenge of the verification-falsification principle on its own grounds. Inevitably such efforts "suffer from the same dependence on a suspiciously narrow use of language" (p. 30). Van Buren proposes that we look at how we extend or stretch the use of words. To understand how a word works we need to know its "home-field." On its home-field, a term works in recognizable ways. To understand how it works after it has been "stretched," we need to know how it plays when it is "home." Then we can understand what is going on when it is playing "away." He gives as an example the term "solid." We know what it means to speak of a rock being solid. We also say that a building is solid, that an argument is solid, that a person is solid, that an institution is solid. We speak of a solid majority, or a solid investment. Yet we cannot extend the term indefinitely, because we would use expressions the meaning of which we could not unpack; such as "Is the world solid?"

When people engage in doing poetry, humor, religion, and metaphysics, they "balance on the edges of linguistic conventions, at the very limits of our language." We push out the limits of our language because there are dimensions of life "in which our . . . rule-governed behavior does not seem to be adequate." Different people push at different places. Christians desire to say all they can about themselves and others, including God, "as persons with a past and a future" (p. 112). When they do so, they engage in a kind of "linguistic extravagance approaching nonsense" (p. 115). Such a "rhetoric of excess" may be the only mode of speech appropriate to talk about the God of excessively abundant grace and love.

To understand Christian language, we have to identify its home-field, the point at which it begins to push at the edges of language. Van Buren identifies its home-field as the covenant between the God of Israel and the Israel of God. "Israel's concern was not simply with conduct, but with the *story* of conduct, not just with Law, but with the history of a Law received, disobeyed, and given again" (p. 122). Christian talk centers, of course, on Jesus Christ, but all its language is borrowed from the covenant between the God of Israel and the Israel of God, as is the very name "Jesus" (which means "Yahweh saves"), and all its stories of him set him in the context of the people Israel in whom he took shape. "Roughly speaking, then, and in the briefest compass, the home-base of Christian discourse begins in the area fixed by the history of Israel, the wider context in which that is set, and the history of Jesus, together with the writings of those who followed him" (p. 129). As Israel engaged in the linguistic extravagance of claiming that the world had been created in order to serve as the context for its election, so the church told its own "tall tale" of Jesus as the very embodiment of the meaning of the call and claim laid by God upon Israel, as the very content of the Torah. Secularity as the criterion of sense-making has been replaced by the "interpreted Bible" (interpreted by Jews as well as Christians) as the sole criterion of theology (*A Theology of the Jewish-Christian Reality*, part 2, 1983, pp. 3-9; hereafter referred to only as parts 1, 2, or 3).

Some people familiar with van Buren's writings wonder what the early van Buren and the later van Buren have to do with each other. Are these two even on speaking terms with each other? The answer is yes. Van Buren's passion for theological sense-making has taken him on an odyssey of discovery, characterized by more than one quantum leap along the way that has landed in a place different from where it began. Although not logically implied by its beginning, where van Buren ends up has everything to do with the hard-headed, but "great-hearted" (James) commitment to sense-making. The good fruit produced by van Buren's theological tree is his theology that emerges in the context and service of the conversation between Jews and Christians.

The home-field of Christian theology is the covenant between the God of Israel and the Israel of God; this is the context in which Christian language "works" or makes sense. The history of the church, however, reflects a turning away from and against this home-field. The anti-Judaic tradition of Christianity (part 2, pp. 9-11) is rabidly Marcionite and views Jews and Judaism as the disconfirming other. Judaism has been relegated to the status of mere prologue to Christianity, hence invisible, or its antithesis, to be negated, or as the scapegoat responsible for having killed Christ. Van Buren directly challenges and reverses this tradition by situating Christian faith within the covenant between God and Israel and insisting that only herein can Christian faith be understood.

The church is that community of Gentiles called by God's grace to join God's people Israel on its walk along the way *(torah)* of faith. Theology is the self-critical conversation that people on the way have with themselves as they discuss where they should walk. Theology is what believers do when we take responsibility for walking the way of faith. Believers are responsible to God, to those who walk with them (including the Jews whose walk we have joined), and to those who will come after them. Believers must take responsibility for their language, recognizing that sloppy use of it has brought untold suffering upon the Israel of God. Taking the covenant as the home-field of theology necessitates recognizing that the covenant with biblical Israel remains in place, that Jews today participate in it. Christian theological conversation is not with a fossil, but with our living neighbors.

Van Buren's theology does not so much differ from other theologies by disagreeing on how this or that doctrine is to be interpreted. It differs by proposing an entirely different paradigm for theology in which everything looks different and in which doctrines, such as the Trinity, have a different value. Whereas the Trinity had stood as a sign for what Jews did not believe, now it is the church's way of articulating that the God by whom it is met in Jesus Christ is the God of Israel.

Whereas Jesus Christ was interpreted as having lived in conflict with Jews and Judaism, taught against Jews and Judaism, and as having been crucified at the hands of Jews and Judaism, only to be raised in victory over Jews and Judaism, now every proper christological statement must make clear that it is done to the glory of the God of Israel and that it affirms the covenant between God and Israel (part 3, pp. xviii-xix).

Let us look briefly at what the anti-Jewish ideology did to Christian theology and doctrine and, just as briefly, outline the new alternative, van Buren's theology of the Jewish-Christian reality. In pre-*Shoah* (before the Holocaust) Christianity, theology was often ideology; anything could be said as long as it served the interest of the church and rendered Jews invisible. God became the God who would displace the people Israel with the church, the God who gave Israel a temporary, inferior covenant and then punished Israel for being faithful to it. Christ became the kind of mediator who would facilitate God's effort in making such an exchange, Christ the displacer. Scripture became a hyphenated, Marcionite scripture with a "New" Testament that fulfills and cancels the "Old" scripture and covenant. The Holy Spirit became a Christian possession, the one who unites believers to Christ but is absent from "carnal" Israel. The church is the replacement community, with whom God has replaced the Jews.

For van Buren, theology becomes not only genuinely self-critical, but must affirm the covenant between the God of Israel and the Israel of God; the work of ideology criticism must be carried on in theology. God is re-envisioned as the faithful One of Israel who seeks out covenant partners (including even Gentiles) for the redemption of the world. Jesus Christ, the re-presentation of *Torah* (Romans 10), is a gift to the church from both the God of Israel and the Israel of God in whom he took shape. The Spirit is now the *Shekhinah*/Spirit, active among Jews and all people in the effort to bind our hearts in love to God and one another. The covenant becomes genuinely inclusive of Jews and Christian Gentiles and the basis for authentic pluralism. Scripture, in which the "Apostolic Writings" are reinserted into the rest of the Bible, becomes "useful light" for walking the way of faith. The kingdom of God remains ahead of both Jews and Gentiles and stands as a sign that God is not yet finished with the church, the synagogue, or human history.

Clark Williamson

Selected Bibliography

1957/1958 *Christ in Our Place: The Substitutionary Character of Calvin's Doctrine of Reconciliation.*
1963   *The Secular Meaning of the Gospel.*
1968   *Theological Explorations.*

1972   *The Edges of Language: An Essay in the Logic of a Religion.*
1976   *The Burden of Freedom: Americans and the God of Israel.*
1980   *Discerning the Way: A Theology of the Jewish-Christian Reality,* part 1.
1983   *A Christian Theology of the People Israel: A Theology of the Jewish-Christian Reality,* part 2.
1988   *Christ in Context: A Theology of the Jewish-Christian Reality,* part 3.

HANS URS VON BALTHASAR
1905–1988

Life and Career

Until recently Hans Urs von Balthasar was known in North America chiefly through smaller, polemical writings, and was often seen as the court theologian of reactionary conservatives. As his important, creative works have been translated into English, this one-sided picture has been changing, revealing much that is timely and valuable.

Born into an old and prominent, devoutly Catholic family of Lucerne, Switzerland, von Balthasar early developed a great love for music and literature. In Vienna, Berlin, and Zürich, he pursued German Studies and Philosophy and was awarded a doctorate from Zürich for his dissertation *The History of the Eschatological Problem in Modern German Literature* (1929).

After a thirty-day retreat in 1927, he decided to enter the Society of Jesus (at the time, still officially banned in Switzerland). Following six more years of philosophical and theological studies, he was ordained a priest in 1936 and worked as a student chaplain in Basel for many years. In 1950 he decided to leave the Jesuit order in order to devote himself to a secular institute (a new kind of Catholic association in which members took vows of poverty, chastity, and obedience while pursuing their different secular professions), which he had founded with Adrienne von Speyr. He remained active as a priest in Basel until his death.

Although a gifted and tireless writer, the author of more than seventy books and hundreds of articles (to say nothing of his work as a translator, editor, and publisher), von Balthasar remained out of the mainstream of his profession. He never pursued a doctorate in theology and was never a university professor. His theology itself is daunting and dazzling because of the enormous literary, cultural, philosophical, and theological breadth one encounters there.

Approach to Theology

Two features, in particular, make his theology appealing and important. First, for von Balthasar, theology and spirituality are intrinsically related. Theology is the loving contemplation in faith upon the personal Word that God has spoken to the world in Jesus Christ. Revelation is not an abstract truth *about* God, but the divine love itself made visible in Christ and communicated historically in and through the church. It is life, not information. Faith is not merely intellectual; it is existential in nature. The speculative, theoretical dimension of theology as a "science of faith" must grow out of a personal surrender to the truth of the divine love that God reveals. As faith seeking understanding *(fides quaerens intellectum)*, theology presupposes both the effort of reason and the effort of Christian discipleship.

Von Balthasar's entire life's work may be seen as the attempt to devise a truly spiritual theology and a solid, theological spirituality. He seeks to overcome the divorce of spirituality and theological reflection that followed the entrance of theology into the university in the twelfth and thirteenth centuries, tellingly described as a change from "kneeling theology" to "sitting theology."

Second, von Balthasar adopts a new approach to theology. Theology, he says, has too long understood revelation as the "truth" to be known or the "good" to be chosen. Instead, he begins with revelation as the "beauty" or "glory" of God. The beautiful, he argues, is what has the power to engage and transform us, to empower and demand a response. Only in the wake of such an experience do the questions about truth and goodness have their real meaning. In this connection, von Balthasar sees the dynamics of revelation and faith as structurally similar to the experience of great art or love.

As the heart of his work, he proposes a theological aesthetics *(The Glory of the Lord)*, a theological dramatics *(Theodrama)*, and a theological logic (as yet untranslated). The aesthetics investigates the analogous relationship between worldly *beauty* and divine glory and presents a theory of theological perception that accounts for how the believer sees the form of God's revelation correctly and how the believer is transformed by it. The dramatics focuses on the *good* of God's self-revelation: the dramatic relationship between human freedom and its ultimate good or end, divine freedom, seen concretely in the person of Jesus Christ. The logic focuses on the *truth* of the event of God's self-revelation in the incarnation of the Logos and the outpouring of the Holy Spirit. It reflects on how divine truth can express itself in finite forms and consequently on the possibility for human beings to speak adequately of the event of God's self-revelation.

For von Balthasar, God does not come to us primarily as a teacher of divine (propositional) truths or moral precepts that are beyond the reach of corrupted human reason. God does not come simply because we sinned and need a redeemer to act for our good. Like John Duns Scotus, von Balthasar sees God as the one whose free plan from all eternity is the outpouring of divine love that gives us a gracious share in God's own life. The glory or beauty of love has no other "purpose" than its surrender to the beloved.

Von Balthasar often emphasizes the nonsystematic nature of his theology, convinced that the inconceivable fullness of God's self-revelation cannot be captured in any system. One can only approach this fullness from fragmentary, partial perspectives. His "method" has been called "theological phenomenology," "inductive convergence," or "infolding." All of these characterizations point to the same thing. For von Balthasar, theology is always the attempt to get to the center, to grasp the whole: the image of the trinitarian love revealed in concrete form in Jesus Christ and communicated in history through the Spirit in the church. Theology must be a contemplative "infolding" into the mystery of God's love before it can be an "unfolding" of its inner depths and implications. The theological enterprise, therefore, is a twofold movement of infolding and unfolding within the richness of the tradition.

The stress upon the contemplative dimension, which is immediately evident in his writing, corresponds directly to the primacy of the object contemplated. In contrast to many contemporary theologians, Balthasar deliberately chooses a different path from the Enlightenment's "turn to the subject," stressing, like Barth, the priority of the concrete form of God's revelation in Christ over the subjective structure of the believing subject. God's revelation cannot be deduced, predicted, or presumed from the human condition. It comes as something utterly free and gracious. It has a power to persuade that comes from its own inner rightness, much in the same way that a classic work of art manifests both an unpredictable "inspiration" and a convincing inner necessity or coherence. (Such power to persuade assumes the possibility of a basic correlation between God's revelation and its human recipient.) The primacy of the "other" who confronts us is the only thing that can account for the truly transformative dimension of all significant aesthetic, personal, and religious encounters.

For von Balthasar, one central, guiding image is the mother whose smile first reveals love, engendering in her child a capacity to love, and eliciting a response of love. Nonetheless, in matters of art, love, and religion specific encounters are often personally but not universally compelling, thus reflecting the complexity of interpreted experience and the inextricable relationship between the objective and subjective moments.

The Triune God

Von Balthasar's doctrine of God is of central importance. For him, the trinitarian nature of God is revealed precisely in the life and mission of Jesus. In Jesus' reference to the Father on the one hand and to the Spirit on the other, we see the anticipation of what would later be called Trinity. Here, the Gospel of John functions as a kind of comprehensive, integrating perspective for the whole of the New Testament and for von Balthasar's particular vision of Jesus. The mission of Jesus and his obedience to that mission are central. Von Balthasar tries to overcome a false opposition between "functional" (what Jesus does) and "ontological" (who

Jesus is) Christologies. Jesus *is,* first and foremost, the one who is *sent.* Person and mission are intrinsically related. One cannot correctly understand Jesus, as portrayed in the New Testament, apart from the Father who sends him or from the Spirit who leads and empowers him and whom Jesus promises to send to his disciples once he has returned to his Father.

For von Balthasar, the conjunction of three elements characterizes the image of Jesus' life-in-mission as a whole and forms the basis of a kind of implicit Christology of the New Testament. The first element is the absolute claim of *authority* made by Jesus ("You have heard that it was said . . . but I say to you" [Matthew 5]; "Those who are ashamed of me and of my words in this adulterous and sinful generation, of them the Son of Man will also be ashamed when he comes in [his] glory" [Mark 8:38]). The second element is the utter *poverty* and defenselessness of his life in surrender to God (faith, prayer, and solidarity with the poor and sinners). And the third element is his utter *self-abandonment* in loving obedience to God. For von Balthasar, the cross is the climax and concentration of a life lived utterly from God and for others. God did not send Jesus to the cross. Jesus prayed to be delivered from it, but refused to turn away from it. He embraced it as the consequence of what he said and did in the name of God. He refused to compromise the values of God's kingdom or to abandon the sinners and poor who have a special place in it. In particular, Christ's obedience means to be the expression of God's loving mercy and radical solidarity with sinners. Jesus chose again and again to be utterly open and faithful to God in a way that allowed the God of love and mercy to be present and active in him for us. Only in this way could he be the revelation of God's own self-surrendering love for the world, a love that shows itself even on a cross. In self-surrendering love we truly see the depths of God's *glory.*

What comes to light in the resurrection is not meant to blind us from the cross and to erase it from our memories, but to let us see in it something more than human evil and tragedy—the revelation of love and a path to true life. Only such a love is worthy of faith.

Only such a love lives and breathes from a Spirit that can be recognized as divine. For von Balthasar, the Spirit is precisely the one who is "over" Jesus, leading and shaping his life-in-mission, and "in" Jesus, empowering him to carry it out. Jesus is the pioneer and model of Christian faith and prayer precisely as one who had to attend constantly to the promptings of the Spirit in order to discern in each new situation the will of the one he called Abba ("Father").

For von Balthasar, the trinitarian structure of the Christ-event is the historical or "economic" revelation of the trinitarian nature of God's "immanent" being as Father, Son, and Spirit. The Christ-event reveals not only that God loves the world, but that God *is* love, a community of love. The self-surrendering love manifest in the life of Jesus is the revelation that God in God's very self is self-surrendering love. Von Balthasar's understanding of God is fundamentally *kenotic* (that is, one of self-emptying love), leading to a conception of the trinitarian persons in a radically relational and paradoxically "selfless" way. Thus, he suggests, the three in God are not so much different "selves," but different modes of divine selflessness.

God is Father precisely as the one who in utter freedom from all eternity expresses Godself in love in the sense that God gives God's very self away in the begetting of the Son. As the perfect expression of the Father's "self" as outpouring love, the Son proclaims and witnesses this love in that he surrenders himself to this love and acknowledges his true "self" as the glorification of the loving Father. This "I-Thou" relationship in which God is Father as Begettor and Son (Word) as Begotten is mutual surrender, "being for the other." The fruit of this loving surrender in its personal unity and miraculous "more" is the Spirit. The Spirit is the "ever-greater love" between Father and Son, the witness of the eternal, inexhaustible fullness of love, which Christians confess to be God. Von Balthasar suggests that we should conceive of God as "infinite comparative" not as static superlative. God's "most" is always "more." This linguistic turn enables von Balthasar to conceive of God in a much more dynamic way than has traditionally been the case. God is ever-greater in God's own essence, not just in comparison to human reason.

Analogous to the love between a man and a woman, which in its utter intimacy and fullness brings forth the miracle of new life, so too, the love between the Father and Son in its absolute intimacy and fullness brings forth the Holy Spirit as the ever-greater "more" of their love. Sexual love is the key metaphor of the Trinity for von Balthasar.

God does not need the world to become love. God freely chooses to create the world in order to share the divine life in love. Creation is an act of self-surrender in love that flows from the self-surrender of the trinitarian persons and has as its climax the incarnation. Thus the concept of the divine self-emptying in love *(kenosis)* is what unifies von Balthasar's whole theology. Trinity, creation, incarnation, and sanctification are seen as the process of God's gracious and loving self-outpouring as Spirit.

The Church

The Spirit of Jesus surrendered on the cross (or breathed from the Risen Lord on Easter, or sent from the right hand of the Father on Pentecost) is the soul of the community of faith. Retrieving a patristic theme, von Balthasar sees the church as born from the pierced side of the crucified Lord. The surrender of the Spirit and the eucharistic outpouring of blood and water is the handing over ("tradition") of Christ's very substance. Thus the church is the Body of Christ. At the same time, the church is the community of human beings for whom the Lord died, and as such, the church is indeed an "other" vis-à-vis Christ, the Bride of Christ. In different ways, these two images express the *unity in difference* between Christ and the church. Seen in the horizon of its origin from the cross, these metaphors come together in the patristic image of the church as the new Eve.

The Spirit, who gave Jesus' life its specific shape and form, informs and transforms the disciples, shaping and enlivening them as the Body-Bride of Christ, and drawing them ever more deeply into the saving mystery and pattern of divine, self-emptying love.

Von Balthasar distinguishes three interrelated dimensions of the church, each symbolized by a figure who had a key position in the Christ-event. The personal, *Marian* dimension, grounded in her yes to God, symbolizes the all-encompassing, receptive, obedient posture of faith. The objective *Petrine* dimension is the form-giving dimension of order and sacrament, which gives enduring mediating form to the Christ-event in history. The subjective *Johannine* dimension is the concrete actualization of the Christ-event in loving communion.

For von Balthasar the eucharist is the center of the church. The mystery of the church and Christian discipleship are seen primarily in terms of our continuing transformation by and participation in the one saving mission of Christ. This subjective transformation in the life of faith is mediated through the objective forms of sacrament, scripture, and church order. This mediation through objective forms is precisely the Spirit's work of glorifying the Son, and for von Balthasar it is most evident in the saints. They are the living, authentic commentaries on the gospel, written by God's own Spirit. In their lives is revealed the glory of divine love in its transforming power.

Like Jesus, the church is sent out to be witnesses of God's love and to encourage men and women to open their hearts to God's life-giving Spirit. Thus, says von Balthasar, the same obedience evident in the life of Jesus ("Not my will, but your will be done") must characterize the lives of believers. The church as a whole owes obedience to the Spirit. Church authority exists to ensure that the community of faith discerns the Spirit authentically in each new situation, acknowledges the gifts and callings that the Spirit bestows and supports, and organizes and deploys them in a way that builds up the whole body. As such, obedience is due it. To be sure, such obedience often involves a painful process of deprivation or self-denial so that one can truly become fruitful "for others." Yet, such an understanding of obedience seems to be based on a very ideal conception of church authority and leaves little room for a responsible theology of dissent and disobedience.

For von Balthasar, therefore, the Christ-event is an act of divine *kenosis* or self-emptying that comes to its climax in the loving outpouring of the Spirit and the communication of divine life in and through the church. Worship, scripture, sacraments, church authority, theology: All of these are the concrete ways in which the divine life of the Spirit is mediated historically. They are not ends in themselves. Everything about the church's practice and "traditions" must be judged in light of this fundamental meaning of Tradition, which is the sharing of divine life.

Salvation

Clearly for von Balthasar, salvation is nothing other than participation in God's own divine life, a process of divinization. To be human means to be fundamentally open, to be capable of being in relationships of love with other persons, and ultimately, with God. However, the world as we know it is deeply marked by our failure to love. As a consequence of sin and its abiding, pervasive effects, human freedom is itself unfree and in need of liberation and transformation by God. This liberation is precisely the work of the Spirit, who as the "form" of divine love and true freedom revealed in Jesus Christ, informs and transforms us, leading us ever more deeply into the paschal mystery. Thus the process by which God shares divine life with us—divinizes us—necessarily involves our redemption from the brokenness of sin. Salvation or divinization is not a once-and-for-all event, but a continuing process that looks toward final consummation through death and resurrection. Yet the process of salvation is not one of steady, easygoing "progress," either individually or cosmically. Indeed, in his later writings, von Balthasar increasingly describes the divine-human drama of sin and grace in apocalyptic terms.

One of the striking characteristics of von Balthasar's eschatology is the prominence that he gives to God's universal saving will. Rejecting any notion of double predestination on the one hand, and a doctrine of universal salvation on the other, he nevertheless insists that Christians can and must *hope* that all men and women will be saved. Biblical language about hell, like that about heaven, should not be understood literally as if it were a divine report about a future that God already knows. Such language expresses, rather, the absolute seriousness of believers' free response to God's self-offer in love. Matthew 25 does not mean that there will in fact be goats at the final judgment; it warns sinners not to allow ourselves to become "goats." The love that provides sinners with salvation cannot save them against their wills, for it would not be love if it ignored human freedom.

For von Balthasar, the hope (as opposed to the knowledge) that all will be saved is based not only on the true nature of love: How could one really say one loves with the love of God and *not* see all people as one's brothers and sisters, *not* hoping that they will be saved? The saved and the damned are not—and cannot be—categories into which faith and hope, if they are truly Christian, divide humanity.

Even more, *Christian* hope is based on the God who is revealed in Jesus Christ, particularly on the cross and in the descent into hell. On the basis of what he believed to be the mystical experience of a surgeon in Basel named Adrienne von Speyr, von Balthasar does not understand the descent into hell as the triumphant appearance of Christ preaching the good news to the just souls awaiting redemption. As the one who "descends into hell," Jesus is the expression of the radical unwillingness of God to abandon sinners, even where by definition God cannot be. Christ's solidarity in hell with all sinners requires Christian hope to be universal in scope.

Von Balthasar speaks of God's erecting the cross in hell and wonders whether God, in the face of the crucified Son, may not have ways of moving even the most obdurate human will, not by force but by the power of love. For von Balthasar, an appropriate image of Christian hope is found in the "throne of grace" (Heb. 4:16). This motif, often portrayed in the history of art, shows the Father seated on a throne, holding the crucified Son on his lap, for the viewer to behold. The Spirit, in the form of a dove, hovers above, sending rays of divine light and grace that enable the eyes of faith to recognize love revealing itself (a love, as Anselm might have put it, "greater than which cannot be conceived").

Here, the cross is not something believers show God to remind God and all persons that the debt has been paid; it is not an emblem that changes or protects from God's wrath. Rather, *God* shows sinners the cross that they may see the depth of God's love for them.

Catholicity

Although many of von Balthasar's writings exhibit a remarkable ecumenical engagement (a profound catholicity in the original meaning of the term), a certain tension characterizes his understanding of the relationship between Christianity and the other world religions. On the one hand, there is a deep conviction that the Spirit blows in places we do not know. In fact, in a striking phrase, von Balthasar calls the Spirit the "Unknown One beyond the Word." On the other hand, he never engaged in any serious or sustained dialogue with other religious traditions. Although he could admit the merits of some forms of Eastern meditation, he maintained a fundamentally skeptical attitude toward them. Perhaps he perceived a certain fascination with the East among Christians who had no idea of the rich resources of their own tradition. In any case, although other religions may well manifest signs of the presence of God's Spirit, they have no real revelatory significance for von Balthasar. It may be that in a given case, contact with another religious tradition helps Christianity see more clearly an insight forgotten or obscured. But the revelation of God in Jesus Christ and its concrete, living historical form in the Tradition is complete and in need of no complement. For von Balthasar, only Christ as God's Word is capable of integrating what is true in the many disparate religious longings and insights of humanity.

John R. Sachs

Selected Primary Works

1968 *Love Alone: The Way of Revelation.*
1971 *The Theology of Karl Barth.*

1982   *The von Balthasar Reader,* ed. Medard Kehl and Werner Löser, trans. Robert J. Daly.

1987   *Prayer.*

1988   *Dare We Hope "That All Men Be Saved"?*

1985-1990 *The Glory of the Lord: A Theological Aesthetics,* 7 vols., ed. Joseph Fessio and John Riches.

1988-1990 *Theodrama: Theological Dramatic Theory I-II.*

1990   *Mysterium Paschale.*

1990   A complete bibliography may be found in *Hans Urs von Balthasar: Bibliographie 1925–1990,* ed. Cornelia Capol.

Selected Secondary Sources

1984   Michael Waldstein, "Hans Urs von Balthasar's Theological Aesthetics," *Communio* 11/1 (Spring):13-27.

1988   Louis Dupré, "Hans Urs von Balthasar's Theology of Aesthetic Form," *Theological Studies* 49:299-318.

1989   David Tracy, "The Uneasy Alliance Reconceived: Catholic Theological Method, Modernity and Postmodernity," *Theological Studies* 50:548-70.

1991   David L. Schindler, ed., *Hans Urs von Balthasar: His Life and Work.*

1992   John O'Donnell, *Hans Urs von Balthasar.*

1993   John R. Sachs, *"Deus Semper Major—Ad Majorem Dei Gloriam:* The Pneumatology and Christian Spirituality of Hans Urs von Balthasar," *Gregorianum* 74/7:631-57.

1994   Edward T. Oakes, *Pattern of Redemption: The Theology of Hans Urs von Balthasar.*

CORNEL WEST
1953–

Life and Career

Cornel West's joint appointment as Professor of Philosophy of Religion and African American Studies at Harvard University reflects the scope of his intellectual interests in devising a multicontextual philosophical, theological, and cultural discourse for engaging a postmodern reality—a world that is increasingly fragmented, diversified, and pluralistic. He is interested in how the contemporary intellectual can participate in the formation of public values that are informed by the best elements of Western intellectual history, especially elements from its prophetic African American Christian tradition.

West graduated from Harvard University *magna cum laude* in 1973, and earned his M.A. (1975) and Ph.D. (1980) degrees at Princeton University. He received his undergraduate degree in Semitic languages and pursued graduate studies in philosophy, becoming the first African American to complete the Ph.D. program in philosophy at Princeton. He has taught philosophy of religion at Union Theological Seminary (New York) and theology at Yale University's Divinity School. Until his most recent appointment, he was Professor of Religion and Director of African American Studies at Princeton University.

Although West's formal specialization is in philosophy, his interests and writings have spanned the philosophy of religion, black theology, social theory, the history of ideas, and cultural criticism. He considers himself to be an African American Christian within the prophetic tradition of Martin Luther King, Jr. He is also a committed "organic intellectual" within that stream of progressive Marxism as expressed by Antonio Gramsci. Throughout his writings he has sought to combine these two influences upon his thought into a vision for social justice.

In developing his perspective, West has appropriated insights from a diverse group of intellectuals, such as W. E. B. Du Bois (an African American social analysis of Euro-American racism), Friedrich Nietzsche (critique of dogmatic values in the struggle for the democratization of cultural sensibilities and norms), Karl Marx (dialectical materialism as a way of understanding the structures and histories of the forces of oppression), Paul Tillich (the method of correlation as an approach for responding theologically to the existential questions that are implicit in our cultural impasse), Reinhold Niebuhr (neoorthodoxy as a form of Christian social critique that is both realistic about the human predicament and yet optimistic about the triumph of good over evil), Martin Luther King, Jr. (African American prophetic Christianity as a form of social critique that is rooted in the continuing struggle for freedom, equality, and liberation), Malcolm X (as a countercultural, Islamic African American voice of social analysis and proposed strategies for liberation), Antonio Gramsci (progressive Marxism that values the religiocultural sensibilities of an organic intellectual), Jürgen Habermas (critique of ideologically coded information and misinformation), Hans-Georg Gadamer (hermeneutics as a way of interpreting the "horizons" of reality in general), Jacques Derrida (deconstructionist strategies for critiquing and challenging hegemonic structures within a given culture), and Michel Foucault (the utilization of certain techniques of discourse analysis in order to disclose hidden meanings and disrupt prevailing notions associated with them as the first step toward innovation and the democratization of values).

As a public theologian, philosopher, and cultural worker, West is committed to a hermeneutics of involvement that compels him to move between the ideologically dense terrain of the academy and the precarious and balkanized environment of popular culture. He seems to do so with relative ease as he continually strives to be both a theorist and a practitioner of the form of prophetic Christianity that he proposes. Like Reinhold Niebuhr, he has the ability to articulate what justice, mercy, and love demand of human beings to provide a moral framework for social change. Moreover, he believes that this conversation should take place in the public sphere as well as within the halls of colleges, universities, divinity schools, and seminaries. In addition, his commitment to a liberationist theological perspective like that of Martin Luther King, Jr., allows him to see political relevance in terms of a biblical emphasis on the plight of the wretched of the earth. Since he sees himself as an intellectual freedom fighter in the African American Christian tradition, ideas become a source of power that can be used both critically and creatively in the struggle for the liberation of all people, especially those who are most marginalized. His own contribution toward this endeavor is to remain organically linked to prophetic movements of a priestly institution, such as the African American church, while taking the life of the mind seriously enough to relate ideas that are generated in the academy to the everyday life of ordinary people.

In the following descriptive analysis, West's thoughts have been placed under traditional theological categories, with the full awareness of the limitations of attempting to classify as strictly theological what he has contributed to both the academy and general public. Such a strategy will benefit those who wish to understand his relevance to Christian theology.

Theological Task

As an African American Christian intellectual, West wants to break out of "the academic cocoon" as a closed system of information dispersal in order to reach the African American community and society at-large by striving to coordinate the activities of the life of the mind with appropriate community activism. For him, the task of theology is to engage the life of the mind and spirit in such a way that this intellectual engagement necessarily includes social praxis. He wants to participate in the public marketplace of ideas as one who is convinced that the Christian message or language of faith is commensurate with other forms of public discourse (e.g., economic, political, juridical). So he utilizes resources outside the traditional Christian vocabulary, though not completely unrelated to it, in order to communicate normative Christian values within a post-Christian and postmodern context.

Like any other intellectual, West has a constellation of issues around which he organizes his thinking. In his case, they include dread, despair, disappointment, and meaninglessness. On the one hand, such existential notions inform his sense of the depth of human anguish, alienation, and potential hopelessness. On the other hand, he wants to present a perspective that is both prophetic and hopeful as an alternative to nihilism. More specifically, he combats the loss of hope and absence of meaning that pervades much of the African American community as well as the broader society. He would like to recapture the dynamic role of the religious community as a vehicle for both individual and social transformation within and beyond the African American community. Therefore, he forms a link between African American religious experience, prophetic Christianity, and the struggle for black liberation that is rooted in a pragmatic revolutionary praxis. The African American prophetic tradition and progressive Marxism are brought together as the primary resources for his own style of theological reflection and social praxis.

West engages in a form of cultural criticism that seeks to analyze, appraise, and critique the present reality while offering an alternative vision to it. He draws extensively from Marxism in order to analyze the structures and histories of oppression that now exist within a developed capitalist society such as the United States. Like Latin American liberation theologians, he appropriates a form of Christian social analysis that sees social oppression as an idolatrous structure purposely set over against the weakest citizens of a given socioeconomic political structure. He advocates revolutionary transformation of oppressive forces in favor of an arrangement that gives privilege to the poor in their struggle for full humanity. Theologically, this change means that the task of the theologian is to proclaim and participate in bringing about God's just kingdom on earth, in word and deed, in theory and practice. His own style of social analysis and cultural critique is not merely one grand synthetic social theory, but a number of local ones that are international in scope and historical in content. It incorporates elements from various modes of social analysis and cultural critique: Weberian, racial, feminist, gay/lesbian, and ecological. Utilizing such diverse methods and perspectives, he makes his own philosophical and theological reflection both multicontextual and multidimensional.

West also sees himself as a radical historicist, one who is immersed, with critical faculties, in the life, ethics, suffering, and hopes of a particular people in particular places without becoming lost in relativism, positivism, or nihilism. He is especially concerned with the particularity of the African American experience and its universal implications for human suffering and the struggle for liberation from oppression. Theory and praxis become intertwined in the ideological and pragmatic struggle for humanization against the dehumanizing "powers and principalities" of a hedonistic, technocratic, capital intensive, and postmodern reality.

Authority (Sources and Method)

As a Christian theologian, West is informed by the Jewish and Christian scriptures, the history of Christian thought, and current trends within Christian theology, especially black theology. At the same time, he is conversant with Enlightenment and postmodern philosophies, especially decontructionism. In this sense, he is akin to Paul Tillich as one who seeks a middle way between philosophy and theology as two traditions that have had a powerful influence upon Western intellectual history. His basic theological stance is a combination of black, womanist, and Latin American liberation theologies. His concern for theologically interpreting the plight of the poor and marginalized is consistent with the style of discourse and social analysis of liberation theologians in general. His appeal for complete human liberation is thus deeply informed by a liberationist theological perspective. Involved in dialogues between black theologians and third world theologians during the mid-1970s to mid-1980s, he agreed that a theological methodology that is employed in light of the oppressed cannot remain abstract, but must become grounded in a hermeneutical circle of reflection and praxis in relation to a specific community.

For West, the prophetic Christian tradition, as a source of his moral vision and ethical norms, follows the biblical injunction to see the world through the eyes of victims. It also yields a christocentric perspective via the lens of the cross while it inspires opposition to existential anguish, socioeconomic, cultural, and political oppression, and dogmatic modes of thought and action. His version of prophetic Christianity, however, is not simply an instrumentalist response to postmodernity's flattening of issues by refusing to address despair and the absurd. Instead, Christian narratives and stories are empowering and enabling precisely because they provide insight into our sojourn on this globe, a way of service and sacrifice, care and love at the center of what it means to be human. While this insight is also found in

Judaism, Islam, and traditional African religions, West seeks to articulate it in a Christian framework.

God and Christ (Theology and Christology)

West's understanding of God (both metaphysically and dogmatically) is informed by his liberationist position. His view of a creating and loving God is balanced by a perspective that views God as just and liberating. This view means that God is both the creator and sustainer of life and the one who initiates a new and revolutionary order in opposition to existing oppressive systems and institutions. As demonstrated in much of the Jewish narrative, God is especially concerned with the plight of the poor and with the responsibility of the faithful to participate in the alleviation of their suffering. Christian responsibility moves beyond occasional acts of charity to a sustained engagement in the analysis, critique, and transformation of the causes of individual and corporate forms of oppression. Here West's philosophical interest in the existential interpretation of the human condition converges with his Judeo-Christian apologetic vision of hope and transformation.

West advances this vision in light of the incarnation, crucifixion, and resurrection in the New Testament narratives of Jesus of Nazareth. Jesus is passionately concerned with the condition of all people, most especially with the wretched of the earth. He demonstrates this concern by his association with the despised persons and groups of his own time. His own death as a criminal of the Roman State epitomizes his stance. The cross thus provides a unique angle of vision for understanding the multidimensionality and universality of human suffering. Correspondingly, it can be inferred from West's writings that the resurrection symbolizes the promise of new possibilities for meaning, in the midst of and beyond the existential sense of dread and despair, as a feasible alternative to meaninglessness or nihilism. Thus, the reality of the cross and the potentialities represented by the resurrection constitute a dialectical demonstration of God's incarnated identification with the tragedy of the human predicament and God's work to create a new humanity and world-cosmic order.

Human Nature, Sin, and Evil

West's theological perspective is most clearly expressed in his understanding of human nature, sin, and evil. He sees within human beings the greatest potential for egalitarian social, political, and economic relationships. These positive potentialities are related to how he perceives traces of the *imago Dei* in the human capacity for creativity, innovation, and altruism. At the same time, he realizes that exploitation and oppression in the forms of imperialism, classism, sexism, racism, xenophobia, and homophobia, for example, thwart those potentialities. In the service of his understanding of essential humanity, he directs his energy as a theoretician, lay preacher, and social activist, sharing his vision of a more just world order.

"Vision" is an important term for understanding and appreciating West's theoretical work. At this level of intellectual activity, he wants to engage some of the most complex and influential minds of the modern and postmodern world in order to situate and establish his own revolutionary interventions in the history of ideas. By way of his own African American idiom (as demonstrated in his sermonic public speeches), he fuels his ideas with an emotive rhetoric that is intended to influence both individual and social behavior. The goal is conversion or the transformation of the individual and society by means of a radical appeal to the best examples of human egalitarianism, both Christian and non-Christian.

The problem of evil is evinced in the prominent life-denying forces in our world. According to West, each form of evil is controlled by a peculiar structure of decadent social logic: economic exploitation (social logic of capital accumulation); state repression (social logic of social augmentation); bureaucratic domination (social logic of administrative subordination); racial, sexual, and heterosexual subjugation (social logic of white male and heterosexual supremacist practices); and ecological subjection (social logic of modern values of scientific manipulation). His view of evil is expressed primarily in terms of sociosystemic relationships. Although West is keenly aware of the individual and personal dimensions of sin and evil, he chooses to speak more directly about their sociostructural manifestations. He emphasizes that the structural forces are historically rooted in the collective lives of individuals, requiring attempts toward transformation that are cognizant of the historical and social determinants of various forms of oppression as well as the need for personal, individual conversions from oppressive to liberating behavior.

Salvation and Hope

As an African American Christian intellectual, West understands the salvific work of Jesus Christ to be the basis of his own engagement (especially in light of the legacy of Euro-American racism) with today's North American culture. His zeal for justice is informed by a realizable concrete eschatology. Strategically, however, West chooses to speak in a language that is primarily philosophical and rhetorical rather than theological and confessional in order to cast as broad a net as possible within the public marketplace. As a public Christian intellectual, he engages a pluralistic context with a compelling sensitivity and dexterity. In the public forum, the influence of the communitarianism of African American Christianity is combined with the egalitarianism of radical Protestantism and democratic socialism. Collectively, these streams flow into a "river of life" from which West draws inspiration for his own eschatological sustenance. In turn, he strives to share this resource with all who participate (or should be allowed to participate) in the making of a truly democratic and egalitarian society.

West believes that the prophetic Christian tradition, as an interpretative resource for addressing the topic of salvation history, provides a synoptic vision that yields insight and power into the multiform character of human existence. This moral vision and its attendant ethical norms propel human intellectual activity to account for and transform existing dogmatism, oppression, and despair. Here again, a hermeneutics of involvement is crucial for grasping the relationship between the Christian message of liberation and the role of Christians as participatory agents of transformation within a given historical context. West's historicist turn in the philosophy of religion helps him to understand the necessity of choice in a rational and critical manner. The process of transformation (via the prophetic Christian tradition) for a better world necessarily involves the revision of theories for living by stressing both human finitude and agency. In other words, he calls us to participate in showing signs of the kingdom of God without arrogantly assuming that we will bring it to full fruition short of God's initiative and cooperation.

West believes that existential suffering and eschatological hope should always be juxtaposed with each other. This juxtaposition is especially clear in the African American context. A collective "Suffering Servant" motif (Isaiah 53) represents the challenge to come to terms with the structural and institutional process that has disfigured, deformed, and devastated African Americans. But left alone, such a perspective is unredemptive and actually induces despair. Therefore, into the historical struggles of African American people one must also bring resources of the collective and critical consciousness combined with moral commitment and courageous engagement to achieve a more promising future. For example, the African American struggle against personal despair, intellectual dogmatism, and socioeconomic oppression on all fronts should foster communities of hope. Of course, such sustained action also requires a bold "leap of faith" into a promised future. Meanwhile, in the present context there is a strong need for race-transforming prophets (of all ethnicities), who never forget the significance of race, but refuse to be confined to it, and who as moralists are concerned about moral development regardless of race, creed, gender, or nation. Such persons must be global citizens whose task is to discern how a Christian (or humanitarian or person of faith of whatever sort) can think and act to diminish the plight of the poor and powerless.

Religious Pluralism

West is not only open to religious pluralism, but convinced that it is indispensable. All forms of censorship and exclusiveness are problematic. Not only should Jews, Christians, and Muslims practice mutual toleration, but also ethnic, class, and gender-based ideological constructs that are oppressive toward others should be demolished. Without diminishing the importance of either individual self-worth or a sense of group identity, West wants to encourage the construction of a social contract that engenders the full participation of all its members. Consequently, his notion of authentic religious pluralism means that the world is a place where diverse ideas and cultural practices are cherished, nurtured, and enhanced to the extent that they contribute to the betterment of all of God's creation.

Will Coleman

Selected Bibliography

1982   *Prophesy Deliverance!: An Afro-American Revolutionary Christianity.*
1982   *Theology in the Americas: Detroit II Conference Papers* (co-editor).
1985   *A Post-Analytic Philosophy* (co-editor).
1988   *Prophetic Fragments.*
1990   *Out There: Marginalization and Contemporary Culture.*
1991   *The American Evasion of Philosophy: A Genealogy of Pragmatism.*
1991   *Breaking Bread*, with bell hooks.
1991   *The Ethical Dimensions of Marxist Thought.*
1991   *Prophetic Reflections.*
1991   *Prophetic Thought in Postmodern Times.*
1993   *Race Matters.*
1993   *Keeping Faith: Philosophy and Race in America.*
1995   *Jews and Blacks: Let the Healing Begin*, with Michael Lerner.

WOMANIST THEOLOGIANS
Jacquelyn Grant, Delores Williams

In 1983 Alice Walker introduced the term "womanist" in her book, *In Search of Our Mothers' Gardens.* The origin of the word lies in the colloquial expression "womanish" that African American mothers use when their young daughters behave "like a woman." For Walker, "womanist" denotes a female who engages in behavior that is "outrageous, audacious, courageous, or willful." She is also

> Responsible. In charge. Serious. Also: A woman who loves other women, sexually and/or nonsexually. Appreciates and prefers women's culture, women's emotional flexibility . . . and women's strength. . . . Committed to survival and wholeness of entire people, male and female. Not a separatist, except periodically, for health. Traditionally universalist. . . . Traditionally capable . . . Womanist is to feminist as purple is to lavender. (p. xi)

Walker's name for a self-possessed, self-defined, community-loving black woman has since been embraced by an emergent movement of African American women theologians. At the forefront of the movement are Jacquelyn Grant, who founded the leadership program Black Women in Church and Society and who teaches at the Interdenominational Theological Center in Atlanta, and Delores Williams, who was formerly on faculty at the School of Theology at Drew University and who now teaches at Union Theological Seminary in New York.

The basic theological sources for womanists are Christian scripture and the lived experience of African American women. The goal of womanist theology is to articulate a Christian basis for liberation that depicts black women's reality and gives authority to their interpretation of scripture and religious life. Grant and Williams agree that a theory of liberation cannot simply do away with Christianity, despite its role in justifying the oppression of women, African Americans, and other ethnic groups, because the Christian tradition remains central for many African American women. They believe that Christian theology can become just and

513

liberating once it reflects African American women's reality. Such a theology is articulated from a historical perspective that honors the continuity of African American women's lives from their origins in Africa, through American slavocracy and the Reconstruction, to the present day. It takes seriously black women's experience of work, family, sexual relations, and moral decision making.

The failure of white feminist and black male theologians to incorporate a historical perspective that includes black women's experiences has provided much of the impetus behind the emergence of womanist theology. Feminist theology has been primarily the domain of white, middle-class women and has tended to ignore the issues of race and class, which have a profound impact on black and poor women. Functioning under the illusion that their experience is representative of the lives of all women, feminist theologians have tended to overlook the extent to which white women have participated in and benefited from the persecution and abuse of African American women from the time of the institution of slavery to the present.

But white women and men have not been alone in using Christian scripture and theology to justify the oppression of black women. Womanist theologians demonstrate that black theology has remained the preserve of men who neglect the impact of class and gender in their work. While black men are able to deconstruct white definitions of black males that are dehumanizing, they have failed to critique their own misogyny and their exclusion of black women from their theologizing. Black male theologians have universalized blackness in the same way that white male theologians universalize gender and that feminists universalize whiteness and middle-class status. In their attempts to wrest control of scripture, doctrine, and theologizing from the hands of white men, white feminists and black male theologians have repeated the traditional theological error; namely, they have presumed to speak for all women and all blacks respectively. Womanists claim equal authority with white and black men and feminists to describe God, to articulate religious experience, and to develop social ethics.

In contrast to other theologians who rely on *either* race *or* gender to ground their work, a womanist theologian includes analyses of gender, race, and class in her theology out of the conviction that each of these social realities conditions an individual's or group's lived reality and relationship with God. Womanists demonstrate how the all-pervasive reality of antiblack and antifemale prejudice in United States culture conditions all human social interactions. In addition, they identify the impact of race prejudice on the self-development of black Americans and of oppressive misogyny both in black communities and churches and in the larger milieu. Furthermore, because a disproportionate number of African Americans live in poverty, classism also undergirds black consciousness and black-white social relationships. Womanists assert that a Christian theology that genuinely represents the will of God for all persons needs to reflect the experience and understanding of those who have been discounted by both traditional and liberation theologies of the past.

Despite their particular stance as African American women, womanist theologians have consistently engaged voices from other theological communities. While critical of white feminists and black male theologians, womanist theologians share many of their methodological techniques and areas of concern. Like most liberation theologians, womanist theologians employ a *contextual* methodology through which they refer to the oral and written traditions of African American women of the nineteenth century to develop a history of black women's personal and communal religious experience. Because enslaved and free black women were usually denied access to the written scripture, general education, and the opportunity to do formal theology, the source of much of womanist content is the literature, music, autobiographies, and lectures of inspired black women like Sojourner Truth, Jarena Lee, and Maria W. Stewart.

Like black liberation theologians, womanist theologians emphasize knowing God as revealed in the Old Testament. Williams and Grant agree that there is a "liberating word" in the Bible, although at the same time they believe that the use of the Bible must be carefully constructed, since, in addition to serving liberation, the Bible has historically served as a tool of oppression against women and ethnic and sexual minorities. Womanists and Christian feminists concur that the Bible is a male story, written by males, about males, and for the edification and advancement of males. Womanists also point out that although black male theologians have readily identified the ways in which Euro-Americans have appropriated the Bible to suit their purposes in showing themselves to be racially and morally superior to blacks, these same male theologians have taken advantage of the ways in which traditional Western theology promotes a belief in the inferiority of women. Despite the difficulties involved in appropriating the Bible for liberative causes, womanists agree with other Christian feminists that the Bible cannot simply be jettisoned by liberationists, because it has been and continues to form the foundation of daily faith and life for many Christian women. The question that must be answered is: How can African American women find support for their particular liberation in the Hebrew and Christian scriptures?

Williams employs the texts about Hagar in the Abraham and Sarah cycle of stories in Genesis to articulate the religious journey of African American Christian women. Since the days of legalized slavery in the United States, African Americans have seen their own history in the plight of the Egyptian maid raped and abused by her slavemaster and his wife. Black slave women especially recognized in Hagar's situation their own experience of slavery in which they were forced to serve as surrogates for white women in all capacities, from being sexual partners of white men to wet nurses (mammies) to white children. These women found in Hagar the hope that God would indeed listen to them and initiate interpersonal relationships with them.

While acknowledging the positive importance of Hagar's life story for black women, Williams confronts the reality that despite God's direct intervention in

515

Hagar's situation, God never liberates her from her slavery to Sarah and Abraham. Indeed, in their first encounter God instructs Hagar to return to the abuse from which she fled. Later, in their second and final confrontation—after Hagar has been forced out into the wilderness—God promises Hagar and her son life, but it is a life of struggle and hard work. The slave woman is never uplifted to the height to which Sarah will be raised by God.

The relationship between Hagar and God points to two of the key issues explored in womanist theology. First, Hagar's life experience represents the reality of black women in America who have historically been forced to serve the needs and agendas of white women and men. Second, God's response to Hagar and Ishmael in the desert is an example of the "non-liberative thread" running through the scripture—the biblical stories in which God seems to condone acts of oppression and genocide. The womanist response to this scriptural reality is to recognize that the Bible is not always friendly to and supportive of efforts by the oppressed to free themselves. In light of such internal contradictions, Williams suggests that black male and womanist theologians take a more critical stance in their use of the Bible as a defense for African-American efforts toward social, political, and economic liberation. Womanists maintain that the Bible is only one source of knowledge of God's will. Personal experience of God's saving grace is an equally valid foundation for theologizing.

Despite the severity of the hardships they face in racist America, and Christianity's role in perpetuating such oppression, African American women and men have always drawn attention to the ways in which their individual and collective burdens are lightened by God. Womanists call on this experience of God's intervention on their behalf in concrete situations to deal with the problems inherent in biblical stories. Although the Bible may depict God as condoning human oppression, the life experience of their relationship with Jesus carries the authority that black women and men need in order to claim that God is all-just. Womanists assume the goodness and justice of God and God's favoritism toward oppressed persons, and they believe that when oppressed groups fail in their attempts to end their suffering, the fault lies in their own praxis or some other human action, not in the will of God. God may not prevent people from treating one another unfairly, but God does intervene to give the persecuted the spiritual means to survive their oppression. Williams refers to this reality as "survival in the wilderness." Using Hagar's situation as an example, Williams conceives that God sends Hagar back to slavery and abuse not because God approves of the behavior of her oppressors, but because in that culture Hagar's best chance for survival existed in her captivity. There, at least, she would be fed and clothed and able to give life to her son. God, Williams concludes, does not stop the oppressor, but God gives the oppressed the means to survive and perhaps to fight the oppressor once again.

Womanists believe that God wills their freedom from three hundred years of oppression, but they recognize that white men and women maintain the political, social, and economic power to obstruct the realization of God's will. Socially constructed webs of relationships that systematically deny the humanity and worth of some persons to gratify the desires of others constitute the source of evil in the world, for evil is a failure or refusal of persons to treat one another as equally valuable. Such marginalization and oppression, womanists contend, runs counter to the will of God. They believe that their methodology is the best approach to doing Christian theology because it is the only one that takes full account of the three primary forms of structural evil: classism, sexism (including heterosexism), and racism.

The propensity for wrong relations notwithstanding, womanists believe that persons are capable of resisting evil and changing oppressive social structures if they emulate what Williams calls the "ministerial vision" of Jesus. Unlike many traditional theologians, Williams explains that Jesus offered humanity a way to salvation not through his bloody death on the cross, but through the example he set in his life and in the ethic he promoted. It was through his ministerial vision of correcting relations between individuals and communities that Jesus made human redemption possible. Persons are called by God to participate in this ministerial vision of righting false relations. But human beings tend to spurn God and seek control of the lives of others. The crucifixion was the response of self-serving persons to Jesus' liberating message. The cross is therefore a symbol of human evil attempting to foil the plan of God, not a symbol of redemption. Ultimately, however, the ministerial vision of Jesus triumphs over the human attempt to destroy it, by means of Jesus' resurrection and the coming of the Spirit.

Just as Jesus' redemptive act did not result in his death but renewed his life, human redemption lies in challenging evil, not submitting to it. Womanists critique other interpretations of the crucifixion that equate Jesus' death with the act of redemption. Limiting redemption to crucifixion creates serious problems for oppressed persons because it sets the precedent that the sacrifice of one's life for the gratification of others is a virtuous act. Williams' theology emphasizes two elements in the oppression that black women have suffered under the domination of white women and men: surrogacy and servitude. She rejects any understanding of Jesus that implies virtue in perpetual servitude or in substituting one person's suffering for another as a means of atonement for sin. Labeling human suffering the route to heavenly rewards "overspiritualizes" it and is nothing more than a foundation for and defense of the status quo that favors some groups at the expense of others. Genuine spirituality as modeled by Jesus does not promote suffering and service; it empowers persons through economic, social, and political revolution.

Womanists, like other Christian feminists, also question traditional theology's emphasis on Jesus' maleness. They are especially critical of black liberation theologians who have been able to speak of a black Christ, but who still fail to accept the idea of a female Christ. Black male liberation theologians maintain that in America blackness is equated with servitude, suffering, and indignity. So in

517

American culture Jesus should be depicted as being black. Womanists ask these African American men to go farther and acknowledge that if "Christ" is whoever suffers most, then Christ must also be a black woman, for on the backs of black women converge the horrors of race, class, and gender oppression.

Acknowledgment of the humanity rather than the maleness of Christ does not lead womanists to negate male humanity or to reject male participation in the Christian community. Instead, it seeks to include women in theological discourse, and it recognizes the effects of sexism and misogyny on the entire African American experience. Because they have suffered oppression due to race as well as gender, womanists recognize the need to defend their ethnic community, their economic class, and their gender. Therefore, womanists cannot take the radical feminist path, because it would negate the importance of ethnicity in the self-definition and experience of African American women. Nor can they simply follow black male theologians, for if black people are to be liberated, they must all be freed, male and female together.

The final message of womanist theologians, as for all liberation and liberating theologies, is that because God is just and good there is hope for improving humanity. God does not intervene directly in human situations to rectify evil structures, but through Jesus' ministry God has revealed a model for just relations and offers the grace that enables groups to struggle for liberation. Womanists demonstrate that African American women can trust in the authority of their experience of God in devising a genuine foundation for self-liberation from race, class, and gender oppression.

Sheilah M. Jones

Selected Bibliography

1979   Frances Beale, "Double Jeopardy: To Be Black and Female," in *Black Theology: A Documentary History, 1966–1979*, ed. Gayraud S. Wilmore and James H. Cone.

1979   Jacquelyn Grant, "Black Theology and the Black Woman," in *Black Theology: A Documentary History, 1966–1979*, ed. Gayraud S. Wilmore and James H. Cone.

1979   Theressa Hoover, "Black Women and the Churches: Triple Jeopardy," in *Black Theology: A Documentary History, 1966–1979*, ed. Gayraud S. Wilmore and James H. Cone.

1983   Alice Walker, *In Search of Our Mothers' Gardens: Womanist Prose.*

1984   Jacquelyn Grant, "Black Response to Feminist Theology," in *Women's Spirit Bonding*, ed. Janet Kalven and Mary I. Buckley.

1989   Jacquelyn Grant, *White Women's Christ and Black Women's Jesus.*

1989   Katie G. Cannon, "Moral Wisdom in the Black Women's Literary Tradition," in *Weaving the Visions: New Patterns in Feminist Spirituality,* ed. Judith Plaskow and Carol P. Christ.

1989   "Womanist Theology: Black Women's Voices," in *Weaving the Visions: New Patterns in Feminist Spirituality,* ed. Judith Plaskow and Carol P. Christ.

1993   Delores S. Williams, *Sisters in the Wilderness.*

1993   Emilie Townes, ed., *A Troubling in My Soul: Womanist Perspectives on Evil and Suffering.*

NOTES ON THE CONTRIBUTORS

Ellen T. Armour teaches at Rhodes College, Memphis, Tennessee. *Sallie McFague.*

James J. Bacik teaches at the University of Toledo, Toledo, Ohio. *Hans Küng.*

Jack Edmund Brush teaches at the University of Zürich, Zürich, Switzerland. *Gerhard Ebeling.*

Lisa Sowle Cahill teaches at Boston College, Boston, Massachusetts. *James M. Gustafson.*

Charles Campbell teaches at Columbia Theological Seminary, Decatur, Georgia. *Hans W. Frei.*

Anne Carr teaches at the University of Chicago, Chicago, Illinois. *Karl Rahner.*

J. Harley Chapman teaches at William Rainey Harper College, Palatine, Illinois. *Robert Cummings Neville.*

Will Coleman teaches at Columbia Theological Seminary, Decatur, Georgia. *Cornel West.*

Elmer M. Colyer teaches at Dubuque Theological Seminary, Dubuque, Iowa. *Thomas F. Torrance.*

M. Shawn Copeland teaches at Marquette University, Milwaukee, Wisconsin. *James Hal Cone.*

Millard J. Erickson is a Distinguished Professor of Theology at Truett Seminary, Baylor University, Waco, Texas, and at Western Seminary, Portland, Oregon. *Carl F. H. Henry.*

John T. Ford teaches at Catholic University of America, Washington, D.C. *Jon Sobrino.*

Chester Gillis teaches at Georgetown University, Washington, D.C. *John Harwood Hick.*

Roberto S. Goizueta teaches at Loyola University, Chicago, Illinois. *Juan Luis Segundo.*

George L. Goodwin teaches at the College of St. Scholastica, Duluth, Minnesota. *Schubert M. Ogden.*

Peter J. Gorday is affiliated with Georgia Institute of Pastoral Care, Atlanta, Georgia. *Raymond (Raimundo) Panikkar.*

David Ray Griffin teaches at the School of Theology at Claremont University, Claremont, California. *Charles Hartshorne.*

Mary Catherine Hilkert is an Associate Professor of Theology at the University of Notre Dame. *Edward Schillebeeckx.*

E. Glenn Hinson teaches at Baptist Theological Seminary, Richmond, Virginia. *Thomas Merton.*

Thomas Hopko teaches at St. Vladimir's Orthodox Theological Seminary, Crestwood, New York. *John Meyendorff.*

Nancy R. Howell teaches at Pacific Lutheran University, Tacoma, Washington. *David Ray Griffin.*

Thomas A. Idinopulos teaches at Miami University, Miami, Ohio. *Nicholas Berdyaev.*

Theodore W. Jennings, Jr., teaches at Chicago Theological Seminary, Chicago, Illinois. *Thomas J. J. Altizer.*

Sheilah M. Jones teaches at Mt. Saint Mary's College, Los Angeles, California. *Womanist Theologians.*

Warren A. Kay teaches at Merrimack College, North Andover, Massachusetts. *Paul Tillich.*

Catherine Keller teaches at Drew University, Madison, New Jersey. *Mary Daly.*

Geffrey B. Kelly teaches at LaSalle University, Philadelphia, Pennsylvania. *Dietrich Bonhoeffer.*

Julian Kunnie teaches at the University of Arizona, Tucson, Arizona. *Desmond Tutu.*

Paul Lakeland teaches at Fairfield University, Fairfield, Connecticut. *Peter C. Hodgson.*

Benjamin C. Leslie teaches at North American Baptist Theological Seminary, St. Paul, Minnesota. *Karl Barth.*

Thorwald Lorenzen previously taught at Baptist Theological Seminary, Rüschlikon, Switzerland. He is pastor at Canberra Baptist Church, Canberra, Australia. *Jürgen Moltmann.*

Dennis P. McCann teaches at De Paul University, Chicago, Illinois. *Reinhold Niebuhr.*

John P. McCarthy teaches at Loyola University, Chicago, Illinois. *David Tracy.*

Otto Maduro teaches at Drew University, Madison, New Jersey. *Leonardo Boff.*

Bruce D. Marshall teaches at St. Olaf College, Northfield, Minnesota. *George Lindbeck.*

Anselm Kyongsuk Min teaches at the Claremont Graduate School, Claremont University, Claremont, California. *Asian Theologians.*

David L. Mueller is Joseph Emerson Brown Professor of Christian Theology (retired) at Southern Baptist Theological Seminary, Louisville, Kentucky. *Emil Brunner.*

Roger E. Olson teaches at Bethel College and Seminary, St. Paul, Minnesota. *Donald G. Bloesch.*

Douglas F. Ottati teaches at Union Theological Seminary of Virginia, Richmond, Virginia. *H. Richard Niebuhr.*

David Pellauer teaches at DePaul University, Chicago, Illinois. *Paul Ricoeur.*

Ted Peters teaches at the Graduate Theological Union and Pacific Lutheran Seminary, Berkeley, California. *Wolfhart Pannenberg.*

Jeffrey C. Pugh teaches at Elon College, Elon, North Carolina. *Thomas C. Oden.*

Carl Raschke teaches at the University of Denver, Denver, Colorado. *Mark C. Taylor.*

Jennifer L. Rike teaches at the University of Detroit-Mercy, Detroit, Michigan. *Langdon Gilkey.*

Jeanette Rodriguez teaches at Seattle University, Seattle, Washington. *Ada Maria Isasi-Diaz.*

John R. Sachs, teaches at Weston School of Theology, Cambridge, Massachusetts. *Hans Urs von Balthasar.*

T. Howland Sanks teaches at Jesuit School of Theology, Berkeley, California. *Avery Dulles.*

Theophus (Thee) Smith teaches at Emory University, Decatur, Georgia. *Howard Thurman.*

Mary Hembrow Snyder teaches at Mercyhurst College, Erie, Pennsylvania. *Rosemary Radford Ruether.*

Volker Spangenberg teaches at Heidelberg University, Germany. D. Dixon Sutherland, trans., teaches at Stetson University, DeLand, Florida. *Eberhard Jüngel.*

Marjorie Hewitt Suchocki teaches at the School of Theology, Claremont University, Claremont, California. *John B. Cobb, Jr.*

Mark McClain Taylor teaches at Princeton Theological Seminary, Princeton, New Jersey. *Gustavo Gutiérrez.*

M. Thomas Thangaraj teaches at Emory University, Atlanta, Georgia. *Gordon D. Kaufman.*

Clark Williamson teaches at Christian Theological Seminary, Indianapolis, Indiana. *Paul M. van Buren.*

Printed in the United States
25975LVS00003B/106-108